Halifax and Its

1749 - 1999

Images From Nova Scotia Archives and Records Management

Co-published by
Nova Scotia Archives and Records Management
and Nimbus Publishing Limited

Nimbus Publishing Limited
PO Box 9301, Station A
Halifax, NS B3K 5N5
(902)455-4286

Design: Arthur Carter
Printed and bound in Canada

Canadian Cataloguing in Publication Data

Halifax and its people
Co-published by Nova Scotia Archives and Record Management.
ISBN 1-55109-292-1

1. Halifax (N.S.) -- History --Pictorial works. I. Nova Scotia Archives and Record Management.
FC2346.4.H34 1999 971.6'225'00222 C99-950210-7

Nimbus Publishing acknowledges the financial support of the Canada Council and the Department of Canadian Heritage.

CONTENTS

PREFACE

It is a very great pleasure for me to welcome readers to *Halifax and Its People 1749-1999*, a joint publication undertaken by Nova Scotia Archives and Records Management with Nimbus Publishing of Halifax. It has been an equal pleasure working with them to produce this book. Together, we hope that those already familiar with the history and development of Halifax, and those who are exploring it for the first time, will find the results of our collective effort an informative and attractive publication.

As a means of commemorating the 250th anniversary of Halifax, the Archives—which has been a keeper of Nova Scotia's documentary heritage for nearly 150 of those years—wanted to contribute a book that would help to define the city across its long history. We recognized early that cities are shaped by their inhabitants, just as much as by their physical location and built environment; accordingly, we decided to focus on the people of Halifax, seen against the ever-changing backdrop of the city. Our focus is a little ambitious, since we also wanted to include the broader possibilities offered by the new Halifax Regional Municipality—and so, for example, we have included the round-up of Sable Island ponies on that isolated electoral outpost of the municipality, paired with their subsequent sale on the Halifax waterfront.

The photographic holdings at Nova Scotia Archives and Records Management are vast—some 500,000 images by the last estimate, covering all aspects of our province's visual heritage. It has been a challenge to select out of these, some 140 images best illuminating the chosen topic. Staff of our Public and Support Services Division are most deserving of recognition for their initiative and commitment to bringing this publication project to fruition. In particular, I extend my thanks to Garry Shutlak and Philip Hartling for their ingenuity in identifying 'the best of the best'—and then creating text to accompany the images; and to Lois Yorke for overall project coordination.

An additional benefit resulting from this collaboration with Nimbus Publishing has been the opportunity to create the Archives' very first 'virtual exhibit'—an electronic version of *Halifax and Its People 1749-1999*. This innovative departure is available on the Archives' web site where, in keeping with our objective of providing expanded and enhanced public access to the institution, it will remain indefinitely as a learning tool, exhibit experience, and resource guide for all who visit.

For those of you already acquainted with the visual history of the Halifax Regional Municipality, it is my hope that you will find 'something new' within these pages. For those of you exploring for the first time, I welcome you to this publication and trust that it will enrich your knowledge of the area—not only during this year of Halifax's 250th, but also for the years ahead, which will bring even greater potential and change to the people who live in and shape this community.

W. Brian Speirs
Provincial Archivist

INTRODUCTION

When asked to write the introduction to *Halifax and Its People, 1749–1999*, I accepted the honour with the greatest of pleasure. On my mother's side, my family can trace its Halifax ancestry to the arrival of Richard John Uniacke in 1774. It proved a most inauspicious beginning, for he first saw Halifax as a prisoner in chains charged with treason. But like so many in our city's 250-year history, he overcame the vicissitudes of life and made Halifax his home.

Halifax itself has undergone many changes of fortune, but hopes ran high on that 21st day of June in 1749, when Colonel Edward Cornwallis and his staff aboard the sloop *Sphinx* first viewed 'Chebookt,' the name the Mi'kmaq had given to the magnificent long harbour that lay before them. Within that harbour would shortly arise a new town, which the settlers named after Lord Halifax. As President of the Board of Trade and Plantations, he had persuaded the British government of the strategic need to establish a fortified town in Nova Scotia to offset the great French fortress at Louisbourg.

Nearly all the 2,500 or so colonists who came with Cornwallis were English, many from London—but among those Londoners there were also Swiss, Irish, Jews, and Germans. As an enticement, the British government had promised all those who would settle in the new town, free land and rations for a year. Such a promise drew disbanded soldiers and sailors and others who proved lawless, lazy, and worthless as settlers—but they would be gone within a year. The call for colonists, however, had also brought to Halifax tradesmen, merchants, and gentlemen anxious to improve their circumstances. Among them were Laurence Collins, Lewis Piers, William Best, John Creighton, and Alexander Keddy, men whose descendants can be found in contemporary Halifax and Nova Scotia.

New Englanders in increasing numbers soon arrived as well, attracted by commercial opportunities and the fishery. Then, in 1751, came the first shiploads of 'Foreign Protestants,' from various German principalities, from Switzerland, and from Montbéliard (a region in the southeast of modern-day France). Most of these settlers would go on to Lunenburg, but those who remained in Halifax made their homes principally in the town's North End, where today the Little Dutch (Deutsch) Church on Brunswick Street, a National Historic Site, commemorates their contribution as "good and industrious people." Early in Halifax's history, the Scots also established themselves in the community, mainly in mercantile and commercial concerns. In 1761, they formed a Scottish Guild of Merchants, out of which in 1767 came the North British Society, the oldest of Halifax's charitable organizations. From its very beginnings, then, Halifax was home to a surprising variety of peoples.

Halifax was founded as a deliberative act of British imperial policy in the ongoing struggle with France for a North American empire, that continued until the fall of Quebec in 1759. Although the French sought the destruction of Halifax, it was the fierce opposition by the Mi'kmaq to the English settlement of their lands that curtailed further settlement in Nova Scotia until a series of peace treaties were devised in 1760. In the meantime, war expenditures resulted in considerable growth within the new town. Following Louisbourg's fall in 1758, and a mere decade after Halifax's founding, Richard Short completed a series of engravings depicting the infant community. The two scenes shown on pages four and five leave us with the distinct impression of an already well-established town, its citizenry going about their daily concerns.

War came again to Halifax with the onset of the American Revolution. Following the declaration of peace and Britain's recognition of American independence, thousands of Loyalist refugees arrived in 1783 and 1784, doubling the province's population and swelling that of Halifax to around 5,000. More significantly for the capital of the colony, the Loyalists—or 'new comers'—by reason of their political influence and often superior attainments, were able to gain an ascendancy within government, which created much resentment among the old inhabitants. Intermarriage and time, however, would see the Loyalists assimilated completely into Halifax society.

Peace was shortlived, for in 1793 the long war with Revolutionary France began, leading into the War of 1812-1814 with the United States. Such were the spoils of privateering and the profits from supplying the army and navy during these years, that it was said that the streets of Halifax were paved in gold. In a delightful watercolour done when the prosperity of war still shone brightly in the community, Joseph Partridge portrays ladies and gentlemen walking in the Grand Parade (page nine), first laid out in 1749, but by 1817 well-leveled, walled up, and fenced in to present an attractive urban setting. English gentility pervades the whole scene.

From the time of Halifax's first settlement, merchants and other early residents owned slaves. Probably 3,000 Blacks freed by the British came to Nova Scotia as Loyalists, and as many as 400 of them were drawn to Halifax by its labour-market opportunities. Of these, however, few remained after the great exodus to Sierra Leone in 1792. During the War of 1812, British military and naval forces occupied the area around Chesapeake Bay. Hundreds of slaves sought refuge and freedom with the British, and between 1813 and 1816, some 2,000 of these were brought north to Nova Scotia, suffering great distress. Most settled at Preston, Hammond's Plains, Refugee Hill, and in Halifax itself. Many Blacks within the bounds of the Halifax Regional Municipality today can trace their ancestry to these Chesapeake refugees from slavery.

Napoleon's defeat at Waterloo in 1815 ushered in a century of peace. It also saw the beginnings of a mass emigration from the British Isles to North America. Although eastern Nova Scotia and Cape Breton Island were heavily settled by Scots, few came to Halifax. It was instead the Irish, many via Newfoundland, who proved to be the largest immigrant group in the growing community. We tend to associate Irish emigration with the Great Famine of 1846–49, but most of the 4,000–5,000 Irish who settled in Halifax after 1815 came in the 1830s. They were predominantly country folk and Roman Catholic. Their integration into a largely Protestant urban population of 20,000 did not come without fierce religious contention, but through these struggles Halifax became a more tolerant society.

By the middle of the nineteenth century, immigration ceased and nearly all Haligonians were now to be native-born. With Halifax's incorporation as a city in 1841 and Dartmouth's in 1873, came much-needed civic improvements to streets, water supply, street railways, harbour ferries—and later, electrification. Other than the establishment of a Board of Commissioners for improving the Halifax water supply, private enterprise remained responsible for establishing and expanding street railways, gas and electrical lighting, and telephones. William O'Brien, for example, founded the first street railway in 1866, with five horse cars. In 1896, the Halifax Electric Tramway Company began a service that gave citizens the means to reach most parts of the city. Many Haligonians can still recall with nostalgia the faithful old trams that ran until 1949, when 'modern' electric trolley cars replaced them. Although a very small boy at the time, I can remember the thrill of being taken by my grandmother on the tram, all the way out to Simpson's Department Store, with its enthralling toy department, at the end of the North West Arm line.

Victorian society is often portrayed as dour, stern, God-fearing, and opposed to any activity that could be classed as frivolous—but Halifax Victorians had great fun. They loved dressing up for fancy-dress balls and skating carnivals. Amateur theatricals thrived. During the last half of the nineteenth century, Haligonians so embraced sports that it was claimed that the city had more admirers of amateur sporting activities than any other city in the Maritimes, if not Canada. There were aquatic carnivals in the harbour, curling on the Dartmouth Lakes, yacht racing in the harbour and North West Arm, tennis at the South End Tennis Club, snowshoeing, rifle shooting at the Bedford Range, horse racing on the Commons, sleigh drives to rendezvouses outside the city, and for children and adults alike, tobogganing and coasting on the many hills.

Halifax would have the first covered skating rink in Canada, after one was constructed inside the Horticultural Gardens (later the Halifax Public Gardens) in 1867, to meet the rising interest in indoor skating. In 1908, a citizens' group founded the Waegwoltic Club on the North West Arm. In those days you could still swim in the Arm. My family were early members of this most family-oriented of recreational clubs. When my mother was a very little girl left at the 'Waeg' one day in the charge of my great-grandmother, Dora, my mother decided to row across the North West Arm, all by herself and without informing anyone. Just as she reached the half-way point, she was glimpsed by my grandmother, with suitable consternation—only to be told calmly by Dora that she need not worry, as she, Dora, was in charge and keeping a watchful eye on her progress.

For those wishing to participate in team sports, Halifax boasted hockey, rowing, football, cricket, and baseball teams, sponsored by clubs such as the Wanderers' Amateur Athletic Association. By the 1890s, businesses and various British regiments also took to sponsoring teams. For those who wished to camp outdoors, hunt and fish, they did not have to go farther than the numerous still-forested areas within Halifax County.

If church-going and participation in church-sponsored activities can be considered a guide, then at no time in Halifax's history has religion been more present in people's lives than in the years leading up to the First World War. Never would the clergy have as high a standing in society as during this period. Although there was always the Poors' Asylum or Poor House, maintained by the City for the utterly destitute, upon the churches fell most of society's responsibility for neglected, homeless, or orphaned children, 'fallen' women and girls, and juvenile offenders. Government provided some financial support, but such institutions as the Protestant Orphans' Home, St. Patrick's Home, St. Joseph's Orphanage, the Home for Colored Children and the Salvation Army Maternity Hospital & Home provided the necessary accommodation, plus some schooling. By the second decade of the twentieth century, government increasingly had to accept that the churches could no longer be expected, nor did they have the resources to continue providing such social services. Nearly all the church-sponsored institutions had accordingly disappeared by the end of the 1960s, with the important exception of the Grace Maternity Hospital.

In the middle of the nineteenth century, through private initiative and provincial financial assistance, two special institutions were established in Halifax for children—schools for the deaf and for the blind; in both cases they were the first such institutions in the Maritimes. William Gray, a deaf mute from Scotland, began working with two pupils in 1855; through the efforts of the Rev. James Cochran and Andrew Mackinlay, provincial and public support allowed for securing a wooden building to house the school. Under the principalship of Charles Frederick Fraser, blind himself since the age of seven, the Halifax School for the Blind became a leading institution in its field; in 1915 King George V bestowed a knighthood on Fraser for his groundbreaking work. The photographs on pages 140 and 142 are especially moving, as we look back at 'special education' in the late Victorian era—young children learning sign language and blind children working at various forms of manual training.

Although the Halifax Medical Society, organized in 1844, pressed the city and provincial governments to establish a public hospital, its efforts proved unsuccessful. Then, in 1859, funds were found to construct a hospital as a charity institution to provide care primarily for the infirm and diseased poor. It, however, did not fulfill the need for a general public hospital with proper medical care available to all Nova Scotians. When a former alderman, William Murdoch, left a sizable bequest for a hospital (he did the same for the School for the Blind), the city decided to proceed with the construction of a facility that could accommodate sixty patients. The City and Provincial Hospital opened in

May 1867 and made possible the establishment of the Halifax Medical College. A photograph taken ca. 1890 on page 139 shows students in the Anatomy Laboratory. On Queen Victoria's Golden Jubilee in 1887, the hospital became the Victoria General. In 1910, when the photograph on page 147 was taken, the facility admitted over 1,500 patients.

In its first half-century, Halifax knew little but war; after the Battle of Waterloo in 1815 and Napoleon's final defeat, Halifax would know only a century of peace. The British Empire spanned the world and Britannia ruled the waves. Haligonians felt themselves to be very much a part of this Empire and imperial sentiment could be seen displayed at every public event. Haligonians turned royal visits into gala occasions with torchlight processions, sporting events, mock battles, and cavalcades through city streets. But the celebrations surrounding Queen Victoria's Diamond Jubilee in June 1897 surpassed all such previous holiday events, lasting a full week. On the city's Natal Day, 21 June, as part of these celebrations, the unveiling of the 'Jubilee' or 'Nymph' Fountain took place in the Public Gardens. In the photograph that graces the cover of *Halifax and Its People*, we see a charming variety of faces of all ages, a classic photograph of its time.

There were few public events in which the army and navy were not present. A substantial garrison and regular Royal Navy visits provided a steady income to Halifax merchants—and a good many husbands for the city's young women. The massive fortress which took three decades to construct astride Citadel Hill exemplified the strategic importance of Halifax to the Empire. Rudyard Kipling expressed that symbolism and sentiment, when in his "Song of the Cities–Halifax," he penned these timeless words:

Into the mist my guardian prows put forth,
Behind the mist my virgin ramparts lie,
The Warden of the Honour of the North,
Sleepless and veiled am I!

As part of the new Dominion of Canada, Halifax's militia contributed the 63rd Battalion for ending the North West Rebellion of 1885. As the ocean gateway to the Dominion, Halifax sent off troops for the Boer War and then welcomed them on their return. But with the sounding of the Guns of August 1914, Halifax was to know war beyond anyone's imagination. The city's enlistment rate became one of the highest in the nation. Patriotic fever soared as regiment after regiment left for France, to the cheers and tears of hundreds. By 1917, German submarines were taking their toll of merchant shipping on Halifax's very doorstep. No vessel could sail except in convoy and the large, protected expanse of Bedford Basin became a gathering place for ships waiting to be escorted across the Atlantic.

On December 6, 1917, the shorelines of Halifax and Dartmouth were literally blown up by the Halifax Harbour Explosion, which occurred when a French munitions ship, the *Mont Blanc*, moving through the harbour Narrows to join a convoy, collided with the Belgian Relief vessel *Imo*—with a devastating loss of life and the total obliteration of Halifax's North End. How ordinary people, given the horrific conditions they then faced, rallied instinctively to provide what assistance they could—often with nothing more than their bare hands—remains the most remarkable and enduring story of the explosion. Although no previous disaster could conceivably prepare people for such a catastrophe, much had been learned from the sinking of the *Titanic* in 1912. Halifax officials, some of whom had been involved with the identification and burial of *Titanic* victims recovered from the ocean and brought to Halifax, now adopted a similar system to that used during the rescue efforts to number the bodies and use temporary morgues to accommodate the hundreds of dead.

Halifax again answered the call to arms in 1939. Six years of war placed unforeseen demands on the city's utilities, an undermanned police force, and the few amenities available for the thousands of troops and naval personnel who came and went. As the war drew to a close in May 1945, there were over 24,000 military personnel in the city. What became known as the V-E Day Riots, involving sailors, soldiers, and civilians, began on May 7, the day Germany formally surrendered. Rioting and looting continued into the next day. By the time order was restored, downtown Halifax was a shambles. If that was not enough, on 18 July an ammunition barge blew up in Bedford Basin, shattering windows in the surrounding communities and sending forth a mushroom cloud. The explosion set fire to nearby exposed ammunition dumps at the Bedford Magazine and only valiant efforts succeeded in containing the fires—though for a time many feared a second Halifax Explosion.

Unlike the end of the First World War, which was followed first by depression and soon after by the Second World War, Halifax in 1945 entered an era of peace and prosperity. For generations, Haligonians had prophesied great benefits from having a bridge across the harbour. With the opening in 1955 of the Angus L. Macdonald Bridge, began a steadily accelerating process of expansion involving the entire metropolitan region.

At the beginning of the 1960s, Halifax's population stood at 110,000. Dartmouth had benefitted quickly and enormously from the Macdonald Bridge—it had now become a city, and with its own amalgamated suburbs had a population of 60,000. Bedford had a little over 2,000, while the total combined population for Lower, Middle, and Upper Sackville was still under 1,000. Halifax, Dartmouth, and the whole region were about to undergo phenomenal industrial and commercial growth. At the end of the 1990s, some 350,000 people reside within the newly-instituted Halifax Regional Municipality.

If somehow we could bring back, for just a moment, even a few of those settlers of 1749, I believe they would feel that the hopes and aspirations they had experienced on first sighting the majestic expanse of 'Chebookt' had been well fulfilled. I would hope that they would see us now as true Haligonians, ready to meet the challenges that the next century and the new millennium will surely bring.

In publishing *Halifax and Its People 1749-1999*, the staff of Nova Scotia Archives and Records Management have sought to commemorate, on this our city's 250th anniversary, the ordinary lives of past generations of Haligonians, via a fascinating series of some 140 images selected from the institution's large photographic holdings. We are privileged to be able to enter into those lives through these photographs, chosen to illustrate such varied themes as Occupations, Entertainment and Social Events, The Life Cycle, Halifax at War, Royal Visits, Education and Institutions, and Sports and the Great Outdoors. We are fortunate that the Archives has succeeded so well in preserving and presenting such vivid imagery of our past. The institution is to be congratulated.

Brian Cuthbertson
Halifax, Nova Scotia
August 1999

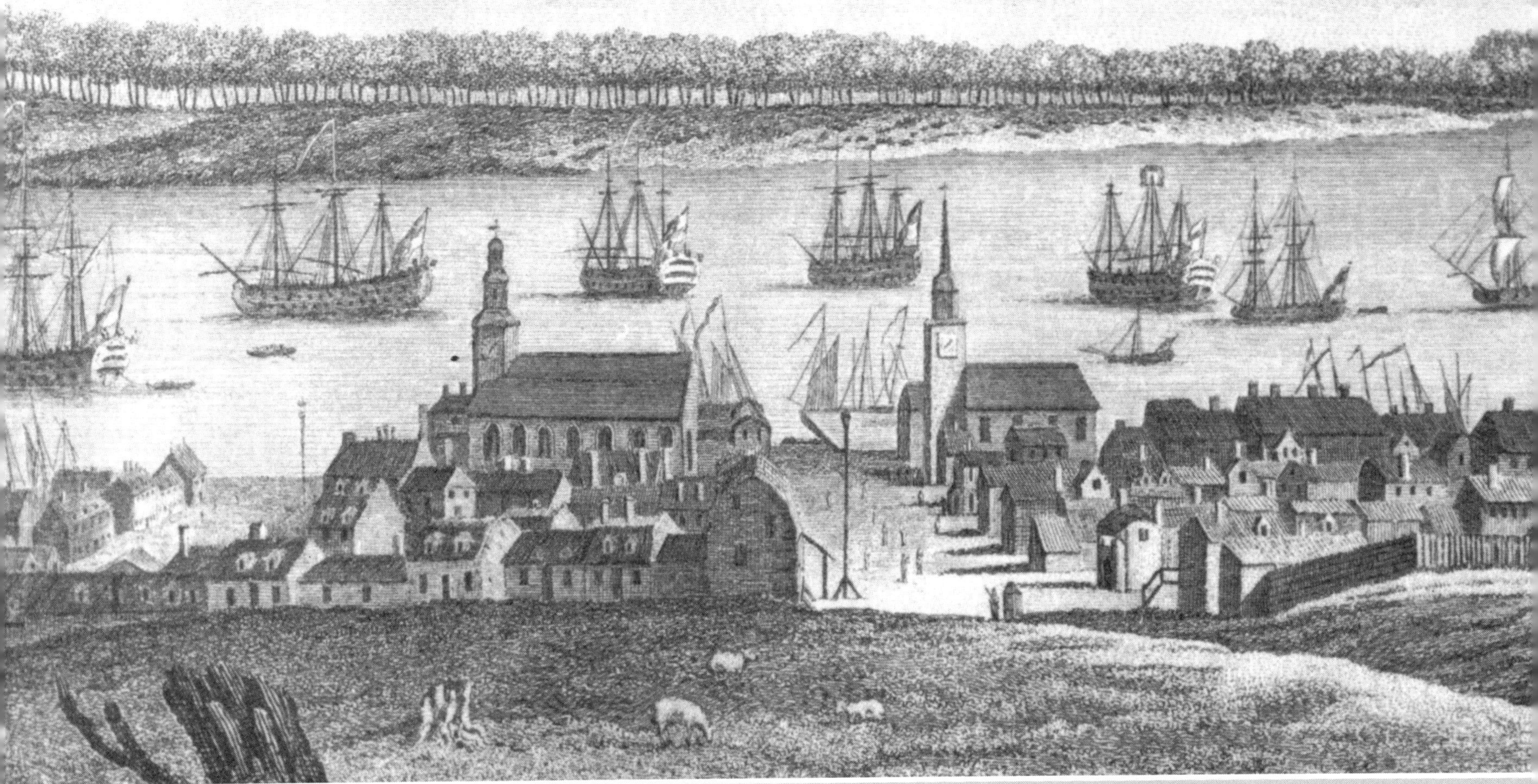

CHAPTER 1

COMPARISON VIEWS

One hundred years ago, the Yarmouth Steamship Company's tourist publication, *Beautiful Nova Scotia: The Ideal Summer Land*, described the capital city of Halifax—then a thriving and picturesque community with about 45,000 inhabitants—as follows:

> *From the summit of Fort George, better known as Citadel Hill, a superb view of the city, the harbor and the surrounding country may be obtained. The older portion of the town lies between it and the water, and the straight cross-streets lead the eye down to the harbor, where vessels bearing the flags of all nations are at anchor. On a clear, sunny morning the scene is one of the prettiest sights imaginable. To the north, shimmering in the summer sun and specked with the wings of pleasure boats, lie the bright waters of Bedford Basin, into which the harbor opens out after passing through the Narrows. To the east are the low hills on the Dartmouth side, and George's Island, green and well-kept....Below and around [Citadel Hill] are the buildings of the town, with here and there a spire rising from among green foliage.*

Regardless of the changes which a century has brought to the urban landscape, the view from Citadel Hill remains a perennial attraction. This particular vantage point, as well as those offered by other strategic locations around the Halifax Peninsula—Fort Needham, Cowie Hill, Georges Island and the Dartmouth shoreline—inspired various eighteenth and nineteenth-century landscape artists passing through the area. Whereas most of British North America remained primeval forest, open prairie or mere clearings in the bush through the last half of the eighteenth century and well into the nineteenth, Halifax was ideal for town-scape painting.

Artists such as Richard Short, Edward Hicks, John Elliott Woolford, R.S.M. Bouchette, Robert Petley, William Egar and William Bartlett—to mention only a few—have left us with a legacy of panoramas and street-scapes, beginning in 1759 and carrying through to the mid-nineteenth century. Probably the most impressive views of Halifax, however, are not these artistic renderings, but instead the large photographic panoramas taken from the eastern side of Citadel Hill by the Notman Studio in 1883 and again c 1892.

Spectacular as the panorama views are, by their very nature they exclude the human figure. It is only with the development of modern photography that the people of the city are—collectively and individually—brought into focus, both as an integral part of the changing city-scape and as its most distinctive and enduring feature.

1. Map of Chebucto Harbour

Inserts: Southern Nova Scotia and its fishing banks. A plan of Halifax and a view of Halifax

1750

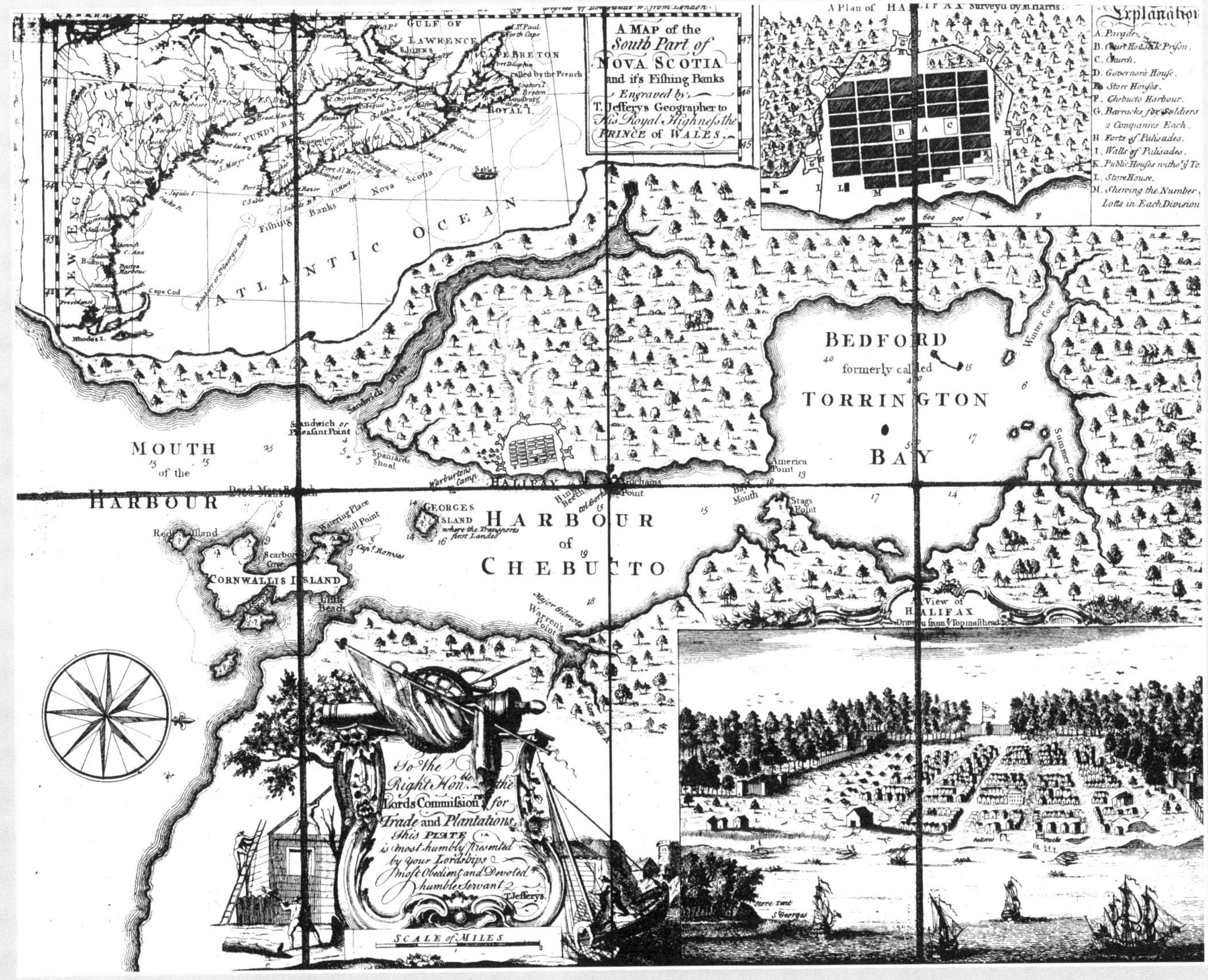

This map first appeared in *The Gentleman's Magazine* for January 1750, a little over six months after the founding of Halifax on June 21, 1749 by the Honourable Edward Cornwallis. The publication noted that the plan of Halifax, inset at top right, and the central map of Chebucto Harbour, plus the top-mast view of the town, inset at bottom right, had been "Drawn on the spot by Moses Harris," while the map of Nova Scotia at the top left was the work of "Mons.[Monsieur] D'Anville, Geographer to the French King." The inset at the top right is a kind of 'master plan' for the new community. It offers a less accurate representation of the actual town than the top-mast view, which shows Halifax as it actually appeared during the latter part of 1749.

2. Part of Halifax town and harbour, looking down Prince Street to the Dartmouth Shore, Georges and Cornwallis islands, Thrum Cap and the sea off Chebucto Head

1759

This sketch, done in May 1759 from what is now the southeast slope of Citadel Hill, was drawn while Richard Short was in Halifax during the Seven Years' War, with the British fleet bound for the siege at Quebec. Short was an amateur artist and the purser on board HMS *Prince of Wales.* The sketch shows at the northern extreme (left side), the Great Pontack Inn at the corner of Duke and Water Streets, and extends as far south as the Governor's Summer Farm, now the site of Government House on Barrington Street.

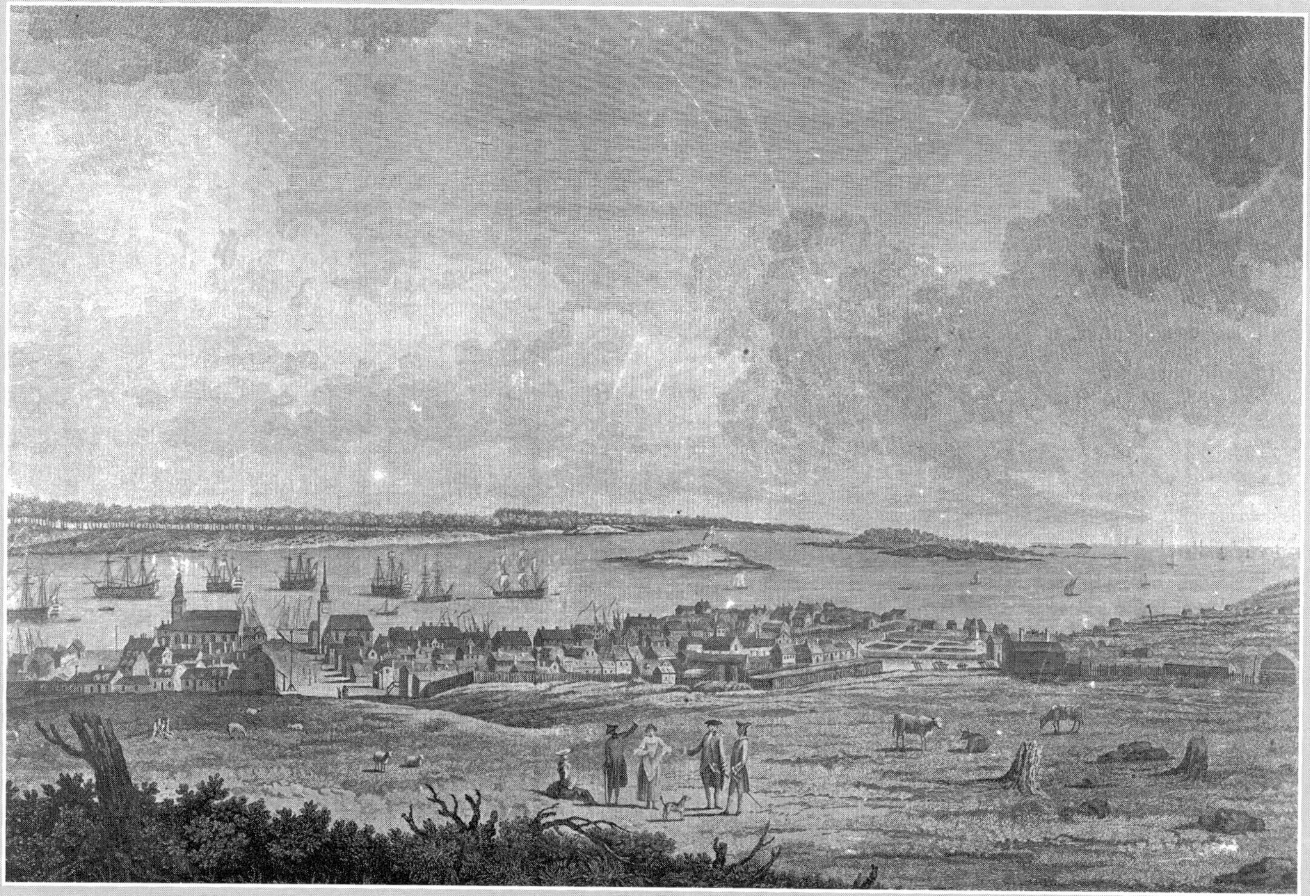

3. The Governor's House and Mather's Meeting House on Hollis Street showing part of the Parade and Citadel Hill
1759

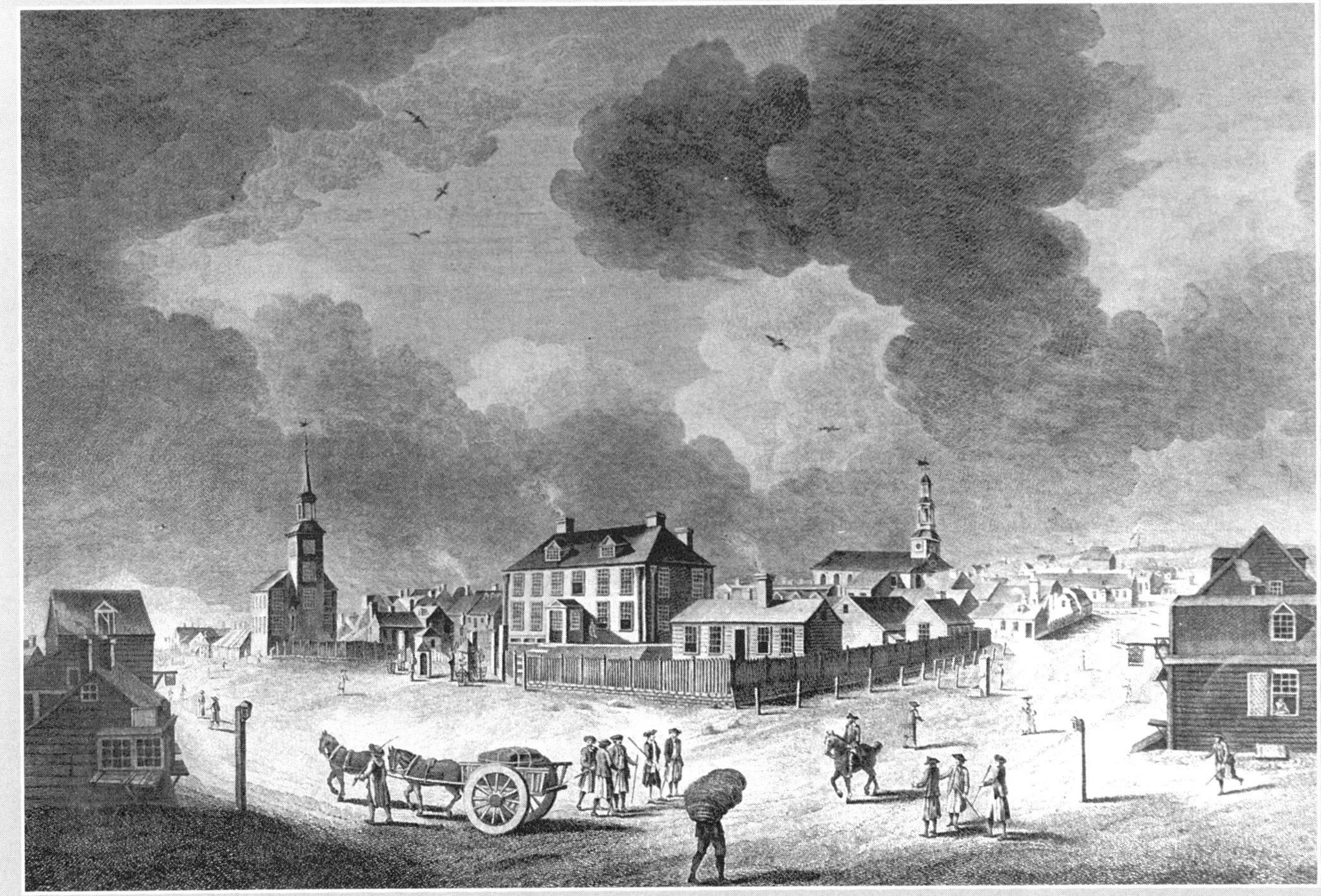

The original Governor's House of 1749 was a small one-storey structure. The frame and material were brought from Boston and the governor took up residence in early October 1749. The new Governor's Mansion shown centre foreground in this engraving was built in 1755 during the tenure of Charles Lawrence. Mather's Meeting House (now St. Matthew's Church), the oldest Protestant Dissenting congregation in Canada, began worship in 1749, and in the following year built the church structure seen to the left of this illustration. The church was used for worship, the basement as a bonded warehouse—until New Year's Day 1857, when a huge conflagration destroyed the church and two adjoining buildings.

4. South Aspect of Halifax from near Point Pleasant Park
c 1780

A view taken from Point Pleasant Battery and Black Rock Point at Point Pleasant, looking north to Citadel Hill (Fort George) and showing Fort Massey, Grand Battery (the Lumber Yard), Camp Hill and, south and west of both Fort Massey and Fort George, the pitched tents of various temporary military encampments. The artist, Lieutenant-Colonel Edward Hicks, was stationed in Halifax from 1778 to 1782 with the 70th Regiment of Foot. His art work graphically documents the posting of thousands of soldiers and sailors to the young settlement during the later years of the American Revolution.

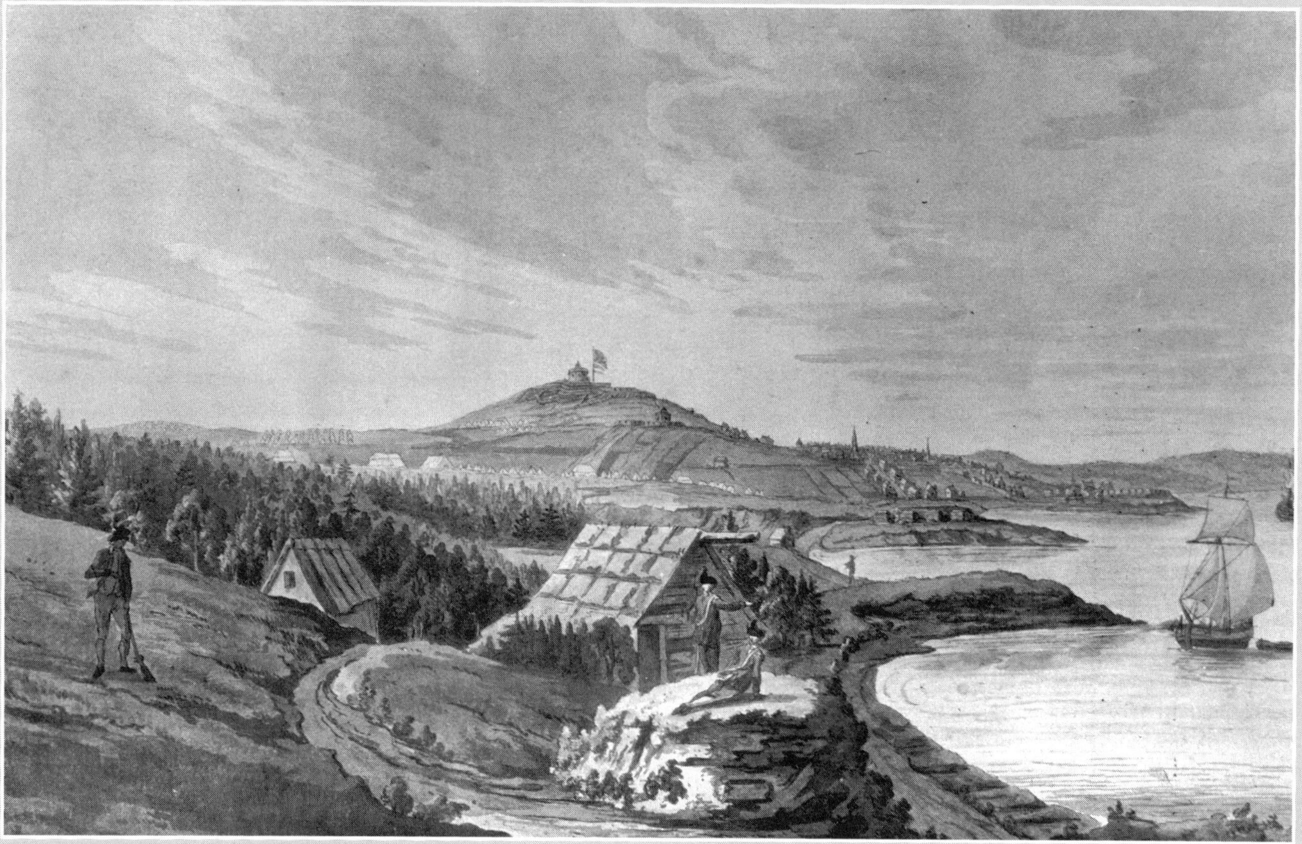

5. Halifax from Fort Needham
c 1780

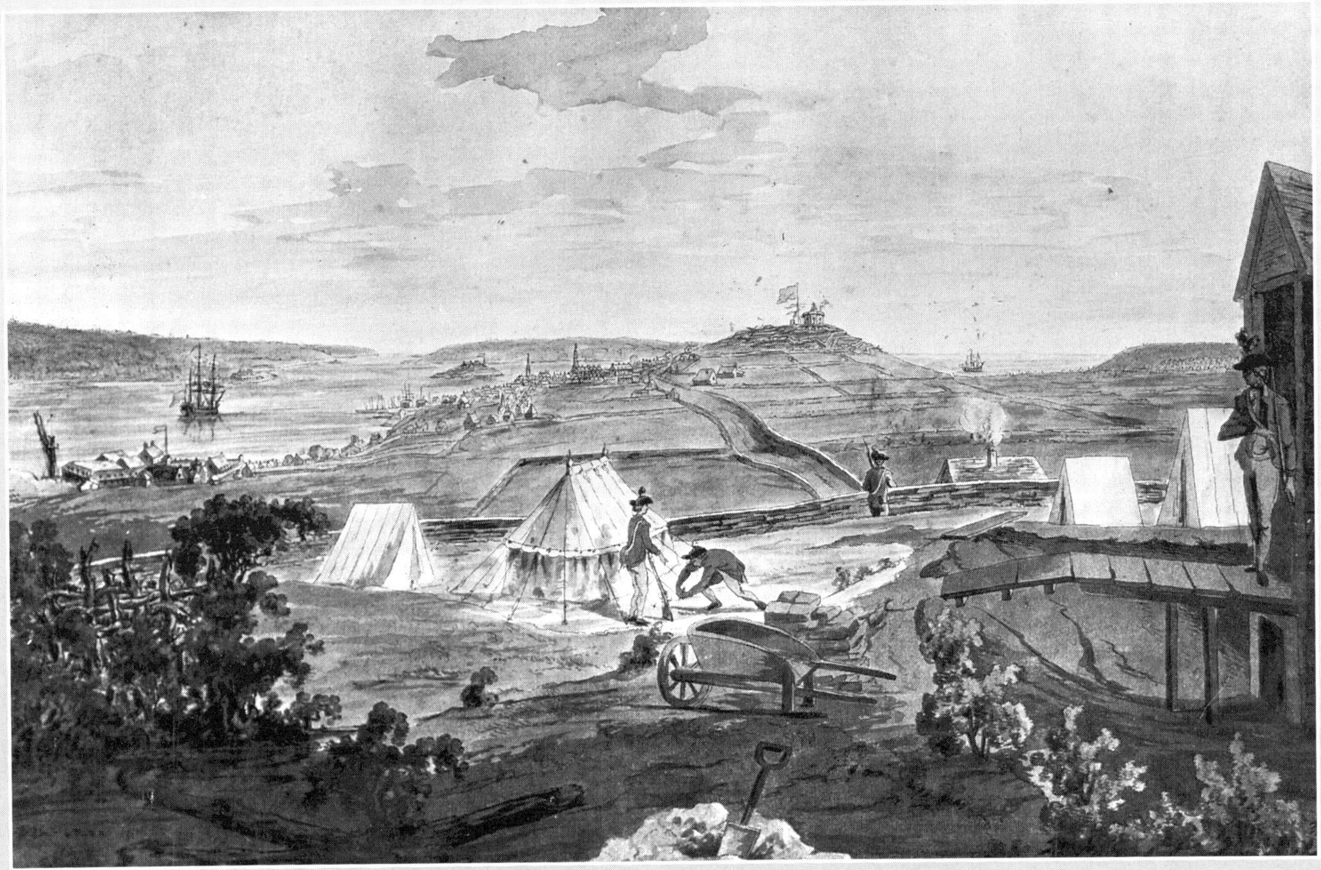

Along the waterfront is His Majesty's Navy Yard, with the adjoining Fort Coote to the far left. This blockhouse was erected in 1775 on a hillock just north of the yard, near the foot of present-day North Street; the fortification was named for General Sir Eyre Coote, a career soldier in the East Indies (India). In the distance is the Citadel (Fort George), considerably enlarged, repaired and strengthened during the 1770s by Captain William Spry, Commanding Officer of the Royal Engineers. Spry's name has come down to us today through 'Spryfield,' his country estate some 8 km. southwest of Halifax, formed out of a crown land grant which he acquired in 1769.

6. "View from Cowie's Hill near Halifax" 1801

Parkyns's view looks down from the height of land above Cowie's Island, an early fishing station on the North West Arm, and then across in an easterly direction to the distant Fort George. The island was purchased by the British military c 1803 and renamed in honour of Henry Dundas (1742-1811), first Viscount Melville and First Lord of the Admiralty (1804-5). A stone prison was immediately erected for French and Spanish prisoners during the Napoleonic Wars, then used for Americans during the War of 1812 and for German internees as recently as World War I. In peacetime it was occasionally used as a temporary receiving station for refugees or transient groups. Among those billeted were African-Americans brought to Nova Scotia by Vice-Admiral Sir Andrew Cochrane during the War of 1812 with the United States, when a proclamation was issued, offering freedom to all southern Blacks who fled to the British forces. As a result, some 2,000 refugees arrived in Nova Scotia between 1813-16, many settling at Preston, Hammonds Plains, Porters Lake, Beech Hill and other areas now within the Halifax Regional Municipality. Later, Foreign Legion volunteers raised in the United States by Joseph Howe to fight in the Crimean War, and inmates from the Poor Asylum after it burnt in 1882, were also housed on the island; and on at least one occasion, in 1847, the military prison was used as a quarantine hospital.

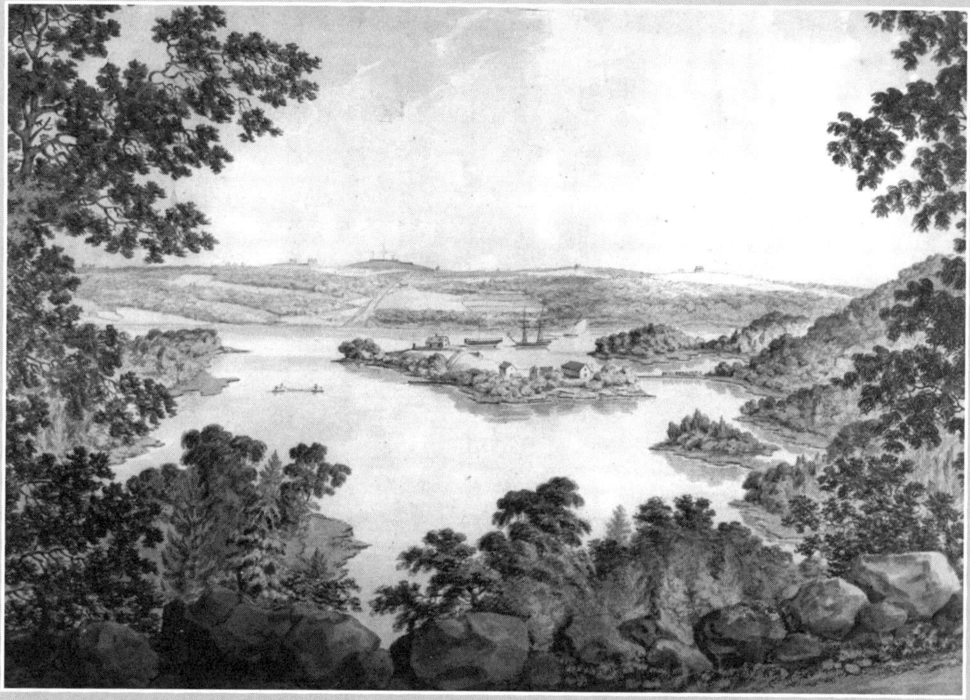

7. National School, Halifax

c 1819

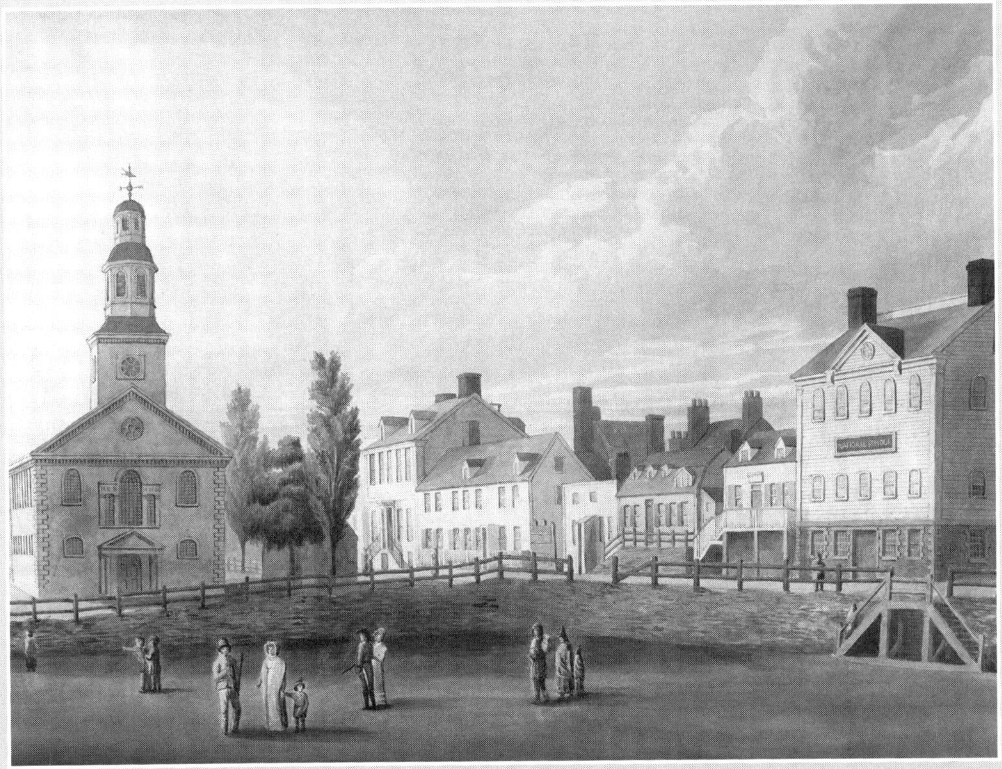

This delightful Joseph Partridge watercolour shows a Halifax street scene still clearly identifiable some 180 years later—a splendid view of the Grand Parade, the Church of St. Paul and the west side of Argyle Street, highlighting the National School (to the far right). The latter, founded under the patronage of the Earl of Dalhousie, then governor of Nova Scotia, opened in 1818, and was intended for children of all social classes, religious denominations and colour—and especially for the children of the poor. For the next 138 years this building was used for educational purposes. The Nova Scotia College of Art and Design was the last such occupant, vacating in 1956; in 1974 the building became the Five Fishermen Restaurant. Moving south along the west side of Argyle Street, the third building from the National School is the new Grand Theatre, later the Theatre Royal. Opened on this site in 1789, it was one of the oldest theatres on the continent when this watercolour was painted. The substantial three-and-a-half storey residence at the end of the Argyle street-scape was St. Paul's Parsonage, completed in 1809 during the appointment of the Rev. Dr. Robert Stanser. It was used as a rectory until sold in 1870, and although greatly altered by time, it remained in place until 1984 when it was razed to make way for a parking lot.

8. View of Halifax from the Red Mill, Dartmouth

c 1853

The Red Mill was a water-driven gristmill adjoining an eighteenth-century windmill built by James Munn and remembered today by Windmill Road in north Dartmouth. The vantage point on a height of land provided a spectacular view across to Halifax, Georges Island and ships in the harbour. At the time this work was executed, the gristmill was still in operation. The ruins remained until 1901, when cleared by the Oland family for a tennis court on their property.

The artist, Robert Wilkie (1827-1904), was born in Halifax and began his painting career here in the 1840s. He emigrated to the United States in 1853 and lived in the Boston area for the rest of his life, a successful painter, illustrator and teacher.

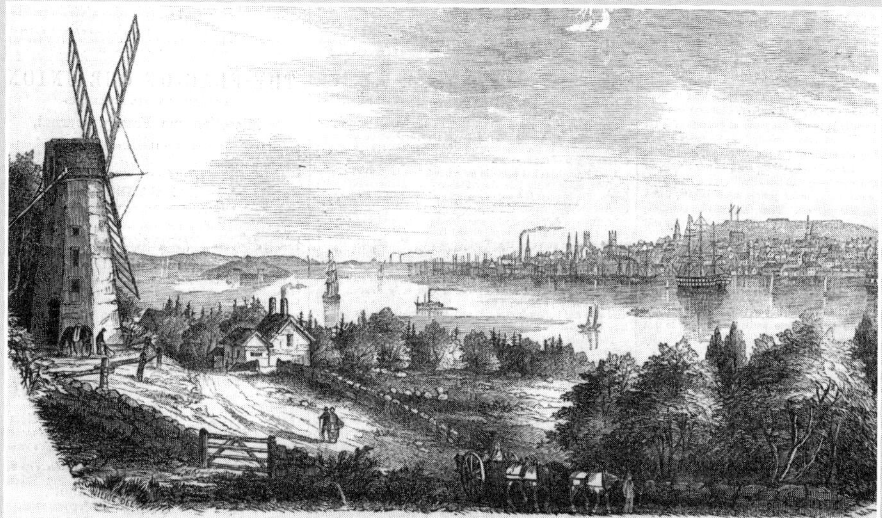

VIEW OF HALIFAX, NOVA SCOTIA, FROM THE RED MILL, DARTMOUTH.

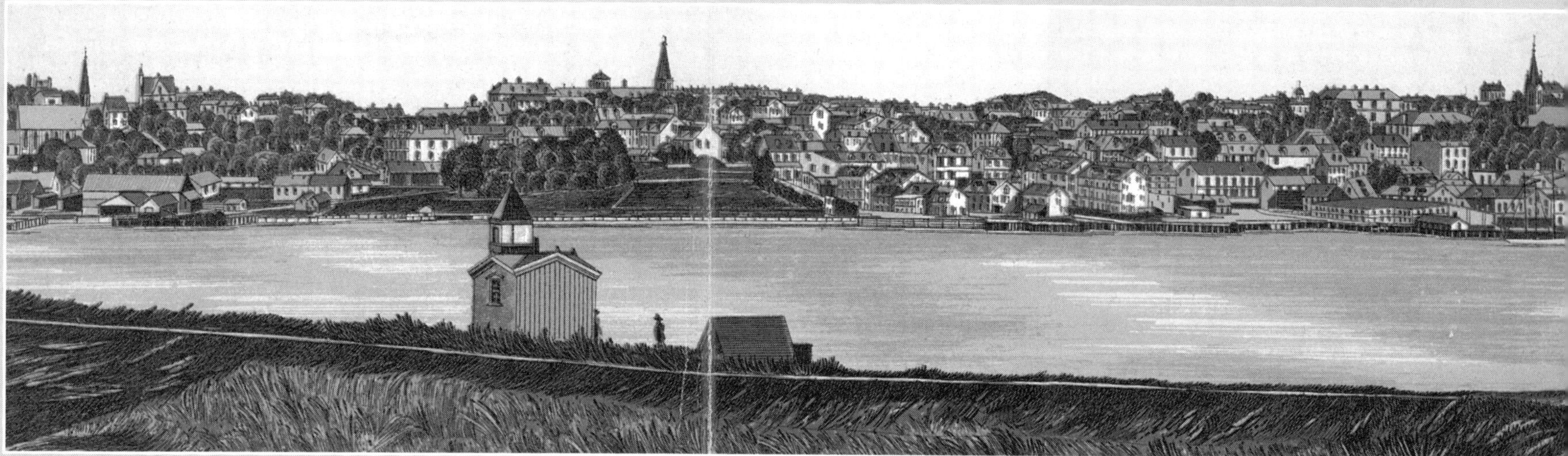

9. *Halifax album*: View of the Halifax Skyline
1880

This fold-out souvenir guide contains 29 images of the City of Halifax, including this panorama view of the waterfront from Georges Island. Souvenir guides such as this were common in the nineteenth century and were produced in many styles and formats, from individual postcards to booklets with pictures and text. Published for and to promote the early tourist trade, they usually extolled the virtues of a particular city or town. They helped create civic pride and were also used to attract trade and industry to the community.

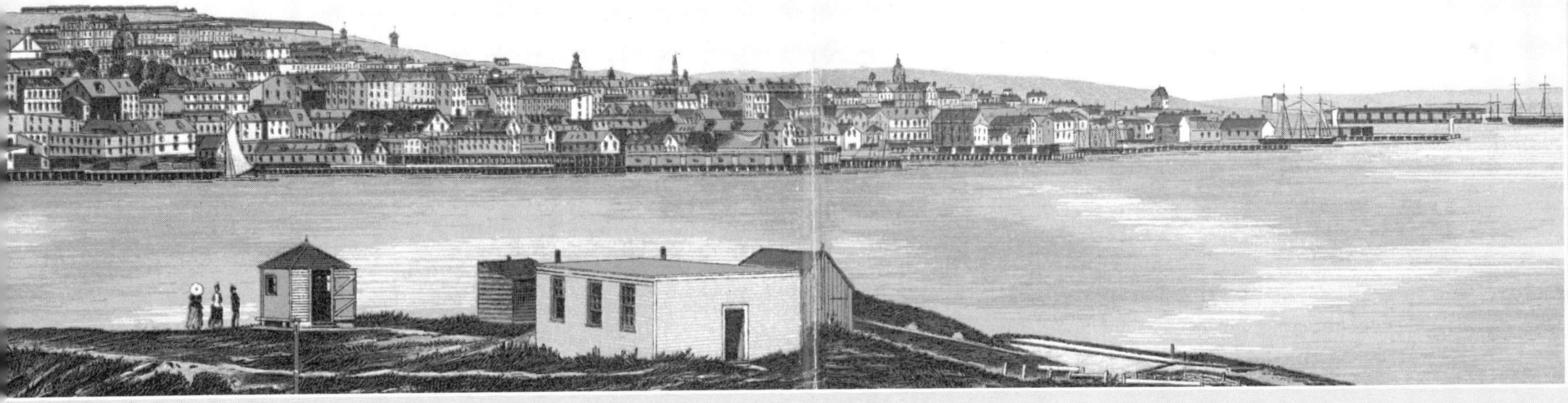

10. Panorama view of Halifax from the Citadel, showing the harbour and the Dartmouth Shore

c 1883

A panorama is an unobstructed and wide view of an extensive area, in all directions. Such photographs were immensely popular in the late nineteenth century, and are often found today in museum or archive collections. They were produced to show a city's progress and to foster civic pride. To devise them, the photographer would find an appropriate place to create the vista and would then set up his tripod and camera. The tripod would remain stationary, while the camera would be moved with enough overlap to splice the images together afterwards, with minimum distortion. This process was continued until the panorama was completed. The spliced prints were then re-photographed to create a negative, and from this prints were made for sale to the public.

This sweeping panorama, taken from the ramparts of the Citadel, shows the downtown core of late Victorian Halifax, beginning north of Jacob Street and travelling in a southerly direction along Brunswick Street to Sackville. At the corner of Brunswick and Duke is Robert Taylor's Boot and Shoe Factory, the Jost Mission and the Central Engine House (i.e., fire station) at the corner of George and Brunswick, all built in 1871. At the head of George Street stands the Town Clock, completed in 1803. At the corner of Brunswick and Prince is the Halifax Visiting Dispensary of 1876, and at the corner of Brunswick and Sackville Streets is the Halifax County Academy, completed in 1879.

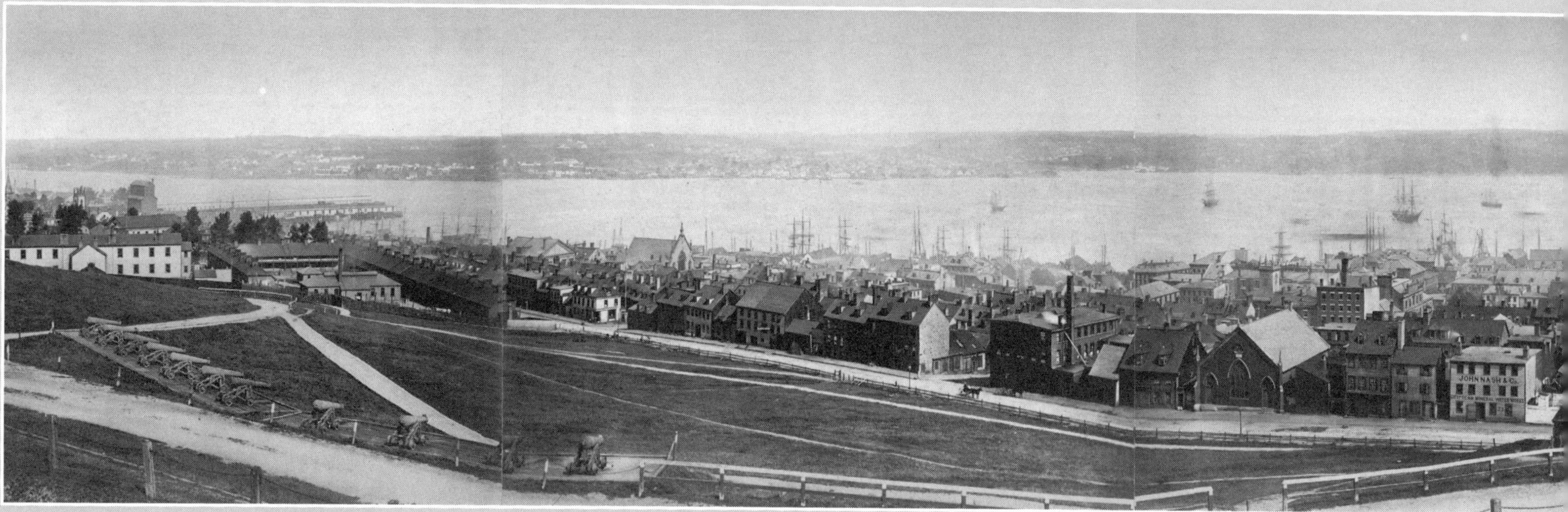

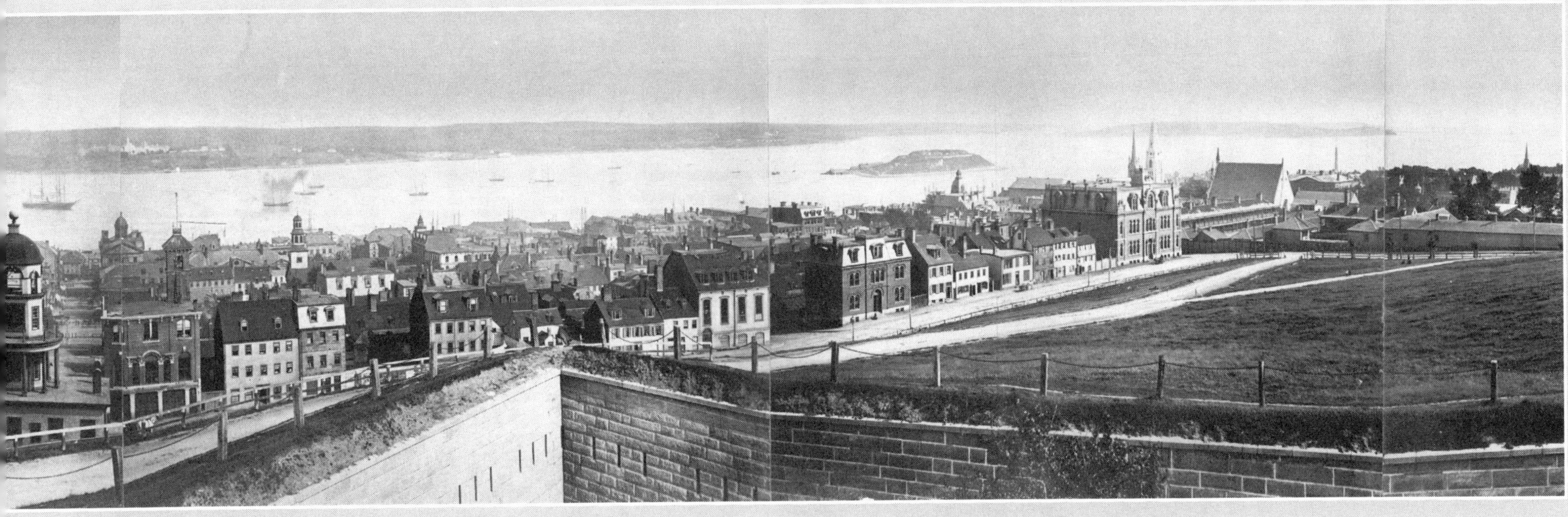

11. Aerial view of the North West Arm, Looking East to Halifax Harbour and the Dartmouth Shore
1949

This oblique-angled aerial photograph taken in Halifax's bicentenary year provides an outstanding view across the southern half of the city: Fleming Park (then outside the city proper), the Memorial or more commonly-known 'Dingle' Tower, the North West Arm, parts of Halifax's residential South End, and the Studley Campus of Dalhousie University, just beginning to expand in the post-World War II boom years.

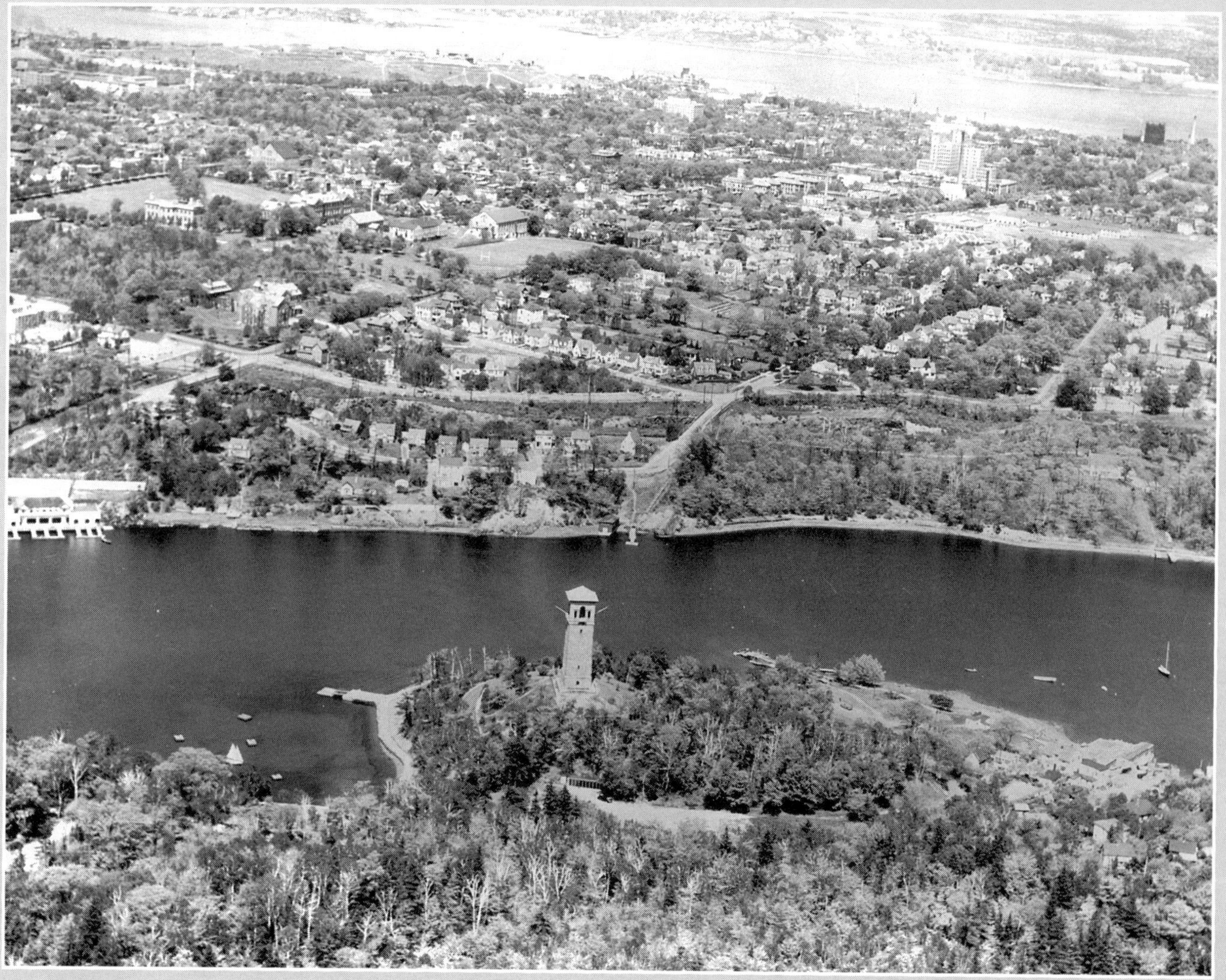

12. "Aerial View, City of Dartmouth October 1988"

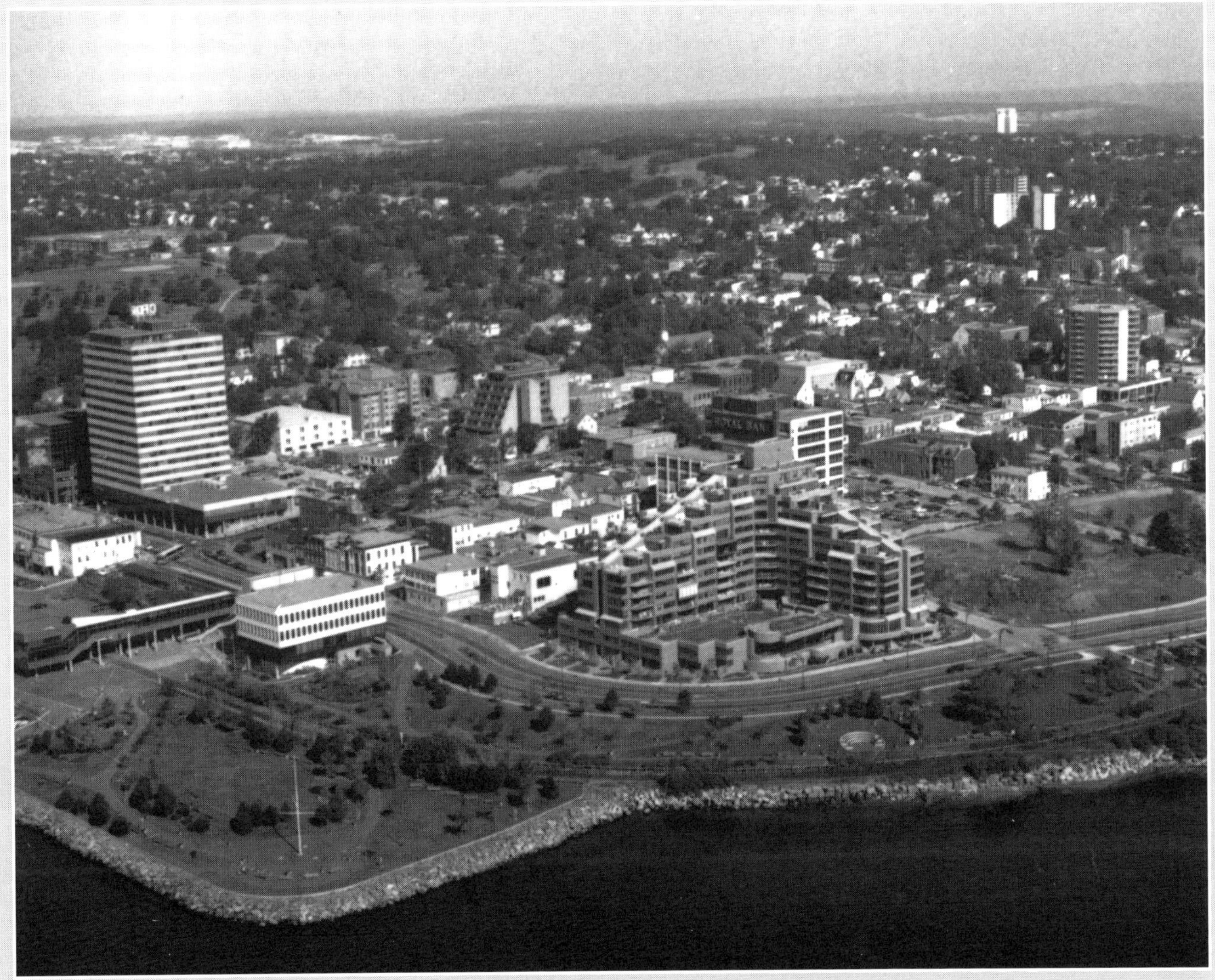

This contemporary view of Dartmouth shows Ferry Terminal Park on the waterfront, adjoining Dartmouth City Hall to the left and several recently-built downtown developments. The high-rise building in the left background is Queen's Square and the apartment tower in the centre foreground is Admiralty Place.

13. "HALIFAX WATERFRONT JULY 1997"

This contemporary aerial view of Halifax's central business district shows the impact of high-rise development grafted on to a 250-year-old urban grid. The Citadel, which once dominated the landscape, now appears discreetly tucked in behind the high-rises of the late twentieth century, successors to the old downtown core with its clusters of wharves, sheds and low-rise commercial buildings.

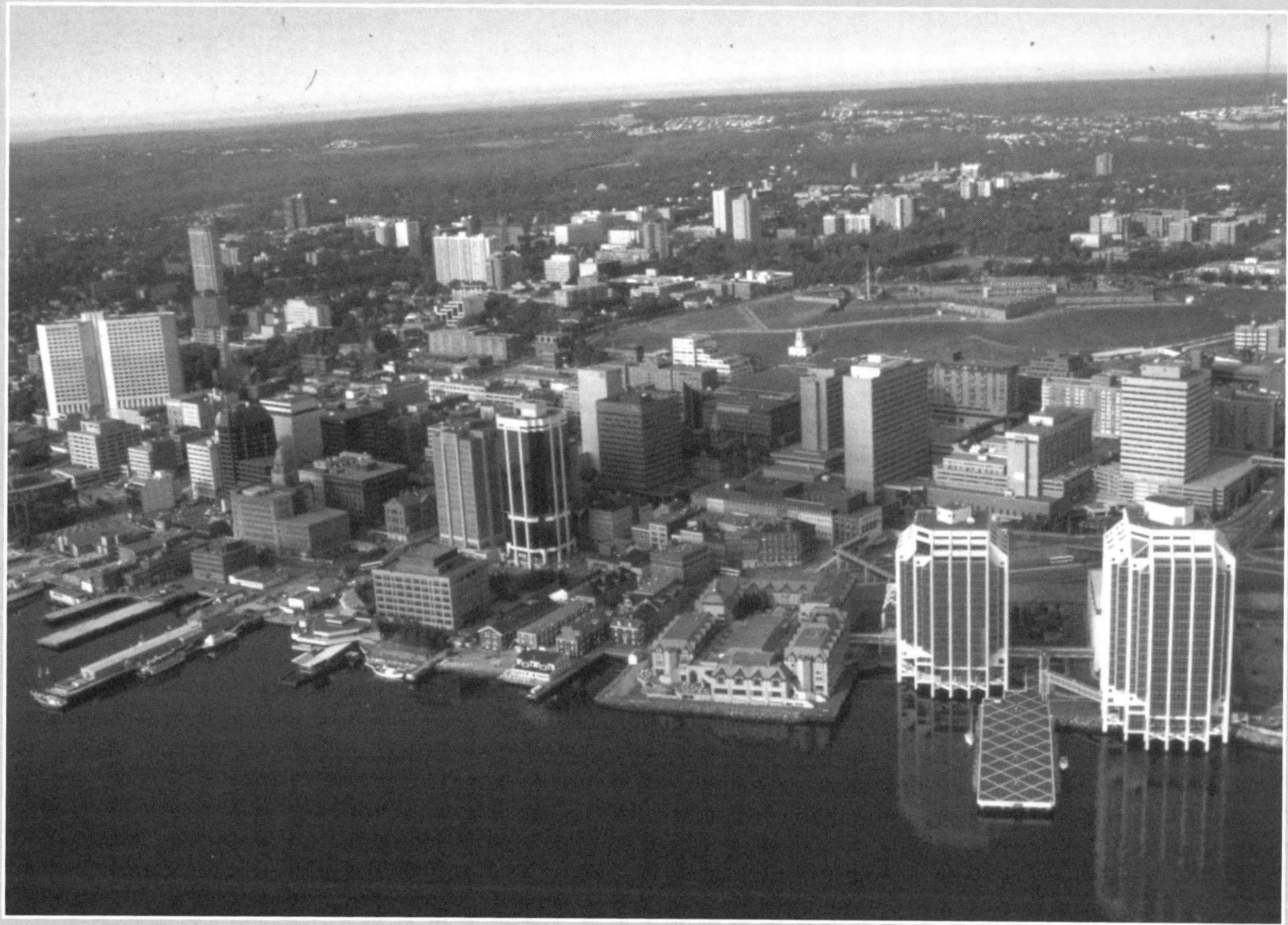

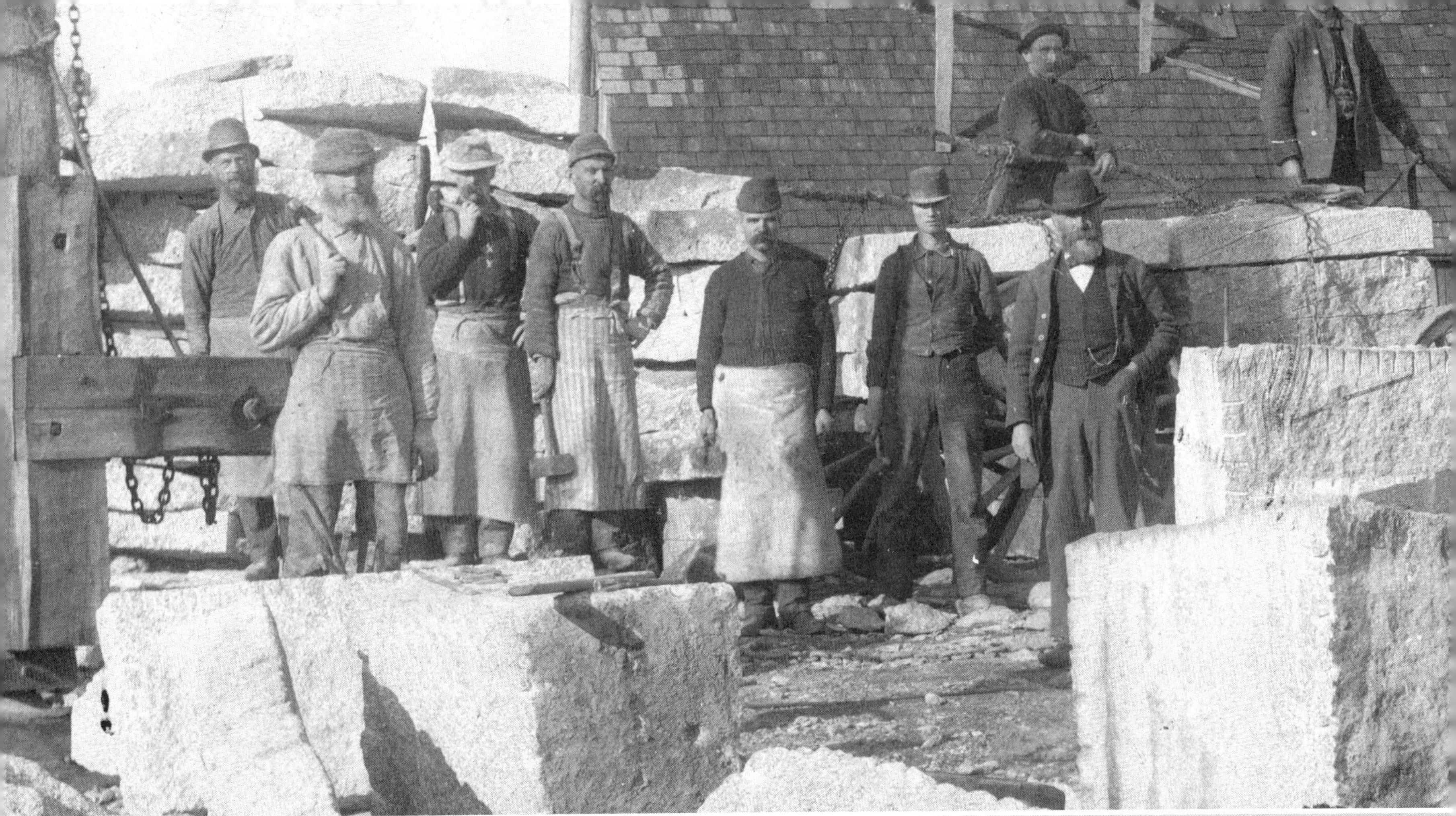

CHAPTER 2

OCCUPATIONS

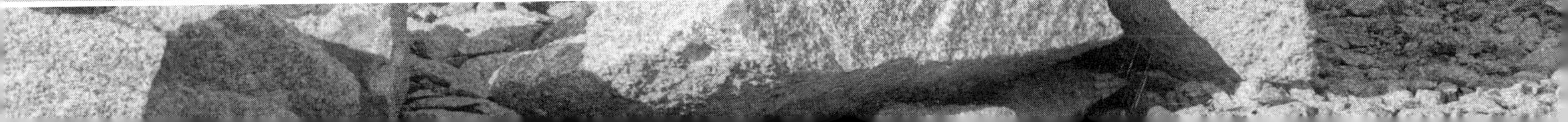

In his bicentenary history of the city, *Halifax: Warden of the North*, Thomas H. Raddall wrote of the eighteenth-century community that:

> *...behind the industry of the merchants and townsfolk flourished the other side of Halifax; the brothels, the drinking dens, the underworld which nourished itself on the vices of the troops and fleet. Already the town was reputed the most wicked in North America. A Yankee settler, writing home to the Reverend Dr. Styles about this Sodom of the frontier, made a famous quip: 'There are 1,000 houses in the town. We have upwards of 100 licensed [drinking] houses and perhaps as many without license, so the business of one half the town is to sell rum and the other half to drink it.' His arithmetic was not quite equal to his wit, and his famous generality ignored the fact that the land and sea forces, who kept most of the taverns going, outnumbered the townsfolk by five or six to one.*

The proportion of drinking establishments to general population had indeed changed dramatically by 1881, when Halifax City and County had only 51 bar-keepers—but 23 brewers and distillers.

The Dominion Census of 1881 listed 12,933 people employed in Halifax city and 10,632 people employed in the county. The statistics were further broken down into those individuals working in agriculture (251 in the city; 3,112 in the county); in commerce (3,293; 849); in domestic employment (2,351; 648); in industry (4,588; 4,533); in the professions (812; 303); and those not classified (1,638; 1,187). Of those employed in the county, 52% were either fishermen (2,466) or farmers (3,086); interestlingly enough, there were 55 women calling themselves the latter. Servants totalled 2014 individuals in the city (262 male; 1,752 female) and 588 in the county (114 male; 474 female). There were 56 physicians and surgeons (44 in the city; 12 in the county) and 72 midwives (65; 7). Government employees numbered only 146 (117; 29), and municipal workers were even fewer (29; 6). The military, a conspicuously large group, were—as usual—absent from the returns, being British in origin, transient in the community, and therefore not enumerated like the permanent population.

From the earliest days, most people living outside the city in what later became Halifax County, were employed in agriculture, lumbering, the fisheries, shipbuilding or other marine-related occupations. However, after gold was discovered at Mooseland in 1858, mining operations were established along the Eastern Shore at Waverley, Montague, Tangier, Moose River, Caribou Gold Mines, Dufferin Mines, Harrigan Cove and other communities, continuing well into the twentieth century.

In 1909, I.J. Isaacs produced, with the approval of the local Board of Trade, a 'booster' booklet entitled *The City of Halifax, The Capital of Nova Scotia, Canada: Its Advantages and Facilities.* Isaacs wrote that Halifax "is the leading manufacturing centre of the Maritime Provinces. The industries carried on here are of a diversified character...." The city's iron and metal-works included a large rolling mill, various foundries, a number of machine shops and several engineering plants. Other manufacturing concerns included large sugar refineries in Halifax and Dartmouth, with 700-800 employees; an extensive cable, rope, and twine factory in Dartmouth; a plant for the manufacture of railway cars; one of the largest clothing factories in the country; a cotton-goods factory; a large boot-and-shoe factory; a paint works; four breweries; a chocolate, coffee, and spices factory; and an extensive manufactory of breads, biscuits, and confectionary.

By comparison, in 1991, exactly 110 years after the 1881 Dominion Census, the metropolitan labour force totalled some 182,310 individuals, working in the following categories: government service (16.52%), retail trade (12.67%), health and social service (10.69%), education (7.53%), manufacturing (6.84%), accommodation, food, and beverage service (6.24%), construction (5.87%), business service (5.63%), wholesale trade (4.89%), finance and insurance (4.82%), transportation and storage (4.44%), communication and other utilities (4.13%), real estate operators and insurance agents (1.68%), fishing and trapping (0.52%), agriculture and related service (0.46%), mining, milling, quarrying, and oil wells (0.35%), logging and forestry (0.22%) and other service industries (6.5%).

1. "Union Engine Company, No. 6 (Alma), in dress uniform, with No. 3 Steam Fire-engine and the old Hand Fire-engine; of about 1855; in front of Queen St. Engine House, 52 Queen St., Halifax, on the occasion of a firemen's tournament c 1878"

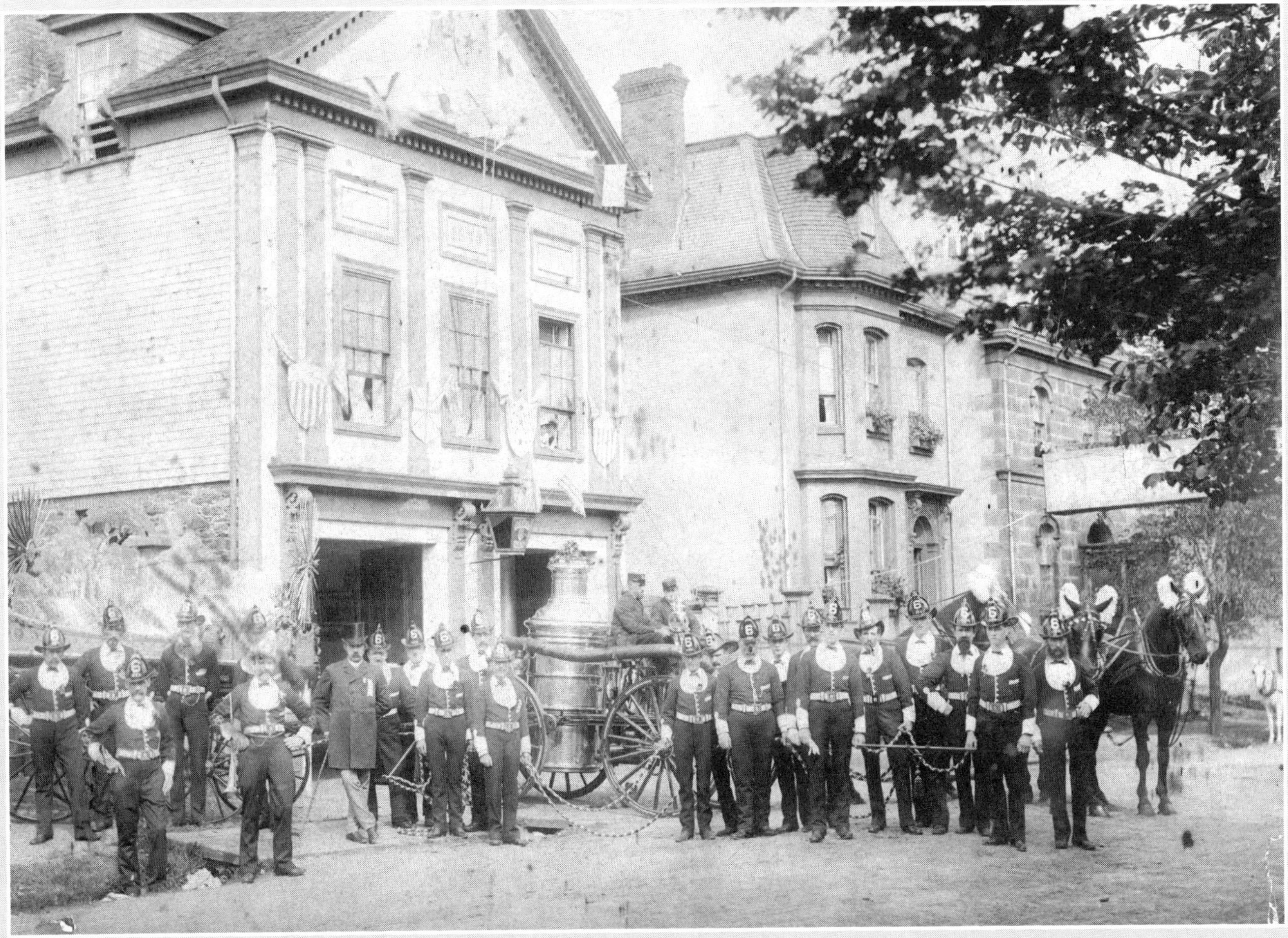

An old, tumbledown building on Queen Street was transformed in 1878 into the Union Engine Company No. 6 Engine House. Designed by the City Engineer of the time, Edward H. Keating, the building still stands today, adjoining the entrance to Fort Massey Cemetery on Queen Street—no longer a fire station, but otherwise not greatly altered on the exterior.

2. CS *MacKay-Bennett* in dry dock, Halifax
between 1885 and 1922

The Cable Ship *MacKay-Bennett*, launched in 1884, was named for two founders of the Commercial Cable Company, John W. MacKay and James G. Bennett. The vessel arrived in Halifax in March 1885, based here to facilitate the at-sea repairs of underwater telegraph cables in the North Atlantic. The vessel is most famous for its part in the RMS *Titanic* disaster, when it was hired by the White Star Line to recover bodies from the mishap. Departing Halifax on April 17, 1912, the *MacKay-Bennett* returned on April 30 having reclaimed 306 bodies, of which 116 were buried at sea and the other 190 brought into port.

The vessel continued at Halifax until 1922, when it was retired to Plymouth, England and used as a cable-storage hulk. Bombed and sunk during World War II, it was refloated and used again as a hulk until 1961, when it was finally scrapped.

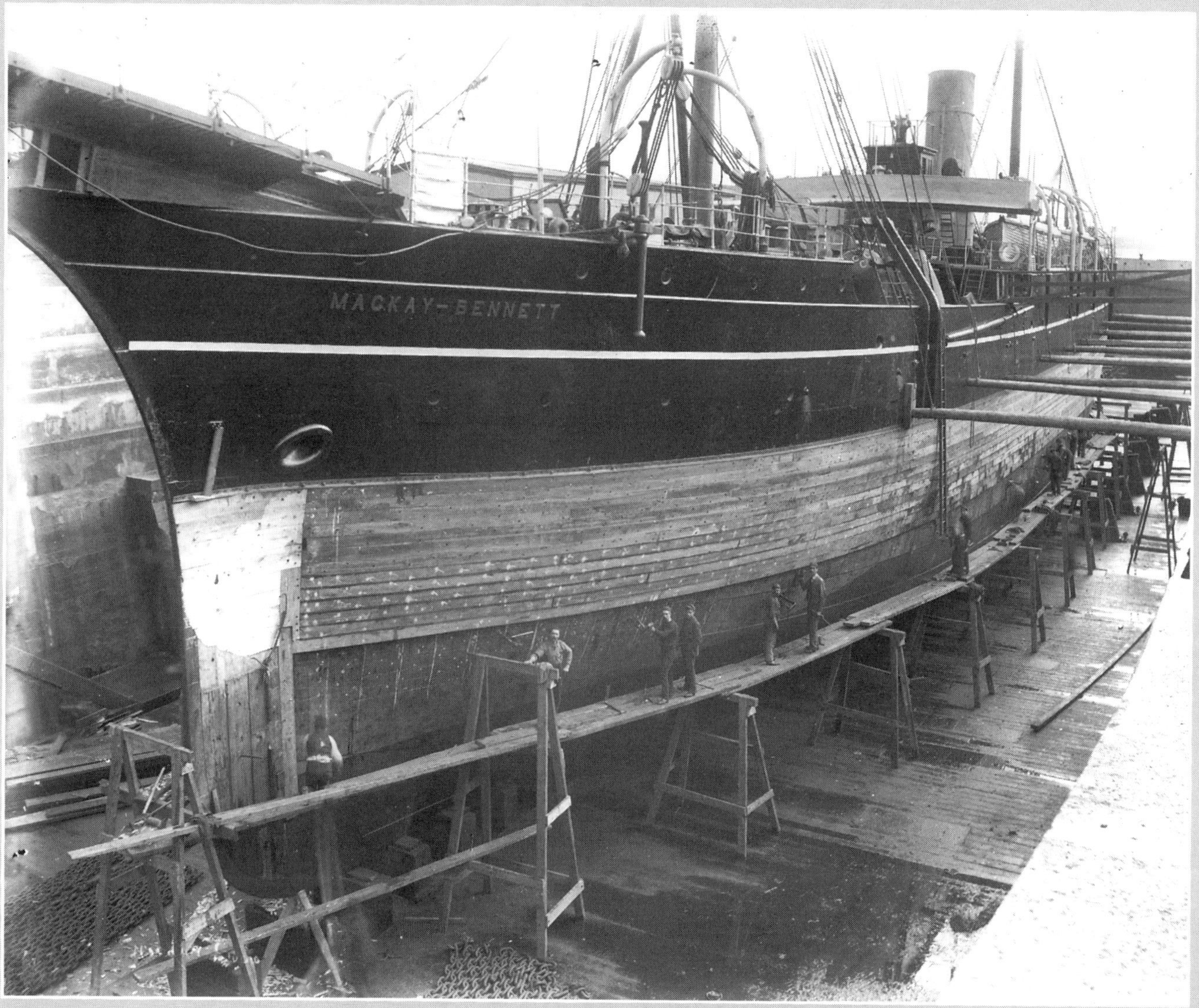

3. "Faders Bros. Market, 8-10 Bedford Row 1885"

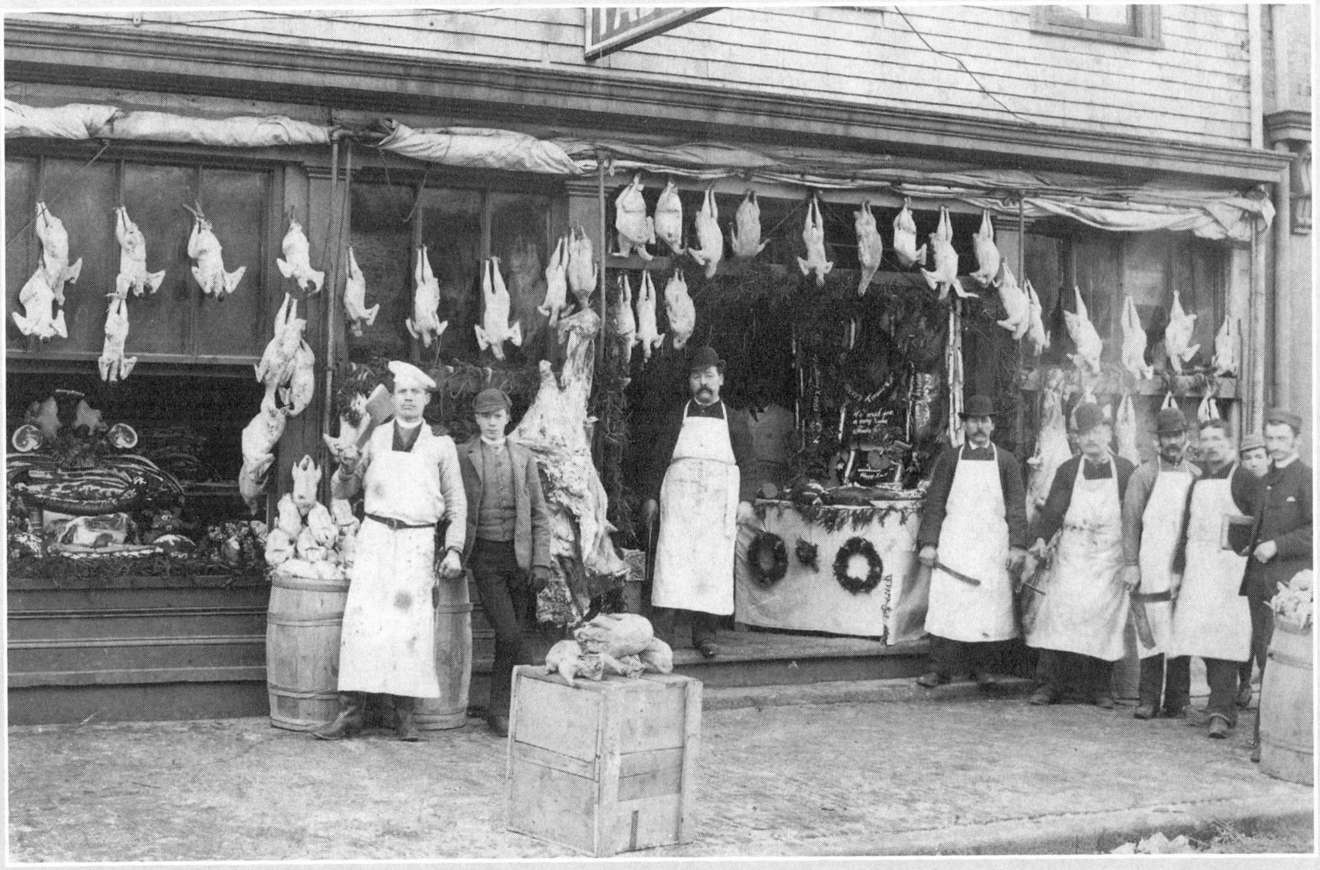

Fader Brothers, wholesale and retail victuallers and dealers in all kinds of meats, vegetables, provisions, etc. was established in 1877 by Albert, John, and Silas Fader. The firm moved to this location in 1885, but went out of business in 1888.

4. "J A Leaman & Co.
8-10 Bedford Row, formerly
owned by Faders Bros., 1890"

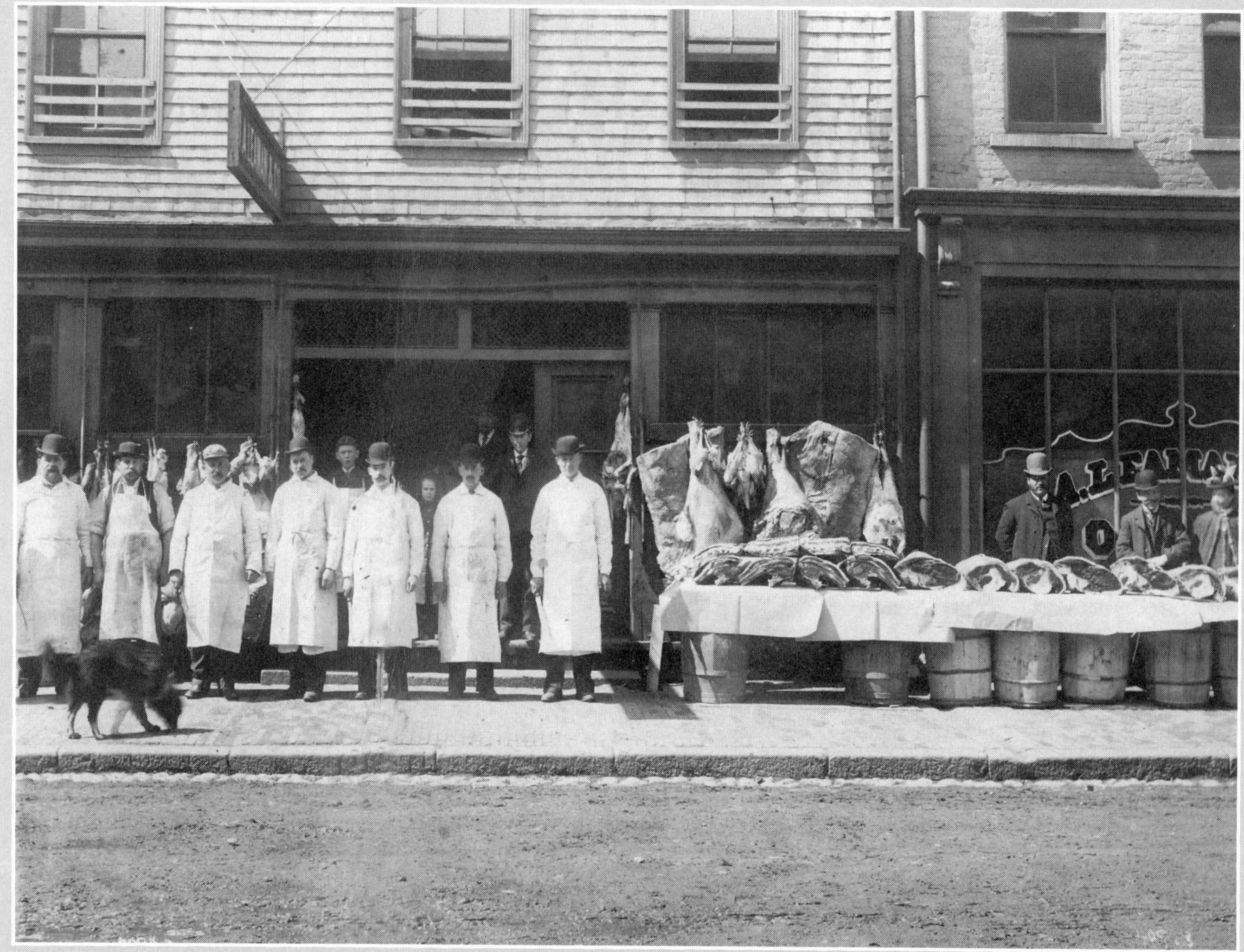

J.A. Leaman & Company was established in 1864. The company's advertisement in *McAlpine's Halifax City Directory* for 1890-91 listed the business as wholesale and retail victuallers, pork packers and manufacturers of canned goods and bologna. The retail stores were at 6-10 Bedford Row, the offices were at number 12, and the packing establishment was across the street at 13-15 Bedford Row.

5. Stiffened Treble Sling Bridge constructed by 18th Co. at Halifax

September 1897

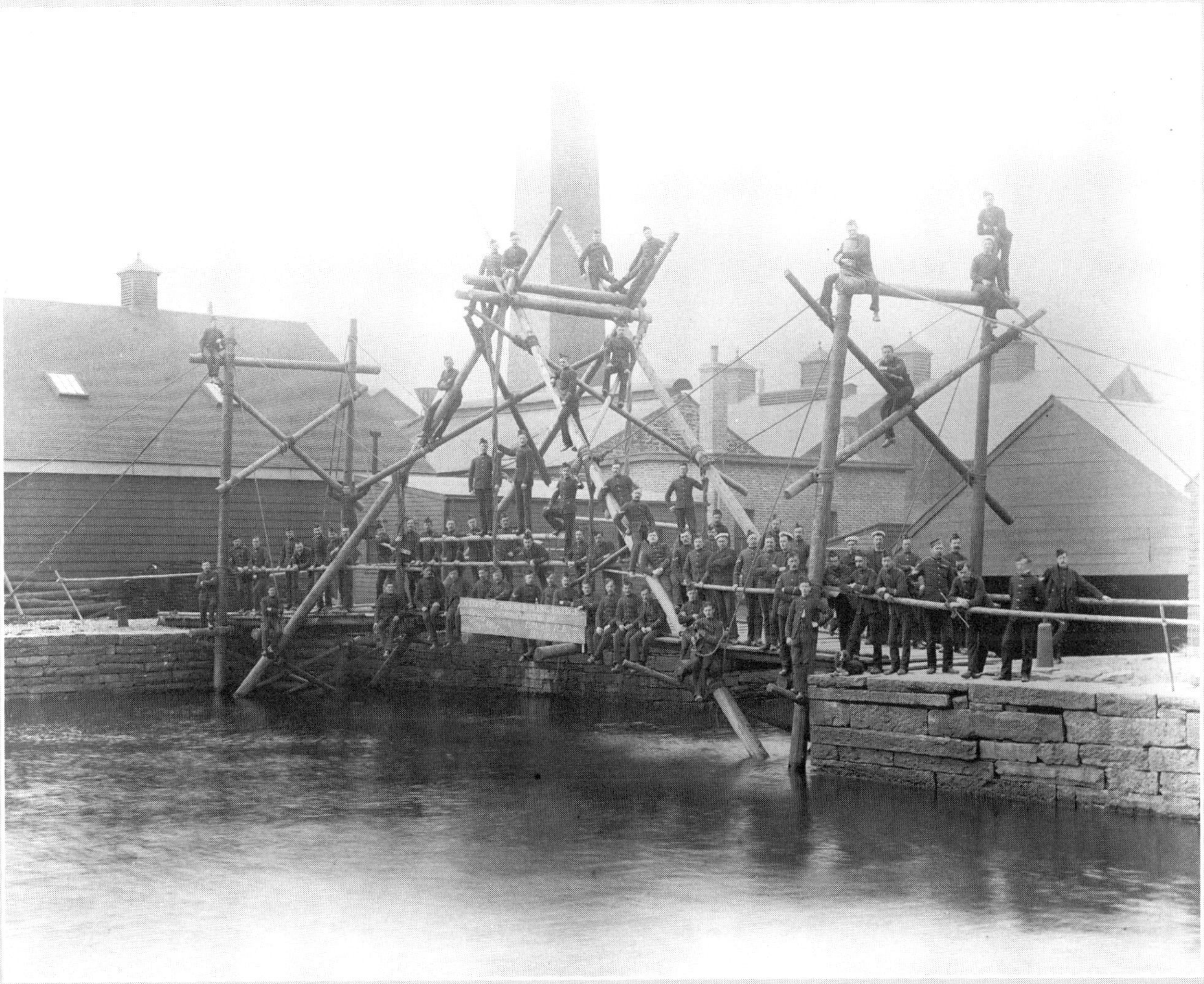

The Royal Engineers provided the surveyors, architects, engineers, builders, and contractors for all British army and navy installations throughout the Empire. From the earliest days of the community until the British forces left in 1906, the Royal Engineers were always represented within the Halifax Garrison.

6. Quarry scene, Spryfield
189–

The reverse of this photograph shows the name 'Andrew Yeadon.' *McAlpine's Halifax City Directory* for 1909 lists Andrew Yeadon, of Yeadon's Quarry, residing at 160 Quinpool Road. On Geological Survey Map Sheet 68 (1908), the Yeadon Granite Quarry is between the Herring Cove Road and Long Lake, Spryfield.

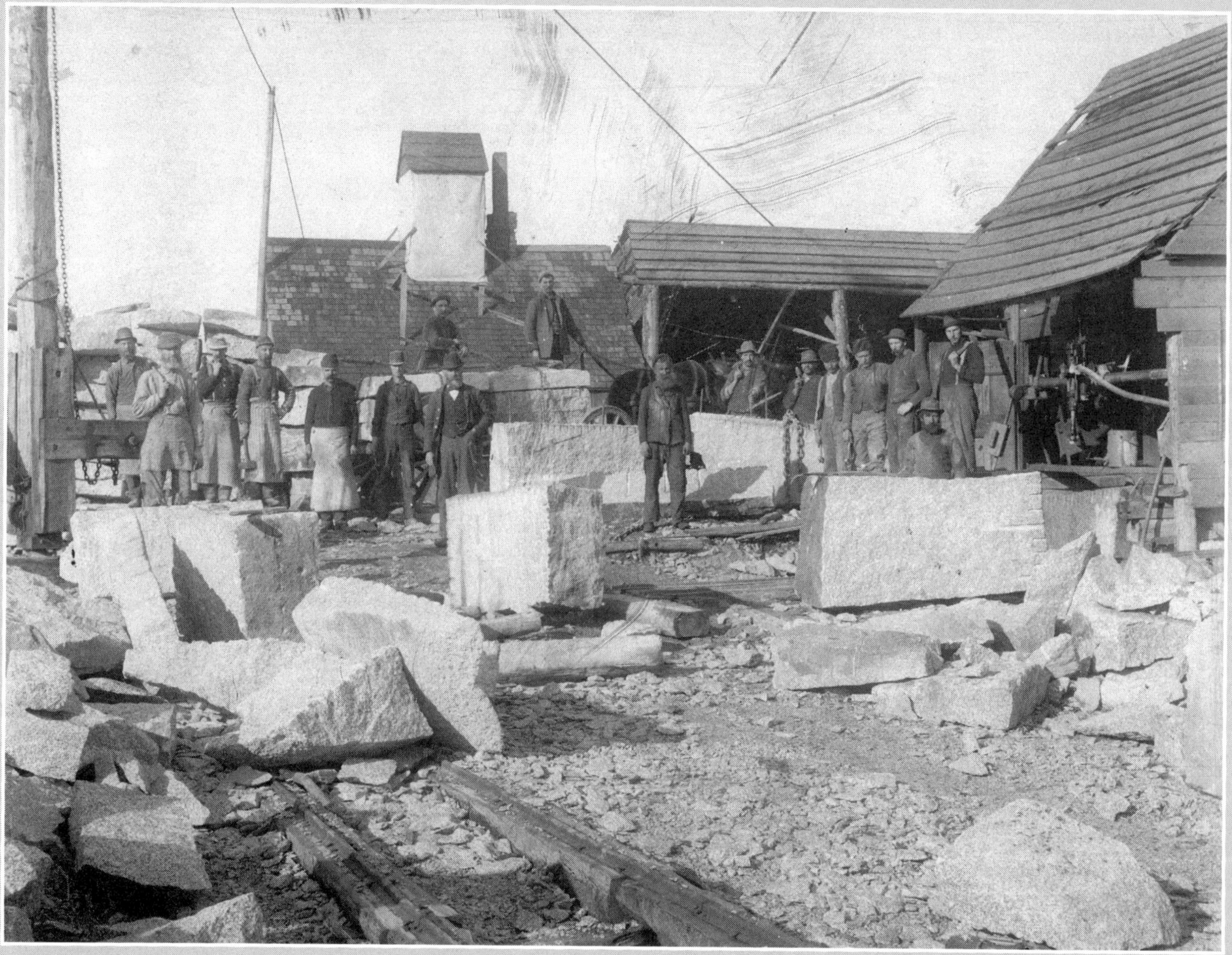

7. From a map of the province of Nova Scotia (City of Halifax Sheet No. 68)

1908

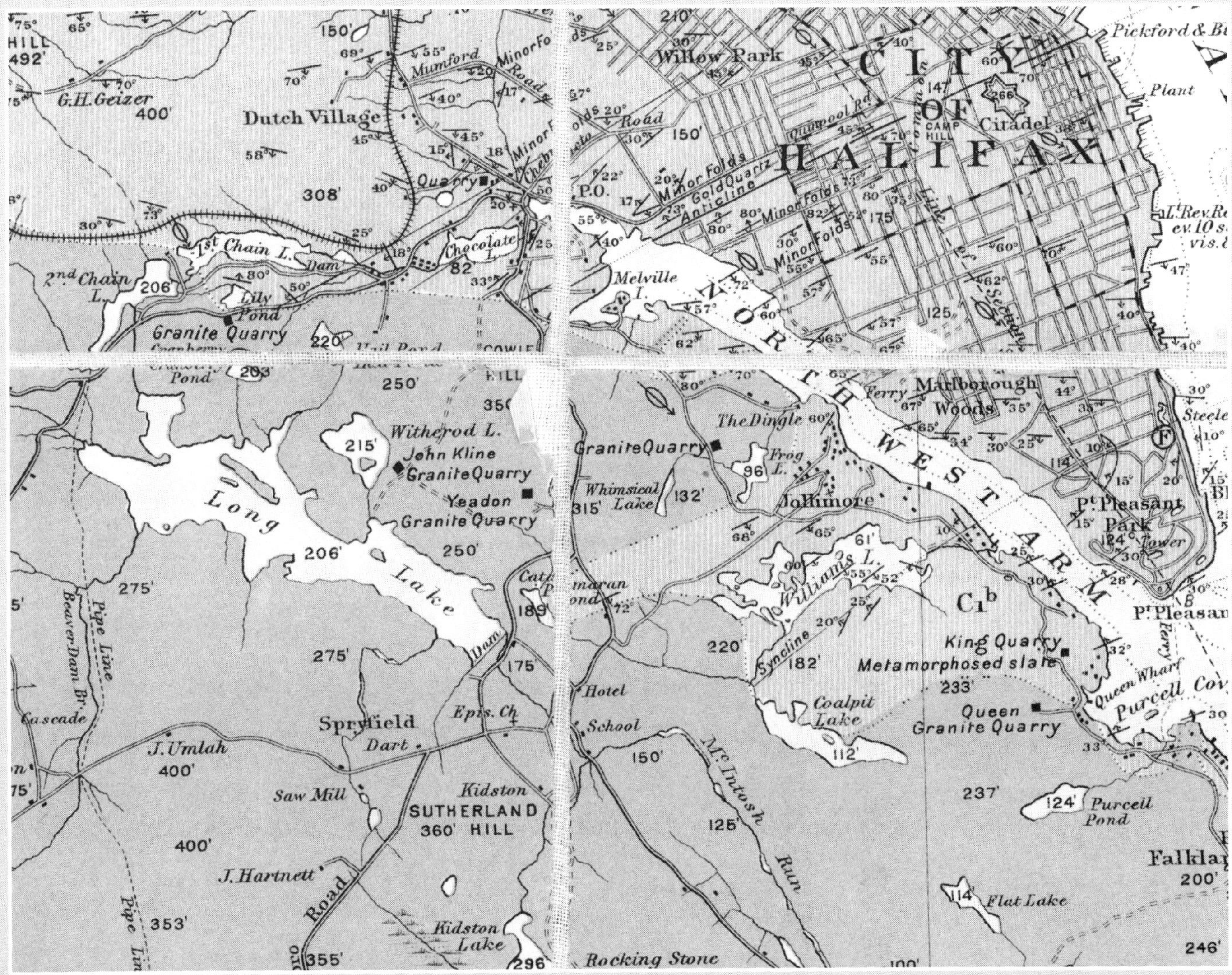

This map identifies a number of granite quarries in the general area of the North West Arm, Purcell's Cove, and Spryfield.

Clayton and Sons, wholesale manufacturers of men's, youths' and boys' clothing of fine and medium grades, was established on Argyle Street in 1869. They manufactured 'A.P.H' brand pants, 'Ladder' overalls and the 'Enn-Ess' clothing label—all products of national reputation. The business moved to Jacob Street in 1875 and a brick building was completed several years later. Another large brick building, fronting Jacob and Barrington, was completed about 1890; and a four-storey brick annex facing Poplar Grove was added about 1897. The three buildings were connected with passageways.

The promotional booklet, *Clayton and Sons, Halifax, Nova Scotia: Thirtieth Anniversary 1869-1900,* includes an illustration similar to this, with the accompanying caption, "Work Room No.1." The booklet noted that this large, well-ventilated room could accommodate 350 employees:

> *In this room are four long tables each containing from 25 to 30 of the most up-to-date machines, many of them made specially for carrying out certain details of boys' and mens' ready-to-wear clothing. All the making up is done in sections and nearly every worker is an expert in his or her special line. This room, as throughout the whole building is kept at an even temperature with hot water heating. Three motors supply electricity for motive power. The electric current is used for lighting the building and also for heating in the Electric Pressing Irons.*

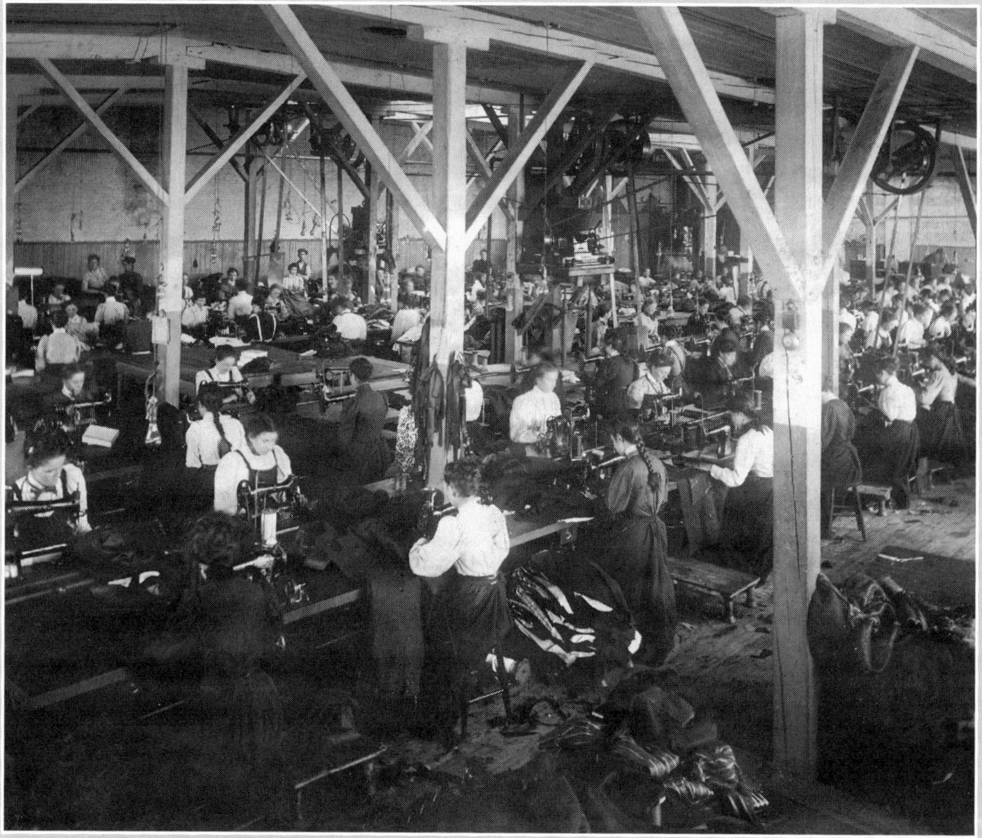

9. Round-up of Wild Sable Island Ponies

c 1900

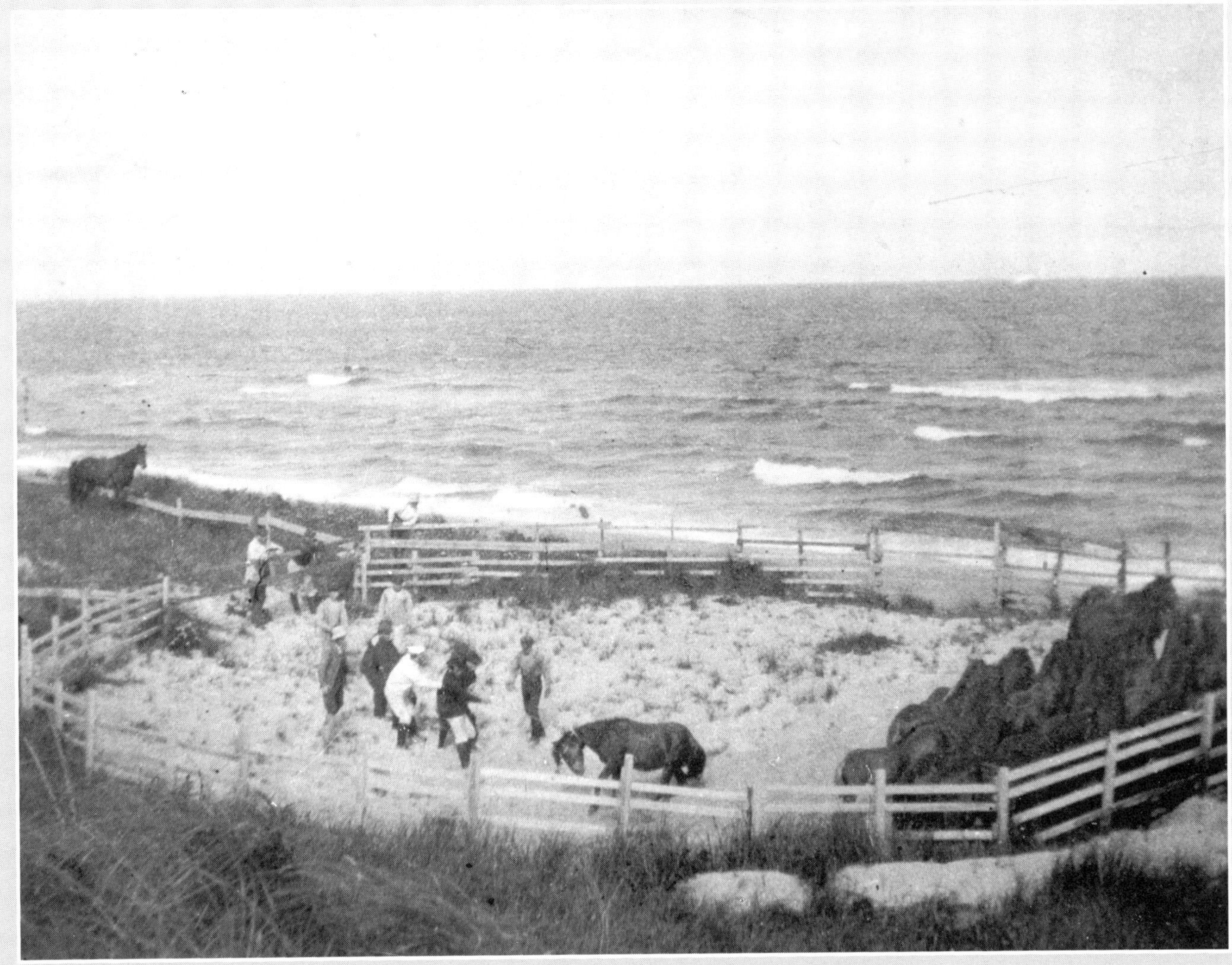

Round-ups of Sable Island ponies commonly occurred twice a year. Since the horses were wild, the work was exhausting and could be dangerous to both man and beast.

10. Sable Island ponies to be sold at auction in Halifax

c 1902

After the appointment of a marine superintendent to Sable Island in 1801, horses were routinely shipped off the island and sold at auction in Halifax, as well as in New England and Newfoundland. Valued for their strength and endurance, these small animals were a familiar sight on the streets of Halifax well into the twentieth century.

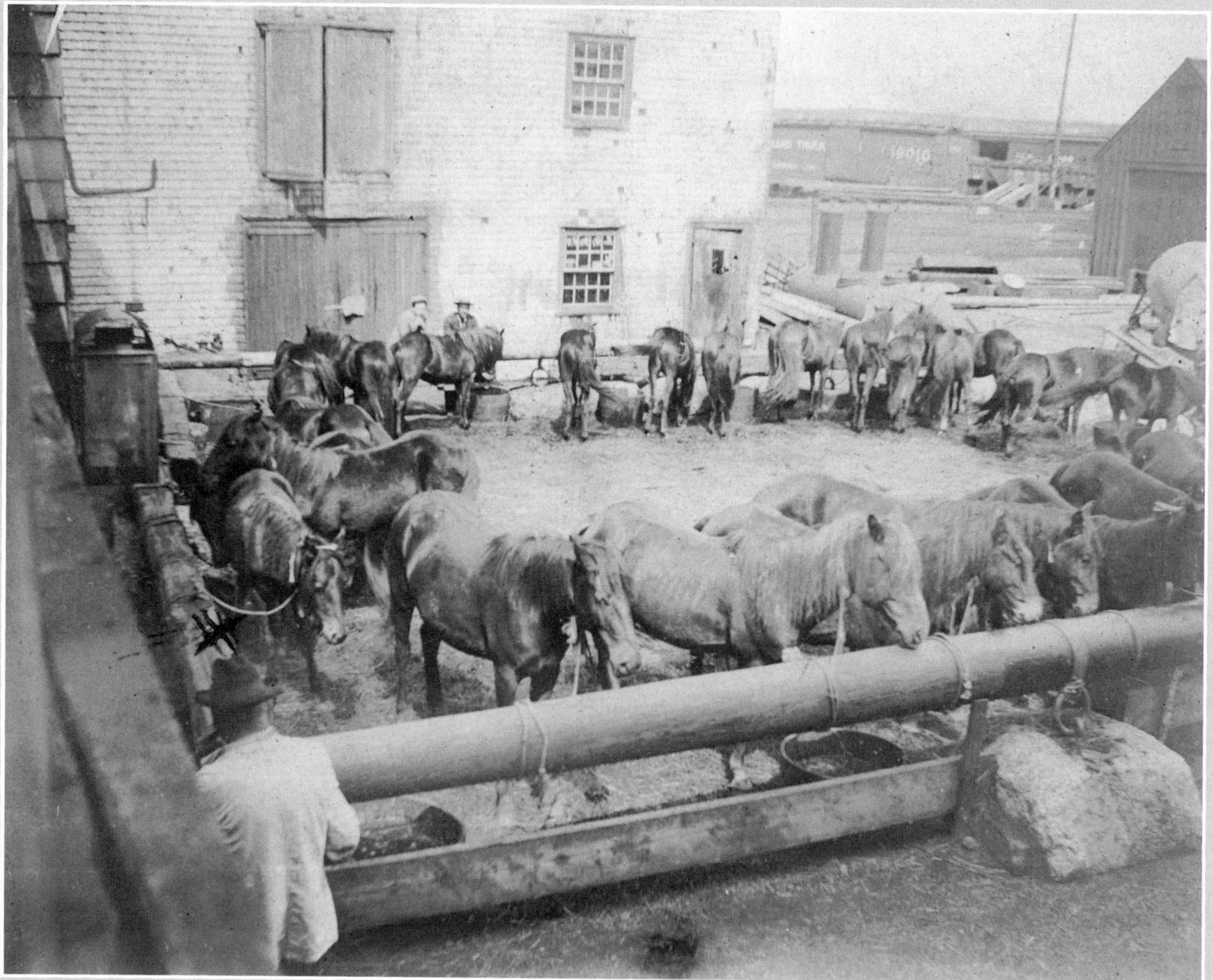

11. Halifax: City Council and Department Heads

1903

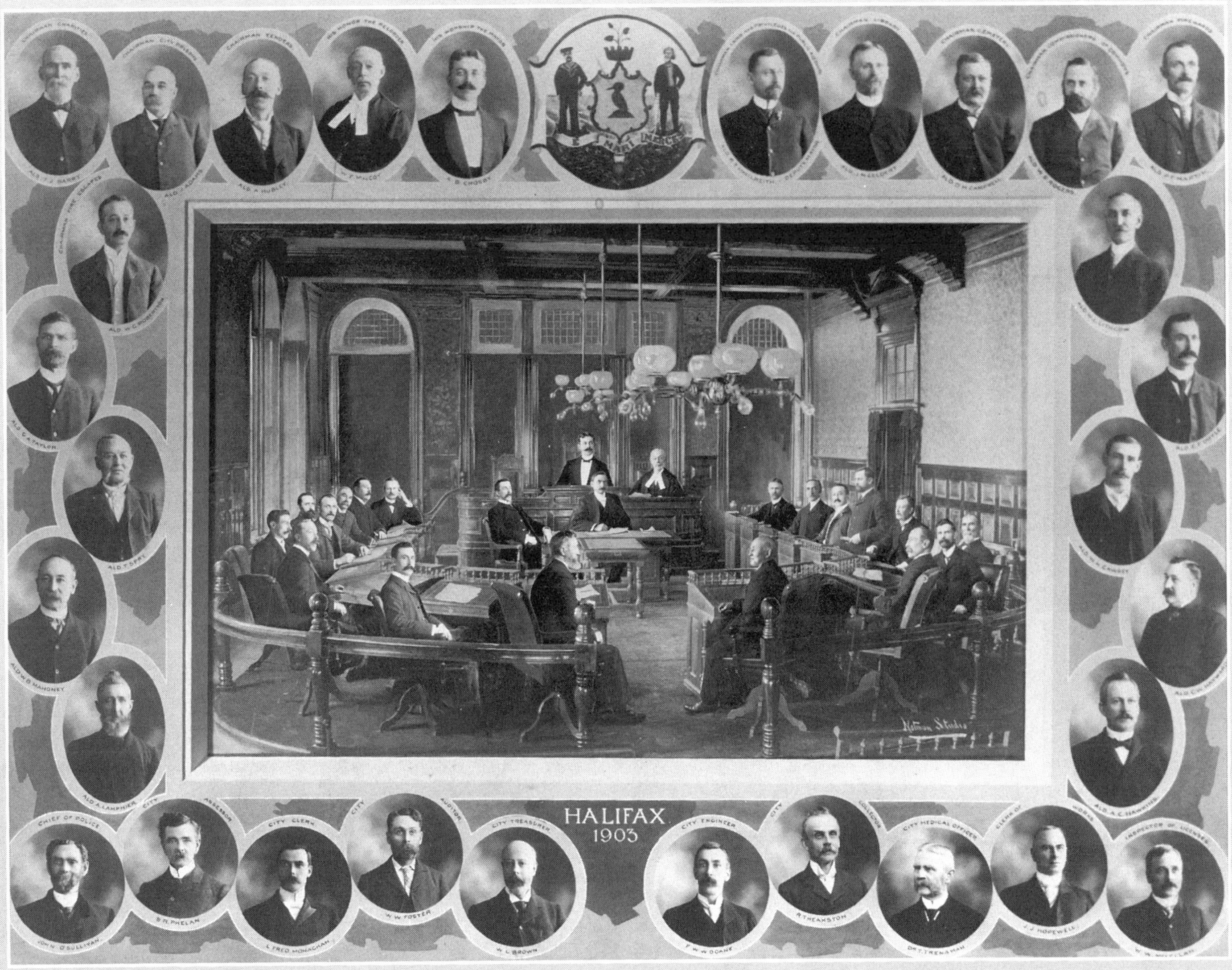

12. Halifax City Police on the Grand Parade 1914

The Halifax Herald for 11 July 1914 reported that:

> *There was a general inspection of the Halifax police force yesterday afternoon on the Parade. The policemen were out in full force with the exception of one or two who are on the sick list. The inspection was by His Worship Mayor Bligh and Controller Harris. Controllers Hoben and Scanlan were also present. Mayor Bligh addrest [sic] the men in a very flattering manner, congratulating them upon the high standard of efficiency which they have attained and assuring them of the protection and co-operation of the Board of Control. Addresses were then heard from Controllers Harris, Scanlan and Hoben in which they offered suggestions for dealing with some of the problems which the police force has to face and pointing out conditions which make it difficult for the law to be properly enforced. Those who have been attending the lectures were given first aid certificates and a large number qualified. Medals were presented those who had successfully completed the gymnasium course at the YMCA....*

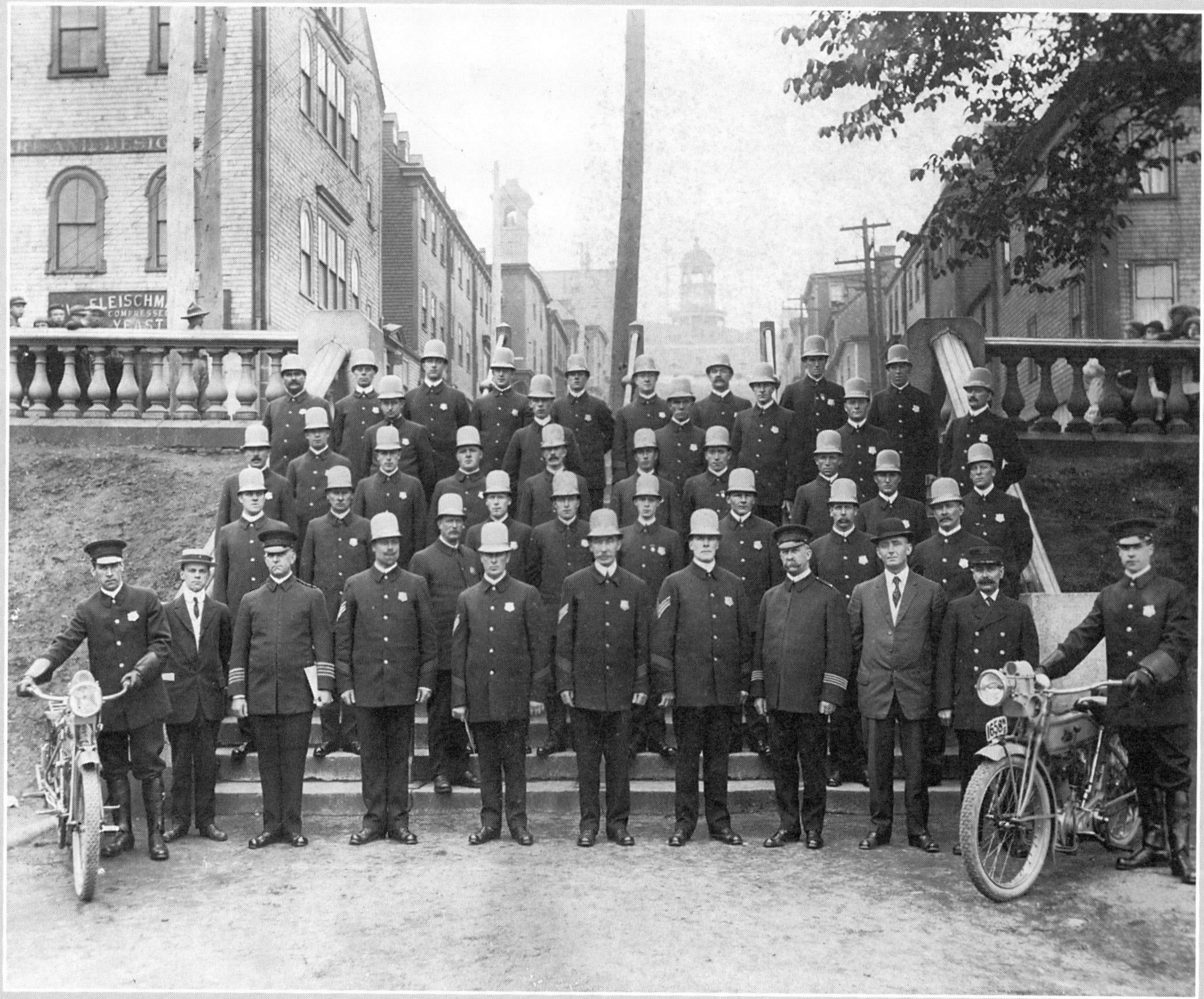

13. Logging Camps near Ingramport, N.S.
193–

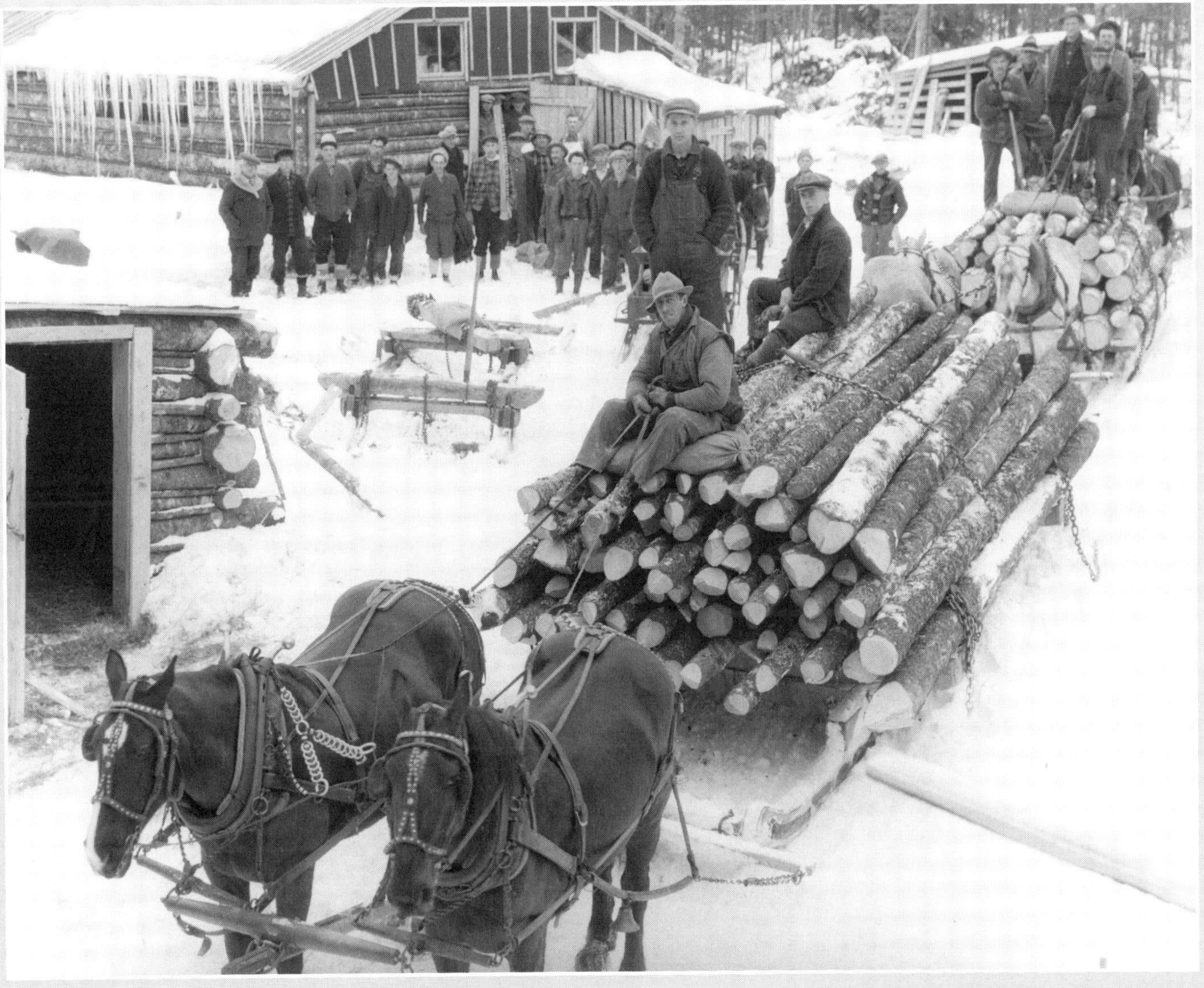

14. Spryfield Volunteer Fire Department
c 1941

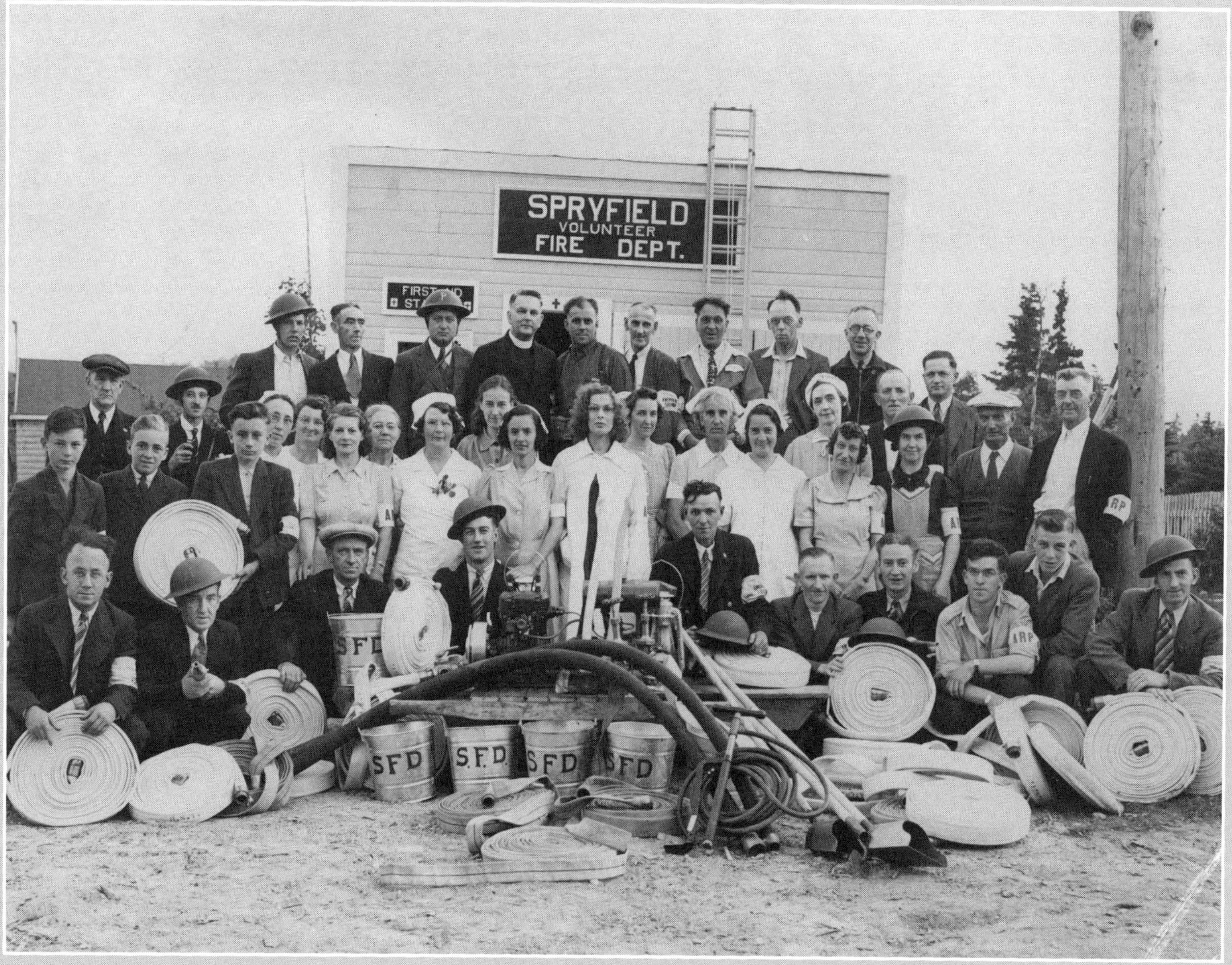

15. Workers filleting fish inside Maritime National Fish Limited Plant, Halifax 1942

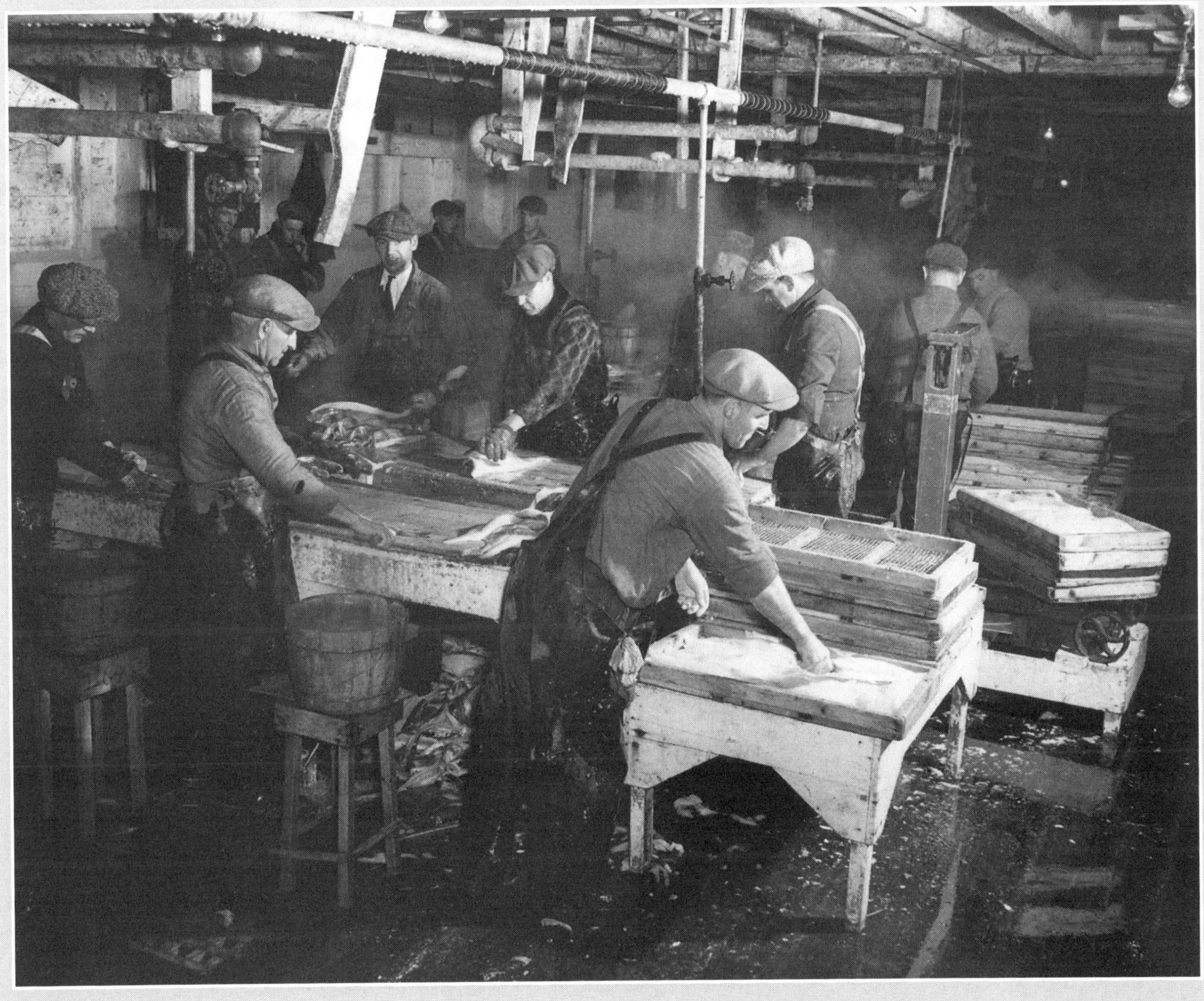

Maritime National Fish Company was located at 35-51 Lower Water Street, just north of Morris on the east or harbour side of the street. The area is now a parking lot.

16. Woman working with Microscope in Atlantic Fisheries Experimental Station, 209 Lower Water Street

January 21, 1947

The woman in the photograph is thought to be Frances E. Dyer, a junior biochemist and the only female scientist known to be working at the Experimental Station in January 1947.

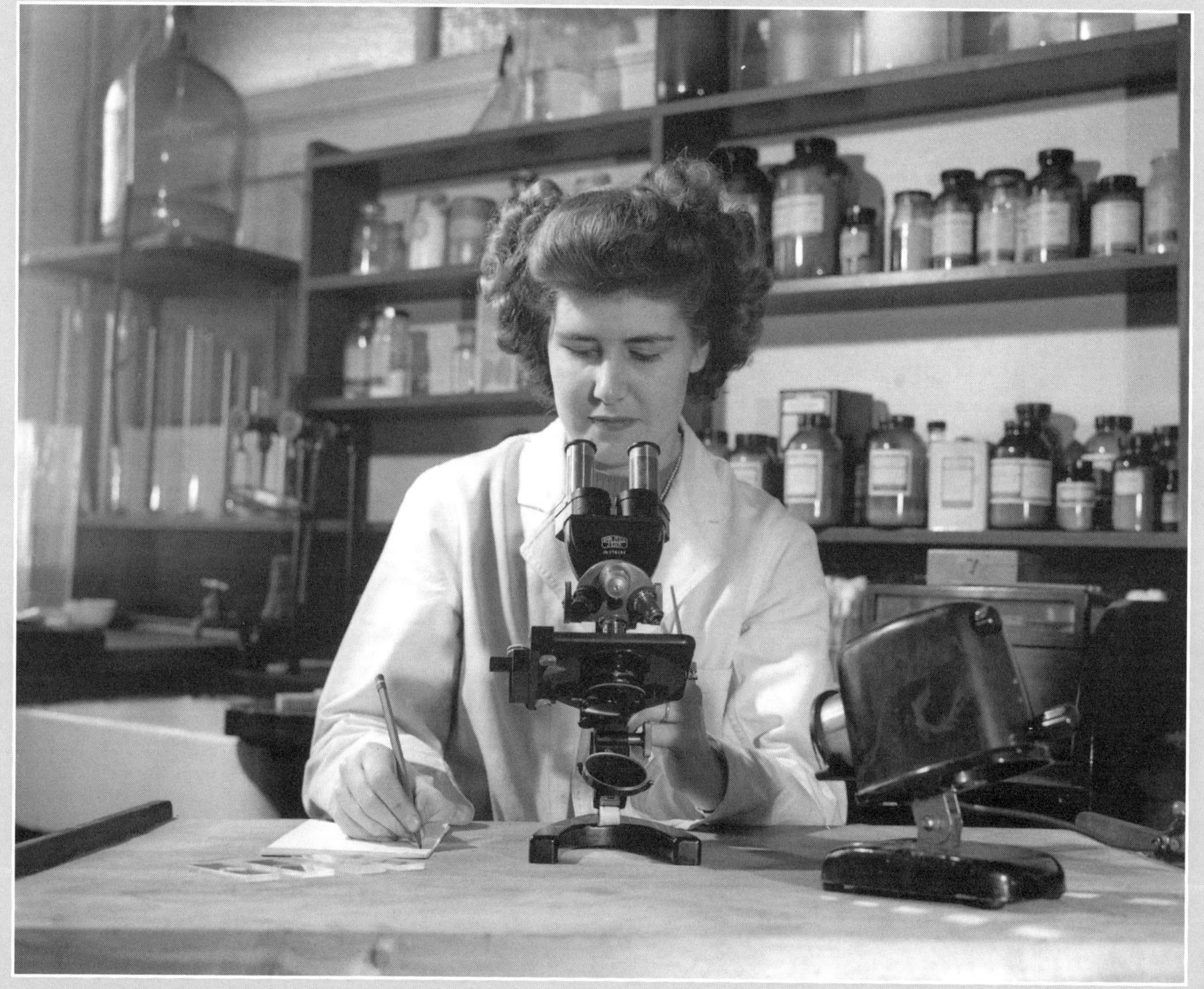

17. Charlie Symonds, a Cooper in Upper Hammonds Plains
1949

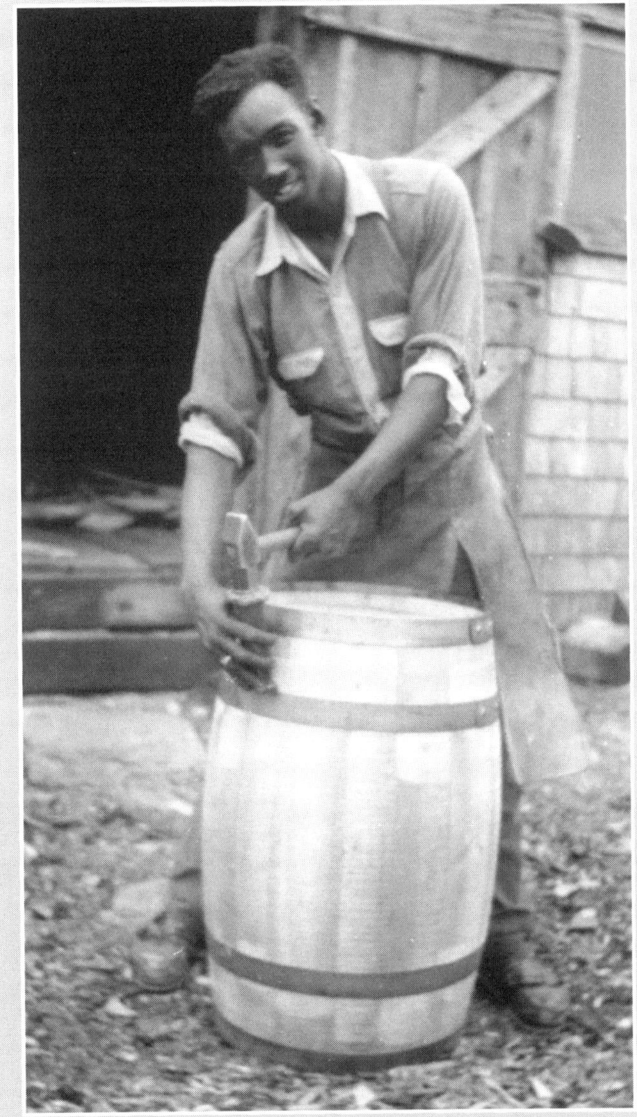

The cooperage shop is behind Mr. Symonds. Charlie made this pickerel barrel in approximately thirty minutes and received $ .30 for his labour. After boring a 'bung' in the side, he blew into it; his breath returning against his face indicated that the barrel was watertight.

18. Cellophane wrapping machine at Moir's Ltd. 1955

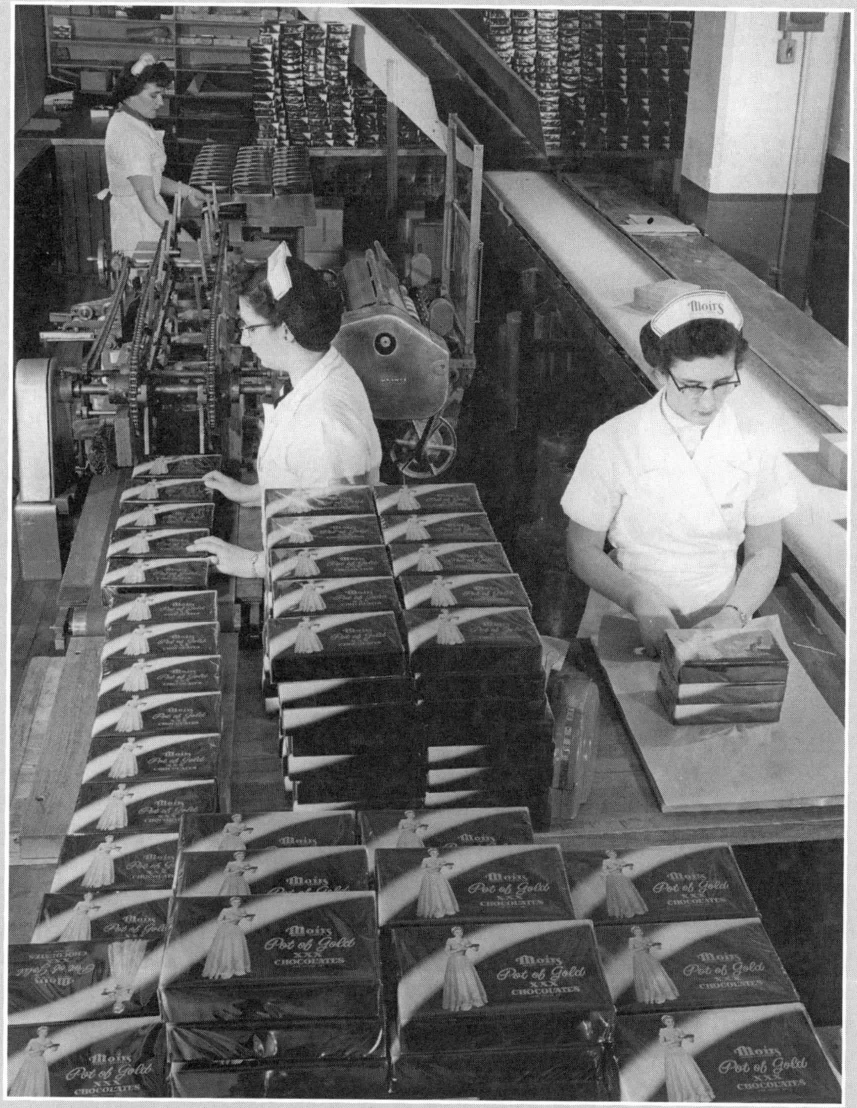

Moir's Limited, manufacturers of biscuits, bread, and confectionery, was founded in 1815 by Benjamin Moir. By the turn of this century, the firm was best known for its high-grade chocolates and candies, its 'XXX' brand being a staple product known and in demand throughout Canada.

19. 'Killocks' (homemade anchors)
Portuguese Cove, N.S.
195–

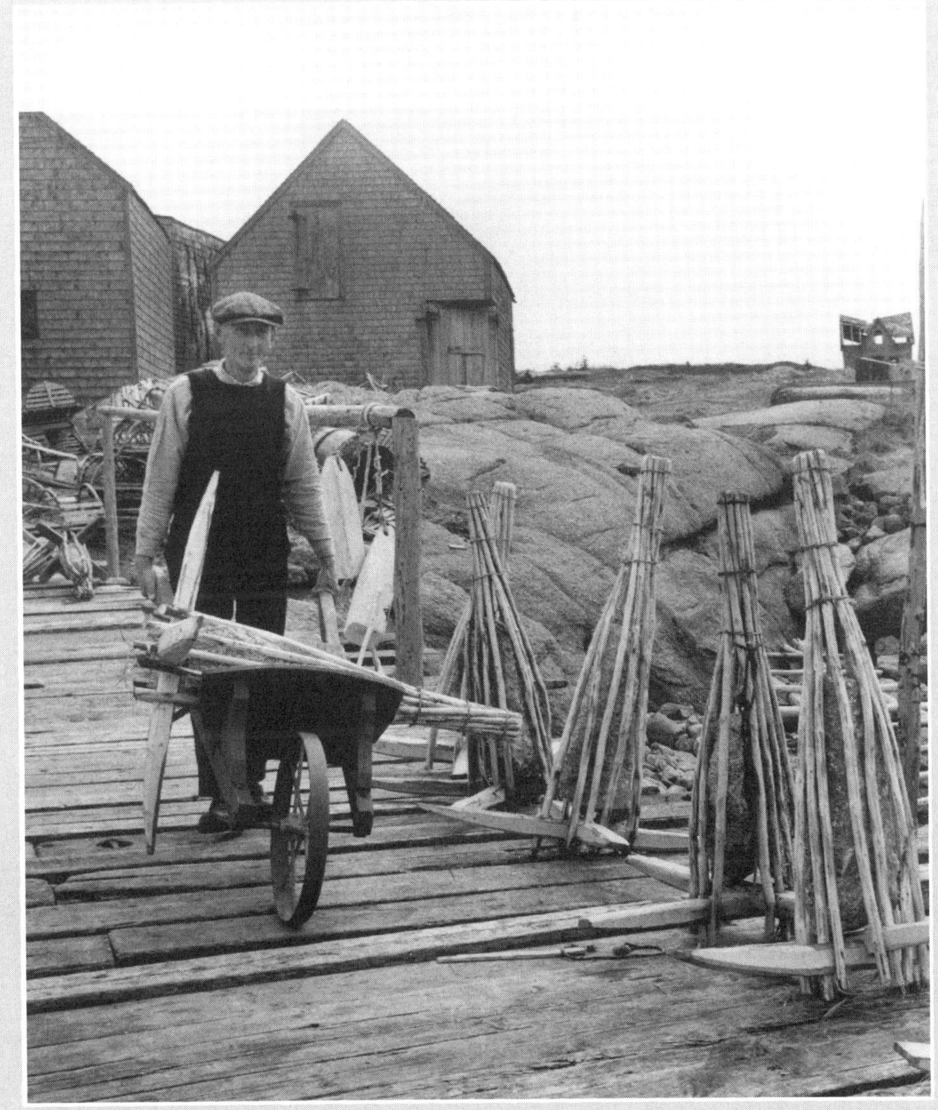

20. Unloading salt cod at Smiths' wharf, Halifax

195–

A. & M. Smith Company were fish exporters and salt importers located at 189 Lower Water Street, adjoining W.M. Robertson & Son Limited, ship chandlers. The Smith buildings were removed and replaced by a modern exhibit wing for the Maritime Museum of the Atlantic in 1981; the storefront of the neighbouring Robertson building has been incorporated directly into the museum's facade.

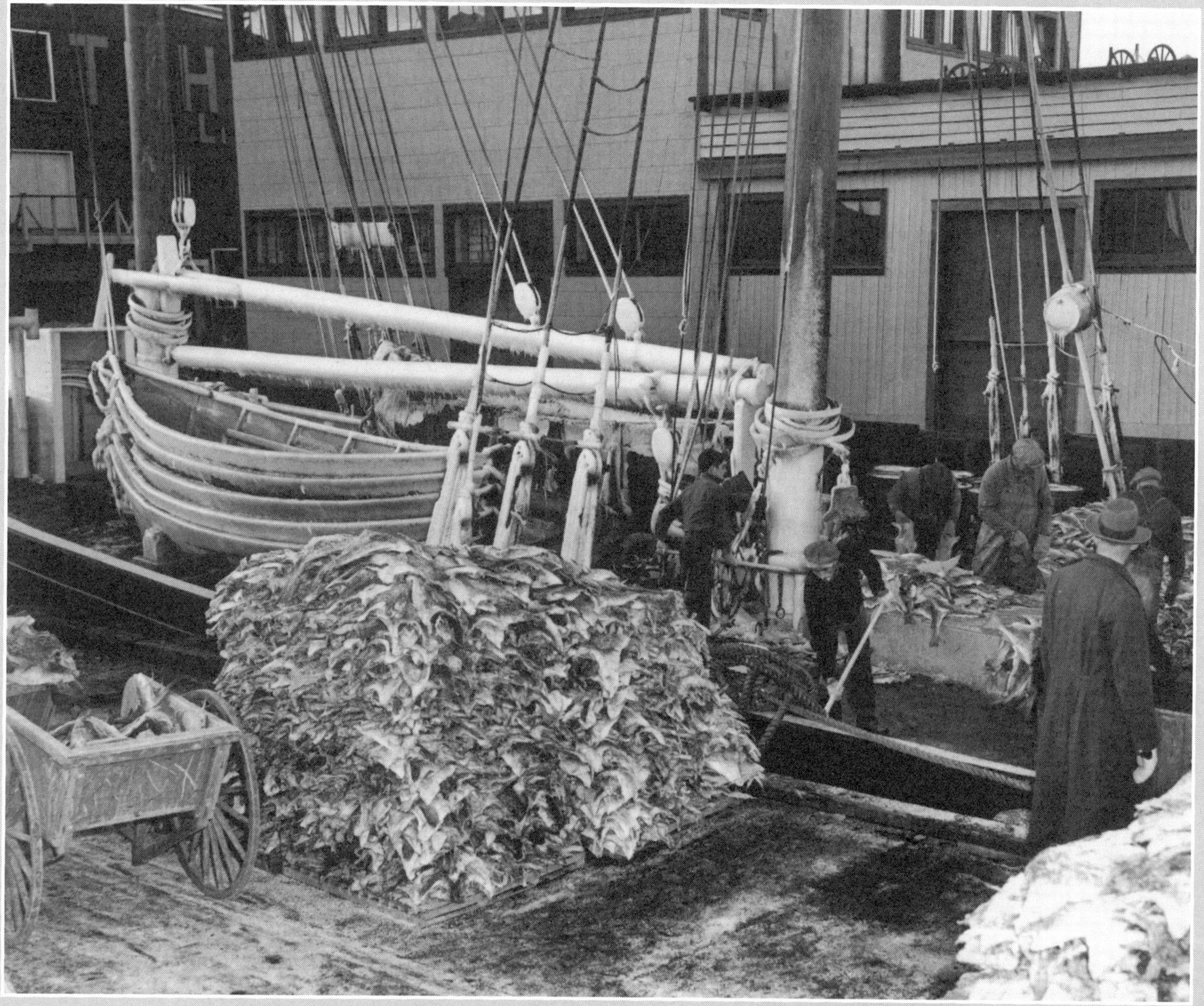

21. "Lathe workers, Halifax Shipyards" 1956

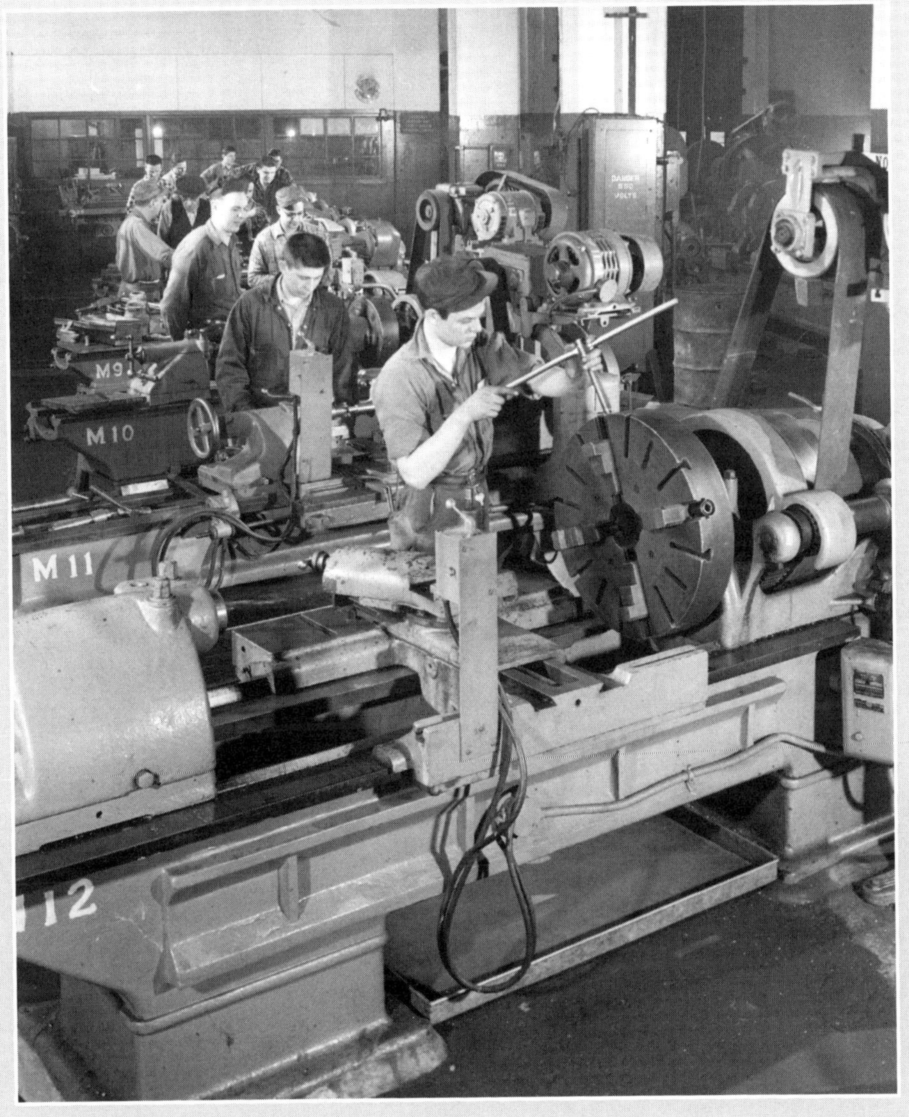

Halifax Shipyards was founded in 1887 as the Halifax Graving Dock Company, providing the city with its first dry-dock facility. Under various ownerships, the facility has continued to repair and/or to build vessels of all kinds for over a century.

22. "Stacking Volvo bodies at Dartmouth"

1963

Volvo opened an assembly plant on the Halifax side of the waterfront in 1967, later moved to a state-of-the-art facility at the new Bayers Lake Industrial Park outside Halifax, but ceased operations in Nova Scotia in 1998.

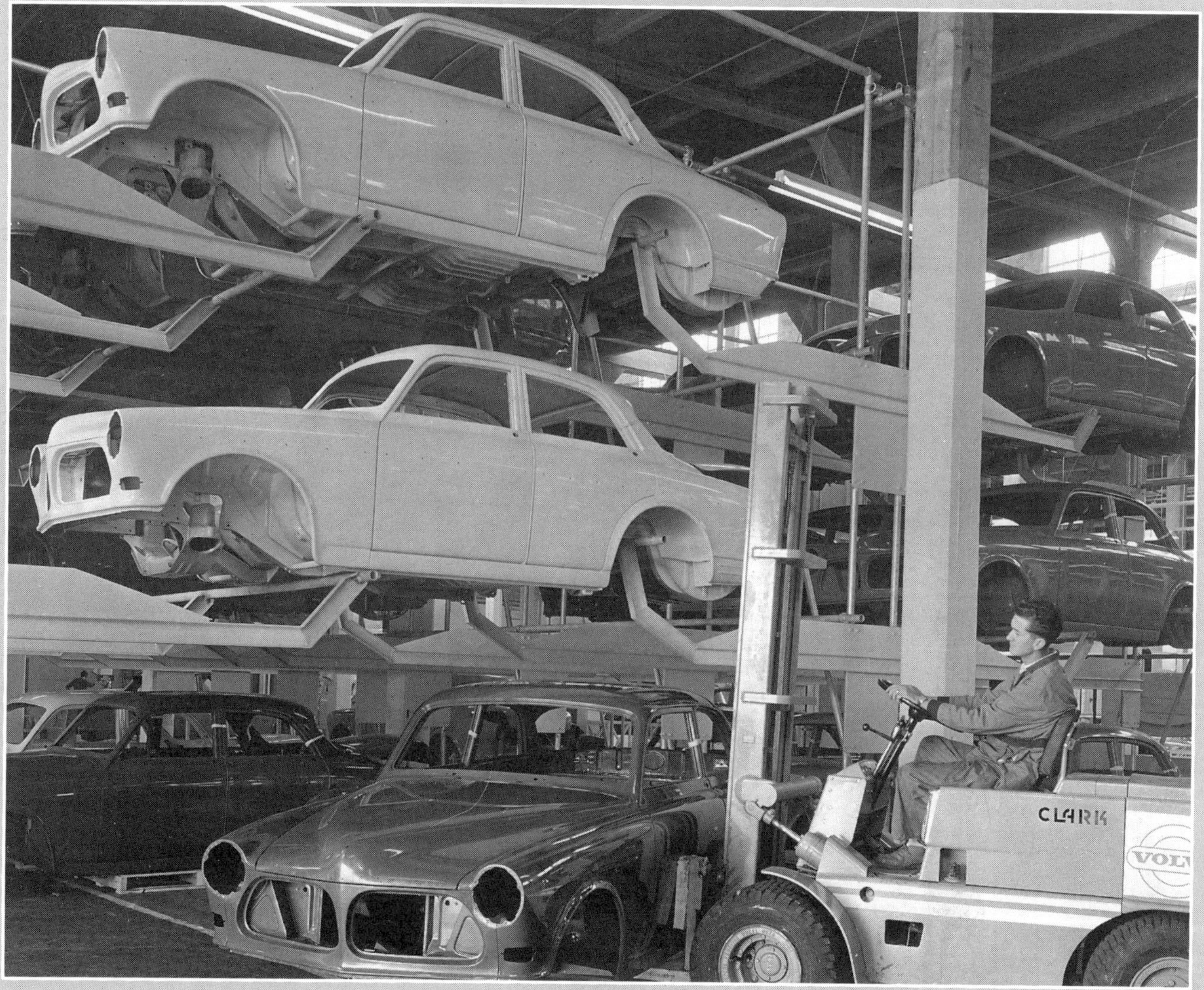

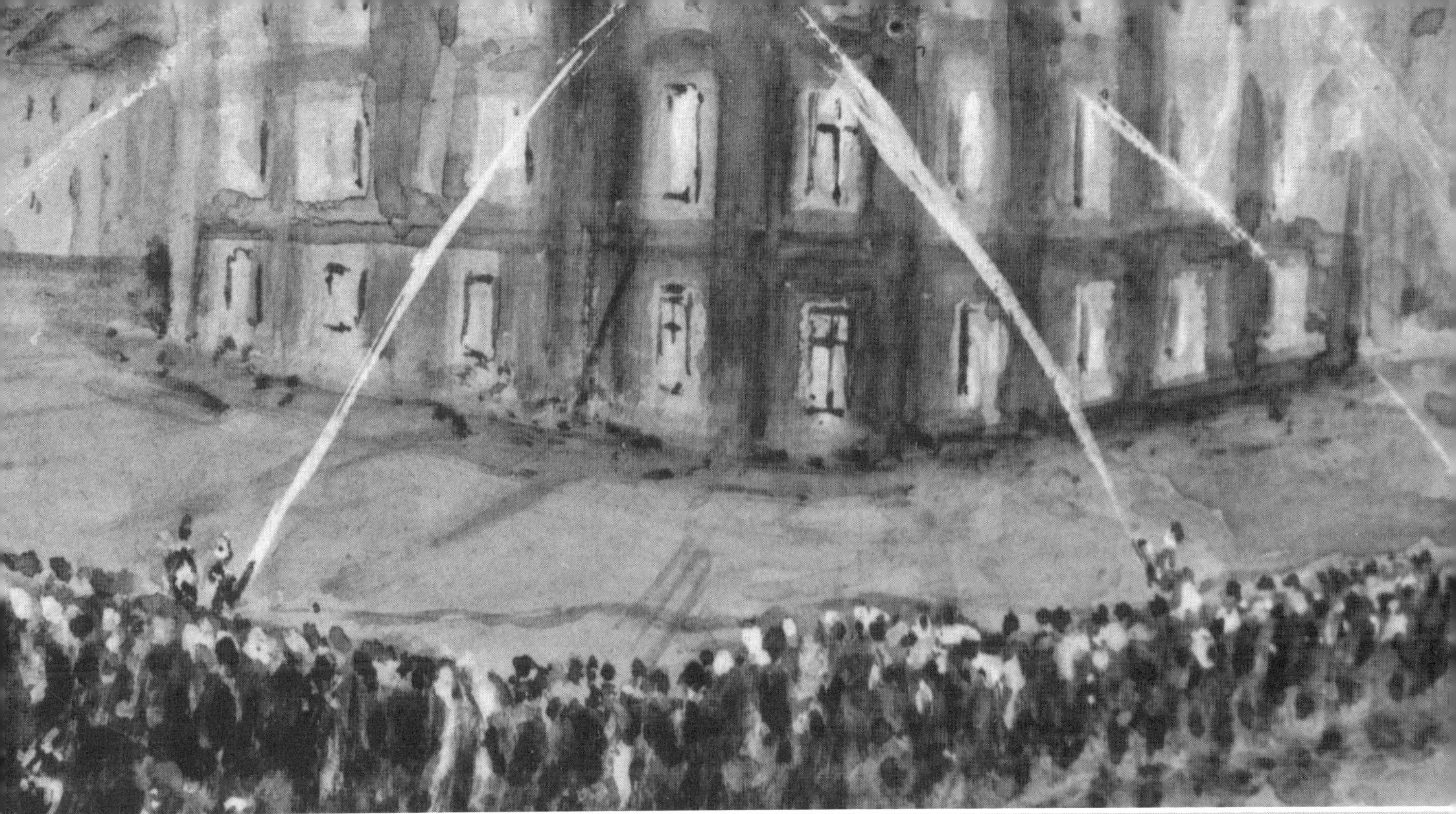

CHAPTER 3

DISASTERS

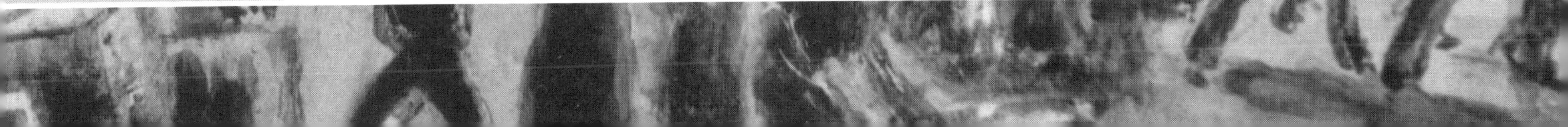

Halifax's chequered history of major catastrophes has brought this municipality international attention and given it the reputation of being disaster prone. Indeed, Halifax has certainly had more than its share of tragedies—on land, under ground, at sea, and in the air.

The painful memories of the crash of Swiss Air Flight 111 off Peggys Cove in 1998 are still fresh. Marine disasters abound, from countless wrecks on the shifting sands of Sable Island—"The Graveyard of the Atlantic"—to the foundering of the SS *Atlantic* off Prospect in 1873, to the aftermath of the RMS *Titanic* in 1912, when Halifax coordinated rescue efforts and buried the dead.

In April 1936, according to the *Canadian Annual Review*, "the attention of much of the civilized world [was riveted] on Nova Scotia for nearly two weeks..." while rescuers struggled to free three men trapped by a cave-in at the Moose River Gold Mine.

Fire is no stranger to any city, and Halifax is no exception. The North Barracks (a military housing complex), along with forty houses, burned in 1850; an entire four acres of development, including some sixty downtown buildings, disappeared in 1859; the Poor Asylum burnt to a shell in 1882, the King Edward Hotel in 1911, and buildings on Barrington Street in 1912. The destruction in 1939 of the Queen Hotel was the greatest disaster in the city since the 1917 Explosion, and is still vivid in the memory of many residents.

The Halifax Harbour Explosion is without doubt the best-known event in Halifax's epic history. On that fateful morning of December 6, 1917, the munitions carrier *Mont Blanc* and the Belgian Relief vessel *Imo* collided in the narrowest part of the harbour, causing the world's largest man-made explosion previous to the Atomic Bomb in 1945. More Nova Scotians died in that single disaster than were killed in World War I. Although less devastating than anticipated, the Bedford Magazine Explosion of 1945 revived memories of 1917 and fears for a similar catastrophe.

Rather than giving in to despair in the face of these disasters, the people of Halifax have always demonstrated great courage, compassion, and resilience, which has earned them international attention and gratitude.

1. "Granville Street Fire Sept. 9, 1859"

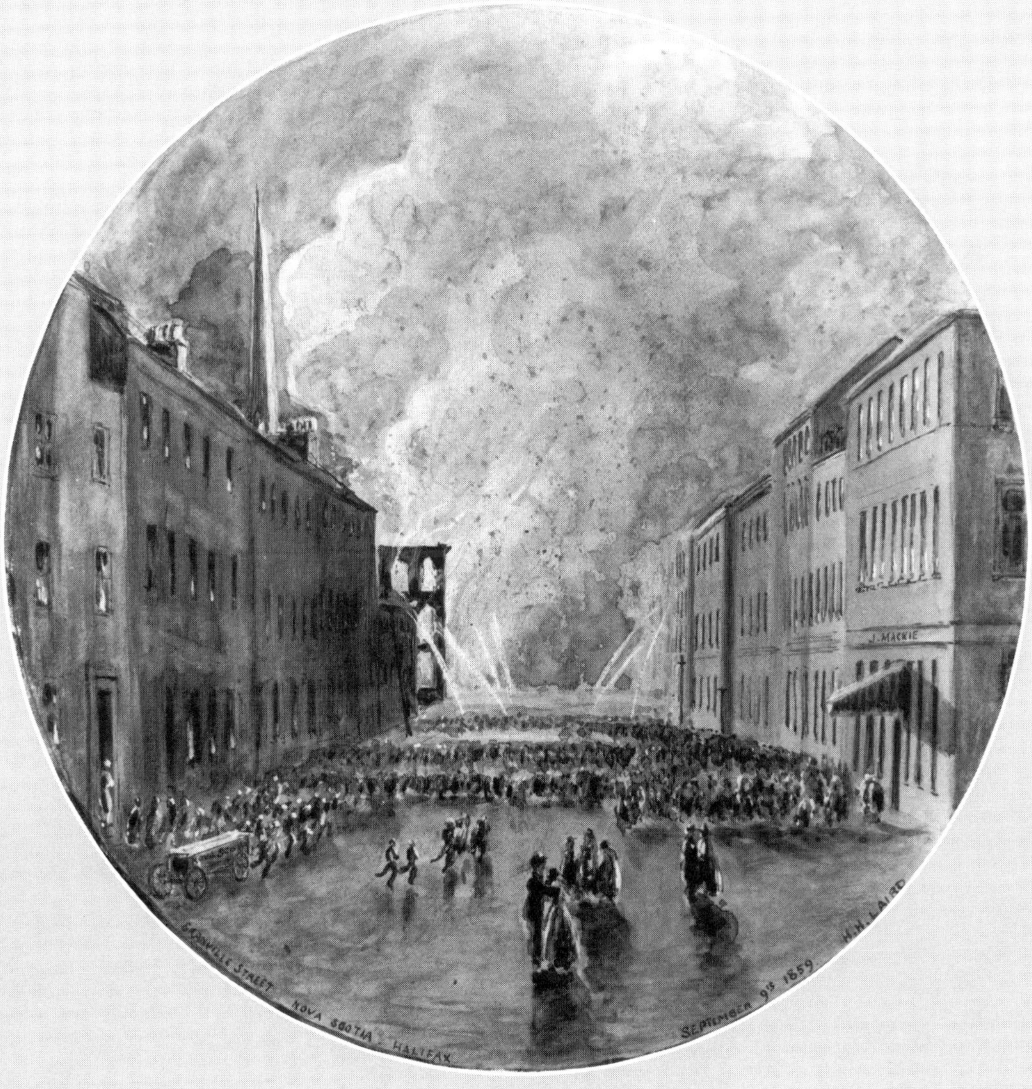

At nine o'clock on the night of September 9, 1859, a fire broke out in the expanding city of Halifax, almost destroying it. *The Illustrated London News* for October 15, 1859, reported that "Houses and stores, wooden, brick, and stone, all alike fed the flames, until, of the two extensive blocks touching on Hollis and Barrington streets, with Granville-street (the Haligonian's paradise), running betwixt them, nothing escaped except one store." Sixty of the finest buildings in Halifax, covering four acres of ground, were destroyed; two lives were lost, and many people suffered severe injuries.

2. "Ordnanace Square Sept. 9, 1859"

This watercolour by H.H. Laird shows the burning of a huge misshapen structure, nicknamed 'The Coffin,' in Ordnance Square. Again quoting from *The Illustrated London News*: "From the brilliant play of colours caused by the combustion of the inflammable materials…and from the danger caused by the proximity of the Ordnance Magazine [army storehouse for explosives], the exitement here was intense."

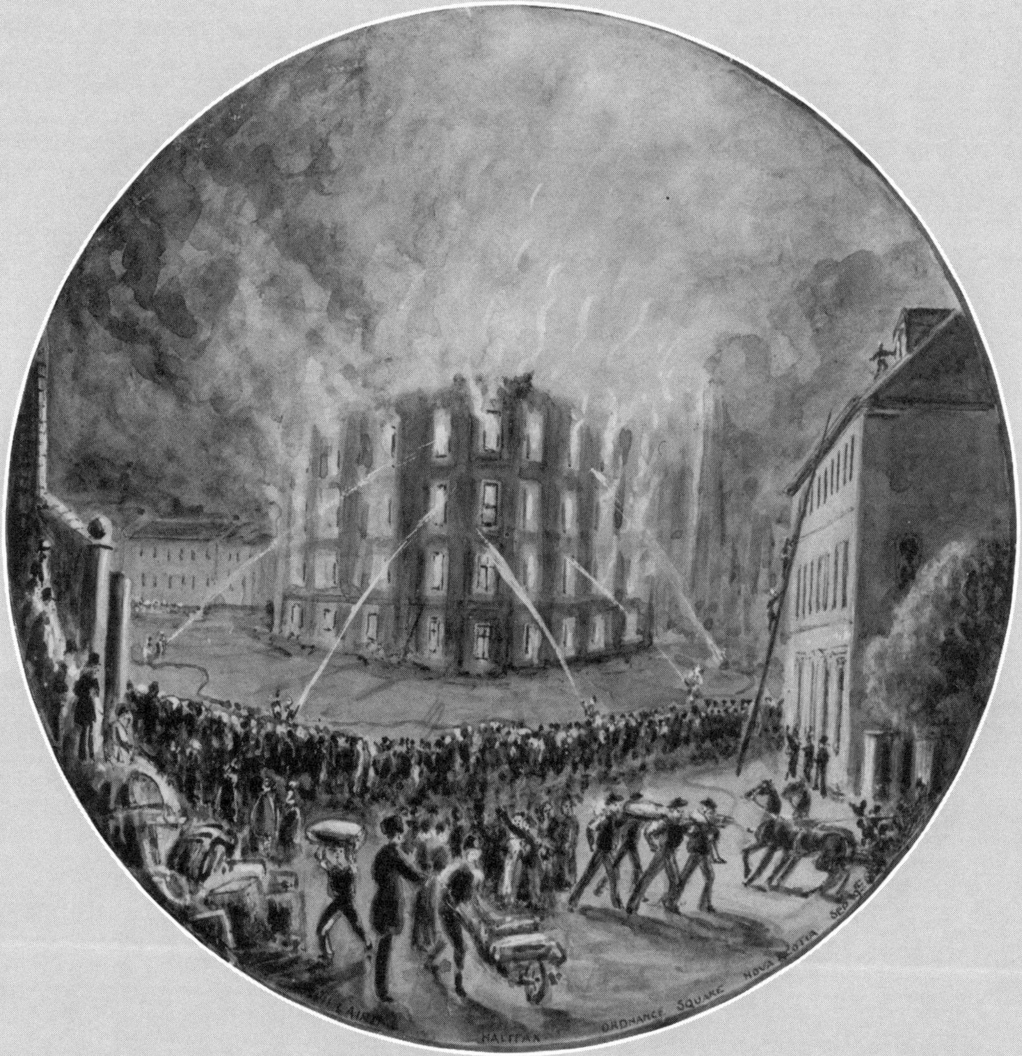

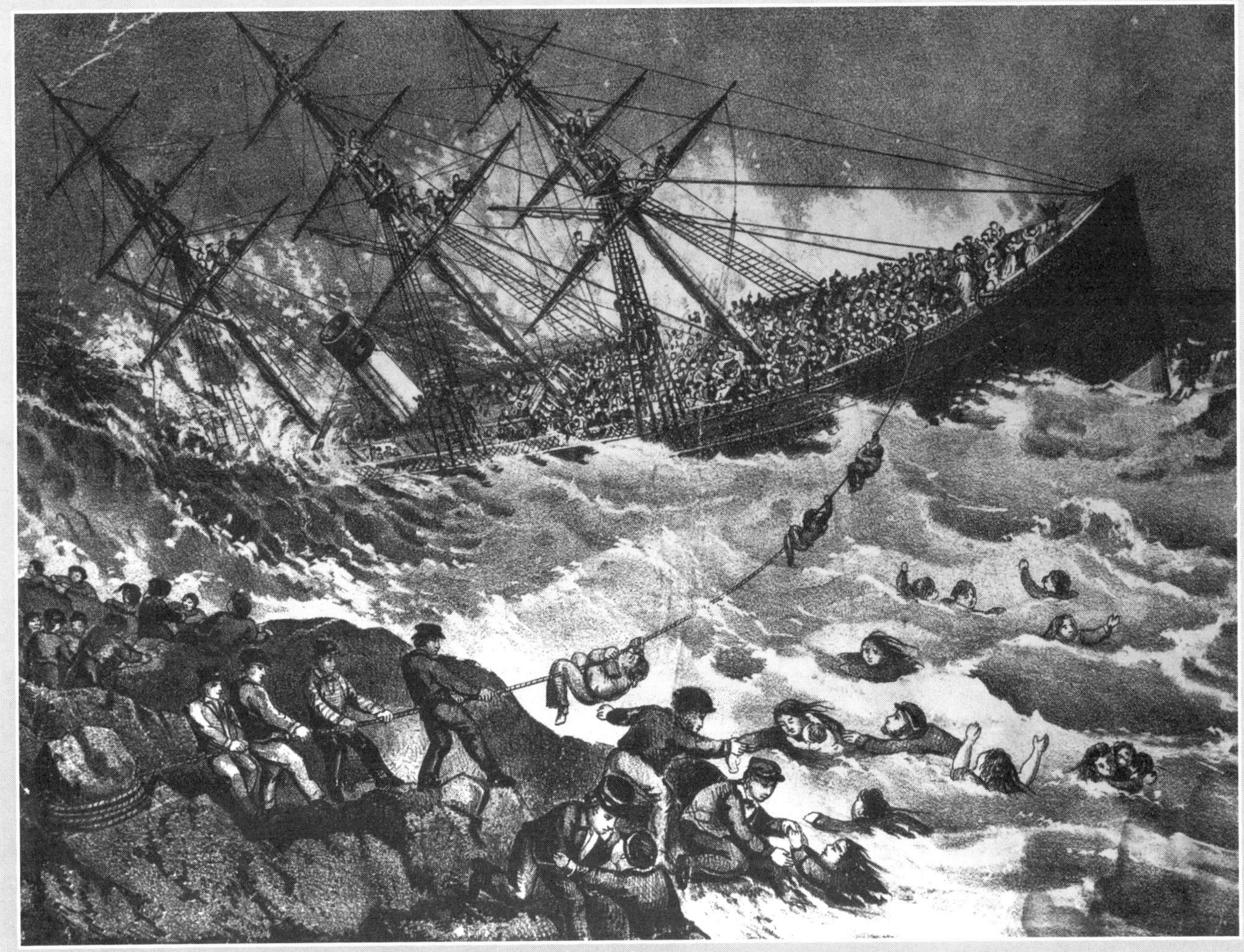

The SS *Atlantic* left Liverpool, England, for New York on March 20, 1873, with 948 people on board, including 790 passengers, 143 crew members, and 15 stowaways. Eleven days later, the captain changed course for Halifax, the nearest port, because the vessel's coal supply was running low. En route, the steamship grounded on Mars Head, near Lower Prospect, in the early morning of April 1. The loss of life was horrendous—565 passengers and crew, including every woman on board and all but one child. The disaster was the world's worst merchant shipwreck known at that time.

4. Actual position of the *Atlantic's* hull April 1873

The international press seized upon the loss of the *Atlantic* with a zeal unsurpassed until the sinking of the *Titanic*, nearly forty years later. The *Canadian Illustrated News* of April 19, 1873, provided on-the-spot coverage of the wreck:

> *The bow, with about sixty feet of the forward part of the ship, is broken sharp off, and lies close to the shore, and at a distance of nearly fifty feet from the rest of the vessel. ... The ship now acts like a breakwater to the small bay in which she lies, occupying nearly the whole of it. The divers and draggers are busy looking with an eager, professional eye to what is coming to the surface in the shape of salvage. Several respectable looking men are watching likewise... . Beneath those iron walls lie the mortal remains of those whose memories are dear to them and occasionally there is something floated upwards that they claim. There are many sad and anxious countenances among that quiet knot of strangers.*

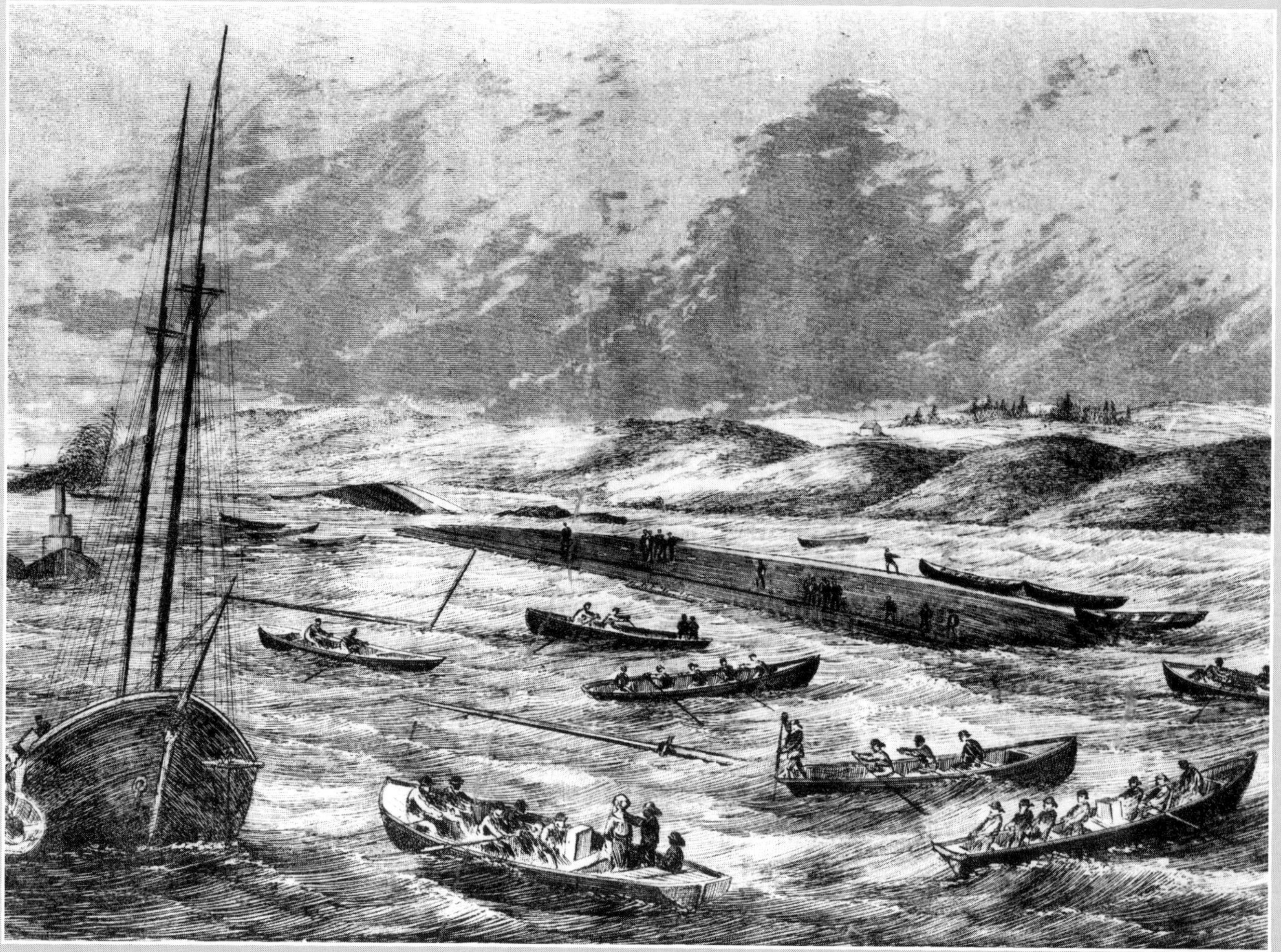

5. Burial service for victims of wreck of S.S. *Atlantic*, at Lower Prospect
April 1873

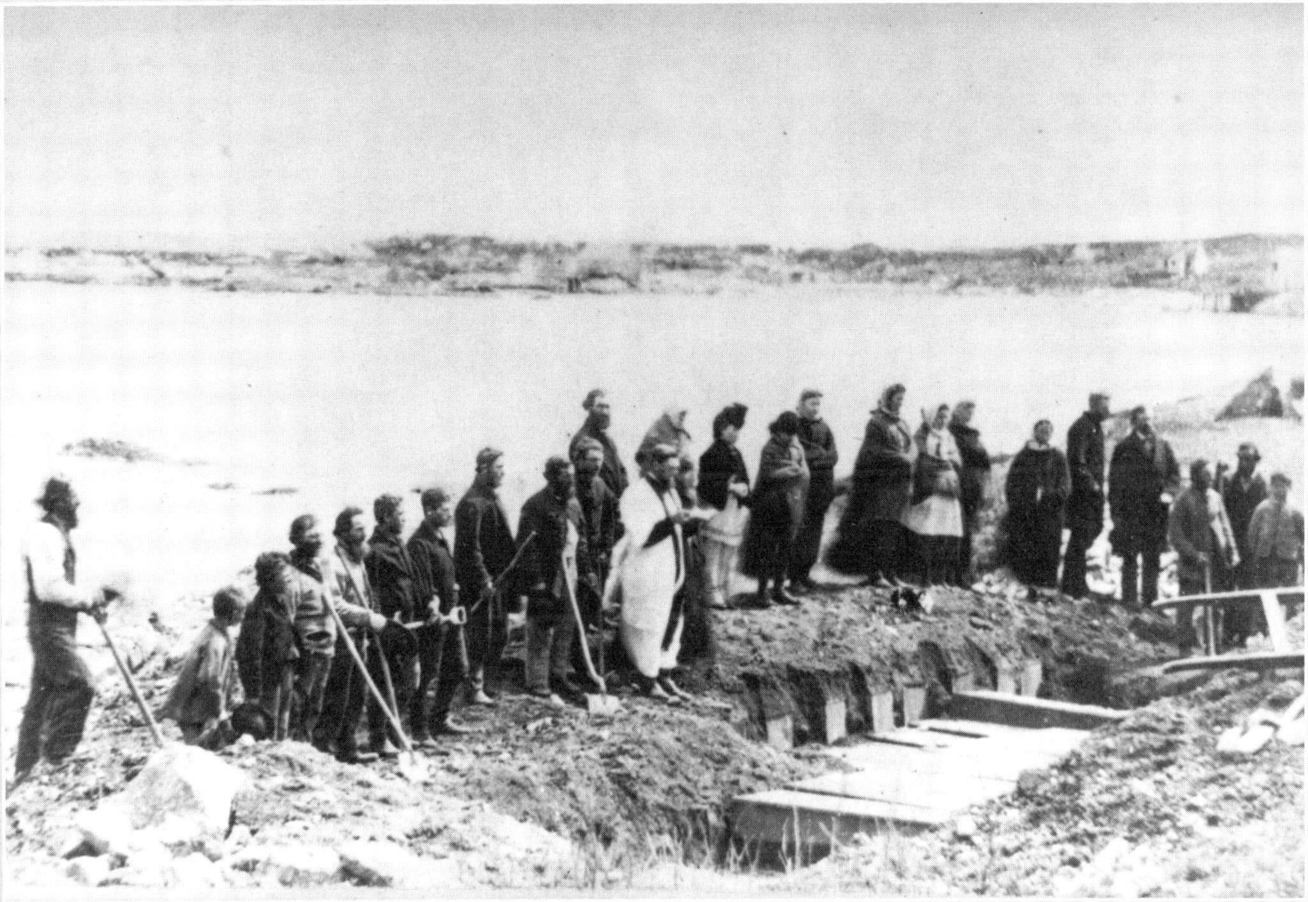

The Rev. William J. Ancient, described as a man "six feet in height and strongly built [with] a genial face, a bright eye, a clear head and a warm heart," attracted worldwide media attention in the aftermath of the *Atlantic* disaster.

Some ten hours after the *Atlantic* grounded, there were still three individuals tied to the rigging—First Officer John W. Firth, a dead woman, and a child. The seas were too rough for boats to approach the wreck, then listing at a fifty-degree angle. Ancient persuaded some fishermen to assist him aboard, and using his seamanship and oratory skills—"Put your confidence in me and the Lord, and move when I tell you!"—made a spectacular rescue effort, which saved the first officer. The child jumped to safety. Ancient, formerly an ordinary seaman in the Royal Navy, was lionized for his achievement which, although thrilling, was merely the climax of a courageous effort by the community of seafarers.

November 7, 1882

The concept of the Victorian workhouse—the Poors' Asylum or Poor House, as it was called in Halifax—has passed entirely from our collective memory, except for Charles Dickens's vivid recreations of life behind the workhouse walls. In Halifax, thirty-one people died on the night of November 6, 1882, when the Poor House burnt to a shell; more lives were lost in that blaze than in any other fire in the city's history. The fire, which started accidentally in the kitchen area of the building, was discovered about 11:30 P.M. It spread quickly through the ceiling to the walls and the elevator, and then from the elevator shaft to the rest of the massive fortress-like structure. Unfortunately, the watchman, fireman, and nurses were of little assistance—they were all inmates who were paid a couple of dollars a month to perform their duties; but because they had been incarcerated mainly for drunkenness, they were scarcely reliable. Many of the 343 inmates were hysterical when the city firemen arrived. When the main door was felled with a fireman's ax, pandemonium erupted. A crowd of inmates streamed outdoors—mothers nursing infants, some fifty to sixty children, elderly women and feeble old men—some partially clothed, others wrapped in blankets, and still others naked. Police, firemen, clergy, reporters, and spectators rushed into the building to assist or to carry the blind, lame, and crippled to safety. Suddenly the building erupted into a raging inferno, with forty or fifty patients still trapped in the infirmary on the fifth floor.

The *Citizen and Evening Chronicle* for November 7 described the gruesome scene: "Far above the roar of flames and crack of bursting slates were heard the cries of the wretched patients… Most of them… were helpless, and could not leave their beds."

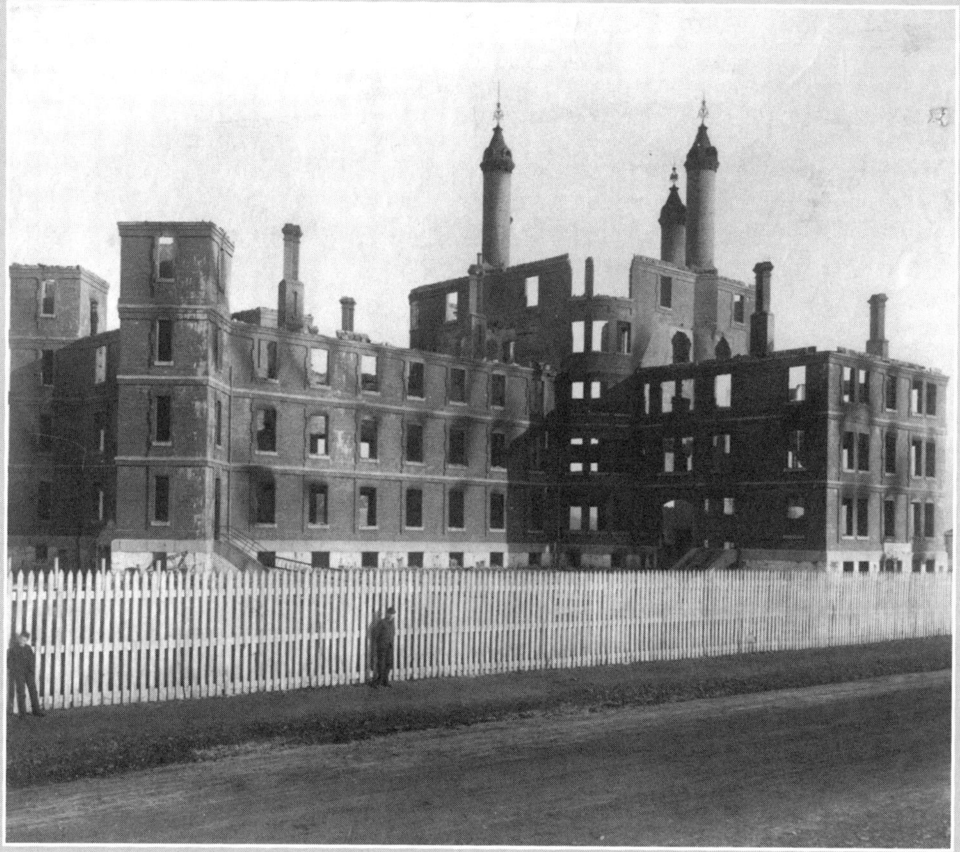

7. Concrete sewer blocks made at the Halifax Poor Asylum

Halifax, 1899

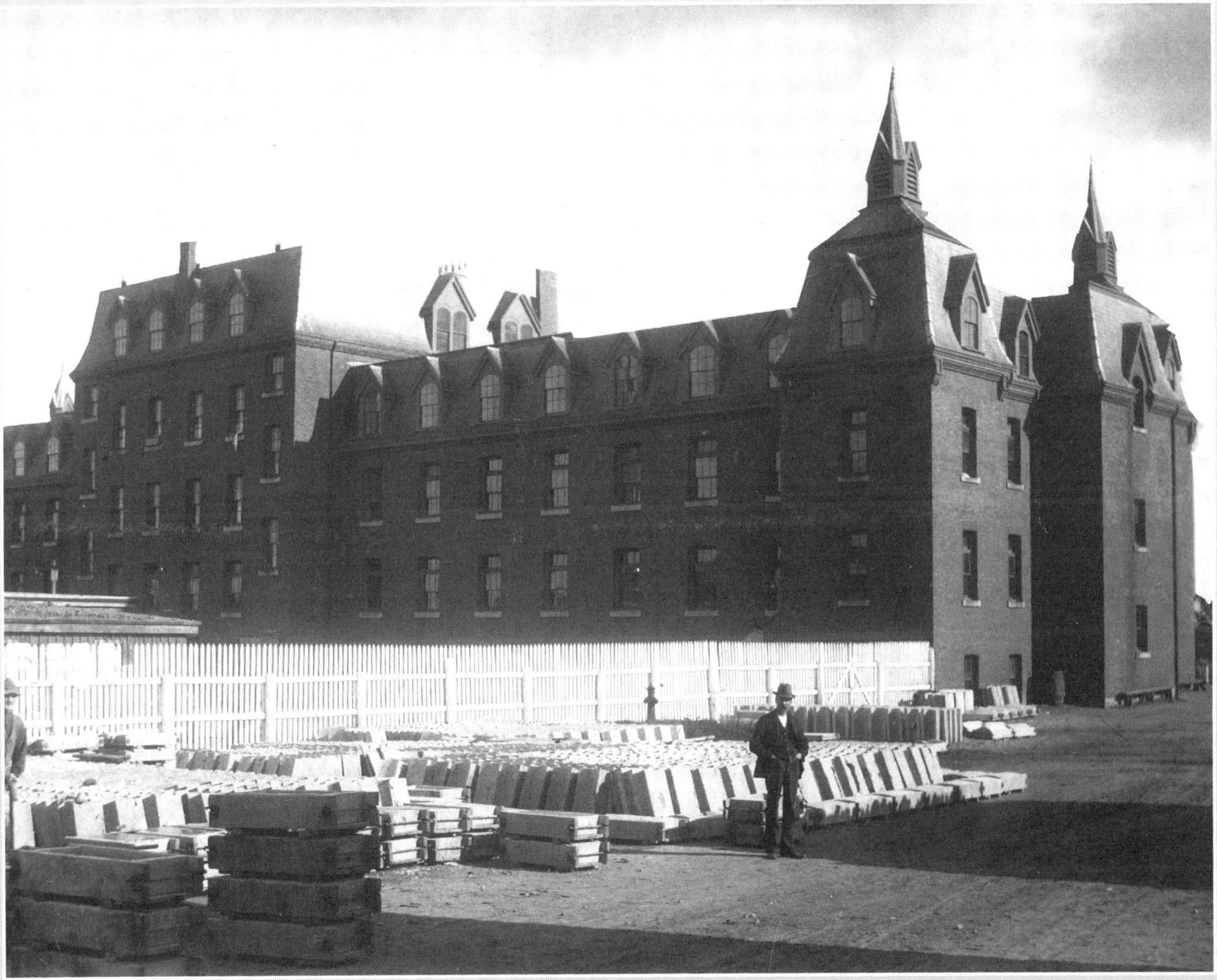

A new Poor Asylum immediately replaced the burnt-out shell on the corner of South and Robie Streets in 1886. True to the concept of the Victorian workhouse, the inmates were employed in revenue-generating activities, which helped to offset operating expenses and brought (perhaps) some sense of contribution by those unfortunate enough to be incarcerated. The Poor House of 1886, altered in purpose but not much in appearance, remained a prominent part of the Halifax landscape until its demolition in 1972.

8. Body of RMS *Titanic* victim aboard rescue vessel CS *Minia*

April or May 1912

The loss of the RMS *Titanic* needs no introduction to anyone living today in the Halifax Regional Municipality. The great liner suffered irreversible damage after a glancing blow from an iceberg opened five water-tight compartments to the in-rushing sea, at 11:40 P.M. on April 14, 1912. At 2:20 A.M. the following day, the technological marvel of the Edwardian Age sank. Of the 2,228 passengers and crew on board, 1,518 lost their lives. Within hours, the RMS *Carpathia* recovered 710 passengers at the scene; five were dead or subsequently died on board and were buried at sea. The Halifax-based cable ships *MacKay-Bennett* and *Minia* were chartered within days, steamed to the site, and recovered the majority of the remaining bodies—306 by the *MacKay-Bennett* and seventeen by the *Minia*.

Altogether, some 337 bodies were plucked from the Atlantic, with the CGS *Montmagney*, the SS *Algerine*, the RMS *Oceanic* and the SS *Ilford* also assisting. One hundred and twenty-eight bodies were buried at sea and 209 brought to Halifax. Of the latter, fifty-nine were claimed and shipped to other locations; the remaining 150 were buried at Fairview Lawn, Mount Olivet, and Baron de Hirsch cemeteries in Halifax.

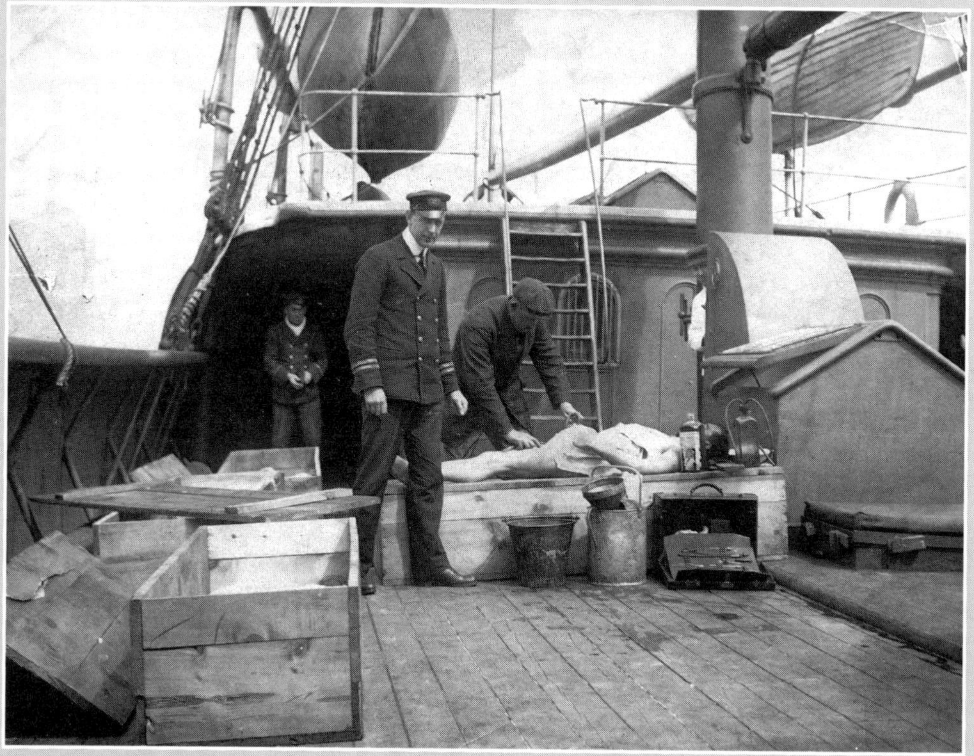

9. HEARSES LINED UP ON HALIFAX WHARF, READY TO TRANSPORT *TITANIC* VICTIMS TO FUNERAL PARLOURS

MAY 6, 1912

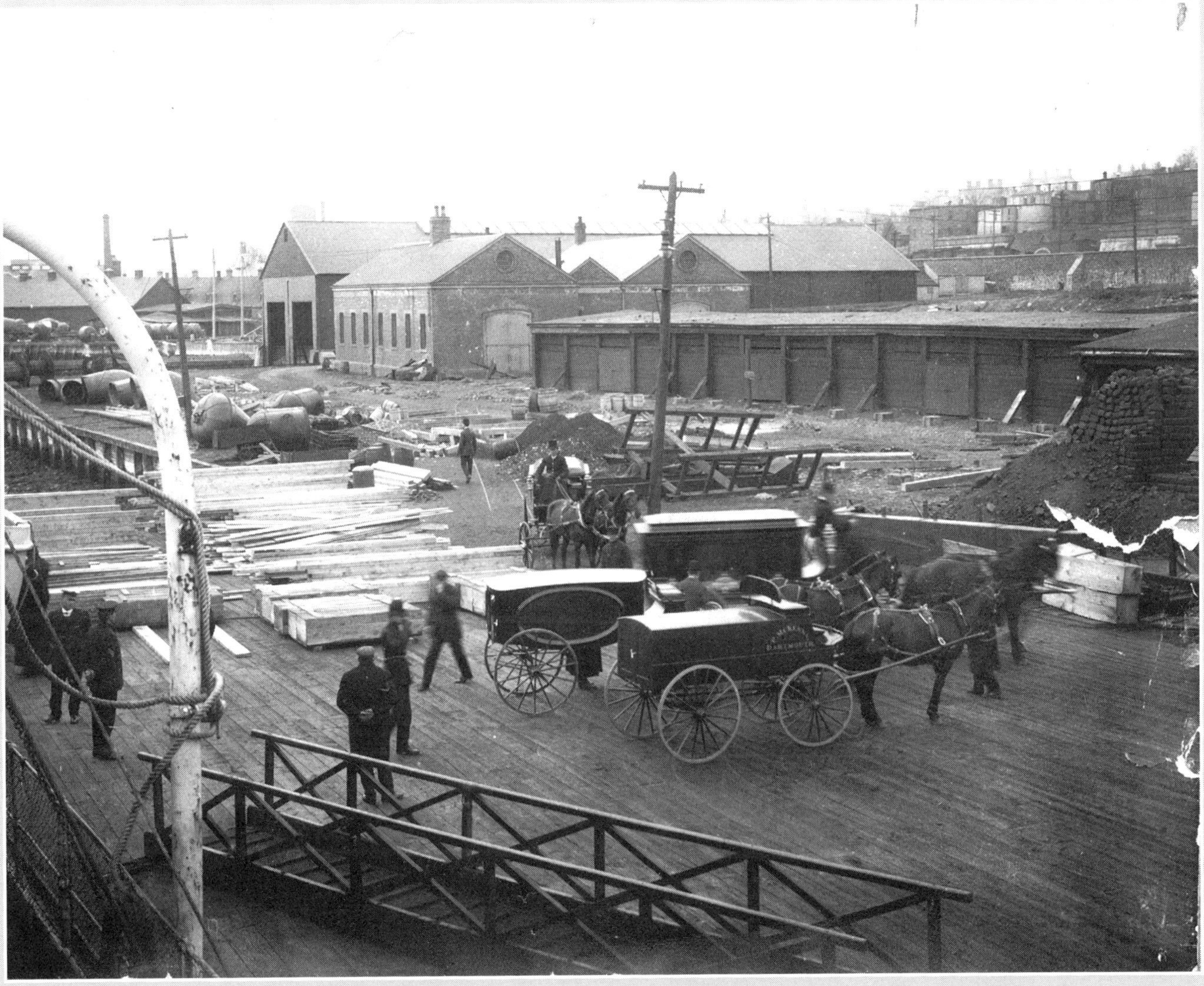

The Anglo-American Telegraph Company's CS *Minia* was chartered on April 21 and went to sea the following day under the command of W.E.S. DeCarteret, with undertaker H.W. Snow and the Rev. H.W. Cunningham (Rector, Anglican Parish of St. George, Brunswick Street, Halifax) aboard. The vessel arrived at the disaster area on Friday April 26, where it joined the *MacKay-Bennett* and remained until May 3. Bad weather hampered the search throughout. After a week, only seventeen bodies had been recovered; fifteen were brought to Halifax to be claimed or interred.

10. William Carbines
Body No. 18
c 1912

This water-stained photograph was used by coroners J.H. Barnstead and Charles W. Benjamin to identify Body No. 18 as Mr. William Carbines of Higher Stennack, St. Ives, Cornwall, England. Carbines was a nineteen-year-old second-class passenger on the *Titanic*. When his body was recovered, this photograph, along with a silver watch and chain, coins, pipe, knife, and personal papers, was found on the body. Carbines was travelling to Calumet, Michigan, to join his brothers. His body was returned to England for burial.

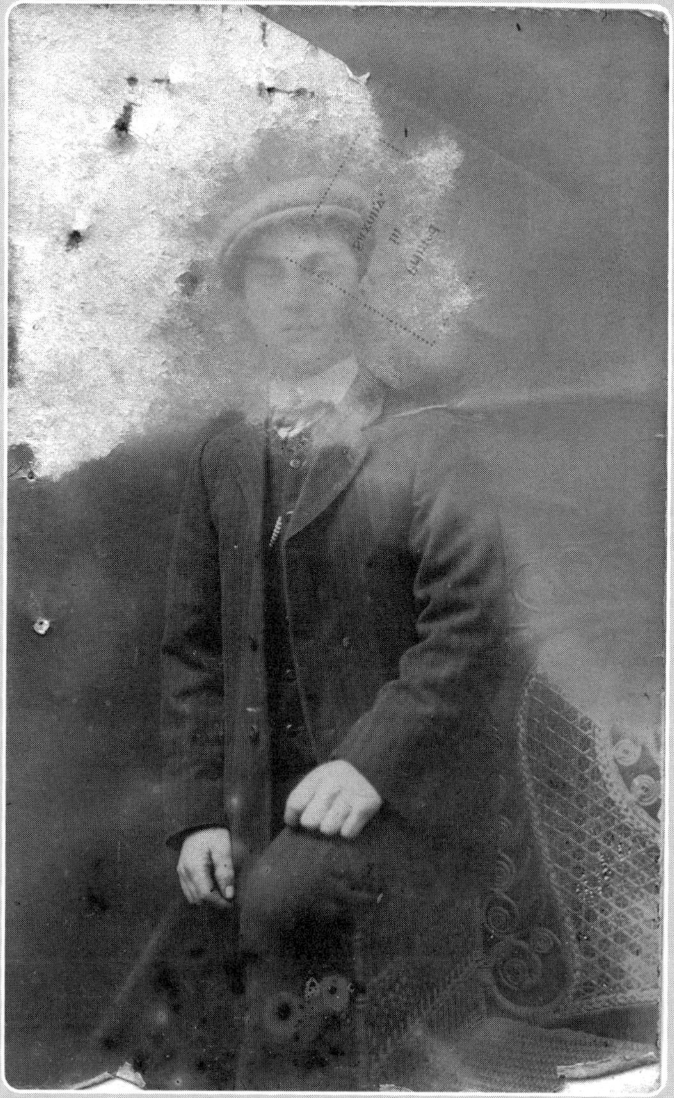

11. Business Card, Mr. Nicola Nasra Uah, Sometimes Known as Nicola Nasser
c 1912

12. Business Card, J.F.P. Clarke
c 1912

13. Business Card, Leopold Weisz
c 1912

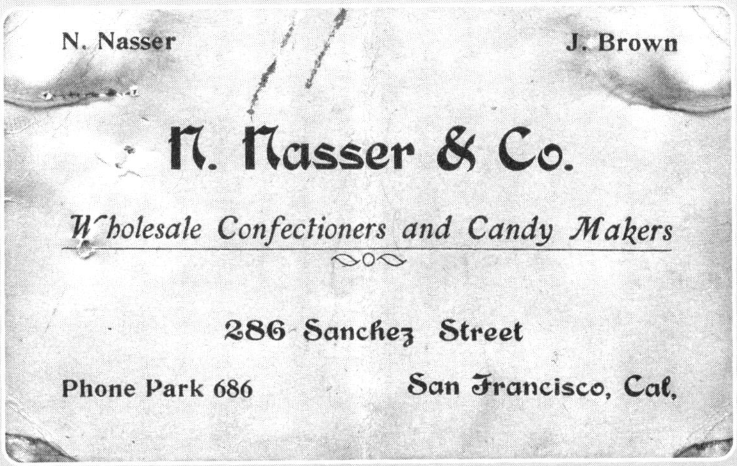

Mr. Nasser, thought to be thirty-two years old, was travelling second class. Among the other effects found on his body was a money belt around his waist, containing £160 in gold.

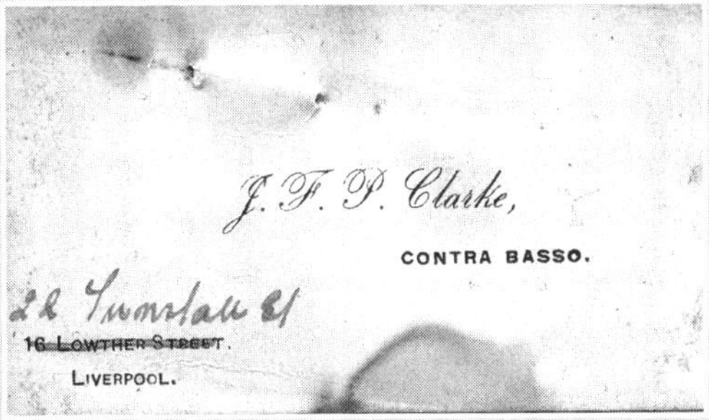

J.F.P. Clarke was one of the members of the Wallace Hartley Band, whose perambulating musical excursions were much appreciated in both the First Class Lounge and the Café Parisian during the *Titanic's* maiden voyage. The band members travelled on second-class tickets and were not technically part of the crew. They are best remembered for playing lively music to calm the passengers as the great liner slowly sank into the North Atlantic. Mr. Clarke is buried in Mount Olivet Cemetery, Halifax.

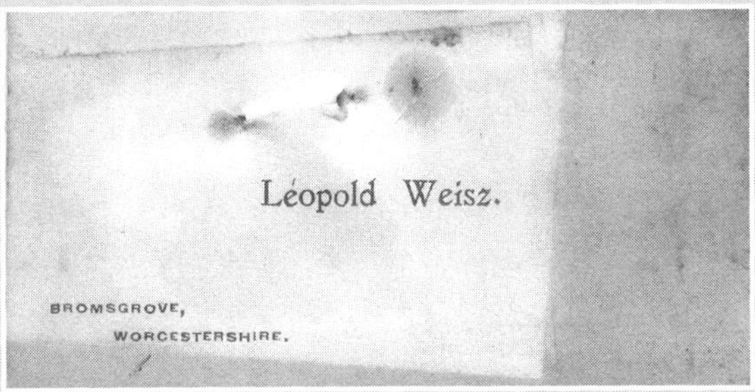

Leopold Weisz was returning to Montreal with his wife Mathilde. The thirty-three-year-old Hungarian-born Jewish stonecutter had $30,000 in currency sewn into the lining of his suit, and was carrying another $15,000 in gold bullion stashed in his pockets. Weisz's body was forwarded to Montreal for burial.

14. Collapsed buildings of Nova Scotia Car Works, Halifax

February 11, 1918

On December 6, 1917, the Norwegian vessel SS *Imo*, carrying Belgian Relief supplies, and the French freighter SS *Mont Blanc*, carrying munitions, collided in Halifax Harbour, creating what at that time was the worst man-made disaster in history. A few seconds before 9:05 A.M., the *Mont Blanc*, with a cargo of 2,500 tons of high explosives and a deck load of monochlorobenzene, blew up, shattering the 3,000-ton vessel and spewing destruction over 325 acres. The explosion killed more than 1,600 people instantly and injured over 9,000 others, in a metropolitan population of 65,000. The catastrophe resulted in over $35,000,000 worth of property damage.

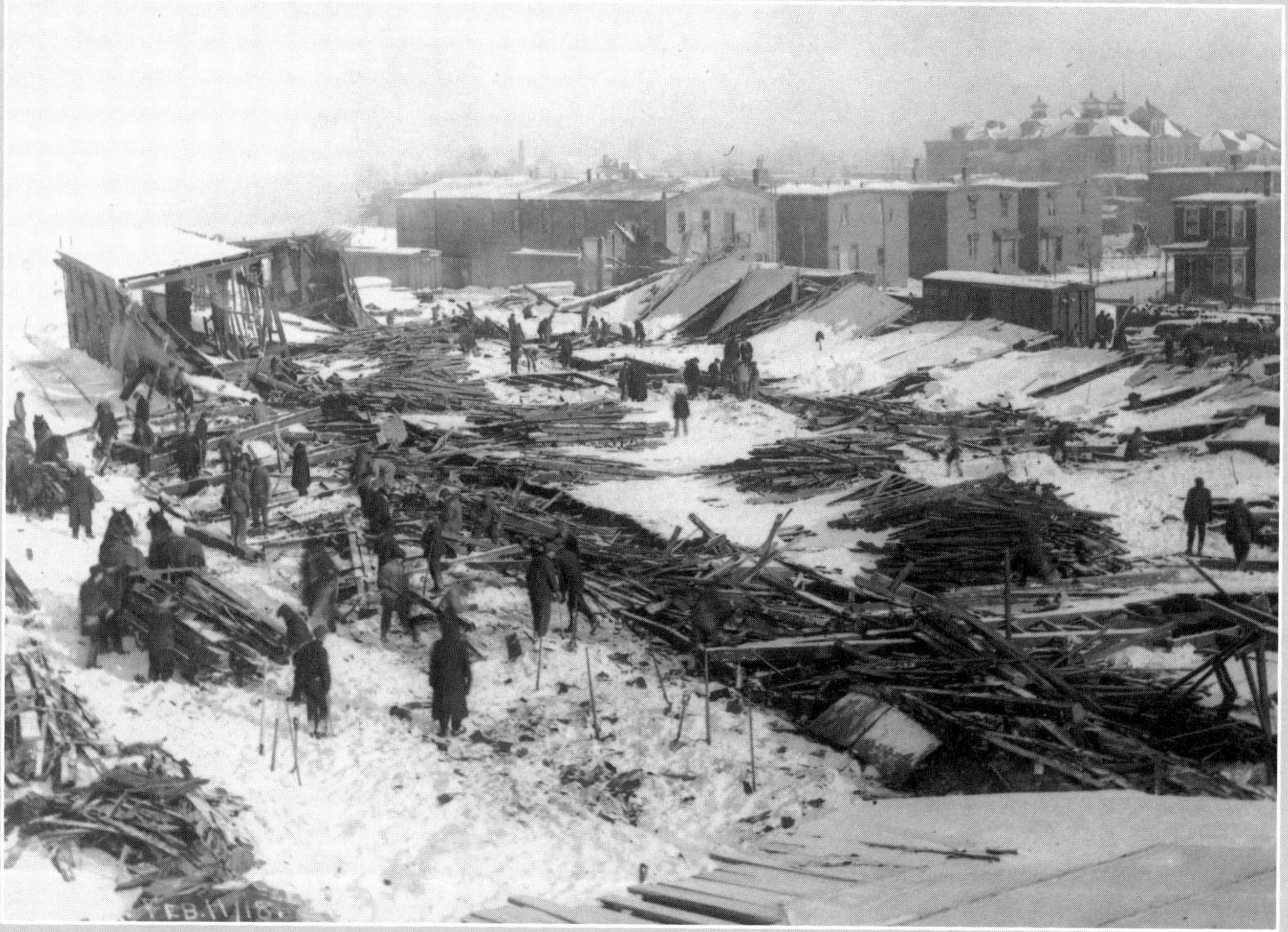

15. Women Walking from Africville towards Halifax, on Campbell Road near Hanover Street
1917 or 1918

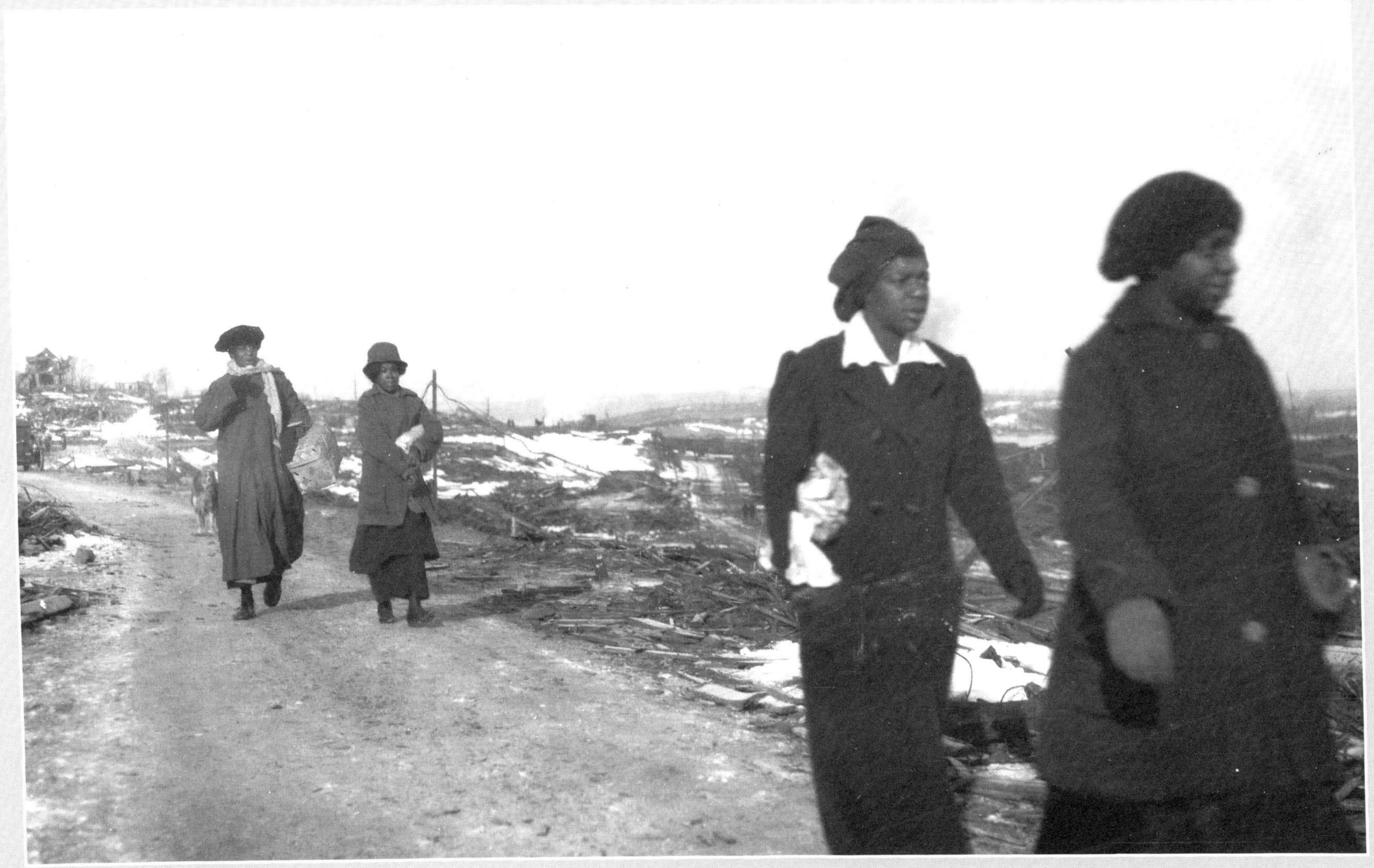

In February 1918, after the explosion, George Ross of the architectural firm Ross and Macdonald, offered his services to the city at a bargain rate. He called for the development of 324 housing units and sixteen shops and offices on West Young Street. Ross's goal was to maximize the aesthetic qualities of the development and to provide fire-resistant and sanitary buildings at a reasonable cost. He decided upon hydrostone (a moulded mixture of gravel, crushed stone, sand, and Portland cement) for the exterior of the houses. To provide variety, he designed six different types of four-unit buildings, as well as a mixture of two-unit houses at the ends of the terraces. He also altered roof designs and the arrangement of timber and stucco, in order to give the buildings an individual appearance. The photograph shows the construction of units on (left) Hennessey Court (now Hennessey Place), and (right) Kane Court (now Kane Place).

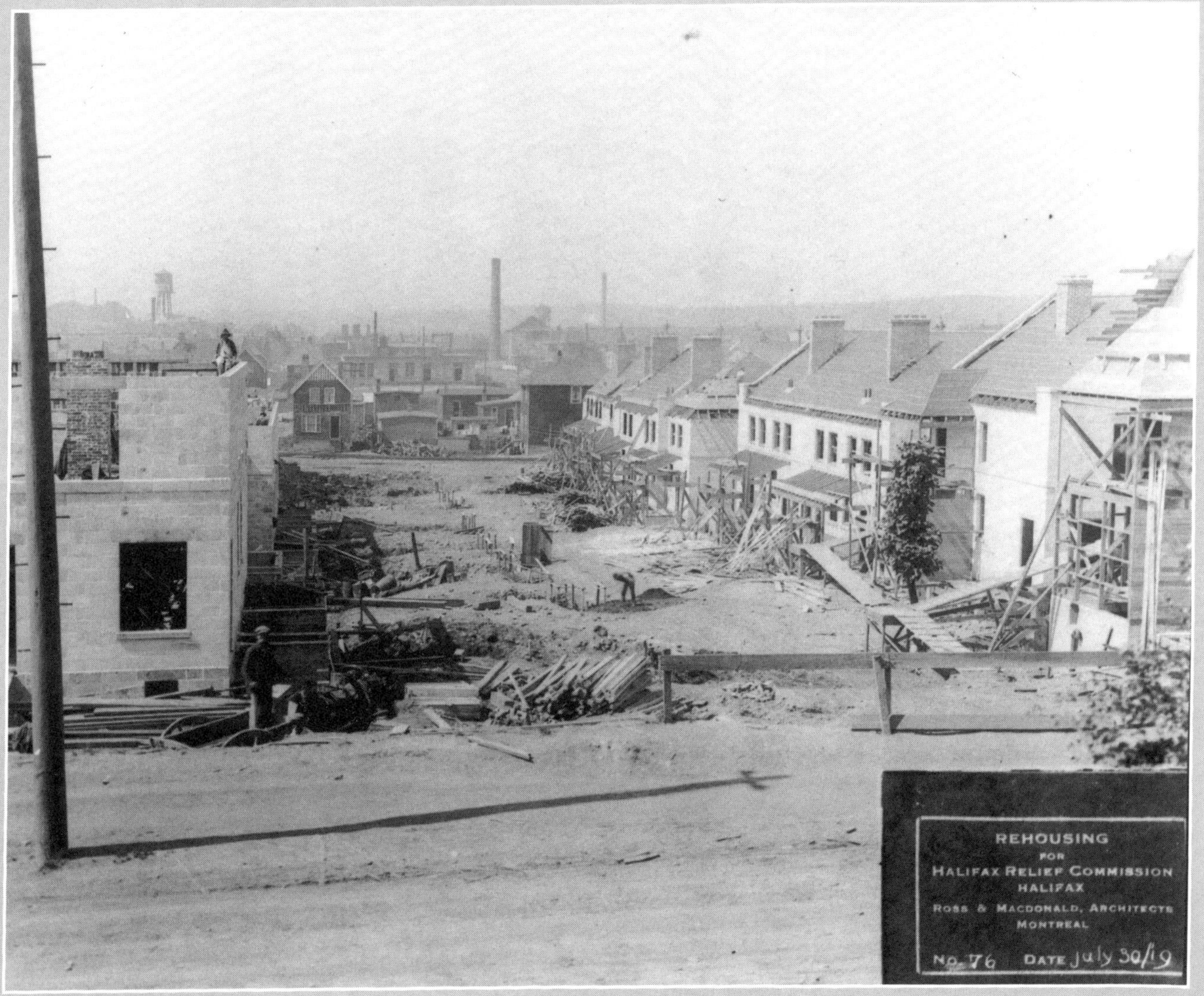

17. J. Allister Bowman, of Maritime Tel & Tel, Using Earphones for Word from Entombed Men in Moose River Mine Disaster

April 1936

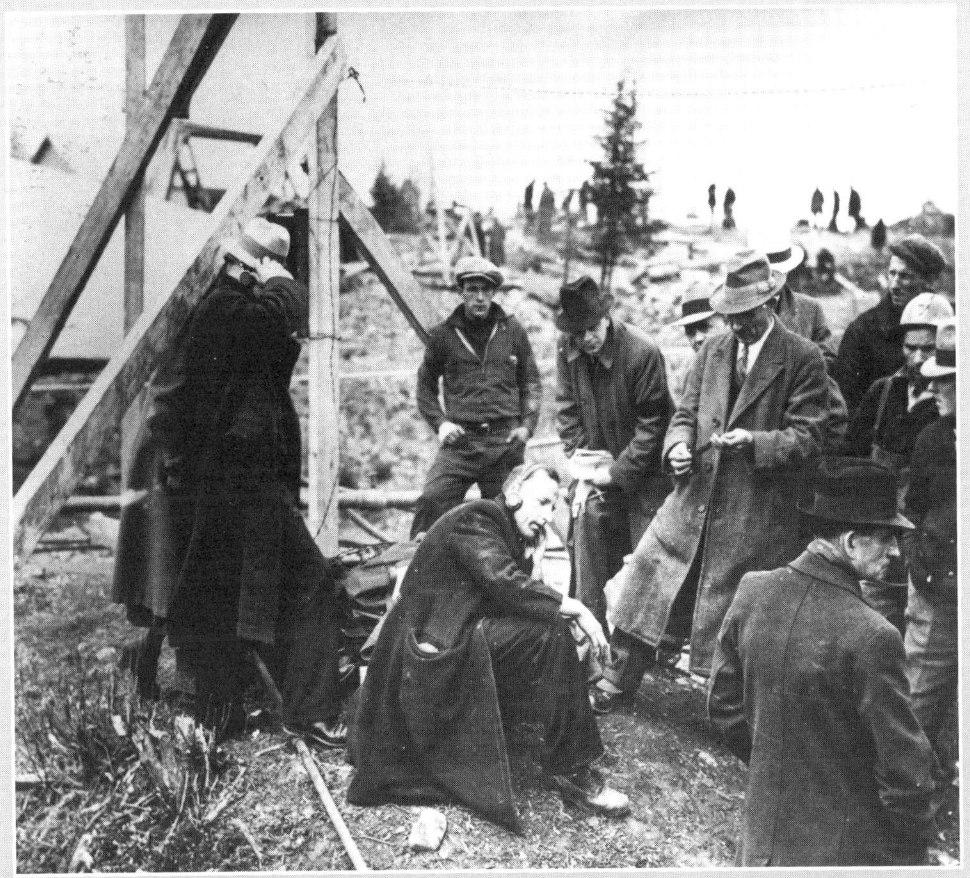

On April 12, 1936, Dr. D.E. Robertson, Herman Magill, and Alfred Scadding were trapped by a cave-in at the 141-foot level of the Moose River Gold Mine, in Halifax County. They remained entombed until rescue miners and draegermen reached them on April 23. Unfortunately, in the interim, Magill died of exposure-incurred pneumonia.

Author Roland H. Sherwood, in his book *Story Parade*, includes a chapter on the disaster. He writes that "two way conversation with the men below was important so the telephone company rushed in wire, men and amplifiers, while back at their workshop in Halifax...a tiny microphone [was built] that would be small enough to be lowered down a pipe...." Reporters converged on the disaster, providing the first-ever live radio news coverage in Canada. Sherwood continues:

The radio broadcasts began on Monday, April 20, at 6 P.M. when two minute bulletins were given out at half-hour intervals. During the course of the broadcasts, 93 two-minute flashes were transmitted. These passed from the radio car at Moose River Mines over covered wire strung along the ground and on the trees, over seventeen miles of built up circuit on the farmer line to Middle Musquodoboit, then on to Halifax, out onto the telegraph lines of the Canadian Pacific to Ottawa. From there it was distributed to fifty-eight stations over the entire network of the Canadian Radio Broadcasting Commission in Canada, and on to the networks of the United States to serve 650 radio stations there. Everywhere on the North American continent, sponsors of radio programs cut their regular shows by two minutes in order that their listeners might receive the radio bulletins from Moose River. This was the largest broadcast hookup originating on this continent, and set a world record for that time.

The Queen Hotel fire was the greatest Halifax disaster since the 1917 Explosion; twenty-eight people died in the inferno. The *Halifax Daily Star* ran this photograph on March 3, 1939, with the caption:

The above picture presents a general view of what is left of the Queen Hotel on Hollis Street, which was levelled by fire yesterday morning... . Note where the hotel wall has collapsed, barely missing one of two automobiles that never will be claimed. Their owners are among the missing. Great difficulty was met by firemen attempting to raise the giant aerial tower and ladder in the foreground.

The Hon. M.B. Archibald, Justice of the Supreme Court of Nova Scotia, was subsequently appointed a one-man commission to investigate fire prevention, fire suppression, and the safeguarding of human lives in Halifax, with particular reference to the Queen Hotel fire. His report (*Journals and Proceedings of the House of Assembly 1940*) noted that:

There was a scarcity of ladders of sufficient length to reach to the upper floors of the building.... [The] aerial ladder is twenty years old, and from the evidence of the firemen and the Chief of the Department, it is apparent that the ladder is unsafe. ...The presence of overhead live wires, combined with the failure to provide the Fire Department with more efficient, up-to-date and speedy wire cutting apparatus, greatly hampered the fire fighters during this fire, and interfered with the work of rescue of occupants of the hotel.

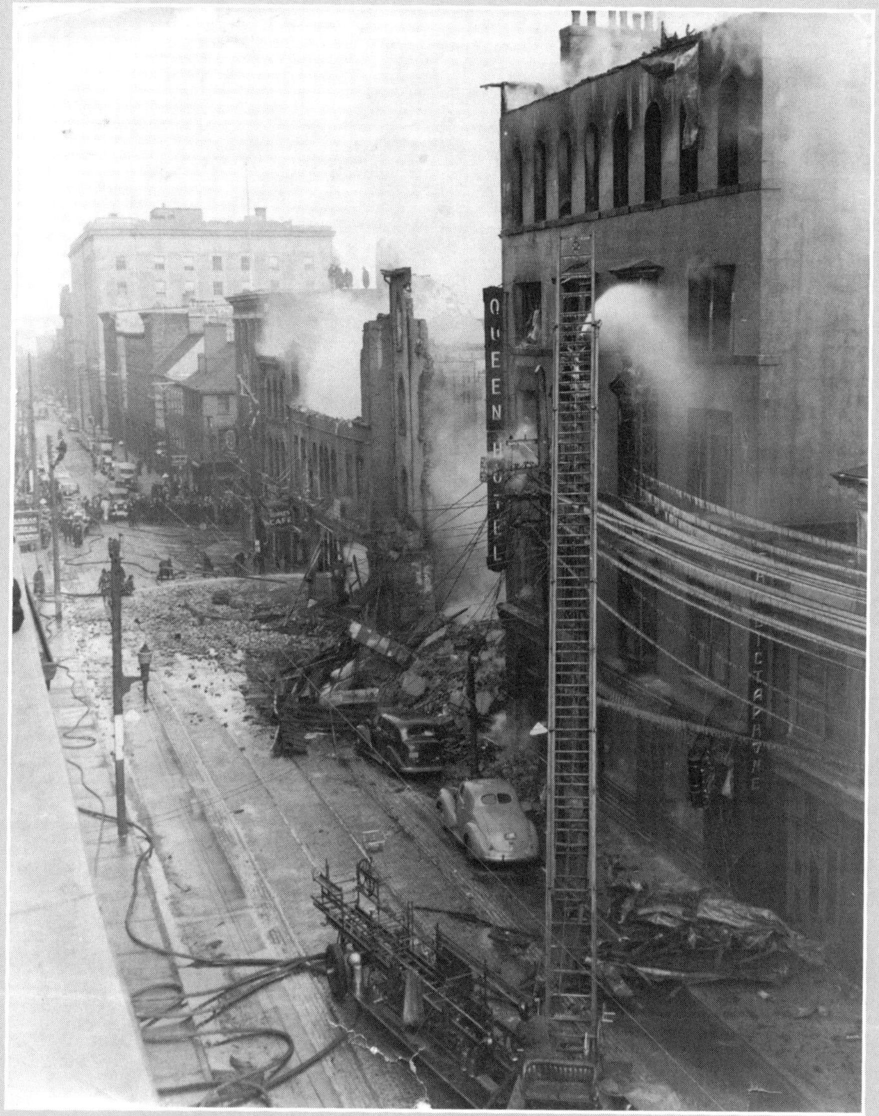

19. Explosion of Munitions at Magazine near Dartmouth
July 18, 1945

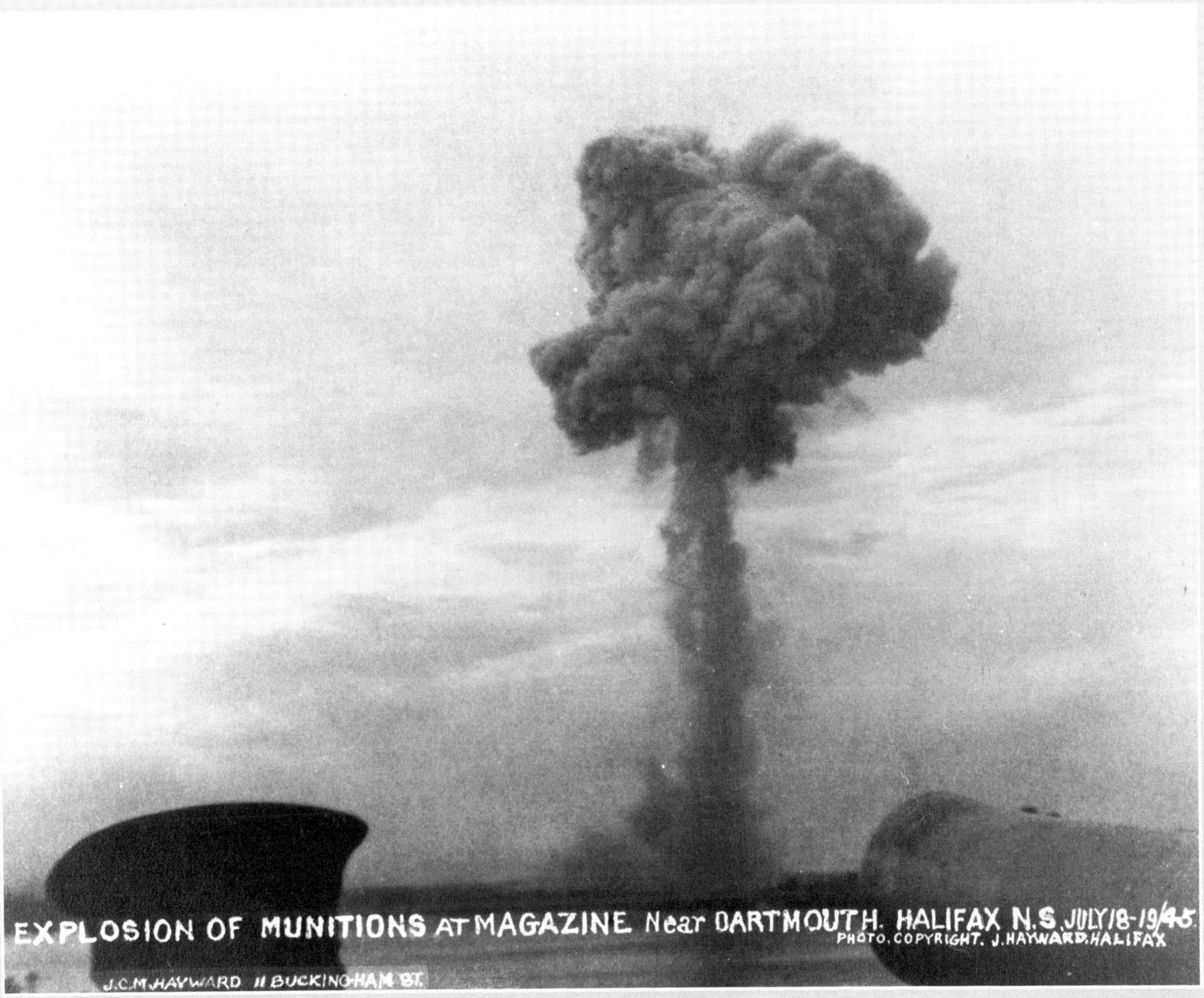

On July 18, 1945, an ammunition barge blew up at the Naval Magazine jetty on Bedford Basin. Fire spread quickly to piles of ammunition. A chain reaction of fire, explosion, and concussion rocked Halifax throughout that day and into the next. Much of the north end of the city was smoothly evacuated on the first day, while the remainder of Halifax went into high alert. However, the Bedford Magazine Explosion came nowhere near the force of the 1917 Halifax Harbour Explosion—although windows shattered, plaster cracked, and minor injuries and one death were reported.

20. Viewing Broken Glass on Barrington Street after the Bedford Magazine Explosion

July 18, 1945

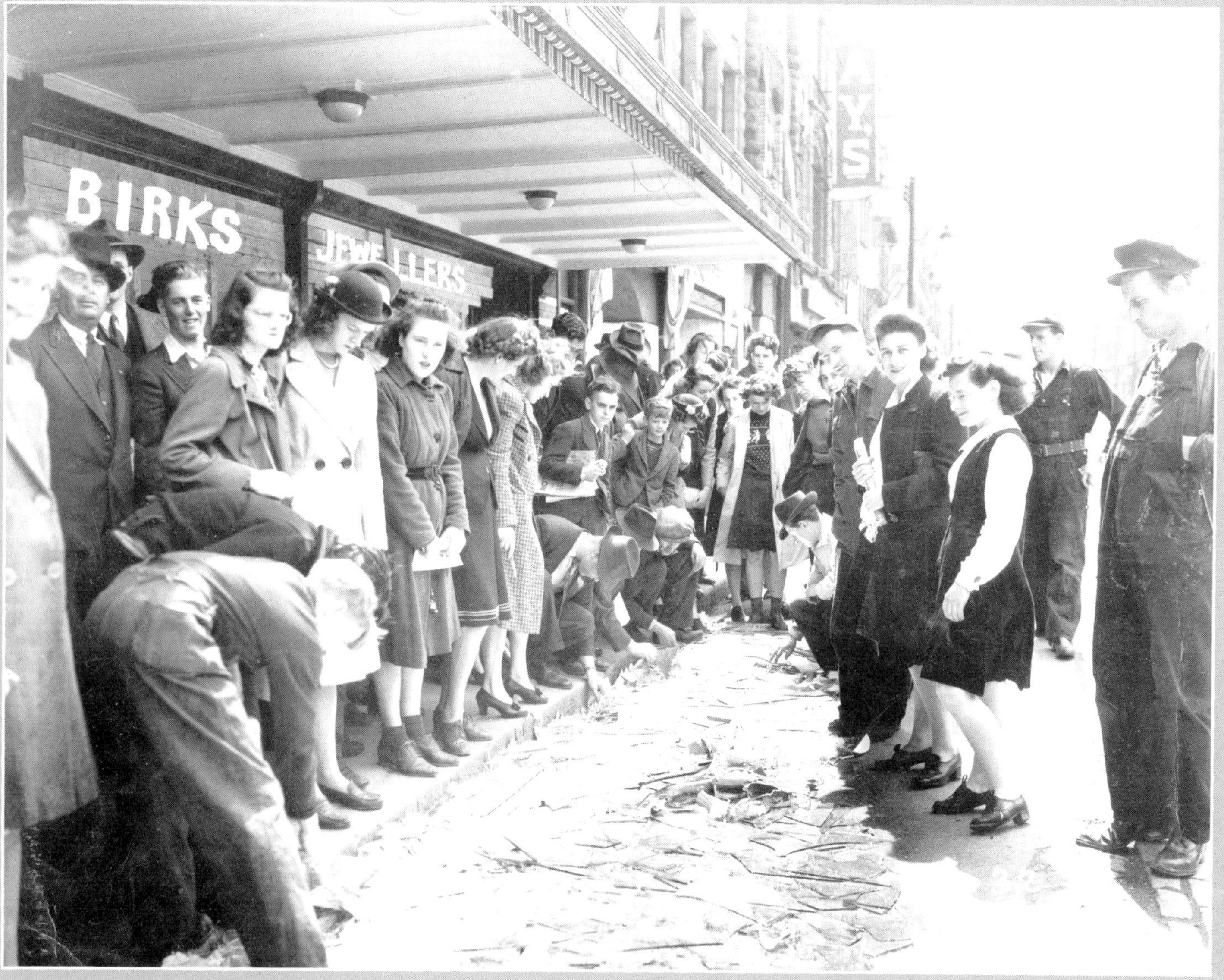

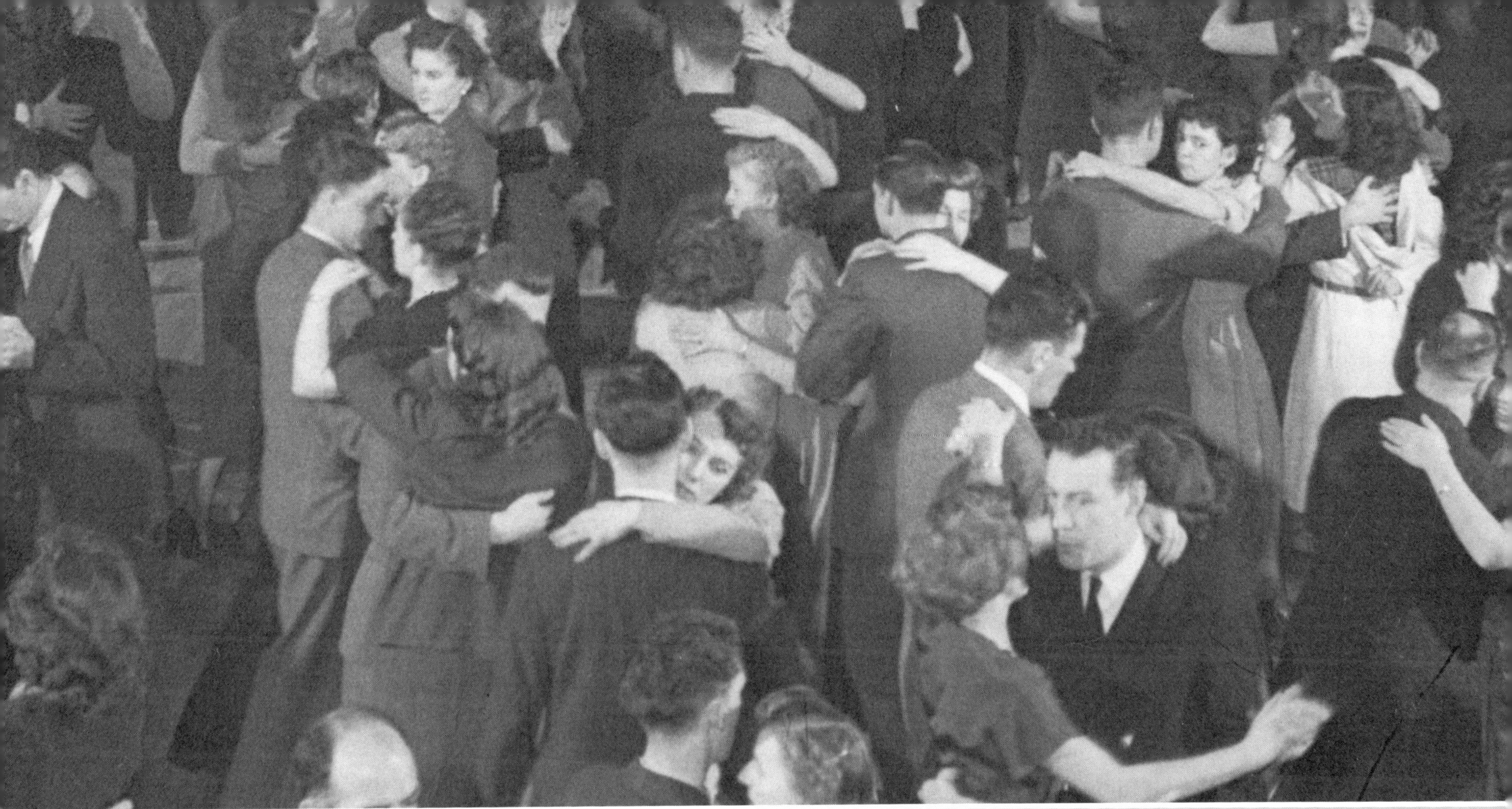

CHAPTER 4

ENTERTAINMENT AND SOCIAL EVENTS

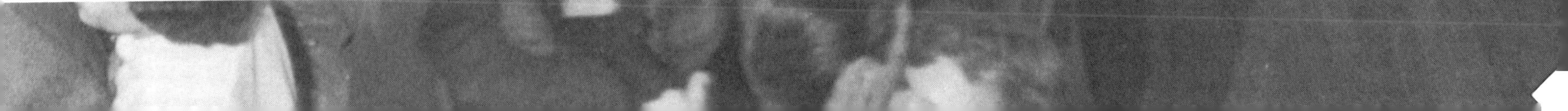

Halifax's reputation as a community which encourages and loves band music dates from the eighteenth century, when the British forces posted to the Garrison City brought their regimental bands and provided stirring music for both troops and civilians. Lieutenant William Dyott, 4th Regiment of Foot, arrived in Halifax in 1787 and noted in his diary that, "There is a square in town called the Grand Parade, where the troops in garrison parade every evening during the summer; and where all the belles and beaux of the place promenade, and the bands remain to play as long as they walk."

Singing, dancing, and music were taught and enjoyed in Halifax from the beginning of the community. Henry Meriton offered dancing lessons to both men and women in 1752, and nine years later, Jacob Althaus advertised that he would teach gentlemen to play various musical instruments. The *Nova-Scotia Gazette*, February 22, 1785, carried the first newspaper reference to a concert, an event held in the Golden Ball, a local coffee-house. Concerts and operas were subsequently performed in the British Tavern, Noonan's Tavern, Mrs. Sutherland's Coffee-House, the British Coffee-House, the Golden Ball, the Grande Theatre and the Theatre Royal.

Mrs. Anna Kearney, describing the evening of August 10, 1795, when she attended the comedy *Ways and Means* and the burletta (a comic opera or musical farce) *Midas*, confided to her diary that:

> *Sir John [Wentworth, the Lieutenant-Governor of the Colony] sent his carriage to conduct me to the Theatre—The Coachman much in liquor & drove so extremely fast that I was near fainting with fear when we got to the Door & trembled from Head to Foot[.] Mrs. George sat also in Sir Johns Box—The Play (which was Ways & means) went off tolerably well with the Scenery pretty & some of the male Voices in Midas extremely fine.*

Late nineteenth-century activities, actively captured by the invention of the camera, reflected typical pursuits and interests of the time: balls and dances, art exhibitions, concerts, plays and lectures, boating and other water-related activities, and family, Sunday School, and group picnics to popular local destinations such as the North West Arm, Bedford Basin, McNabs Island, Cow Bay, and the Rocking Stone in Spryfield. Another local novelty was the skating rink at the Exhibition Building on Tower Road, officially opened in 1880. Ice carnivals were held there regularly, attracting upwards of 3,000 spectators to watch hundreds of costumed skaters.

1. Fancy-dress ball given by Gen. Sir Patrick L. MacDougall, K.C.M.G., Commander of H.M. Forces, at 'Maplewood,' Northwest Arm

sometime between 1878 and 1883

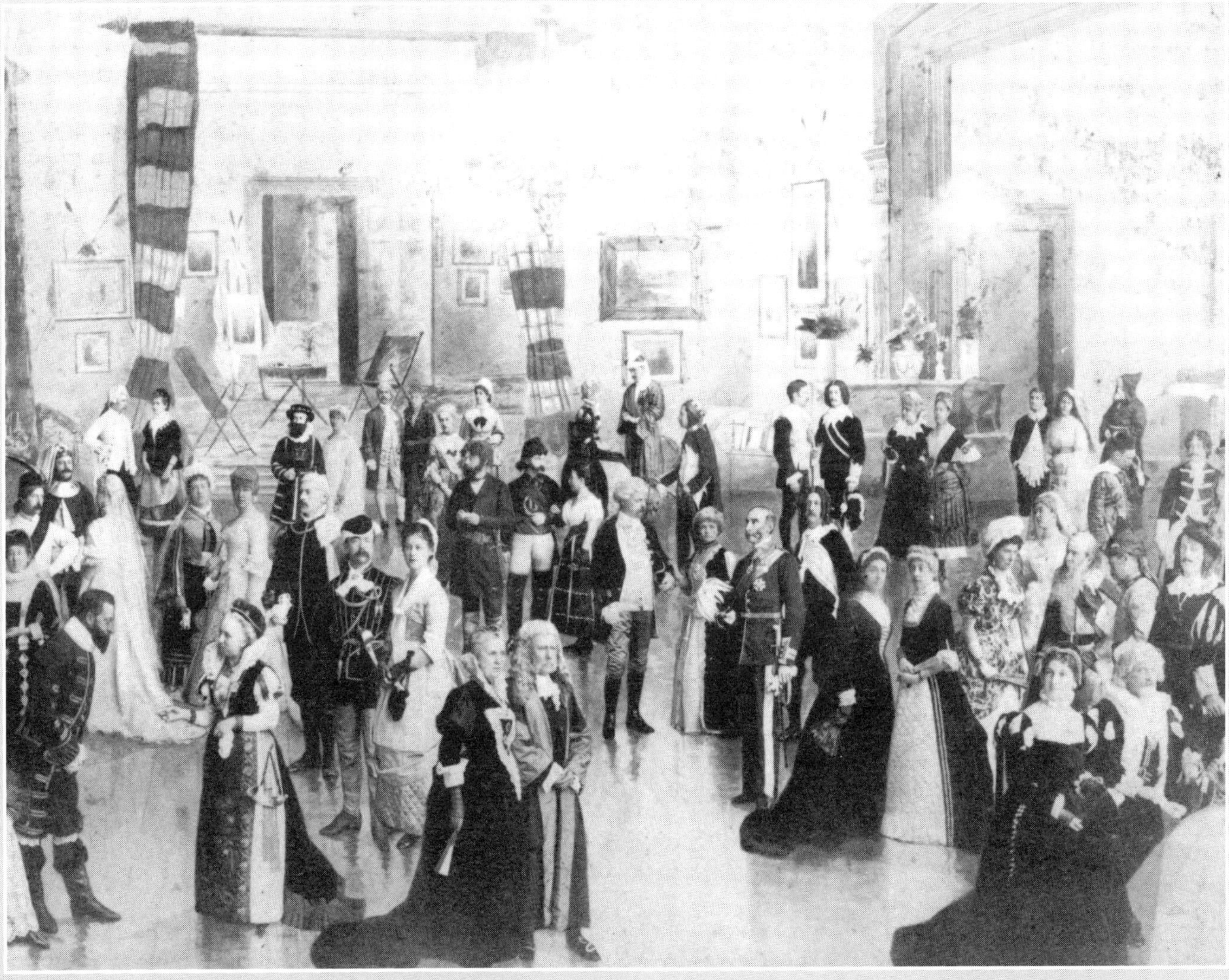

'Maplewood' was a magnificent eight-acre property on the North West Arm; the residence was described in *The Citizen* (Halifax), April 4, 1872, as "large and commodious containing fourteen rooms. Besides kitchens, cellars, bathroom....stables, barns, root house, fowl house, [and] ice house, there is also a small conservatory and gardener's dwelling." The property, leased in the summers, 1878-83, to General Sir Patrick MacDougall, Commander-in-Chief of Her Majesty's Forces in Canada, was ideally suited for the extensive entertaining which went along with Sir Patrick's position as military chief and a leader of Halifax society.

Amateur theatricals were a favourite leisure activity for officers of the regiments stationed in Halifax, joined by members of the local gentry. This cast was photographed in the Lieutenant-Governor's garden on Barrington Street, across from Government House and adjoining St. Paul's Cemetery (now known as the Old Burying Ground).

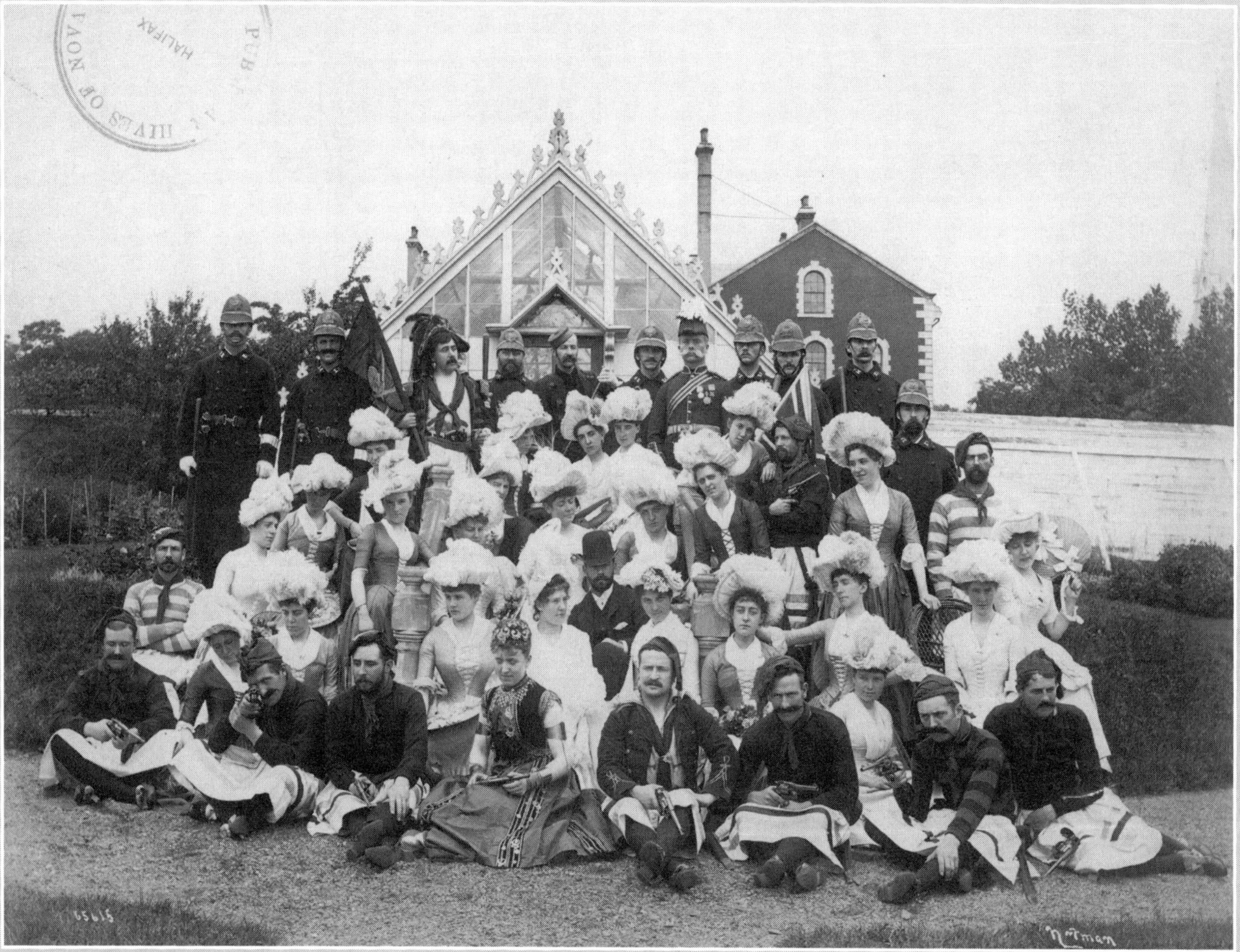

3. "Carnival, Old Exhibition Rink, Feb. 1899"

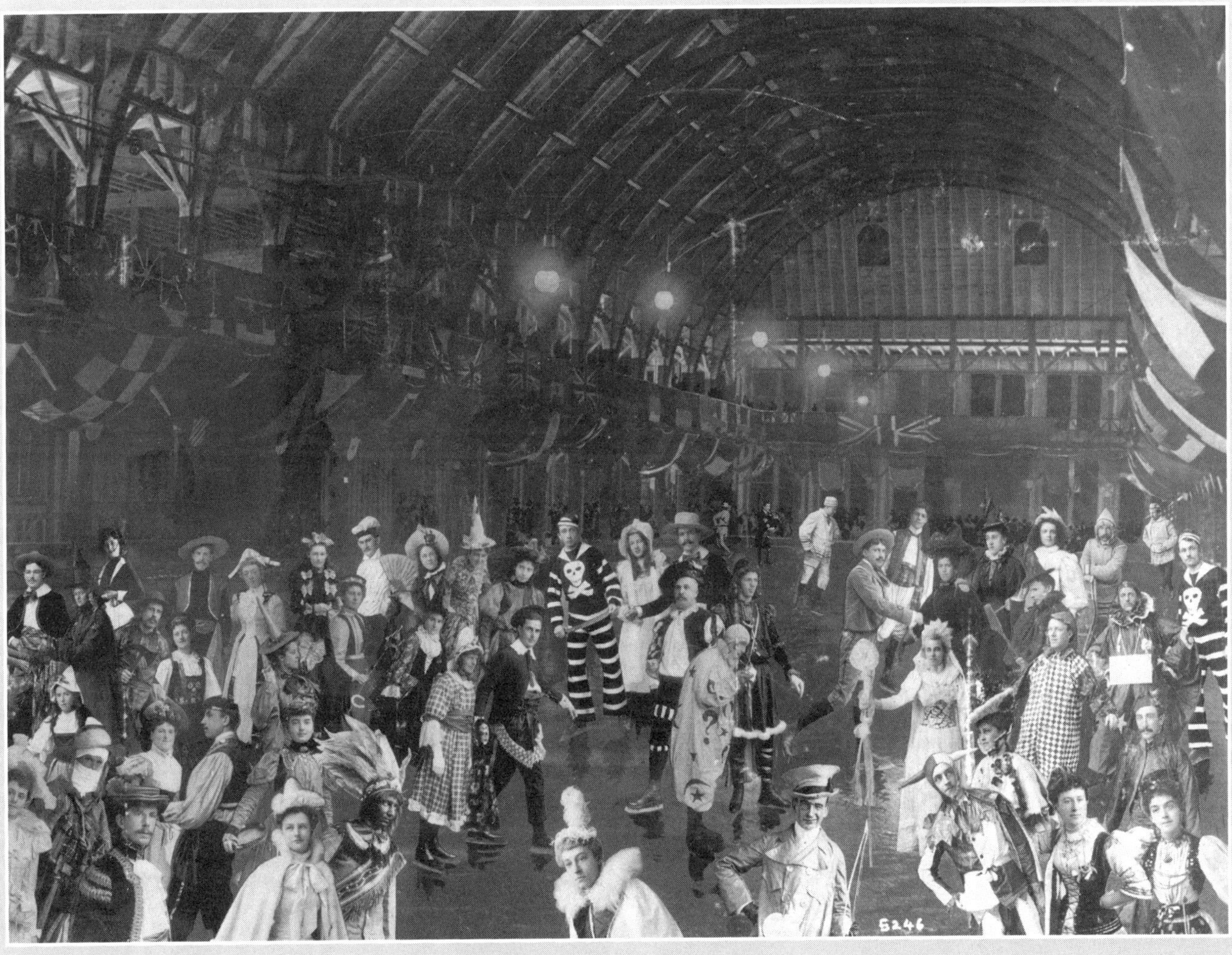

About 200 skaters and 1000 spectators attended the Carnival held in the South End Exhibition Rink in February 1899. The *Halifax Daily Echo* for February 7 described the participants:

> *The Royal Canadian regiment and St. Patrick's bands rendered a splendid programme, including many waltzes, which the skaters and spectators enjoyed. The ice was never in better condition, and one well known skater said he had never seen a better sheet in his life. There was nothing very strikingly new in the costumes, though nearly all were very neat and some very pretty. There was only one group noticeable—the Geisha girls (Frank Stephen, D'Arcy Weatherbe and C. Grant) who were made up to represent three very presentable maidens. A lampshade costume, worn by Mrs. Green, was of crimpled paper arranged with pretty effect....Another costume that attracted notice was that of the Daisy, worn by a lady whose name was not among those registered. On a dark green dress were worked daisies, and she wore a little cape with a yellow centre near the neck and the petals falling over the shoulders.*

4. Frances Gwendolyn Castens in her Noah's Ark costume
189–

5. "Hesslein & Anderson"
c 1885

Frances Gwendolyn Castens was the daughter of Sarah Jane and Gilbert W. Francklyn and the granddaughter of Sir Samuel Cunard. Her somewhat unusual headpiece is complemented by a gown sporting appropriate fish, fowl and wildlife. The family resided at 'Emscote,' a large property on the North West Arm, and gave their name to Francklyn Street and the Francklyn Park sub-division.

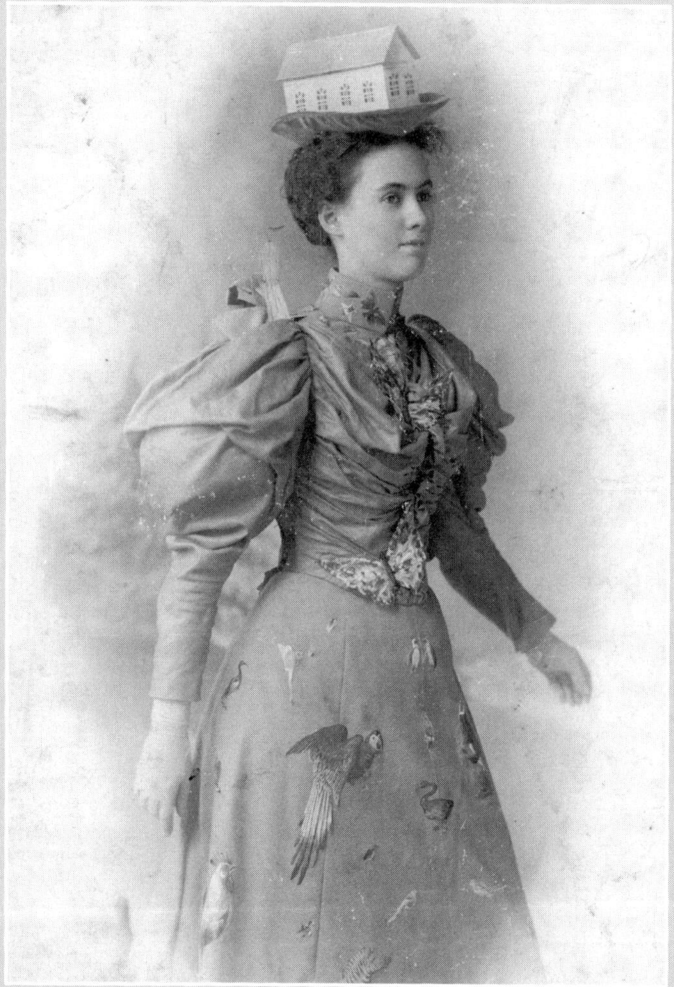

Messrs. Louis J. Hesslein and Gibson Anderson are dressed in oriental attire for a skating carnival. Mr. Hesslein and his brother A.G. Hesslein were proprietors of the Halifax Hotel on Hollis Street, the largest hotel in the Maritime Provinces at the time.

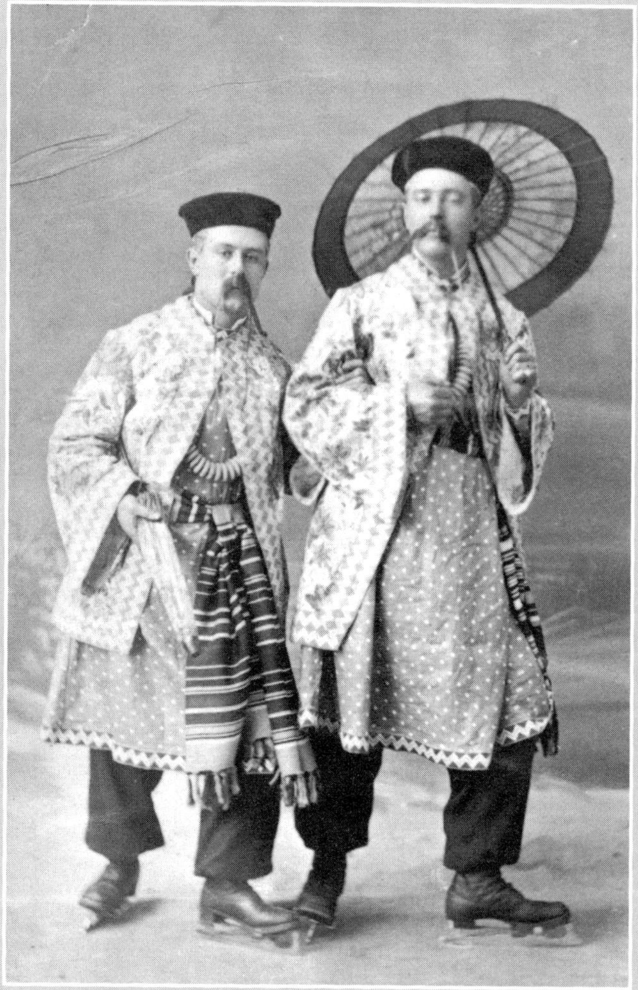

6. Missionary Loan Exhibition, Halifax

January 1903

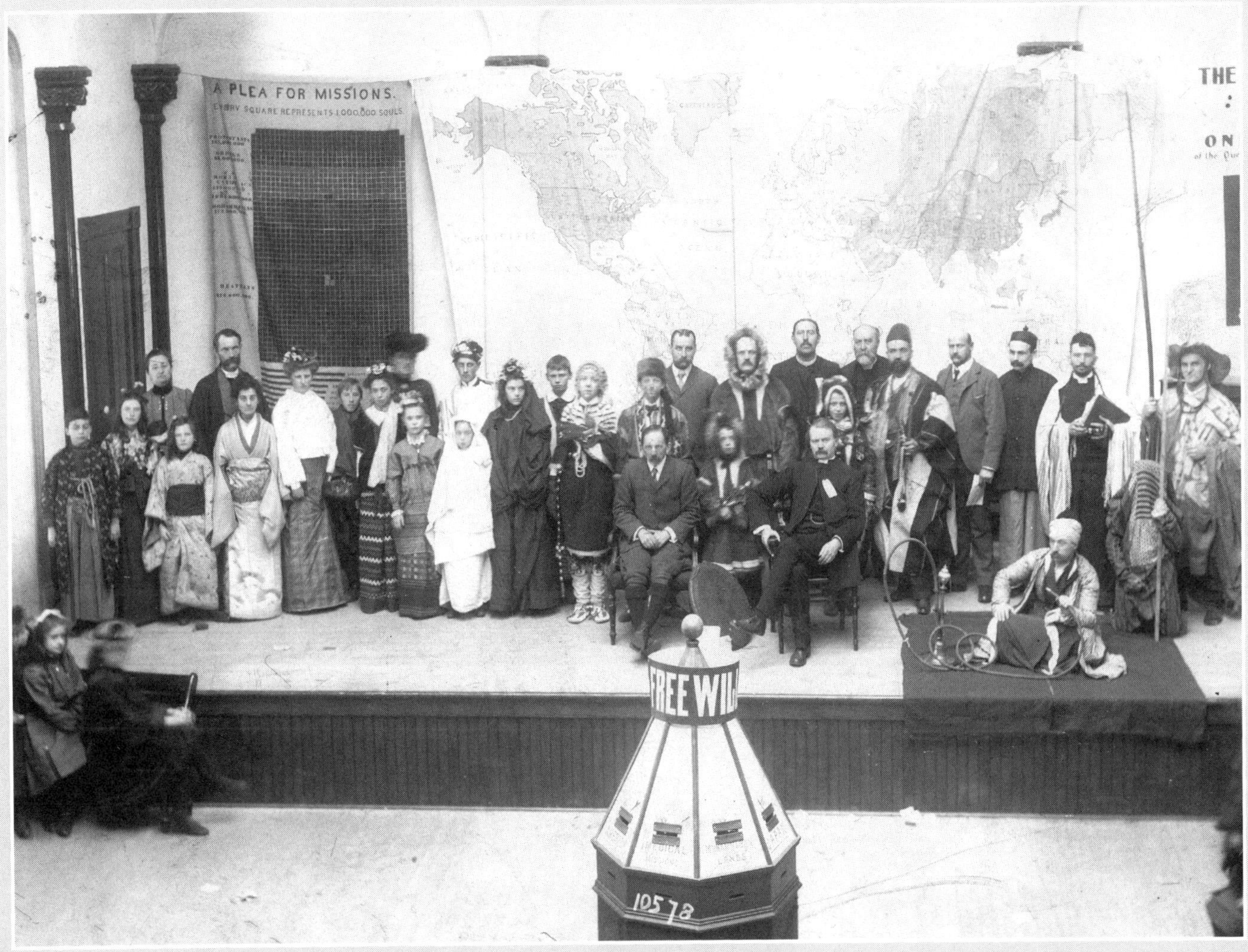

Lieutenant-Governor Alfred G. Jones and the Anglican Bishop, Frederick Courtney, formally opened the Missionary Loan Exhibition held in St. Paul's Parish Hall from January 20-24, 1903. The exhibition included examples of silver, stone, and woodwork from missions in Africa, Asia, South America, and the South Seas. Tea was served daily at 5 p.m. and half-hour concerts were performed in the evenings. Organized by Major J. C. Thorpe, it was the first function held in the newly-renovated hall, designed by architect W. Critchlow Harris. The exhibition was conceived to foster interest in foreign missions, to be both entertaining and instructive. Those manning the booths dressed in the attire of the ethnic groups they represented, and upwards of ten thousand people visited the exhibition.

7. Spectators Watching Boating on the North West Arm in front of the Waegwoltic Club
c 1910

In 1908, a group of private citizens purchased 'Bloomingdale,' which had been the residence of Alfred G. Jones (1824-1906) from 1860 until his appointment as Lieutenant-Governor in 1900. His family included daughters Frances (later Bannerman), a noted artist and poet, and Alice, a well-known author, both of whom later moved overseas. The purchase price for 'Bloomingdale' was $10,000, and the citizens' group subsequently founded the Waegwoltic Club, a name derived from the Mi'kmaq word for the North West Arm. The house and property remain intact today, a thriving private recreational facility and Halifax landmark.

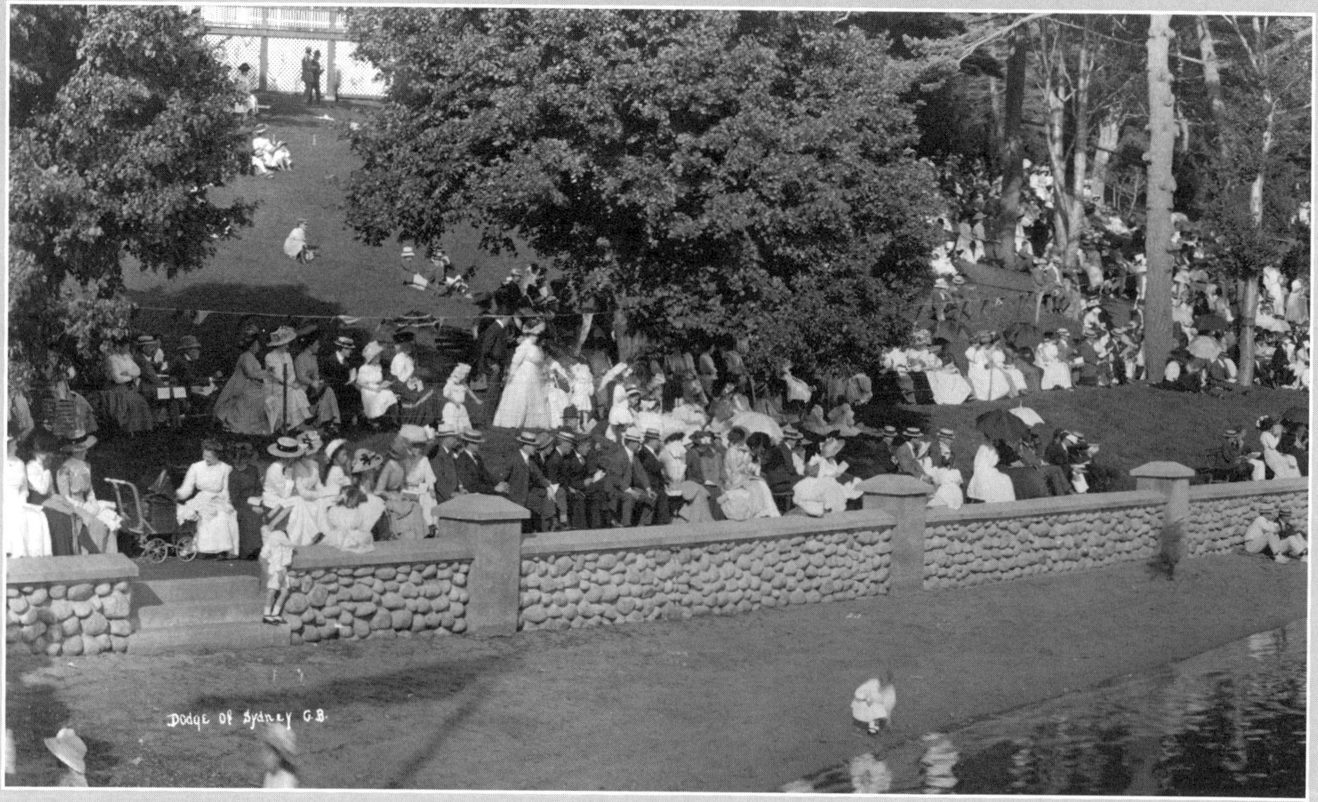

8. "Scene from the movie *Evangeline* shot in the garden of Billman Residence, Melvillewood, Armdale, now called 17 Herring Cove Rd." 1913

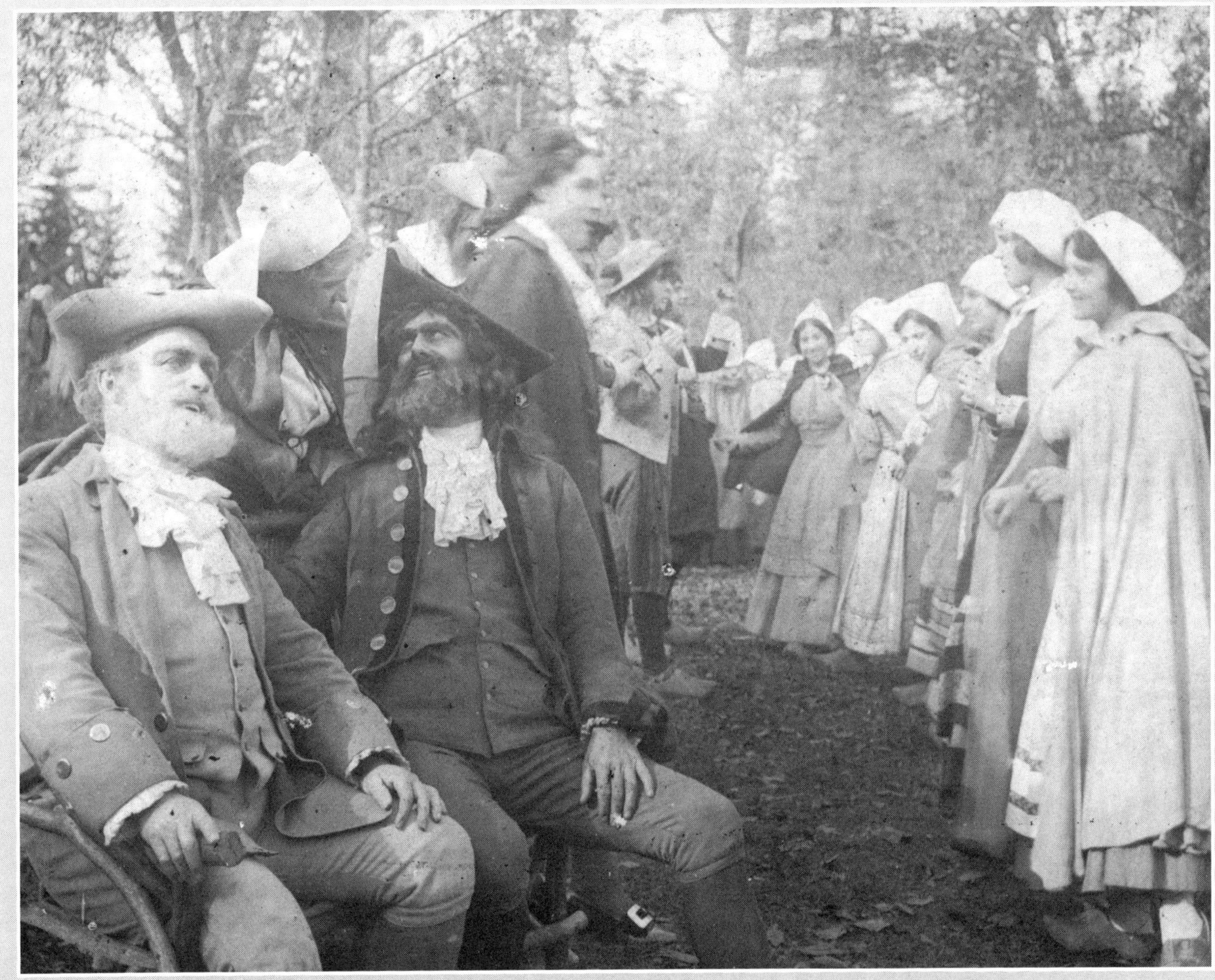

Evangeline was a film based on Henry Wadsworth Longfellow's epic poem of the same name. It was both the first Canadian feature-length motion-picture and the very first film shot on location in Canada. *Evangeline* was produced by the Canadian Bioscope Company, founded in 1912 by H.H.B. Holland, with its headquarters at 108-118 Pleasant Street (now the Foundry Building on Barrington Street, near Inglis). The company went on to produce seven widely varied films for the Canadian market—none of which has survived; with the outbreak of World War I, Canadian Bioscope went out of business.

9. "The Commercial Club luncheon, 1925, given by Moir's Ltd., on the old Bedford Road, now part of Moir's Ltd."

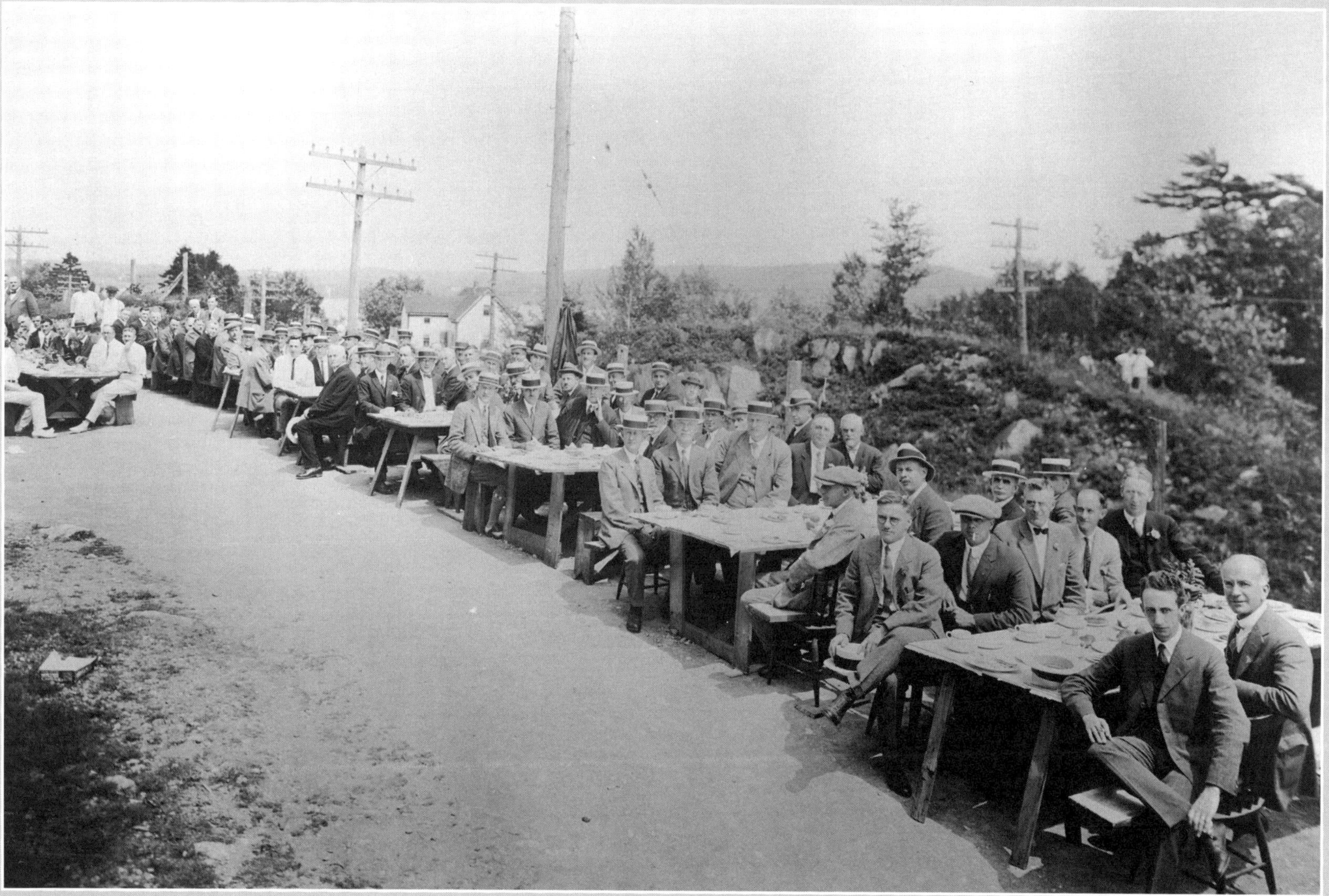

10. Canadian actor Austin Willis and Dick Fry perform from the CHNS Studio, Lord Nelson Hotel

c 1939

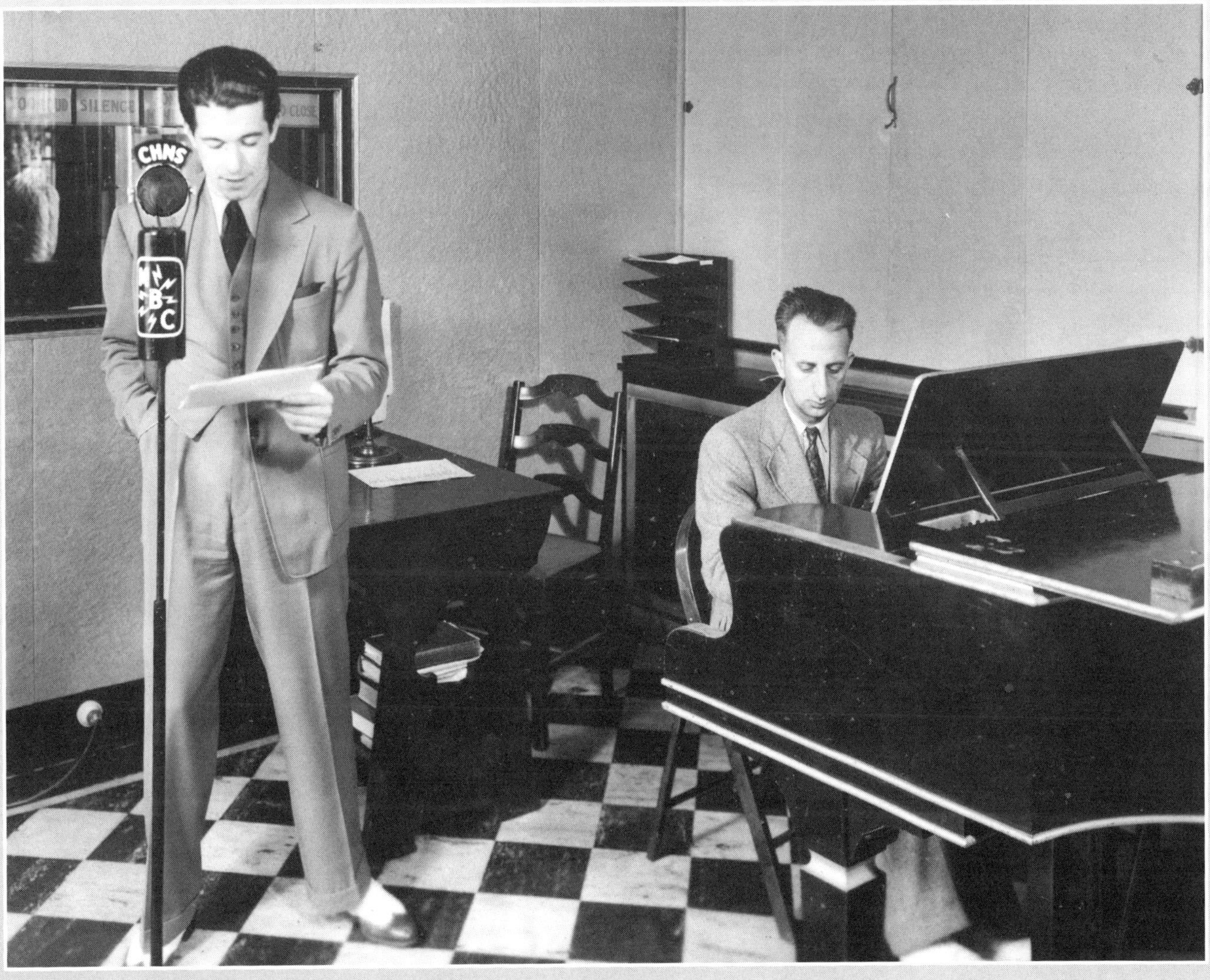

Maritime Broadcasting Limited began broadcasting as Radio Station CHNS in 1926 from the Carleton Hotel, corner of Argyle and Prince, with a 100-watt transmitter. Two years later, the station moved to the penthouse of the Lord Nelson Hotel, this time with a 500-watt transmitter.

The *Halifax Daily Star* for April 27, 1931, carried this photograph and reported that:

> *Here we have the ballet of the minstrel show to be presented at the Capitol Theatre tonight by the Commercial Club of Halifax under the direction of Miss Frances Foster. According to the press agent, these 'girls' will be a riot. They are garbed as senoritas, an old Spanish custom with Commercial Club minstrels. Left to right, they are: Ald. W.E. Donovan, F.G. Balcom, C.E. Dowden, H.M. Laurence, Murray Ryan, W.R. Moore, J.E. Hudson, R.O. Cutler, E.A. Young, W.E. Godding, H. Montgomery.*

The Capitol Theatre, located on Barrington Street at the foot of Spring Garden Road, was designed in 1929 by noted Toronto theatre architect, Murray Brown. Opening to the public in 1930, it was a thematic or atmospheric movie-house, designed to be reminiscent of a medieval castle. It was demolished in 1974.

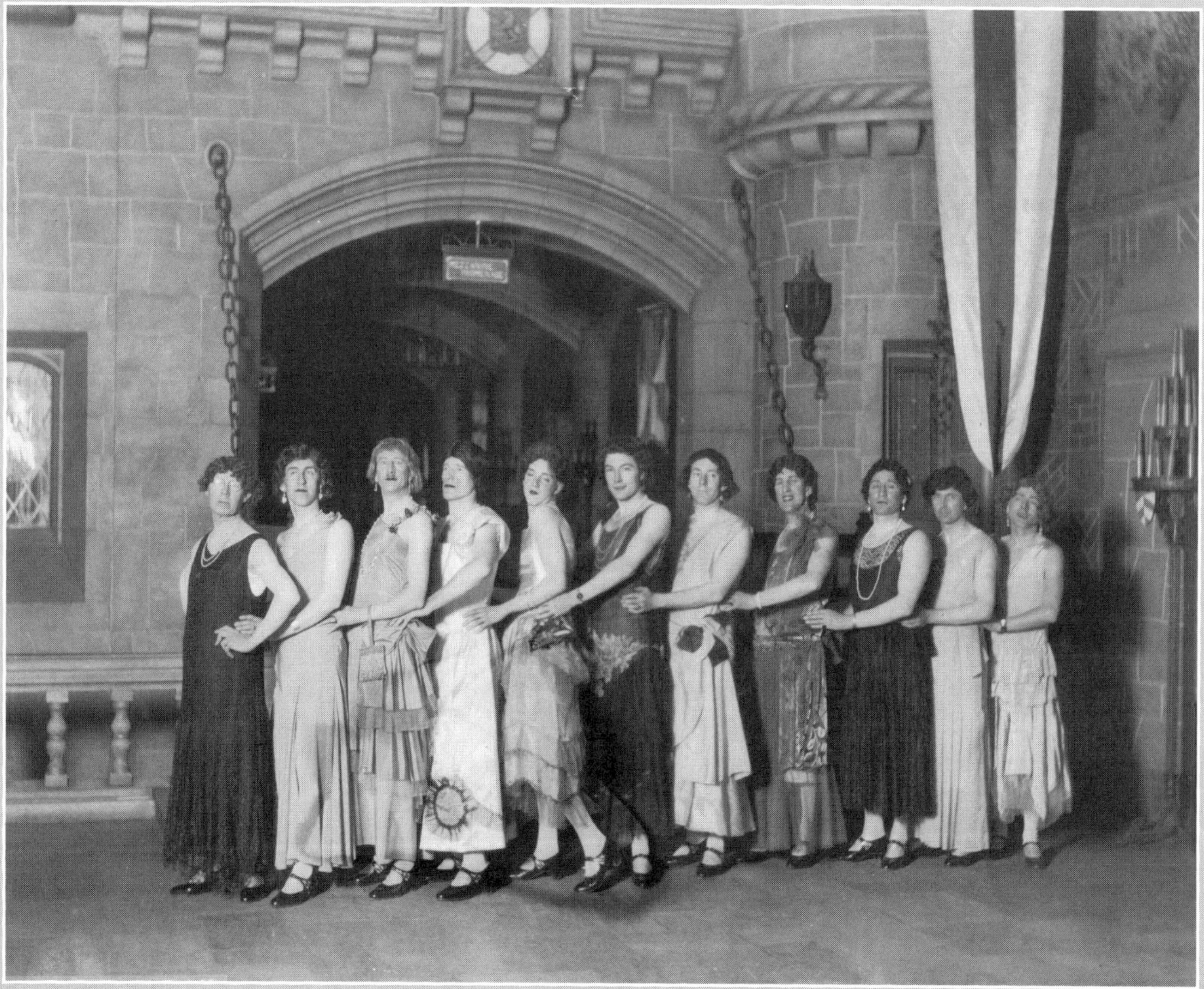

12. "Minstrels of '31" programme

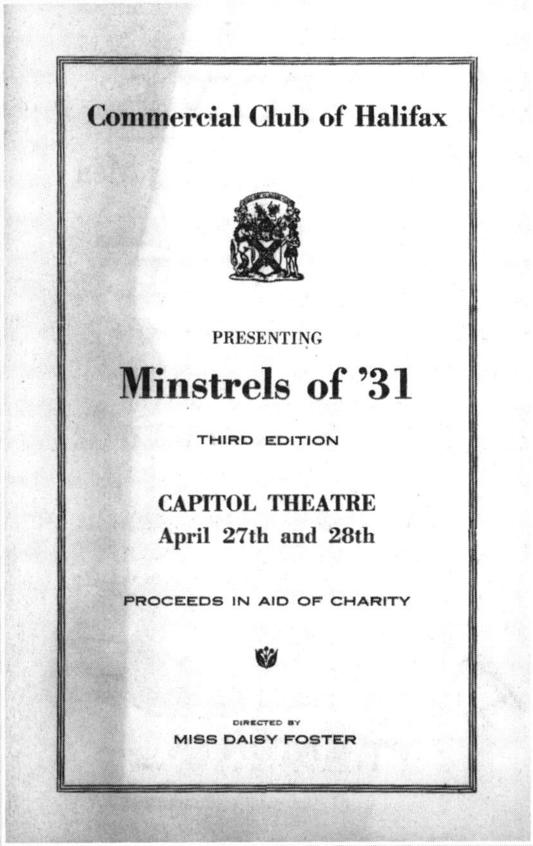

Commercial Club of Halifax

PRESENTING

Minstrels of '31

THIRD EDITION

CAPITOL THEATRE
April 27th and 28th

PROCEEDS IN AID OF CHARITY

DIRECTED BY
MISS DAISY FOSTER

The *Halifax Daily Star*, April 28, 1931, reported that the show was a success: "Well muscled 'Senoritas,' wise-cracking endmen, and the bull fight that happened in Monterey, filled the theatre with laughter."

13. Letter from R E. Inglis, to Members of the Commercial Club of Halifax, requesting them to sell tickets

March 12, 1931

The Commercial Club of Halifax

Halifax, N. S.,
March 12th, 1931.

Dear Sir:

The Commercial Club of Halifax, with a record of two outstanding successes in the amateur Minstrel Show field during recent years, is now preparing under the able direction of Miss Frances Foster, the capable directress of their former successes, to present at the Capitol Theatre a Minstrel Show which in beauty of conception and magnificence of production bids fair to far eclipse all former efforts.

This elaborate production will be staged, as intimated, at the new Capitol Theatre on April 27th and 28th. Exchagge tickets are to sell at the popular price of $1.00 each, the proceeds to be entirely devoted to charity.

To make this show a success, each member is asked tc dispose of tickets. Your tickets are numbers.........to ...., and are enclosed herewith.

The exchange office at the Capitol will be open from 10.00 a .m. until 6.00 p. m. on April 22nd, 23rd and 24th. Additional exchange tickets, and a limited number of logue tickets at $1.50 each, may be secured from the undersigned, to whom all returns are to be made.

It is hoped that each member of this old Club, with its splendid record of present and past achievement, will spare no effort to make this Show as successful from a monetary standpoint as it undoubtedly will be from a pleasure giving and artistic point of view.

The Commercial Club assure you of two evenings of unalloyed pleasure. Will you do your utmost to co-operate by disposing of these tickets?

Yours truly,

R. E. INGLIS,
On Behalf of the Ticket Committee.

P. S. Please make your returns as promptly as possible
R.E.I.

14. Olympic Gardens Dance Hall, Hunter Street, Halifax

c 1948

The Olympic Gardens was opened to the public c1948 by Victor Beed. It was a popular dance hall in the city for many years.

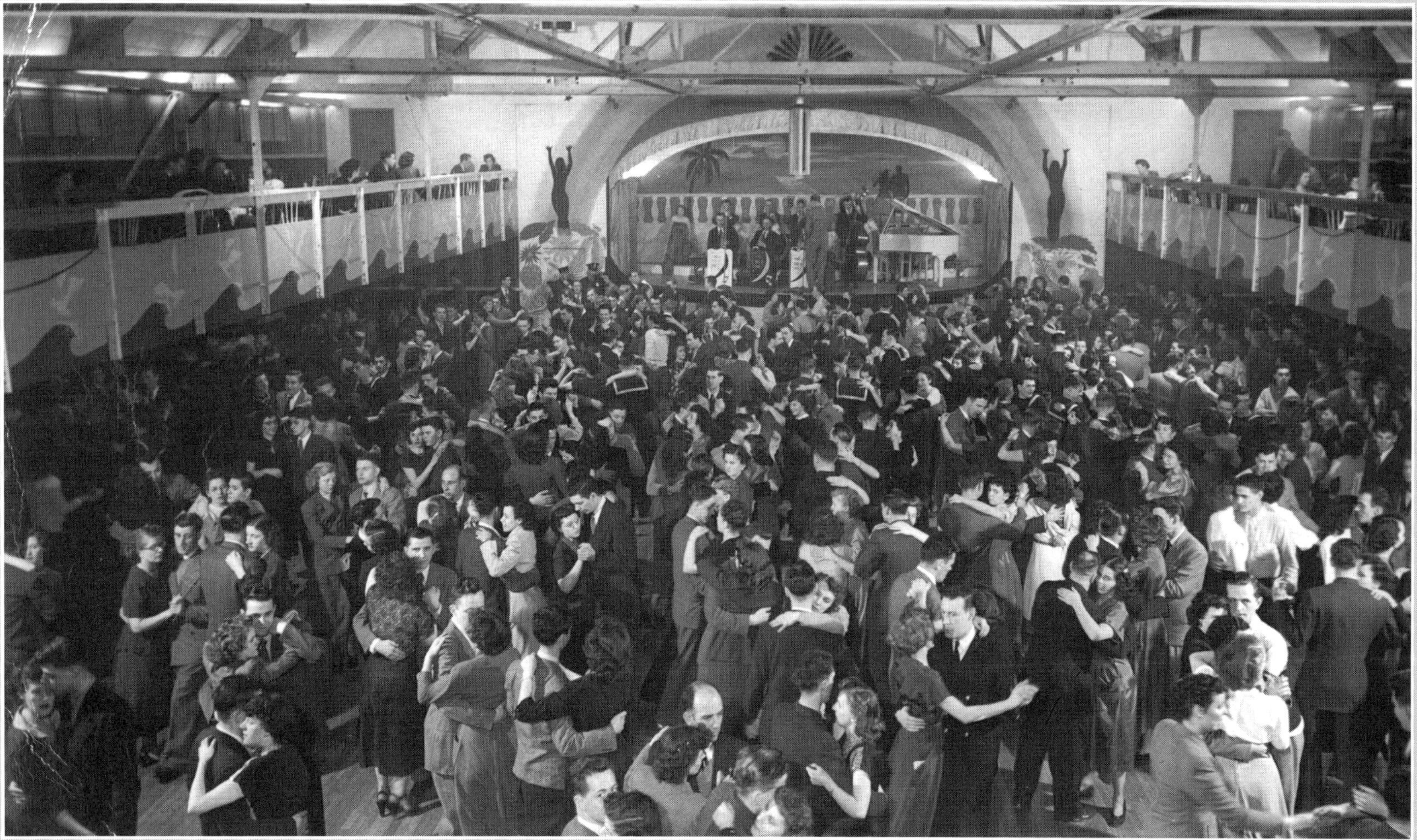

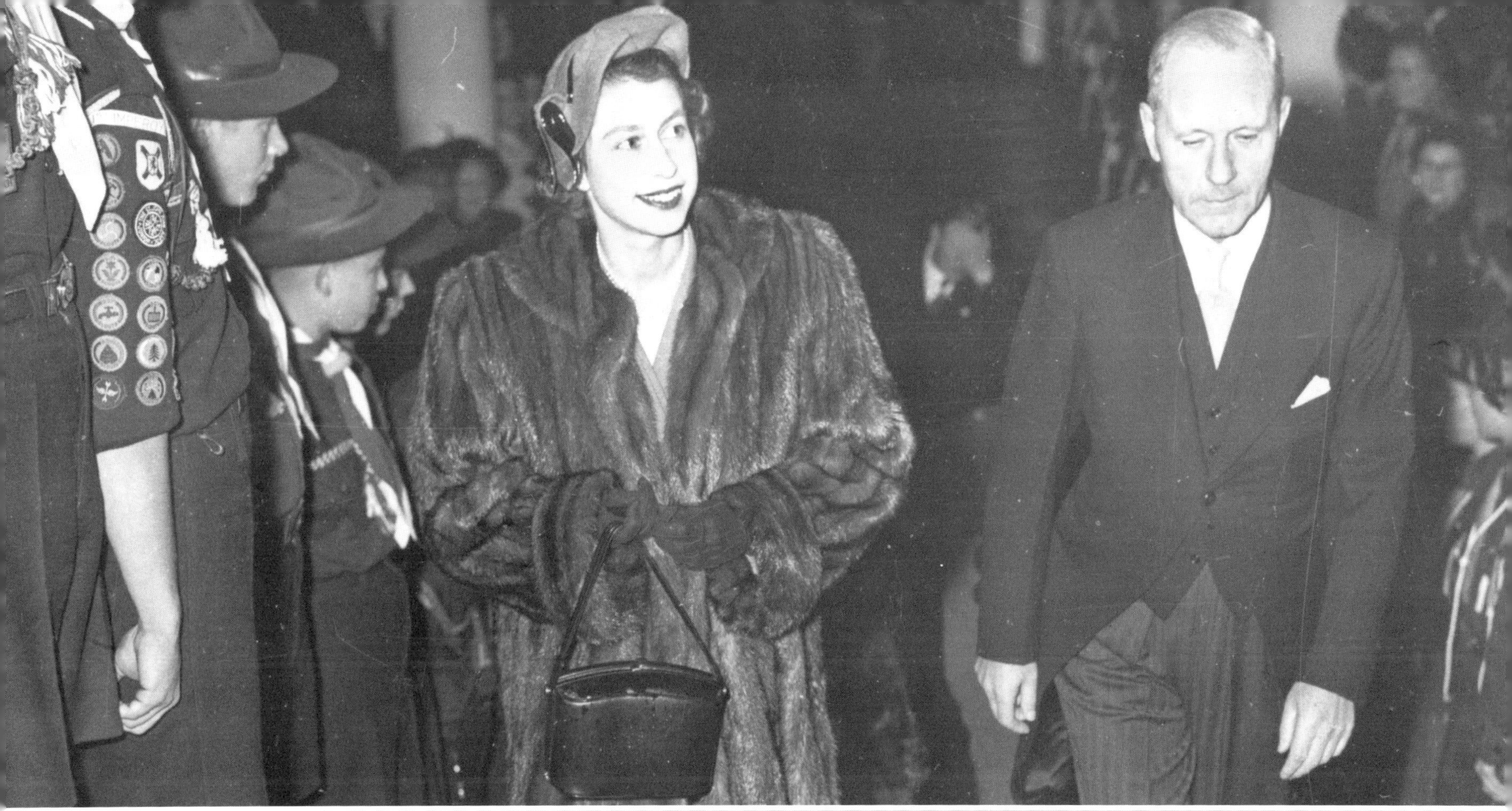

CHAPTER 5

ROYAL VISITS AND SPECIAL EVENTS

With its long history as a significant naval port and military garrison for the strategic defence of British North America, it is only natural that Halifax has been a stopping-off point on various royal itineraries over the years. In 1786 and 1787, Prince William Henry (later King William IV), then captain of HMS *Pegasus*, called in port on several occasions. During the 1790s, his brother, HRH Prince Edward, Duke of Kent, came to the city as Commander-in-Chief of His Majesty's Forces in British North America, bringing with him his mistress, Madame St. Laurent, who both charmed and mortified the local gentry, some of whom refused to attend gatherings where she would be present.

The duke's grandson, HRH Prince Albert Edward, Prince of Wales, visited the Garrison City in 1860; Phyllis R. Blakeley described this event in her book, *Glimpses of Halifax 1867-1900*:

> *Day after day the future King Edward VII received addresses and read replies, reviewed volunteer troops, drove through cheering crowds on streets bedecked with bunting, held levees and attended dances and luncheons.... The streets and gutters had been swept until there 'was not a dead cat, a broken bottle, or an old boot to be seen. Even the dirty pieces of paper, the favorite embellishment of our sidewalks and gutters, especially in the upper streets, had vanished for the nonce.'*

Indeed, no dead cats, broken bottles or old boots can be seen in the photographic record of the visit, one of the earliest surviving examples of outdoor photography produced in the city.

HRH Prince Arthur, Duke of Connaught and later the Governor-General of Canada (1911-16), stopped off in the city in 1869. His sister, Princess Louise, was the first female member of the Royal Family to visit Halifax; she accompanied her husband, the Marquis of Lorne, who in 1878 took the oath of office as Governor-General of Canada, in the city. The most memorable Royal Visits of this century have been those of King George VI and Queen Elizabeth in 1939; HRH Princess Elizabeth and Prince Philip, Duke of Edinburgh in 1951; and HRH Prince Charles, Prince of Wales and Diana, Princess of Wales, in 1983.

Other notable visitors have also drawn large crowds to the old port city over the years. Most recently, the eyes of the world were on the city in June 1995 when the leaders of the industrialized nations held their annual G-7 (21st) Economic Summit in Halifax, using the waterfront as backdrop.

1. Inauguration of the Welsford-Parker Monument, Halifax

July 17, 1860

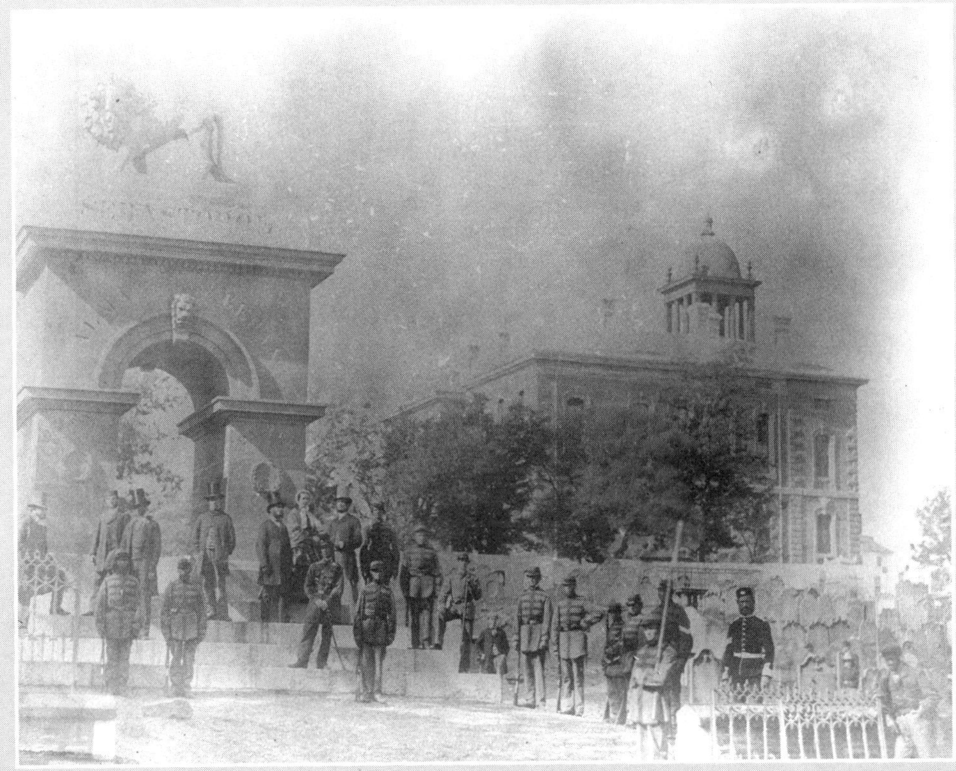

This well-known monument, located in Halifax's Old Burying Ground, was erected by citizens in memory of Captain William Parker and Major Augustus Welsford, Nova Scotians who died in the Crimean War. The *Acadian Recorder* for July 21, 1860 reported that:

> *The afternoon was clear, but uncomfortably warm. A little after 2 o'clock, the procession formed on the Grand Parade. It consisted of all the Halifax and Dartmouth Volunteer Companies, a large number of the Masonic body, and various public officials. These, paraded by bands of music, marched down Barrington Street to the old Cemetery, where detachments of the Regular troops of the garrison were already stationed. The military portion of the assemblage formed a hollow square around the Monument, within which ticket holders were admitted. A large assemblage, especially of the fair sex, were present to witness the proceedings; and the gloomy old grave yard for once presented a gay appearance. The ceremonies commenced with prayer by the Rev. John Scott. His Excellency the Lieutenant Governor, Lord Mulgrave then addressed the assemblage at some length and, in concluding, introduced the Rev. George Hill, the Orator of the day.…A great deal of cheering was done and the proceedings concluded by the Volunteer Artillery under the command of Captain Tremain, firing 13 minute guns, and by the bands playing and the whole assemblage singing the National Anthem. We find that while the ceremonies were going on, Chase, the clever photographer succeeded in taking an excellent photographic view of the whole scene, a copy of which we have no doubt many people will hasten to secure, as a memento of the day and the event.*

The reporter for the *Acadian Recorder* was obviously fascinated by the photographer's activities. Outdoor photography was still a novelty, and this is one of the very first surviving examples taken in Halifax. In the background of the photograph is the Court House, designed by William Thomas of Toronto—brand-new then and still standing today.

2. General Trollope's Arch in honour of the visit of the Prince of Wales, designed by Col. Nelson, R.E.

1860

HRH Prince Edward, Prince of Wales, arrived in Halifax on Monday, 30 July 1860. At noon the prince left his flagship, HMS *Hero*, and was greeted by dignitaries in the Dockyard. Then a procession formed and travelled southward to Government House, passing under numerous arches and greeted by throngs of Haligonians. On Tuesday morning, Prince Edward's standard was lowered at Government House and the prince, accompanied by his personal retinue, plus the Earl of Mulgrave (Lieutenant-Governor of Nova Scotia), General Charles Trollope (Commander-in-Chief of HM Forces in Nova Scotia) and various staff members, proceeded via Pleasant (Barrington) Street and Spring Garden Road to the western end of the Horticultural (Public) Gardens and on to the Halifax Commons. *The British Colonist* of 2 August gave a detailed account, describing the arch on Spring Garden Road near the Court House as:

...the grandest object amongst all our displays, in or around the city, outside of the Province Building..... It is the most splendid thing of the kind we have ever seen, here or elsewhere, and evinces on the part of its designer, not only much taste but real genius. First there are eight immense columns, 25 feet in length, three or four feet diameter at the base, and tapering to about 15 inches at the top. These columns are formed of small spars bound together with hoops. These eight columns support two immense arches, on the outside of which are two smaller arches, supported on lesser pillars of the same description. Each outside large column is capped with a Prince's feather, and above the central arch another, all perfect plumes formed of evergreens, and above the latter, floated the British ensign at a height of 71 feet. The distance between the large columns is 17 feet at the base— and the depth from the outside, parallel with the street, 13 feet.— From the street to the top of the plume is over 48 feet. Over the small arches are various inscriptions.

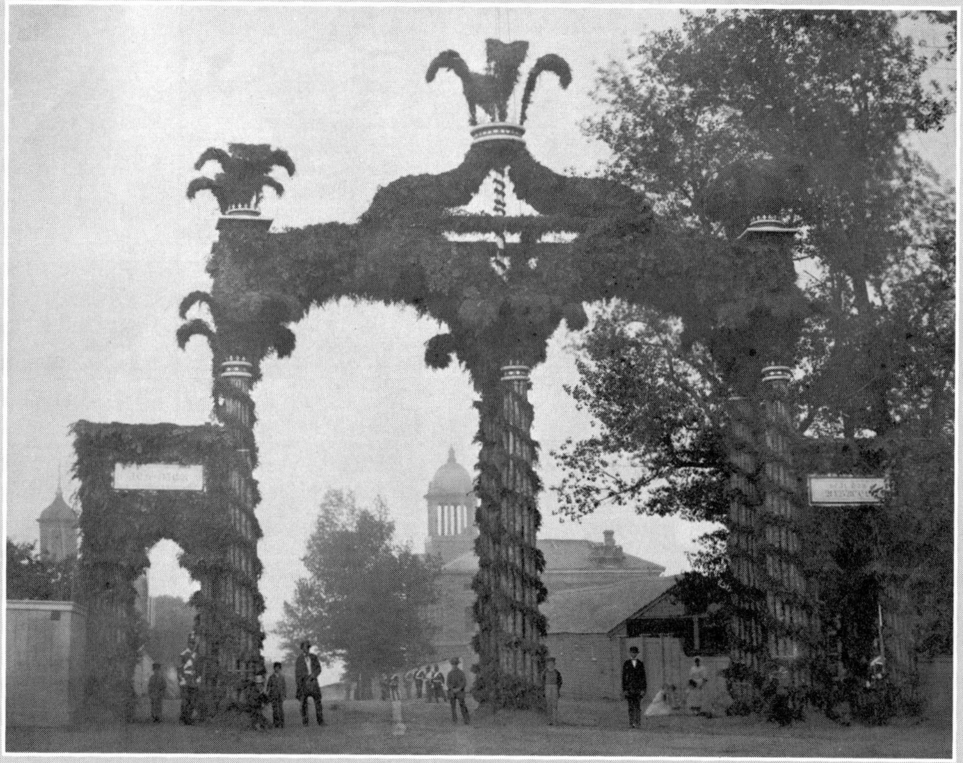

3. Presentation of Mi'kmaq to the Marquis of Lorne, in the Council Chamber of the Provincial Building, Halifax

November 26, 1878

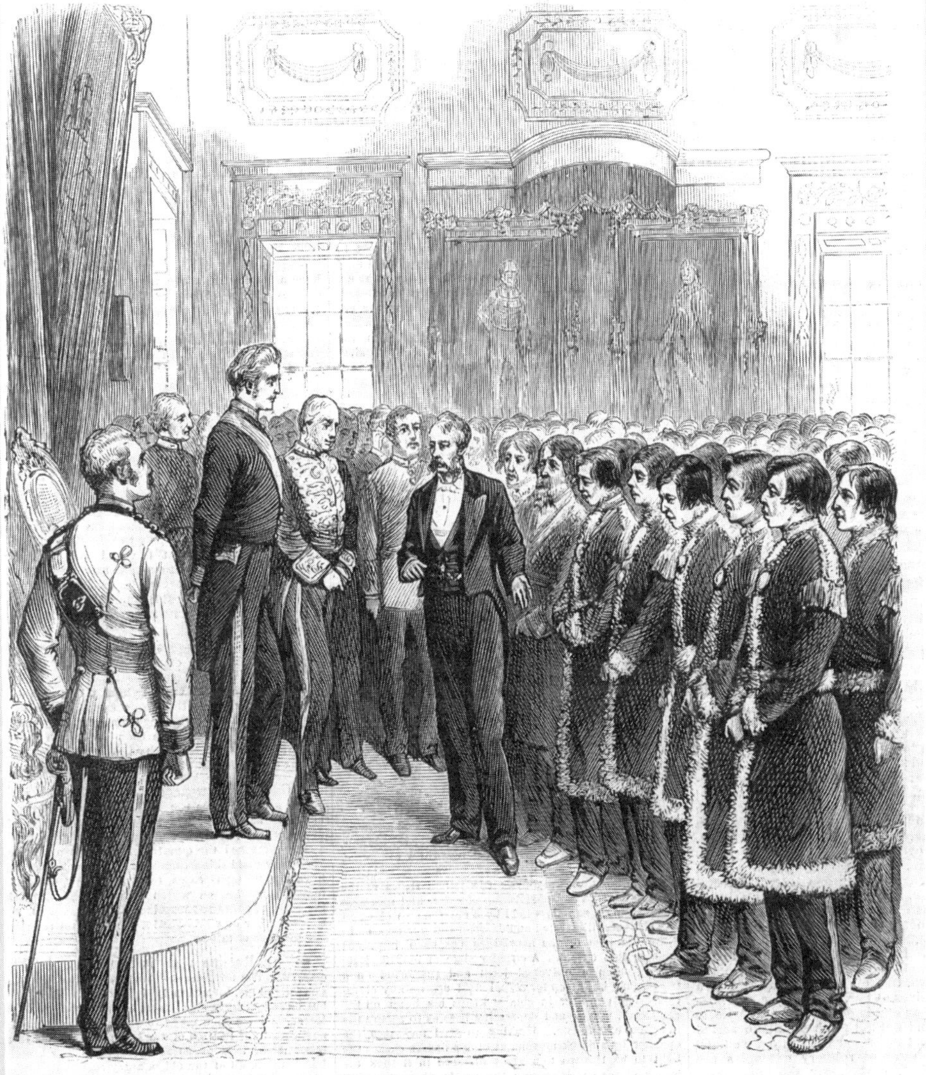

PRESENTATION TO THE MARQUIS OF LORNE OF MICMAC INDIANS, IN THE COUNCIL CHAMBER OF THE PROVINCIAL BUILDING HALIFAX, NOVEMBER 26TH.

In 1871, Princess Louise Caroline Alberta, Duchess of Saxony and daughter of Queen Victoria, was married to John Douglas Sutherland, Marquess of Lorne and 9th Duke of Argyll. Sutherland was subsequently appointed Governor-General of Canada in 1878 and was sworn in at Province House, Halifax, in the Red Room, on November 25. At 33 years of age, he was Canada's youngest Governor-General.

4. School children at unveiling of fountain, Public Gardens, Halifax, Jubilee week
1897

The 'Jubilee' or 'Nymph' Fountain commemorated Her Majesty Queen Victoria's Diamond Jubilee, the sixtieth anniversary of her reign. The fountain was unveiled by Ishbel, Marchioness of Aberdeen and Temair, the wife of John Campbell Gordon, 7th Earl of Aberdeen and Governor-General of Canada (1893-98).

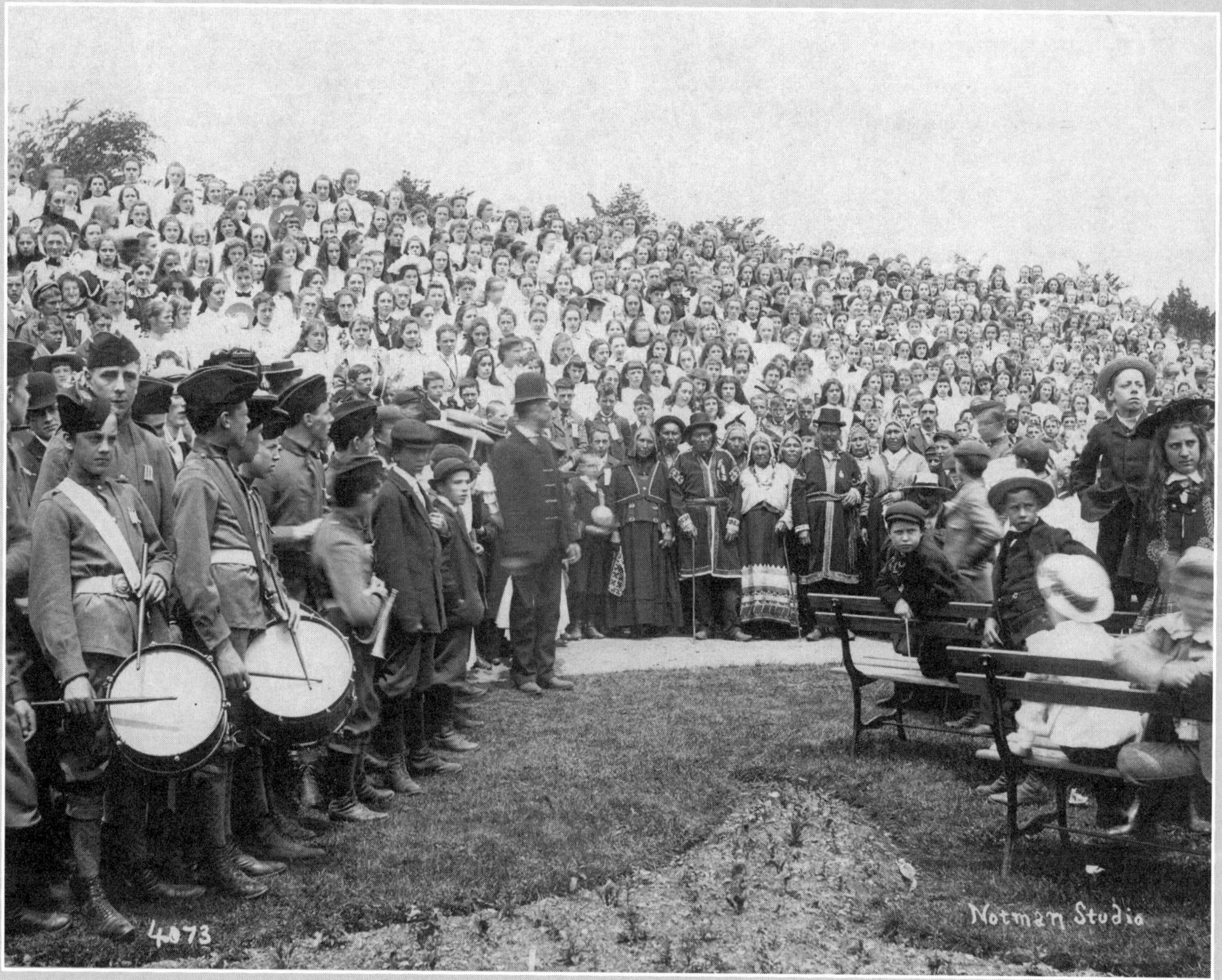

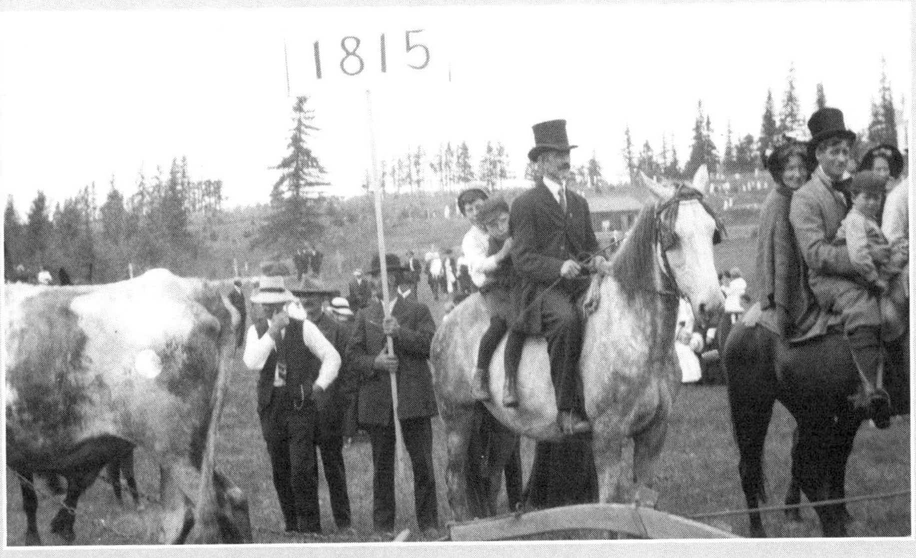

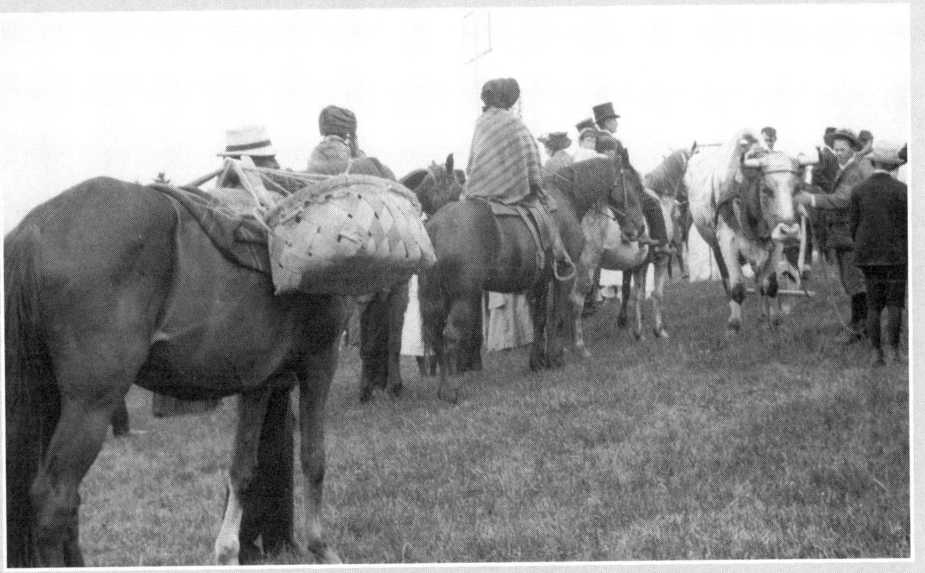

The Presbyterian Church celebrated its centenary in the Musquodoboit Valley in 1915. *The Truro Daily News*, July 14, reported that church services had been held throughout the valley on Sunday July 11. The next day, Monday, was a "real gala day" with an "Antique Procession" in Middle Musquodoboit. The newspaper explained that:

> *This was a sort of pageantry depicting the costumes of the people of 1815 in contrast to those costumes in vogue today. Leading the procession was the ox-drawn plow of 1815, and concluding it was the automobile of today. Between these representations of their age were the methods of travel, men and women gowned in the costumes of 1816 and thereabouts mounted on horseback. There were the swains of that day and the brides and the children. Then followed the procession of farm implements now in use, evidencing the advanced methods adopted by the people of Musquodoboit.*

The day concluded with amusements on the Exhibition Grounds, lectures, temperance addresses and a concert.

6. "H.R.H. Prince of Wales, Halifax, N.S. Aug. 18th, 1919"

Edward, Prince of Wales, arrived in Halifax on HMS *Renown* on Sunday, August 17, 1919. The following morning he visited Province House, the North End Military Hospital, and Camp Hill (Veterans') Hospital; toured the area in North End Halifax devastated by the 1917 Explosion; and then attended a luncheon at the Waegwoltic Club, hosted by the Government of Nova Scotia. The photograph shows him at this function, accompanied by Lieutenant-Governor McCallum Grant (front left). Later in the day, the Prince laid cornerstones for Dalhousie University's Shirreff Hall and for the Navy League's Home for Sailors; then went on to a public reception at Government House, where the crowds of people waiting to meet him were so large that the entry doors had to be closed. The crowds remained outside, however, clamouring to see him, so Edward later went out to greet and thank the assembled throng. A state dinner and dance followed in the evening at Government House. Later the Prince returned to his battleship, which then steamed for Prince Edward Island.

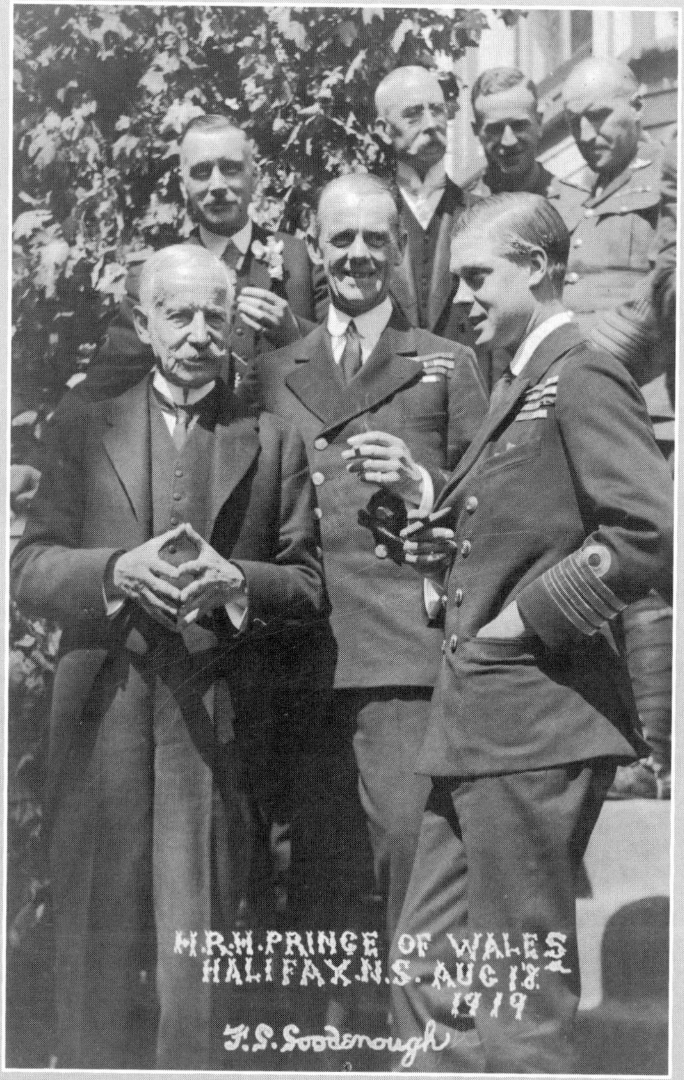

7. King George VI and Queen Elizabeth's visit to Halifax
1939

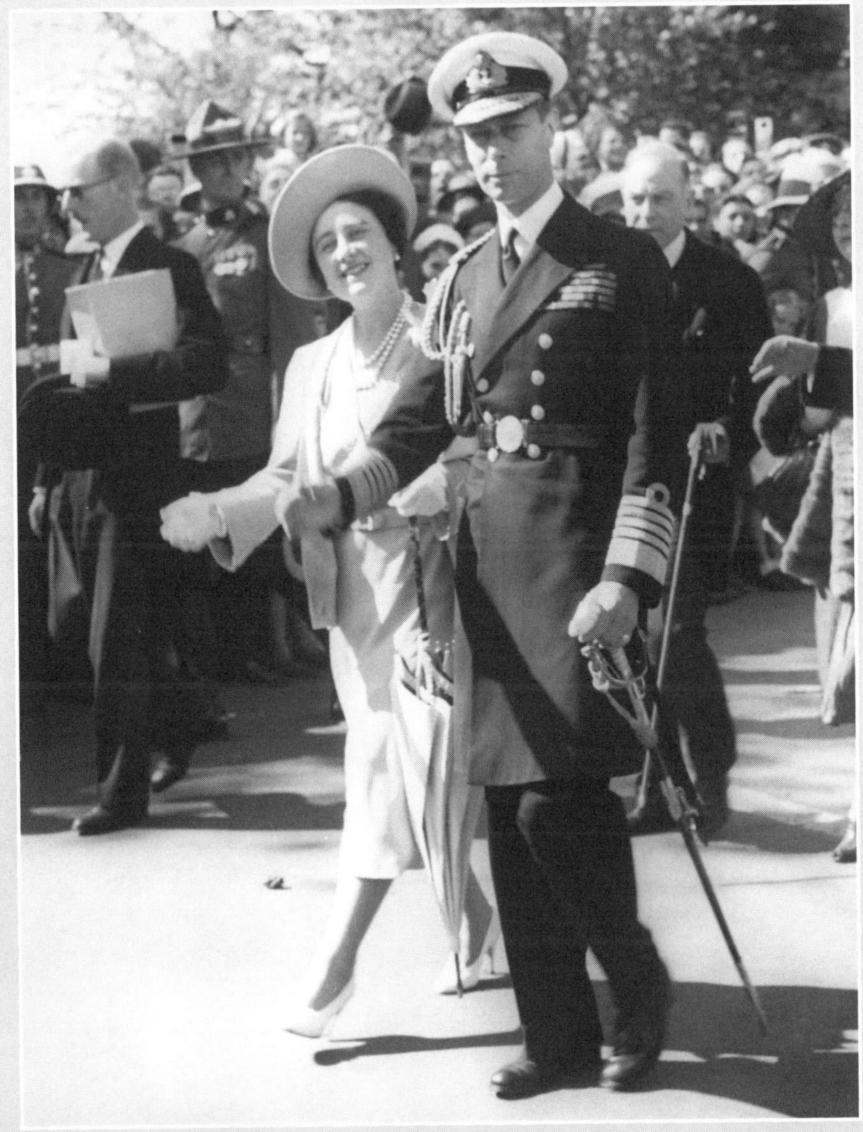

Photograph taken as the King and Queen left the Garrison Grounds to walk to the Public Gardens, where a tree was planted in honour of their visit.

8. Halifax Bicentenary Parade on Quinpool Road, Looking East near Oxford Street 1949

Halifax celebrated its bicentenary in 1949, and *The Standard* (Montreal) of July 16 commented that "Like a tired but happy old lady playing hostess at the biggest party of her life, Halifax laid out the welcome mat June 21 for a summer-long whirl of parades, fun-making and pageantry to mark the city's 200th birthday."

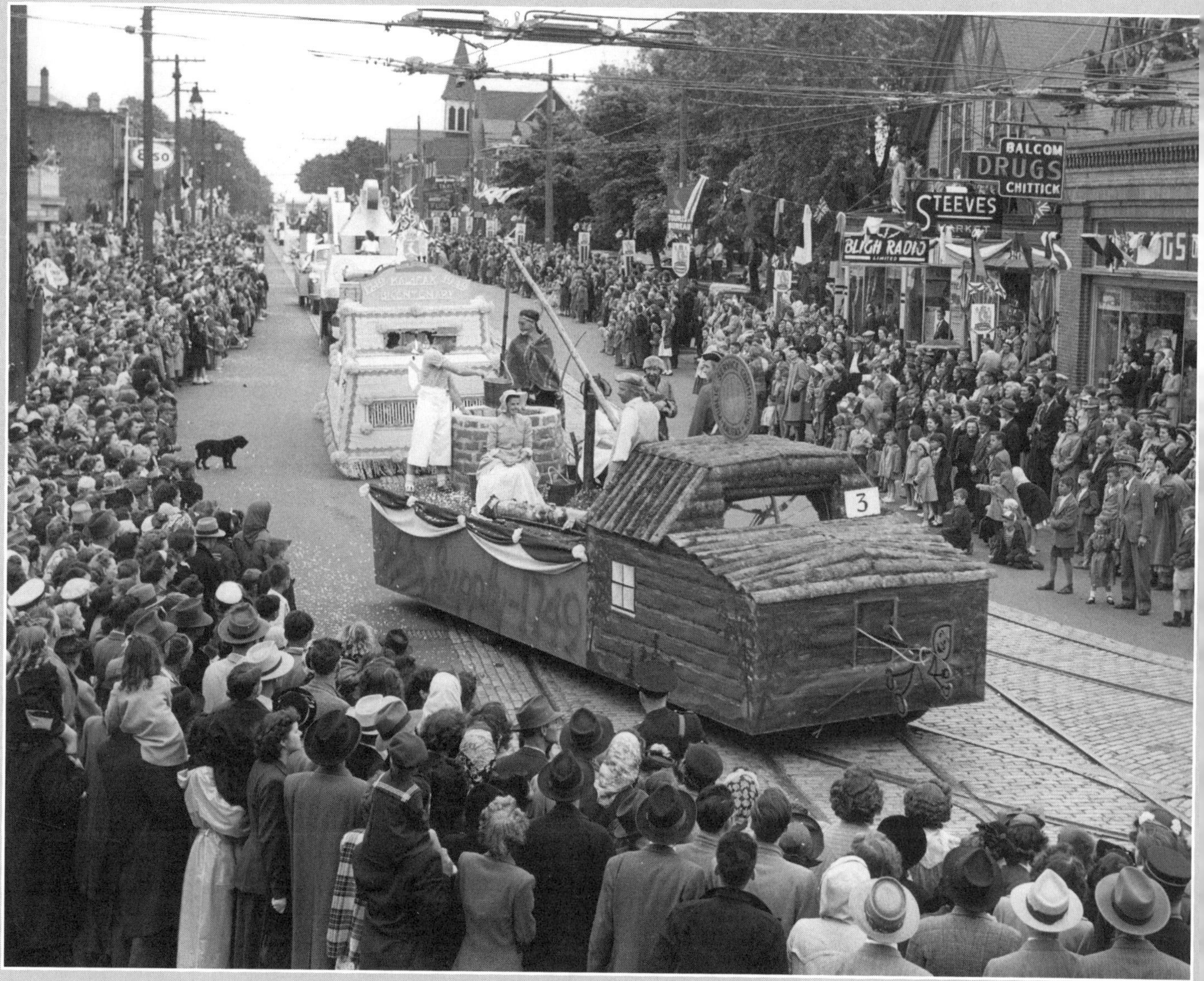

9. HRH Princess Elizabeth and Premier Angus L. Macdonald walking between Boy Scouts and Girl Guides in Province House
1951

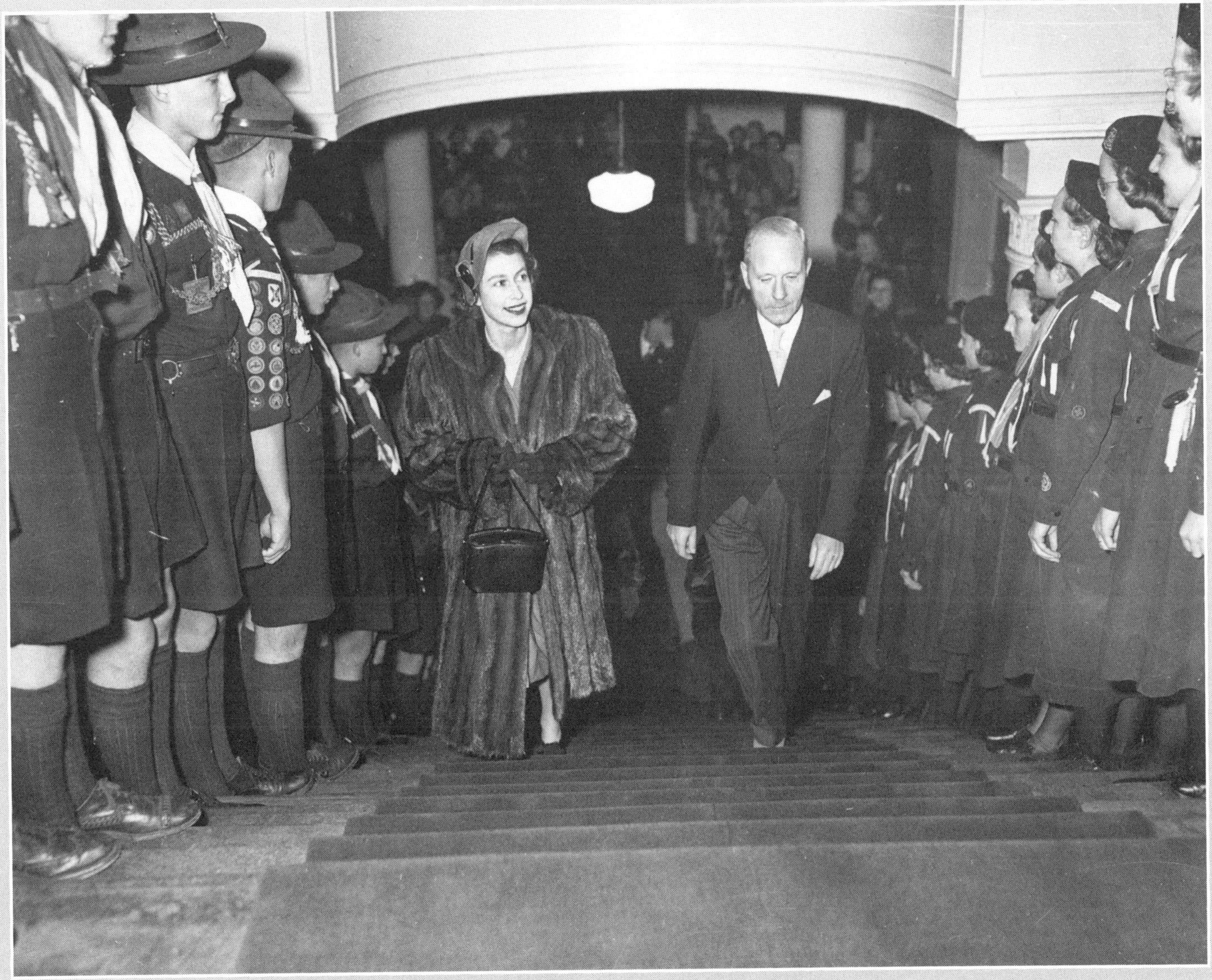

10. President William Jefferson ("Bill") Clinton greets onlookers during the G-7 Economic Summit held in Halifax
June 15, 1995

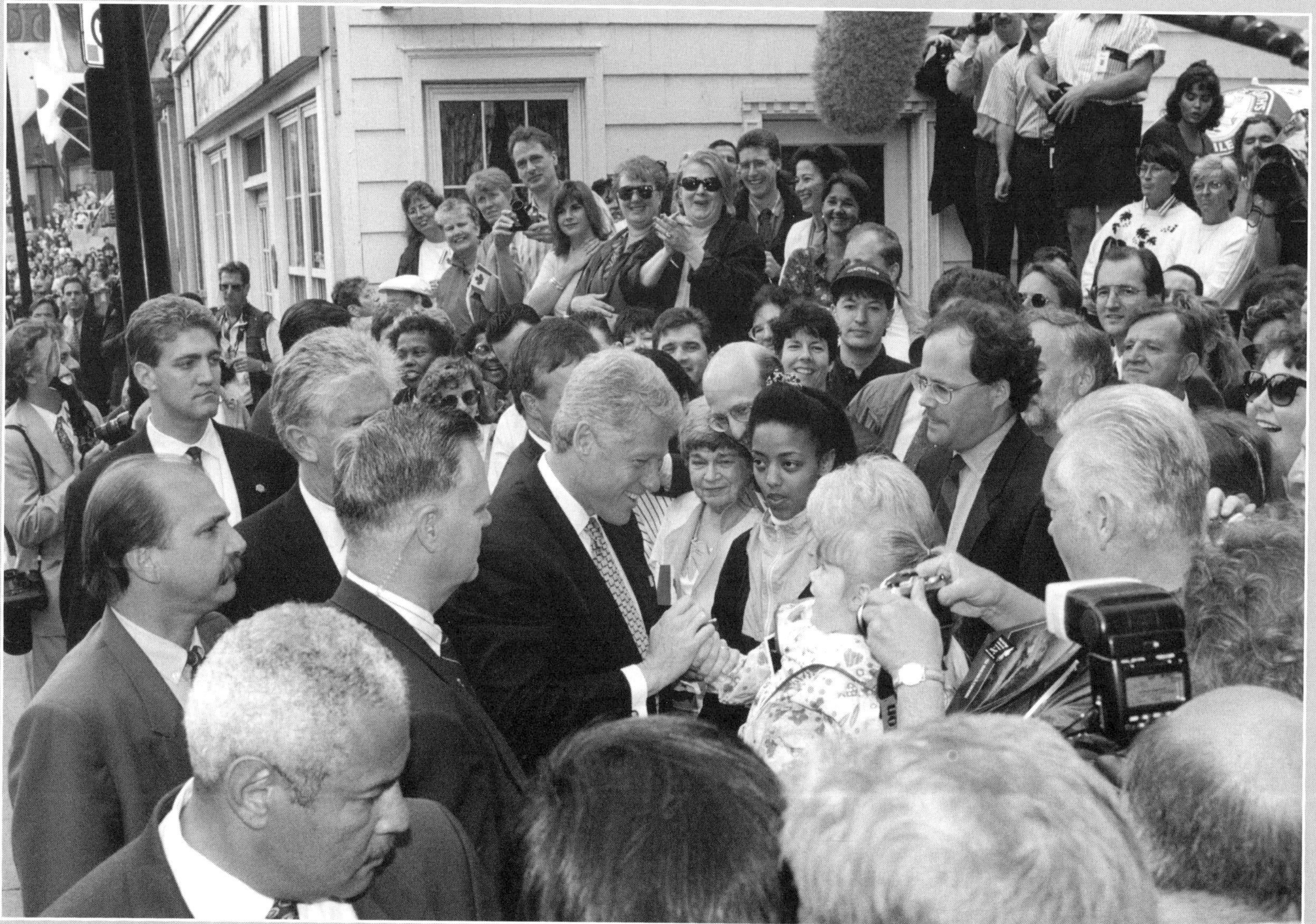

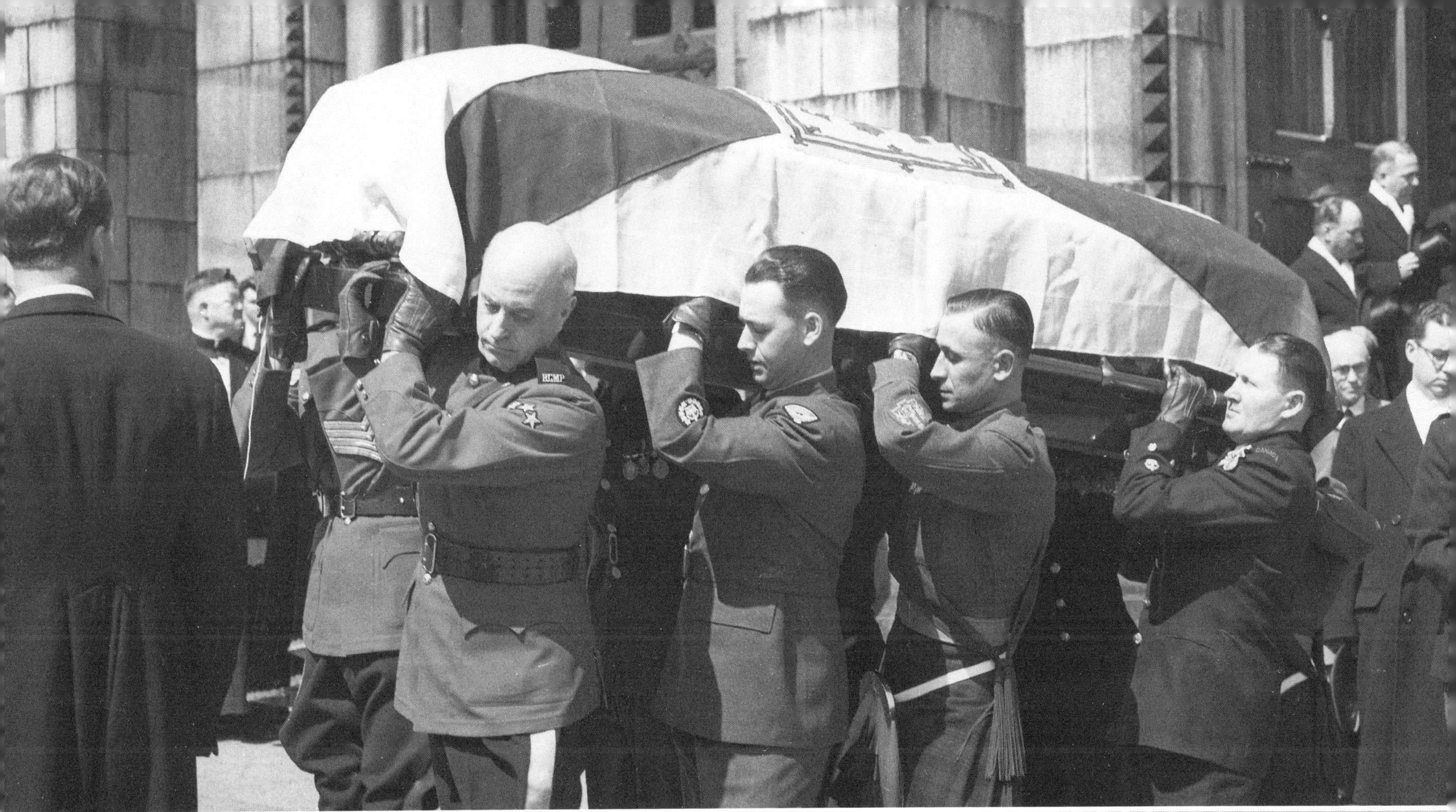

CHAPTER 6

THE LIFE CYCLE

Birth, marriage, and death are the most conspicuous markers within the cycle of human life. Church and state invariably keep records of these significant events, but apart from the official record, we—as individuals and families—have consistently commemorated these special events and rites of passage that mark the life cycle: baptisms, first communions and bar mitzvahs, graduations, birthdays, marriages and anniversaries, family reunions, and leave-takings. Two hundred years ago, the well-to-do captured the essence of their individuality in formal portrait paintings; today, we do the same via studio photo-portraits, through our own still photography, and, in the late twentieth century, with that latest recorder of the modern world, the video-camera.

1. DEAD CHILD
c 1867

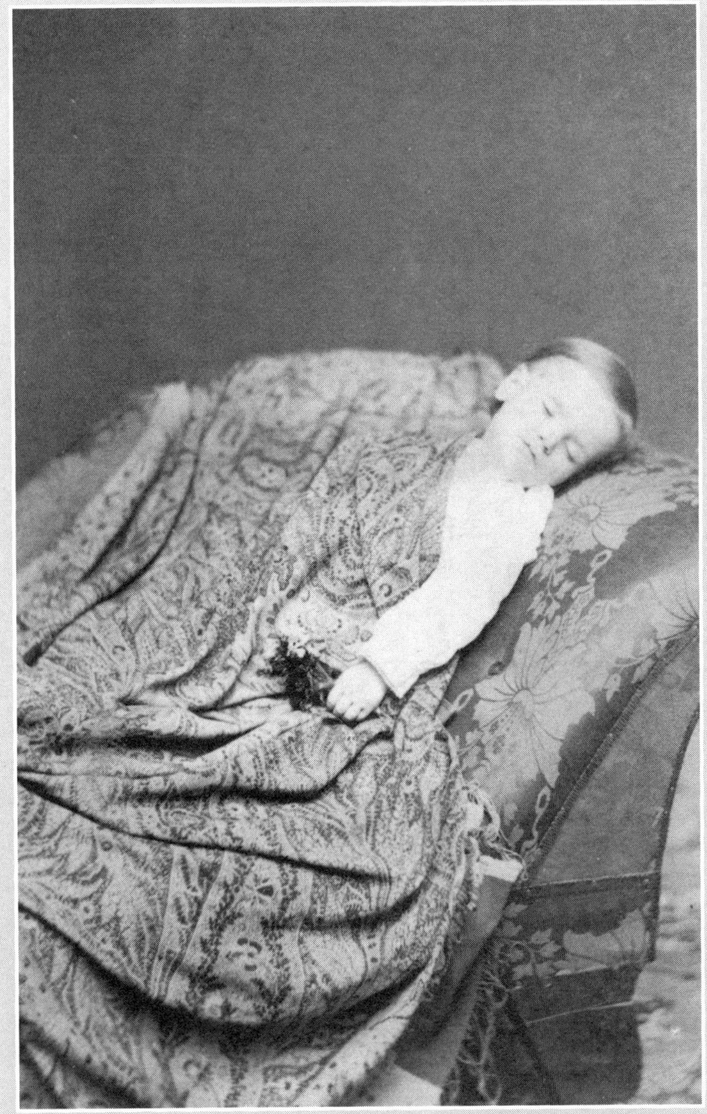

Infant mortality was a reality of life in Victorian Halifax. A recognized custom of the time was for parents to have their dead child photographed as if the youngster were sleeping, for a *memento mori*.

c 1880

William J. Kinnear and Isabella L. Ryan were married in Halifax in 1869. Kinnear was a book-keeper by profession. By about 1880, the entire family—including doll—went to the Notman Studio for a formal portrait sitting, forever fixing in time a typical Halifax family of the late Victorian period.

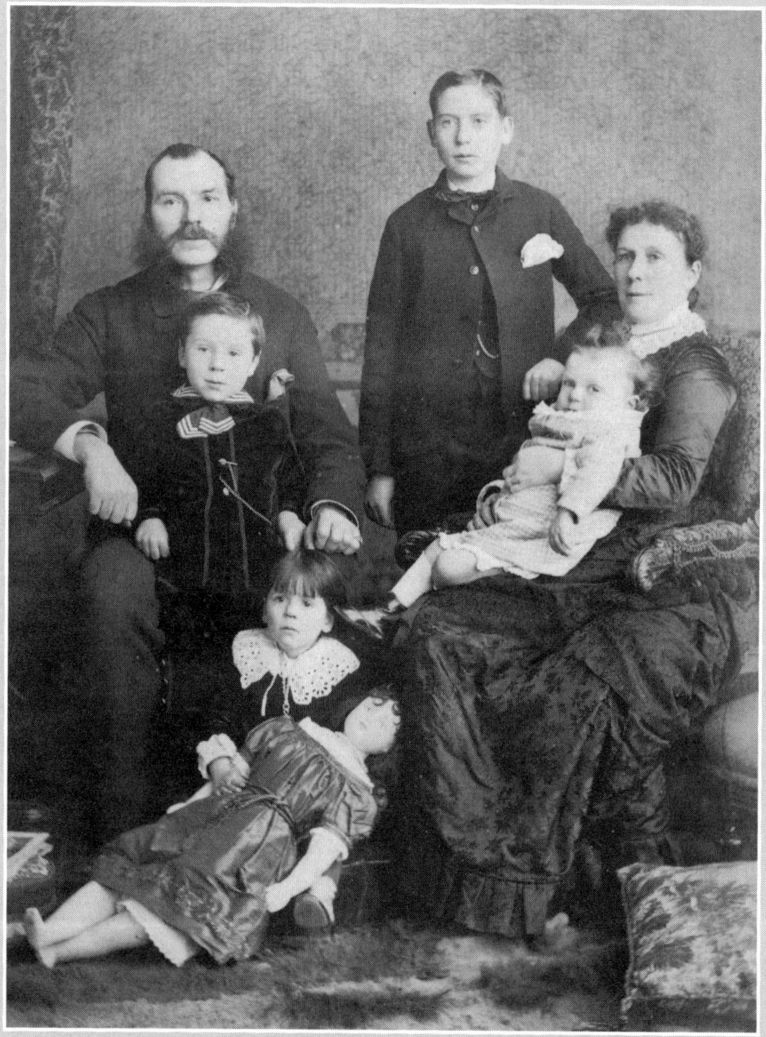

3. Wedding of Miss Mary Borden and Mr. Richard Tynes, Dartmouth
1898

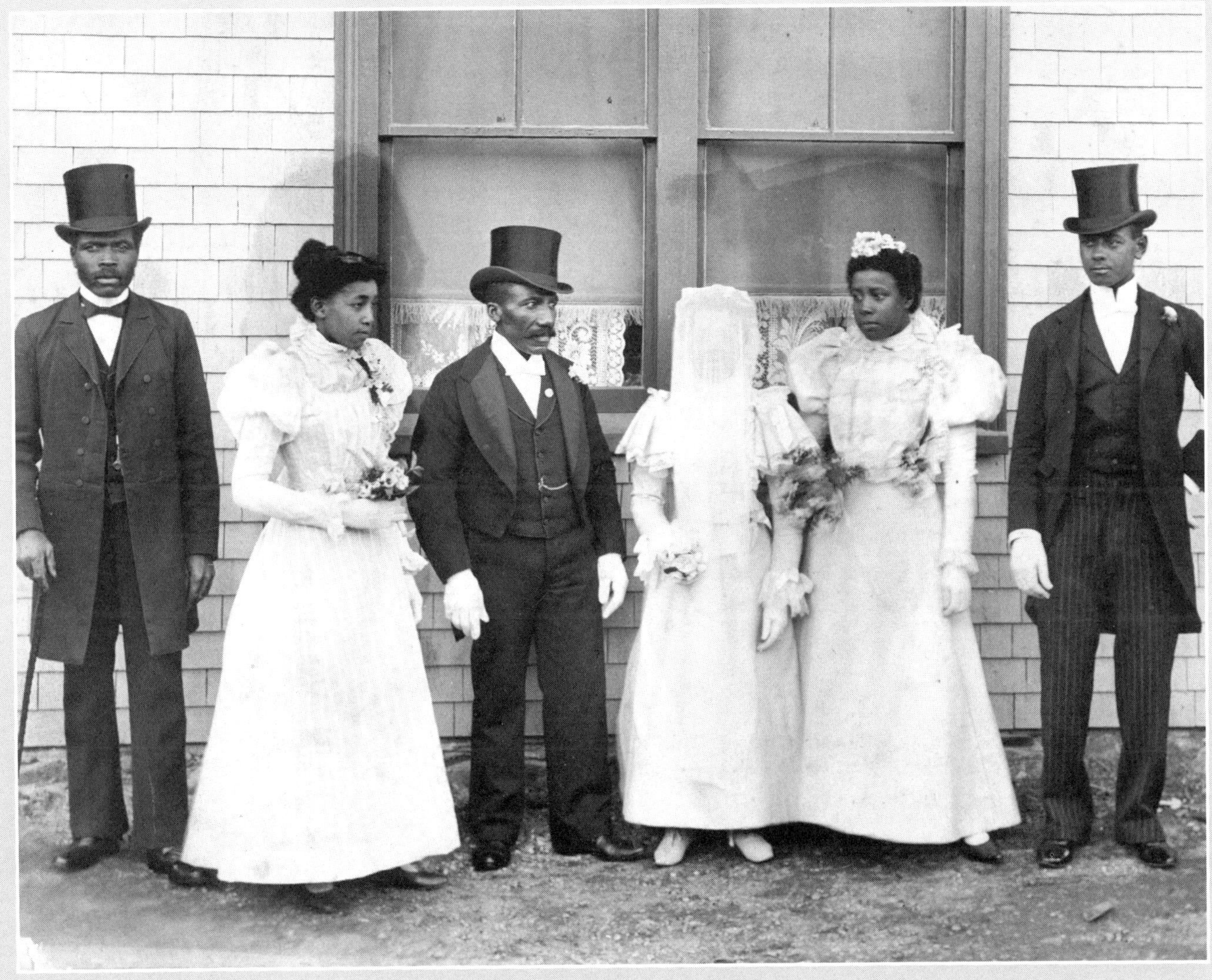

The *Atlantic Weekly* for June 18, 1898 aptly described the wedding:

> *Promptly at 7.30 the party arrived in four carriages, each drawn by a pair of grays. Some five or six other carriages conveyed friends and relatives of the happy couple. Before entering the [Lake Baptist] church the participants and guests had a group photo taken. The bride looked charming attired in blue silk, with chiffron [sic] trimming, veil of orange blossoms, and hat to match. She was given away by her father, and as the couple entered the church the choir, under the leadership of James Tynes (of E.M. Walker's staff), rendered appropriate music. The Misses Hannah and Lena Lee were bridesmaids dressed in white muslin and pink silk respectively, each carrying a bouquet, and presented a most becoming appearance. Willie Saunders and Charles Bowden assisted the groom. After the ceremony the happy couple, with about 100 guests, partook of a sumptuous, enjoyable supper at the residence of the bride's perents [sic], and an enjoyable evening [was] spent.*

4. Wedding of Rev. Willoughby Goddard-Fenwick and Miss Ella Major, Sackville 1912

The Halifax Herald, September 27, 1912, reported that:

> *St. John's Anglican Church, Sackville, N.S., was...the scene of a pretty wedding.... Miss Major looked thoroly [sic] charming in her wedding gown of white satin, with pearl trimming, and wearing the conventional veil and orange blossoms. The bridesmaid's gown was of pale blue, the little flower girl wearing a dainty white silk frock. The ceremony was followed by a reception and wedding luncheon at the residence of the bride's parents....*

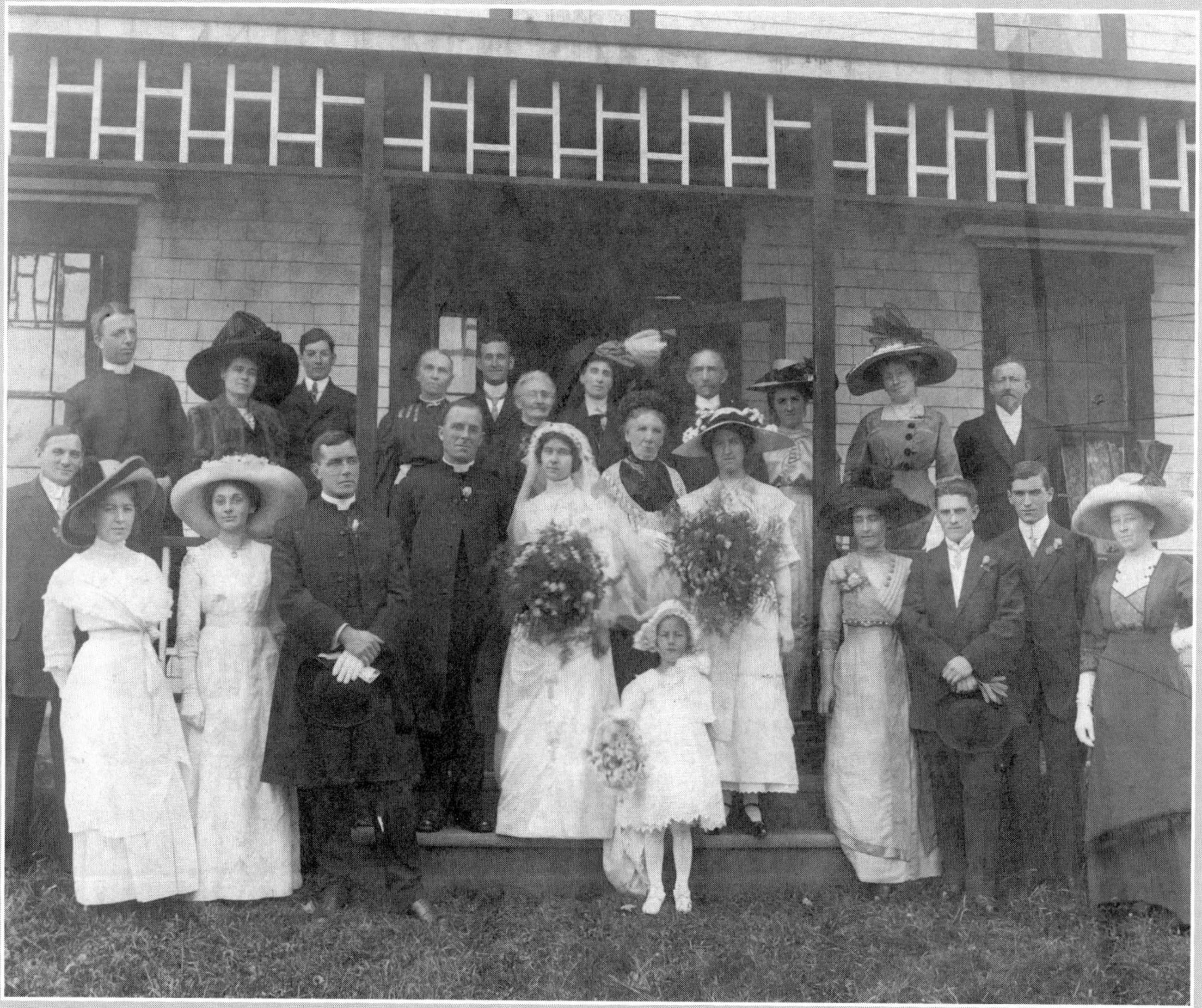

5. First Communion:
Group of Boys and priests
St. Mary's Cathedral, Halifax
193–

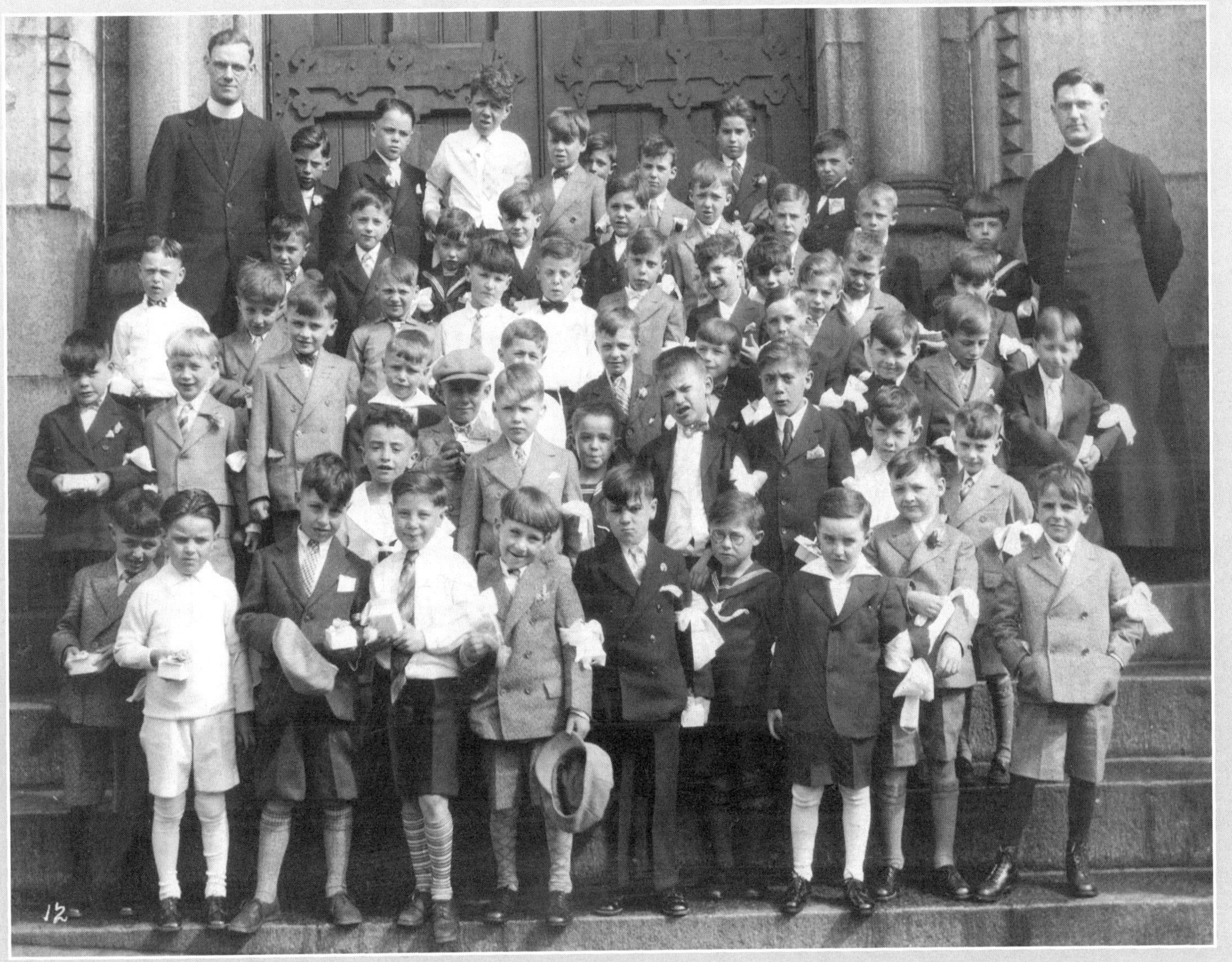

The body of Premier Angus L. Macdonald lay in state in the Red Room of Province House, April 15-19, 1954. Thousands filed by the casket to pay their last respects, and thousands lined city streets to view the funeral cortege. On Easter Monday, servicemen pulled the gun carriage up George Street, along Barrington, and up Spring Garden Road to the Basilica. After the Requiem Mass at St. Mary's, the late premier was interred in Gate of Heaven Cemetery, Lower Sackville.

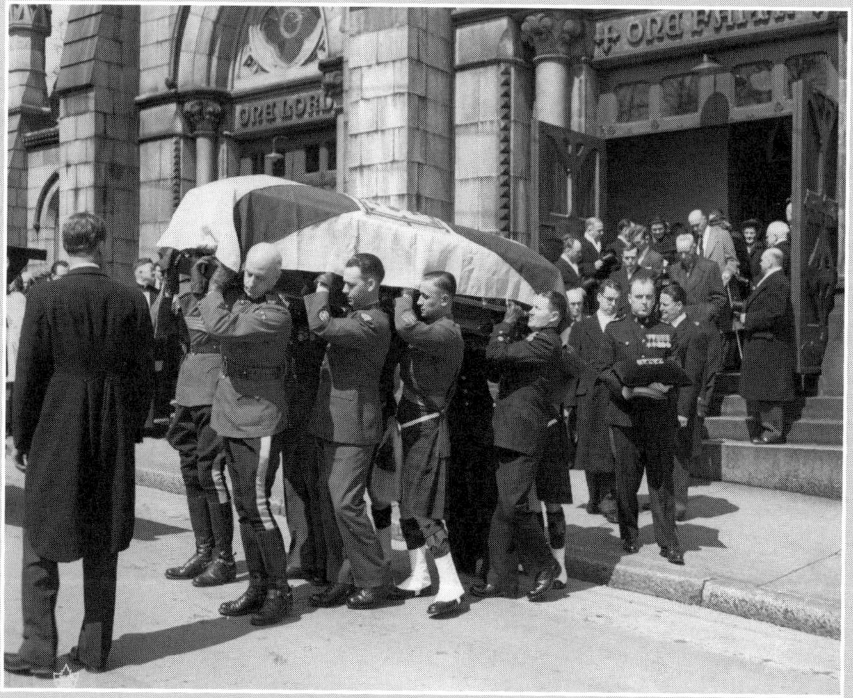

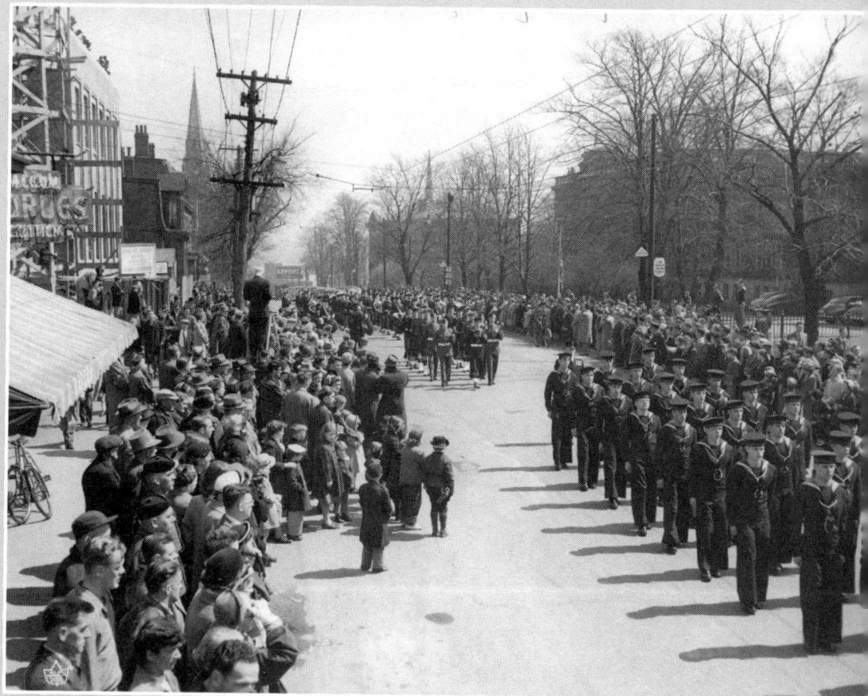

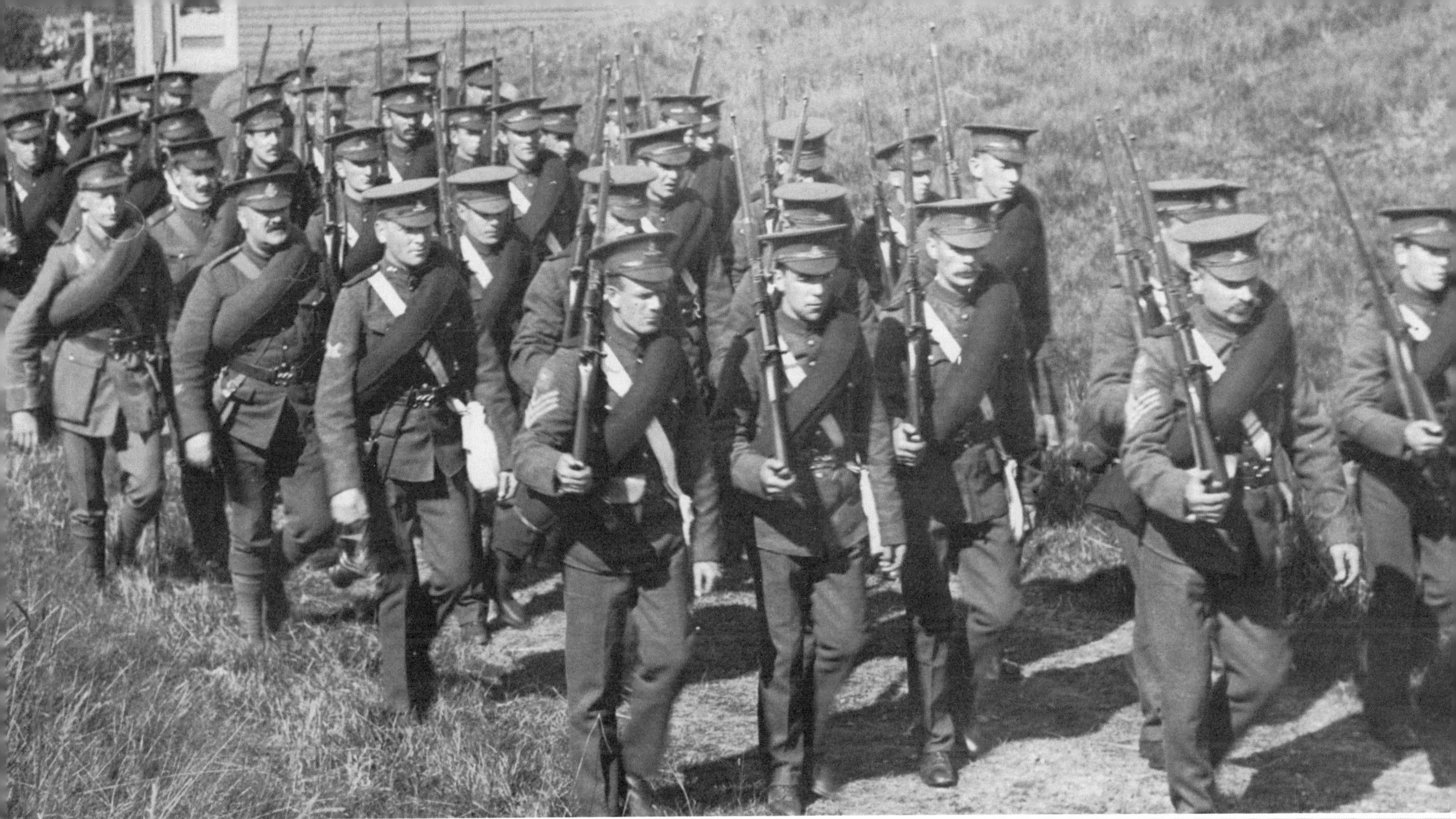

C H A P T E R 7

HALIFAX AT WAR

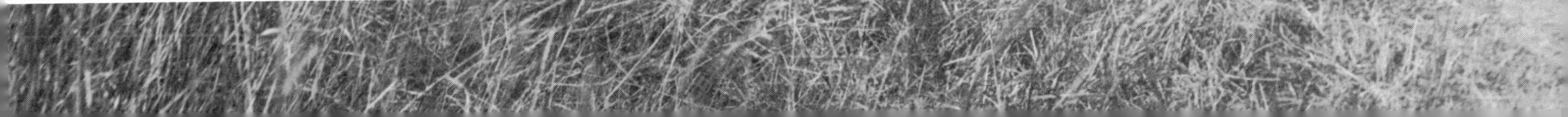

Halifax has always been a 'garrison city' and continues so to this day, with much of the local economy still dependent upon the military presence. In earlier times, the fortunes of the city rose and fell with the tide of political circumstances unfolding across the Atlantic. For example, massive expeditions launched against the French military garrisons and naval bases at Louisbourg (1758) and Québec (1759) were conceived in England, but were organized in and sailed from Halifax. Indeed Halifax was founded by British forces in 1749, largely to offset the growing French presence in eastern North America.

During the War of the American Revolution, the Napoleonic Wars and the War of 1812, privateers routinely sailed in and out of Halifax Harbour, fortunes were made on their booty, and both French and American prisoners-of-war were held on Melville Island and elsewhere in the city. For most of the nineteenth century, however, Halifax's strategic importance within the British Empire languished. Although naval vessels and military regiments came and went, the garrison city was essentially an outpost and an imperial backwater. Nevertheless, the British remained until the turn of this century, leaving only in 1905-06 when they transferred the Halifax Defence Complex (the Citadel, York Redoubt and the various harbour defence stations) to the new Canadian Army. Many Haligonians, however, can still remember the old Glacis Barracks which survived at the bottom of Citadel Hill until the late 1950s, a tangible reminder to all of the British garrison in its heyday.

During World War I, Halifax was again an important naval base: this time the Royal Canadian Navy, in its infancy, patrolled the coast, and the port was a strategic trans-shipment point for troops mobilized for overseas active service in war-ravaged Europe. On December 6, 1917, the Norwegian vessel SS *Imo*, carrying Belgian Relief supplies, and the French freighter SS *Mont Blanc*, carrying a lethal load of munitions, collided in Halifax Harbour. The explosion which resulted triggered both death and destruction on a massive scale throughout Halifax and Dartmouth. The memory of that day has never been erased from either the physical landscape or from our collective identity as a community.

Halifax again became a centre of wartime activity after Canada declared war on Nazi Germany in 1939. Once more the port became a strategic mobilization and trans-shipment point. Throughout World War II, a total of 17,593 vessels passed through the port, safely brought in through the submarine nets deployed across the harbour mouth, then temporarily moored in Bedford Basin where they were formed into huge convoys to transport troops and supplies across the Atlantic. Meanwhile, Halifax Shipyards repaired some 7,000 vessels damaged in submarine warfare during the Battle of the Atlantic.

When the German surrender became official on V-E Day in May 1945, Halifax went wild—servicemen and civilians alike. Pent-up emotions, accumulated through six years of rationing, over-crowding, the constant threat of attack, and quiet friction between transient military and settled population, boiled over all at once. Naval personnel stormed a streetcar, cleared out the driver and passengers, then set the vehicle ablaze. Thomas H. Raddall, remembering the day in *Halifax: Warden of the North,* wrote that "Bacchanalia followed. Two shops were set afire, and all along the downtown streets sailors, waterfront toughs, and women of all sorts from giddy young girls to wizened hags could be seen smashing bottlenecks on the curbs, drinking themselves senseless, and lolling among the strewn merchandise on the sidewalks and in the gutter." Raddall also noted that photographers took pictures of the riot and he commented that "One filthy harridan, staggering along Barrington Street at the height of the riot with her arms full of stolen finery, shrieked again and again, 'Never had so much fun in my life!' "

1. Members of the 63rd Battalion, Halifax Rifles

c 1890

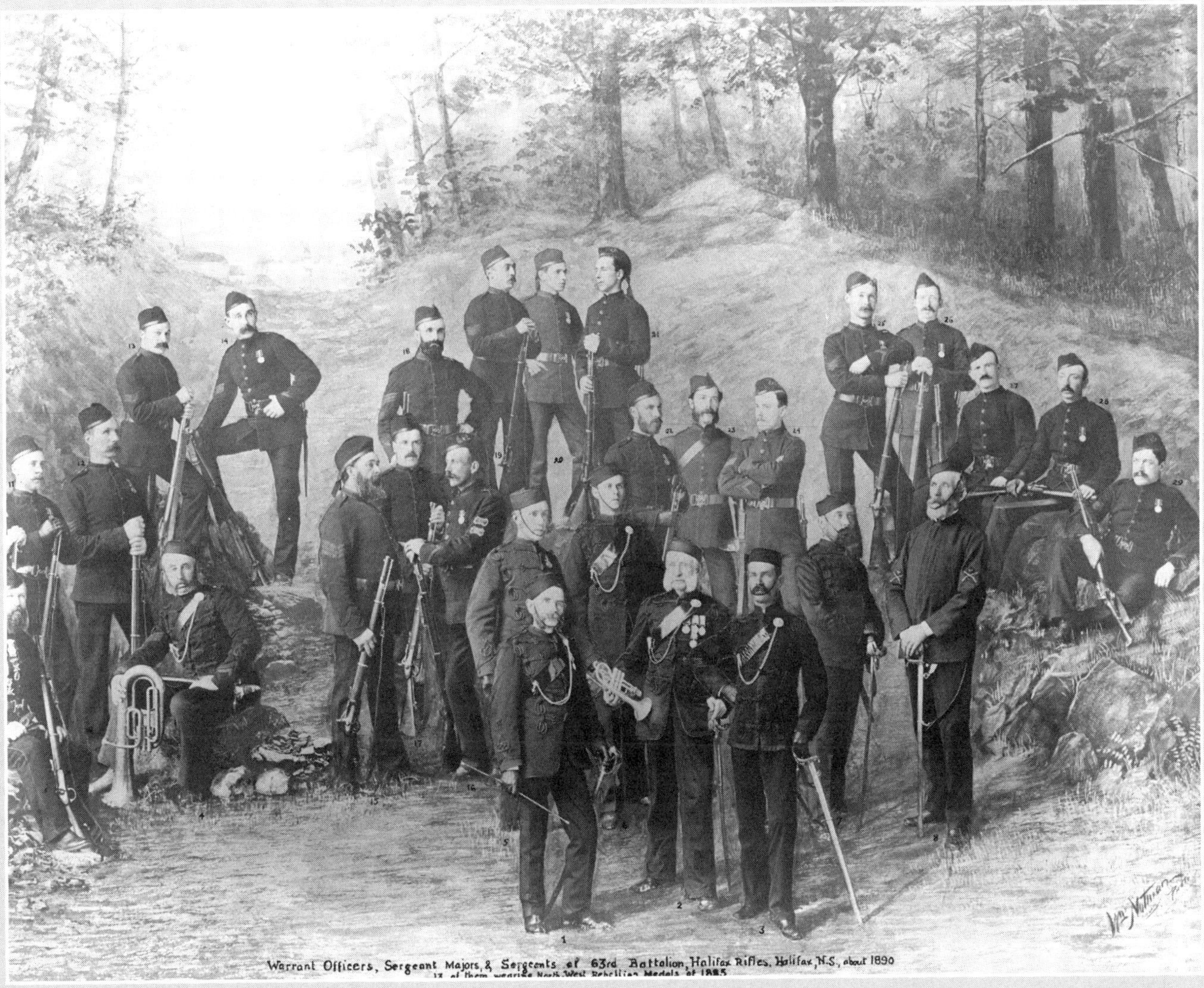

The North West Rebellion of 1885 was the culmination of discontent on the part of Métis, Indians and white settlers, which had simmered since the Red River Rebellion of 1869/70. In Ottawa, the government reacted swiftly, mobilizing troops—nearly all militia units—to assist in putting down the insurrection. The 63rd Battalion of the Halifax Rifles was the only Nova Scotian unit to take part.

2. Coaling HMS *Charybdis* at HM Dockyard, Halifax

189- or 190-

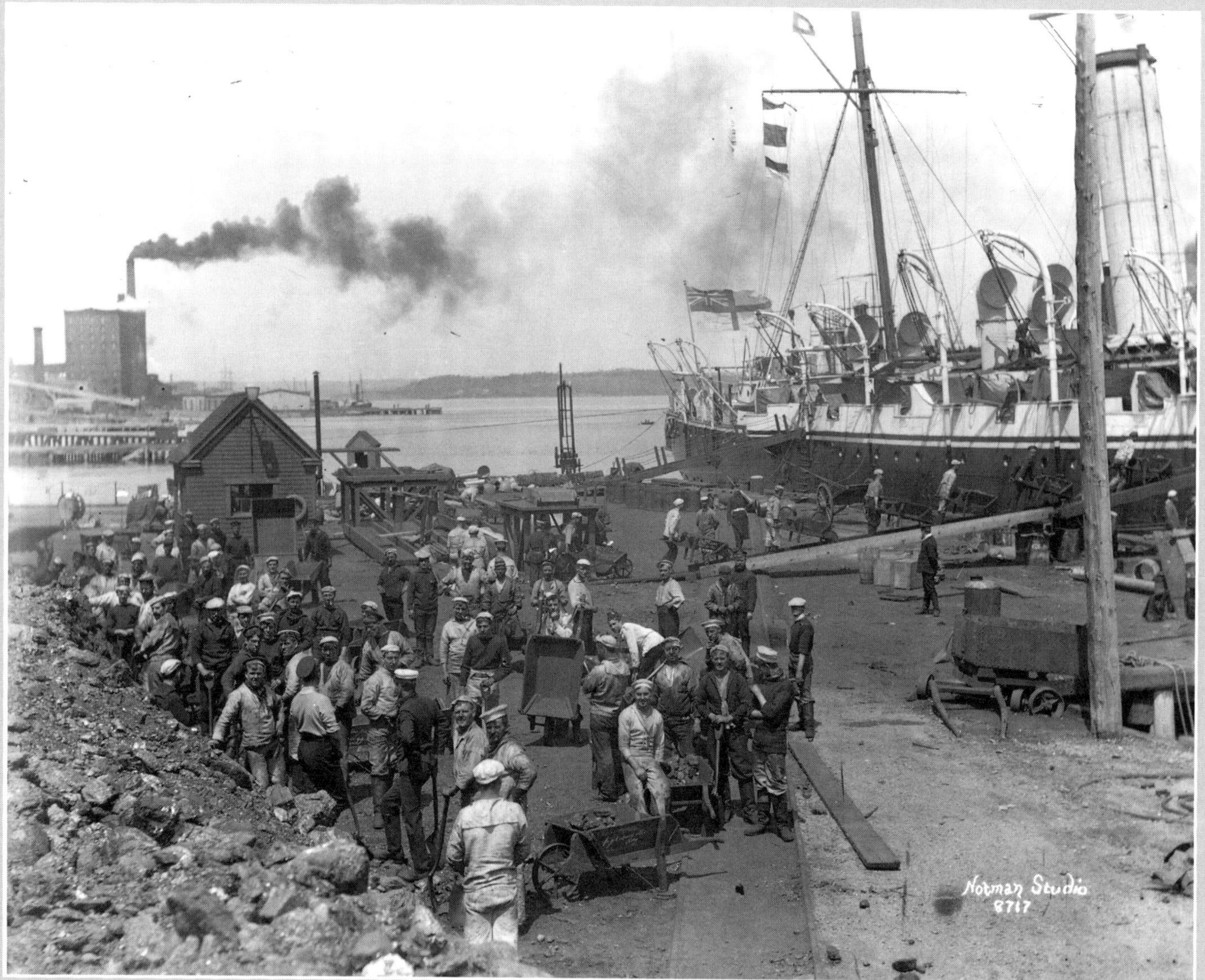

3. Troop transport Ship *Idaho* disembarking Boer War troops, Halifax
1900

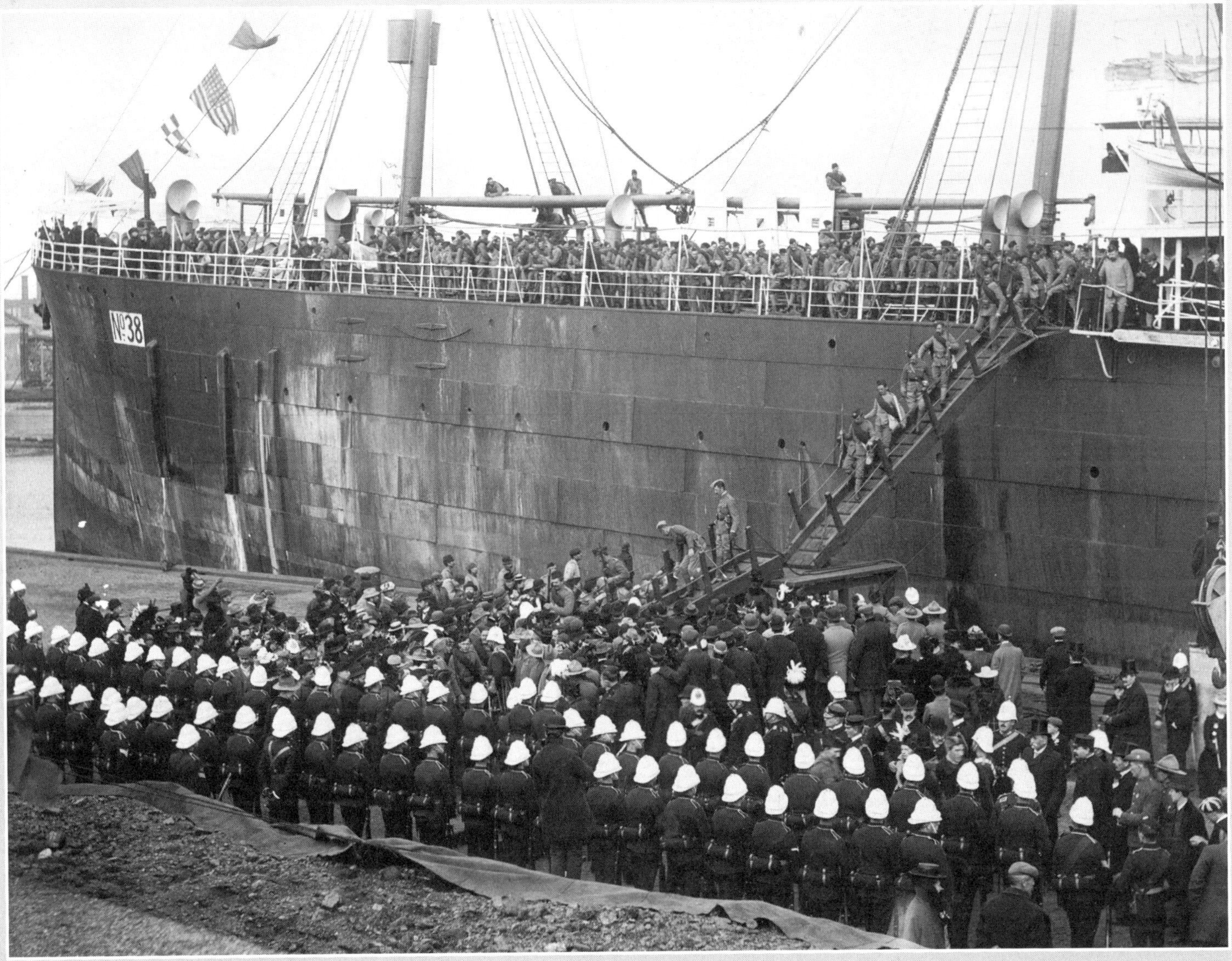

4. "Patriotic concert for Belgian Relief Fund by staff of Mahons Limited: Tableau Britannia"

between 1914 and 1918

Mahon Brothers Limited was founded in 1873 as a dry goods and general notions business. It was located in its early days at 97-103 Barrington Street, at the corner of Prince. The Belgian Relief Committee was organized internationally in 1914 to provide relief to the people of Belgium, invaded by the Germans during World War I.

The photograph includes: [back row] B. Doley, J. Gillis, Rose Kline; (third row) E. Anasty, A. Condon, Elaine Hanrahan, C. Daine; (second row) Annie Delany, Amanda Nicolle, D. Hatton, Della Nauss, Margaret Carew, Sadie Woodley; (first row) Maud Inglis, Georgina Hubley.

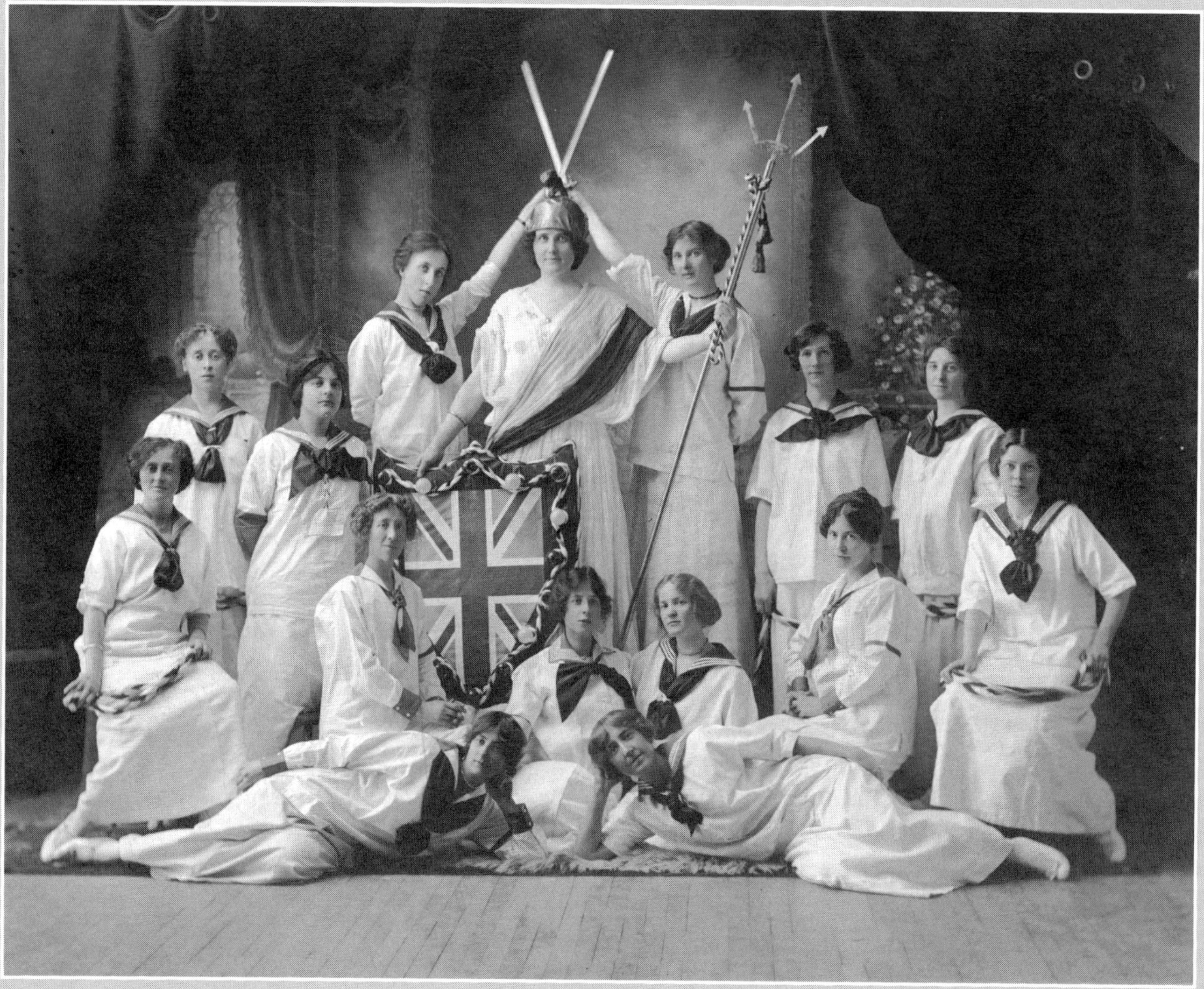

5. "Detachment No. 4 Co'y. 1st Regt. Canadian Garrison Artillery, Fort Charlotte, Halifax" 1914

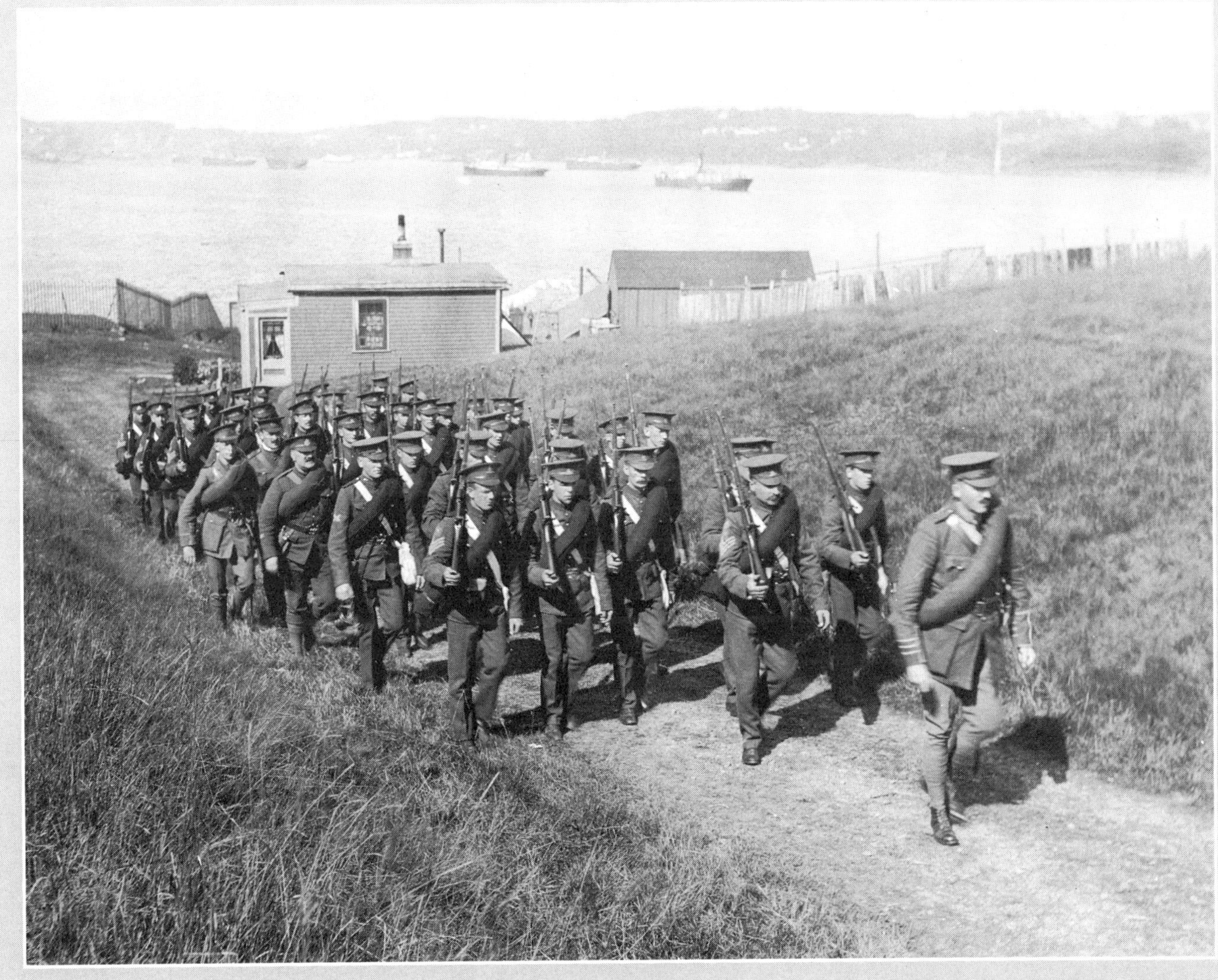

The Canadian Garrison Artillery was mobilized in August 1914 and the regiment was immediately detailed to occupy various defence posts around Halifax Harbour. During the war, nearly seven hundred officers and men from the regiment volunteered for overseas service. Those remaining were stationed in the damp, unsanitary and long-disused fortifications around the city—including those on Georges Island. This regiment assisted civilian authorities after the Halifax Harbour Explosion in December 1917.

6. Prisoners of war, Halifax Citadel
c 1917

Prior to the opening of a permanent prisoner-of-war camp in Amherst in 1917, internees were housed at the Halifax Citadel from October 1914 to September 1917. It proved to be as uncomfortable for the prisoners as it was for the Canadian Garrison Artillery.

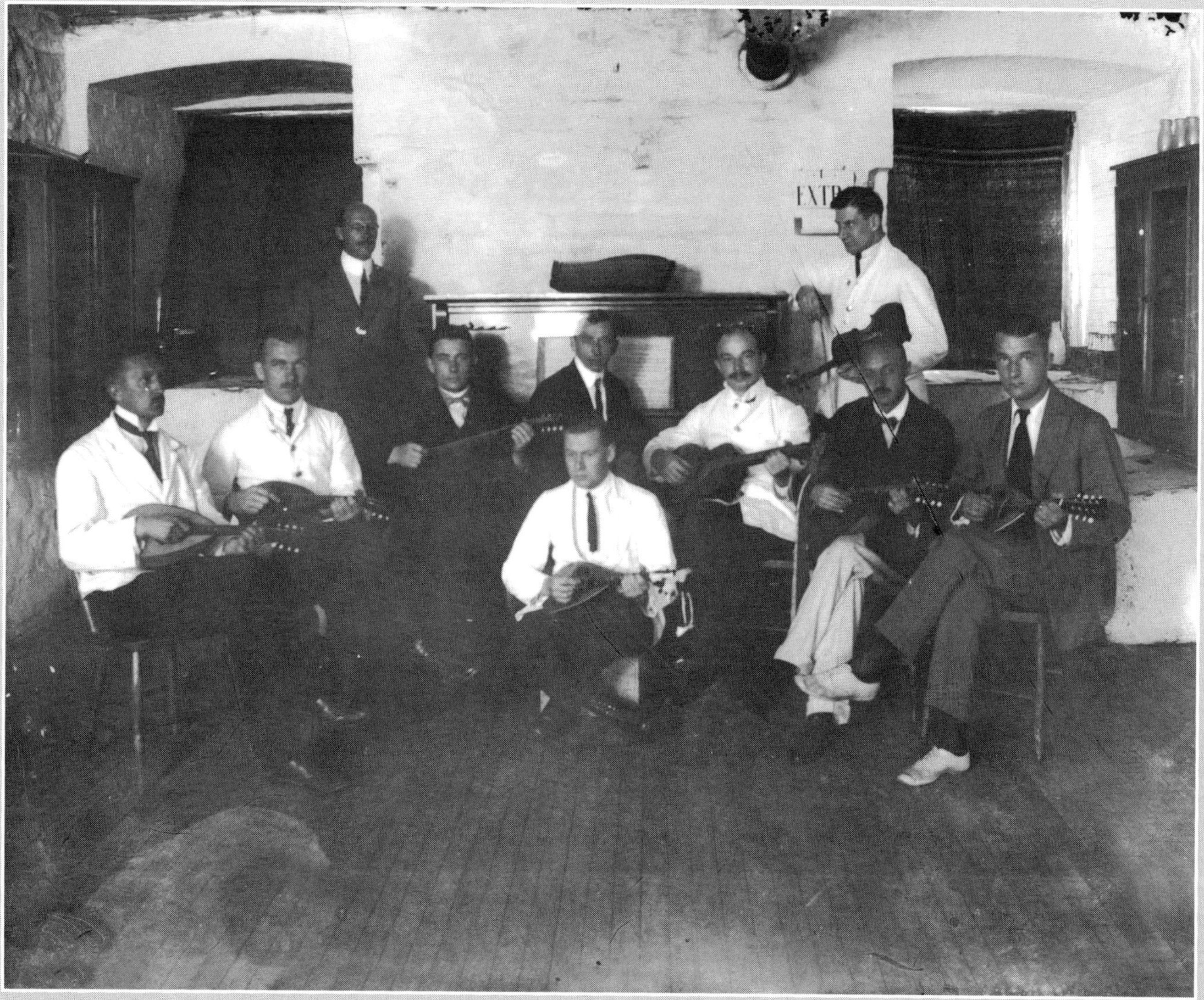

7 & 8. MAUD FOLEY, STREET-CAR CONDUCTOR IN SUMMER UNIFORM AND WINTER UNIFORM, HALIFAX 1917 OR 1918

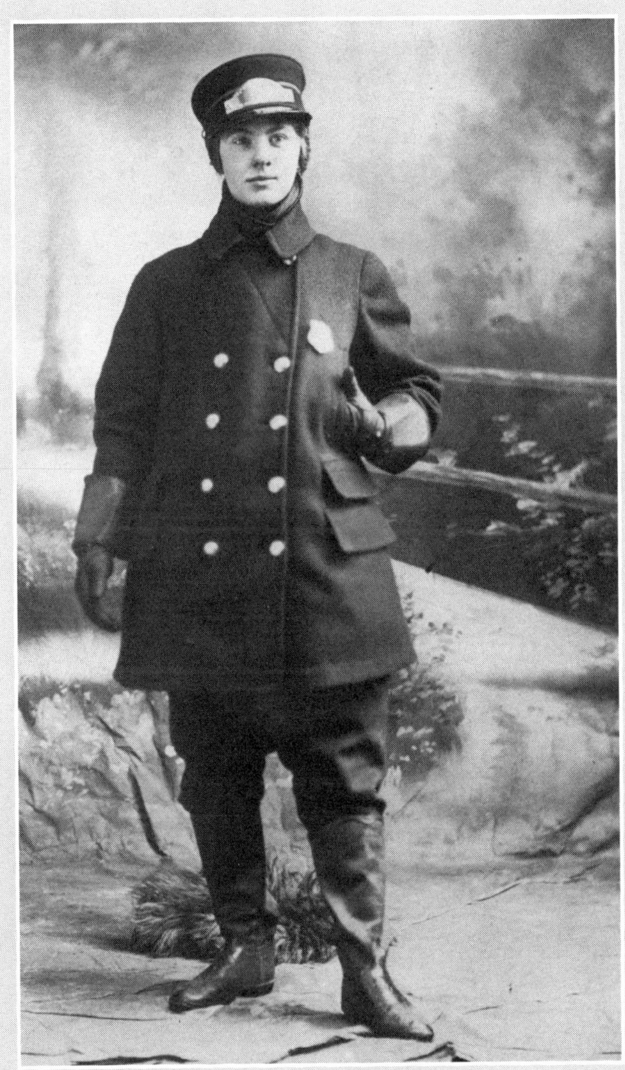

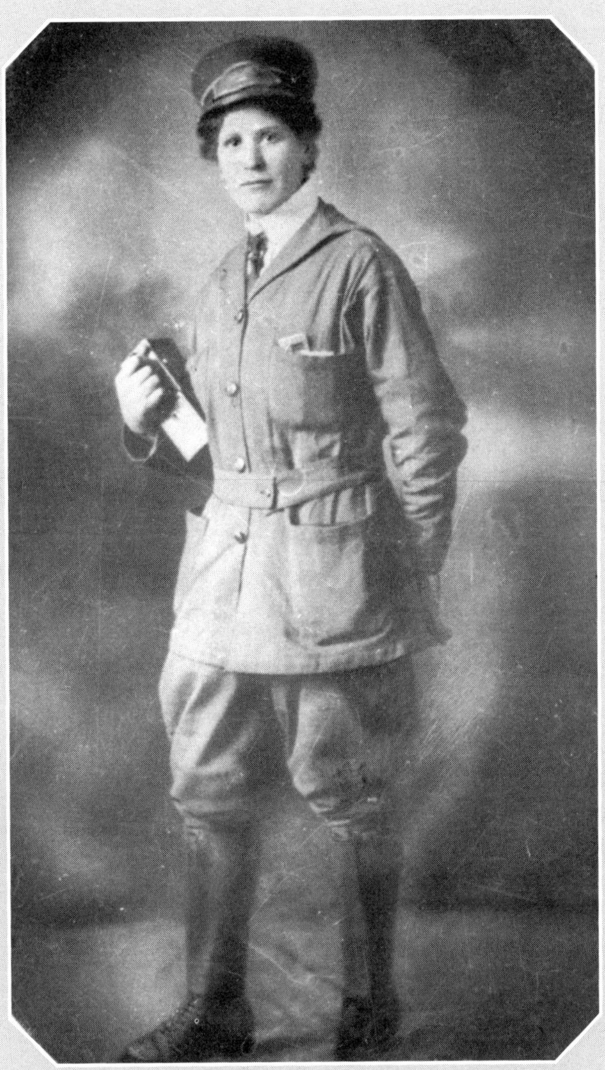

During World War I and especially after the Halifax Harbour Explosion, there was a shortage of male workers in the city. Maud Foley was one of a dozen women street-car conductors hired after the Explosion to operate the city's electric tram-cars. These women gave commendable service but were replaced by men when the war ended. Mrs. Foley made about $. 45 an hour for an eight-hour shift; the pay was considered good. The summer uniform was khaki and the winter uniform was blue/gray, with accompanying boots, leggings, voluminous trousers and three-quarter-length coat. During the summer, the conductor stood with the money-box on the outside running-board. Carl Moulton, a Connecticut native passing through Halifax briefly before going overseas in 1918, wrote to his girlfriend that "It seems strange to see girls running the elevators and acting as trolley car conductors. I saw a girl walking on the outside of a car and fixing the pole just like a man. What are we coming to anyway?"

9. British evacuee children arriving in Halifax
1941

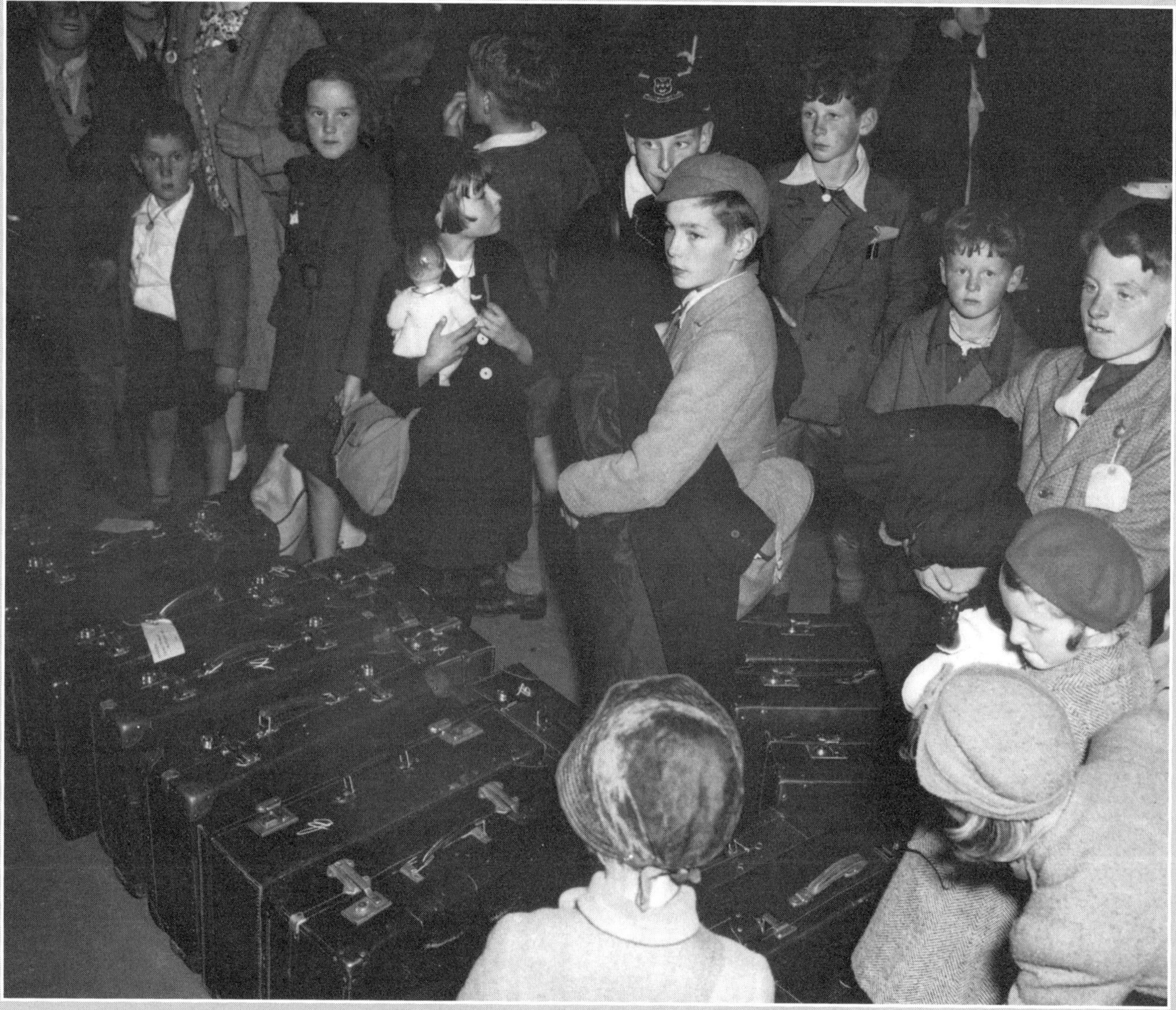

At the beginning of World War II, Britain initiated a plan to evacuate British children to Canada and other British Dominions. However, after two vessels carrying 'Guest Children' were destroyed by German U-boats, participation in the plan was seriously eroded. In all, about 3,000 children were sent to Canada in 1940-41.

10. "Store with War Savings Stamps"
1942

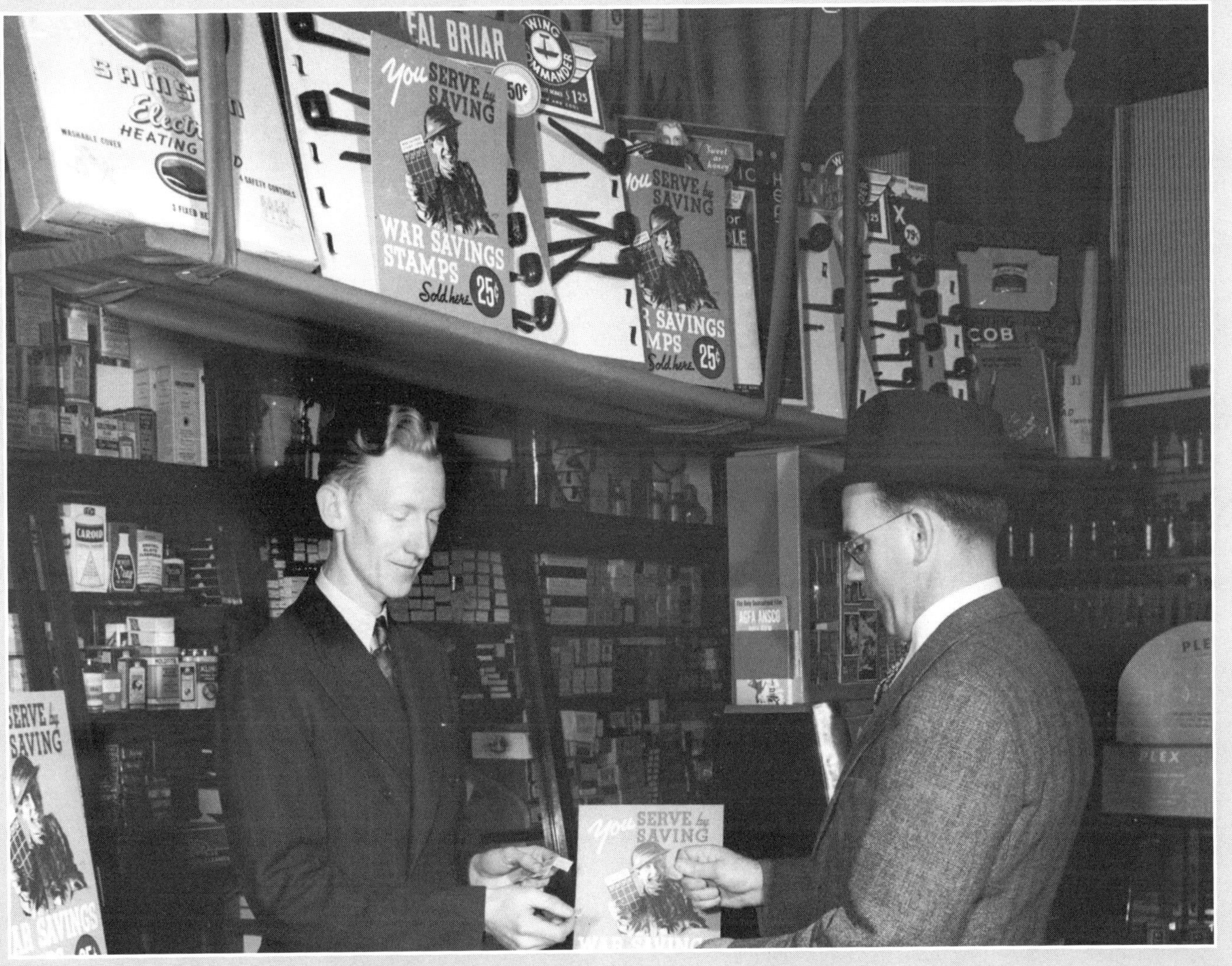

Customer purchasing War Savings Stamps at an unidentified Halifax pharmacy.

11. V-E Day rioters walking along Salter Street between Hollis and Barrington Streets

May 1945

Halifax's celebration of the formal end to war in Europe on May 8, 1945 started off peacefully and in an orderly fashion—but ended up in rioting and general disorder beyond the control of both civilian and military police. Windows in over two hundred businesses were smashed and as the day progressed, widespread looting took place.

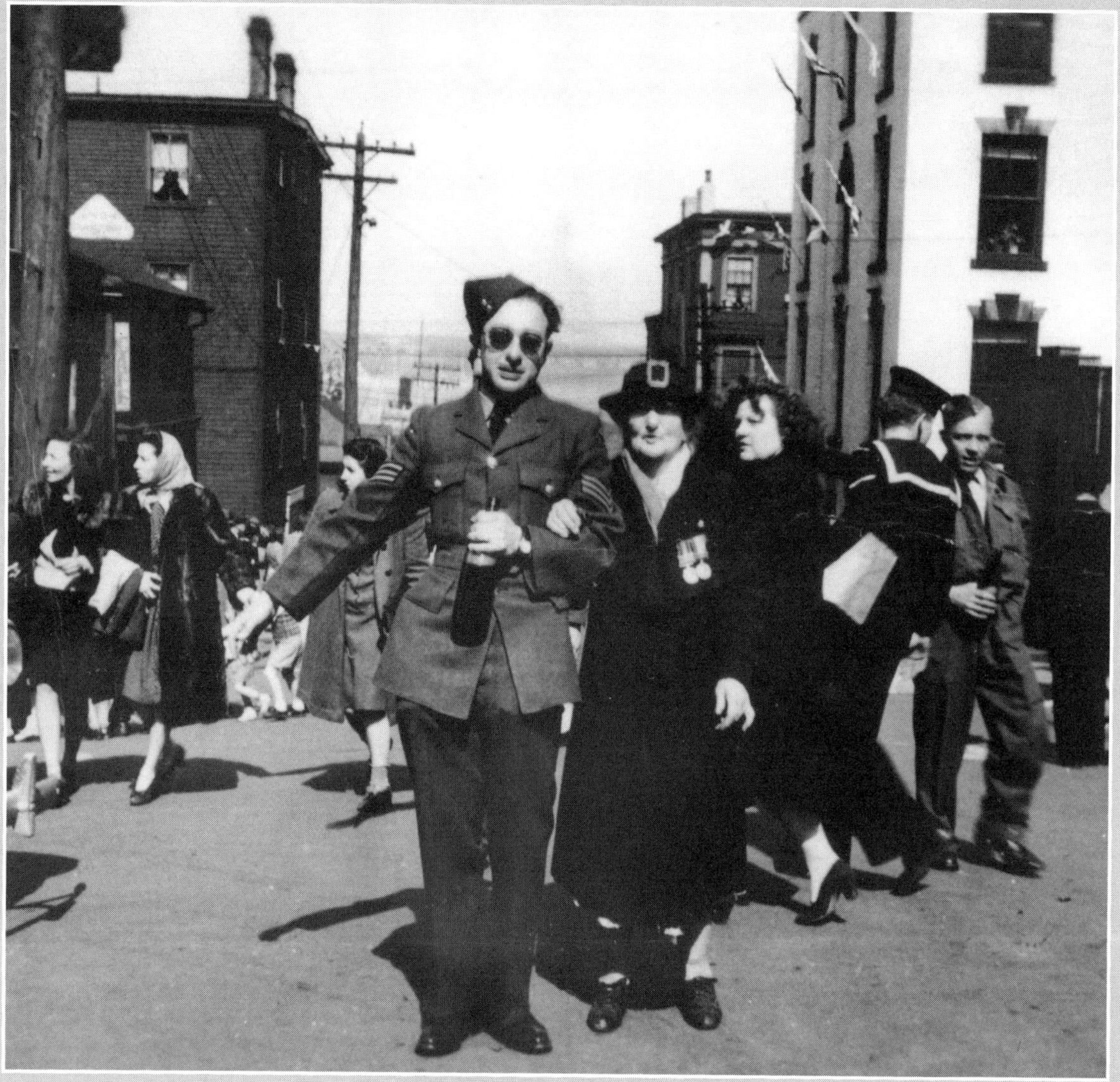

12. V-E Day rioters on Hollis Street looking north towards Salter Street
May 1945

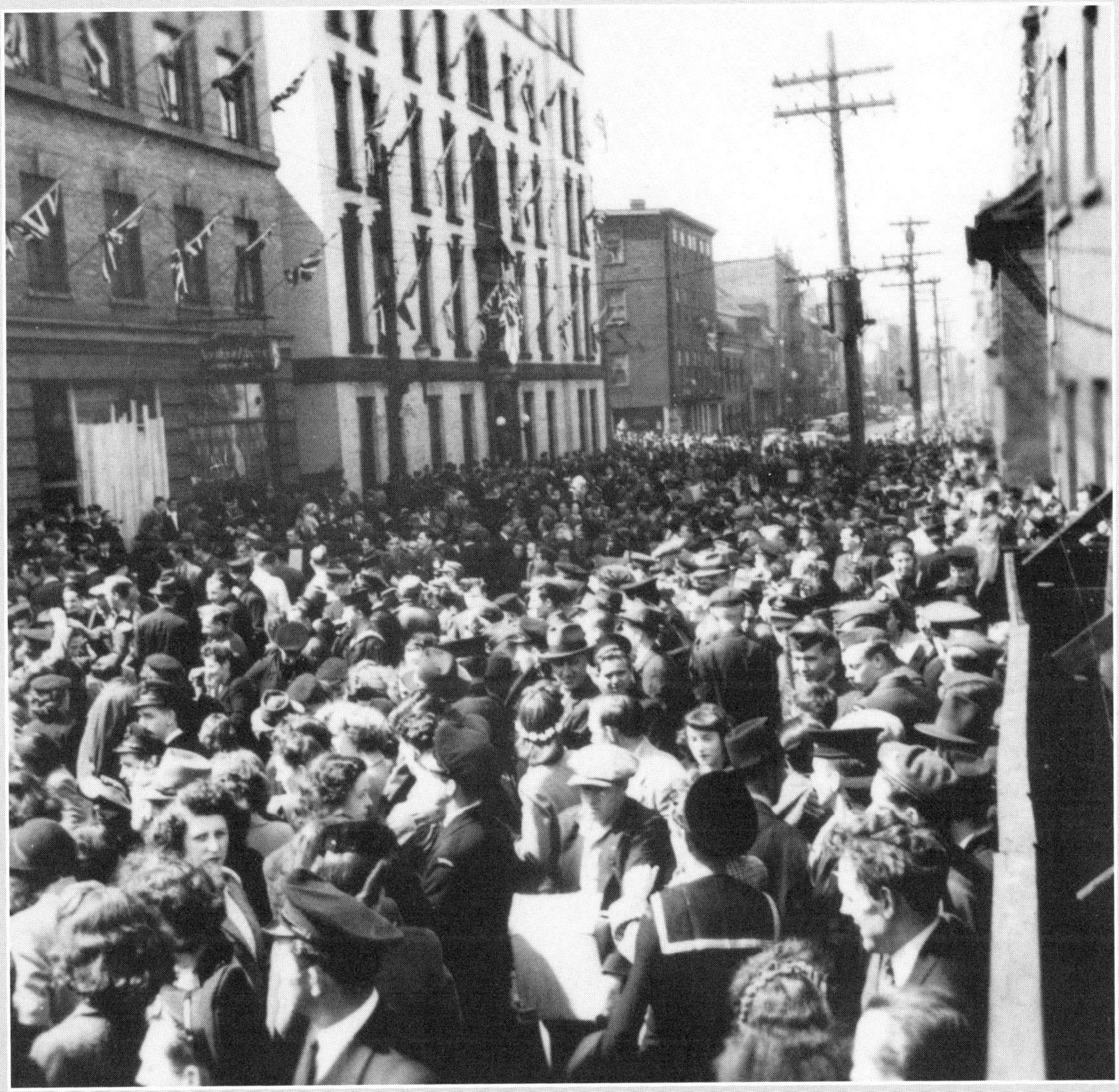

13. War brides arrive on the Liner SS *Scythia*

March 26, 1946

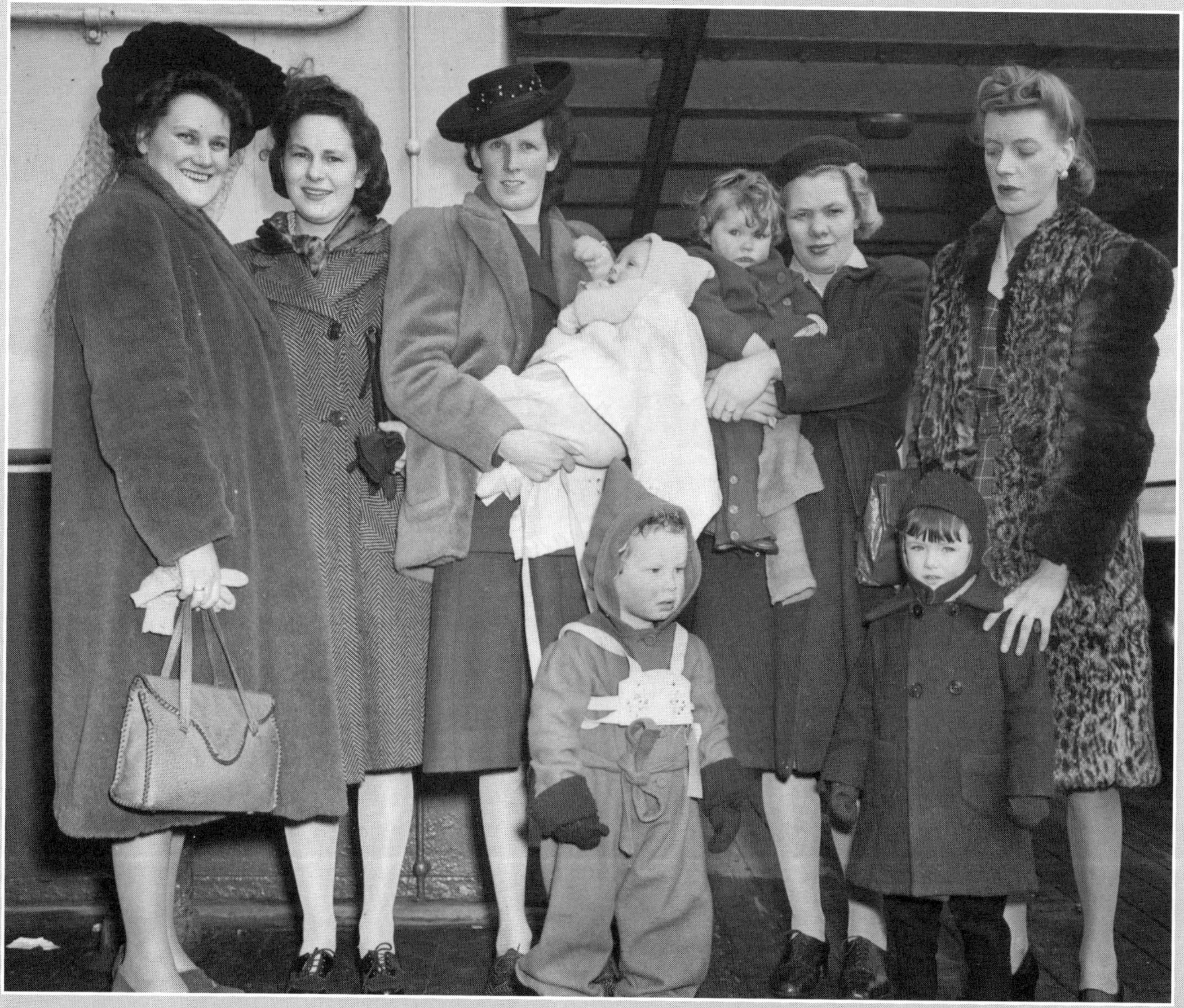

More than five hundred British war brides en route to their future homes in Newfoundland arrived in Halifax on the liner SS *Scythia* on March 26, 1946. The group (left to right) included: Mrs. H. R. Stone, Labrador; Mrs. Guy Frazer, St. John's; Mrs. A. J. Brown, baby Lawrence and David, St. John's; Mrs. Jean Day and son Peter, Trinity Bay; and Mrs. Marion House and daughter Marion, Saint Barbe.

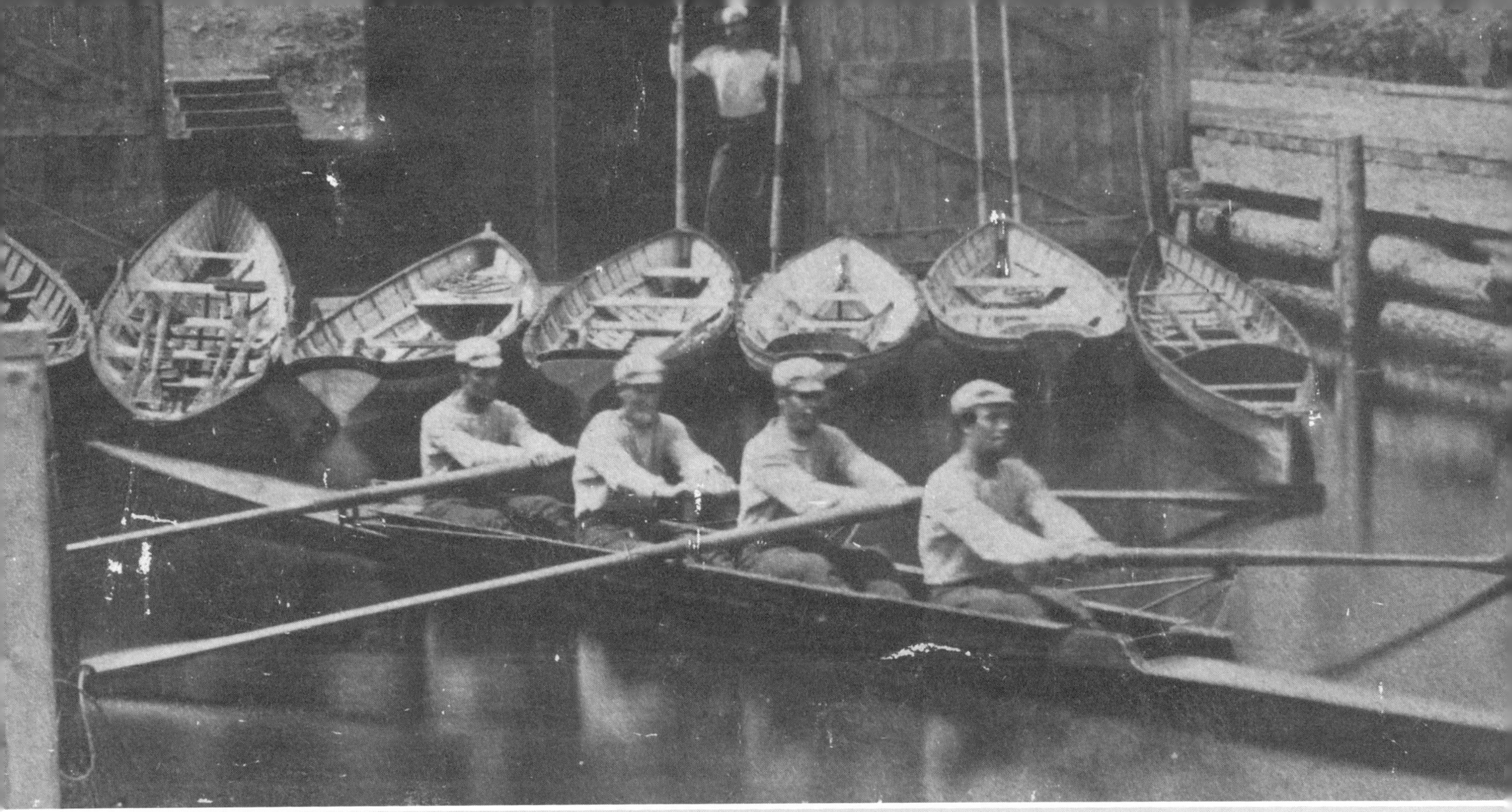

CHAPTER 8

SPORTS AND THE GREAT OUTDOORS

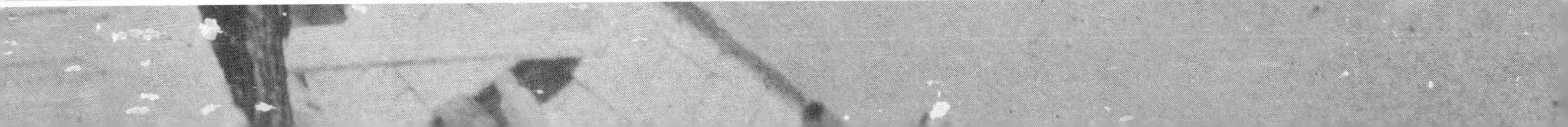

In October 1850, student John B. Young wrote to his "Dear Papa," George R. Young, telling him about a big sporting event he had recently attended at the Garrison, including 150-yard, 250-yard, and half-mile races. A highlight was climbing the greased pole: "Several tried it but none suceeded till a man of war sailor threw of his jacket ascended the pole and carried of the prize [.] this in a manner which would make any person laugh [.] by means of his hand he scraped of the grease and conferred it [on] his trousers...." The prize was $2.00 and a leg of mutton.

Haligonians either participated in or observed a wide array of summer and winter sports offered locally: baseball, quoits, football, tennis, cricket, archery, boxing, swimming, rowing, sailing, yacht racing, horse racing, polo, fishing, hunting, skating, hockey, curling, coasting, and snowshoeing—to enumerate only the more obvious. Although most present-day sports were introduced in the first half of the nineteenth century—often by the British forces stationed here—wage-earners worked long hours and had few holidays so only a small proportion of the population was able to participate. At the time of Confederation, sporting events were informal and games were played between amateurs. However, in the last quarter of the nineteenth century many athletic clubs were formed locally, and sporting events came to be organized in a more professional manner.

Regardless of the season, sporting activities in Halifax have traditionally focused on the water. The first harbour regatta was held under the auspices of Admiral Lake in 1826. Yachting, rowing, schooner racing, and swimming all developed into highly competitive activities. Skating was especially popular as a winter sport for everyone, favourite locations being Chocolate Lake, the North West Arm, the Dartmouth Lakes, and Bedford Basin when sufficiently cold enough to be safe. Curling was also played on ponds near Tower Road in Halifax and on the Dartmouth Lakes.

1. THE NOTED PRYOR CREW, TRAINING FOR GREAT AQUATIC CARNIVAL IN HALIFAX HARBOUR

AUGUST 31–SEPTEMBER 1, 1871

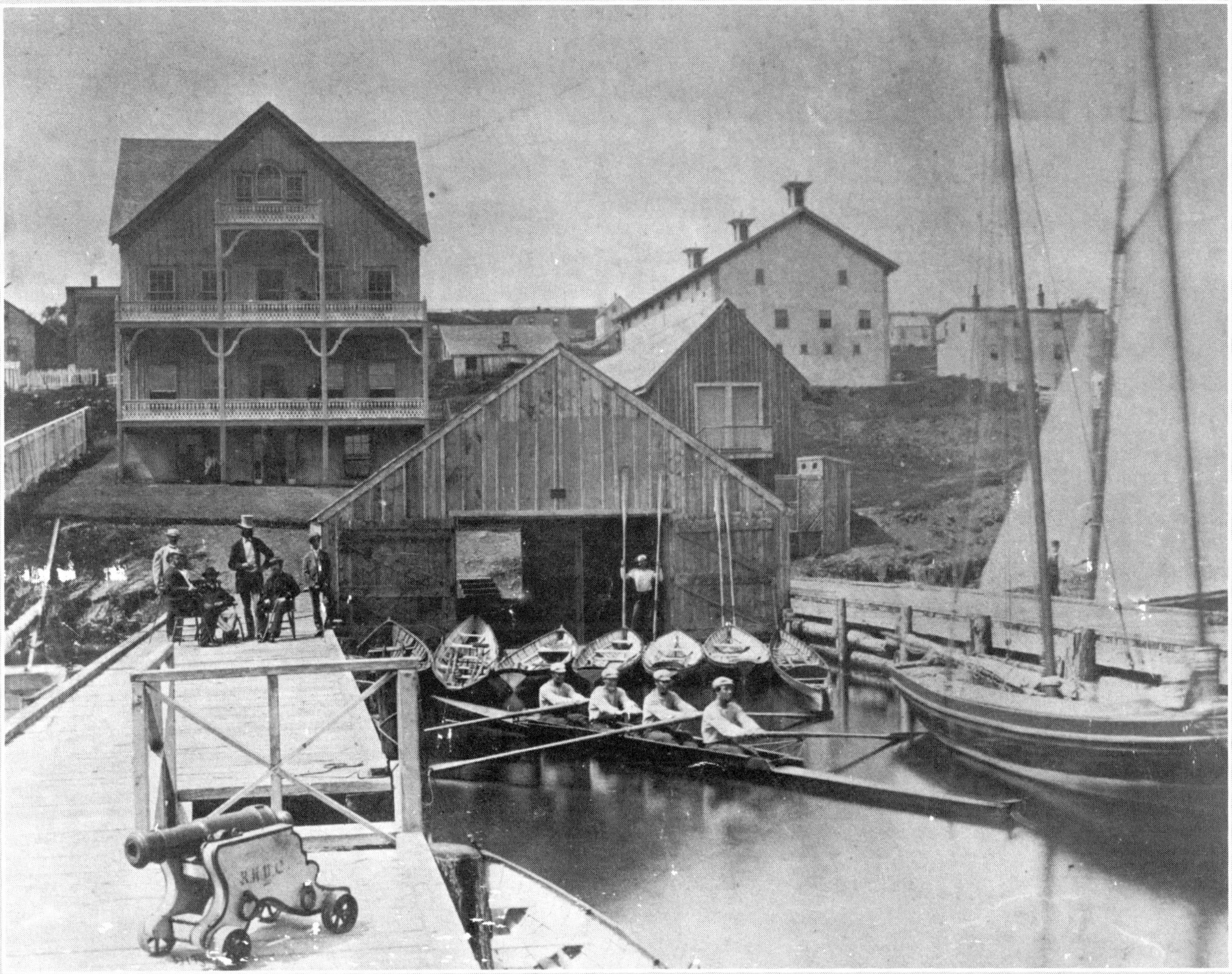

The Pryor Crew included (left to right): the internationally famous oarsman George Brown, Herring Cove; Thomas Hayes, Herring Cove; Warren Gray, Sambro; and Charles W. Nickerson, Sambro, all seated in shell; and James McGrath, Prospect (the spare), standing with oars in boat-shed doorway (centre), near the Royal Halifax Yacht Club House (upper left). The Yacht Club—now the Royal Nova Scotia Yacht Squadron—was located then on the Halifax waterfront, near the foot of Hanover Street in an area which is now part of Halifax Shipyards. When this photograph was taken, the clubhouse had only recently been completed.

2. "Polo team at Fort Needham"

c 1885

Polo was introduced into Canada with the organization of a club at Halifax by the officers of the 20th Regiment in 1878. It was played at 'Brucefield' on Quinpool Road (the present location of the Quinpool Court complex) and at Fort Needham in the North End. The game was not played exclusively by the military, and many of the players came from old established Halifax families: Duffus, Laurie, Morrow, Anderson, and Stairs, to name but a few. After 1893, the local popularity of polo declined and it ceased to be played in the area.

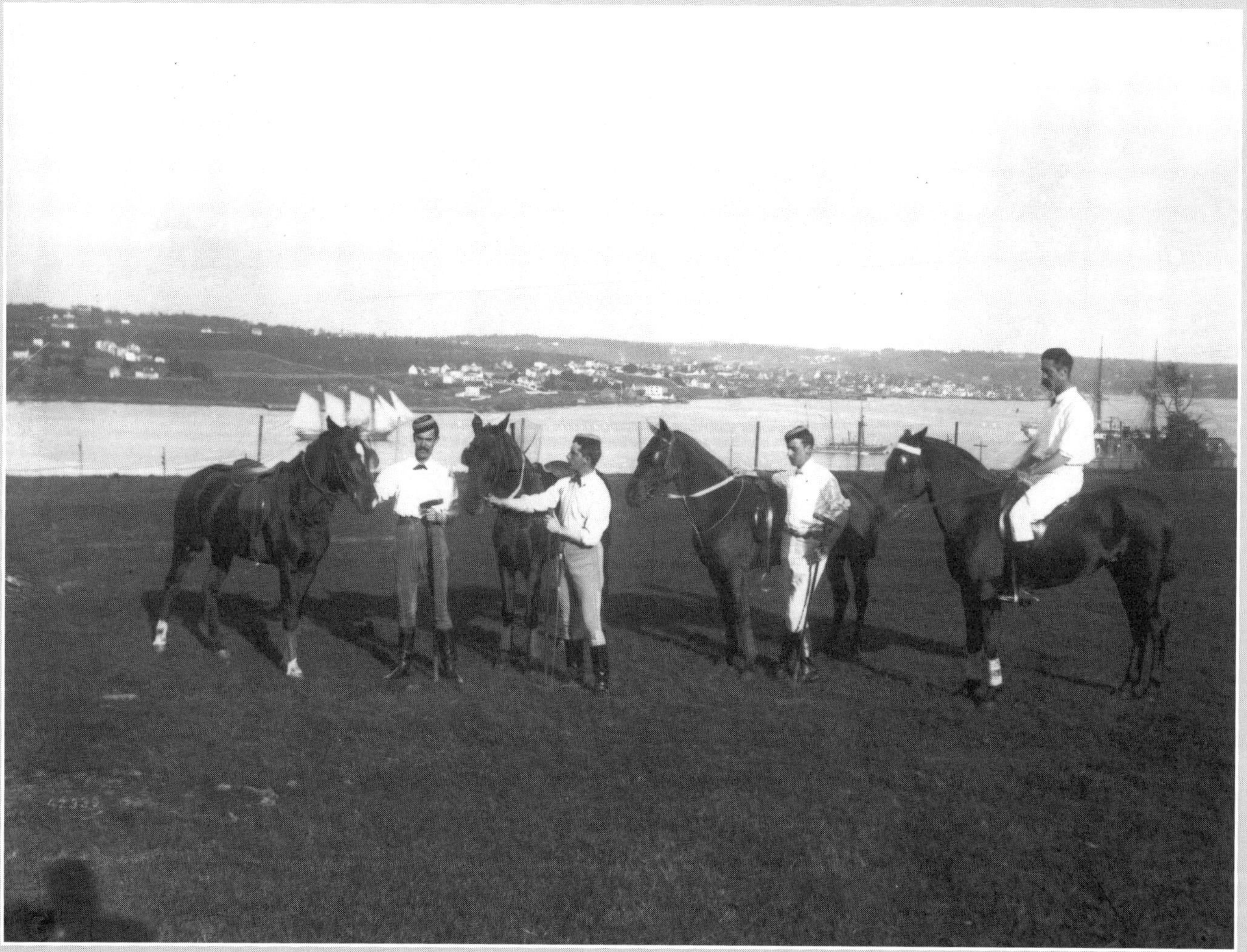

3. Red Cap Snowshoe Club, Halifax

c 1890

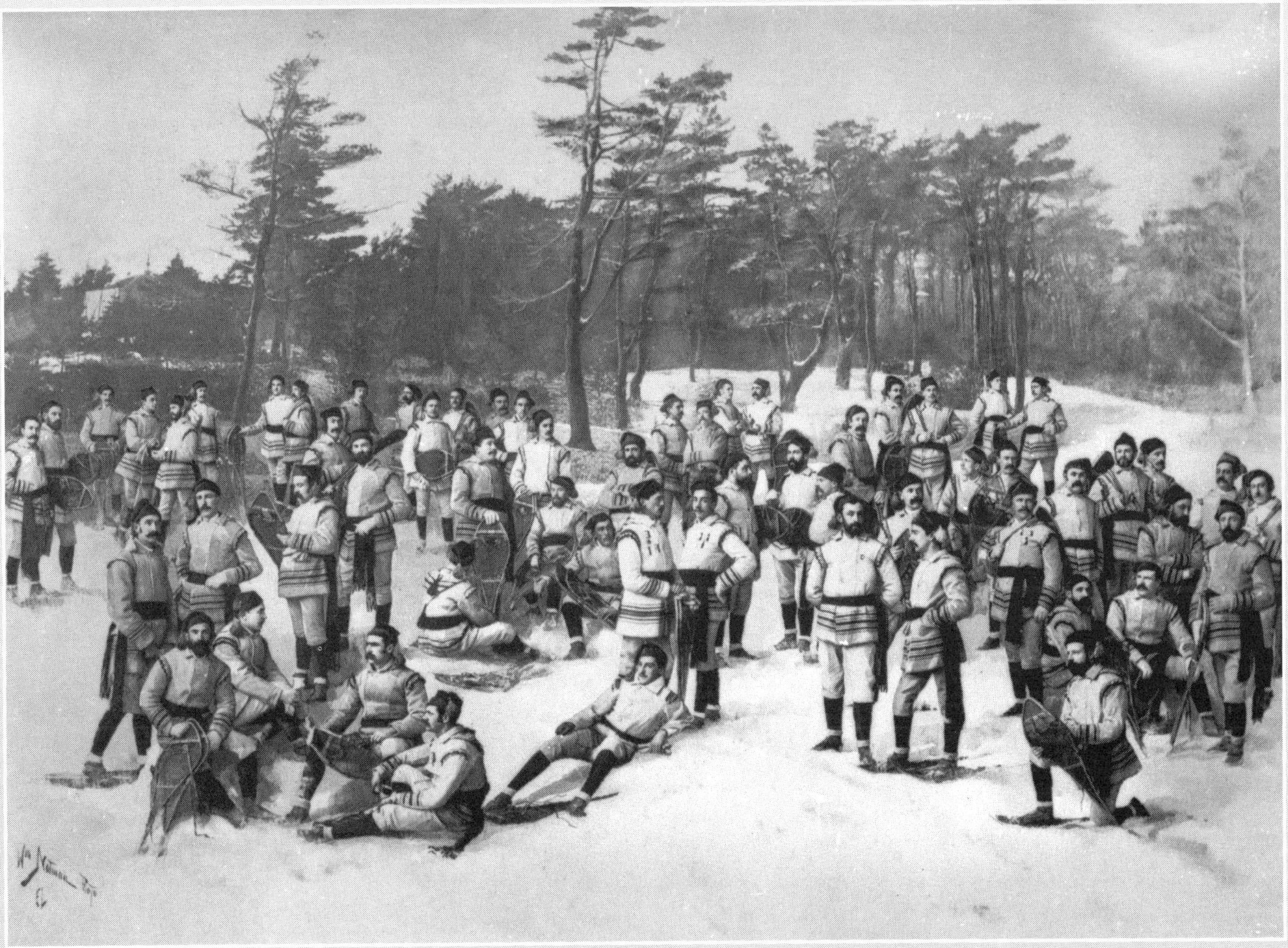

The Red Cap Snowshoe Club was established in 1874 to encourage a taste for the exercise sports of snow-shoeing and snow-shoe racing. The society would later amend its by-laws to include all winter sports activities. For this early group photo, the Notman Studio photographed each member individually or in small groups and then constructed a large composite photograph of the entire club.

4. "Rocking Stone," Spryfield
c 1895

During the nineteenth century, the Rocking Stone in Spryfield was a popular destination for the weekend rambler. First described in 1828, the 162-ton granite rock resting on a pivot of the same material, could be easily moved with a lever. It is still a well-known local landmark, although it stopped rocking in 1963.

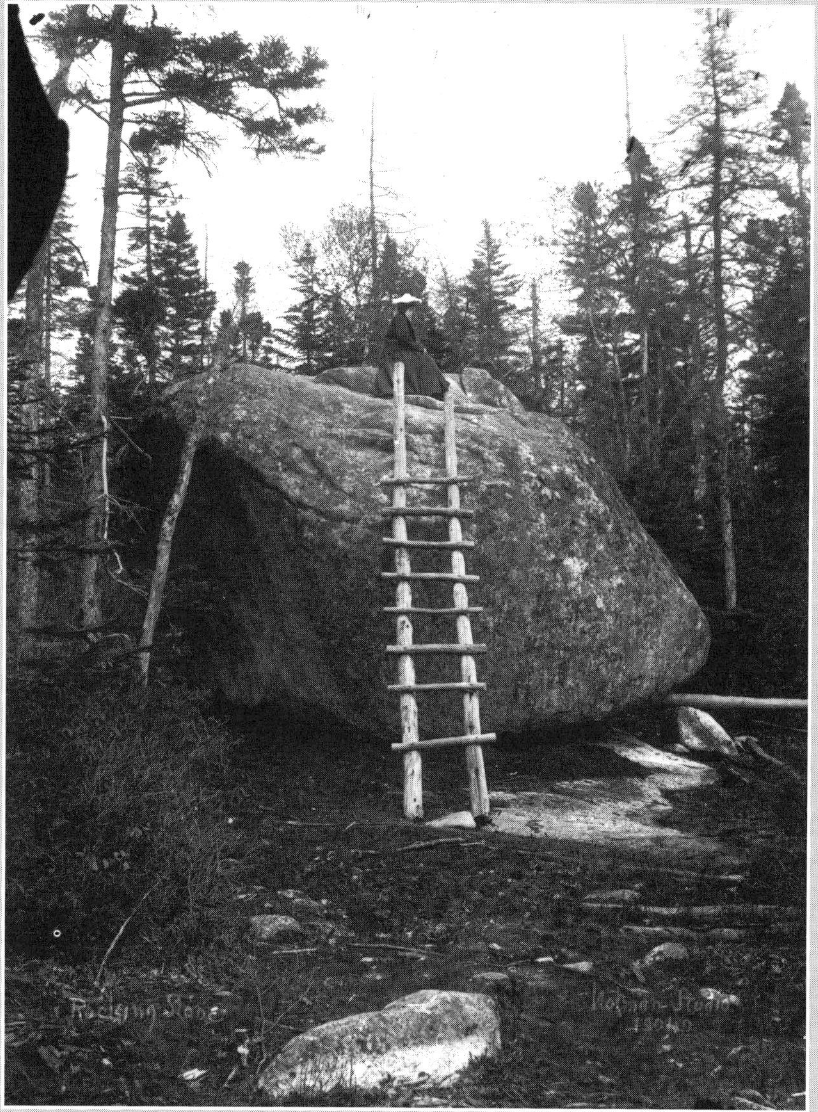

5. CURLING ON THE DARTMOUTH LAKES
C 1897

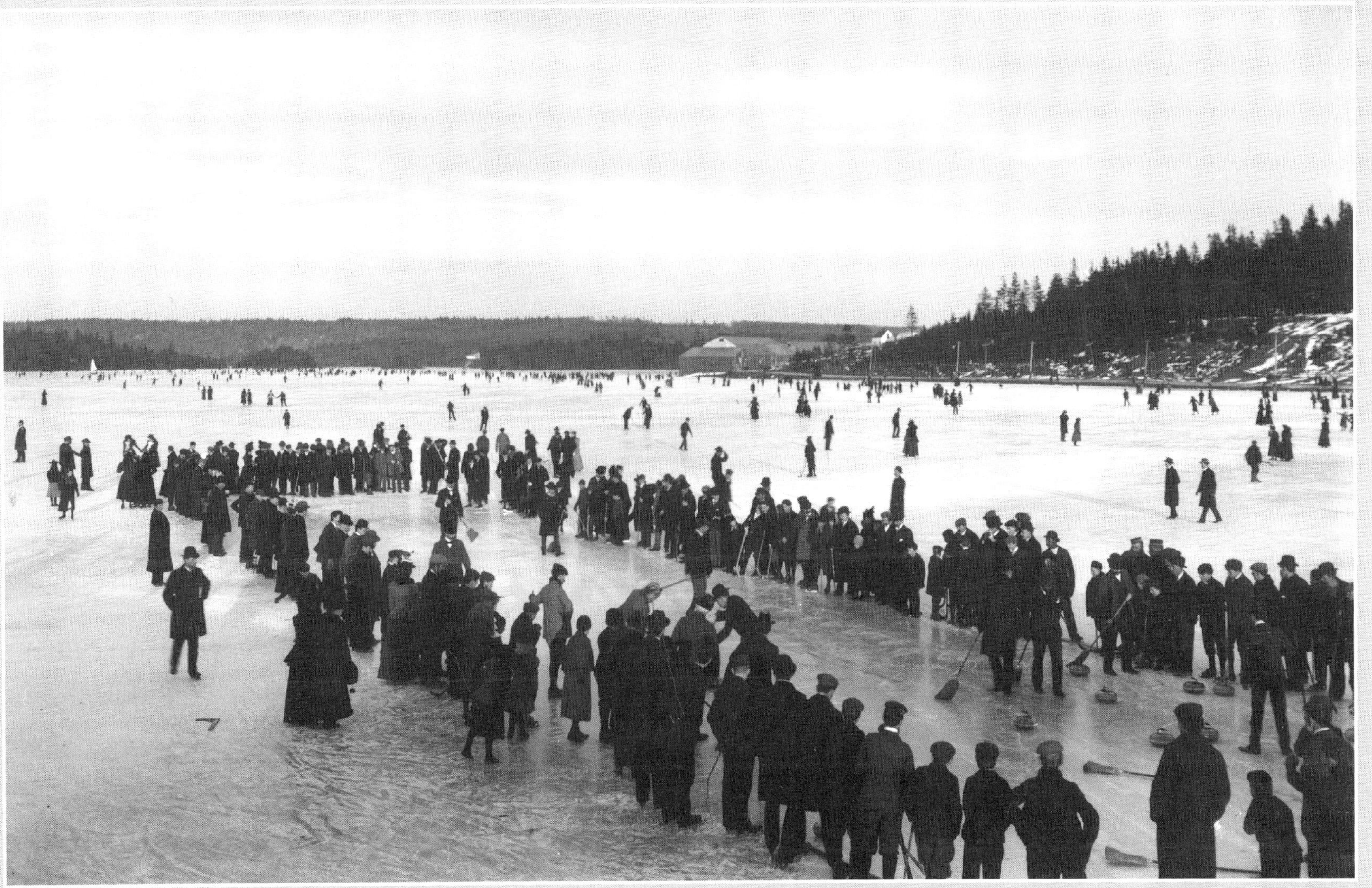

6. "Camp, head of Baker's Lake"
c 1900

The collection featured here includes several photographs of a fishing expedition in Halifax County, c 1900. Harry M. Rosenberg, noted artist and principal (1898-1910) of the Victoria School of Art and Design (now the Nova Scotia College of Art and Design), was in the party.

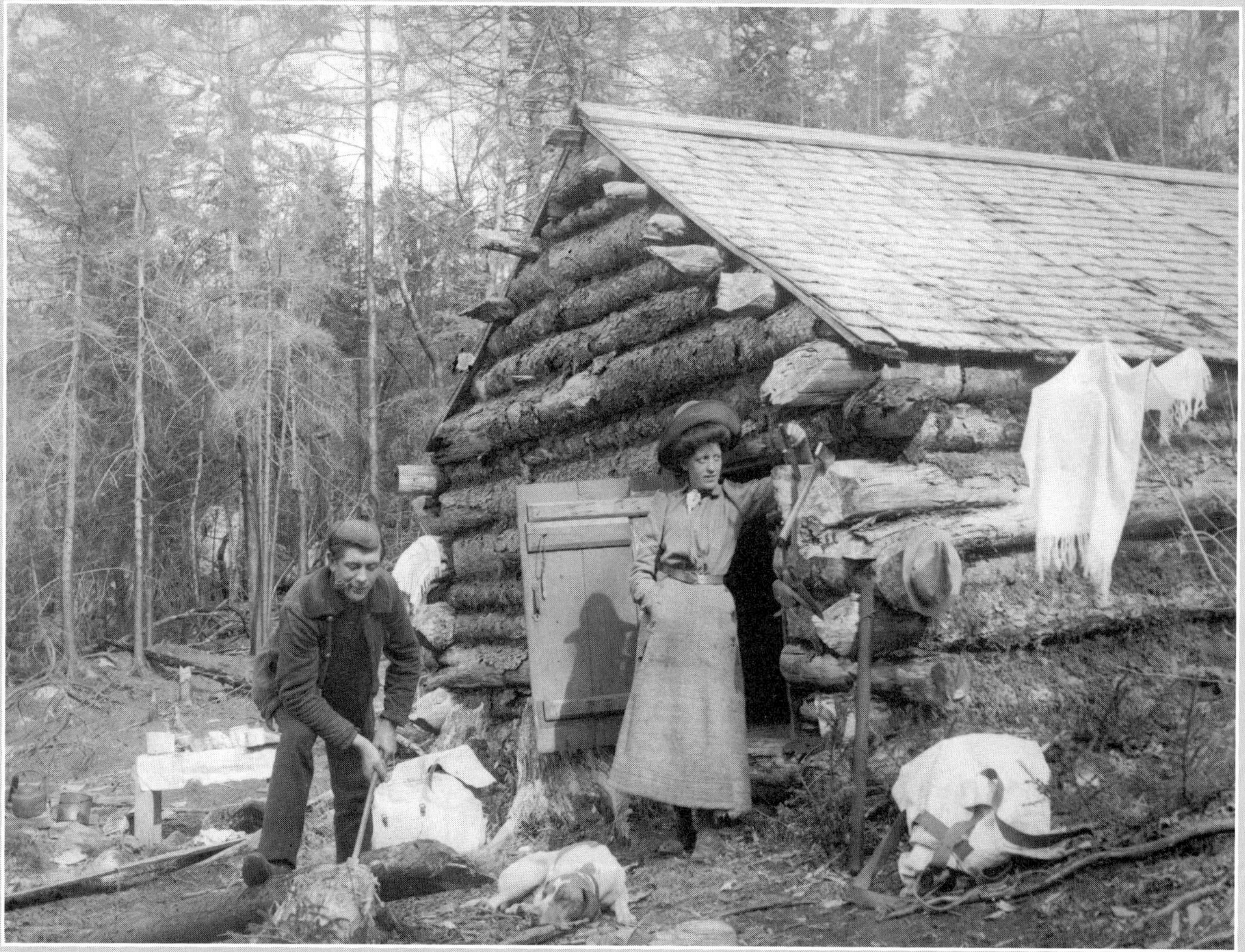

7. "Frances and Mater [Mother] at Sue's place"
c 1900

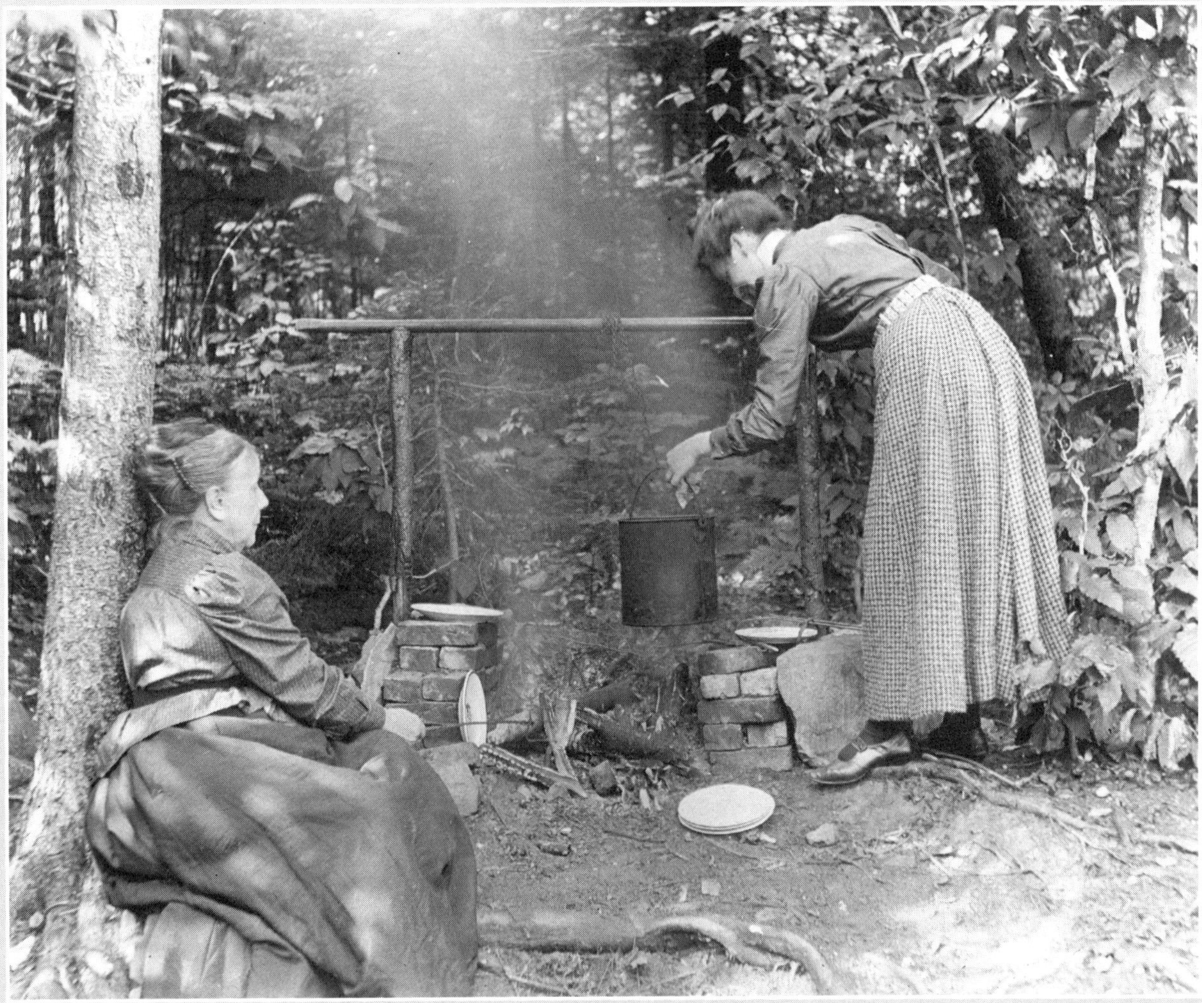

8. Woman fly-fishing

c 1900

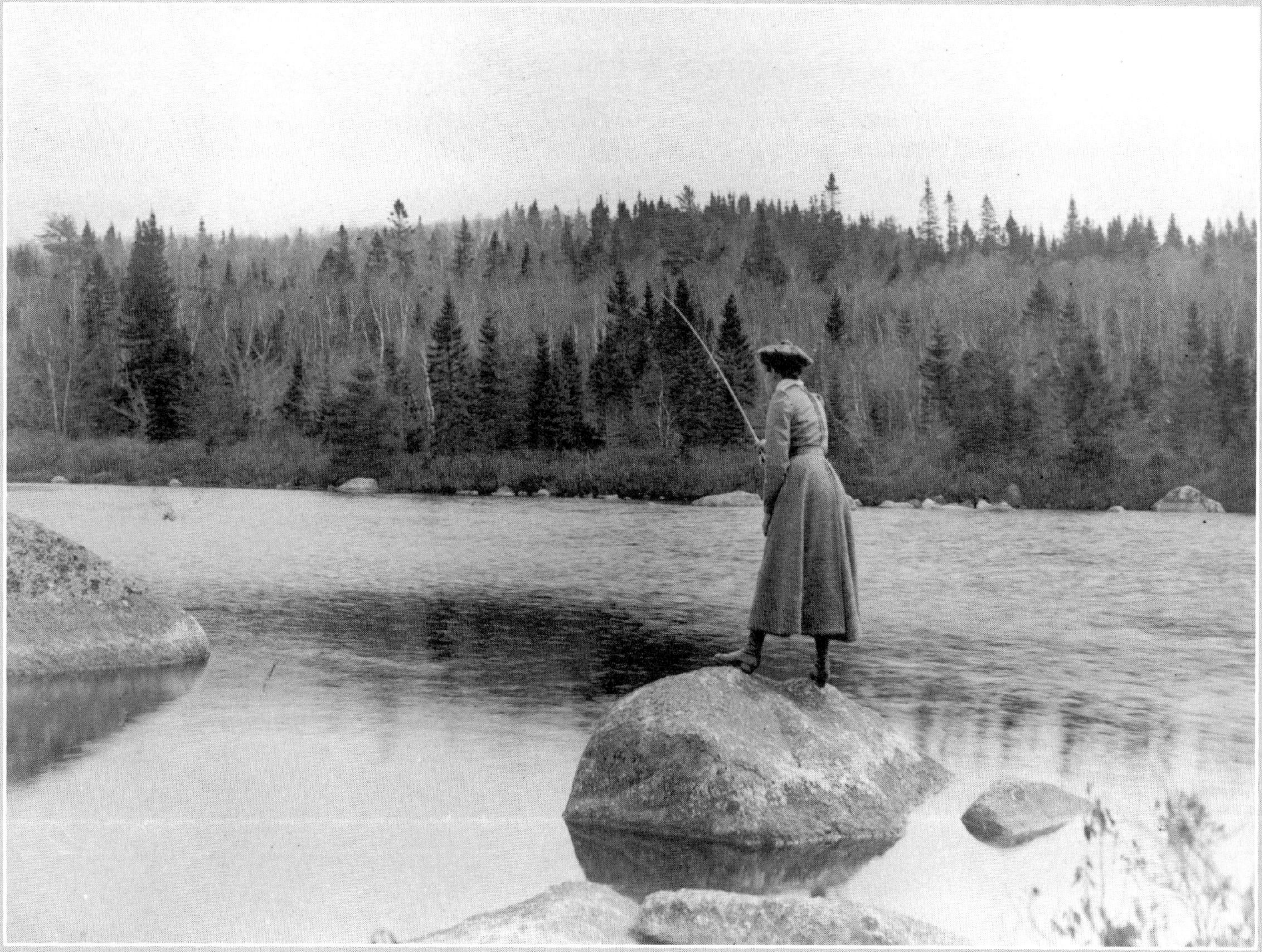

9. “H. M. Wylde’s yacht” sailing in Halifax Harbour c 1900

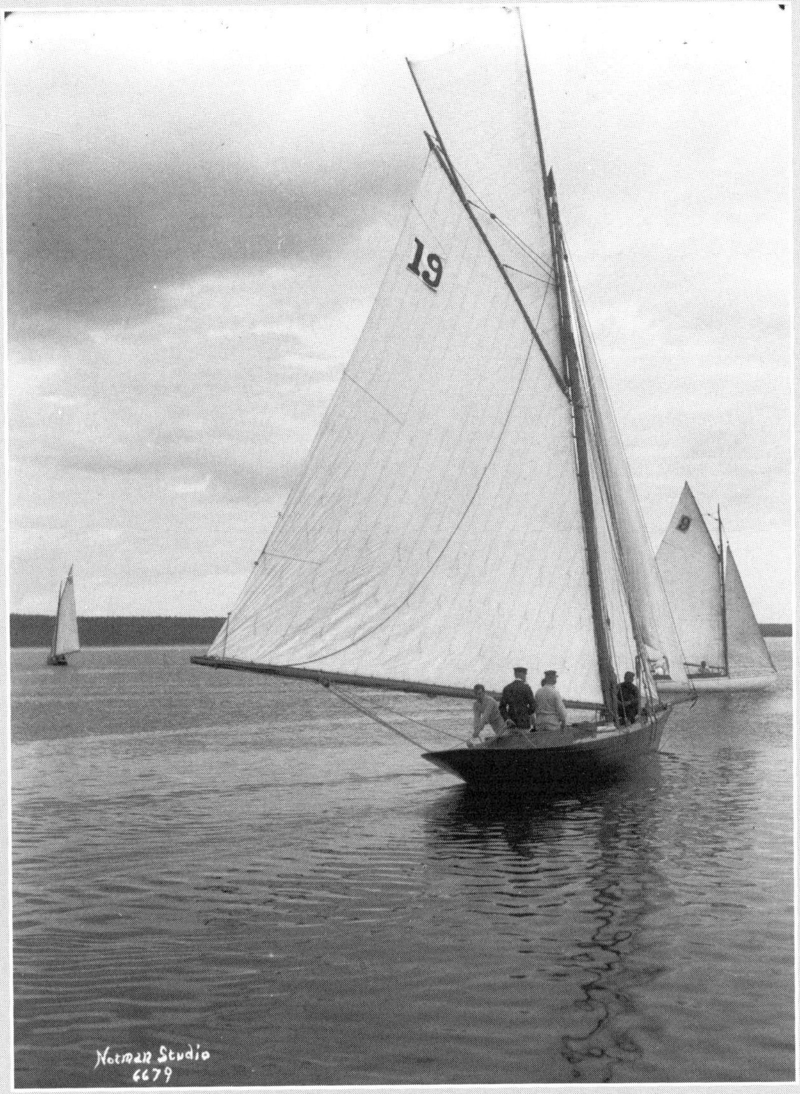

Harry Wylde’s 26-foot cutter *Youla* was designed by William Fife and built by Reuben Harlow at Dartmouth. The yacht was a successful racer for both Mr. Wylde and subsequent owners.

10. South End Lawn Tennis Club, Halifax

c 1900

Tennis was played in Halifax as early as 1876 and the first lawn-tennis court in Canada was located on the archery ground on the west side of the Public Gardens. The South End Tennis Club was formed in 1890 and is now one of the oldest such private facilities in Canada. The club originally leased a portion of the J. S. MacLean property facing on Young Avenue; this same property was later purchased and the club is still located there, over a century later.

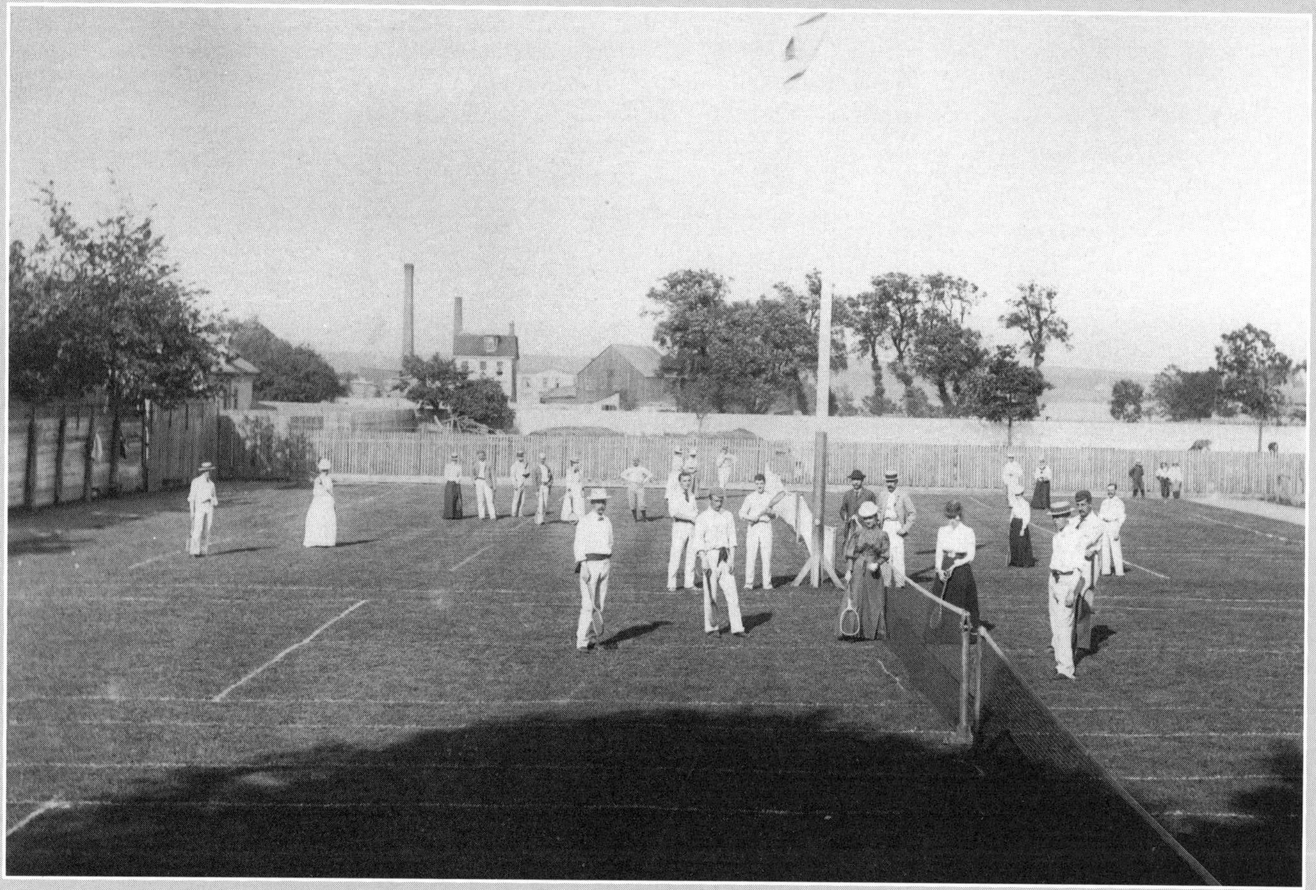

11. NOVA SCOTIA RIFLE ASSOCIATION MEETING, BEDFORD
AUGUST 1911

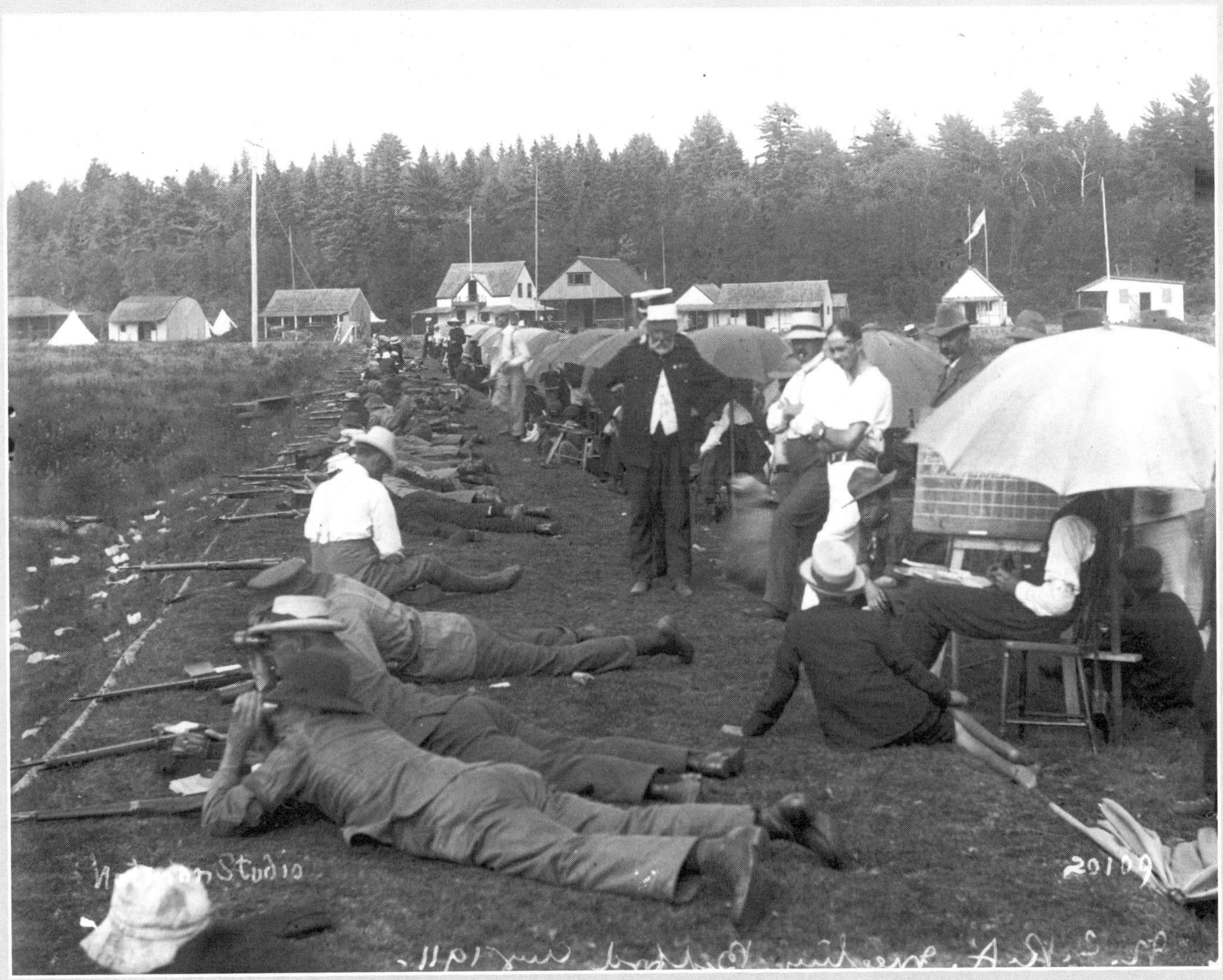

12. Boxing match on the Wanderers' Grounds, Halifax
192-

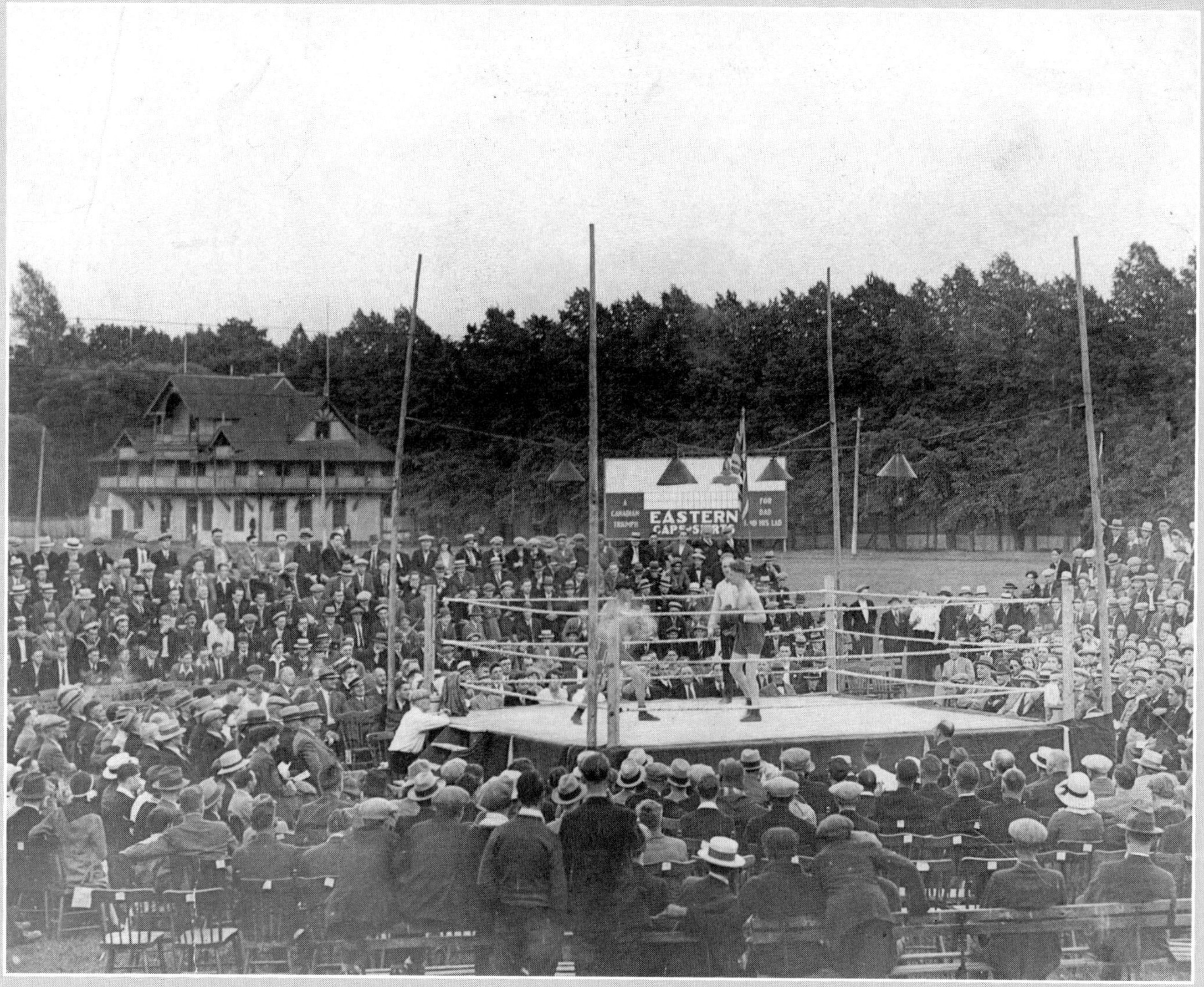

13. Ice Hockey, Anglican Church, Peggys Cove
195–

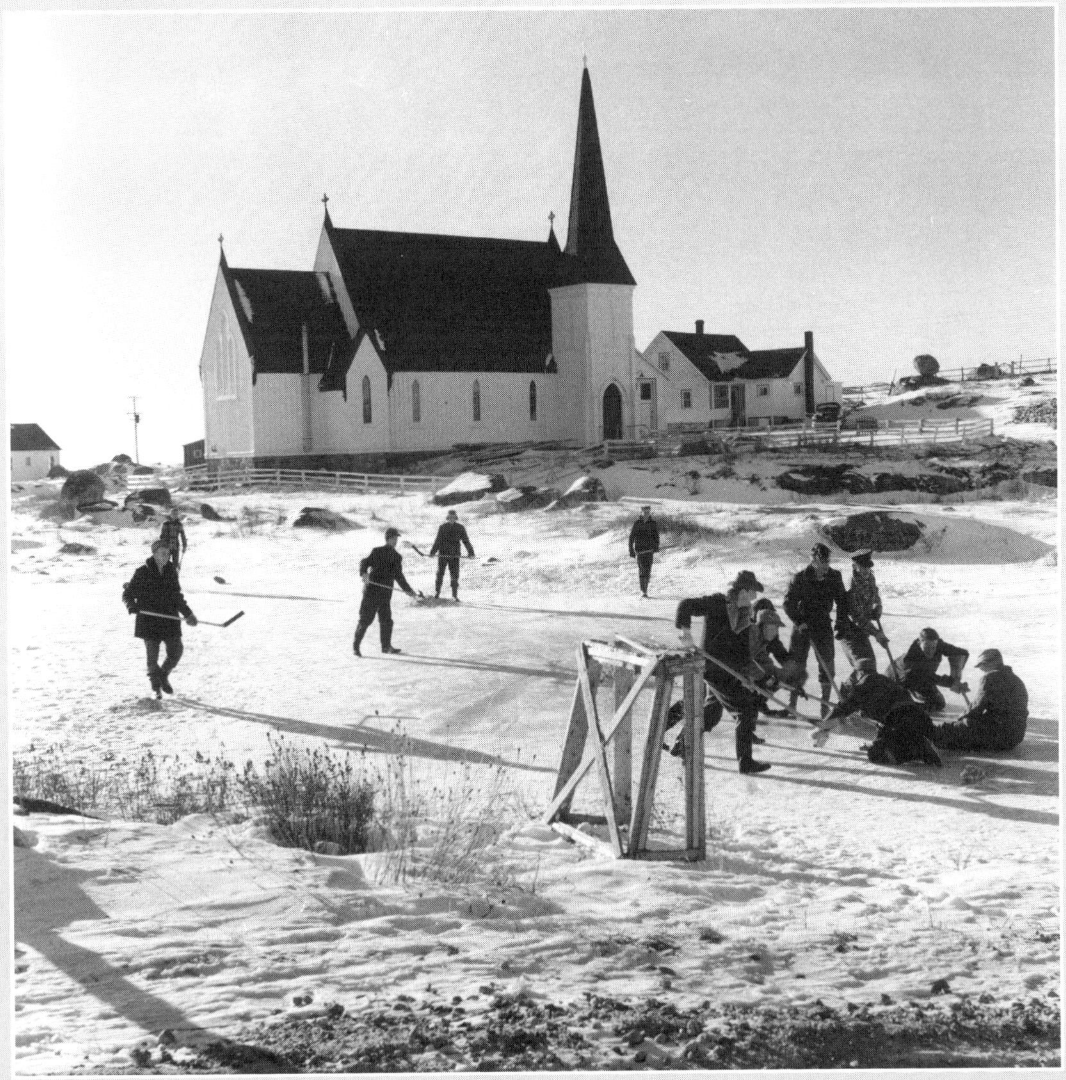

14. Polar Bear swim on New Year's Day, Halifax

between 1986 and 1988

This annual event started in 1976, when Halifax business-man and cable-television personality Bill Maden and a few friends decided to take a dip in the harbour at Black Rock Beach. The rest, as they say, is history....

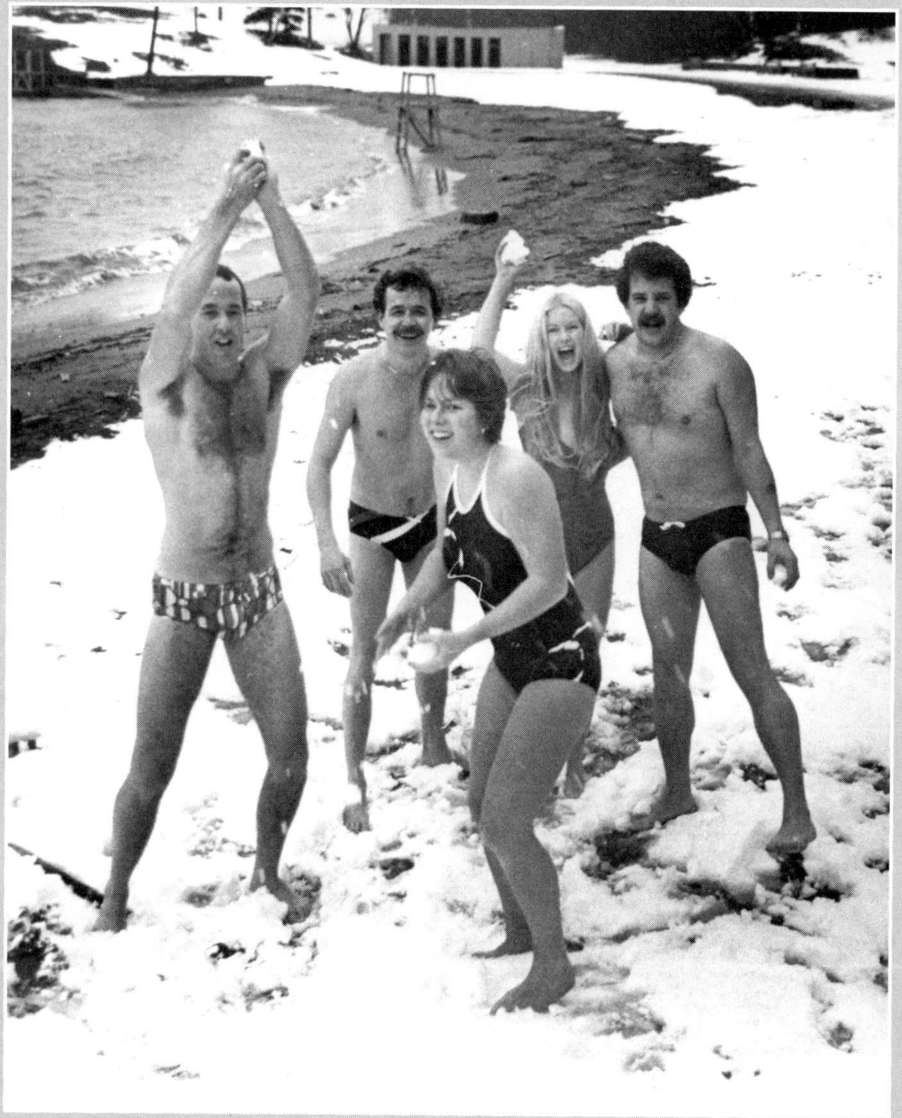

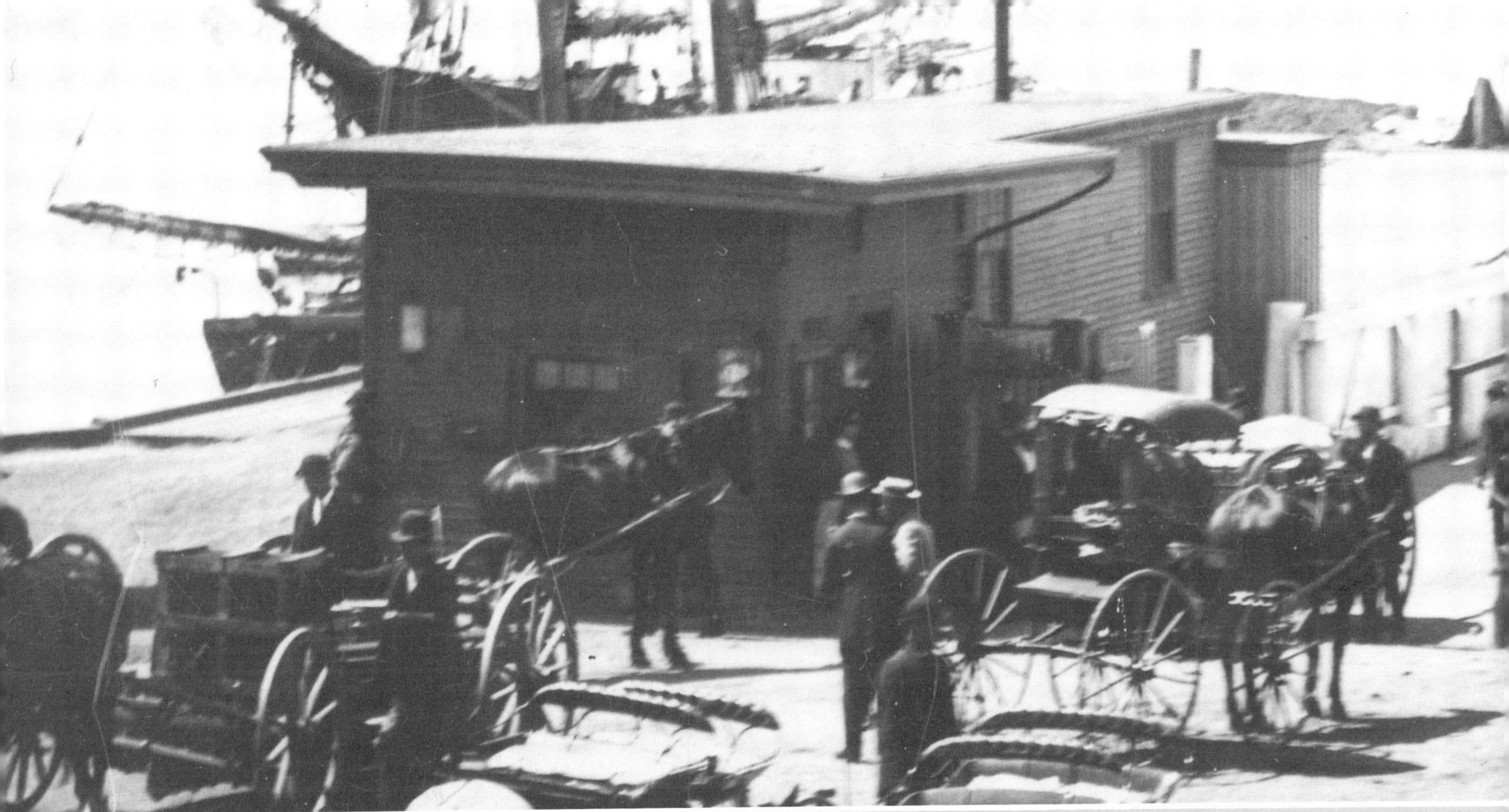

CHAPTER 9

TRANSPORTATION AND COMMUNICATION

In July 1750, the early settlers of Halifax were ordered to clear the streets in front of their respective lots. However, as T.B. Akins later noted in his *History of Halifax City,* as late as 1780 the main thoroughfares were still in rough condition, while less-travelled streets were impassable to carriages, due to protruding tree stumps and rocks. Between 1820 and 1824, street commissioners were appointed for the town and they began gradually to 'macadamize' (pave) the streets.

William D. O'Brien's horse-car railway commenced operations along Water Street, from Richmond in the north to the site of the present-day Ocean Terminals in the south, in 1866. Over the following thirty years horse-car service improved, with larger vehicles and extended routes. Improvements came again in 1896, when the Halifax Electric Tramway Company introduced the first electric tramcars over one-and-a-half miles of track on Barrington Street. This service soon extended to all parts of the city.

The 'keep-to-the-right' rule of the road was introduced to Nova Scotia in 1923—and necessitated an immediate change in the location of the door and the driver in all Birney tramcars then operating in the city. The army nicknamed this particular and distinctive vehicle model the 'Mustard Can', while the navy referred to them as the 'Banana Fleet'. Prior to World War II, some 58 Birney tramcars carried an average of nine million passengers per year in Halifax. This number, however, skyrocketed to more than thirty-one million passengers annually during the war. Twenty-three additional trams were purchased from all over North America, but during the bicentenary year, 1949, a new electric trolley-coach service was commenced, resulting in the nostalgic 'retirement' of the old and familiar Birney cars.

Ferry service has been continuous across Halifax Harbour since 1752. After at least three earlier attempts to span the water with some sort of structure, two permanent bridges now link the two largest communities within the Halifax Regional Municipality—the Angus L. Macdonald (1955) and the A. Murray MacKay (1970). Until this century, travel through Halifax County was primarily by stagecoach over rough roads, or by sailing vessel or coastal steamer. By the turn of the century, the Halifax and South-Western Railway linked the city with South Shore communities, and in 1916 another rail-line officially opened between Dartmouth and Upper Musquodoboit. The opening of an airport on Chebucto Road in 1931 signalled that the city was ready to encourage commercial aviation, and the present-day Halifax International Airport officially opened in 1960.

1. Ferry Wharf at Dartmouth with Ferry SS *Chebucto* in the dock. Ticket office (centre), waiting room and Ferry Co's office at left
c 1885

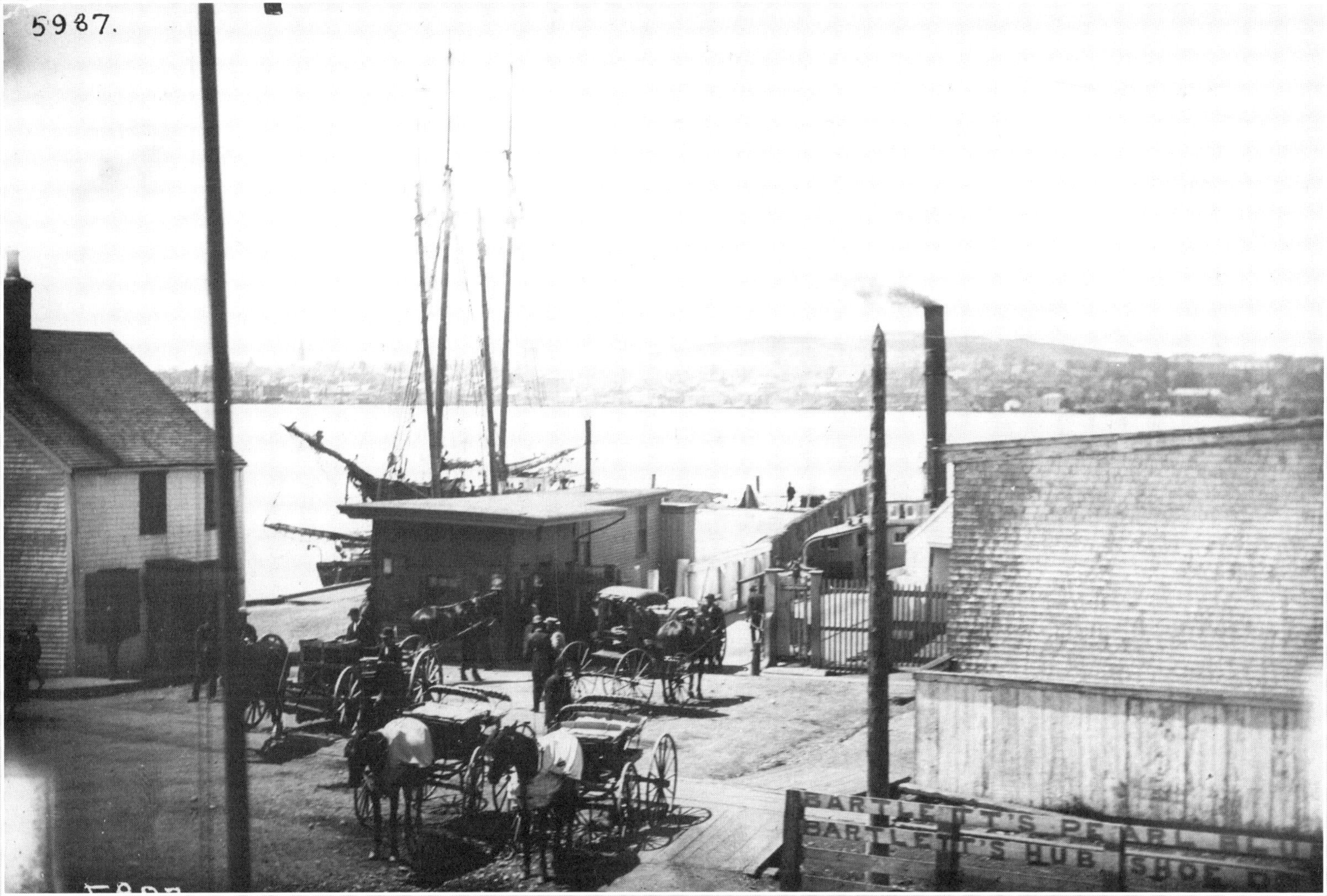

Manager James Adams and most of the conductors and drivers, with two open (summer) horse cars, Halifax Street Railway Co., in front of the company's car barn, southeast corner of Campbell Road (Barrington Street) and Hanover Street in the Richmond district, Halifax.

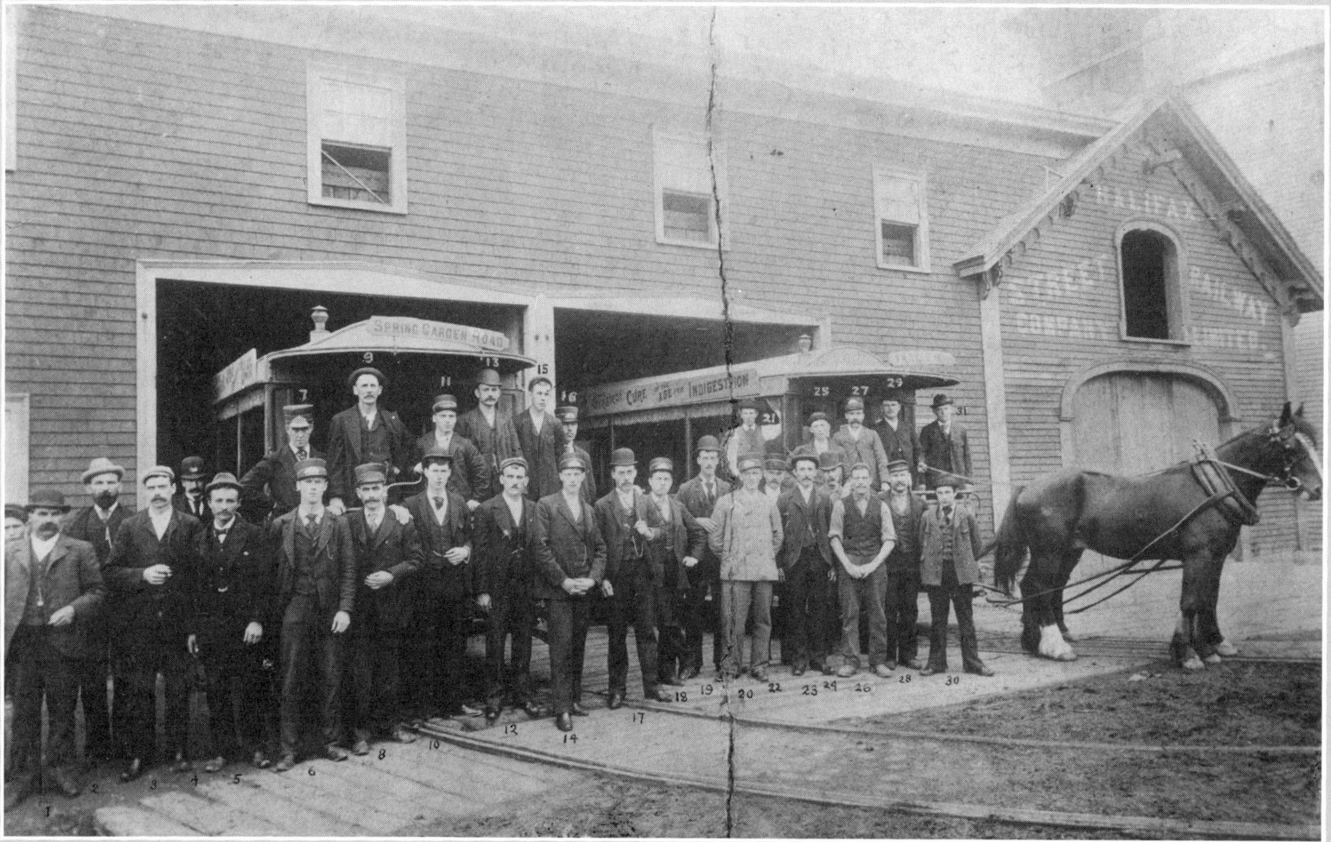

3. Sewer and water trenches, Burton's Hill, Portland Street, Dartmouth, Looking east

c 1900

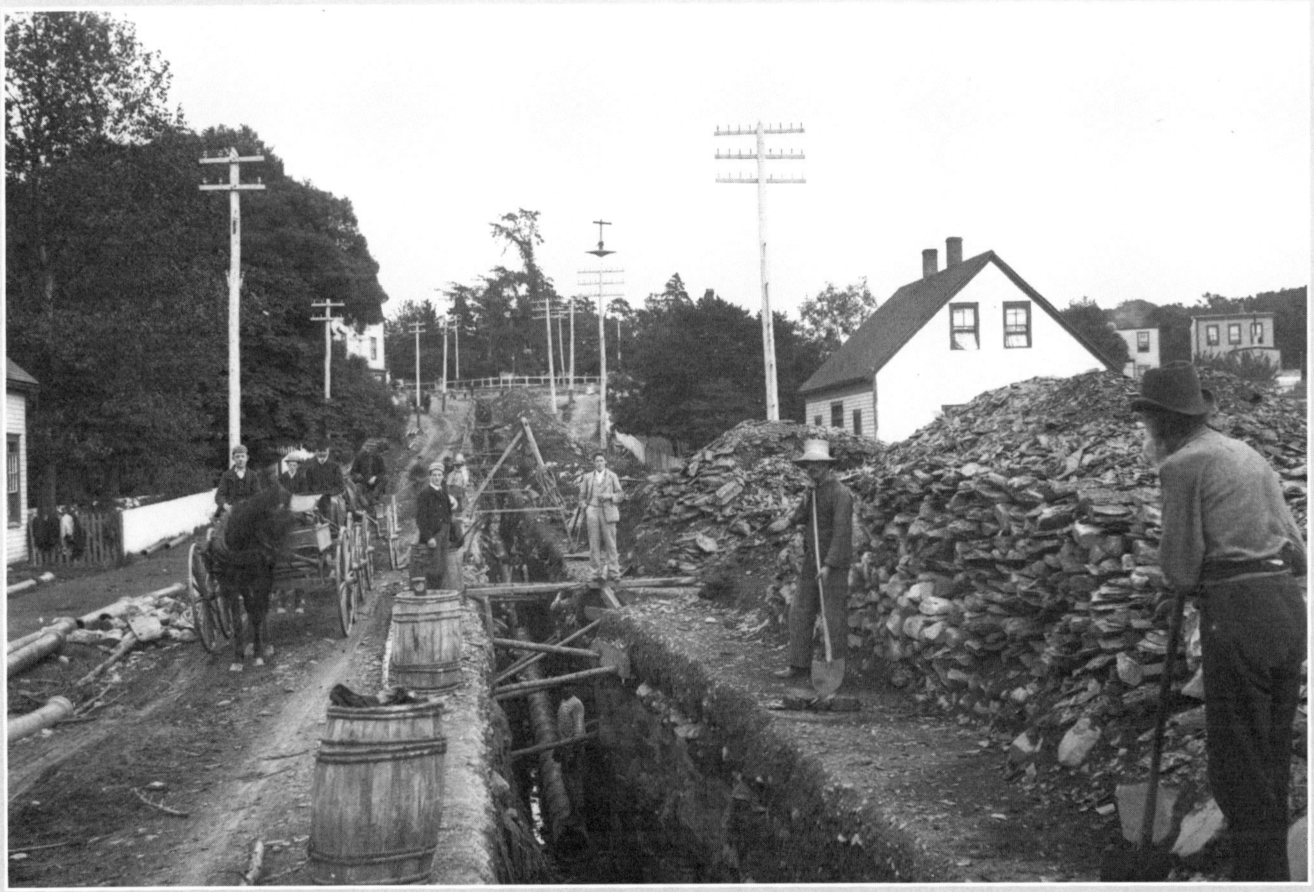

Burton's Hill is that section of Portland Street between Prince Albert Road and the Five Corners, at the intersection of Pleasant, Portland, and Albert Streets.

4. LAYING DOUBLE TRACK FOR HALIFAX ELECTRIC TRAMWAY, POSSIBLY QUINPOOL ROAD
BETWEEN 1906 AND 1912

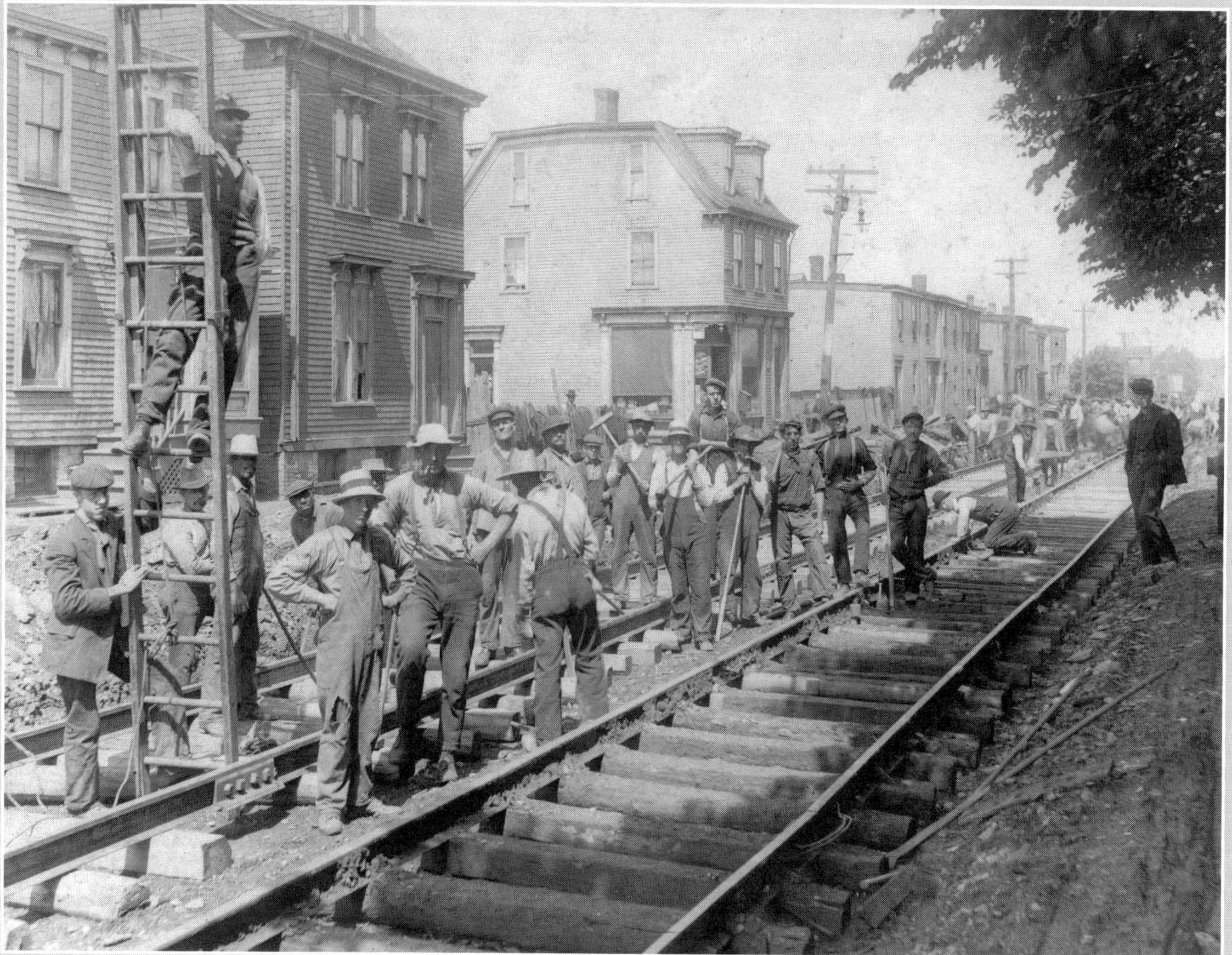

5. Steamer *Dufferin* at the Government Wharf, Port Dufferin, with Smiley & Company's lobster crates awaiting Transport to Halifax
c 1910

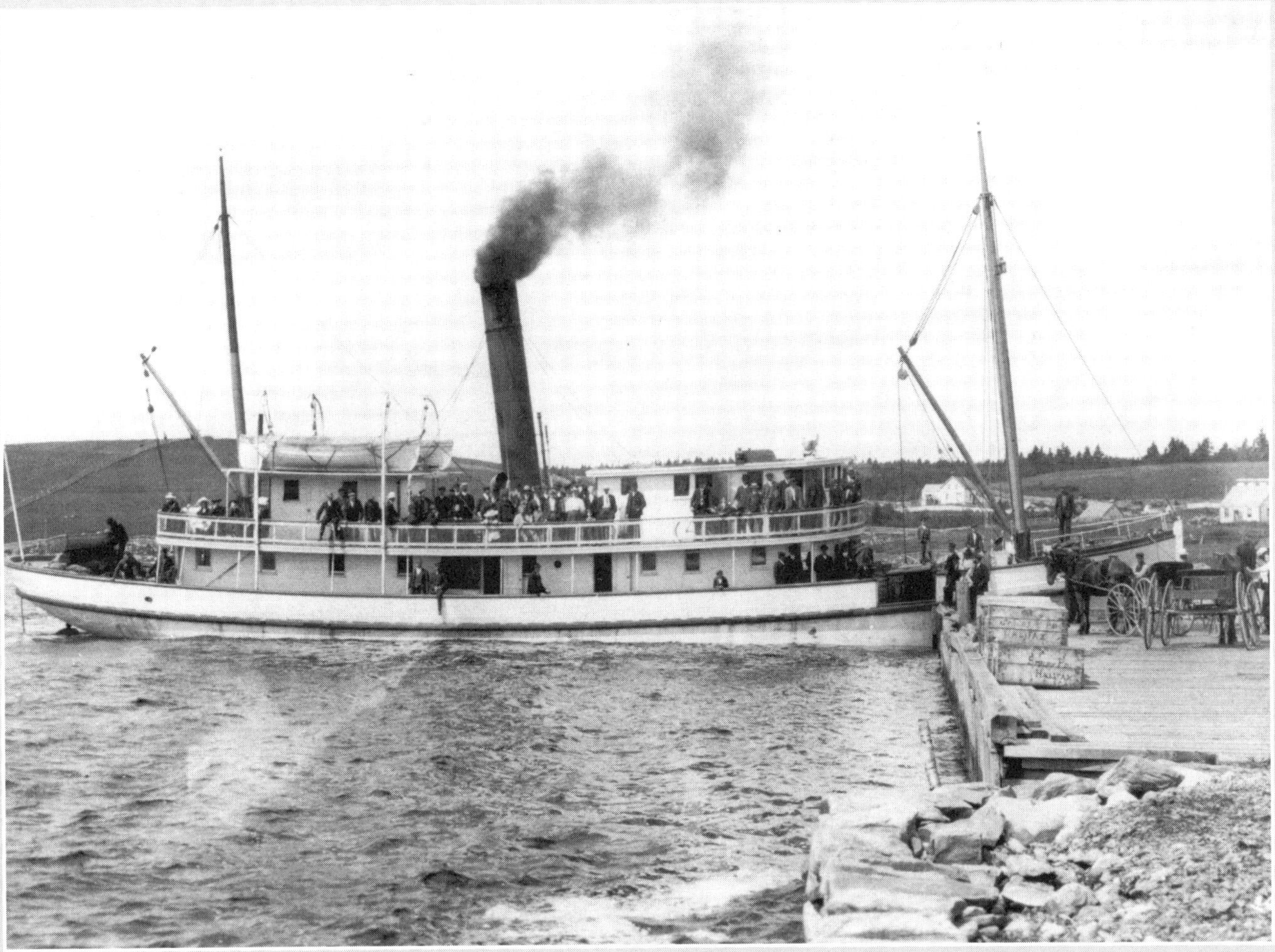

Stage coaches travelled the rough Eastern Shore post-road and vessels sailed along the coast in the nineteenth century. Steamer service to Sheet Harbour began about 1890 and in subsequent years the *City of Ghent, Wilfrid C, Strathcona, Dufferin, Margaret, Scotia, Chedabucto,* and various other streamers called at Eastern Shore ports. The 211-ton *Dufferin* began service in 1905; the steamer left Halifax every Thursday at 10 p.m. and arrived in Port Dufferin the next morning at 5:30 a.m., weather permitting. It then called at Moser River, Ecum Secum, and Guysborough County ports. The *Dufferin* carried passengers and a general cargo usually consisting of feed, hay, kerosene, and groceries. On the return trip to Halifax, it called at the same ports, collecting quantities of lumber and lobsters in the spring. On arrival in Halifax, the crates of lobsters were dumped into the water until the next morning, when they were transported by the Dominion Atlantic Railway to Yarmouth and then on to Boston.

6. First bus operated by the Eastern Shore Bus Co-op
c 1939

Ted Ogilvie and Carl Anderssen began their bus route between Sherbrooke and Halifax in 1939.

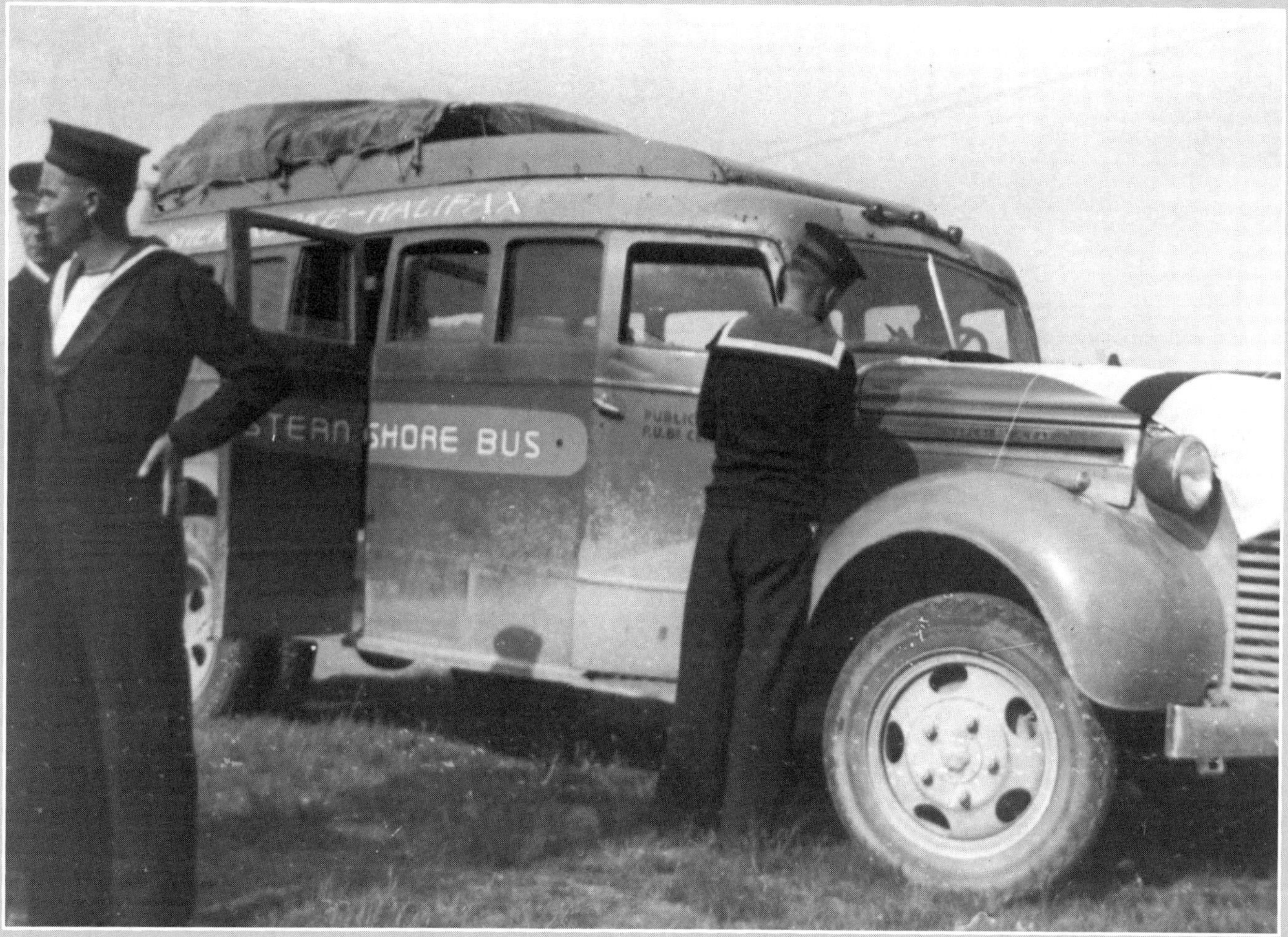

7. Photographer, with a camera and tripod, photographing a decorated Birney streetcar, marking the end of Tramcar service in the main part of Halifax

March 26, 1949

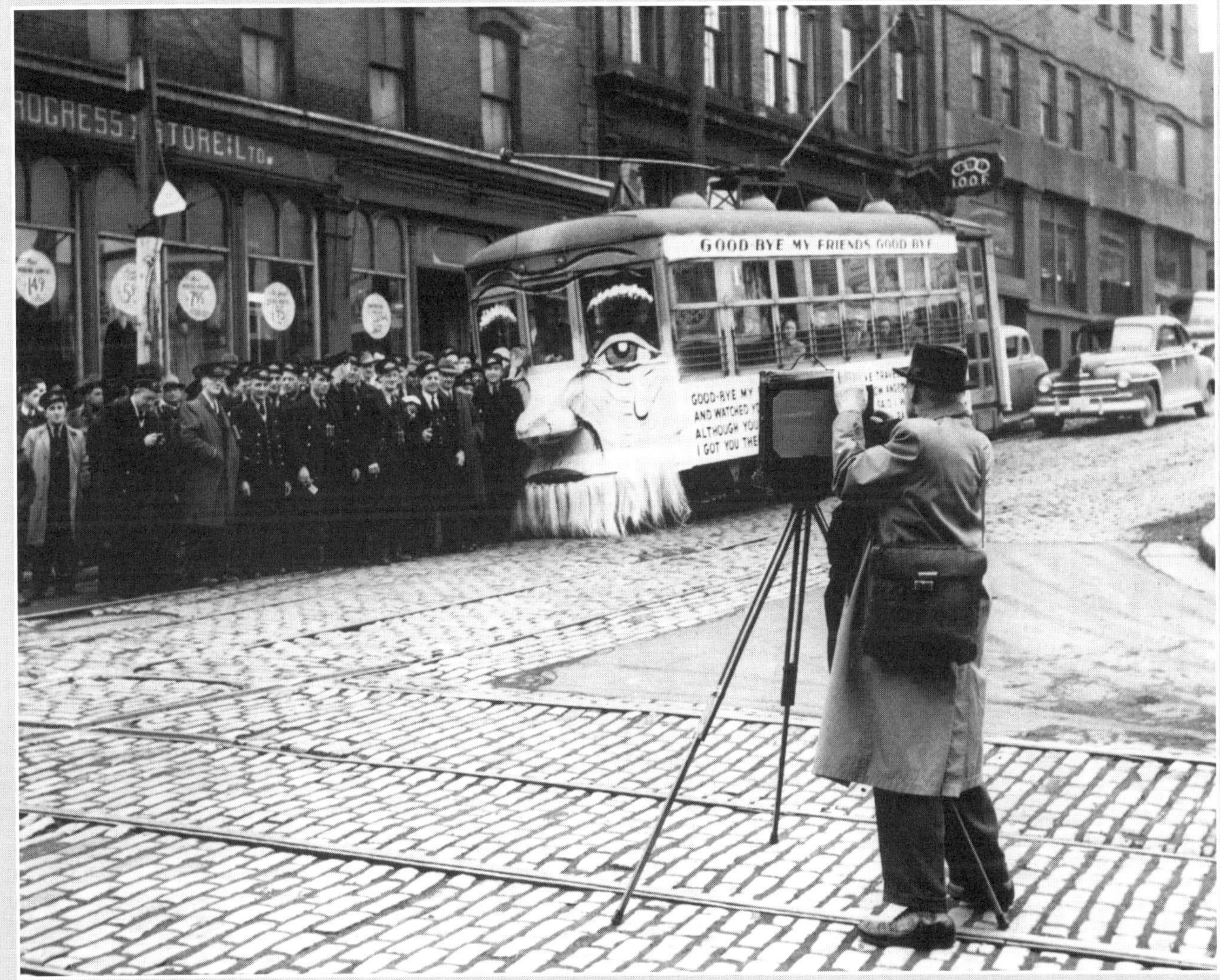

The photographer is standing in the intersection of Buckingham and Barrington Streets, looking towards the Progress Stores Ltd. and the Independent Order of Oddfellows Temple at 10 and 16 Buckingham Street, respectively. Russ Lownds's *Trams & Tracks:'The Birneys' of Halifax, Nova Scotia*, describes the last run:

> *On March 26, 1949, the Birneys ran downtown for the last time, and Car 177 was de-corated for the occasion with a tearful, bewhiskered face painted on the front and farewell messages painted on the side panels and rear of the car. The verses on the tram were composed by Miss E.H. Doyle, then Assistant-Secretary of the Nova Scotia Light and Power Company.*

8. Motorcade inaugurating service on Angus L. Macdonald Bridge
April, 1955

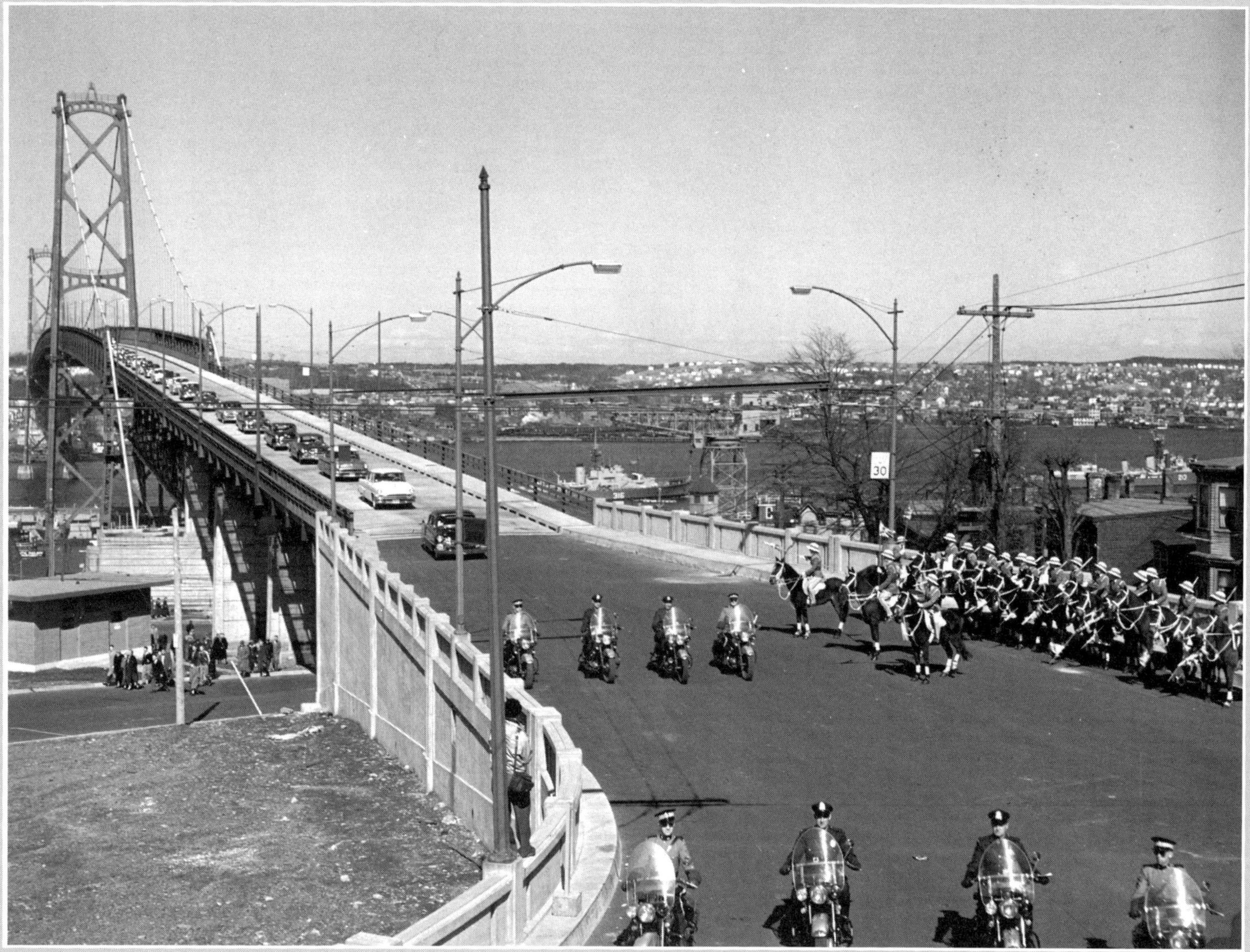

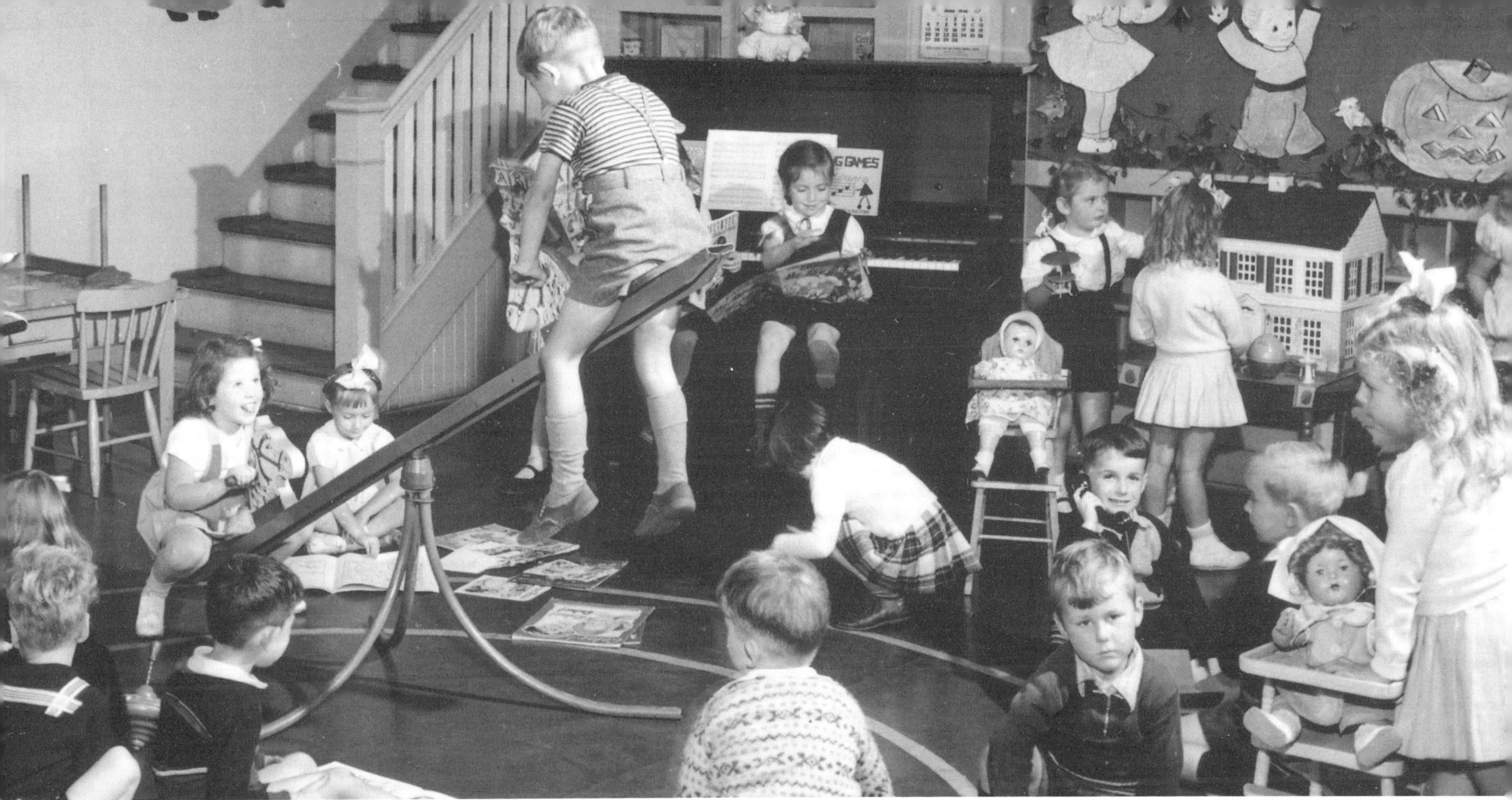

CHAPTER 10

EDUCATION AND INSTITUTIONS

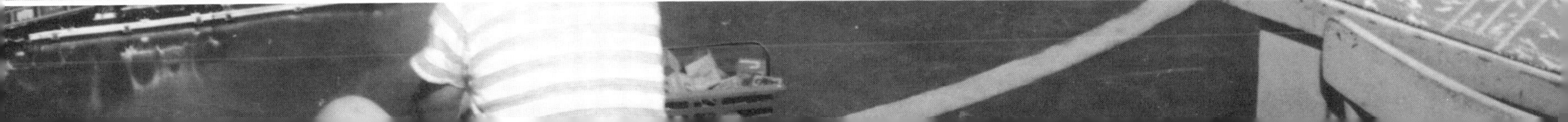

The Church of England's quaintly-named "Society for the Propagation of the Gospel in Foreign Parts" sponsored the first schools in Halifax, soon after the founding of the community. In 1789, the Halifax Grammar School opened, intended to provide higher education for children of the well-to-do. Over the following decades, various private and church-sponsored schools—all of them requiring the payment of some kind of fees for most pupils—came and went in the city, prior to the *Free School Acts* of 1864 and 1865. In the latter year, 700 children attended city schools.

Addressing the Halifax City Board of School Commissioners in 1866, Dr. T. H. Rand, the Superintendent of Education, complained that there were still serious problems within the local system:

> *At present most of the schools in the city are merely miscellaneous gatherings. In the same room may not infrequently be heard the alphabet class and the class in the higher departments of English grammar, the class in Addition and the class in Exchange or Alligation; in short, the pupils throughout the city are not as a whole, pursuing a systematic course of instruction. Every teacher is pursuing his own course. If he prefers geography to grammar, or arithmetic to reading, the pupils under his charge will be found partaking of the same one-sidedness; their scholarship will lack symmetry; it will, in fine, be mere half-work.*

The superintendent concluded with his vision for public education in Halifax: "The system of schools I propose for the city embraces a series of ascending grades, having accommodation for 5,000 pupils or over, at the outset; and a prescribed course of instruction adapted to each step in the series, covering a period of eleven or twelve years." Three years later, some 5,065 students were enrolled in Halifax's 21 public schools.

A combined school and orphanage was started in the city as early as 1750. In subsequent years, various specialized institutions were established throughout the city and surrounding area: St. Joseph's Orphanage, the Home of the Guardian Angel, the Protestant Orphanage, the Halifax Infants' Home, the Nova Scotia Home for Colored Children, the Halifax Industrial School and St. Patrick's Home. The School for the Deaf was opened on Gottingen Street in 1857 and the School for the Blind on Morris Street in 1871.

The Halifax Regional Municipality presently has a wide variety of post-secondary learning institutions: the Atlantic School of Theology, Dalhousie University and DalTech (formerly the Technical University of Nova Scotia), Mount Saint Vincent University, the Nova Scotia College of Art and Design, St. Mary's University, The University of King's College, and three Nova Scotia Community College campuses.

1. "Protestant Orphans' Home, North Park Street, Halifax"

May 1874

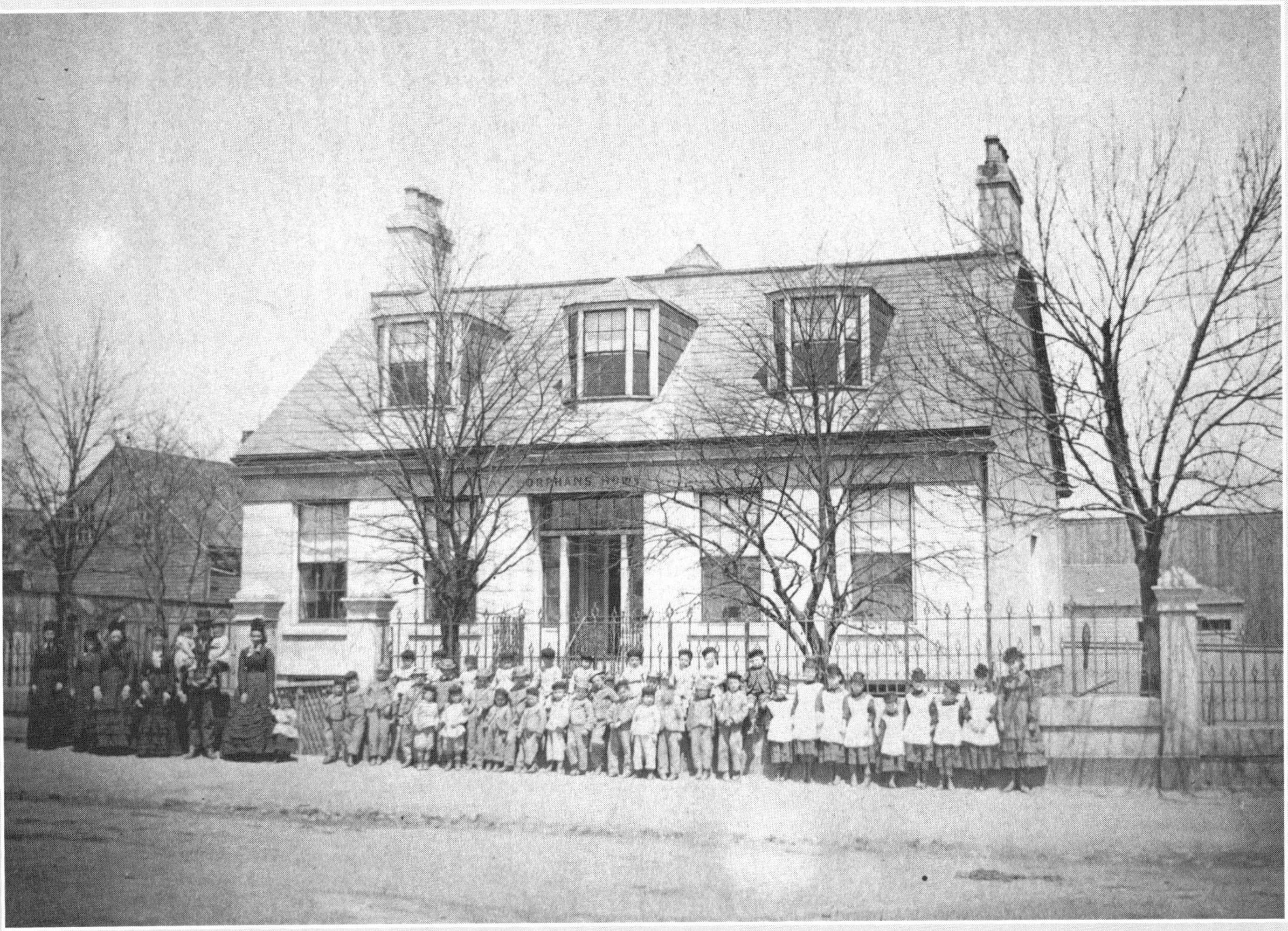

The Seventeenth Annual Report of the Protestant Orphans' Home (1874) reported that during that year, almost 80 children had passed through the home, 28 had been formally admitted, 33 had been adopted in the town and country, but 40 were still residents. The report raised concern that:

> *The time...has clearly arrived for making some better arrangements to meet the requirements of sickness among the children. At present it is almost impossible to prevent diseases of an infectious and contagious character from spreading rapidly, and the necessity for better means of isolation must be evident to all who consider the character of the Institution...it will be better to obtain another site and erect a new building designed purposely for an 'Orphanage'....*

2. "Industrial School, Quinpool Road, Halifax"
c 1880

This building, designed by Henry F. Busch, first opened to residents in 1871. In 1880, thirty-eight boys resided in the Halifax Protestant Industrial School, which had been founded in 1867 to provide basic vocational training for truant and wayward boys from the local community. The regimen also included eight hours of rudimentary general education a week, since many boys could not read or write when institutionalized.

Although the school's 1880 *Report* gave glowing accounts regarding the progress of many "inmates," the report began by stating that "The material given us to work upon is invariably of the roughest description, and therefore the best adapted to our purposes, being chiefly boys sent by the Stipendiary, or such as have passed beyond parental control." Many of the boys were taught boot- and shoemaking in Amos A. Bliss's workshop [Bliss advertised in *McAlpine's Halifax City Directory*, 1879-80, as a "manufacturer of and dealer in all kinds of hand-made boots and shoes" at 96 Gottingen Street]. Others cleaned carpets and cut kindling wood. In 1880 the boys earned $1434.73 for the school: $889.92 from Mr. Bliss for their work, $403.11 from the sale of kindling, $137.70 for cleaning carpets, and $4.00 for "drumming" broom handles.

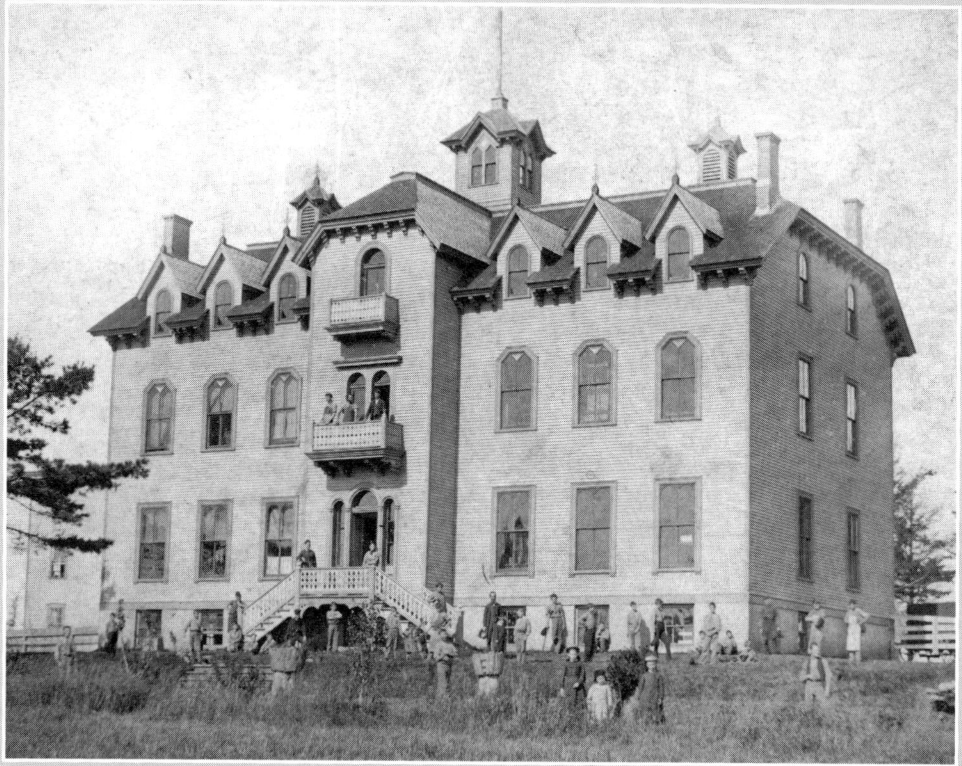

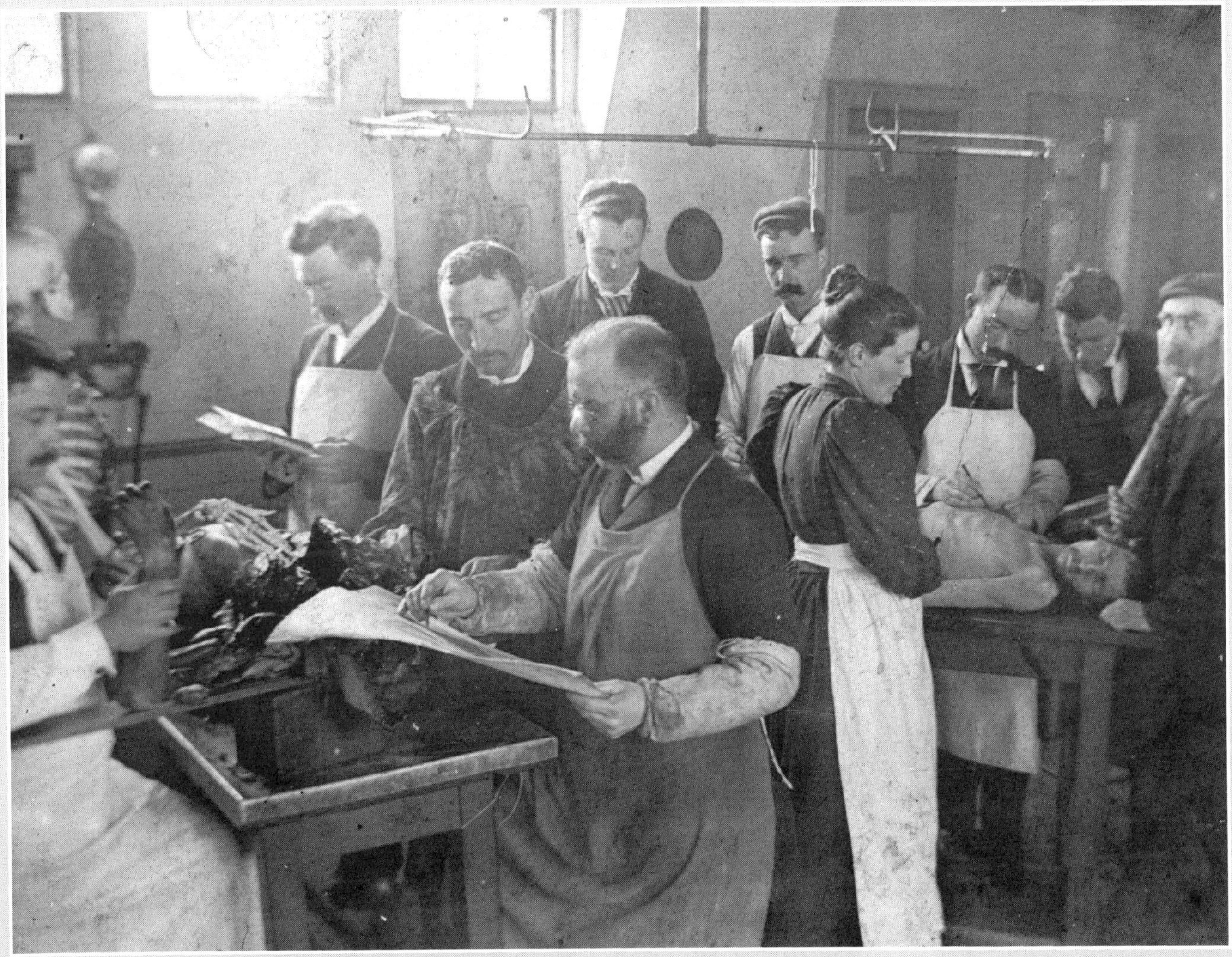

The Halifax Medical College was established in 1867 as the Medical Department at Dalhousie College. In 1875 it became a separate corporation and constructed a building on the corner of Carleton and College Streets from designs by Henry F. Busch. In 1889, the two institutions united again, Dalhousie having recently completed the Forrest Building just across the street from the Medical College.

Enid Johnson MacLeod, in *Petticoat Doctors*, has identified the woman in the Anatomy Laboratory as Clara Mary Olding, the third woman to graduate (1896) from the college.

4. STUDENTS LEARNING SIGN LANGUAGE, HALIFAX
1893

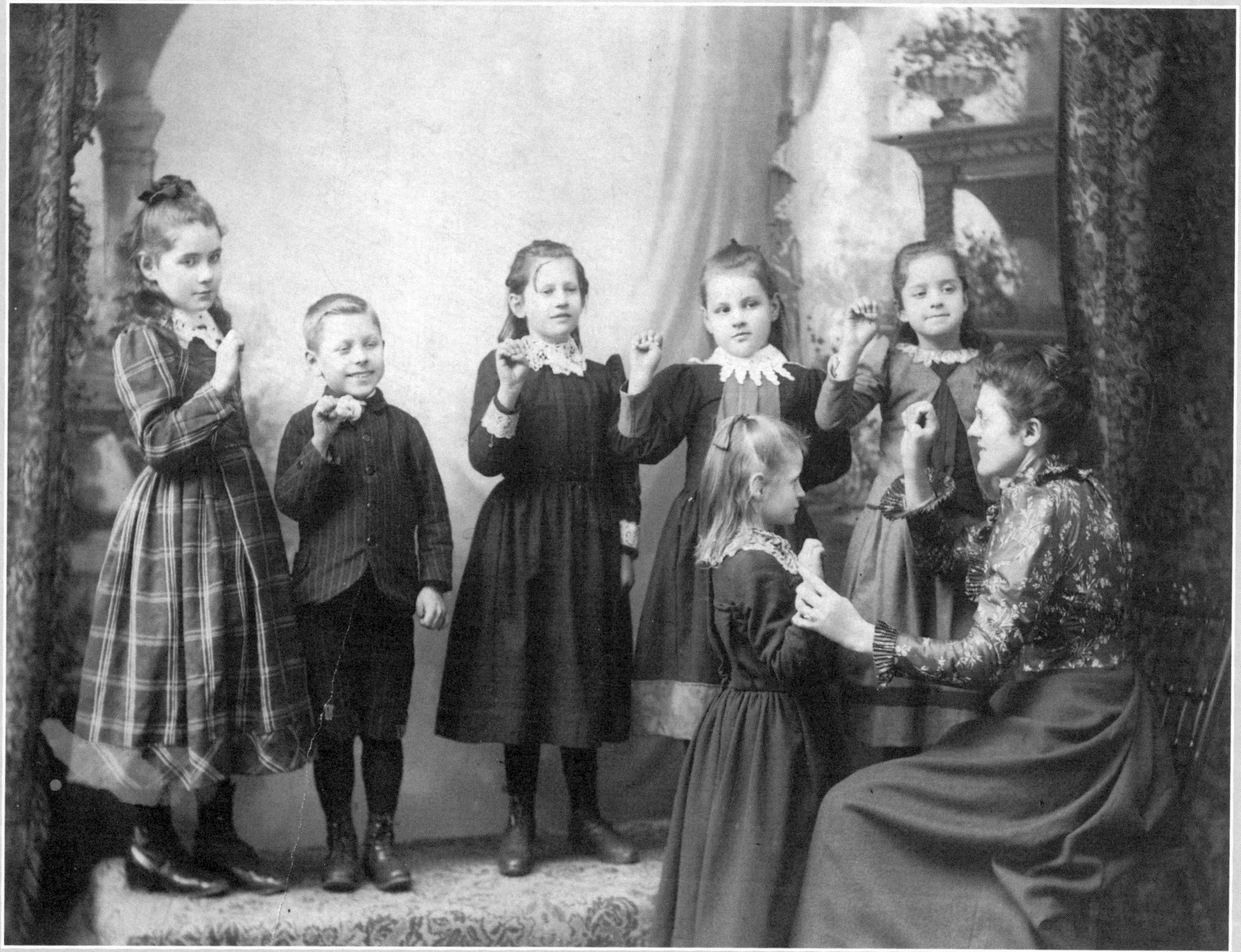

5. Evening Technical Class, Instructor standing is Geo. H. Holder
February 27, 1911

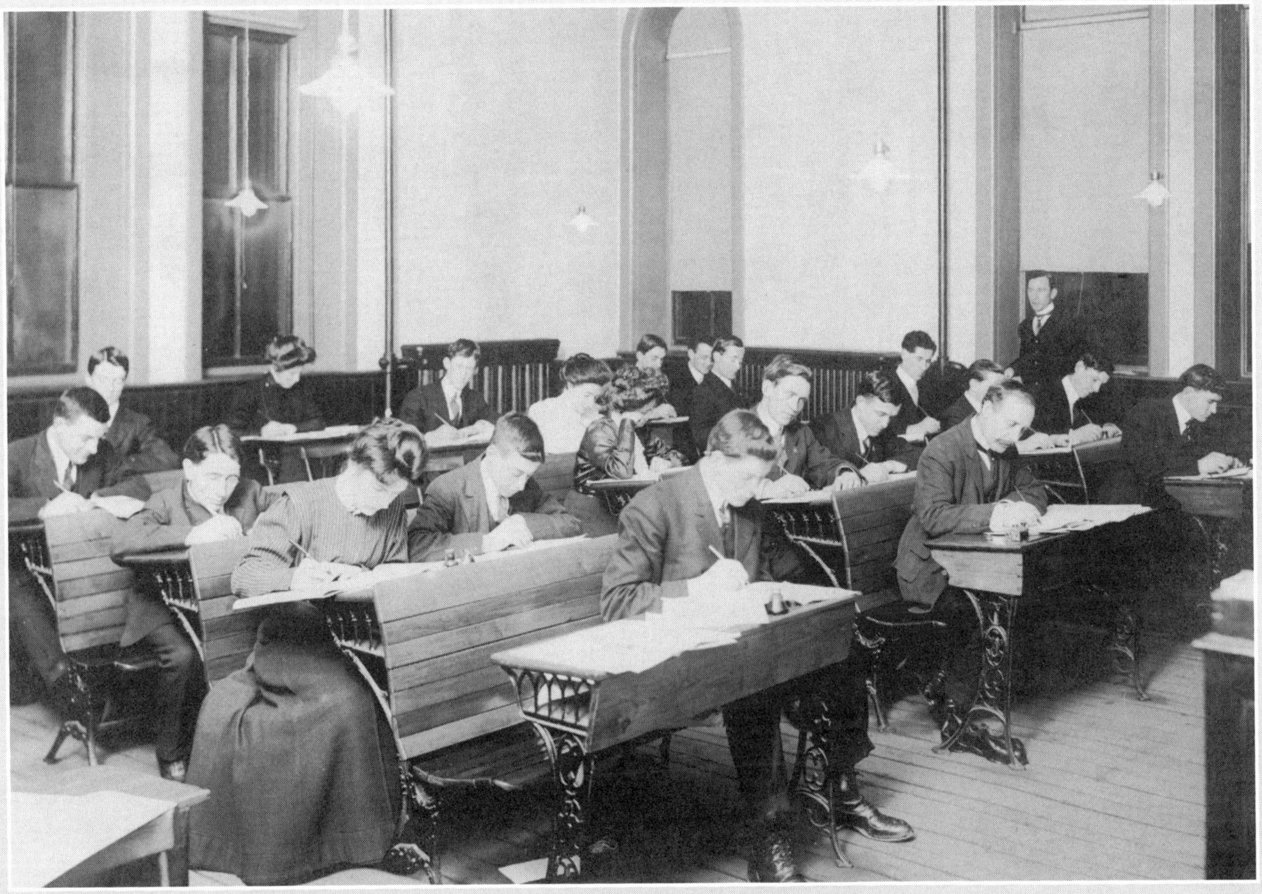

During the academic year 1911-12, there were 670 students enrolled in the Evening Technical School; 147 were studying book-keeping. The *Report of the Board of School Commissioners for the City of Halifax*, 1910-11, noted that:

> *The rapid growth of the Evening Technical School from 125 students in 1907, the first year of the program to 670 in 1911 shows that these classes are meeting a great need among the wage earners in the community. The instruction must be effective because tangible results have already been achieved. A number of voluntary testimonials have been received from students who have attended the technical classes to the effect that these individuals have received substantial promotions and increases in salary which are attributed to the increased technical knowledge.*

6. Halifax School for the Blind: Girls' manual training class engaged in machine sewing, chair caning, weaving, basketry, needlepoint, and knitting 1921

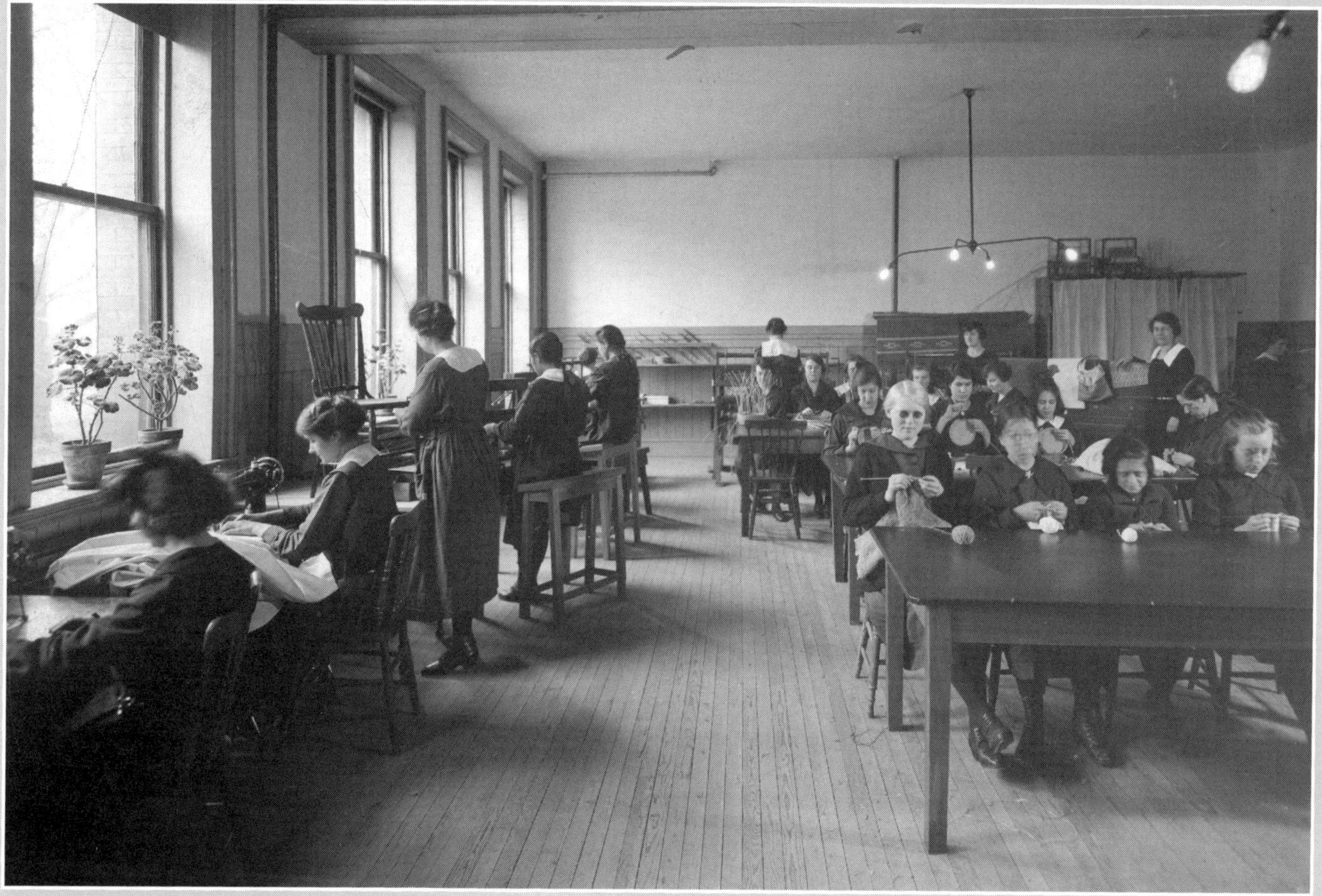

The School for the Blind formally opened in 1871. Between 1868 (when construction began) and 1903, the building was enlarged and renovated three times, in order to accommodate a growing number of pupils who came from throughout Atlantic Canada in response to the progressive education which the school offered to the visually challenged. Located on the south side of Morris Street between South Park and Tower Road, the building was a Halifax landmark until its demolition c 1983.

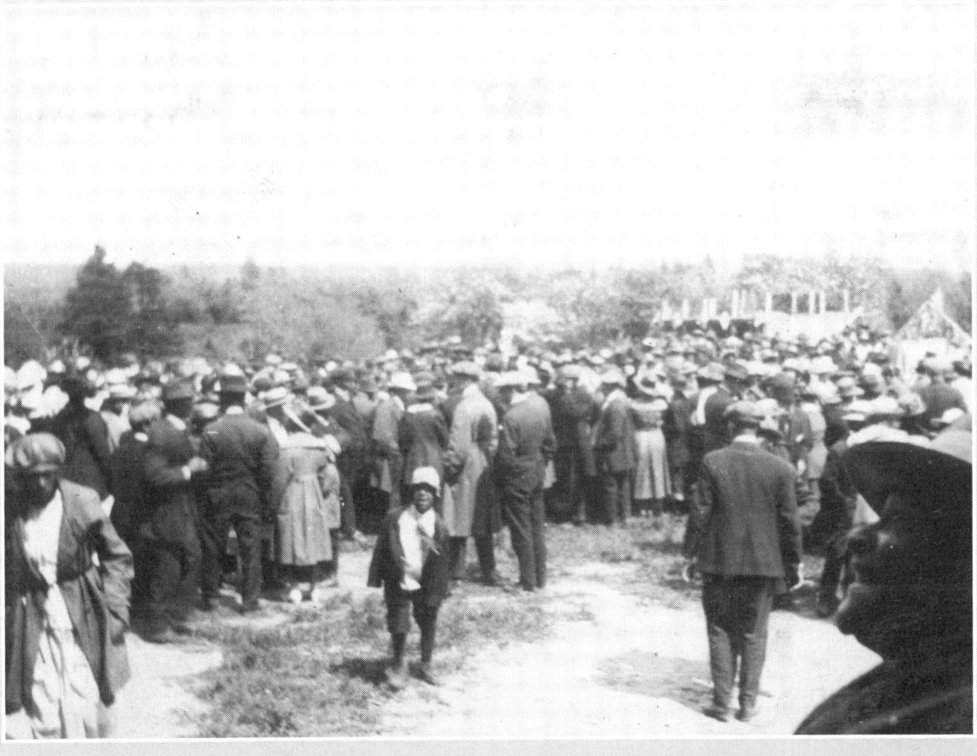

Approximately 3000 people gathered at Knox's Farm prior to marching in procession to the Home for Colored Children, three-quarters of a mile distant. Private Arthur Wyse led the march, followed by the Salvation Army Band, then the executive of the African United Baptist Association, members of the local Masonic Lodge, and carriages with dignitaries. The Industrial School's Fife and Drum Band also participated. African Methodist Episcopal Boy Scouts and Girl Guides formed an honour guard as the procession arrived at the stage. The official opening included sacred music, speeches, a concert, and refreshments. Charles R. Saunders wrote in *Share & Care*, that "All the speakers underscored the importance of the occasion. However, it was the eloquence of J.A.R. Kinney, then secretary of the Board of Directors, that came closest to capturing the day's true meaning when he called it 'the greatest event in the history of the colored people of Nova Scotia'. "

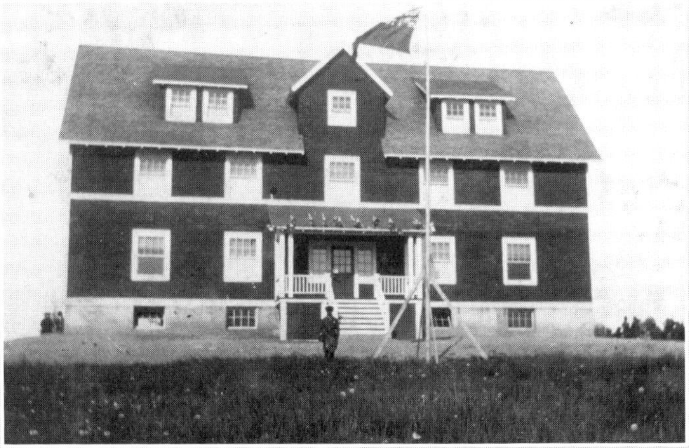

9. Kindergarten and Grade One, St. Thomas Aquinas School, Halifax

October 15, 1948

This elementary school is located on the north side of Watt Street. It was built initially as a Roman Catholic facility within the city's educational system, which provided separate schools for Protestant and Roman Catholic children.

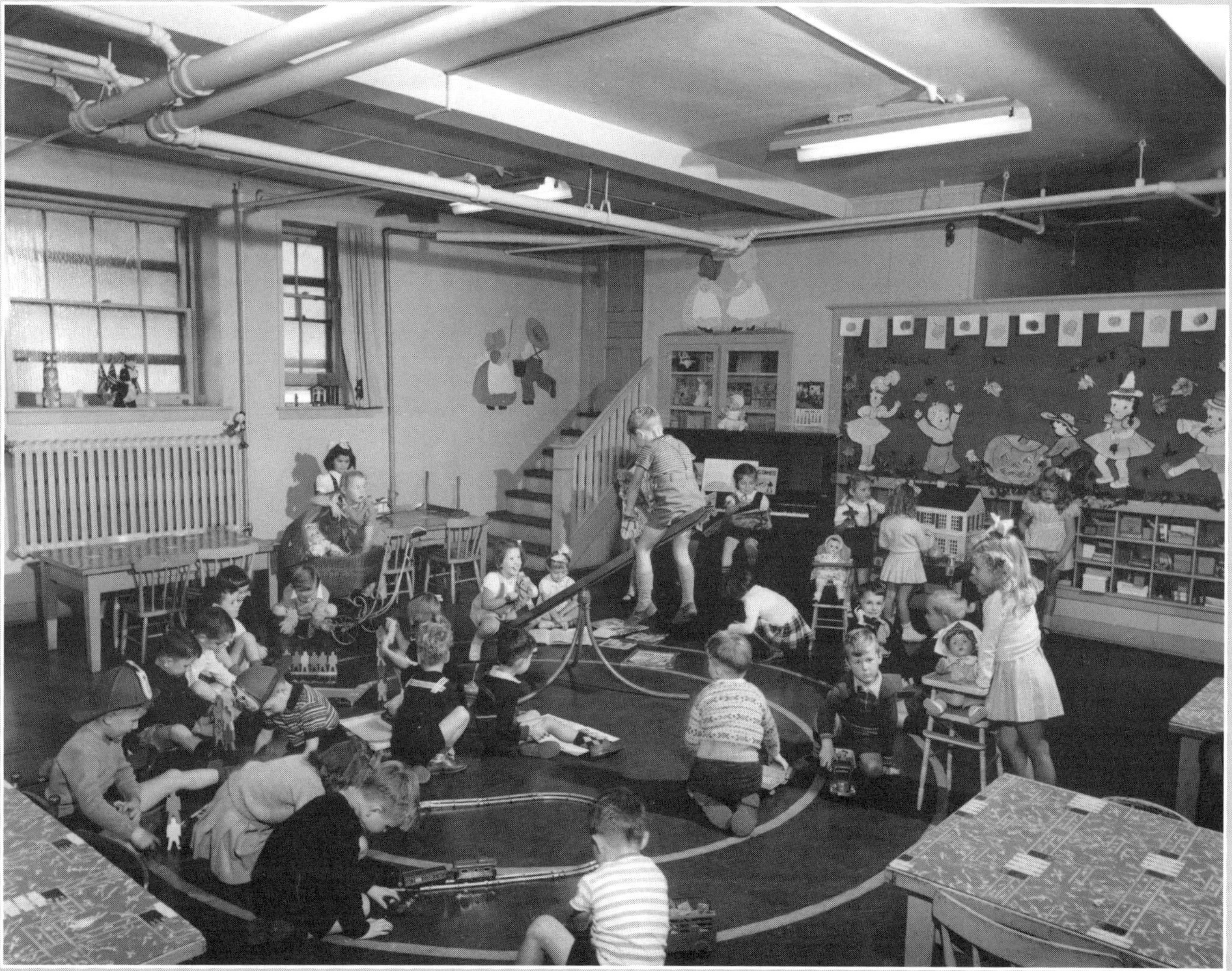

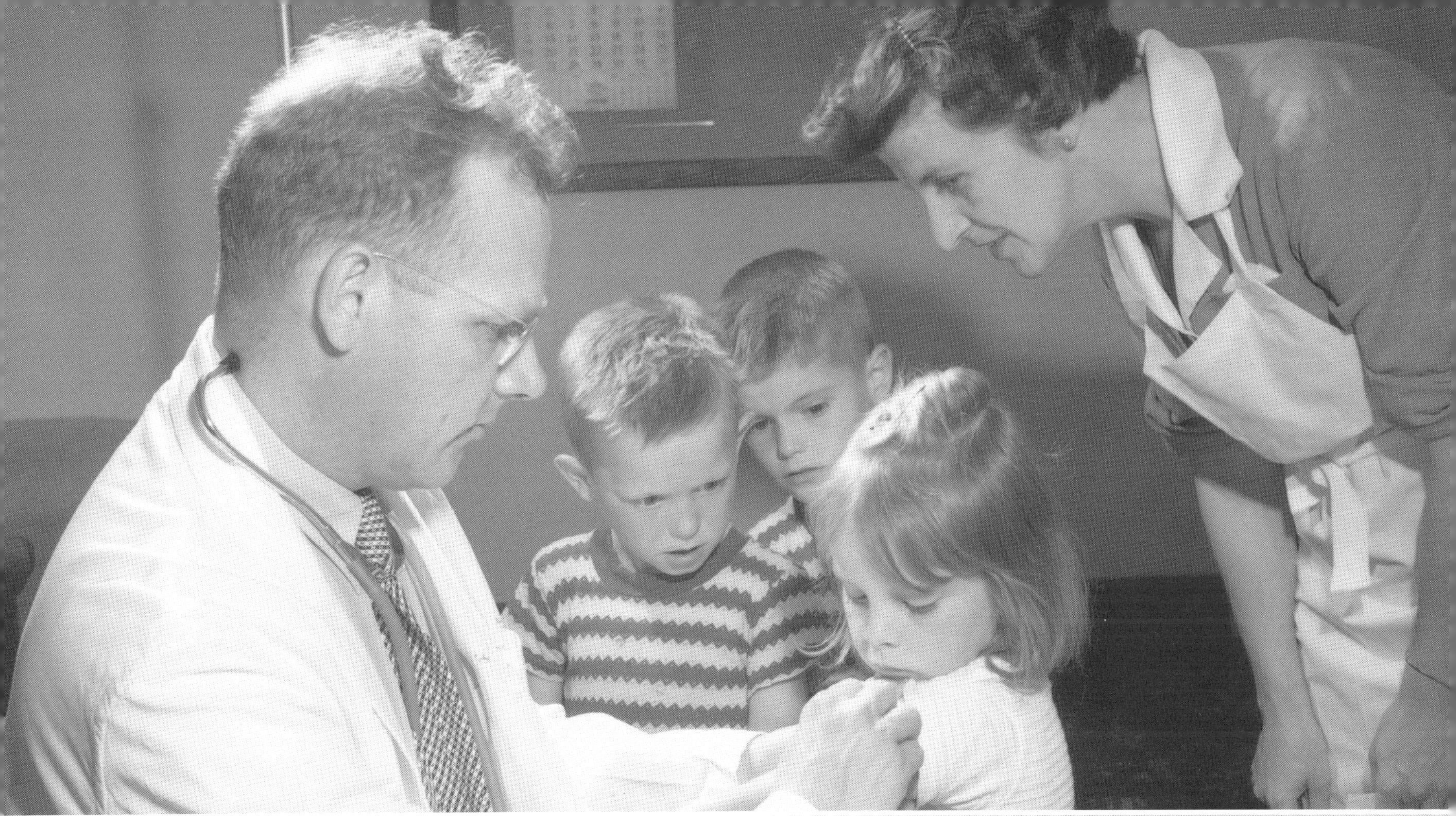

CHAPTER 11

HEALTH

As Haligonians prepared to celebrate the 200th anniversary of the city's founding, Dr. Allan R. Morton, the Commissioner of Public Health and Welfare, wrote in *The Official Bicentennial Guide Book 1949* that "Halifax is adequately supplied with Hospital and Health facilities. Dalhousie University, with the only medical school in the three Maritime Provinces, is situated here, and a number of hospitals are practically on the campus of the University. These hospitals are all utilized for teaching purposes, and this requires that the standard of our hospitals must be high, as the medical school is classed as Grade A."

The city's medical facilities then included the Victoria General Hospital (which began as the City Hospital in 1859), the Halifax Infirmary (begun in 1886 and operated by the Sisters of Charity), the Salvation Army's Grace Maternity Hospital (1898), the Children's Hospital (1909), the Tuberculosis Hospital (1921), the Halifax Hospital for Communicable Diseases (1928), Camp Hill Hospital (1917), and the Royal Canadian Naval Hospital at HMCS *Stadacona.* Across the harbour in Dartmouth was the Nova Scotia Hospital, founded in 1856 as Mount Hope Asylum. In addition to the Medical School at Dalhousie, begun in 1868, there was a Public Health Clinic (1924), a Pathology Laboratory and a Bacteriological Laboratory.

We often forget that basic survival was a challenge for every Nova Scotian in the eighteenth and nineteenth centuries. In the late eighteenth century, for example, average life expectancy was 49 years; by 1981, some 200 years later, this had risen to 75 years. Allan Marble, writing about "Epidemics and Mortality in Nova Scotia, 1749-1799," reminds us that "Of the 4,348 persons who died in [the province] during the period 1780 to 1799, 1,328 [or 30.5%] are known to have been infants or children under the age of sixteen years."

One hundred years later, infant and child mortality remained extremely high, even given the advances of Victorian medicine. The Dominion Census for 1881 listed (for the previous year, 1880) 662 deaths in the city and 507 deaths in the county. Those under 11 years of age accounted for 49.5% of deaths (city) and 48.9% (county). Of these, 19.8% and 17.9% respectively, were children under one year of age. The census reported causes of death by province-wide statistics, and the five leading causes of mortality were consumption (tuberculosis; 15.9%), diphtheria (13.3%), lung disease (5.6%), old age (3.9%), and heart and blood diseases (3.1%).

Twenty years later, in 1901, the census listed only 836 deaths in the city and county combined. However, infant mortality was still high: 130 deaths (15.6%) were under one year of age, and 30.5% of the deceased were 14 or younger. The main killers in 1901 were tuberculosis (17.5%), senile debility (11.4%), bronchitis and pneumonia (11.2%), diseases of the heart (6.6%), and apoplexy and paralysis (5.9%). Diphtheria and croup accounted for 2.8% of all deaths.

In the half-century since the bicentenary in 1949, amalgamation, rationalization and general progress in the treatment of various diseases have changed the shape and delivery of medical services throughout the Halifax Regional Municipality. But the faces looking out at us from these earlier photographs are a reminder of the human needs and fears which have guided the community response to health care over the years.

1. Ward 42,
Victoria General Hospital
1910

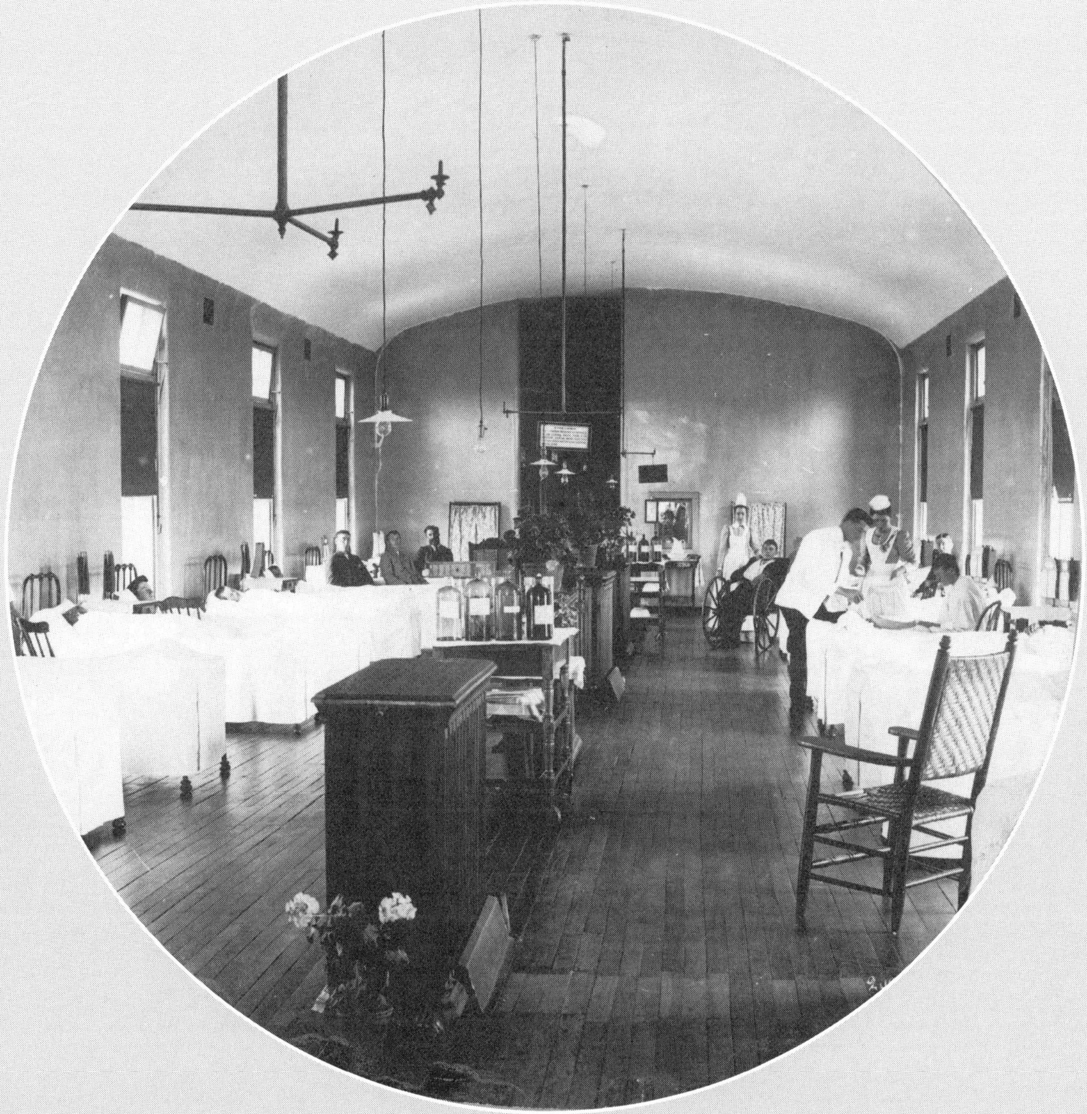

2. Pageant given in honour of return of Caravans, Halifax 1920

Surplus money from the Halifax (Explosion) Relief Fund was used by the Red Cross to send two public health caravans around Nova Scotia in 1920. Each caravan had three ambulances, a truck with moving-picture equipment and a touring car for doctors and nurses who provided professional services. Dr F.W. Woodbury asked Helen Creighton to drive an ambulance. In the pouring rain on July 12, the Very Rev. John P.D. Llwyd, Dean of All Saints Cathedral, pronounced a blessing, and photographs and moving pictures were taken. In her autobiography, *A Life in Folklore*, Creighton summarized the work. The group gave 221 public health talks, held 41 public meetings with moving pictures, hosted 20 clinics, treated 927 dental patients, examined 615 tuberculosis patients, operated on 172 individuals and provided advice on throat ailments and general illnesses to 652 patients.

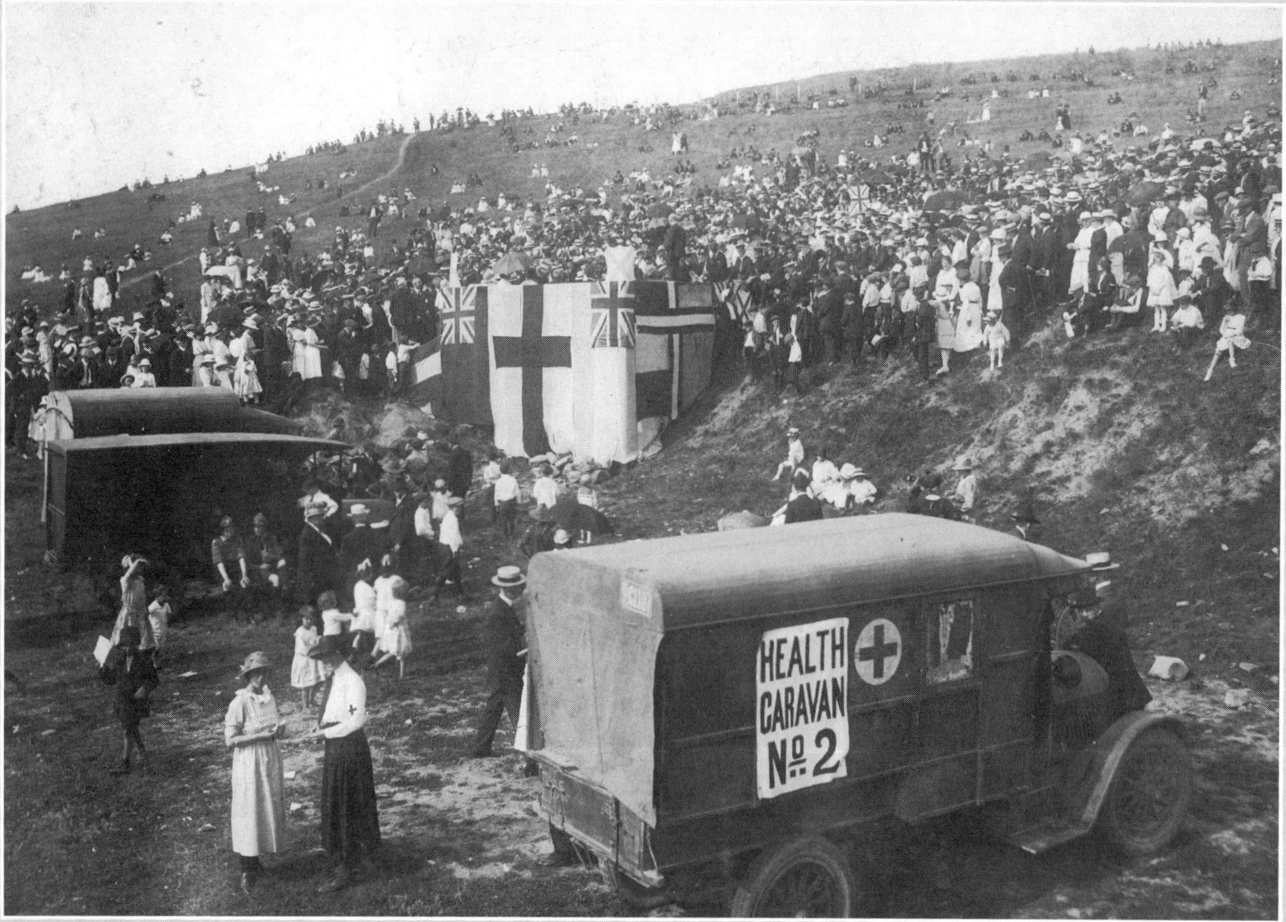

In late August, the two caravans returned to a reception on Citadel Hill which lasted for two hours. On that occasion, 27 choirs sang as the vehicles took their positions. Lieutenant-Governor McCallum Grant and others spoke, the band played and the Rev. Dr. J.A. Clark pronounced the invocation. Creighton continued, "It seemed somewhat superficial, perhaps because we were too tired, had seen too many people in need, and did not feel one bit heroic, although perhaps we were. Few of us got paid more than food and lodging, and we worked our heads off. Yet we had been a happy group...."

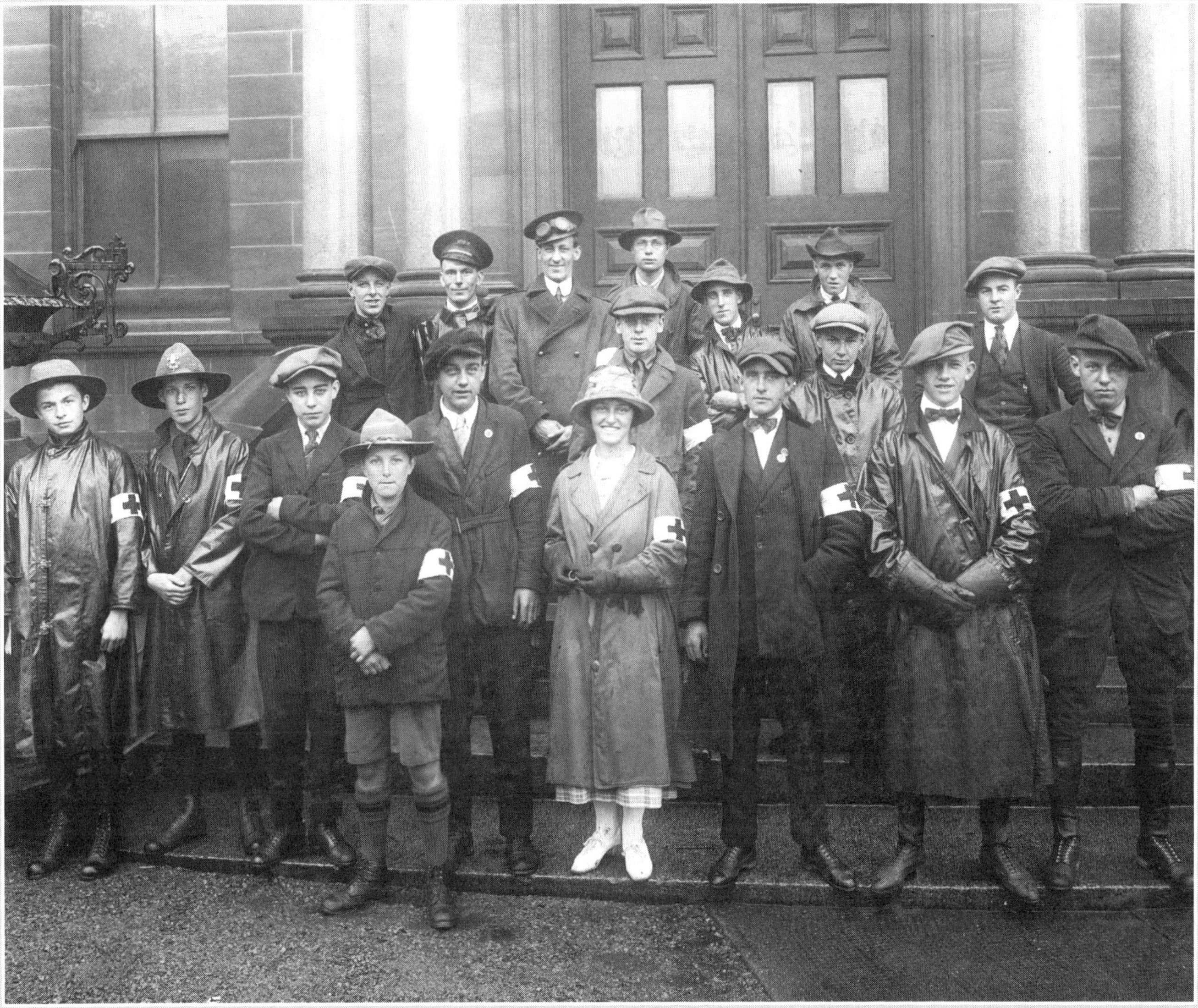

Helen Creighton standing, front centre, on steps of City Hall, Halifax.

4. "Children's Hospital,"
group of young patients,
Halifax
1948

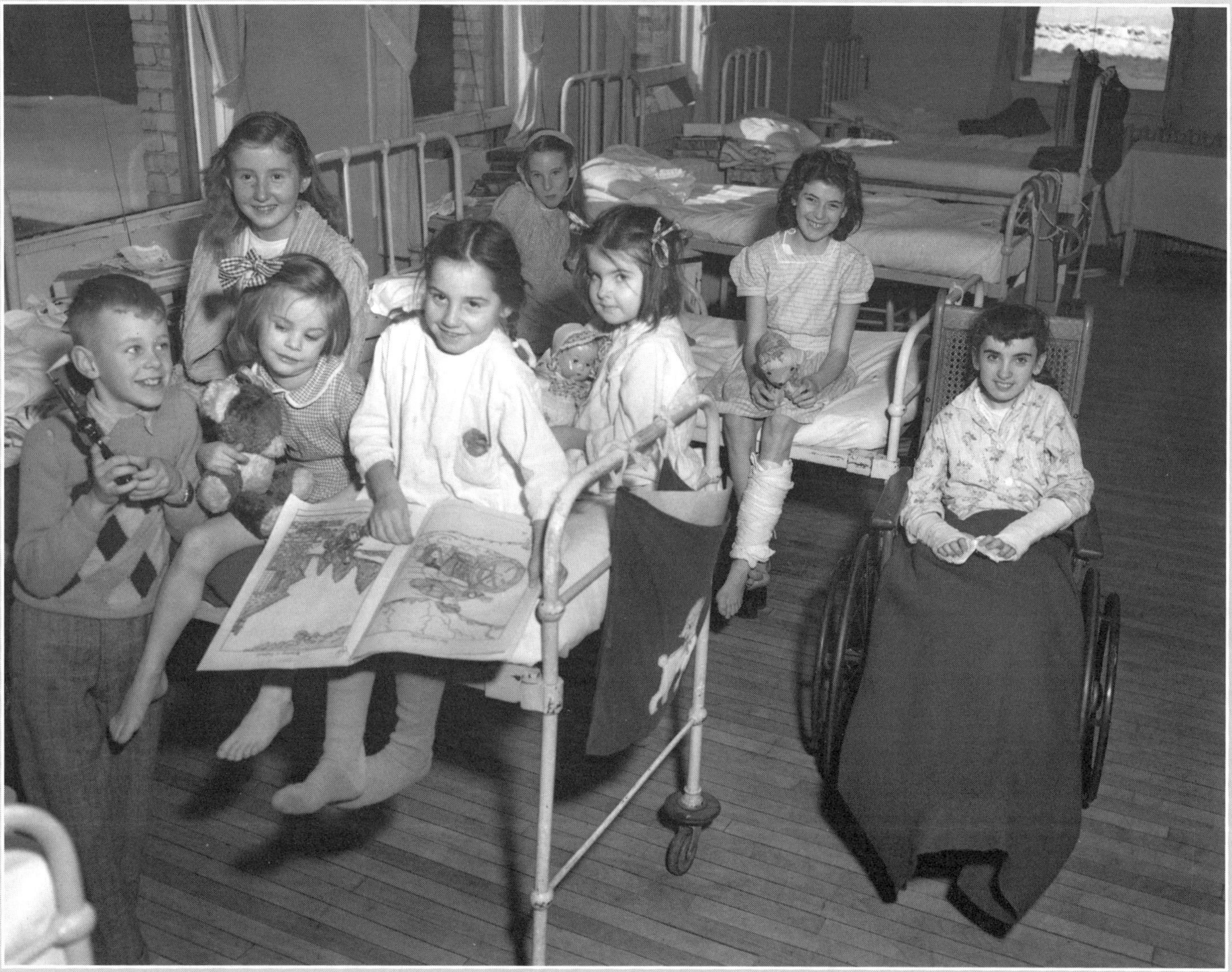

5. Immigrant Children with Red Cross Port Workers, Pier 21
1948

6. Immigrant woman with Baby, Pier 21
1948

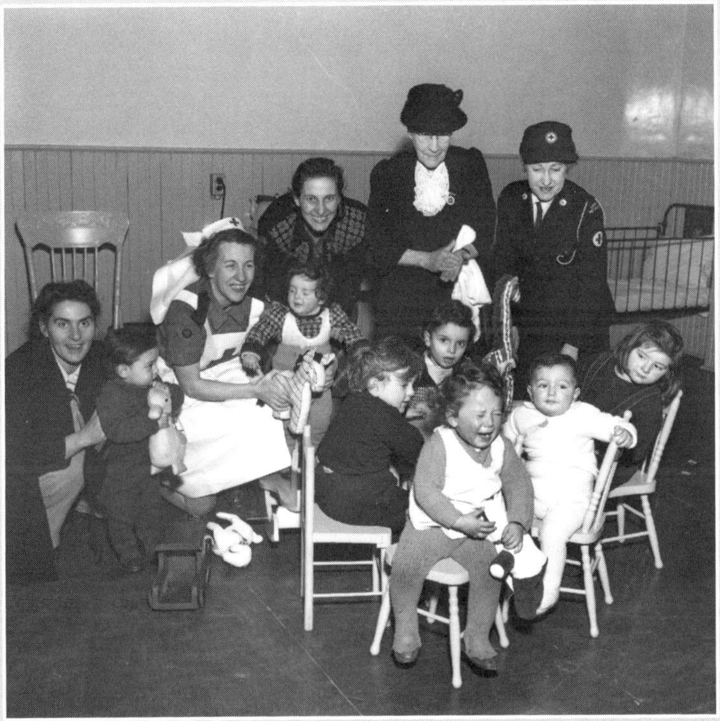

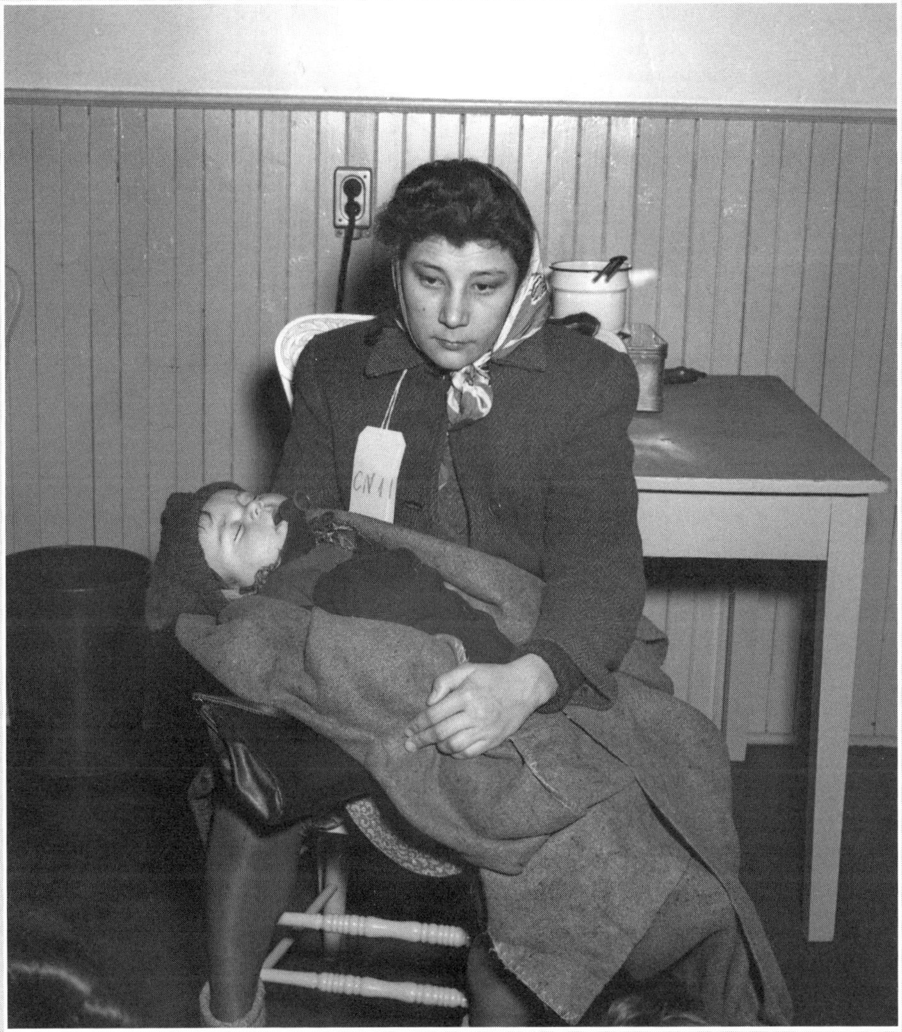

The physician wielding the needle is Dr. Allan R. Morton, City Commissioner of Health and Welfare. He may be administering the new Salk polio vaccine, or booster shots to protect against diphtheria, whooping cough and tetanus. It is also possible that he is administering the new intradermal tuberculin test, which he introduced to city schools in 1955 to replace the former patch test. None of the recipients look happy about these advances in modern preventive medicine.

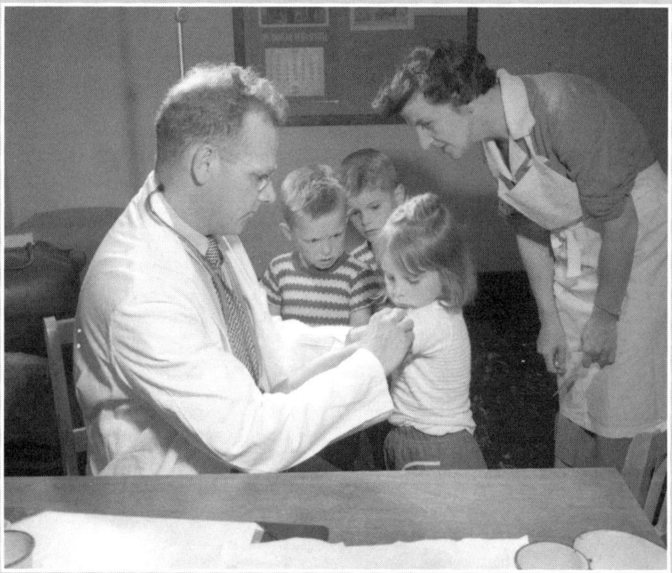

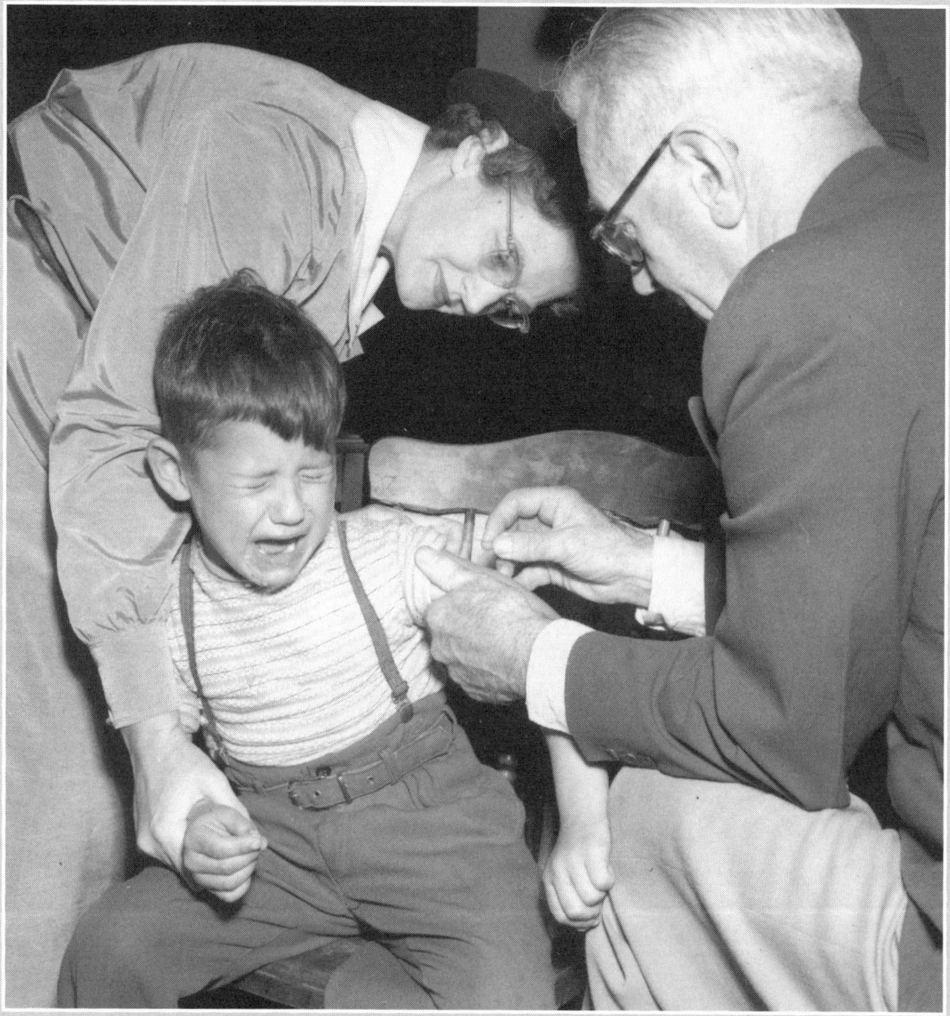

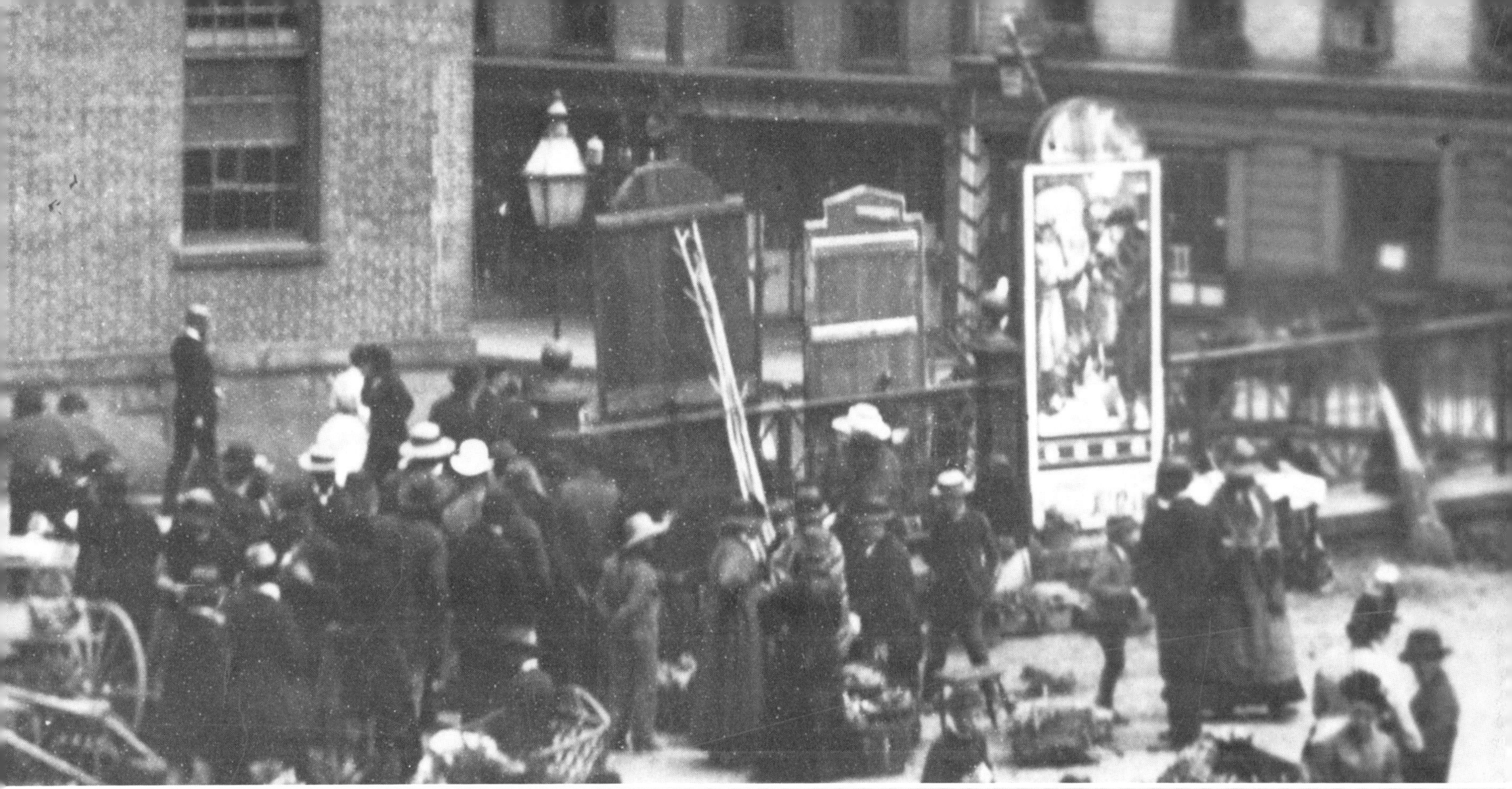

Chapter 12

Glimpses of a Lost Halifax

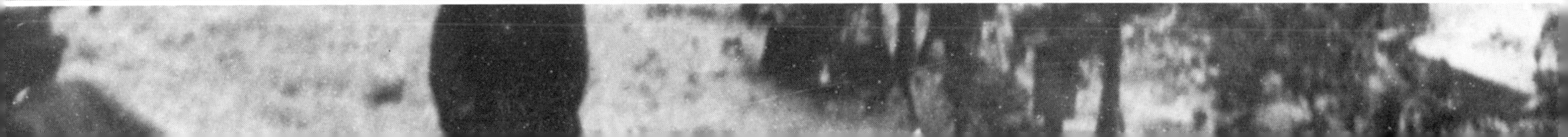

In 1749, Halifax was a rough settlement of wood-frame buildings hastily thrown together behind a palisade that stretched between Citadel Hill and the harbour. These early structures gradually gave way to a Victorian downtown, constructed largely of brick and stone—commercial establishments, shops, government and private offices, churches, small manufacturing concerns—and an inner community of wooden structures, home to seamen, longshoremen, labourers, shop assistants, tradesmen, and their families. The face of downtown Halifax began to change again, drastically, after the city's bicentenary, and continues to change today as large numbers of surviving Victorian buildings, and even entire street-scapes, have been demolished and replaced by the glass-and-steel office towers and high-rise apartment buildings that are the trademarks of the late twentieth century.

Other areas of the present Halifax Regional Municipality, beyond the old downtown core, have also experienced complete transformations over time. North End Halifax was totally redeveloped after the Explosion of 1917. The Mi'kmaq community at rocky Turtle Grove, just outside the old town of Dartmouth, was a landmark on the harbour until it, too, was devastated by the Explosion. And the old established Black community of Africville, on the south shore of Bedford Basin, survived the Explosion—only to fall victim to city officialdom, who decreed its destruction and the relocation of its residents to modern public housing in the 1960s.

As the city continues to grow and evolve in an age of rapid change, a cursory glance at our colourful past quickly reveals that the horse and wagon have given way to the automobile, the horse-drawn streetcar to Metro Transit, the telegraph to the cellular phone, and the typewriter to the computer. For better or for worse, time marches on, with the one constant being the faces of the people who make up our collective identity as Haligonians.

1. Mi'kmaq encampment near Halifax 1812

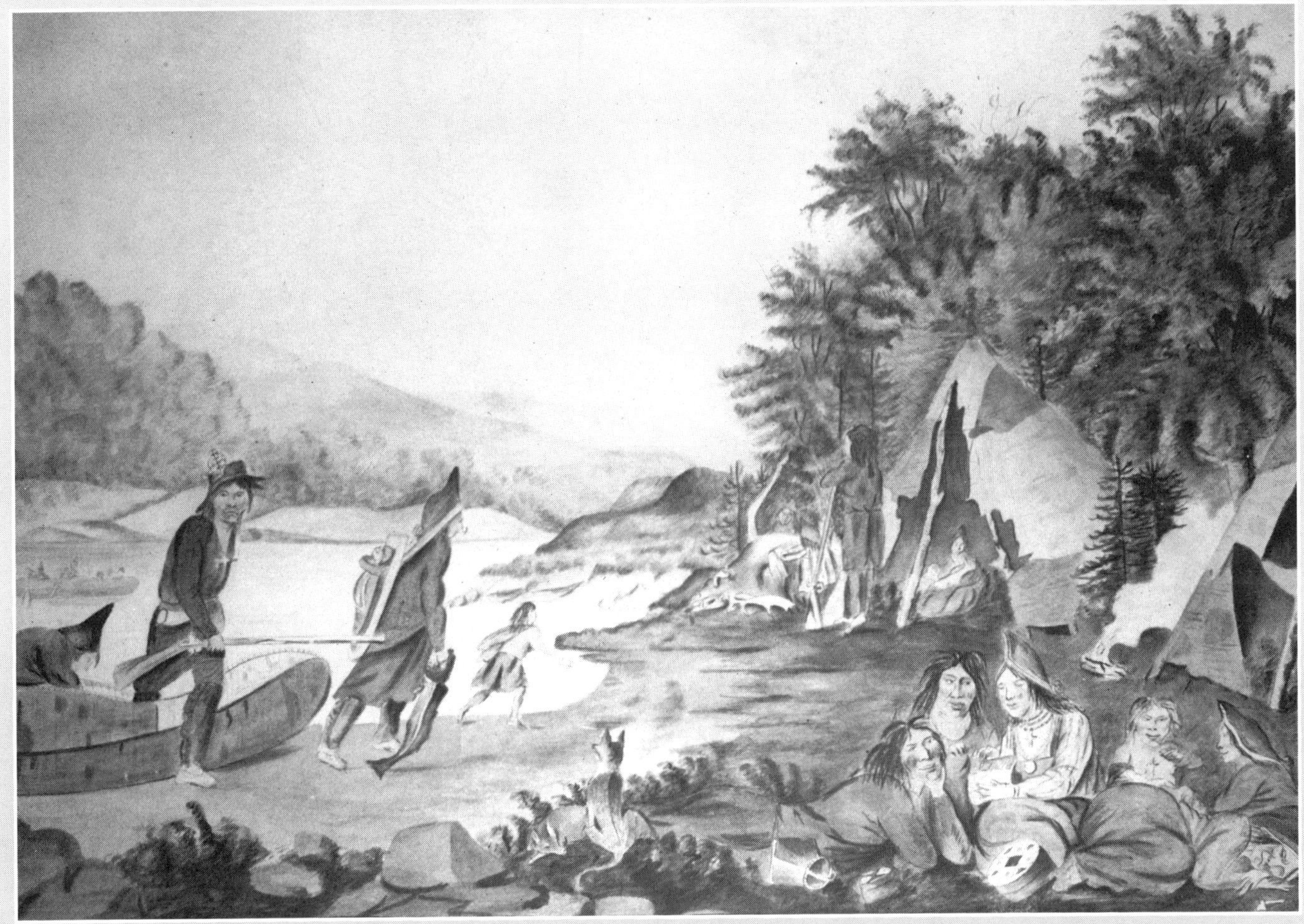

This is a version of a frequently reproduced watercolour by Hibbert Binney; the original is dated 1790 and titled *A Family of Micmac Indians with their Chief in Nova Scotia*.

2. "NEW GOLD-DIGGINGS IN NOVA SCOTIA: GOLD-STREET, TANGIER"

1861

Lieutenant C. L'Estrange discovered gold at Mooseland while moose hunting in 1858. Two years later, John Pulsifer found gold in the same place and reported his discovery in Halifax. W. Malcolm provides additional details in his book, *Gold Fields of Nova Scotia*: "In October, 1860, Peter Mason discovered some auriferous quartz in the bed of a brook a short distance north of Rush Lake. As soon as the fact became known a number of people flocked to the locality to search for the source of gold, but as the ground was frozen, and as Mr. Mason was unwilling for them to prospect on his land, little was done until the following year." Malcolm continues: "In April, 1861, the district was proclaimed and William Anderson proceeded to lay off mining lots measuring 50 feet across and 20 feet along the supposed course of the leads. Nearly one hundred of these lots were soon leased, at an annual rental of $20, and in a short time about 600 men were engaged in mining or prospecting."

In subsequent years, discoveries were reported in various Halifax County locations and in other areas of the province. Throughout the late nineteenth century and continuing into the twentieth, gold mines were in operation at Caribou Gold Mines, Dufferin Mines, Harrigan Cove, Montague Gold Mines, Moose River, Waverley and elsewhere. Piles of waste rock are usually the only remaining evidence of an active and more prosperous past.

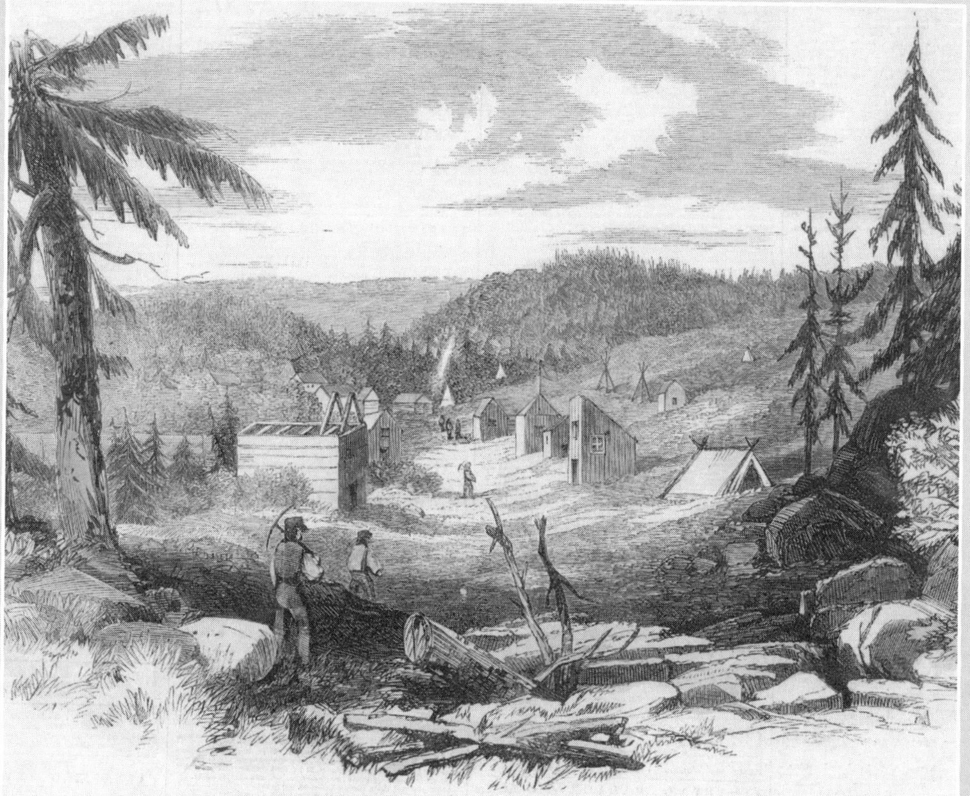

NEW GOLD-DIGGINGS IN NOVA SCOTIA : GOLD-STREET, TANGIER.

3. Mi'kmaq at Tufts Cove, Dartmouth
c 1871

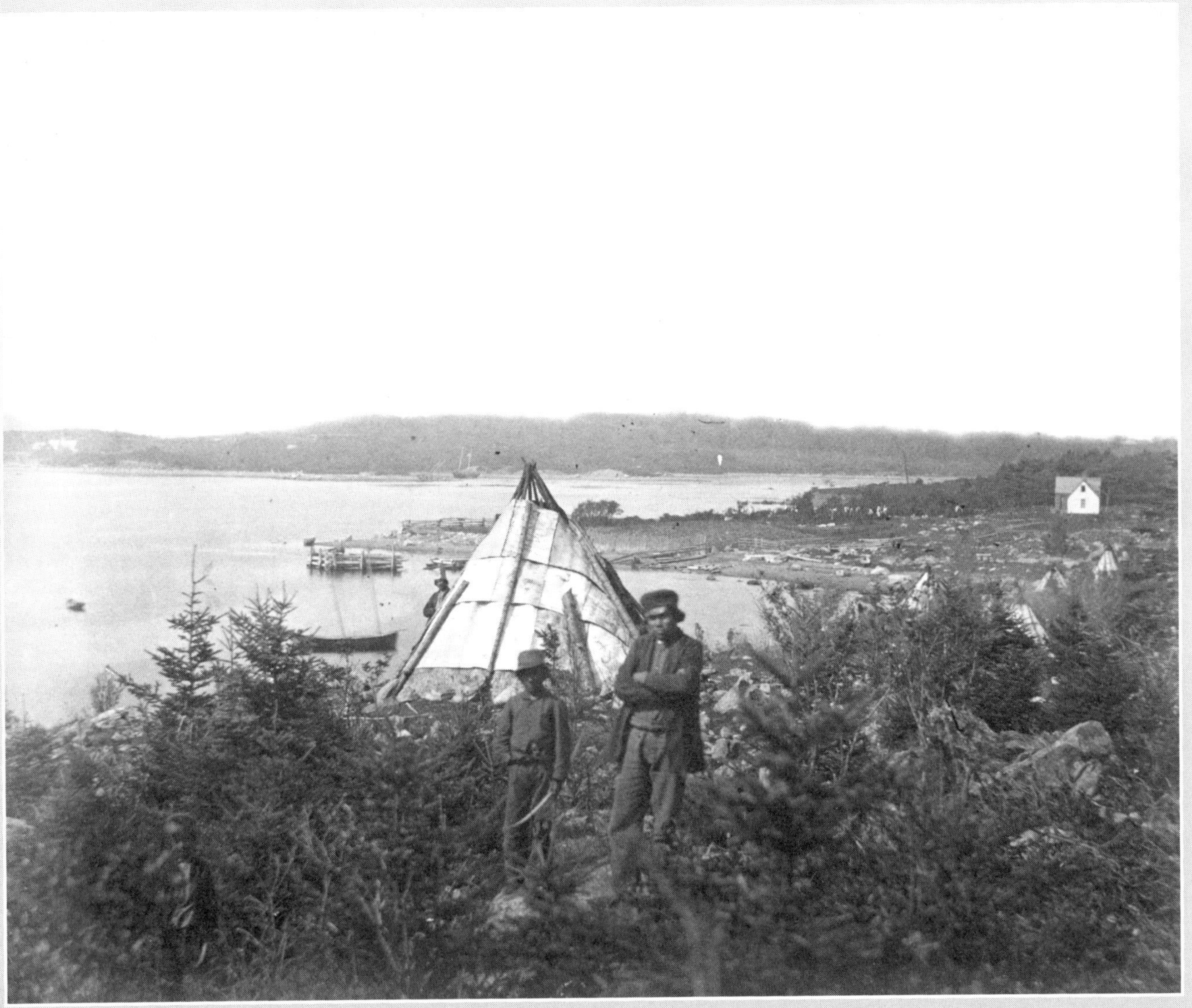

4. 'Jock' (William) Craig, 81, who for 54 years was the letter-carrier of the General Post Office

August 1, 1871

William Craig (c 1790-1874) was a noted Halifax character who wrote under the signature "Will the Ranter of Craig Lee." His publications included *Rich Men: A Lecture by Will the Ranter, at the New Market Hall, Oct. 9, 1863* and *Verses* (1869). Craig's rhyme, "The Champion of Nova Scotia," which appeared in *Verses*, criticized Joseph Howe's political switch from Anti-Confederate M.P. to Conservative cabinet minister: "What has come o'er our champion Joe/ That he has been converted so/ Why should he go and join the foe.../ Go with the traitors one and a';/ You've sold yourself to Ottawa...."

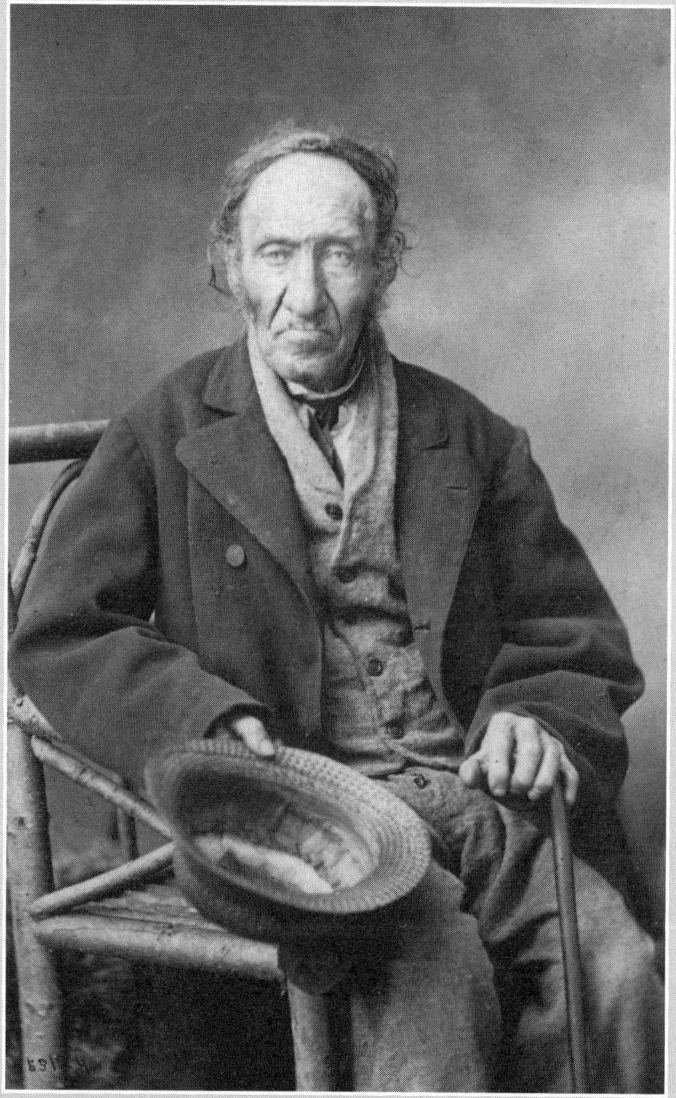

5. F.H. Baker, Editor of the *Mayflower*
c 1878

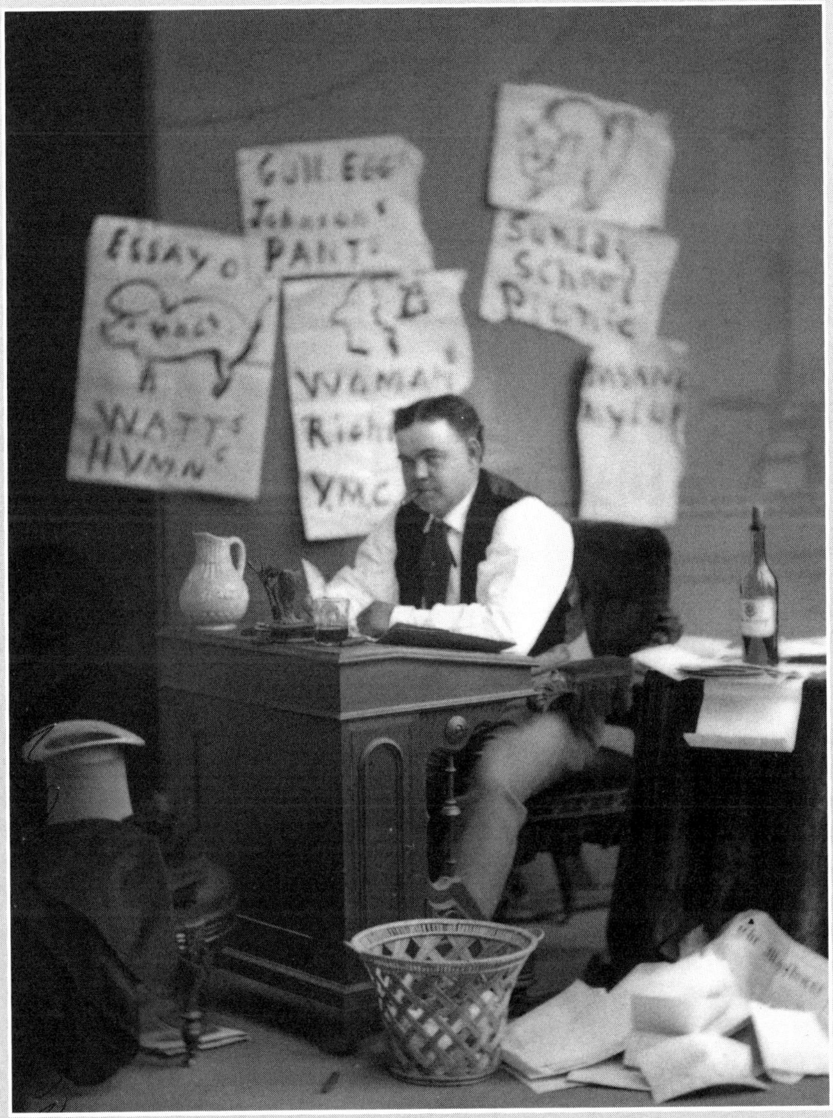

The *Acadian Recorder* for October 24, 1885 gave a lengthy biography of Baker on the occasion of his death, noting that he:

> *was perhaps more generally known as he appeared on our streets several years ago, than any other resident, because he was pointed-out as 'Baker, of the Mayflower,' and more people read that journal while it lasted than ever acknowledged to doing so. He came to Nova Scotia some twenty years ago, to engage in lobster-canning, and had large factories on the coast, paying out much money in wages, and engaging in extensive operations in the line of business in question. During this time he became the proprietor of a weekly journal called the 'Mayflower,' which had been started for literary purposes in this city, and made it a personal organ. It to a large extent ventilated any scandals that were being discussed or whispered in public, and held up sundry individuals to ridicule because of peculiarities. He was a great foe to snobbery and 'exquisite'ness, and with a most copious pen slashed right and left, often in the most impassioned language. At one time the paper had a great circulation, extending all over the Province and even abroad. Everyone who decried it seemed to have 'one in their pocket' which they would show to their friends, and expatiate on the turpitude of the writer of certain articles therein.*

6. Halifax Police Court & City Hall (formerly Exchange Coffee House), City Market House (built 1851 or '58), and Market Square, at corner of Bedford Row & George Street

July 1886

The Halifax Police Court and City Hall (to the left) was built in 1810 as the County Court House; the court occupied the main floor, with the Exchange Coffee House on the first and attic floors. In 1841 the building became Halifax's first City Hall. The City Market Building (to the right) was erected in 1854 from the designs of architect William Findlay. It later housed various city offices until the new City Hall was built on the Grand Parade. Then as now, Saturday mornings brought crowds of people to the Market.

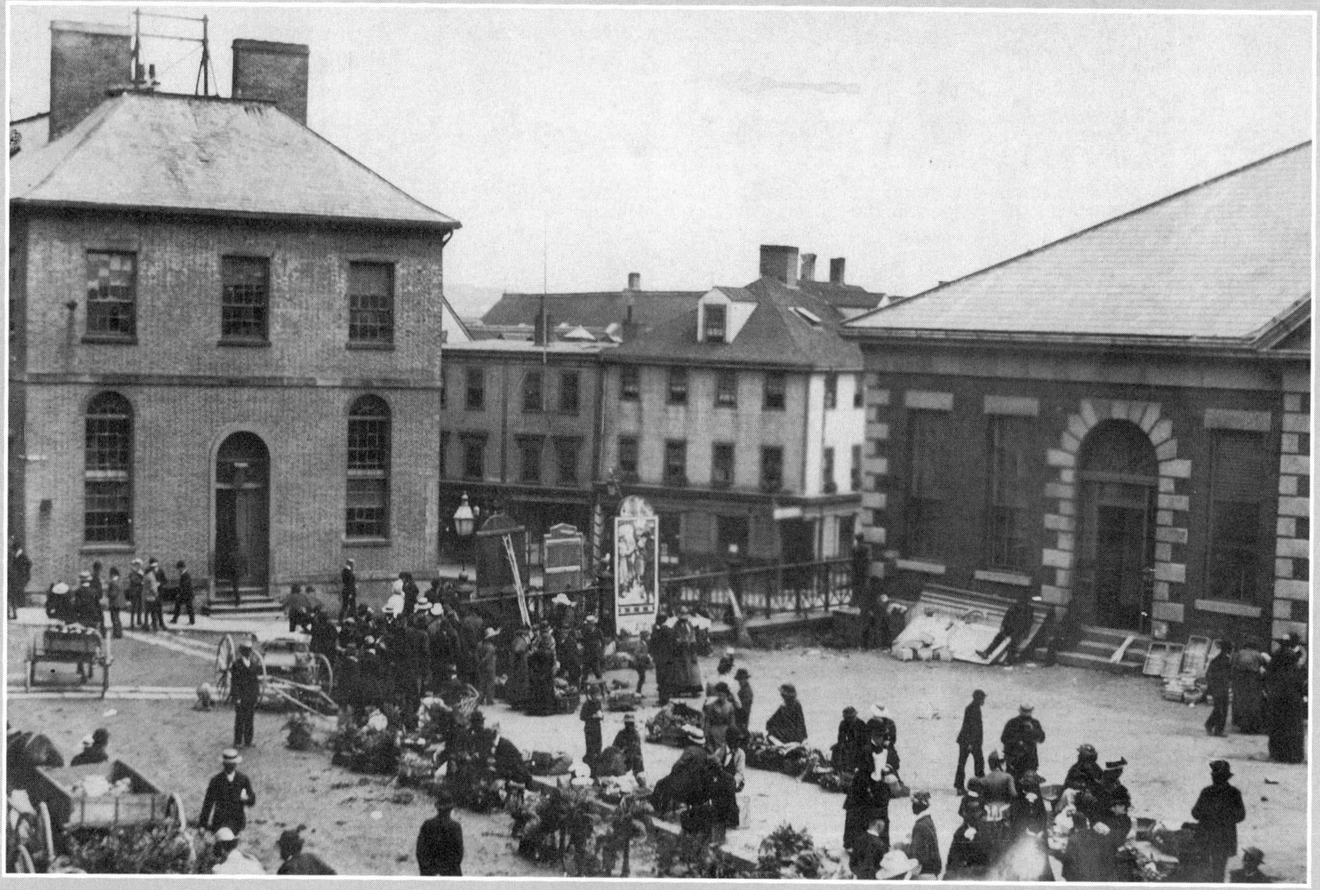

7. Gabriel Hall, 94, who came to Canada as a slave on board the *Chesapeake*
1892

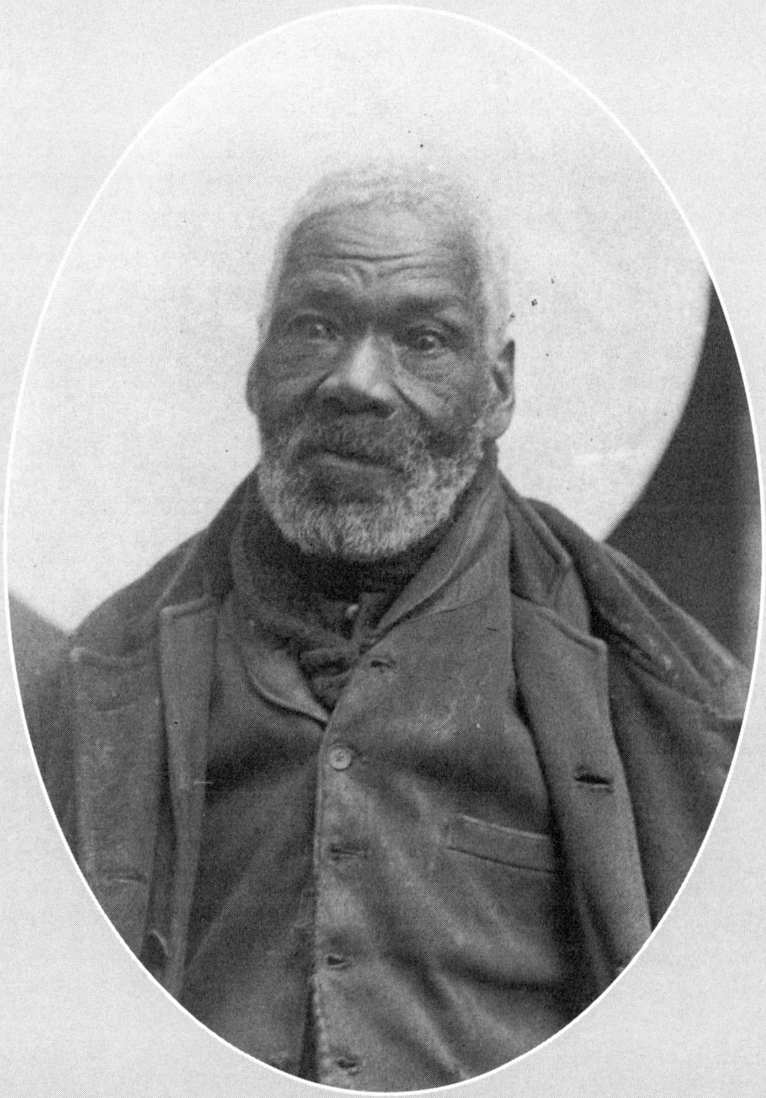

Hall was listed as a farmer in Preston when he was enumerated for the Dominion Census of 1871. The *Chesapeake* was an American frigate captured by HMS *Shannon* and brought triumphantly into Halifax as a war prize in 1813, during the War of 1812.

8. The Canadian Atlantic and Plant Steam Ship Company Wharf and Building, "After the fire at T.J. Egan's, [177 Lower] Water Street"

after September 15, 1904

The firm of Thomas J. Egan sold guns, fishing tackle, and sporting goods, and it was in this building that the fire began. The Plant Line was located at the foot of Sackville Street, on the waterside of one of the numerous downtown 'arches' leading from street to wharf, all of them now long gone from the urban landscape. The Plant Line, established in the city since 1889, offered the only direct (i.e. non-stop) shipping and passenger service between Halifax and Boston, and thus captured the majority of business traffic along this important sea route. The firm advertised its service as "the most desirable way to travel, only one night is spent at sea. There are no changes to make, no dust or dirt, no scurrying for meals, a comfortable trip on a floating hotel."

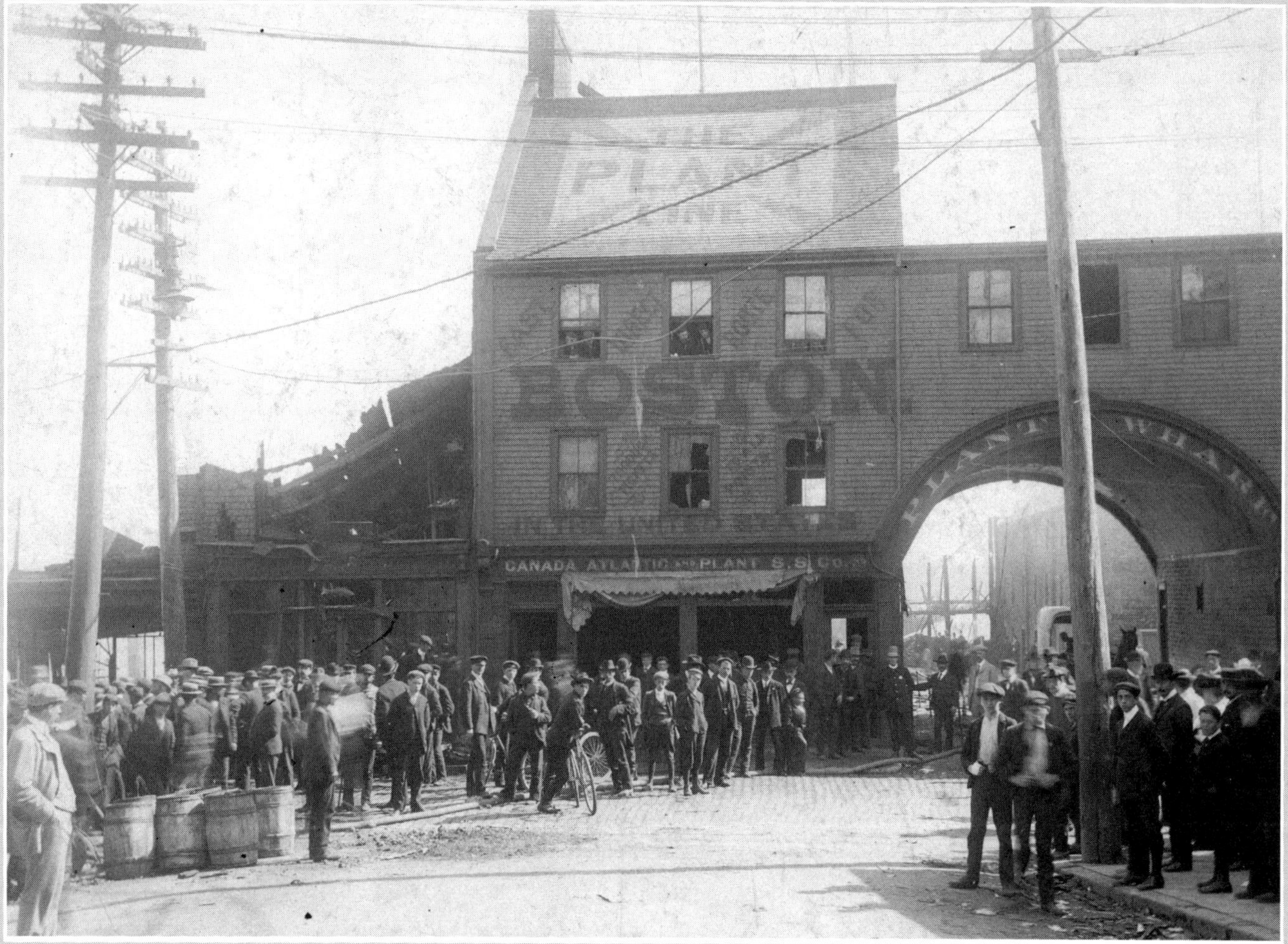

9. Christmas trees on Hollis St., Halifax
c 1947

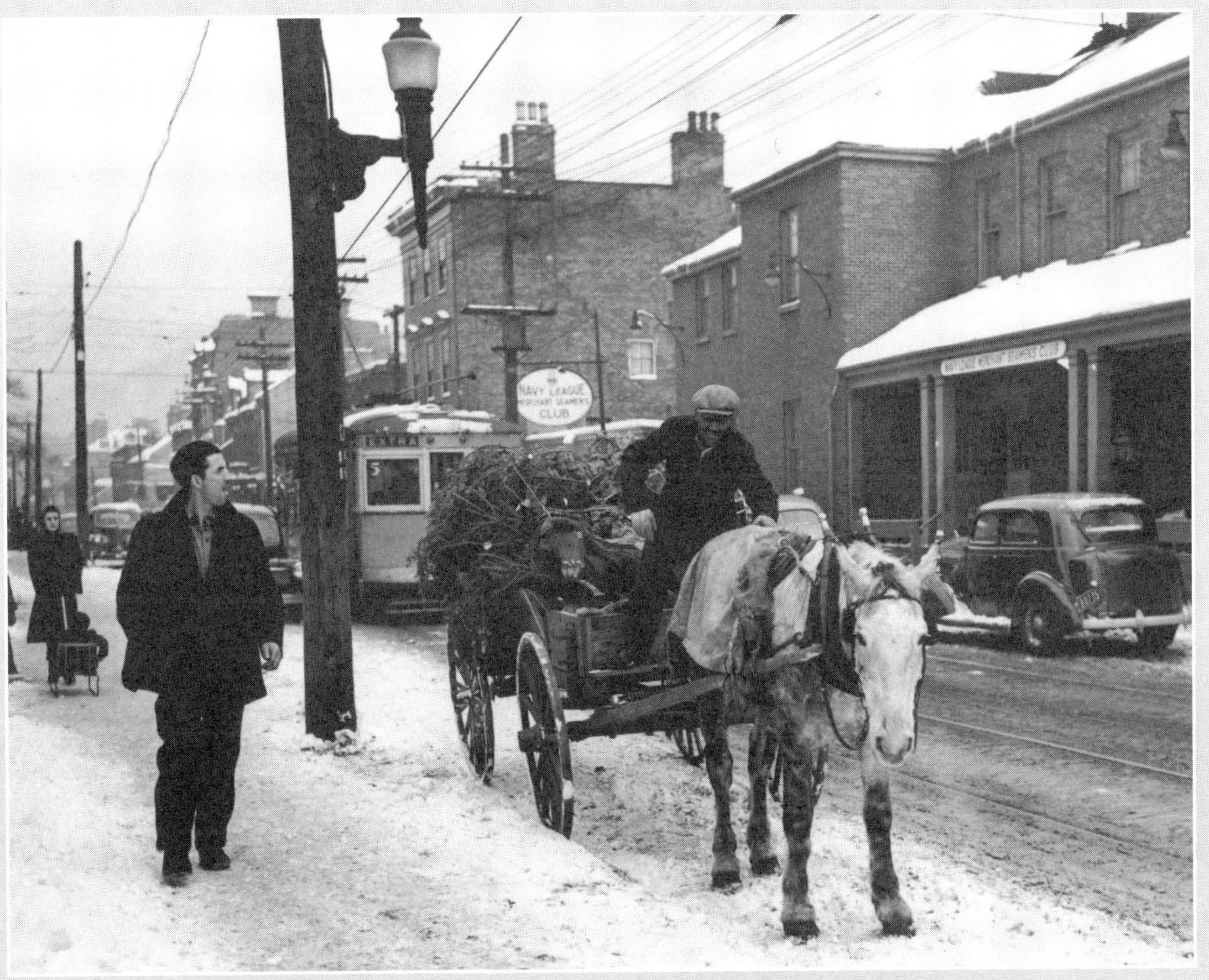

The photographer was looking north on Hollis Street between Morris and Bishop Streets.

10. City of Halifax Stray Animal Patrol Van
195–

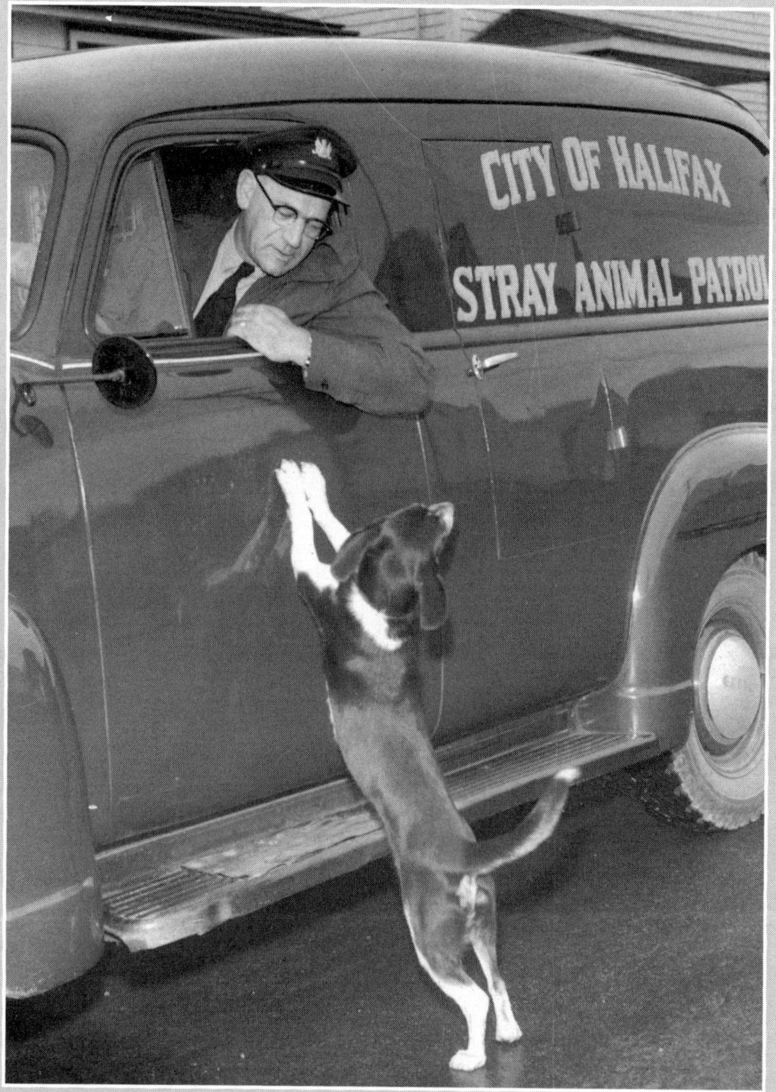

11. "Outside old City Market, Halifax, N.S."

c 1953

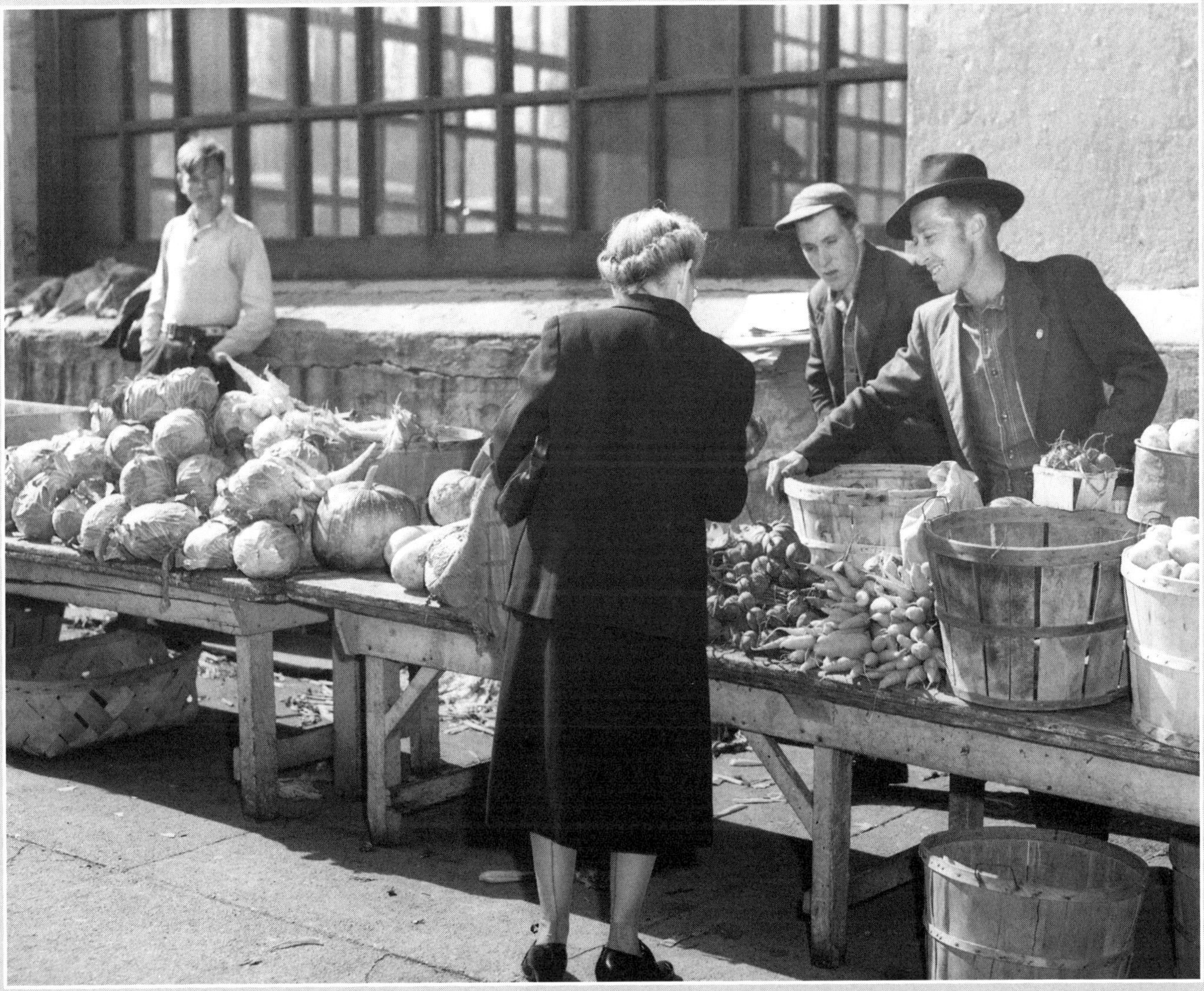

The City Market has resided in many locations throughout downtown Halifax during its long life. In 1953 it was located at 148 Market Street, a building purpose-designed in 1913 by architect S. P. Dumaresq. By 1953, however, most of the building had been taken over by the Halifax Police Department.

12. Africville Relocation Meeting, Seaview Baptist Church, Halifax

c 1962

Writing in *Africville: A Spirit that Lives On*, Donald Clairmont observed that:

> *In the early 1960s total relocation finally occurred. At that time Africville was home for eighty families, some four-hundred persons (all but a handful of whom were black).Compared to other Haligonians, black and white, the Africville residents had very low incomes and were very underemployed. Sewerage, piped water, paved roads and public lighting were conspicuously absent....There was still enough community spirit to initially reject the idea of relocation as it had been rejected in the past in favour of community development approaches. But City officials were adamant: Africville had to go. Equally important was the fact that local, and even national, community and civil rights leaders concurred with that assessment. Believing the stereotypes of Africville, they decried segregation and poor living conditions. The actual relocation took place between 1964 and 1967. The City spent about $400,000 for the lands and the homes; another $200,000 were budgeted for welfare assistance, furniture allowances and the waiving of unpaid taxes and hospital bills. Relocation planning had called for education and training programs and, in general, the creation of new and better opportunities for the relocatees. In actuality, virtually none of these programs ever happened.*

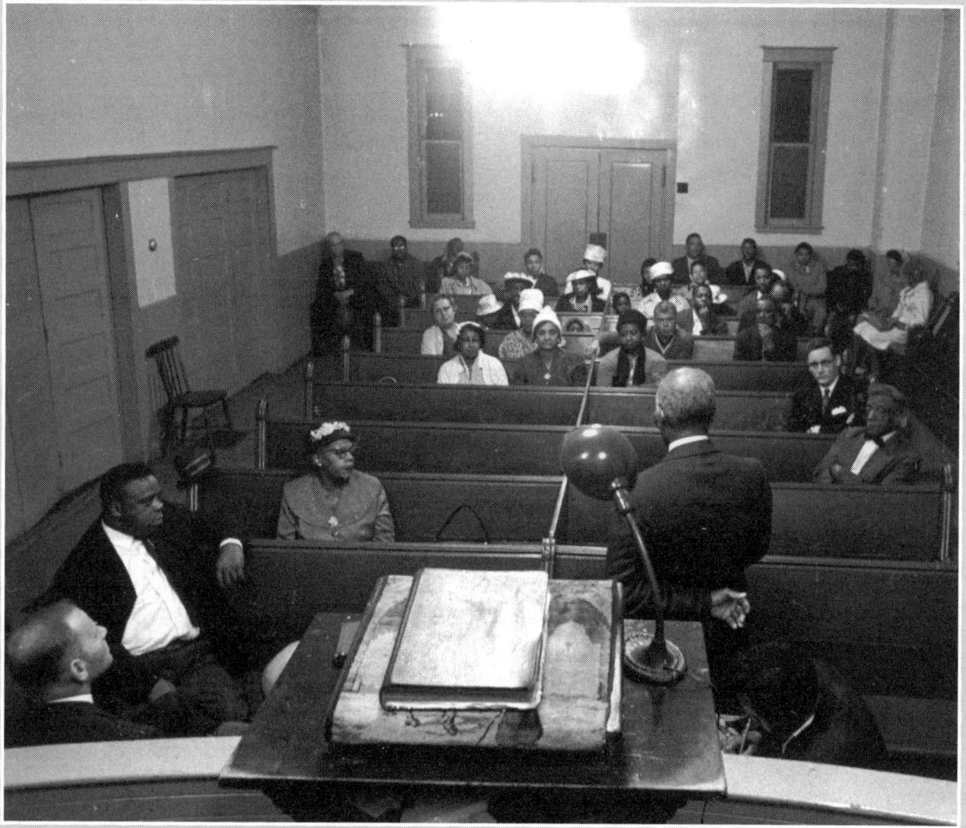

APPENDIX:
SOURCES AND REFERENCES

Chapter One: Comparison Views

No. 1
Harbour of Chebucto, with inserts: "A Map of the South Part of Nova Scotia and it's [*sic*] Fishing Banks..."; "A Plan of Halifax Survey'd by M. Harris"; and "A View of Halifax Drawn from ye Topmasthead," 1750

Artist: Moses Harris and D'Anville; published according to an Act of Parliament, 25 January 1750; printed for T[homas] Jefferys, St Martin's Lane, Charing Cross [London, England]
1750
Medium: engraving, 31 cm. x 42 cm.
Fonds/collection: Maps
Reference: S.B. 4
Copy negative number: O/S N-0371

No. 2
"Part of the Town and Harbour of Halifax in Nova Scotia looking down Prince Street to the Opposite Shore shows the Eastern Battery, George & Cornwallis Islands, Thrum Cap, & c. to the Sea off Chebucto Head," 1759

Artist: Richard Short, 1759; described & published by Short, 1 March 1764, London, England, James Mason, engraver; subsequently painted by D. Serres and published by John Boydell, London, 25 April 1777
1777
Medium: engraving with etching, 33 cm. x 50 cm.
Reference: accession no. 1979-147.171
Location: 42-14
Copy negative number: N-3931.

No. 3
"The Governor's-House and St. Mather's Meeting House in Holles [*sic*] Street, looking up George Street shews Part of the Parade and Citadel Hill at Halifax in Nova-Scotia," 1759

Artist: Richard Short, 1759; described & published by Short, 1 March 1764, London, England, Aveline, engraver; subsequently painted by D. Serres and published by John Boydell, London, 25 April 1777
1777
Medium: engraving with etching, 36 cm. x 51 cm.
Reference: accession no. 1979-147.169
Location: 42-14
Copy negative number: N-4215

No. 4
South Aspect of Halifax from near Point Pleasant Park, c 1780

Artist: Edward Hicks; engraved and published, London, England, c 1782
[c 1780]
Medium: aquatint with line etching (sepia tone), 38 cm. x 52 cm.
Reference: accession no. 1979-147-611
Location: 42-52
Copy negative number: N-6462

No. 5
Halifax from Fort Needham, c 1780

Artist: Edward Hicks; engraved and published London, c 1782
[c 1780]
Medium: aquatint with line etching (sepia tone), 31 cm. x 53 cm.
Reference: accession no. 1979-147.614
Location: 42-52
Copy negative number: N-0505

No. 6
"View from Cowie's Hill near Halifax," 1801

Artist: drawn, engraved and published by George I. Parkyns, London, England
29 April 1801
Medium: coloured aquatint; 37 cm. x 59 cm.
Reference: accession no 1979-147.167
Location: 42-14

No. 7
"National School at Halifax, NS," c 1819

Artist: Joseph Partridge
[c 1819]
Medium: water colour with touches of pencil and ink, 27 cm. x 39 cm.
Reference: accession no: 1979-147.178
Location: 42-14
Copy negative number: N-0328

No. 8
"View of Halifax, Nova Scotia from the Red Mill, Dartmouth, c 1853"

Artist: Robert D. Wilkie; P. Mayor, engraver
[c 1853]
Medium: engraving
Reference: *Gleason's Illustrated Magazine*, 10 September 1853
Location: 59-1

No. 9
Halifax Album, 1880

Photographer: Notman Studio; manufactured by Charles Frey, Portland, Maine; published by the Canada Railway News Co., Ltd., Montreal, PQ
1880
Medium: lithograph, 15 cm x 144 cm
Fonds/collection: Album 15B
Reference: accession no. 1958
Location 31.1.1

No. 10
Panorama View of Halifax from the Citadel, showing the Harbour and the Dartmouth Shore, c 1883

Photographer: Notman Studio, O.M. Hill, Manager
[c 1883]
Fonds/collection: Notman Studio
Location: 47-7

No. 11
Aerial view of the North West Arm, Looking East to Halifax Harbour and the Dartmouth Shore, 1949

Photographer: Royal Canadian Navy
1949
Fonds/collection: Royal Canadian Navy, no. 1391

No. 12
"Aerial View, City of Dartmouth, October 1988"

Photographer: Nova Scotia Information Service
1988
Fonds/collection: Nova Scotia Information Service #36043
Reference: unaccessioned
Negative number: NSIS #36043

No. 13
"Halifax Waterfront, July 1997"

Photographer: Visual Nova Scotia, # 17- 4
1997
Reference: courtesy Communications Nova Scotia

Chapter Two: Occupations

No. 1
"Union Engine Company, No. 6 (Alma), in dress uniform, with No. 3 Steam Fire-engine and the old Hand Fire-engine 'Alma' of about 1855; in front of Queen St. Engine House, 52 Queen St., Halifax, on the occasion of a firemen's tournament, c 1878"

Photographer: anonymous
[c 1878]
Fonds/collection: anonymous

Reference: Photo Drawer - Places - Halifax - Fire Department - Union Engine Co.

No. 2
CS *MacKay-Bennett* in Dry Dock, Halifax, between 1885 and 1922

Photographer: Notman Studio
[between 1885 and 1922]
Fonds/collection: Notman #1113
Copy negative number: N-5142

No. 3
"Faders Bros. Market, 8-10 Bedford Row, Halifax, N.S.,1885"

Photographer: anonymous
1885
Fonds/collection: Fader
Reference: accession no.: 1972-21, no. 24

No. 4
"J A Leaman & Co., 8-10 Bedford Row, Halifax, N.S., formerly owned by Faders Bros., 1890"

Photographer: anonymous
1890
Fonds/collection: Fader
Reference: accession no. 1972-21, no. 25

No. 5
"Stiffened Treble Sling Bridge — constructed by 18th Co.y RE — Halifax, N.S., Sept. 1897"

Photographer: Gauvin & Gentzell
September 1897
Fonds/collection: H.E. Smith
Reference: accession no. 1988-21, no. 2
Copy negative number: N-9494

No. 6
Quarry Scene, Spryfield, 189-

Photographer: Gauvin and Gentzell
[189-]
Fonds/collection: Jean Holder
Reference: accession no. 1980-195, no. 28
Copy negative number: N-0181

No. 7
"Province of Nova Scotia. Halifax County (City of Halifax, Sheet No. 68)," 1908

Author: E.R. Faribault for Canada. Department of Mines. Geological Survey Branch
1908
Reference: V10/ Sheet 68
Copy negative number: N-9495

No. 8
"Clayton & Sons, Halifax, N.S. — Work Room, about 1900"

Photographer: anonymous
[c 1900]
Fonds/collection: Jean Holder
Reference: accession no.: 1980-195, no. 24
Copy negative number: N-0172

No. 9
"No. 2 Pound Round up wild Sable Island Ponies," c 1900

Photographer: Beatrice Boutilier
[c 1900]
Fonds/collection: Beatrice Boutilier
Reference: accession number 1984-430, no. 96
Copy negative number: N-7935

No. 10
"Sable Island Ponies after being unloaded from Steamer, to be sold at Auction — Halifax, N.S. about 1902"

Photographer: anonymous
c 1902
Fonds/collection: Beatrice Boutilier
Reference: accession number 1984-430, no. 70
Copy negative number: N-7176

No. 11
"Halifax, 1903": City Council and Department Heads

Photographer: Notman Studio
1903
Fonds/collection: Notman O/S [#100,053]

No. 12
"Halifax City Police" on the Grand Parade, 1914

Photographer: Cox Bros. Co.
10 July 1914
Fonds/collection: R. V. Harris
Reference: accession no. 1992-415, no. 5

No. 13
"Logging camps — Near Ingramport, Hfx. Co., N.S.," 193-

Photographer: Robert Norwood
[193-]
Fonds/collection: Robert Norwood
Reference: accession number no. 1987-480, no. 279
Copy negative number: N-6970

No. 14
Spryfield Volunteer Fire Department, c 1941

Photographer: anonymous
[c 1941]
Fonds/collection: Blair Beed
Reference: accession no. 1984-342, no. D.3

No. 15
Workers Filleting Fish inside Maritime National Fish Limited Plant, Halifax, 1942

Photographer: E.A. Bollinger
1942
Fonds/collection: E.A. Bollinger
Reference: accession no. 1975-305, 1942 no. 562-W
Negative number: accession no. 1975-305, 1942 no. 562-W

No. 16
Woman Working with Microscope in Atlantic Fisheries Experimental Station, 209 Lower Water Street, Halifax, 21 January 1947

Photographer: E.A. Bollinger
21 January 1947
Fonds/collection: E.A. Bollinger
Reference: accession no. 1975-305, 1947 no. 472-3
Negative number: accession no. 1975-305, 1947 no. 472-3

No. 17
Charlie Symonds, a Cooper in Upper Hammonds Plains, 1949

Photographer: C. R. Brookbank
July 1949
In: C. R. Brookbank's "Afro-Canadian Communities in Halifax County, Nova Scotia" (MA thesis, University of Toronto, 1949), p. 38
Reference: NSARM Library: HT431/ B871/ A259
Copy negative number: N-6940

No. 18
"Celopane [*sic*] wrapping machine at Moir's Ltd., Halifax," 1955

Photographer: Nova Scotia Film Bureau
[1955]
Fonds/collection: Nova Scotia Information Service, #9118
Reference: unaccessioned
Negative number: NSIS #9118

No. 19
" 'Killocks' — 'Home[made] anchors' — Portuguese Cove, N.S.," 195-

Photographer: Robert Norwood
195-
Fonds/Collection: Robert Norwood
Reference: accession no. 1987-480, no. 42-1
Negative number: accession no. 1987-480, no. 42-1

No. 20
"Unloading Salt Cod at Smiths [Wharf], Hfx., N.S.," 195-

Photographer: Robert Norwood
195-
Fonds/collection: Robert Norwood
Reference: accession no. 1987-480, no. 241
Negative number: accesion no. 1987-480, no. 241

No. 21
"Lathe workers, Halifax Shipyards," 1956

Photographer: Nova Scotia Bureau of Information
1956
Fonds/collection: Nova Scotia Information Service #9145
Reference: unaccessioned
Negative number: NSIS #9145

No. 22
"Stacking Volvo bodies at Dartmouth," 1963

Photographer: Nova Scotia Bureau of Information
1963
Fonds/collection: Nova Scotia Information Service #16172
Negative number: NSIS #16172

Chapter 3: Disasters

No. 1
"Granville Street Fire, Sept. 9, 1859"

Artist: H.H. Laird
[n.d.]
Medium: watercolour; 23 cm. diameter
Reference: accession no. 1979-147.24

No. 2
"Ordnance Square Fire, Sept. 9, 1859"

Artist: H.H. Laird
[n.d.]
Medium: watercolour: 23 cm. diameter
Reference: accession no. 1979-147.25

No. 3
"The Wreck of the *Atlantic*, 1873"

Photographer: copied by E.A. Bollinger
1952
Artist: originally published by Currier and Ives
Reference: Photo Drawer - Transportation & Communication - Ships & Shipping - Atlantic
Copy negative number: E.A. Bollinger #5257

No. 4
"The *Atlantic* disaster - actual position of the hull," April 1873

Artist: from a sketch by E.J. Russell
Copy print from wood engraving
From: *Canadian Illustrated News*, April 19, 1873, p. 249
Borrowed for copying from Charles P. de Volpi Collection, Special Collections, Dalhousie University Libraries
Copy negative number: N-7590

No. 5.
"Burial service of Victims of Wreck of S.S. *Atlantic*, at Lower Prospect, Hx. Co., N.S., April 1873. Shows the Rev W J Ancient, C. of E. rector of Turns [Terrence] Bay, reading the service before an open trench in which can be seen about 14 rough wooden coffins while gathered by are fisherfolk of the district & a very [*sic*] visitors from Halifax. Enlarged from a carte-de-visite photo by W. Chase of Halifax, N.S."

Photographer: W. Chase
1873
Copy print from a copy photograph
Reference: Photo Drawer - Transportation & Communication - Ships and Shipping - Atlantic
Copy negative number: N-719

No. 6.
"Ruins of Poor House burnt Nov. 7, 1882; photo taken Jan., 1884 (on present site, viz. corner Robie & South Sts.)"

Photographer: anonymous
January 1884
Copy print from original photograph
Reference: Photo Drawer - Places - Halifax - Buildings - Poor House
Copy negative number: N-877

No. 7
"Concrete Sewer Blocks made at the Halifax Poor Asylum, Halifax, N.S., 1899, over 1000 barrels of Citadel Brand of cement used, manufactured by St. Lawrence Portland Cement Coy., Montreal, Quebec"

Photographer: J.M. Margeson
1899
Copy print from original photograph
Fonds/collection: Anonymous
Reference: accession no. 1992-411

No. 8
"Body of *RMS Titanic* victim aboard rescue vessel [*CS Minia*] being made ready for make-shift coffin," April or May 1912

Photographer: attributed to William J. Parker
[April or May 1912]
Copy print from original photograph
Reference: Photo Drawer - Transportation & Communication - Ships & Shipping - Titanic, no. 2
Copy negative number: N-715

No. 9
"Hearses lined up on Halifax wharf (near the present Jetty 4 of HMCS Dockyard) to carry *RMS Titanic* victims to funeral parlours," 6 May 1912

Photographer: attributed to William J. Parker or William Mosher
[6 May 1912]
Copy print from original photograph
Reference: Photo Drawer - Transportation & communication - Ships & Shipping - Titanic, no. 3
Copy negative number: N-332

No. 10
William Carbines, Body No. 18, c 1912
Coroners' Reports. RG 41, vol. 75, no. 18

No. 11
Business card, Mr. Nicola Nasra Uah, sometimes known as Nicola Nasser, c 1912
Coroners' Reports. RG 41, vol. 75, no. 43

No. 12
J.F.P. Clarke, Business Card, c 1912
Coroners' Reports. RG 41, vol. 76, no. 202

No. 13
Leopold Weisz, Business Card, c 1912.
Coroners' Reports. RG 41, volume 76A, no. 293

No. 14
Collapsed buildings of Nova Scotia Car Works on Clifton Street near St. Albans Street, Halifax, with Bloomfield School in background at right, 11 February 1918

Photographer: Gauvin & Gentzel
February 11, 1918
Copy print from original photograph
Fonds/collection: Charles Vaughan (copied through the courtesy of Mrs. Shirley Vaughan)
Copy negative number: N-7035

No. 15
Women walking from Africville towards Halifax, on Campbell Road near Hanover Street, 1917 or 1918

Photographer: James & Son
[1917 or 1918]
Copy print
Fonds/collection: James 2451 (courtesy of the City of Toronto Archives)

No. 16
"Rehousing for Halifax Relief Commission, Halifax, Ross & Macdonald, Architects, Montreal, No.76," July 30, 1919

Photographer: Gauvin & Gentzel
July 30, 1919
Copy print from original photograph
Fonds/collection: Charles Vaughan (copied through the courtesy of Mrs. Shirley Vaughan)
Copy negative number: N-7038

No. 17
J. Allister Bowman, district plant superintendent, Maritime Tel & Tel, using earphones for word from entombed men in Moose River Mine Disaster, N.S., April 1936

Photographer: anonymous
April 1936
Copy print from copy photograph
Reference: Photo Drawer - Places - Moose River - Mine Disaster, 1936
Copy negative number: N-318

No. 18
Queen Hotel Fire, Hollis Street, 1939

Photographer: attributed to Roy Tidman, *Star* staff cameraman
[March 2, 1939]
Copy print from original photograph
Fonds/collection: John F. Rogers
Reference: accession no. 1995-370, no. 6
Copy negative number: N-9453

No. 19
"Explosion of Munitions at Magazine near Dartmouth, Halifax, N.S., July 18, 1945"

Photographer: J.C.M. Hayward
July 18, 1945
Copy print from original photograph
Fonds/collection: Yarmouth County Historical Society
Reference: accession no. 1981-517, no. 1
Copy negative number: N-639

No. 20
Crowd viewing broken glass outside Henry Birks & Sons Limited, Barrington St., Halifax, after the Bedford Magazine Explosion, July 18, 1945

Photographer: J.C.M. Hayward
[July 18, 1945]
Copy print from original photograph
Reference: Photo Drawer - Places - Halifax - Explosion, 1945 - Damage - Barrington St.

Chapter Four: Entertainment and Social Events

No. 1
"Fancy-dress Ball given by Gen. Sir Patrick L. MacDougall, K.C.M.G., Commmander of H.M. Forces, at 'Maplewood', Northwest Arm, Halifax, N.S., sometime between 1878 & 1883, composite photo by W. Notman, Halifax"

Photographer: Notman Studio
between 1878 and 1883
Fonds/collection: Notman, Oversize #45760

No. 2
Amateur Theatre Cast of *Pirates of Penzance*, c 1885

Photographer: Notman Studio
[c 1885]
Fonds/collection: Notman #65615
Copy negative number: N-1323

No. 3
"Carnival, Old Exhibition Rink, Feb. 1899"

Photographer: Notman Studio #5246
February 1899
Reference/collection: Captain Ferdinand James Odevaine
Reference: accession no. 1992-306, no. 15

No. 4
"Mum [Frances Gwendolyn (née Francklyn) Castens] in her Noah's Ark costume, worn when skating," 189-

Photographer: Notman Studio
[189-]
Fonds/collection: Mary K. Sterling
Reference: accession no. 1995-122, no. 1
Copy negative number: N-8544

No. 5
"Hesslein & Anderson," c 1885

Photographer: Notman Studio
[c 1885]
Fonds/collection: Notman Studio #93576

No. 6
Missionary Loan Exhibition, Halifax, January 1903

Photographer: Notman Studio
January 1903
Fonds/collections: Notman #10578
Copy negative number: N-6989

No. 7
Boating on the North West Arm in front of the Waegwoltic Club, Halifax, c 1910

Photographer: Harry O. Dodge (Gauvin & Gentzel)
c 1910
Fonds/collection: H.O. Dodge
Reference: accession no. 1987-73, no. 3

No. 8
"Scene from 'Evangeline' (movie) 1913, garden of Billman Residence, 'Melvillewood', Armdale, later called 17 Herring Cove Rd."

Photographer: anonymous
1913
Fonds/collection: James Billman
Reference: accession no. 1981-295, no. 1
Copy negative number: N-1652

No. 9
"The Commercial Club Luncheon, 1925, given by Moir's Ltd., on the old Bedford Road, now part of Moir's Ltd."

Photographer: Climo
1925
Fonds/collection: Climo
Reference: accession no. 1987-72, no. 11
Copy negative number: N-9492

No. 10
Canadian Actor Austin Willis and Dick Fry Perform from the CHNS Studio, Lord Nelson Hotel, Halifax, c 1939

Photographer: anonymous
[1928]
Fonds/collection: CHNS Radio Studio
Reference: accession no. 1992-396, no. 6

No. 11
"Gay 'Senoritas' to dance tonight," April 1931

Photographer: J. C. M. Hayward
[April 1931]
Fonds/collection: Commercial Club of Halifax
Reference: MG 20, volume 78

No. 12
Minstrels of '31 Programme, Commercial Club of Halifax

1931
Fonds/collection: Commercial Club of Halifax
Reference: MG 20, volume 78

No. 13
Letter from R E. Inglis, Ticket Committee, to Members of the Commercial Club of Halifax, 12 March 1931, Requesting Them to Sell Tickets

March 12, 1931
Fonds/collection: Commercial Club of Halifax
Reference: MG 20, volume 78

No. 14
Olympic Gardens Dance Hall, Hunter Street, Halifax, c 1948

Photographer: anonymous
[c 1948]
Fonds/collection: Blair Beed
Reference: accession no. 1984-342, no. E.1

Chapter Five: Royal Visits and Special Events

No. 1
Inauguration of the Welsford-Parker Monument, Halifax, 17 July 1860

Photographer: W. Chase
[July 17, 1860]
Fonds/collection: Wellington Chase Collection, no. 8
Reference: unaccessioned
Copy negative number: N- 9491

No. 2
"Court House, Halifax, Spring Garden Road, looking east, 1860. Arch of General Trollope in honour of the visit of the Prince of Wales, designed by Col. Nelson, R.E."

Photographer: W. Chase
1860
Fonds/collection: W. Chase, no. 6
Copy negative number: N-1253

No. 3
"Presentation to the Marquis of Lorne of Micmac Indians, in the Council Chamber of the Provincial Building, Halifax, November 26th," 1878

Artist: from sketches by H.A. Ogden
1878
In: *Frank Leslie's Illustrated Newspaper*, December 21, 1878, p. 264
Fonds/collection: Prints Old and Rare
Reference: accession no. 1997-233, no. 6

No. 4
"School children at unveiling of fountain, Public Gardens, Halifax, Jubilee week, 1897"

Photographer: Notman Studio
1897
Reference: Notman #4073
Copy negative number: N-0337

No. 5
"Musquodoboit Centennial Celebrations," 11-13 July 1915

Photographer: anonymous
[1968], copy print
Copy prints from copy photographs
Fonds/collection: William A. Fisher Collection
Reference: Photo Drawer - Places - Musquodoboit, Middle - Churches - Presbyterian Centenary, nos. 2, 4

No. 6
"H.R.H. Prince of Wales, Halifax, N.S., Aug. 18th, 1919"

Photographer: F.G. Goodenough
August 18, 1919
Photograph in postcard format
Reference: Photo Drawer - People - Edward, Prince of Wales (Edward VIII)

No. 7
King George VI and Queen Elizabeth's visit to Halifax, 1939

Photographer: John Kanelokas
[1939]
Fonds/collection: Jean C. Cuthbert
Reference: Photo Drawer - People - George VI - Visit, 1939

No. 8
Halifax Bicentenary Parade on Quinpool Road, Looking East near Oxford Street, 1949

Photographer: Nova Scotia Bureau of Information
[1949]
Fonds/collection: Nova Scotia Information Service #3906
Negative number: NSIS #3906

No. 9
HRH Princess Elizabeth and Premier Angus L. Macdonald Walking between Boy Scouts and Girl Guides in Province House, 1951

Photographer: The Halifax Herald Ltd.
[1951]
Fonds/collection: Girl Guides of Canada. Nova Scotia Division
Reference: accession no. 1981-352, no. 25

No. 10
President William Jefferson ("Bill") Clinton Greets Onlookers during the G-7 Economic Summit held in Halifax, June 15, 1995

Photographer: MCPL M. Ray, CFB Halifax
June 15, 1995
Fonds/collection: G-7 21st Economic Summit [courtesy Canada. Department of National Defence]
Reference: accession no. 1996-178, no. 8

Chapter Six: The Life Cycle

No. 1
Dead Child, c 1867

Photographer: The People's Gallery
[c 1867]
Fonds/collection: Album no. 5, #74
Copy negative number: N-9372

No. 2
"W.J. Kinnear's Grp [group]," c 1880

Photographer: Notman Studio
[c 1880]
Fonds/collection: Notman Studio #48479

No. 3
Wedding of Miss Mary Borden and Mr. Richard Tynes, Dartmouth, 1898

Photographer: O. Bertram Stubbs
[1898]
Fonds/collection: Joan Payzant
Reference: accession no. 1983-396
Copy negative number: N-9286

No. 4
Wedding of the Rev. Willoughby Goddard-Fenwick and Miss Ella Major in Sackville, NS, 1912

Photographer: Gauvin & Gentzel
[September 24, 1912]
Reference: Photo Drawer - Miscellaneous - Costumes - Weddings - Sackville

No. 5
First Communion — Group of Boys and Priests on the Steps of St. Mary's Cathedral, Halifax, 193-

Photographer: J. C. M. Hayward
[193-]
Fonds/collection: Eveleen L. Burns
Reference: accession no. 1995-85, no. 26

Nos. 6 & 7
"Leaving St. Mary's Cathedral"and "Proceeding along Spring Garden Rd.," Funeral of Premier Angus L. Macdonald, 19 April 1954

Photographer: Royal Canadian Navy, National Defence
Nos. 30274, 30290
April 19, 1954
Reference: Photo Drawer - People - Macdonald, Angus L. - Funeral

Chapter Seven: Halifax at War

No. 1
"Warrant Officers, Sergeant Majors & Sergeants of 63rd Battalion, Halifax Rifles, Halifax, N.S., about 1890. 13 of them wearing North-West Rebellion Medals of 1885"

Photographer: Notman Studio
c 1890
Fonds/collection: Notman [#100,059]
Copy negative number: N-9493

No. 2
Coaling HMS *Charybdis* at HM Dockyard, Halifax, 189- or 190-

Photographer: Notman Studio
[189- or 190-]
Fonds/collection: Notman #8717

No. 3
Troop Transport Ship *Idaho* Disembarking Boer War Troops, Halifax, 1900

Photographer: O. Bertram Stubbs
[1900]
Reference: Photo Drawer - Army - Boer War
Copy negative number: N-1959

No. 4
"Patriotic Concert for Belgian Relief Fund by Staff of Mahons Limited: Tableau Britannia," between 1914 and 1918

Photographer: Climo
[between 1914 and 1918]
Fonds/collection: Joan Galloway
Reference: accession no. 1989-222, no. 3

No. 5
"Detachment No. 4 Co'y. 1st Regt. Canadian Garrison Artillery, Fort Charlotte, Halifax," 1914

Photographer: Climo
1914
Fonds/collection: Schooner Books
Reference: accession no. 1992-409
Copy negative number: N-6963

No. 6
Prisoners of War, Halifax Citadel, c 1917

Photographer: Notman Studio
[c 1917]
Fonds/collection: Notman #47

Nos. 7 & 8
Maud Foley, Street-Car Conductor in Summer Uniform and Winter Uniform, Halifax, 1917 or 1918

Photographer: anonymous
1917 or 1918
Fonds/collection: Nova Scotia Light and Power Co.
Reference: MG 9, volume 226, pp. 27-28

No. 9
British Evacuee Children arriving in Halifax, 1941

Photographer: E. A. Bollinger
1941
Fonds/collection: E. A. Bollinger
Reference: accession no. 1975-305, 1941 no. 419-B
Negative number: accession no. 1975-305, 1941 no. 419-B

No. 10
"Store with War Savings Stamps," 1942

Photographer: E. A. Bollinger
1942
Fonds/collection: E. A. Bollinger
Reference: accession no. 1975-305, 1942 no. 618-A
Negative number: accession no. 1975-305, 1942 no. 618-A

No. 11
V-E Day Rioters Walking along Salter Street between Hollis and Barrington Streets, May 1945

Photographer: anonymous
[May 1945]
Fonds/collection: David Hall
Reference: accession no. 1981-412, no. 8
Copy negative number: N-1404

No. 12
V-E Day Rioters on Hollis Street between Blowers and Bishop Streets, May 1945

Photographer: anonymous
[May 1945]
Fonds/collection: David Hall
Reference: accession no. 1981-412, no. 11
Copy negative number: N-0638

No. 13
War Brides Arrive on the Liner SS *Scythia*, 26 March 1946

Photographer: Canadian Army Photo
March 26, 1946
Fonds/collection: H.B. Jefferson
Reference: accession no. 1992-304, no. 25
Copy negative number: N-6965

Chapter Eight: Sports and the Great Outdoors

No. 1
"The noted 'Pryor Crew', Aug. 1871, training for great Aquatic Carnival, Halifax Harbour, 31 Aug. - 1 Sep. 1871, trained by Jerry Holland," August 1871

Photographer: anonymous
August 1871
Reference: Photo Drawer - Sports -Rowing - Pryor Crew, 1871
Copy negative number: N-0097

No. 2
"Polo Team at Fort Needham," Halifax, c 1885

Photographer: Notman Studio
[c 1885]
Reference: Notman #42939
Copy negative number: N-1200

No. 3
Red Cap Snowshoe Club, Halifax, c 1890

Photographer: Notman Studio
[c 1890]
Fonds/collection: Notman #66169

No. 4
"Rocking Stone," Spryfield, c 1895

Photographer: Notman Studio
[c 1895]
Fonds/collection: Notman #13040
Copy negative number: N-5945

No. 5
Curling on the Dartmouth Lakes, c 1897

Photographer: W. L. Bishop
[c 1897]
Fonds/collection: W. L. Bishop
Reference: accession no. 1983-240, no. 12
Copy negative number: N-6977

No. 6
"Camp, Head of Baker's Lake," c 1900

Photographer: anonymous
[c 1900]
Fonds/collection: W.C. Dunlop
Reference: accession no. 1992-398, no. 12
Copy negative number: N-2487

No. 7
"Frances and Mater at Sue's place," c 1900

Photographer: anonymous
[c 1900]
Fonds/collection: W.C. Dunlop
Reference: accession no. 1992-398, no. 15
Copy negative number: N-2328

No. 8
Woman fly fishing, c 1900

Photographer: anonymous
[c 1900]
Fonds/collection: W.C. Dunlop
Reference: accession no. 1992-398, no. 23
Copy negative number: N-2459

No. 9
"H. M. Wylde's yacht" sailing in Halifax Harbour, c 1900

Photographer: Notman Studio
[c 1900]
Fonds/collection: Notman #6679
Copy negative number: N-5098

No. 10
South End Lawn Tennis Club, Halifax, c 1900

Photographer: anonymous
[c 1900]
Reference: Photo Drawer - Sports - Tennis, c 1900
Copy negative no.: N-5544

No. 11
"N.S.R.A. [Nova Scotia Rifle Association] Meeting, Bedford, Aug. 1911"

Photographer: Notman Studio
August 1911
Fonds/collection: Notman #20109

Large Print for

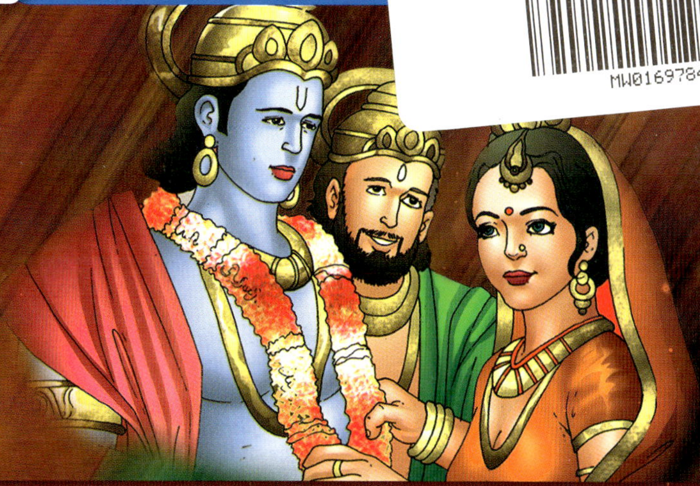

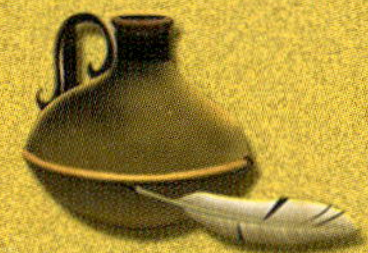

TALES FROM Ramayan and MAHABHARAT

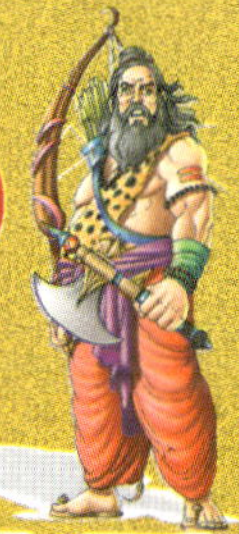

ANURAG MEHTA

Nita Mehta Publications
Enriching Young Minds

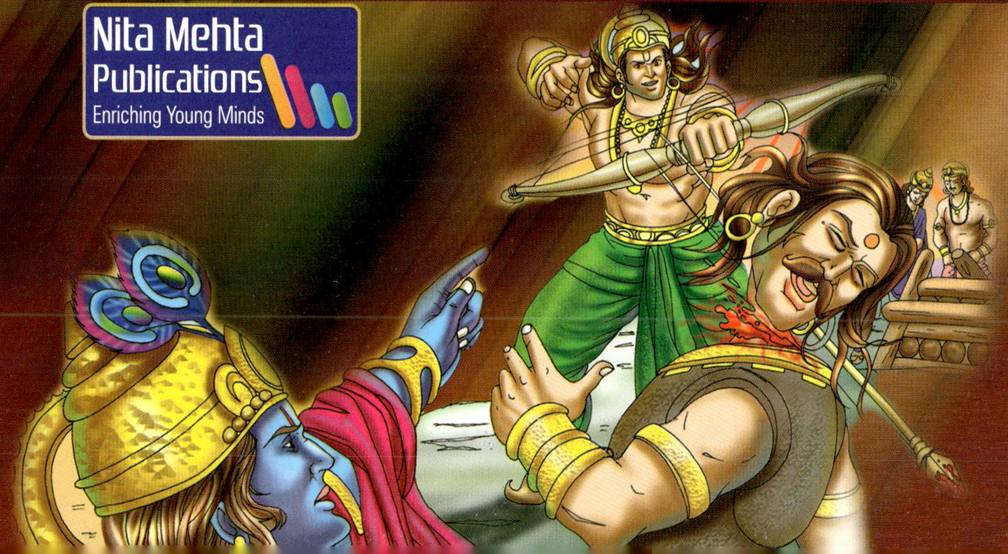

The Three Princesses

King Shantanu of Hastinapur and his wife Satyawati had two sons, Chitrangada and Vichitravirya. Bhishma, Shantanu's other son, was their guardian. One day, Satyawati asked Bhishma to find brides for Vichitravirya. Bhishma went to Kashi where a swayamvara was being held for the three daughters of the king. Bhishma brought the three princesses to Hastinapur. But the first princess, Amba, said that she wanted to marry Prince Shalva and thus the other sisters, Ambika and Ambalika were married to Vichitravirya.

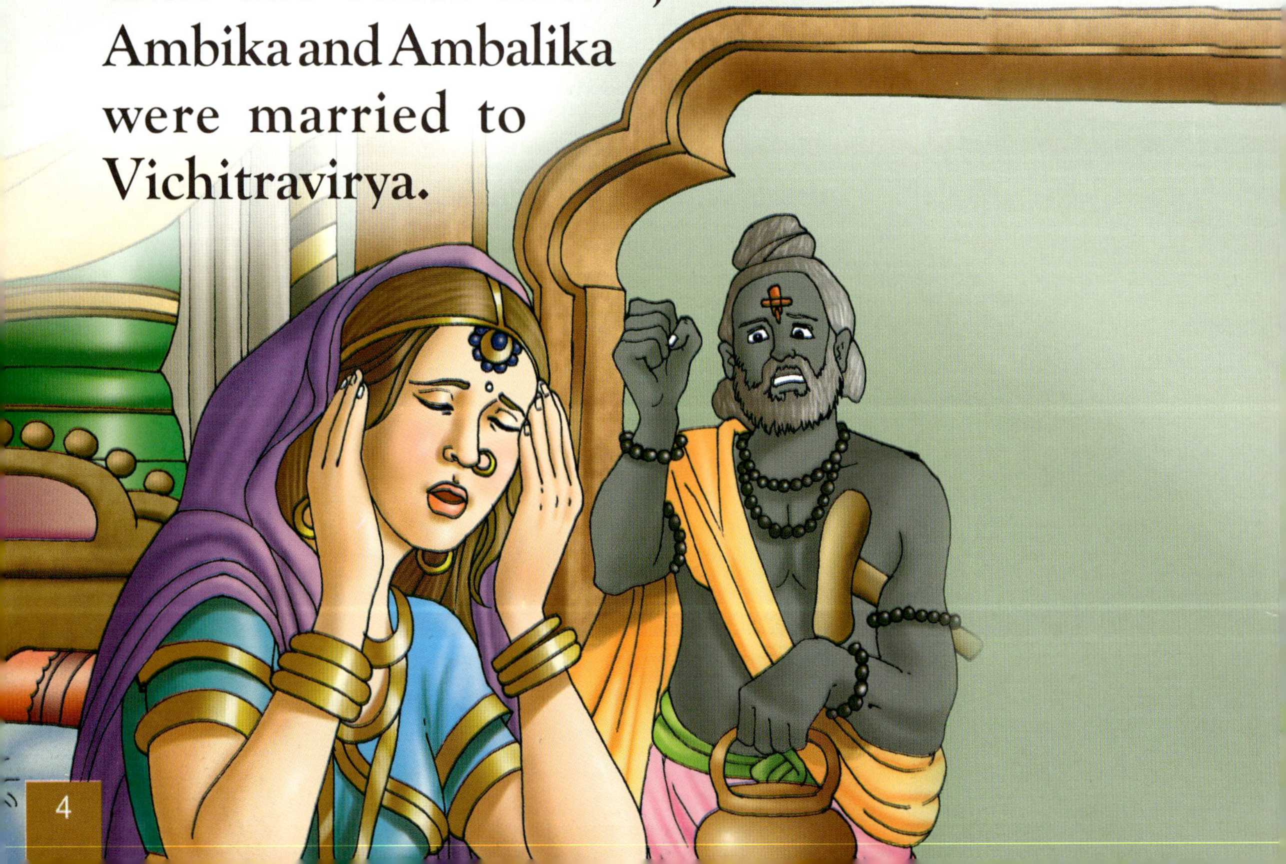

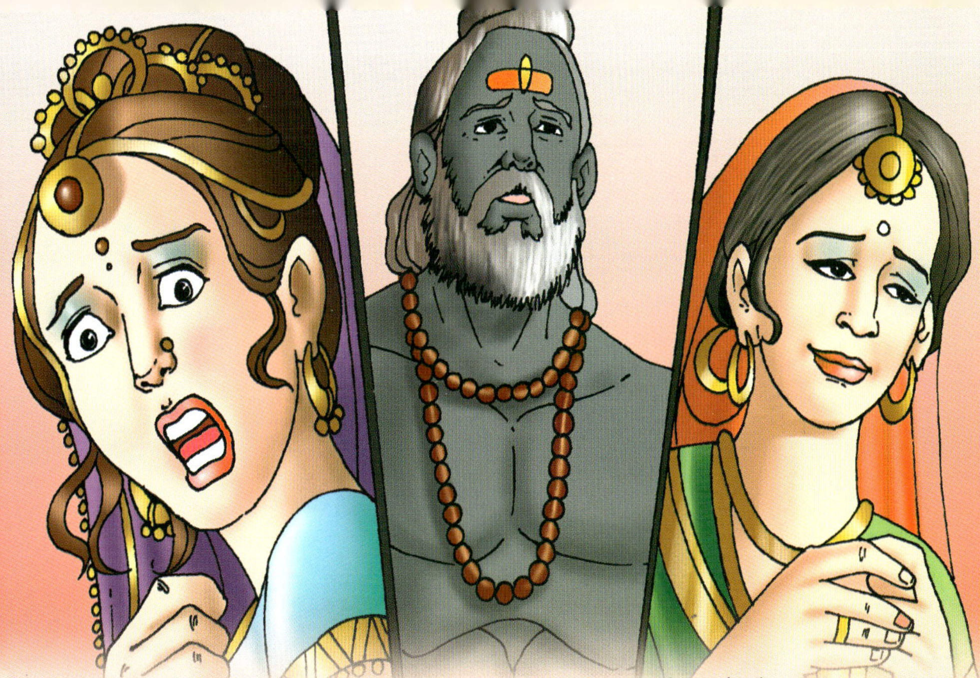

One day, Ambika and Ambalika went with their maid to visit the very ugly, Sage Vyasa. Seeing his face, Ambika closed her eyes while Ambalika turned pale. Vyasa cursing them said, "Ambika shall give birth to a blind son and Ambalika will give birth to a pale and weak son." When the maid looked fearlessly at the Sage, he blessed her saying that a very intelligent son would be born to her. As time passed, Ambika gave birth to Prince Dhritarashtra, who was strong but blind. Ambalika's son Pandu grew to be a great shooter but was weak. Due to his blindness, Dhritarashtra was not crowned the king. Instead Pandu was enthroned. The maid's wise son, Vidura, was made a minister in the court.

Sita's Swayamvara

King Janaka of Mithila had organized a grand swayamvara for his beautiful daughter, Sita. Swayamvara was the ritual where kings and princes from different lands would visit the king's court asking for the princess's hand, but only the bravest would be selected.

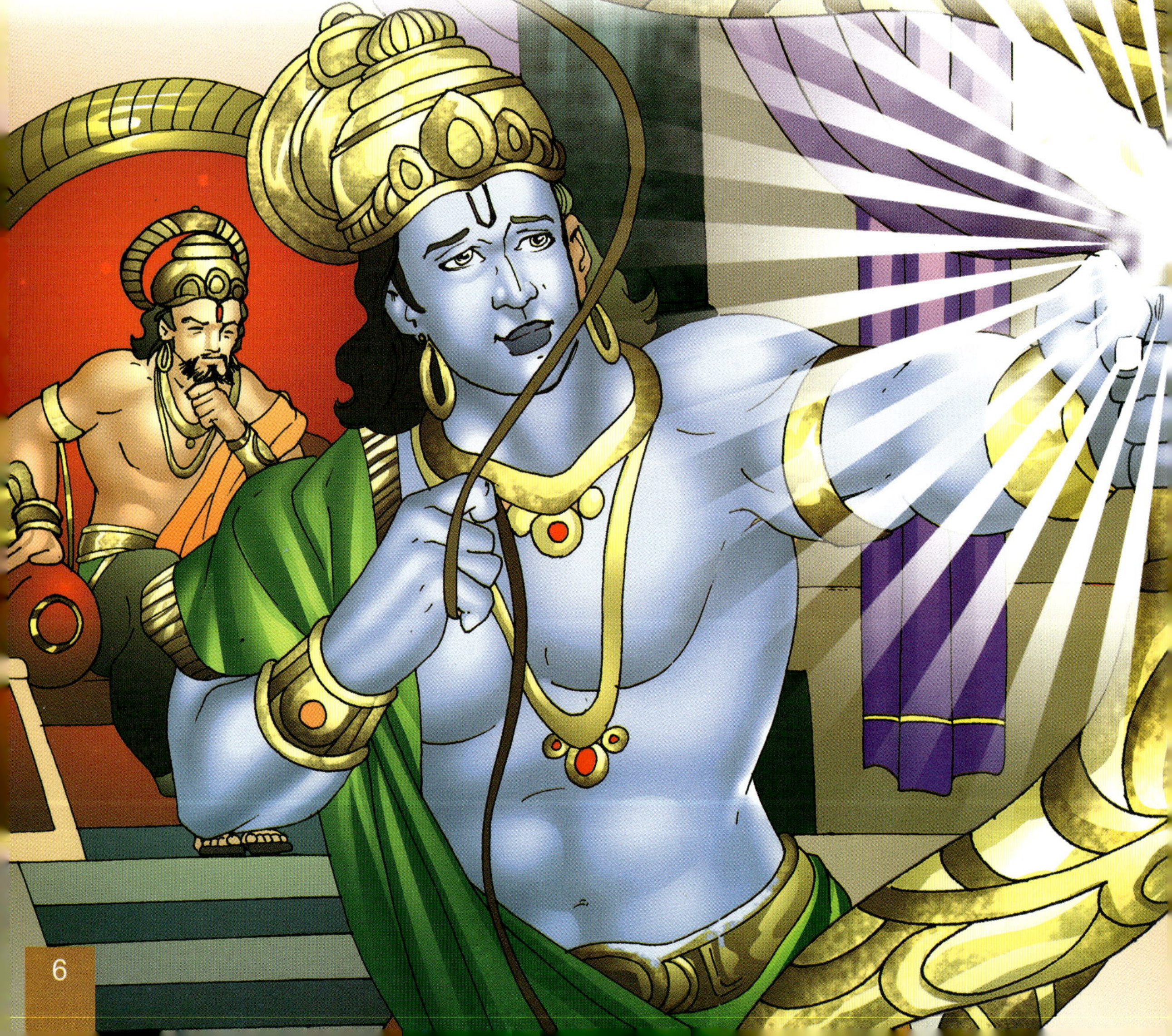

King Janaka announced that he had a mighty bow, blessed by Shiva. The one who could string the bow would marry Sita.

Many princes tried in vain but nobody could even lift the bow. Rama and Lakshmana were also present. Rama, to their amazement bent down and lifting the formidable bow, snapped it into two.

King Janaka proclaimed, "My beloved daughter Sita is to be wedded to Rama." Sita walked up to Rama and garlanded him.

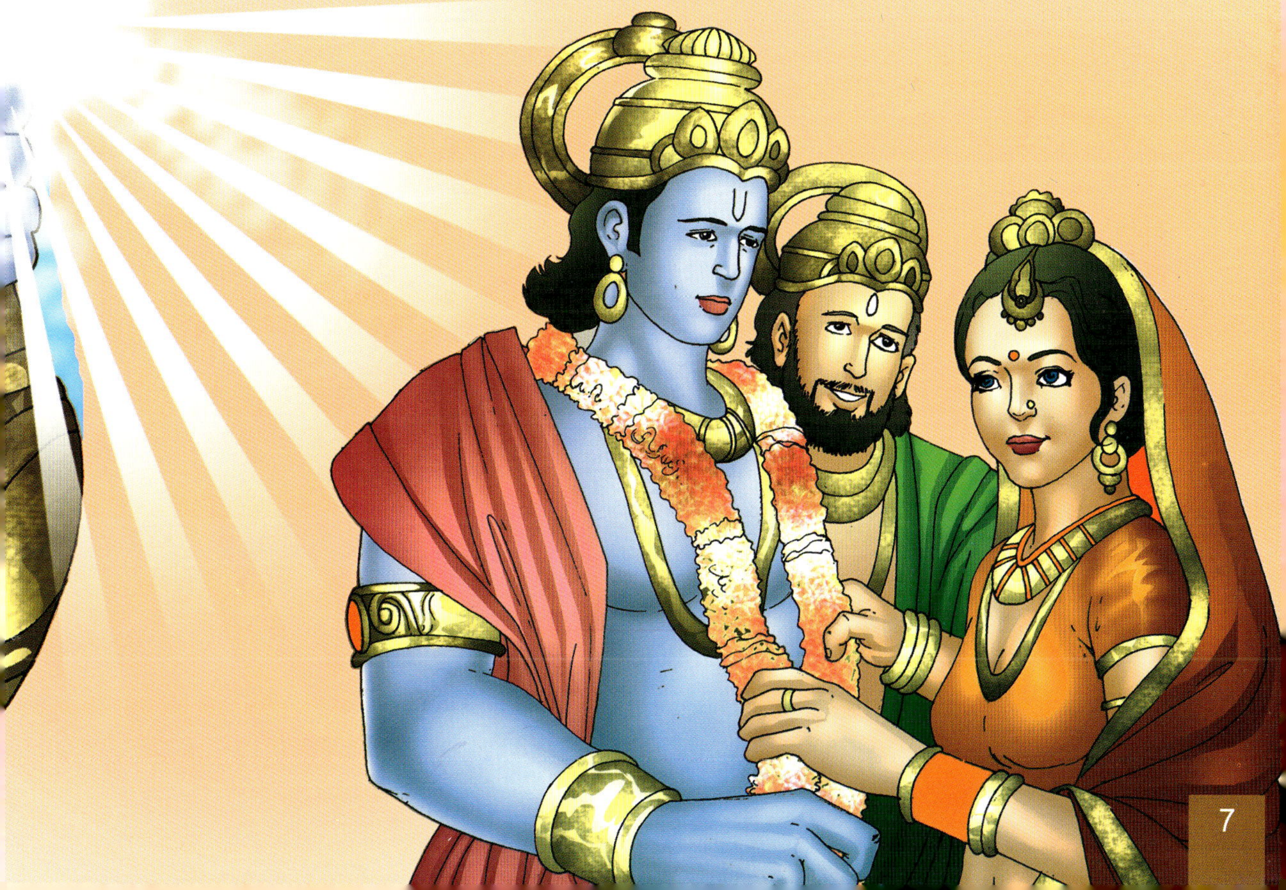

The Birth of Kauravas

Gandhari, the princess of Gandhara kingdom, was chosen as the bride for blind Dhritarashtra. Not wanting to be better than her husband in any respect, Gandhari tied a silk bandage on her eyes and pledged never to remove it.

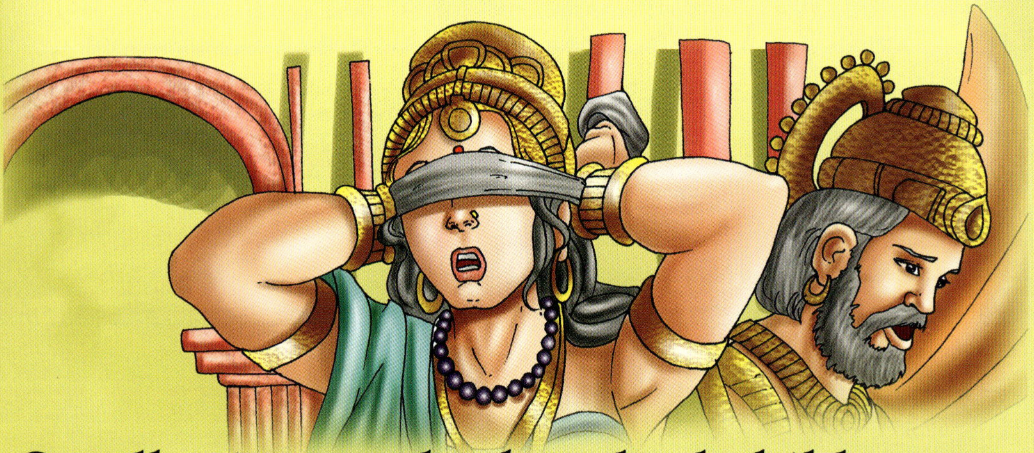

Gandhari wanted a hundred children so she prayed to Sage Vyasa who granted her this boon. But she gave birth to a lump of flesh.

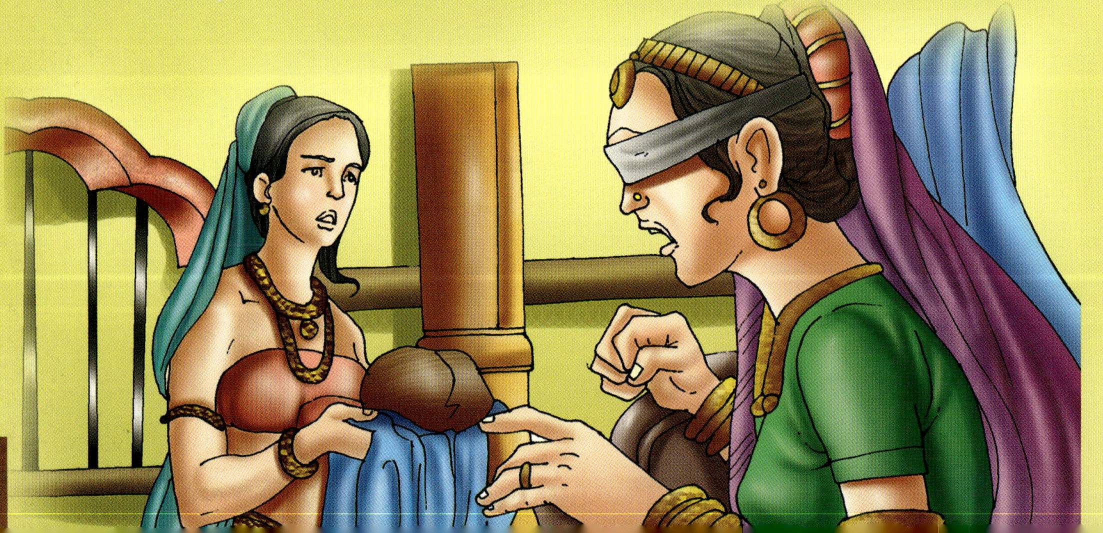

Just then sage Vyasa appeared, and taking the shapeless mass of flesh, he divided it into a hundred and one pieces. One by one, he placed each piece in a jar. In nine months, in one of the jars, a baby appeared. As soon as he was formed, the day became night and a wailing wind rattled the rooftops. “This child will destroy the world,” everyone said, terrified. “Leave him in the forest where the beasts will destroy him.”

But Dhritarashtra refused, and brought his son home. The child was named Duryodhana. A month later, ninety-nine other princes came forth. From the last jar was born Gandhari’s only daughter, Dushala. Thus were born Gandhari’s hundred sons who were called the Kauravas.

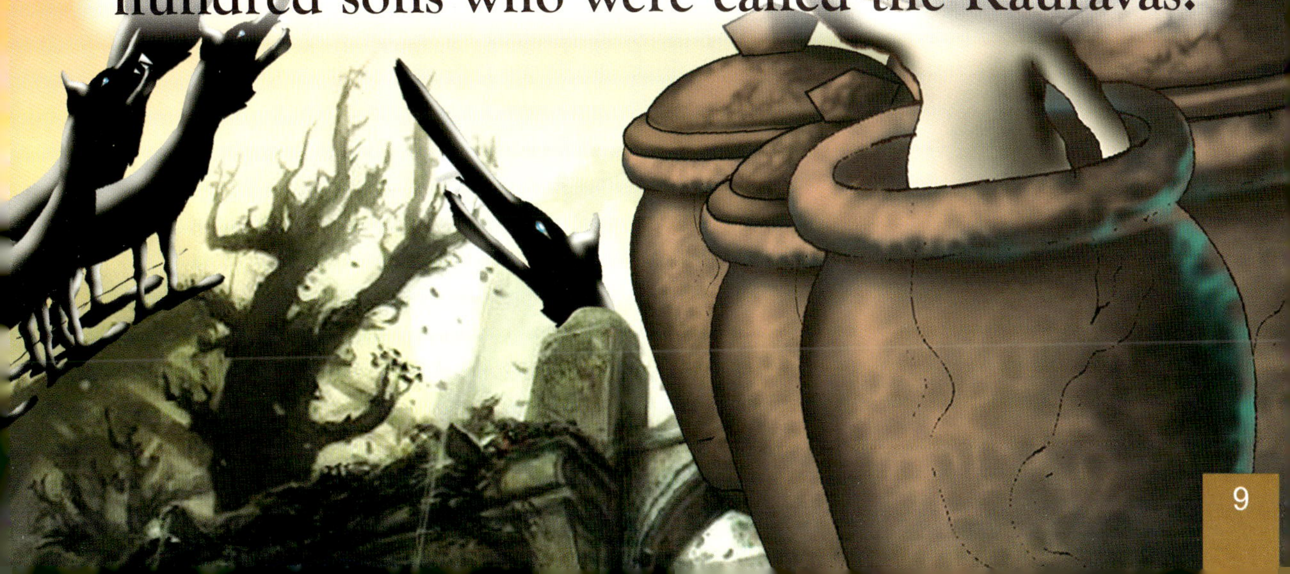

Birth of Draupadi

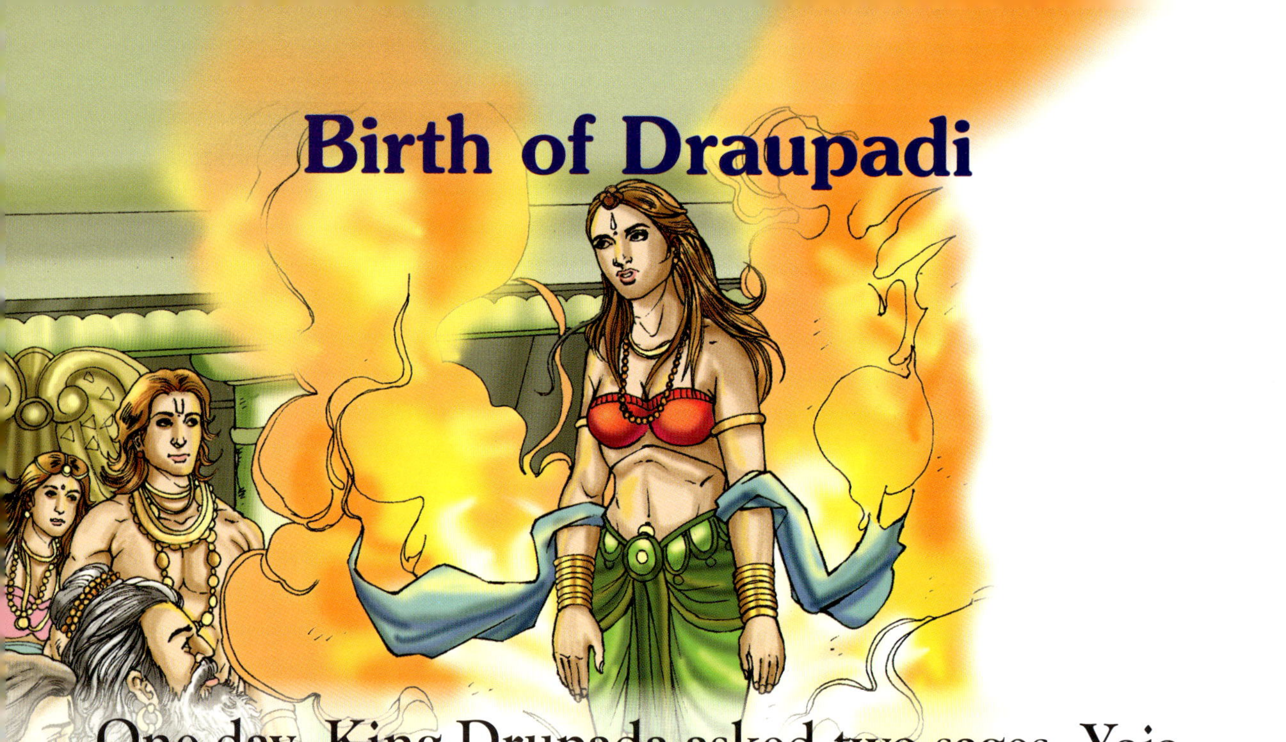

One day, King Drupada asked two sages, Yaja and Upayaja, to perform a yagna. When the yagna was over, the sages offered the prasada to Drupada's wife. At that moment, the queen had something in her mouth so she asked the sages to wait. Angered, Yaja put the prasada in the yagna fire. Suddenly from the fire emerged a young warrior. Similarly Upayaja also put the prasada in the fire from which emerged a beautiful woman. A voice was heard from the sky, "This woman has taken birth to become the cause of destruction of those who are evil." The woman came to be known as Draupadi after her father Drupada and the warrior was called Dhrishtadyumna.

Parashurama

Parshurama, the sixth avatar of Vishnu, had a violent temper. On hearing about Rama breaking the bow at Sita's swayamvara, he became furious. Being a proud Brahmin priest, he disliked the idea of 'Kshatriya,' a man belonging to the warrior class, emerging victorious. He decided to meet Rama and challenge him. Wielding his famous axe, Parashurama promptly attacked Rama. Rama, on the other hand, countered it with his kondanda bow, and a fierce battle ensued.

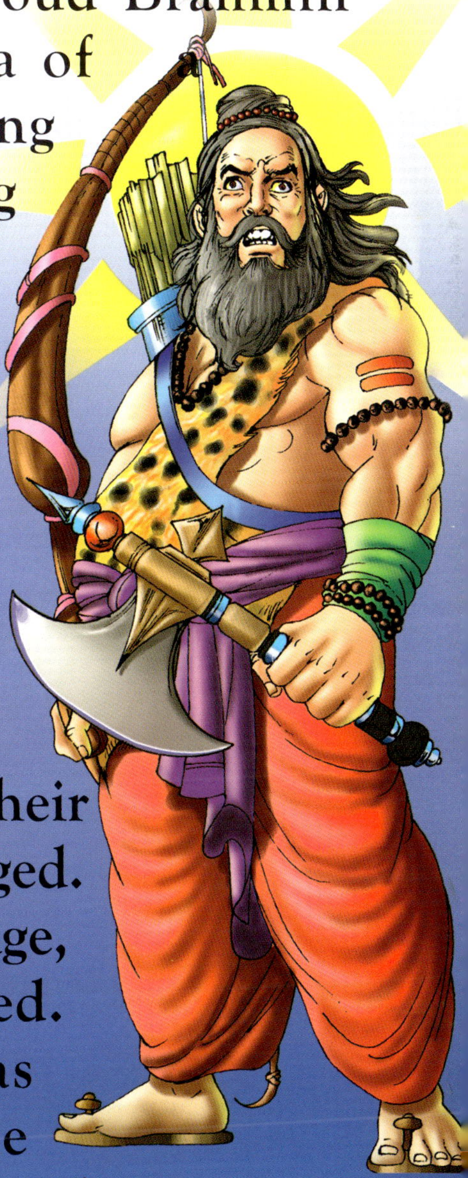

While the battle continued, their eyes met and everything changed. There was love in place of rage, and respect instead of hatred. Recognizing each other as different forms of the same supreme Vishnu, they threw their weapons and embraced each other.

The Great Teacher

One day as the princes of Hastinapur were playing together, their ball fell into a well. Then a ring, too, fell into the well. The princes peered into the well wondering how to retrieve them.

Drona, standing nearby, said, “It is a shame that princes like you are not able to do such a small task.” He picked up a blade of grass and shot it at the ball in the well. The blade got stuck to the ball. Then he shot another blade, which stuck to the end of the first blade. In this way, he made a chain of grass blades, reaching the top of the well.

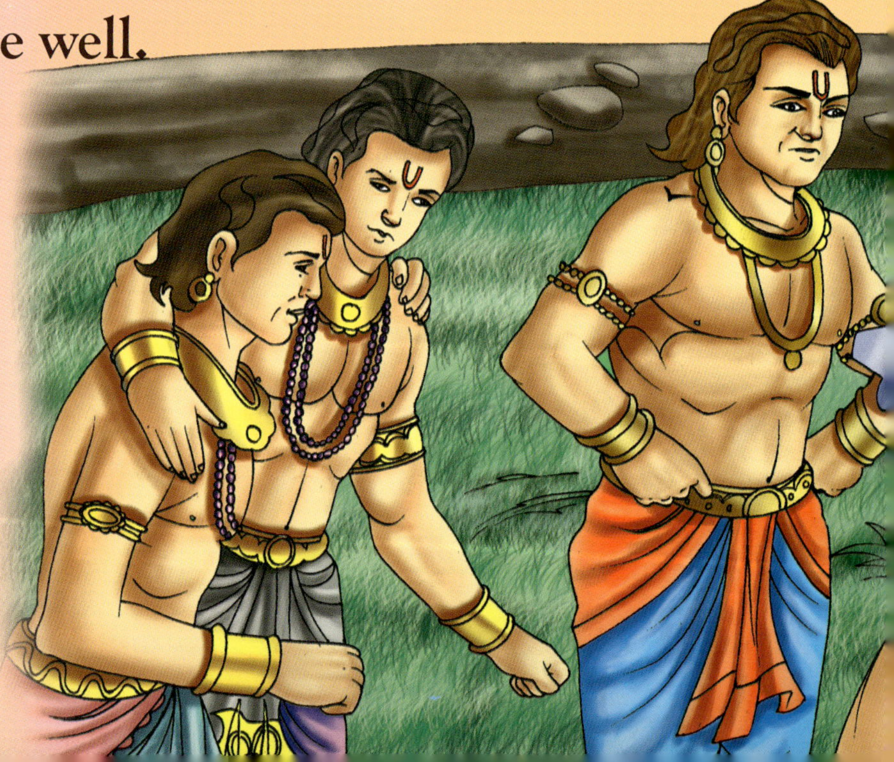

He then pulled out the ball with it. Then he shot an arrow at the ring in the well. The arrow sprung back, and brought the ring with it. The princes were amazed. They related the incident to their great grand uncle, Bhishma.

Bhishma felt that Drona was skilled enough to teach the princes archery and warfare and later made him the princes' teacher.

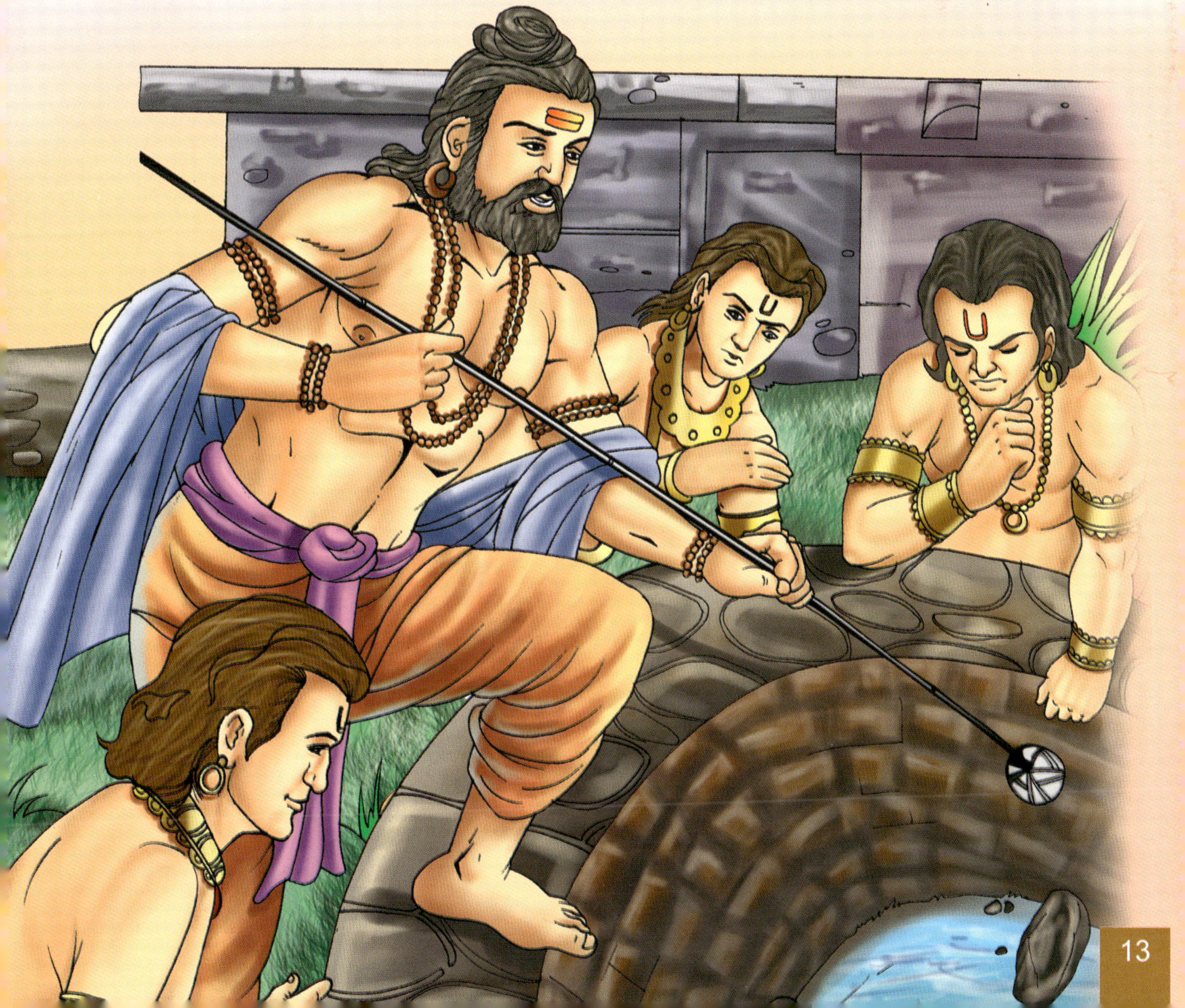

Bharata, the Ideal Brother

Hearing about Rama's exile because of his own mother, Bharata left for Dandaka forest with an entourage to find Rama. There he fell at Rama's feet and begged forgiveness for his mother's behaviour and informed Rama about their father's death. The news greatly saddened Rama, Lakshmana, and Sita. Bharata then pleaded, "Please accept the throne which lies empty without you." Rama answered, "I am only fulfilling our father's wish." Realizing that Rama would not return to Ayodhya, Bharata asked Rama to give his sandals to him. "I shall place them on the throne and serve them faithfully till you return." Rama gave Bharata his sandals and they were placed on the throne till Rama's return.

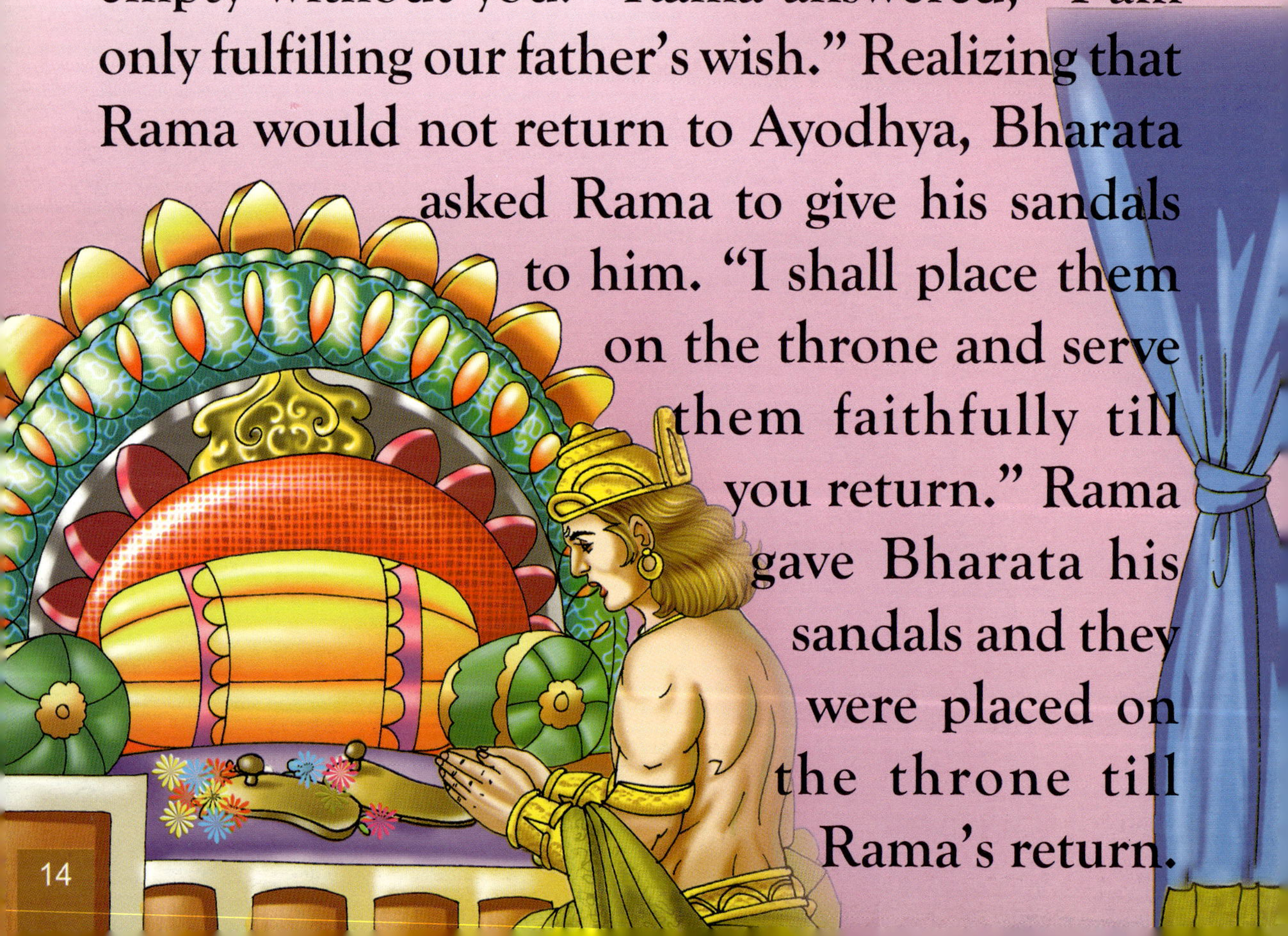

Poison Kills Poison

One day, Duryodhana, the eldest Kaurava with the help of his uncle Shakuni, made a devious plan to kill his cousin Bhima. He invited Bhima for a picnic near the bank of river Ganga. Duryodhana had poisoned some of the laddoos that were served and offered them to Bhima, who loved food. As soon as Bhima ate them, he fainted. Duryodhana pushed him into the river. In the river, many poisonous snakes bit Bhima. It is said that 'poison kills poison.' The poison from the snakes counteracted the effect of the poison from the laddoos. Thus Bhima was saved.

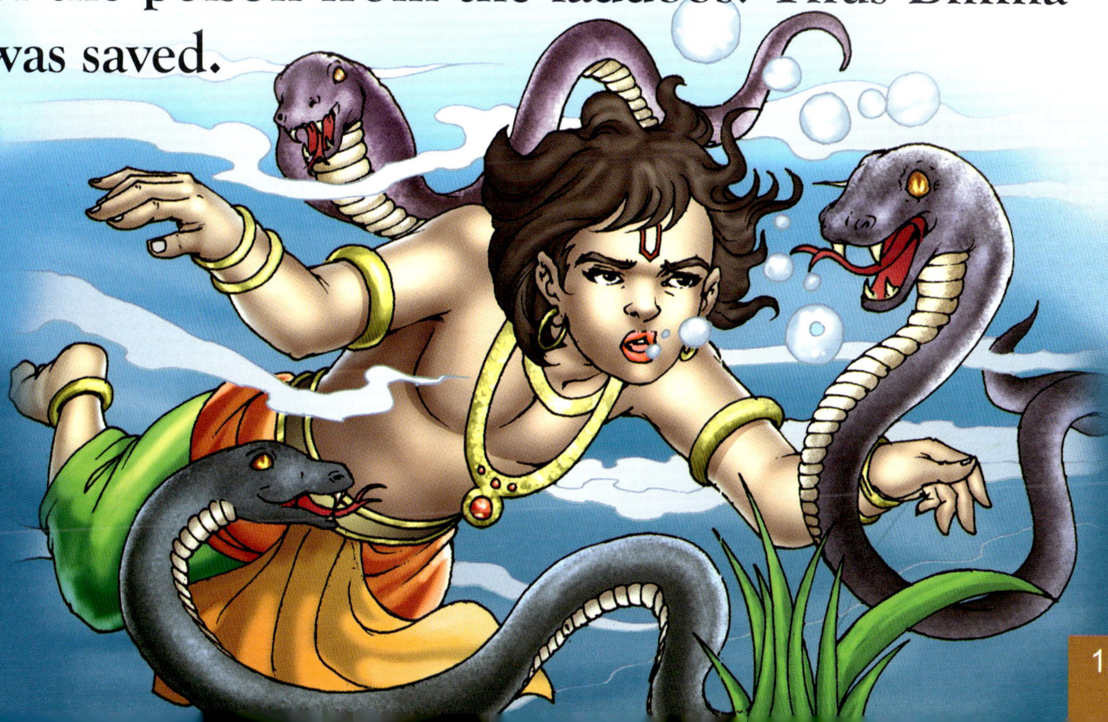

Viradha & Rama

In the forest, Rama along with Sita and Lakshmana chanced upon a man-eating monster called Viradha.

The monster lifted Sita in an attempt to abduct her.

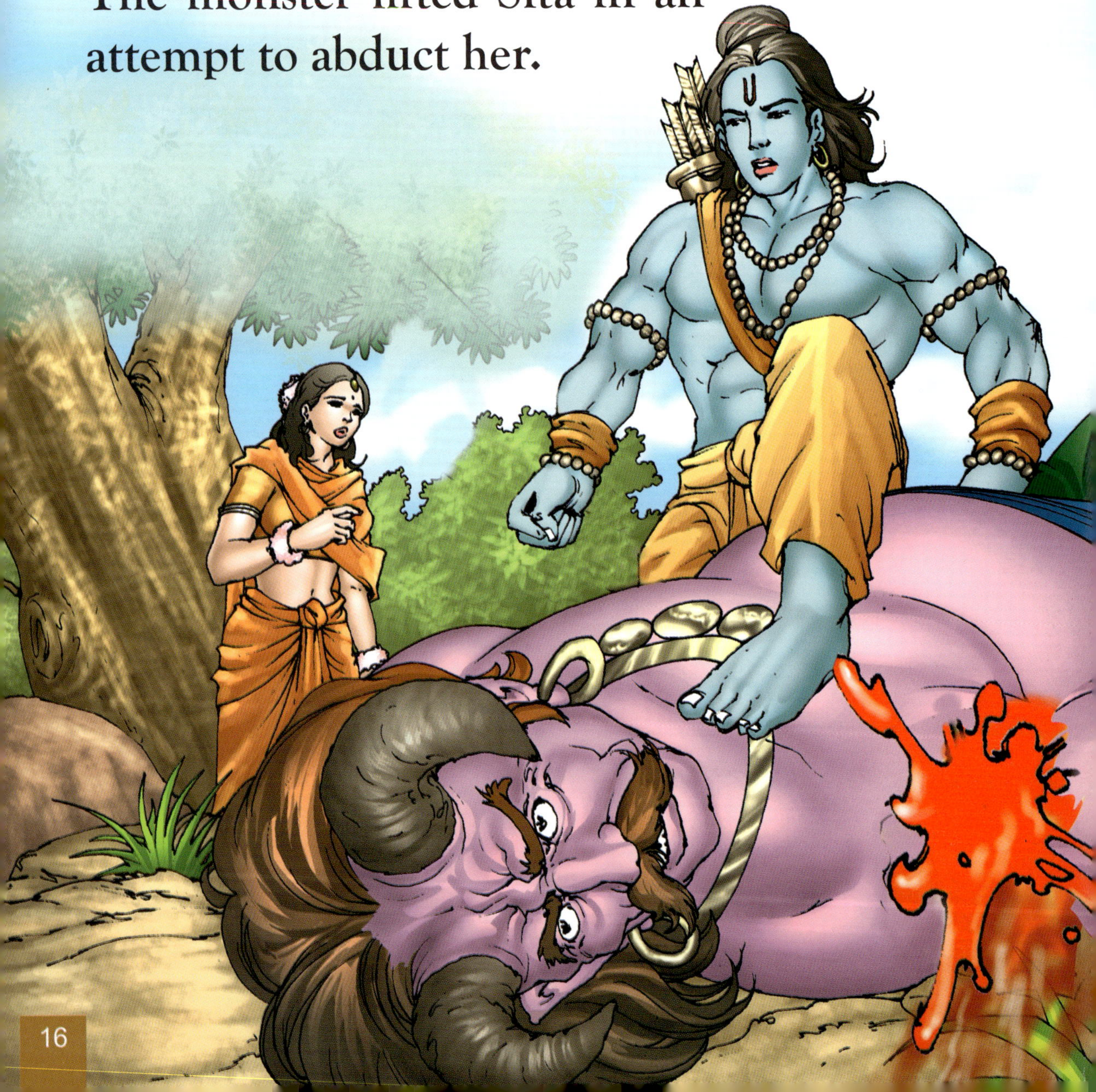

Realizing the futility of using bows, Rama and Lakshmana, with great gusto wrenched off Viradha's arms and threw him on the ground. Rama immediately planted his foot on Viradha. The touch had a wondrous effect. Viradha's eyes softened, and with folded hands

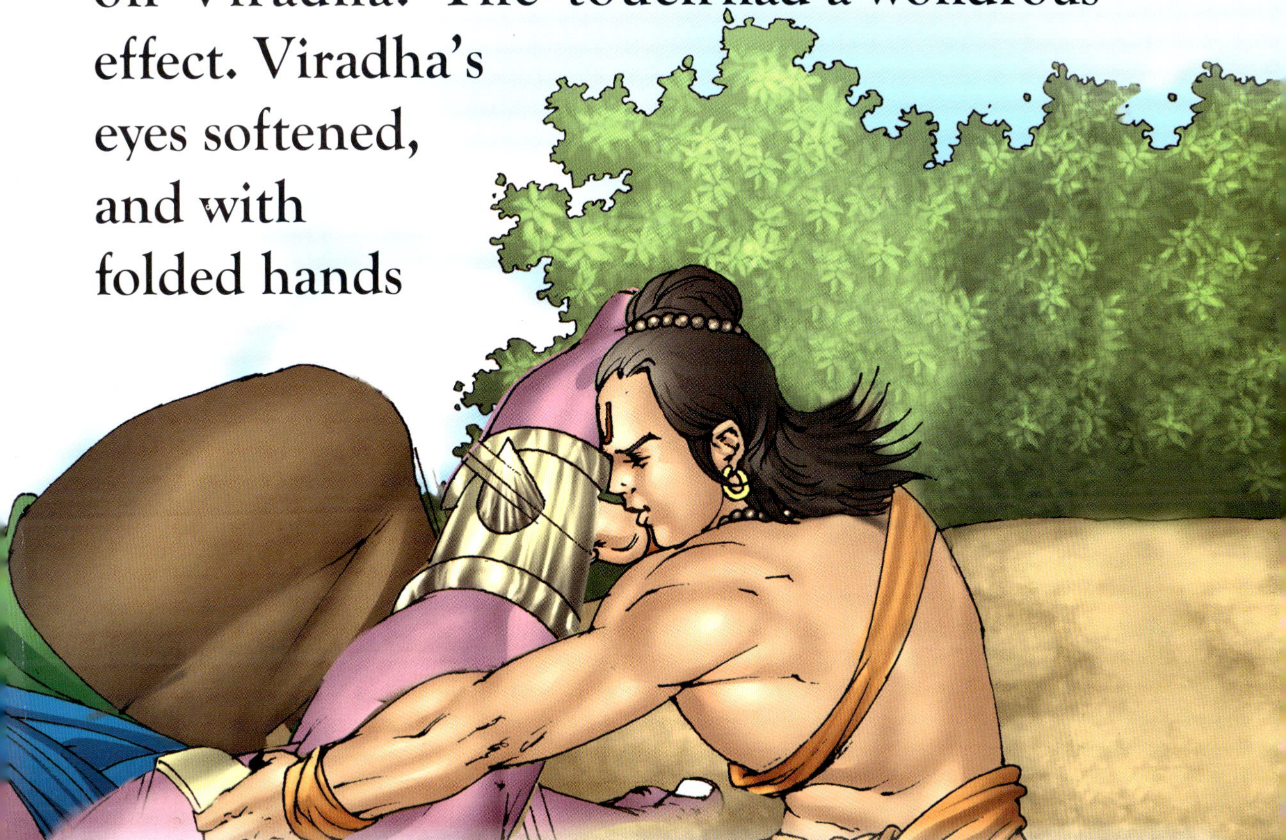

he said, "Your touch has purified me. I am a gandharva (nature spirit), and not a monster. Please kill me and relieve me of my curse." Accepting Viradha's request, Rama killed him. The monster's body then changed into a gandharva and soared up to the skies.

Jatayu

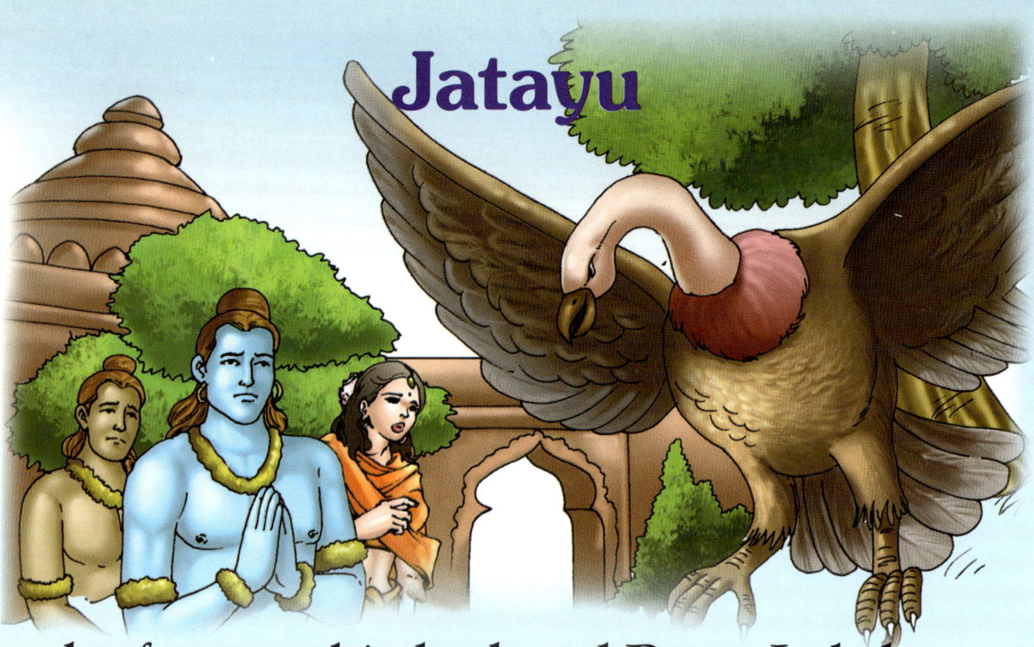

In the forest, a bird saluted Ram, Lakshmana, Sita and said, "I am Jatayu, King Dasharatha's friend." Jatayu told them that he had protected Dasharatha during a battle with a fierce enemy. Rama welcomed his father's saviour. Jatayu then mentioned that he was the grandson of Sage Kashyap and his father Arun, was the charioteer of the Sun God, Surya. He also narrated how his elder brother Sampati had burnt his wings while trying to save him from soaring towards the sun. Jatayu had come to the forest of Panchavati where he was entrusted with the kingship of vultures. Jatayu then promised Rama to protect them with all his might.

Bhima & Hidimba

Once, the Pandus were in the forest when a she demon, Hidimba, spotted them. As soon as Hidimba saw the handsome Bhima, she fell in love.

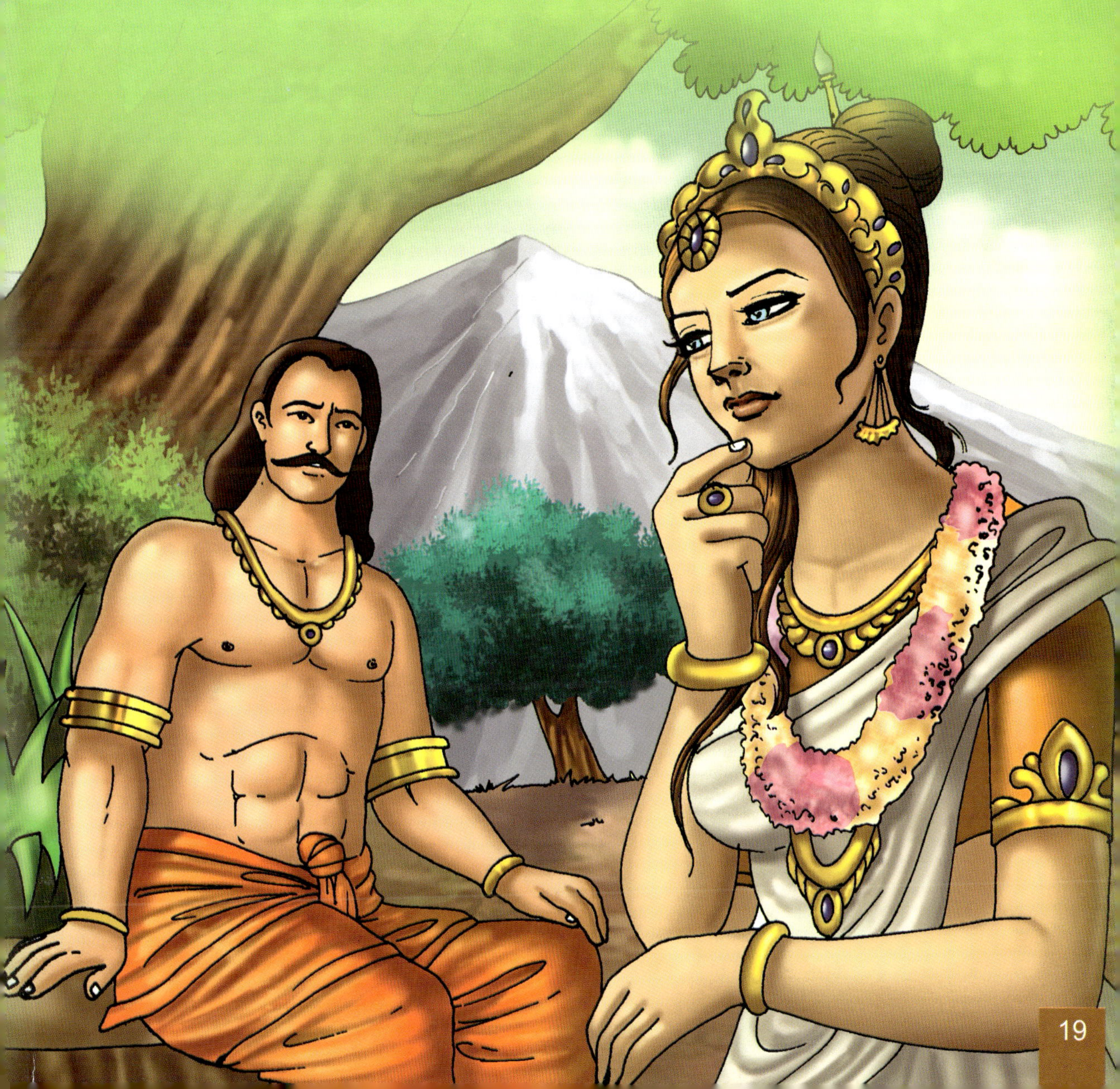

Assuming the form of a beautiful woman, she said, "I am Hidimba, my brother is a demon, he will eat all of you." Bhima smiled and replied, "Don't worry, I am strong enough to defeat your brother."

When Hidimba did not return, Hidimb, her brother, went looking for her. He saw her talking to Bhima. He shouted furiously, "I sent you to kill the human and you are talking to him. I will kill him myself." Saying so, he attacked Bhima. A fierce fight ensued and ended with Bhima killing Hidimb. Later Bhim married her. Soon Hidimba gave birth to a son named Ghatotkacha.

As time passed, the Pandavas decided to leave the forest. They took leave of Hidimba and Ghatotkacha, who had grown up to be a strong

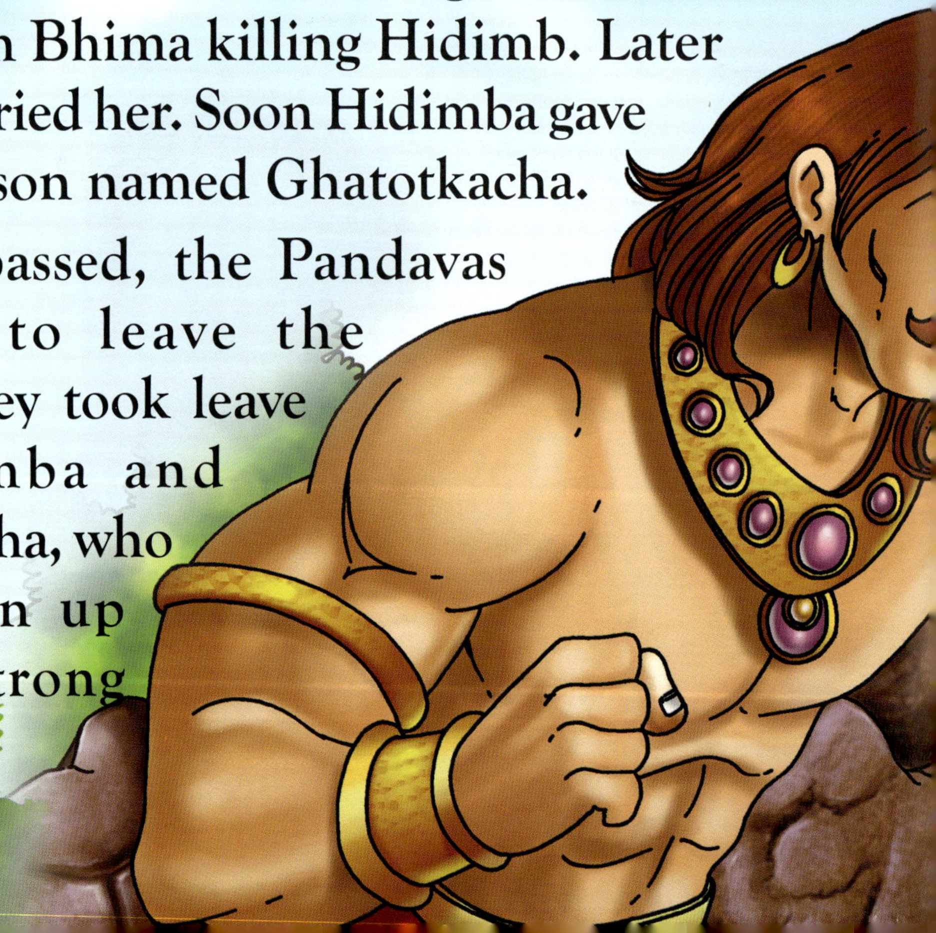

boy. Ghatotkacha promised the Pandavas that he would come to them, whenever they needed him.

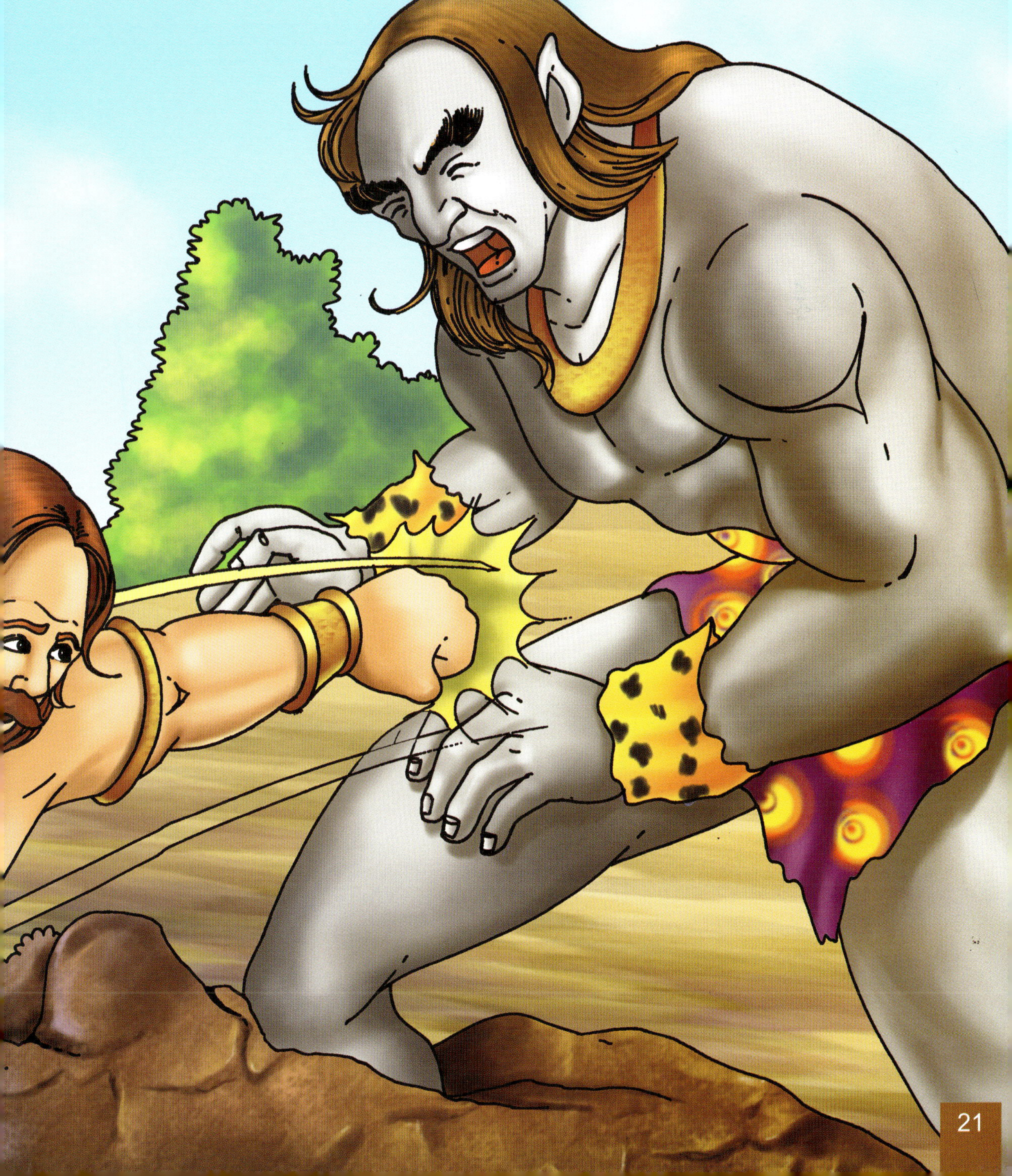

Shurpanakha

Shurpanakha, Ravana's sister fell in love with Rama.

Shurpanakha was very ugly and in order to attract Rama, she transformed herself into a beautiful maiden and approached him saying, "I am Shurpanakha, I want to be your wife." He refused saying that he was already married.

Shurpanakha then spotted Lakshmana and she

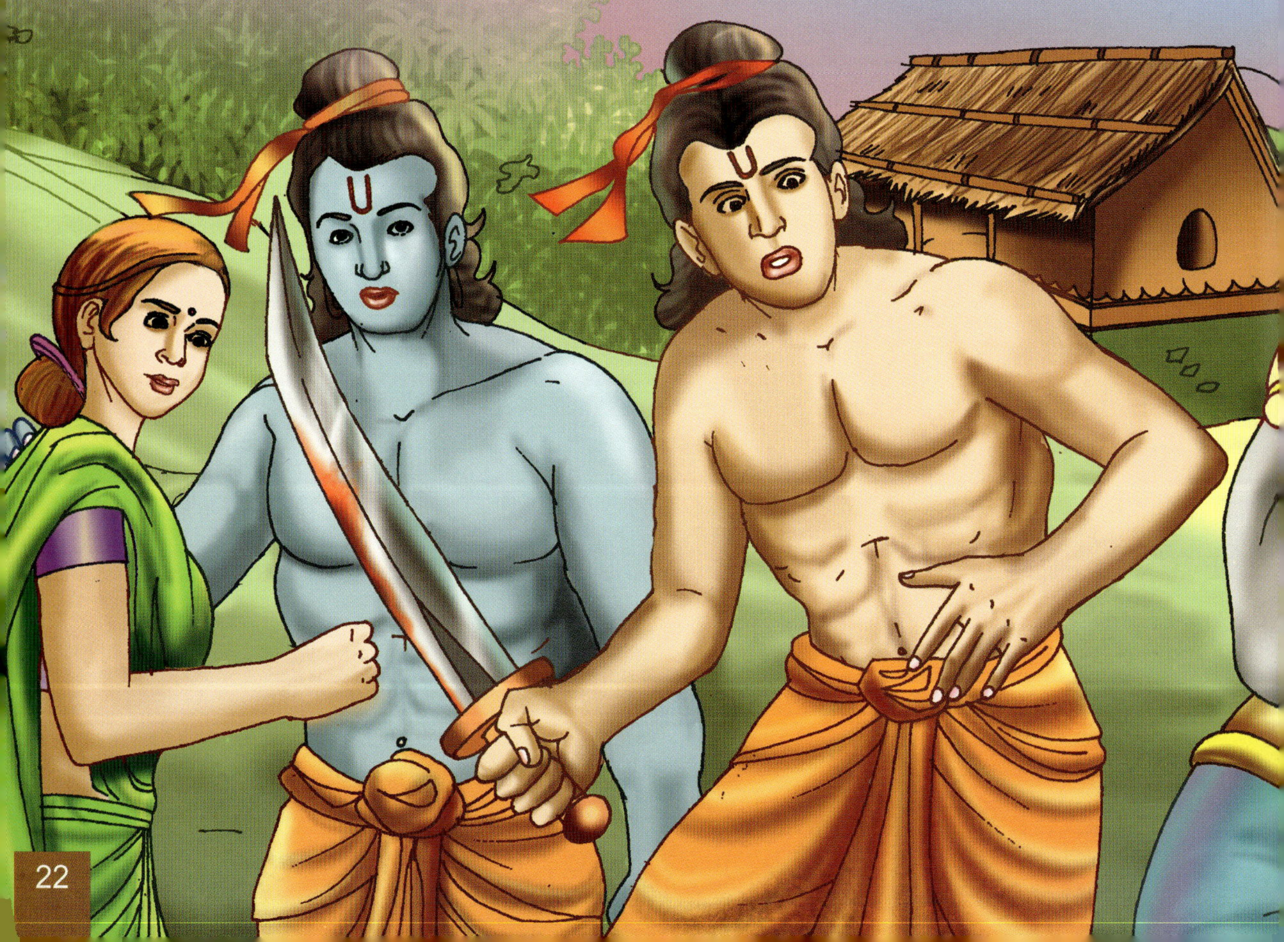

asked Lakshmana to marry her. Lakshmana also rejected her offer.

Unable to bear this insult, Shurpanakha, assuming her true form of a demoness, attacked Sita. This angered Lakshmana and he took a sword and cut off Shurpanakha's nose.

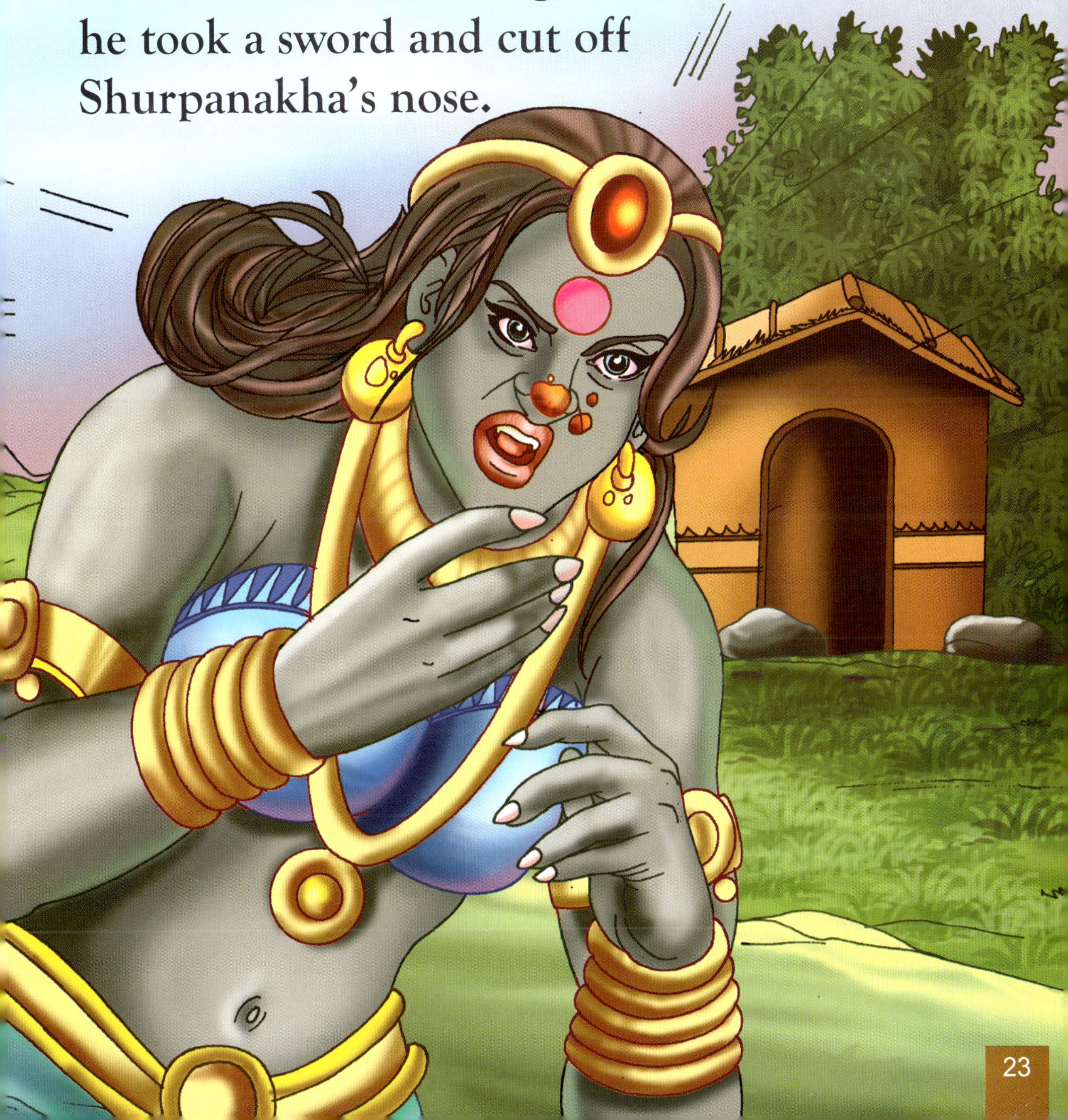

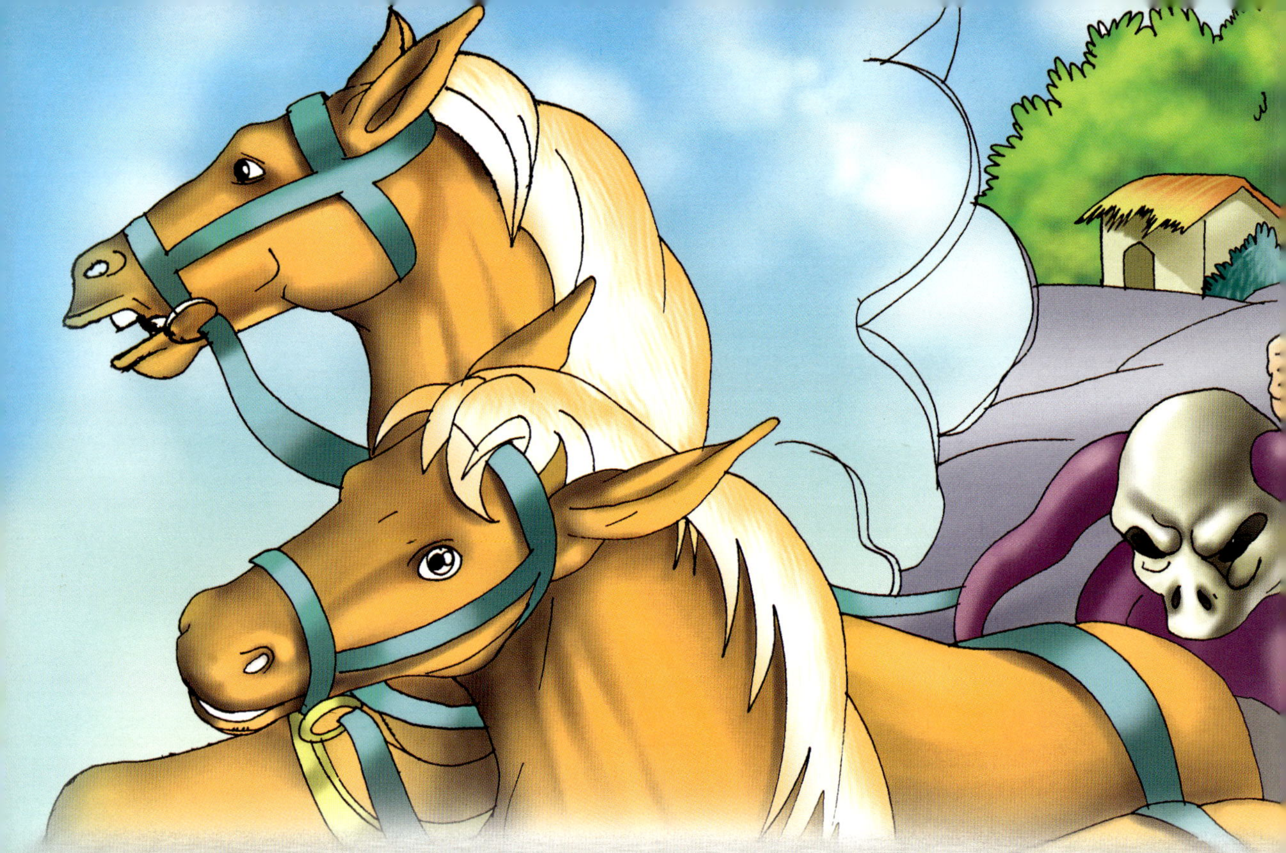

Jatayu Fights Ravana

When Ravana was taking Sita away to Lanka in his flying chariot, Jatayu, the wise old bird, was resting in the forest. Hearing Sita's helpless screams, Jatayu flew to Ravana's chariot.

Being a great devotee of Rama, Jatayu challenged Ravana's strength, fully aware that he would get killed by obstructing Ravana's path. Jatayu decided to save Sita from the clutches of Ravana at any cost.

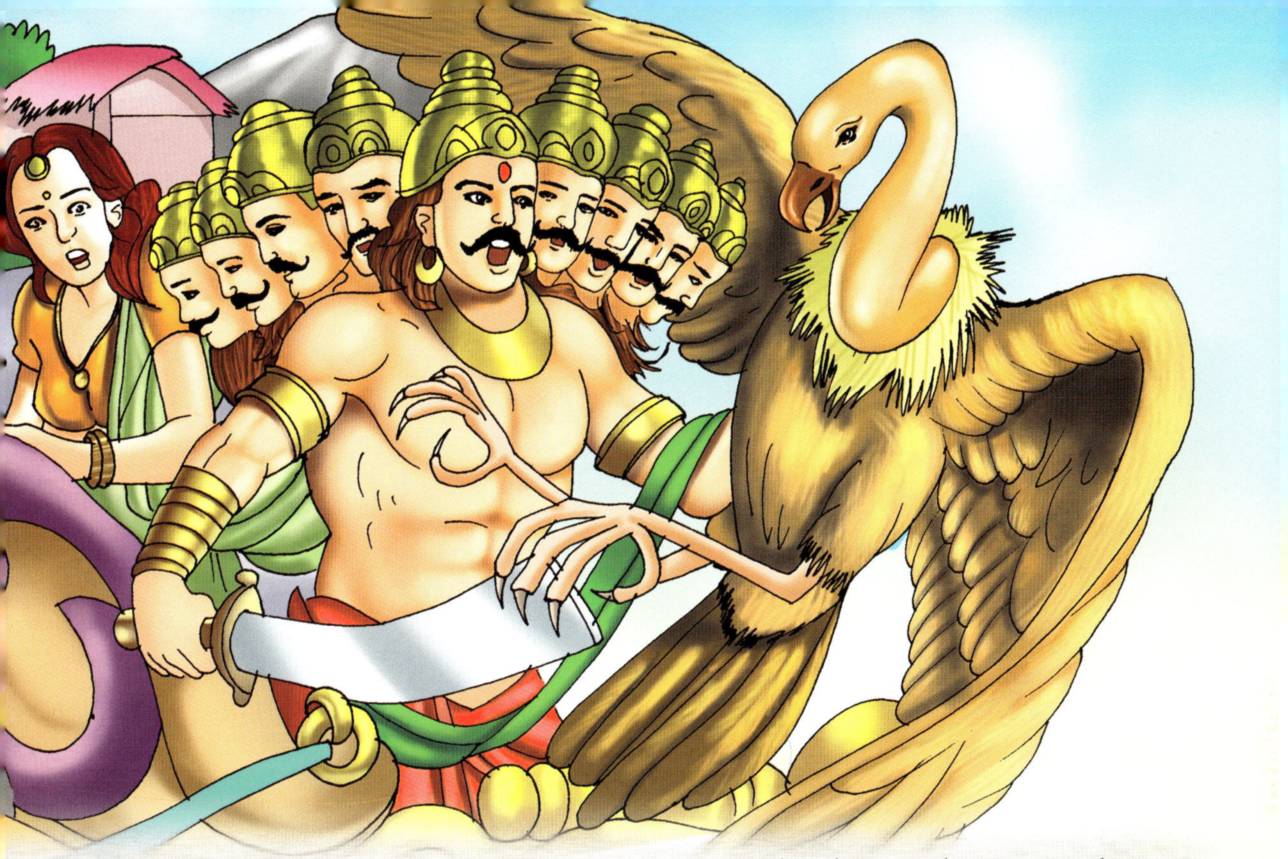

Jatayu attacked Ravana with his sharp claws and hooked beak.

Ravana took out his diamond-studded arrow and fired at Jatayu's wings. As the arrow hit, one frail wing tore off and fell, but the brave bird continued fighting. With his other wing, he bruised Ravana's face and tried to pull Sita from the chariot. The fight continued till Jatayu was bleeding from the wounds all over his body.

Finally, Ravana took out his sword and struck Jatayu's other wing. As it hit, the bird fell on the ground, bruised and battered.

Jatayu Helps Rama

Rama and Lakshman were anxiously searching through the forests, for Sita, who was missing. That is when they chanced upon the injured bird, Jatayu. Writhing in pain, the bird just managed to tell them about Sita's abduction and pointed to the direction in which Ravana had gone. With folded wings, he bid farewell and breathed his last.

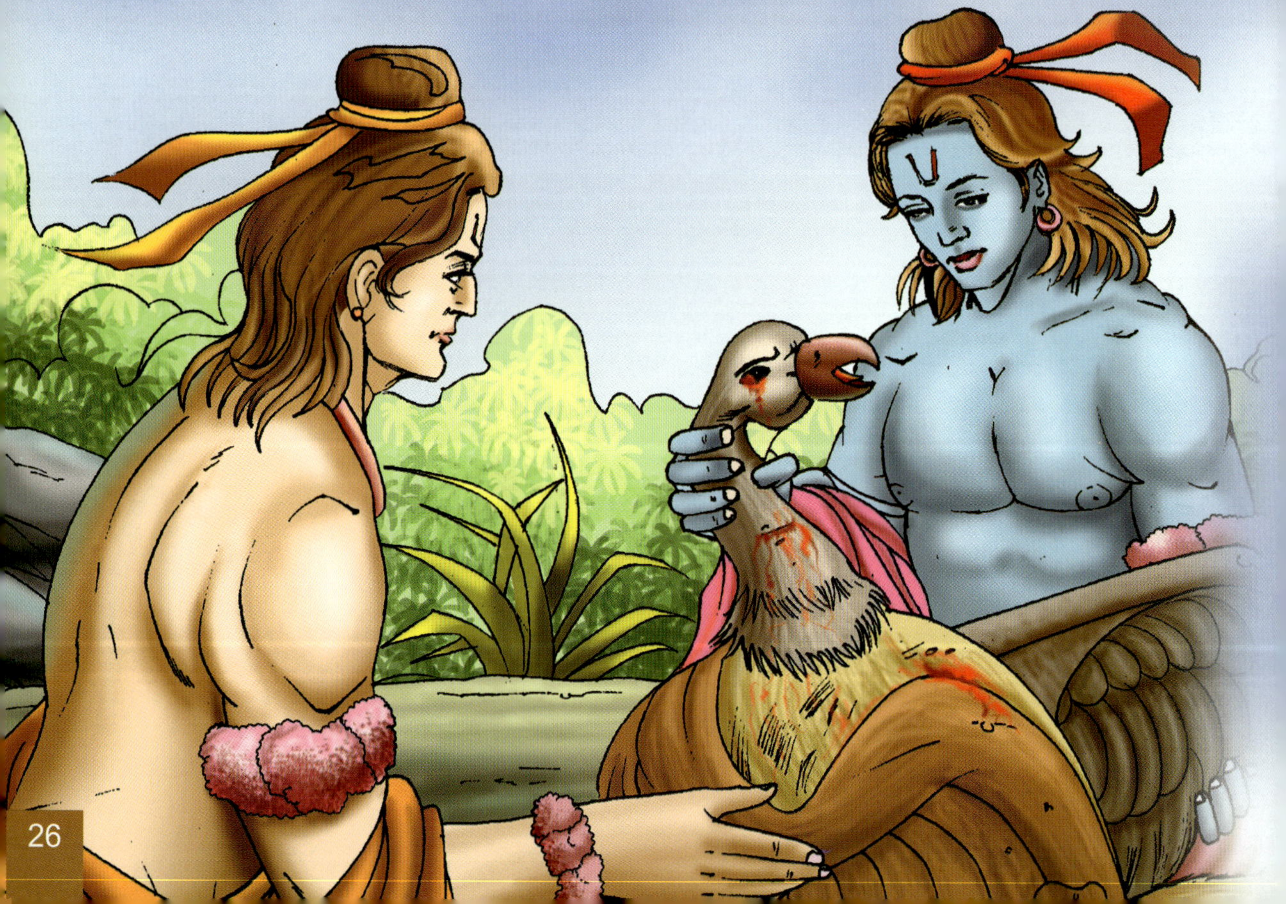

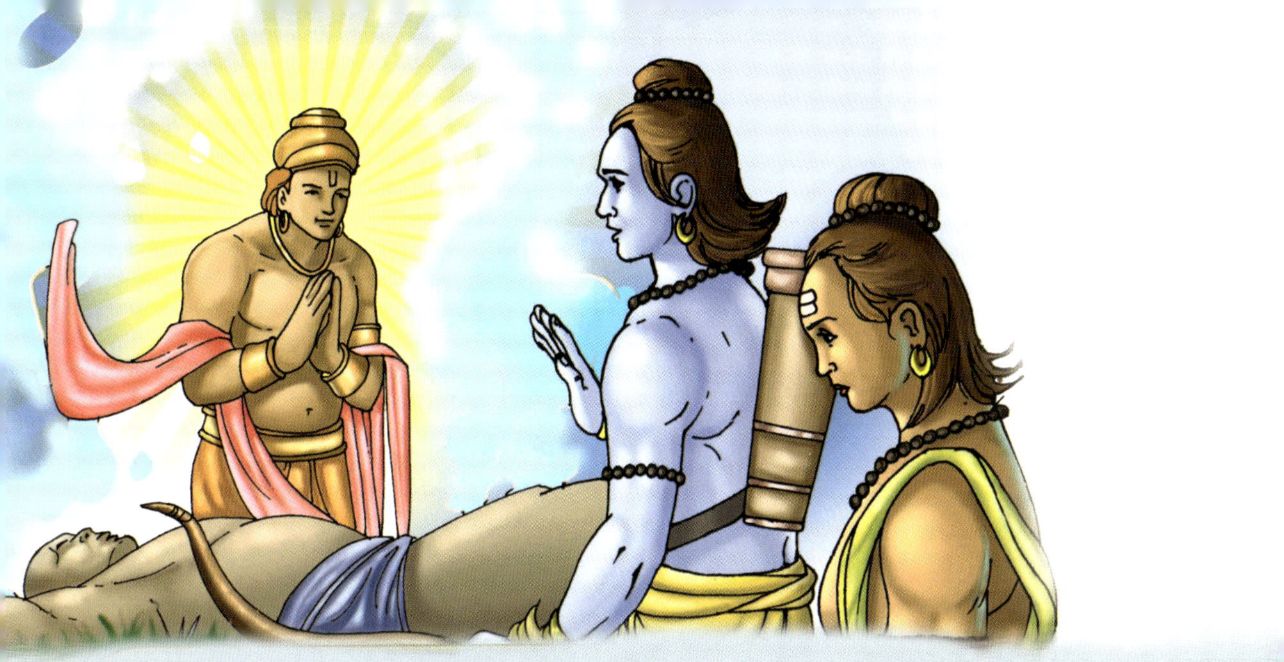

Kabandha Meeta Rama

While searching for Sita, Rama and Lakshmana saw a ferocious demon in the forest named Kabandha.

The hungry demon caught hold of them and was about to devour them, when the brothers fired arrows and cut off his arms. Dying Kabandha bowed in reverence and told them his story. "Brahma had cursed me to change into a demon for my misdeeds and only if Rama would kill me would I get back to my earlier form." Kabandha then begged Rama to end his life. As his body burnt to ashes a beautiful figure emerged from it.

Bhima and Kichaka

The Pandavas along with Draupadi were serving as help in the palace of Viratnagar, disguising their true identities; fulfilling the condition of the bet they had lost to Duryodhana. Draupadi was living in Viratnagar as the Queen's maid. Kichaka was the Queen's brother.

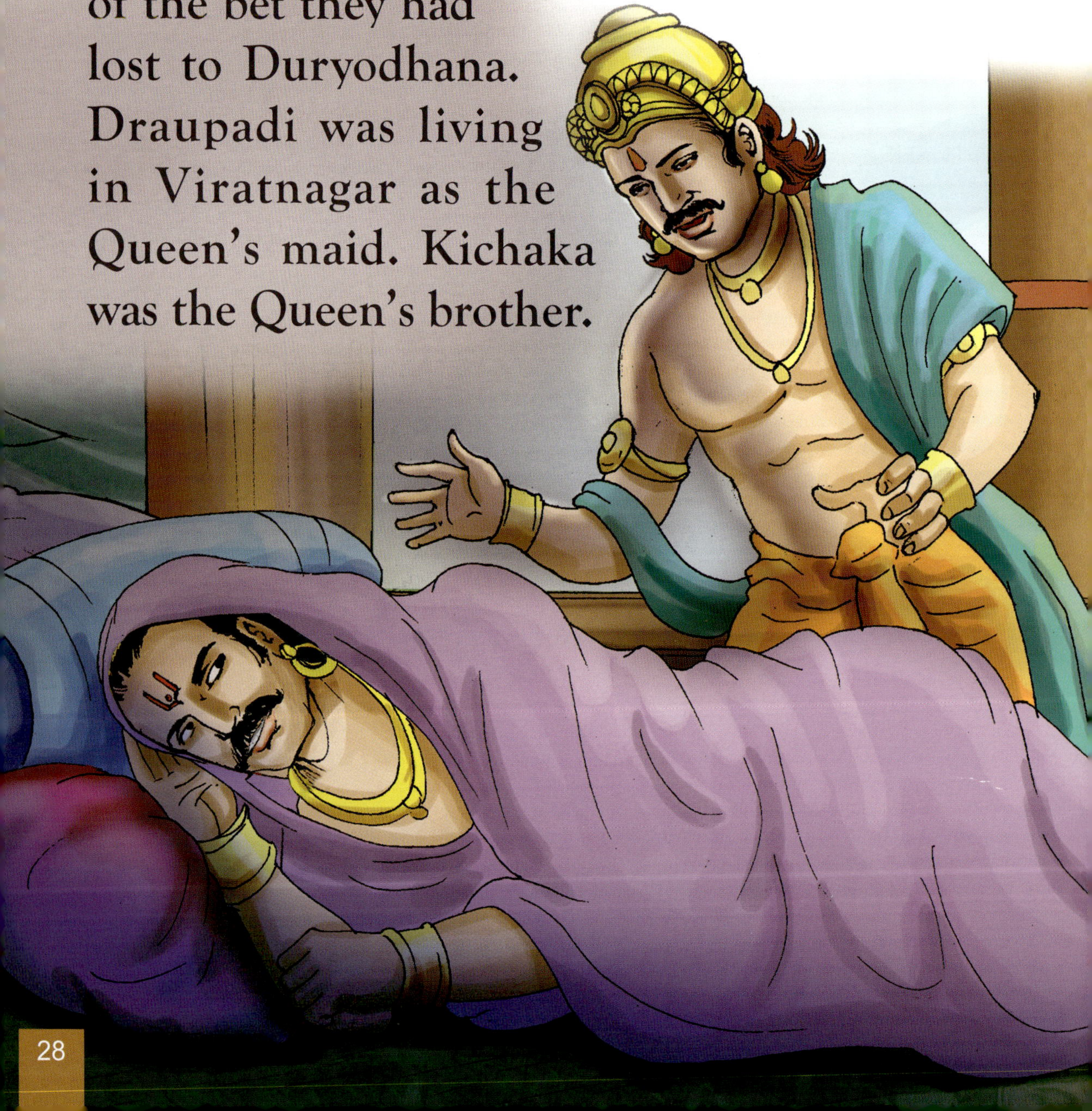

One day, Kichaka saw Draupadi and fell in love with her, and seeing she was one of the Queen's maids, offered to marry her. Draupadi warned, "Do not trouble me." Angered by her boldness, Kichaka dragged her to the king's court. He kicked and insulted her. Crying Draupadi rushed to Bhima, who was working as the royal cook and asked him to kill Kichaka. In the darkness of the night, Kichaka approached an apparently sleeping Draupadi. But to his dismay, the blanket fell off and it was revealed that the unknown person was none other than Bhima! Bhima jumped up, overpowered him and killed him. The news of the death of Kichaka, who was a great warrior, spread like fire. Eventually, Duryodhana came to know about it and realized that the Pandavas who were thought to be in hiding were in Viratnagar.

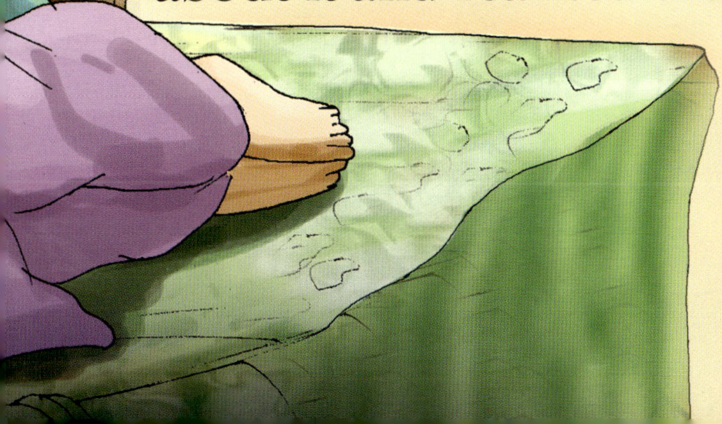

Bali and Sugreeva

The son of Indra, Bali, was the monkey king of Kishkindha. His younger brother was Sugreeva. The kingdom had a sworn enemy called Manyavi. Tired of the demon's attack, Bali decided to settle the score. When Bali and Manyavi entered a cave during their fight, Sugreeva was ordered to keep a watch outside till Bali emerged victorious.

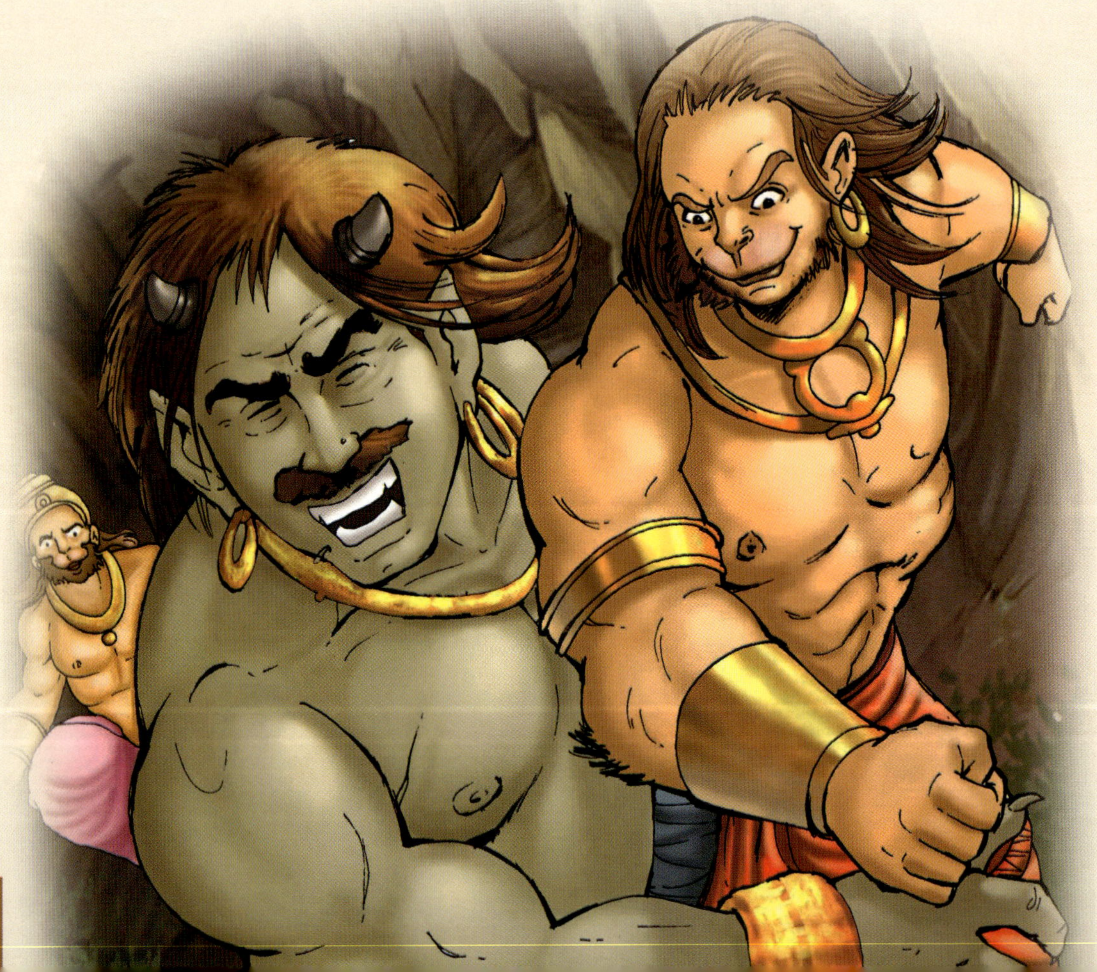

Time passed and after nearly a year's wait when neither Bali nor the demon came out, Sugreeva assumed both were dead. Sugreeva went back and crowned himself the king. However, Bali returned and seeing Sugreeva as king, felt betrayed. Though Sugreeva tried to explain the misunderstanding, Bali attacked him, forcing him and his team of monkeys to flee Kishkindha. Bali regained his kingship but became Sugreeva's enemy forever.

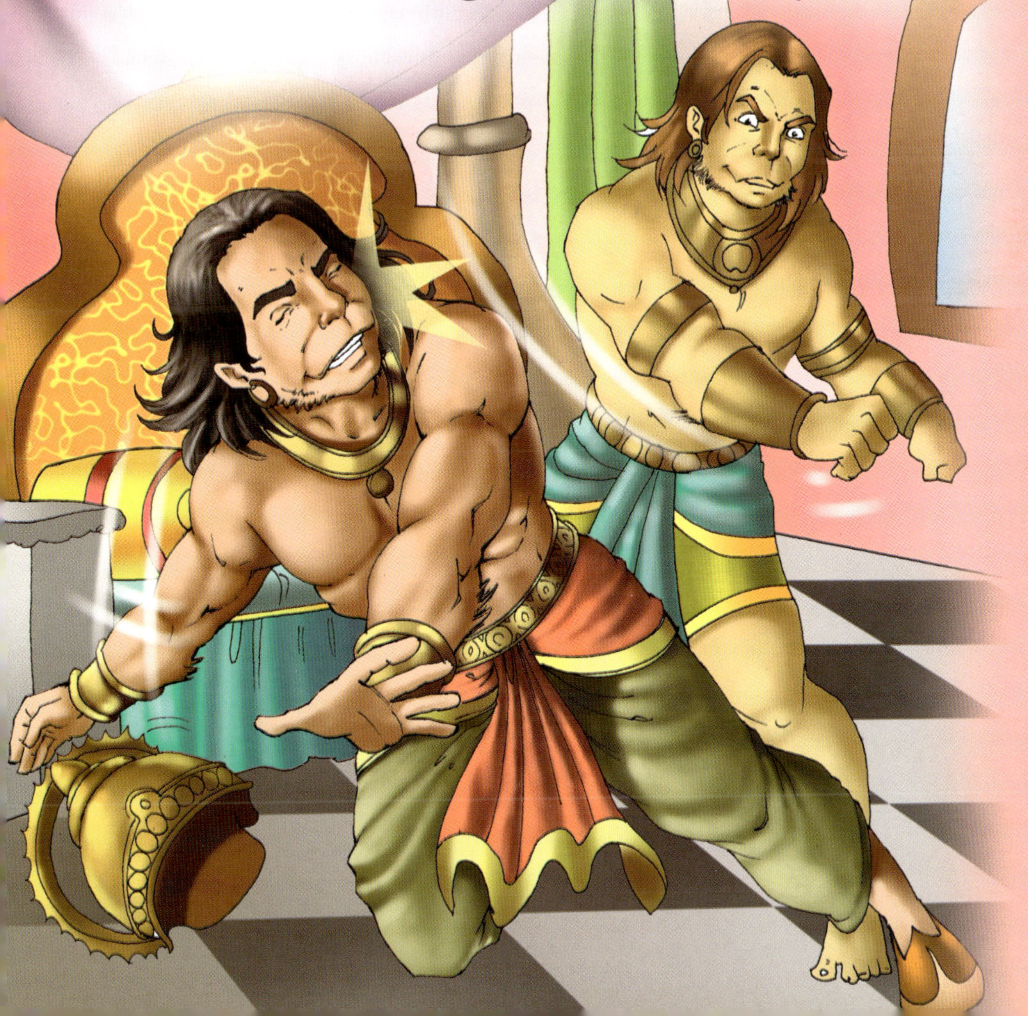

Arjuna's Prey

During the Pandavas' exile, Arjuna went to Mount Kailash to pray to Shiva for divine weapons. Just then, a demon, Mooka, attacked Arjuna in the form of a wild boar. Arjuna shot an arrow which struck the boar. But he saw another arrow in the body of the boar. He said, "Who dare shoot my prey?" Shiva, in the hunter's form, said, "I shot the

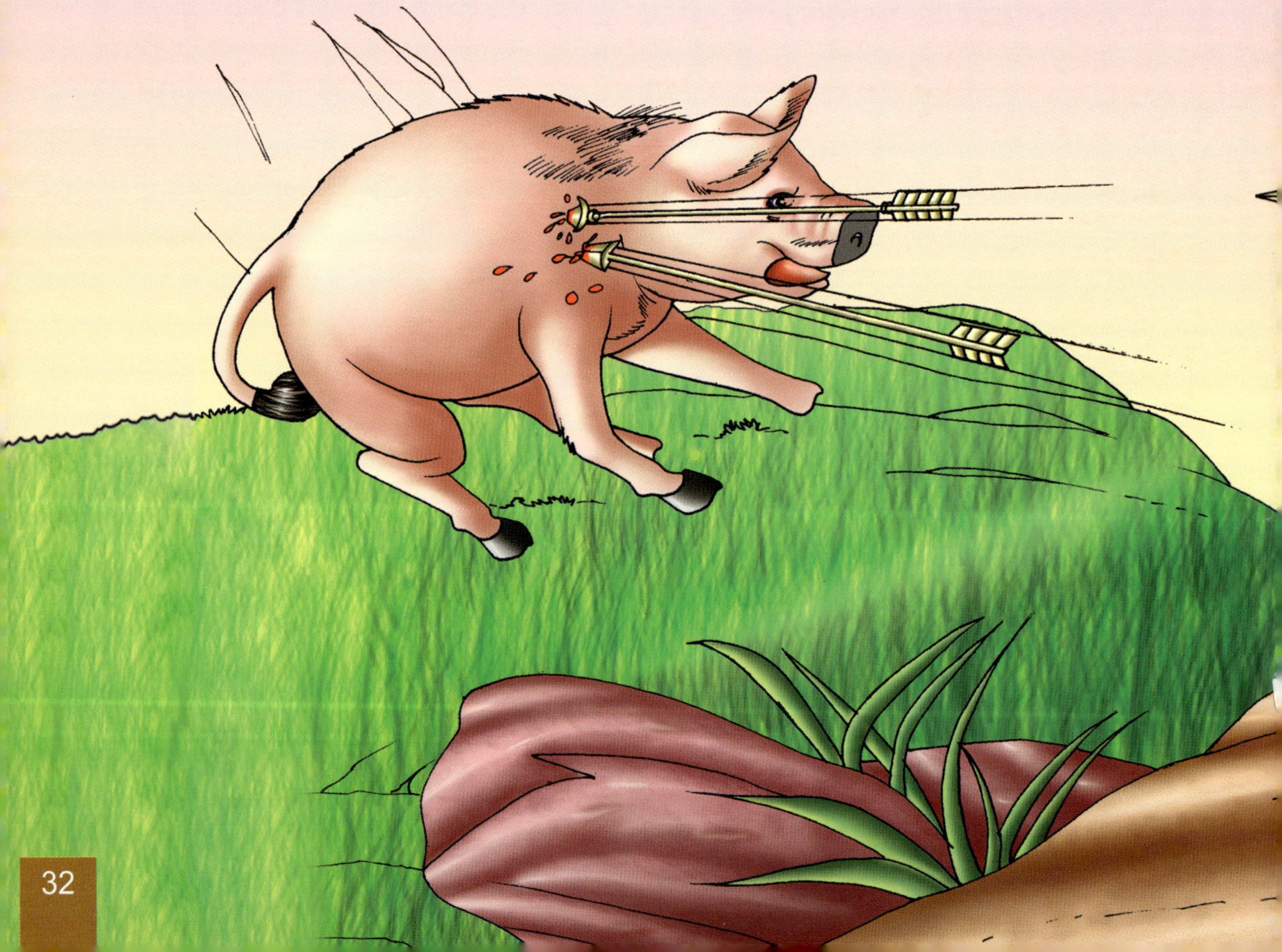

arrow. This is my prey." A long fight ensued between the two and Arjuna grew tired. "I will fight after my prayers," said Arjuna. Arjuna made a Shivalinga and put a garland around it. But suddenly found the garland around the hunter's neck. Arjuna understood that the hunter was Shiva. He fell at the hunter's feet. Shiva assumed his real form and bestowed upon him the divine weapon, the Pashupatastra.

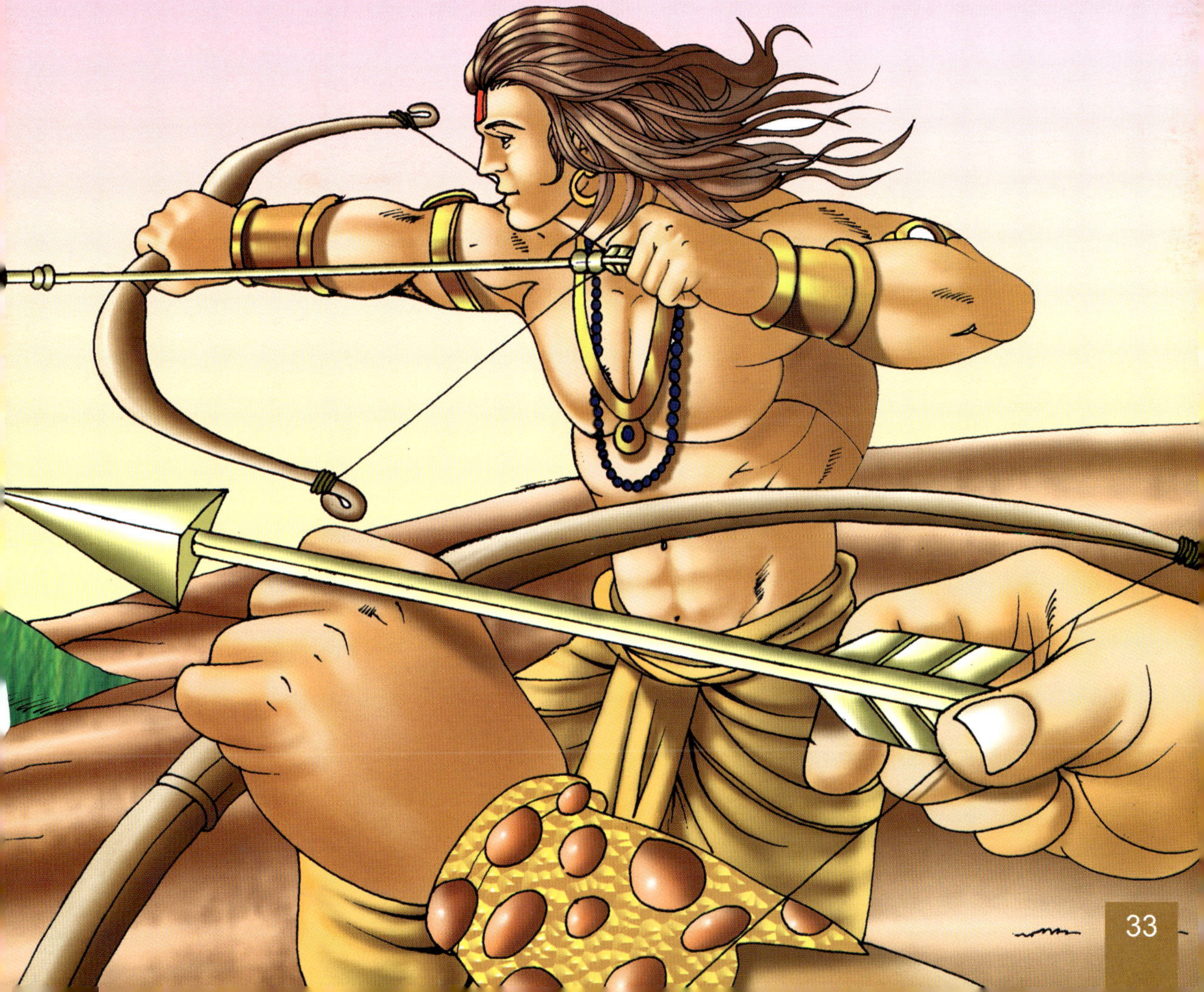

Curse on Bali

Bali had killed a demon named Dundubhi. Sugreeva showed Rama the demon's carcass and told Rama the reason about making Rishyamooka his hiding spot.

He informed Rama that the famous Sage Matanga lived in the Rishyamooka mountains. When Bali had swung the battered body of Dundubhi from Kishkindha, it fell inside the Sage's ashram.

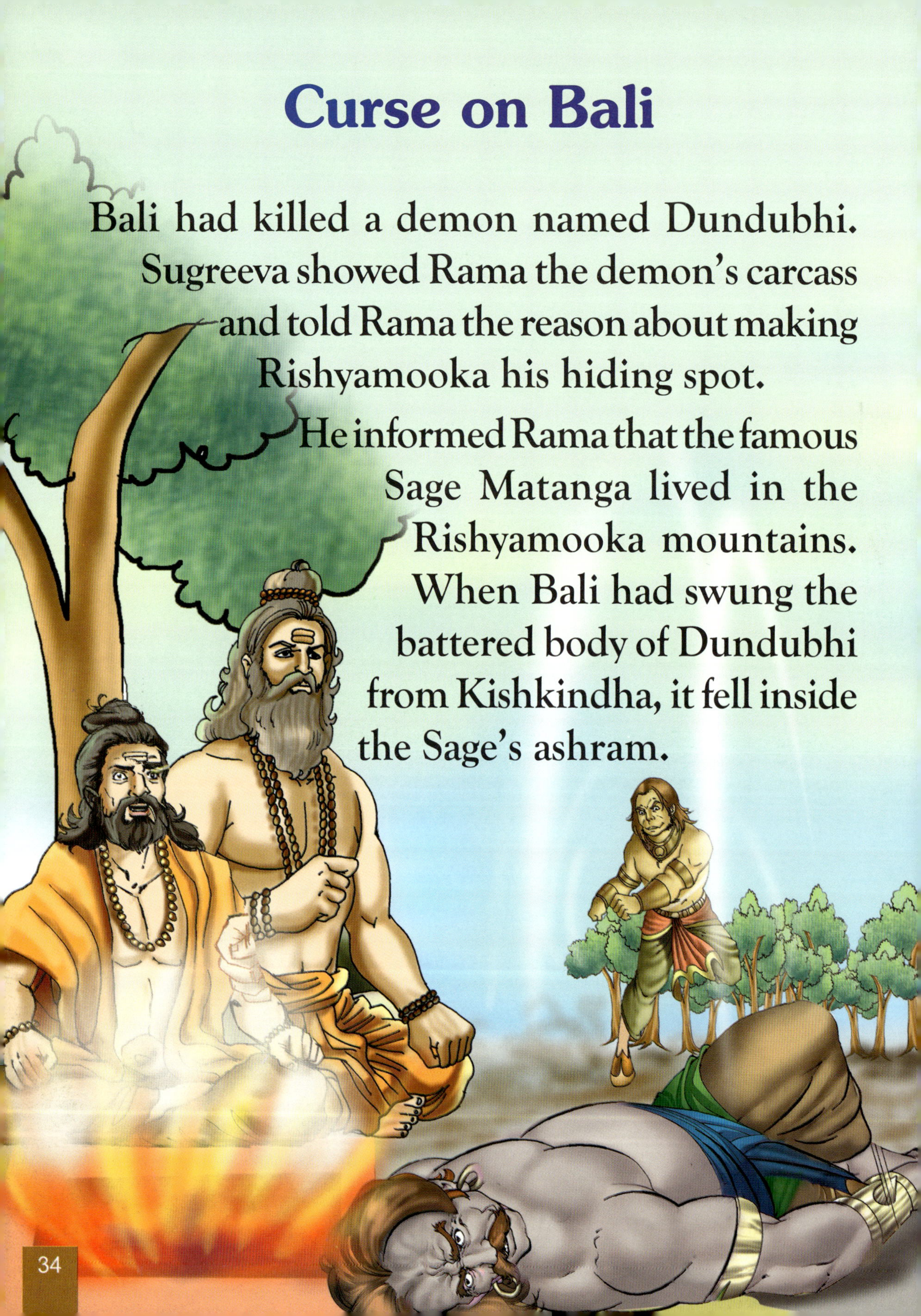

The sage was enraged ! Sage Matanga roared, "Who dares to tarnish my ashram with a blood-smeared corpse?" When no answer came, he sat down in deep meditation and discovered Bali's name. In a fury, the sage cursed Bali and his men to be destroyed if they ever entered the forests of Rishyamooka. Sugreeva thus added that because Bali would hunt him down wherever he went, he took shelter in these forests knowing that Bali could not enter it.

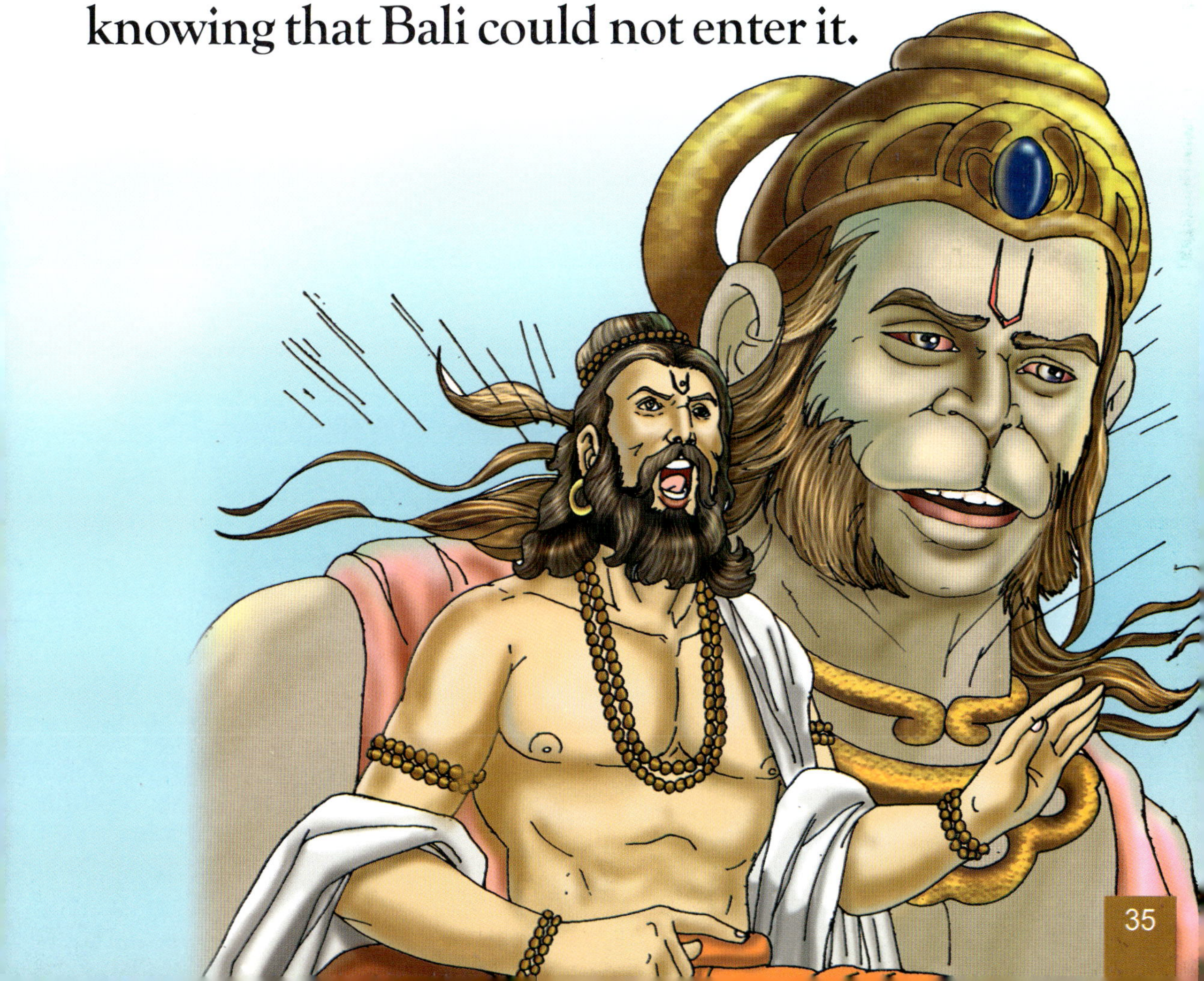

Hanuman Crosses the Sea

The vulture Sampati, Jatayu's older brother spotted Sita under the Ashoka tree in Lanka. The monkeys decided to immediately start for Lanka, but a problem arose.

Who would fly across the huge ocean?

The monkeys reminded Hanuman of his strengths.

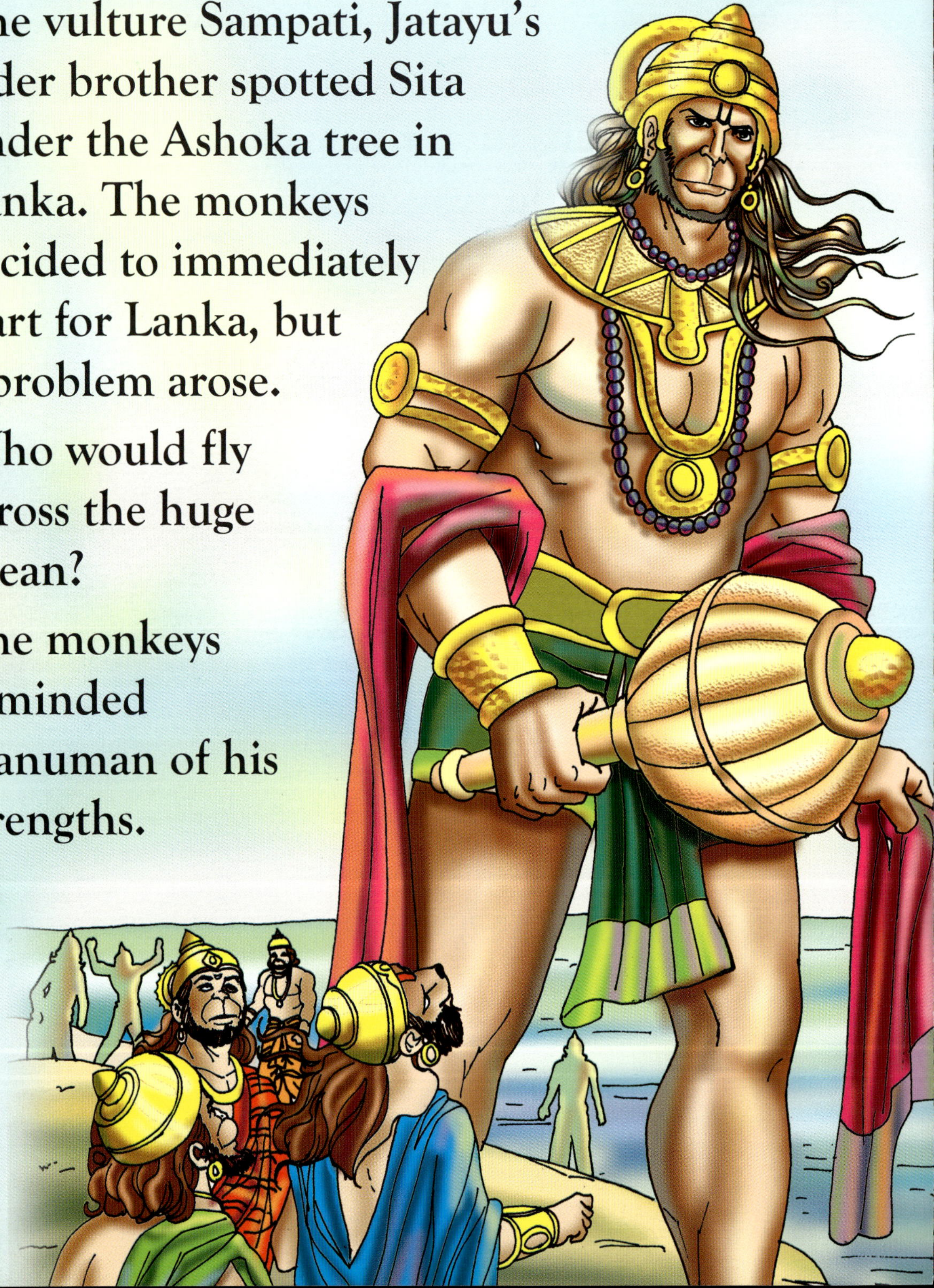

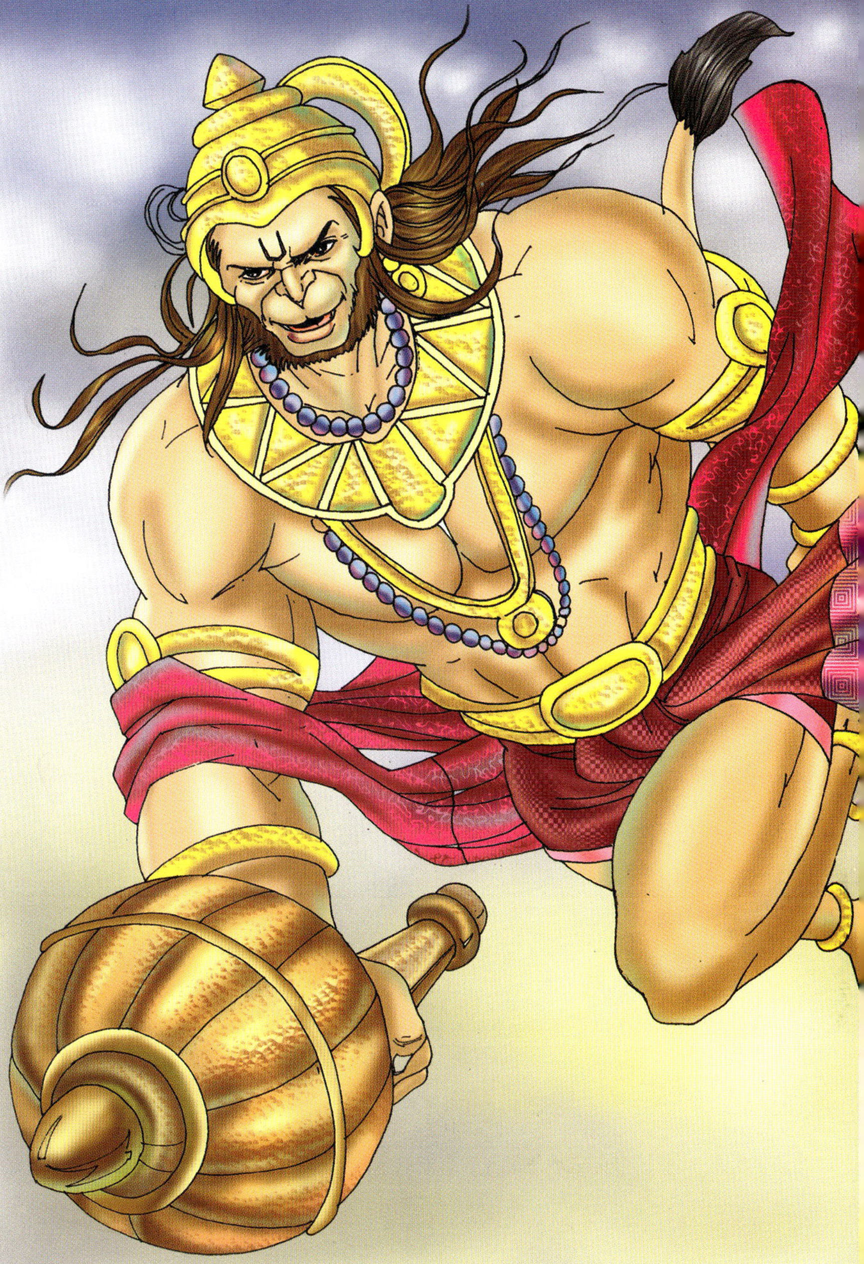

Inspired by their words, Hanuman offered his prayers and set off on the journey.

He assumed his full, gigantic form and with a great roar, leapt up to the skies. With one jump, he reached the peak of a mountain. Within a minute, he was airborne, on his way to find Sita in Lanka.

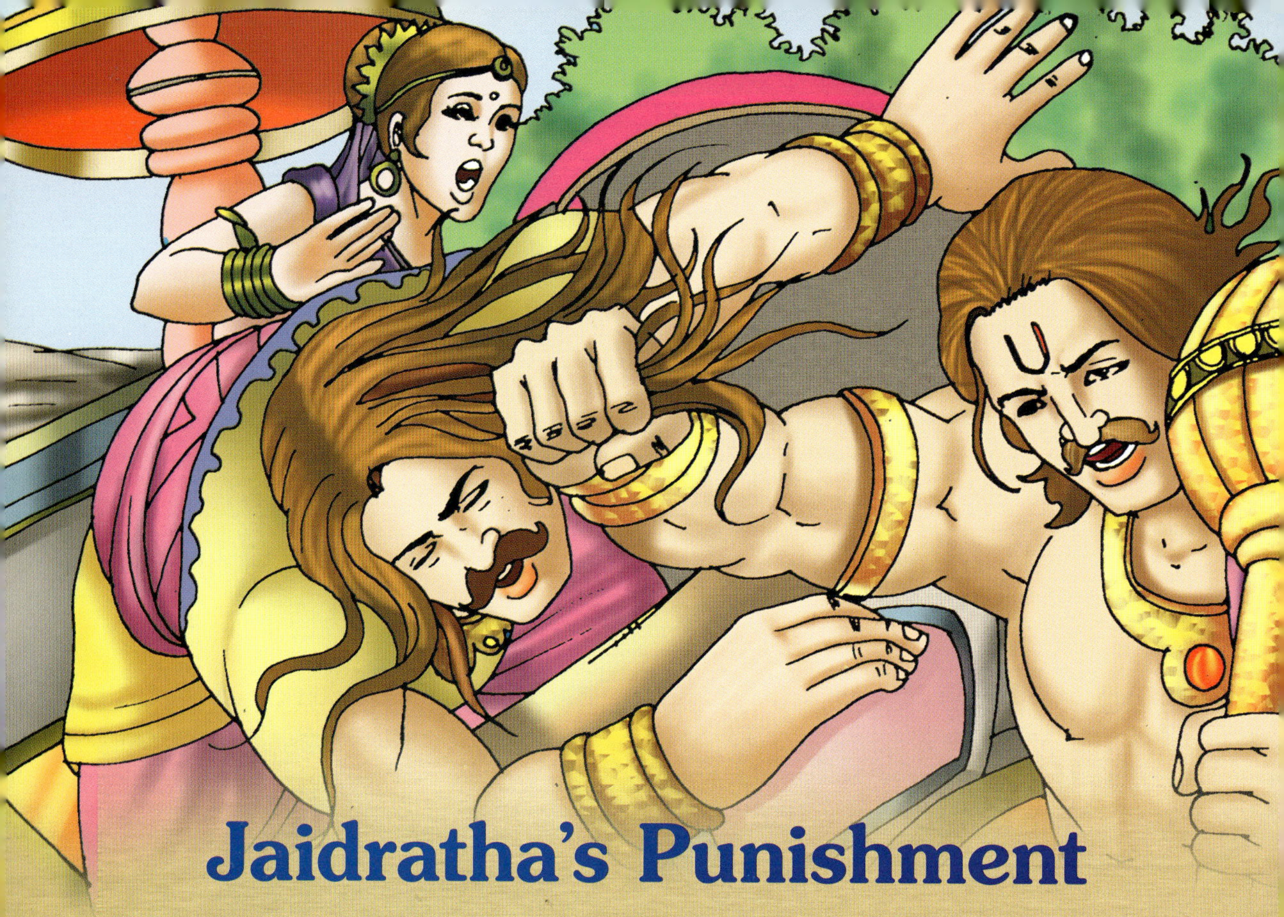

Jaidratha's Punishment

While they were exiled, one day, the Pandavas had gone hunting and their wife, Draupadi was alone in their hut. Jaidratha, the king of Sindhudesha passed by the hut and saw Draupadi. Fascinated by Draupadi's beauty, he approached her and introduced himself. Draupadi remembered he was the husband of Dushala, Duryodhana's sister. Seeing he was a relative, she invited Jaidratha into the hut. "You are so beautiful. Come with me, I will make you my queen," urged Jaidratha.

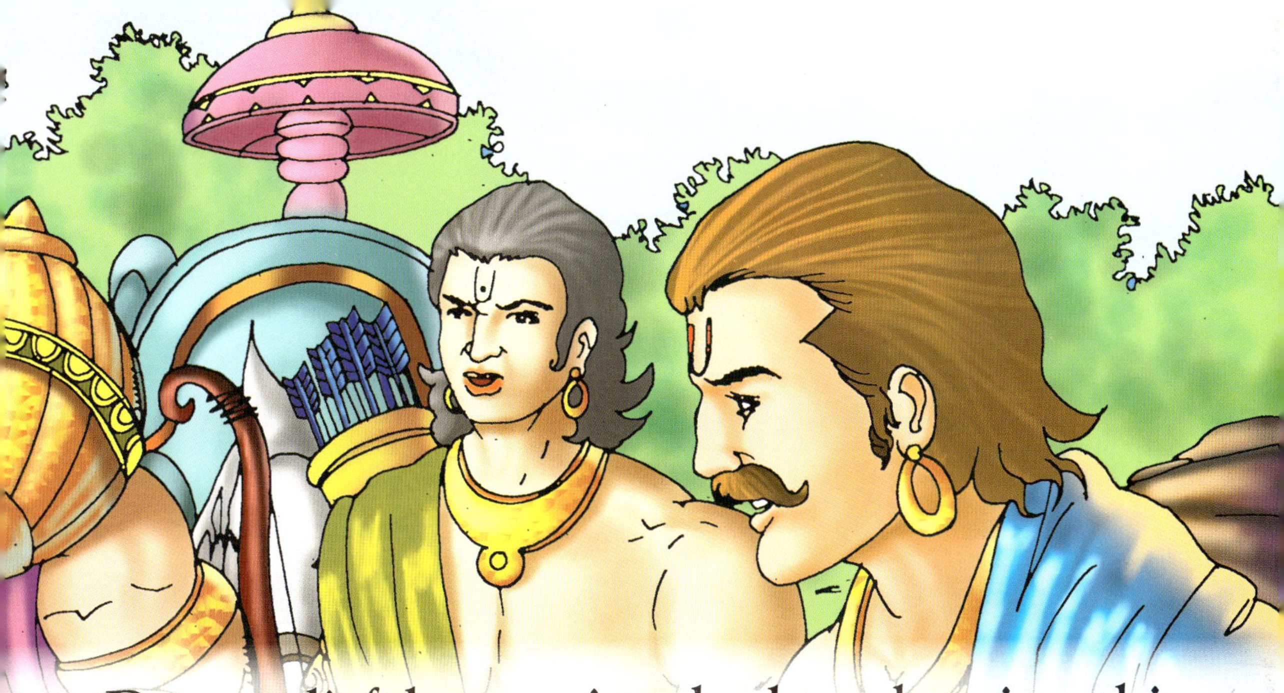

Draupadi felt very insulted on hearing this and rebuked him. Jaidratha, however, forced Draupadi into his chariot, taking her away. Soon the Pandavas returned to their hut and found Draupadi missing. Bhima took his chariot and followed Jaidratha. He captured Jaidratha. Draupadi was crying bitterly. Seeing this, Bhima asked his elder brother's permission to kill Jaidratha. Yudhisthira said, "Jaidratha is our sister's husband. If we kill him, our sister would be widowed. Let us punish him suitably but spare his life." Thus, Jaidratha's head was shaved leaving only five tufts of hair on it.

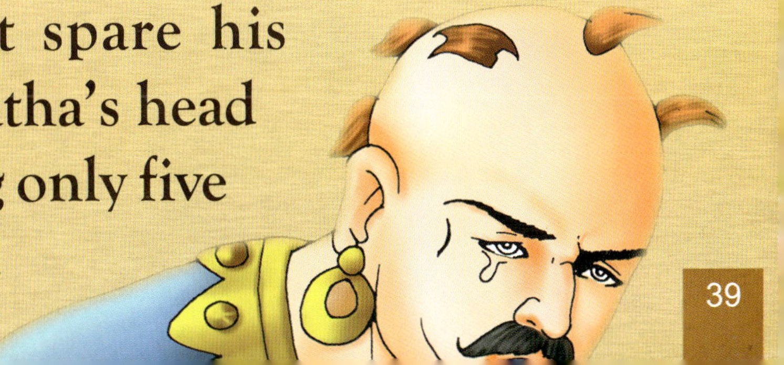

The Pandavas Save Duryodhana

Duryodhana had come to the forest where the Pandavas were spending their years in exile. There, Chitrasena, the king of the Gandharvas imprisoned him. On hearing this, Yudhisthira said to Arjuna, "An outsider has captured our cousin. It is a question of our clan's honour. Go and rescue him."

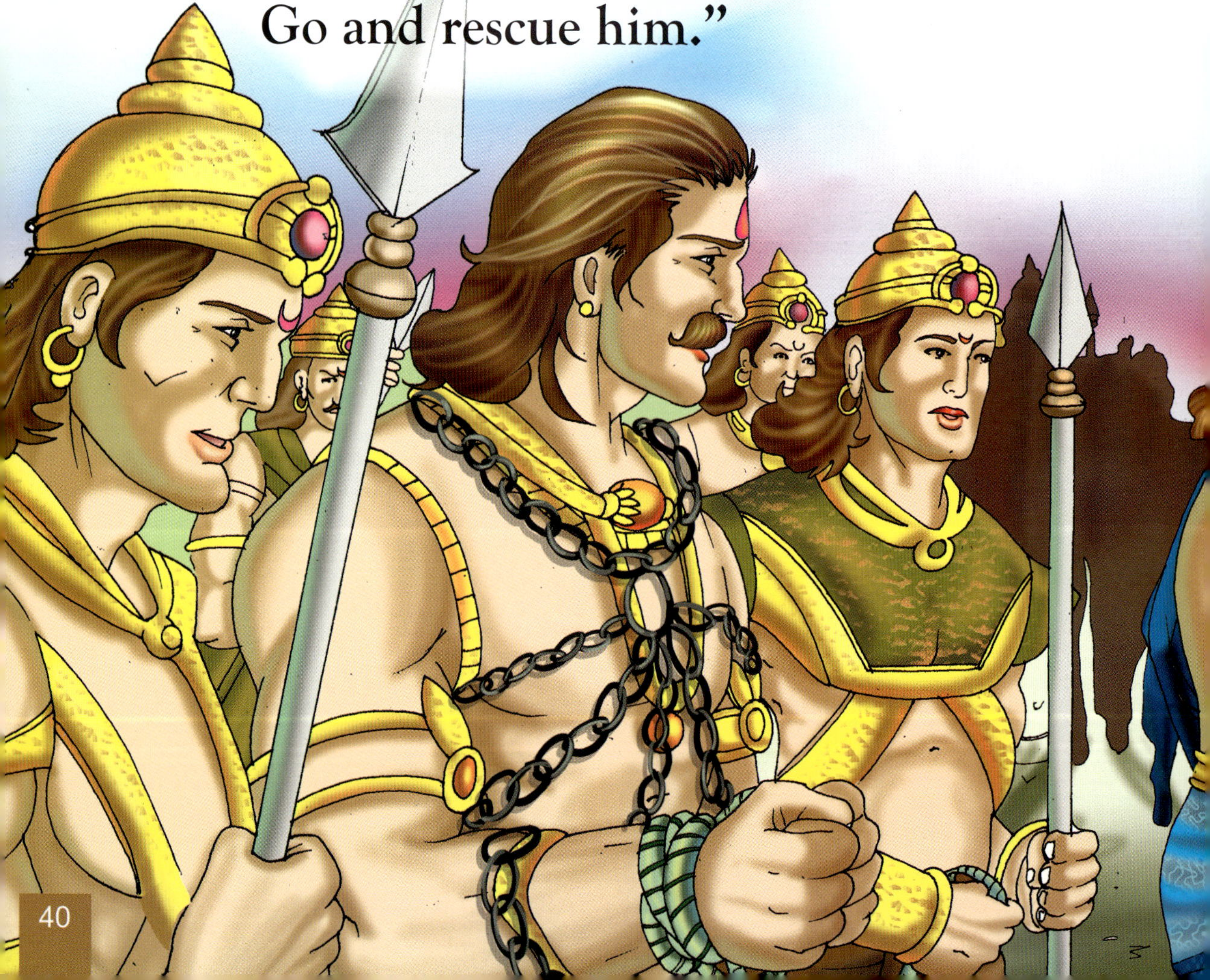

Arjuna defeated Chitrasena's soldiers and Chitrasena was forced to descend from heaven. He was Arjuna's friend.

He told Arjuna, "Indra had ordered me to punish Duryodhana and his friends for ridiculing you." Arjuna took Chitrasena to Yudhisthira. "We thank you for your concern for us. But please release Duryodhana now," said Yudhisthira. Chitrasena agreed and released him. Duryodhana felt very humiliated because his most hated enemies, the Pandavas, had saved his life.

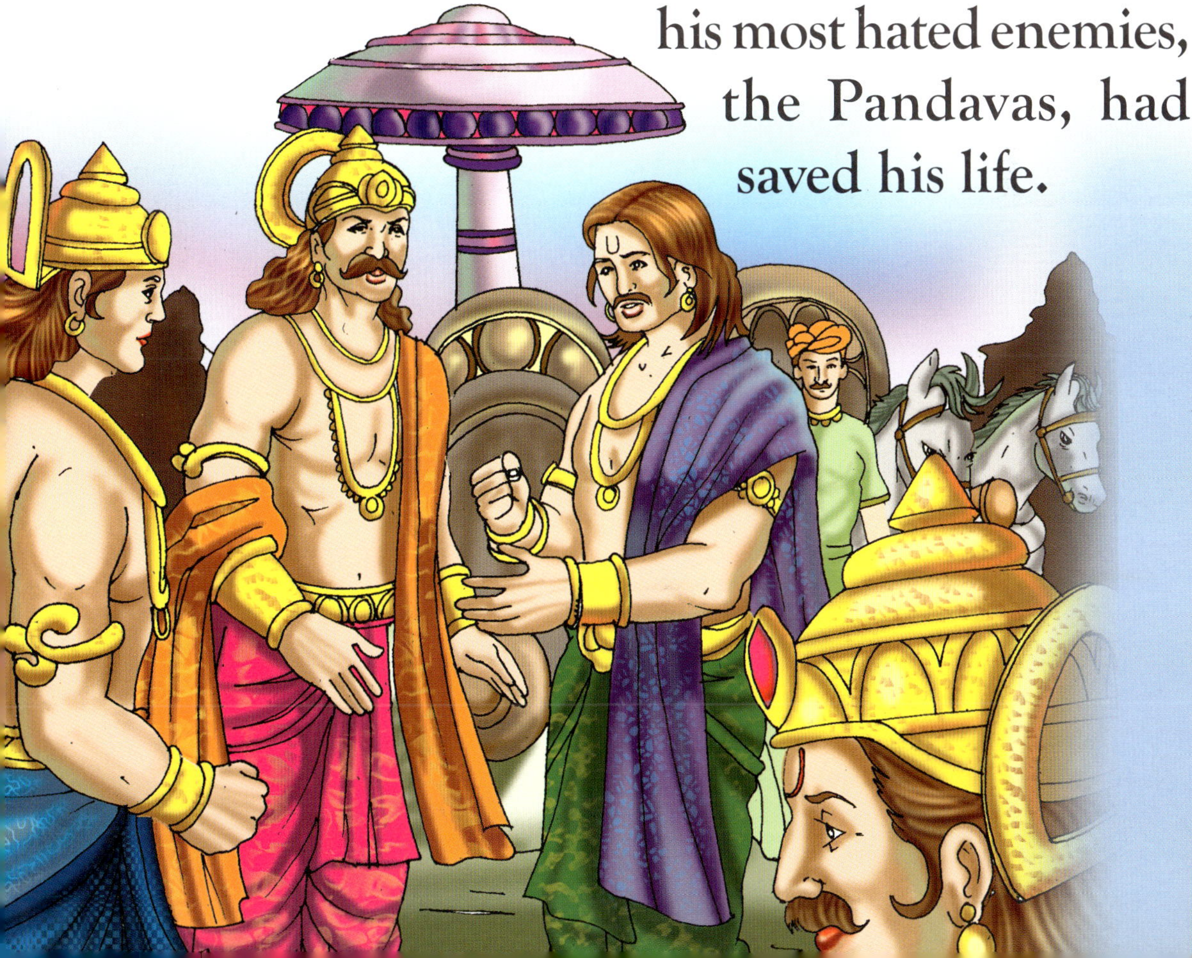

Vibhishana Meets Rama

Ravana expelled his younger brother Vibhishana from Lanka when he discouraged Ravana from fighting with Rama. Vibhishana decided to seek Rama and help him.

Like a loyal servant, Vibhishana told Rama about Ravana's strengths and weaknesses and also about the boon of immortality granted to Ravana by Brahma.

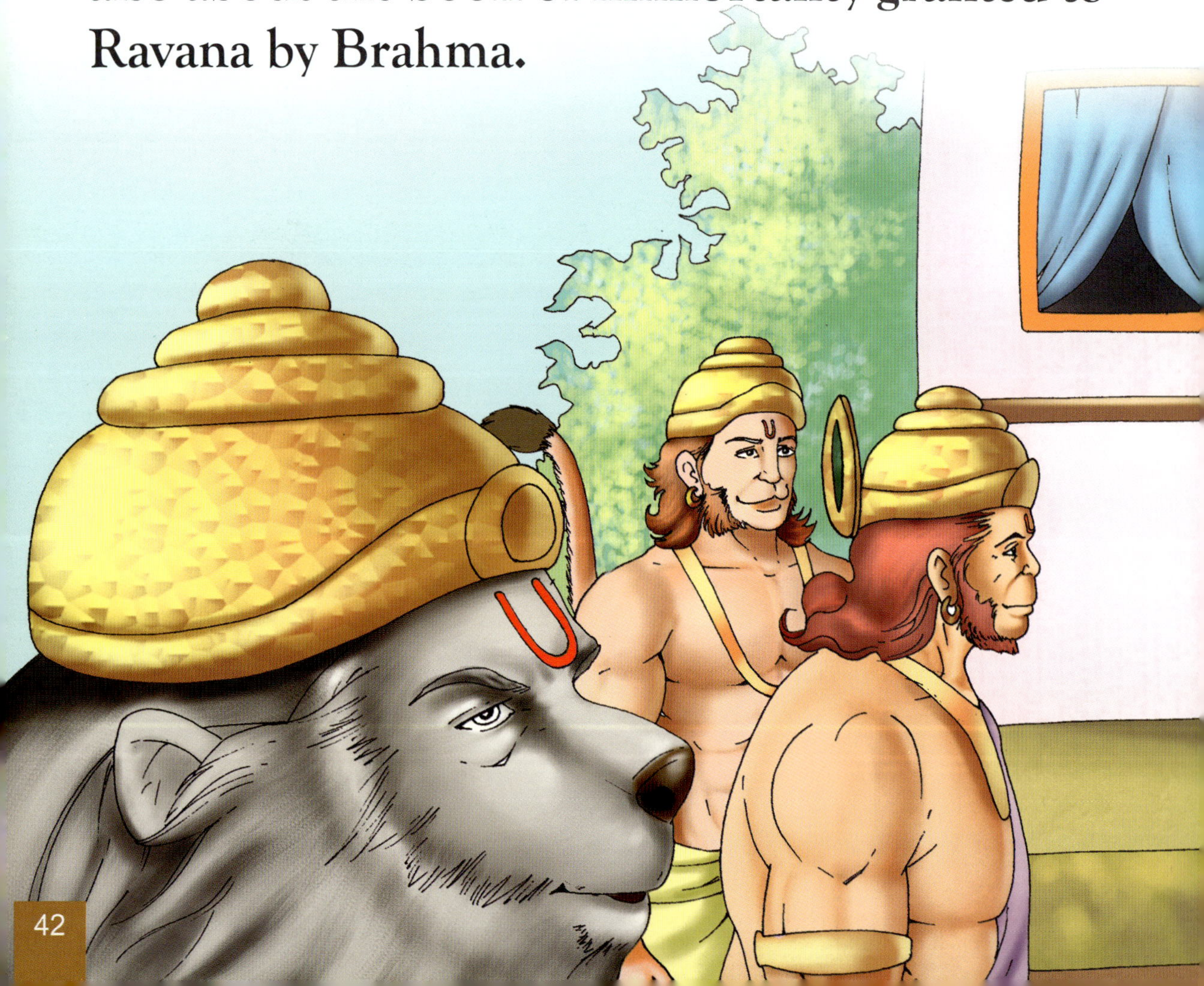

He gave Rama all the details of Ravana's weapons, soldiers, army, and methods of warfare, including Meghnad's gift of invisibility while fighting his enemy.

This valuable information helped Rama organize his army and fight Ravana. Rama warmly hugged Vibhishana and thanked him for all his help promising him protection and the crown of Lanka after defeating Ravana and freeing Sita from his clutches.

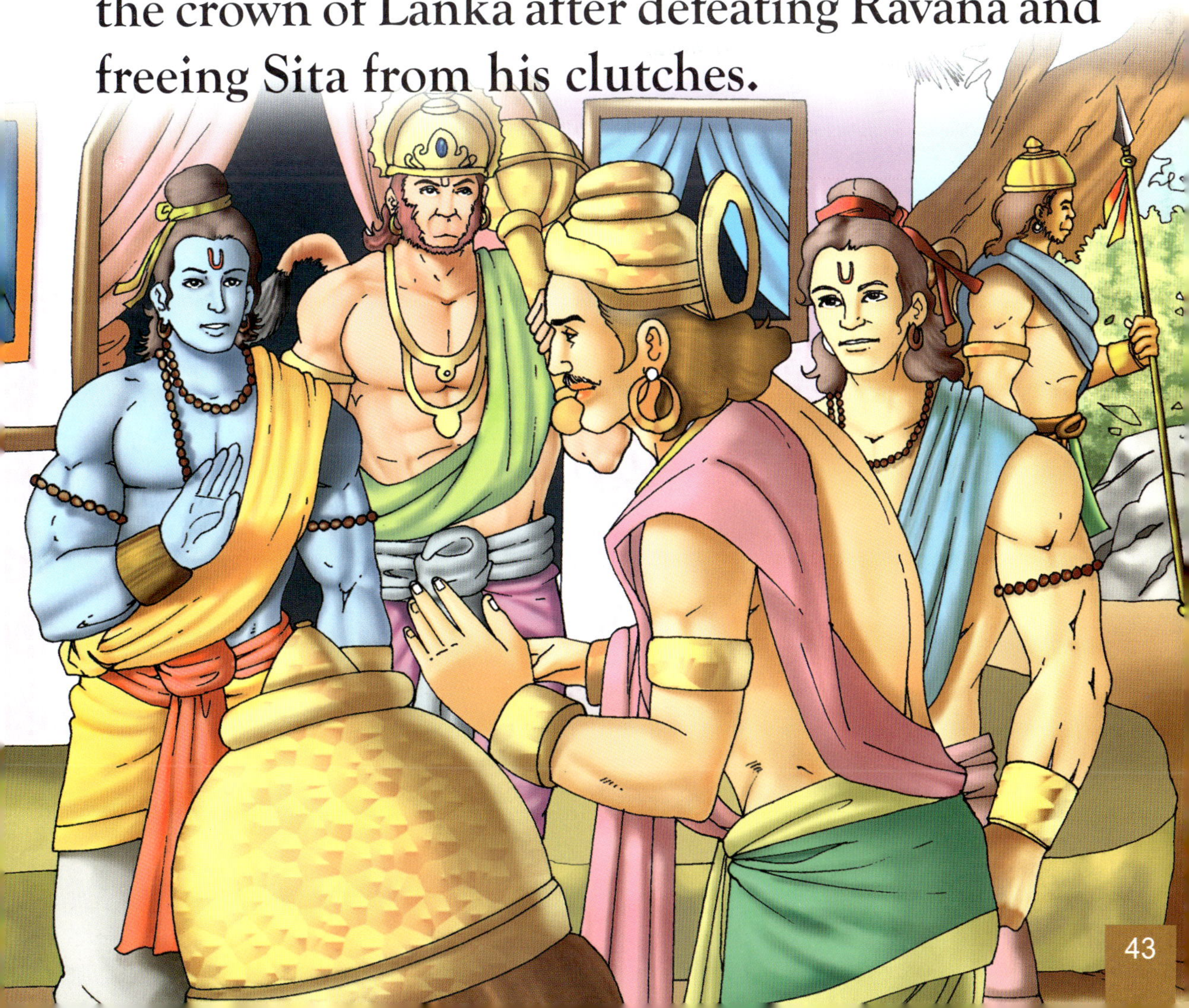

The Curse of Parashurama

Karna realized that he also needed a guru as great as Drona in order to master the entire field of archery to successfully challenge Arjuna, when the time arose. In his mind, he decided to approach Drona's one time Guru, Parashurama. "If Parashurama comes to know that I am a Kshatriya, he will refuse to teach me. Everyone knows Parashurama's hatred towards Kshatriyas," Karna mused. Deciding to disguise himself as a Brahmin, Karna approached Parashurama. The elderly Guru liked Karna and agreed to school him further in the arts of war.

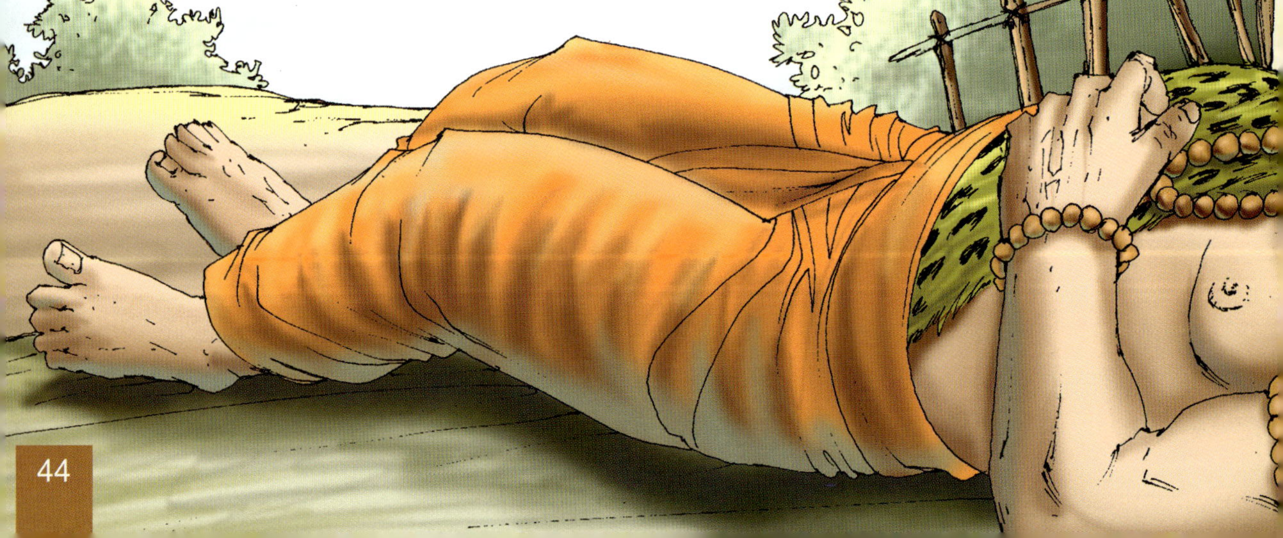

Karna's secret remained hidden for a long time, until one day. That day, Parashurama was sleeping, with his head resting on Karna's lap. Suddenly, Karna was bitten by a Scorpio. The bite was so bad that pools of blood sprung out. Agonized by pain, Karna however, kept silent because he did not want to disturb his guru.

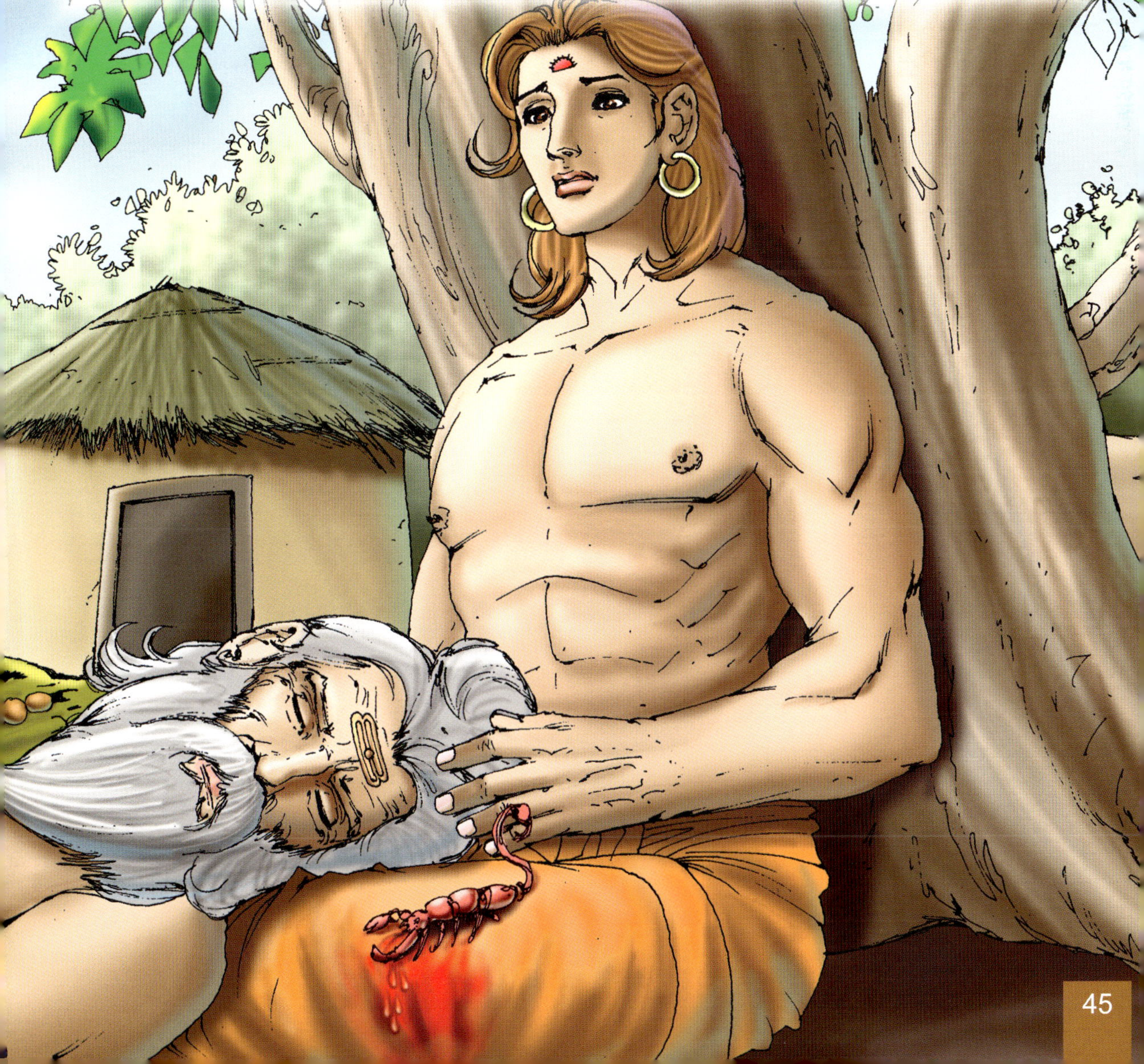

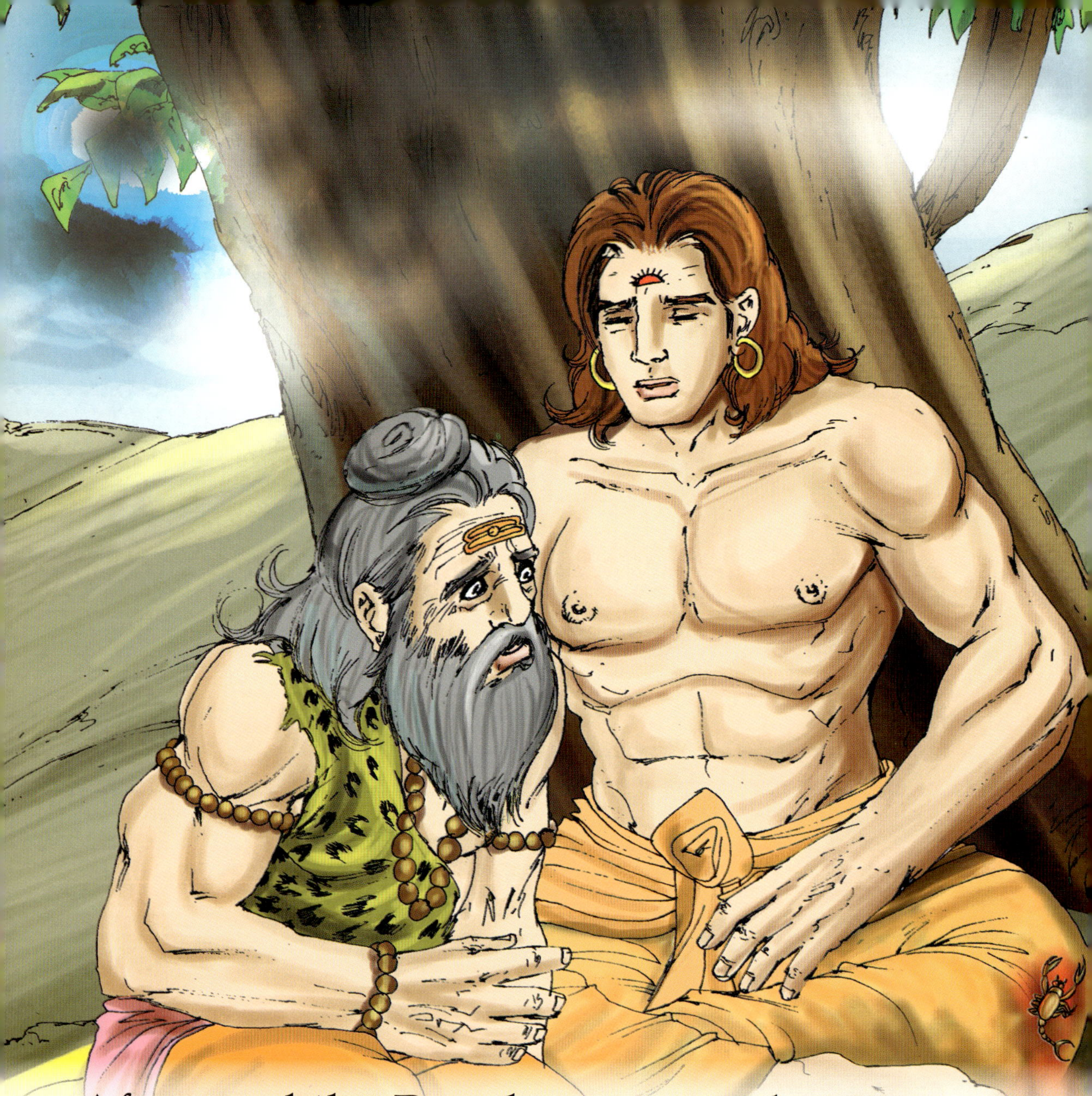

After a while, Parashurama awoke. He was shocked to see Karna tight lipped controlling his pain. 'The endurance to such agonizing pain can only come from a Kshatriya,' thought Parashurama and realized that he had been cheated.

The enraged Guru cursed him, "You will forget everything I have taught you." Karna groaned and fell to the Guru's feet, desperately asking for forgiveness and begged him to take the curse back. "I cannot take my curse back, but I can amend it. The knowledge I have imparted to you, will fail you, when you need it the most." Karna left the ashram, feeling sad at this turn of events.

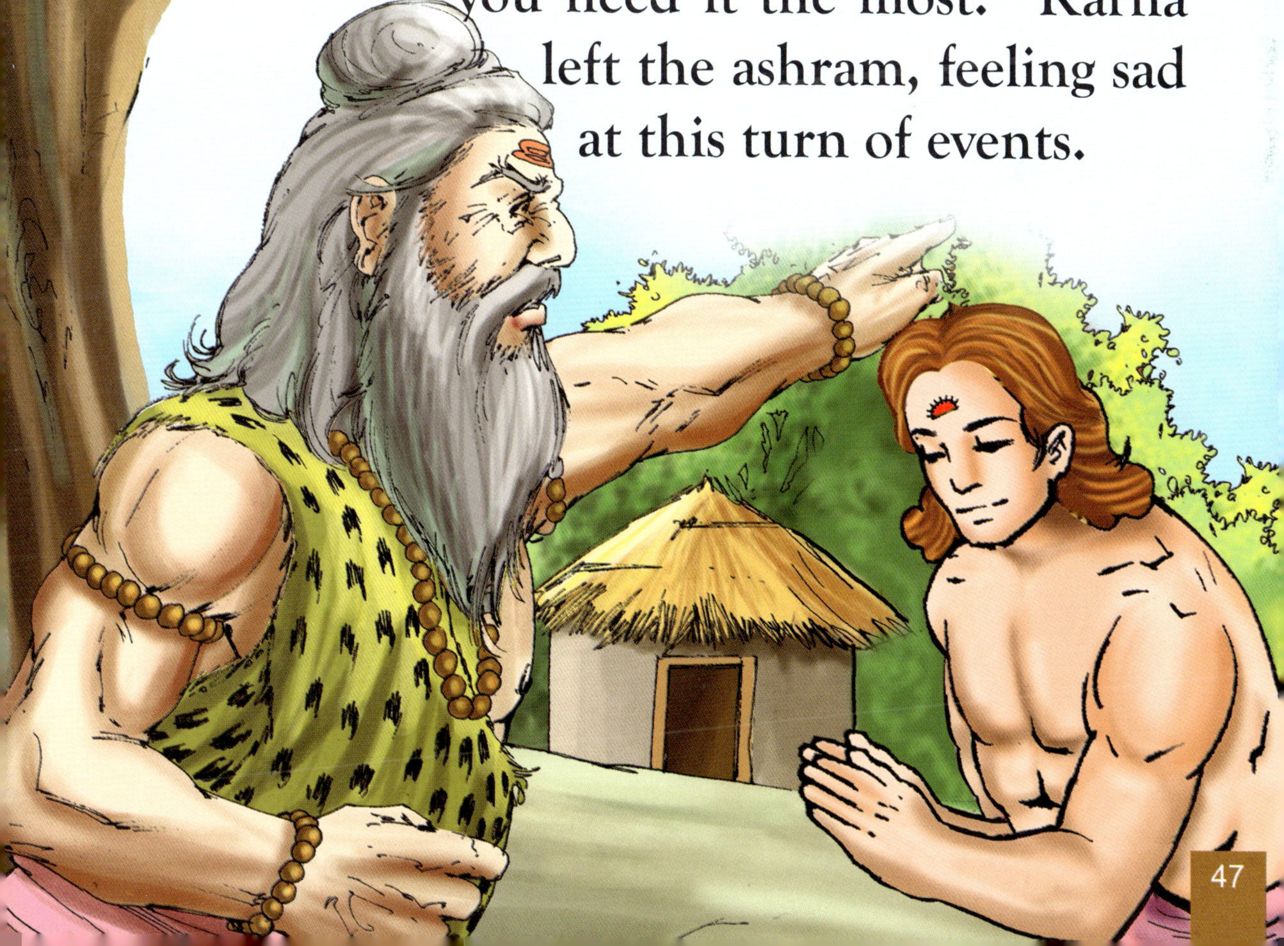

Rama & the Squirrel

Rama and his army started building a bridge on the ocean to reach Lanka. The Sea God had promised that would keep the rocks afloat. Rama's entire monkey army began building the bridge by placing boulders.

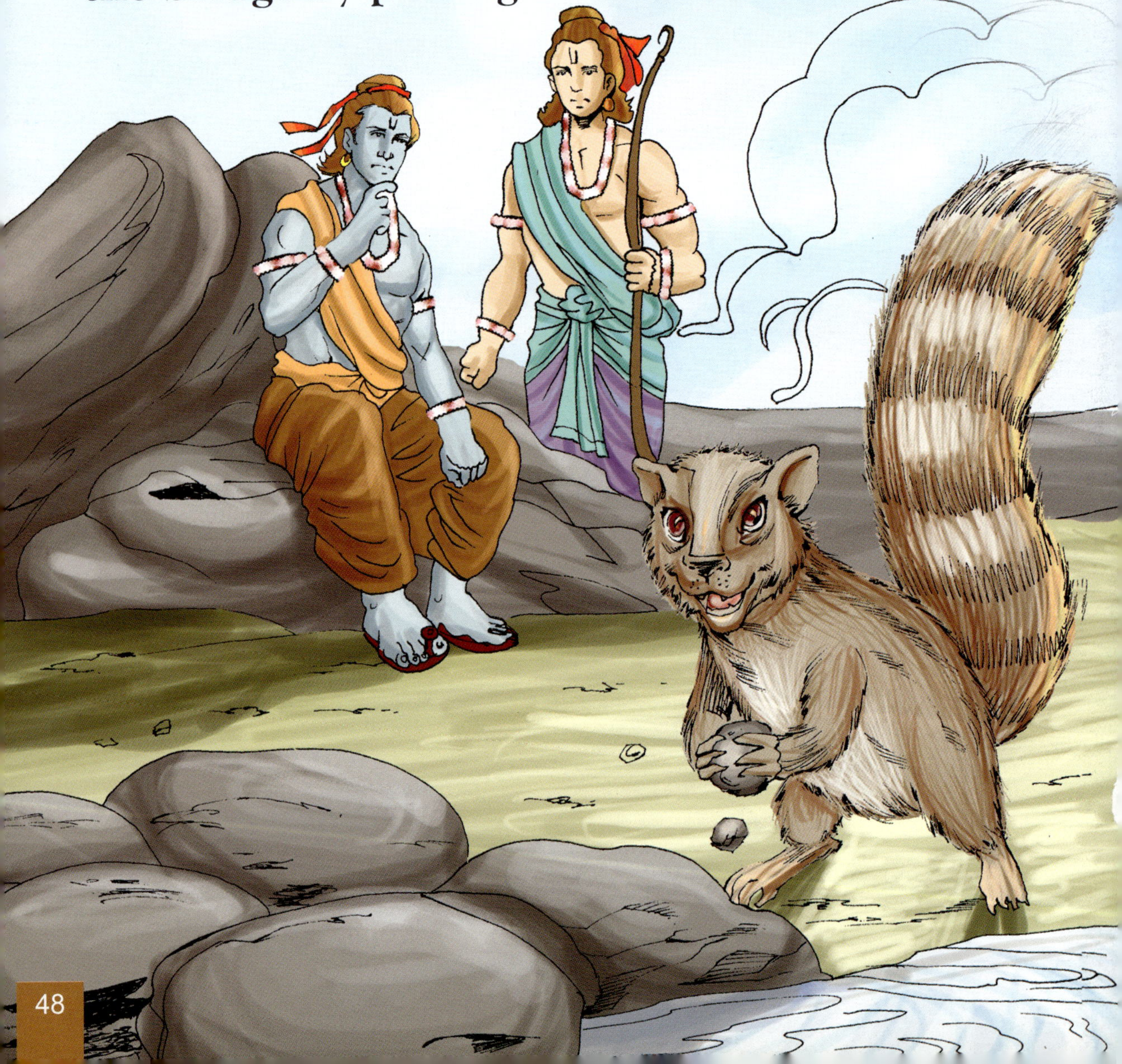

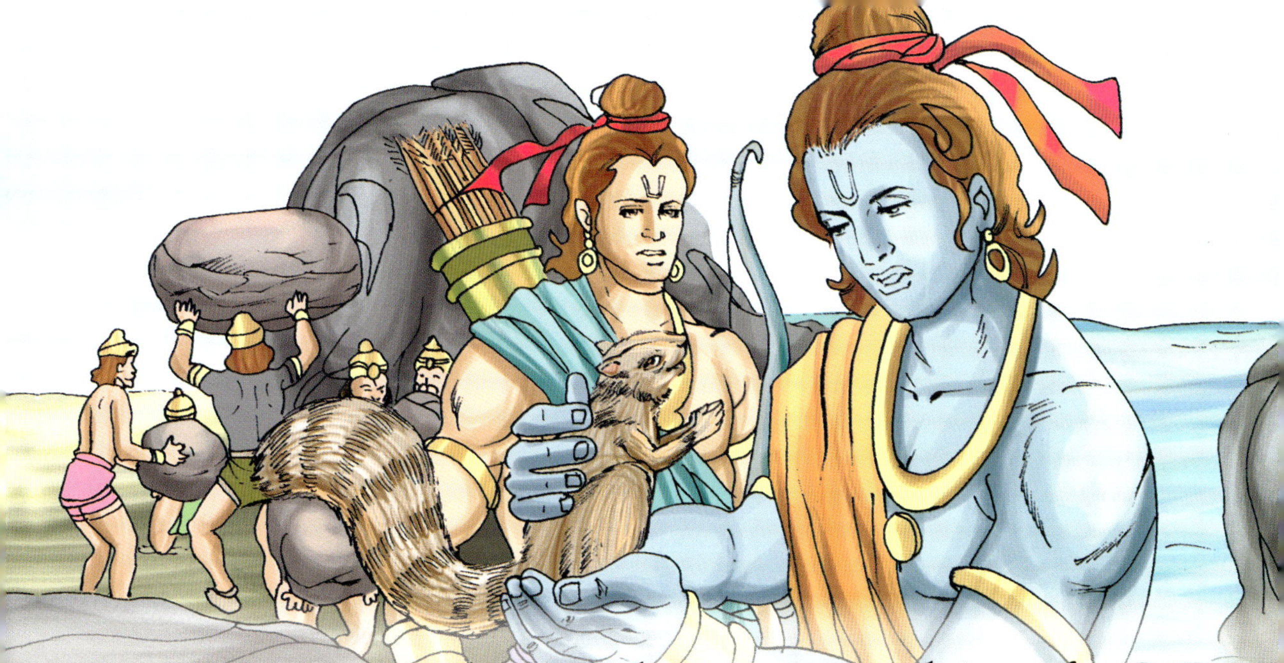

A tiny squirrel, watching everything from her burrow decided to help Rama. She began picking sand and scattered twigs, scurrying back and forth from the shore to the sea. Noticing the dedication of this tiny creature, Rama picked her up on his palm, and warmly stroked the animal with his three fingers. It is believed that the three lines which appear on a squirrel's back are due to Rama's blessings.

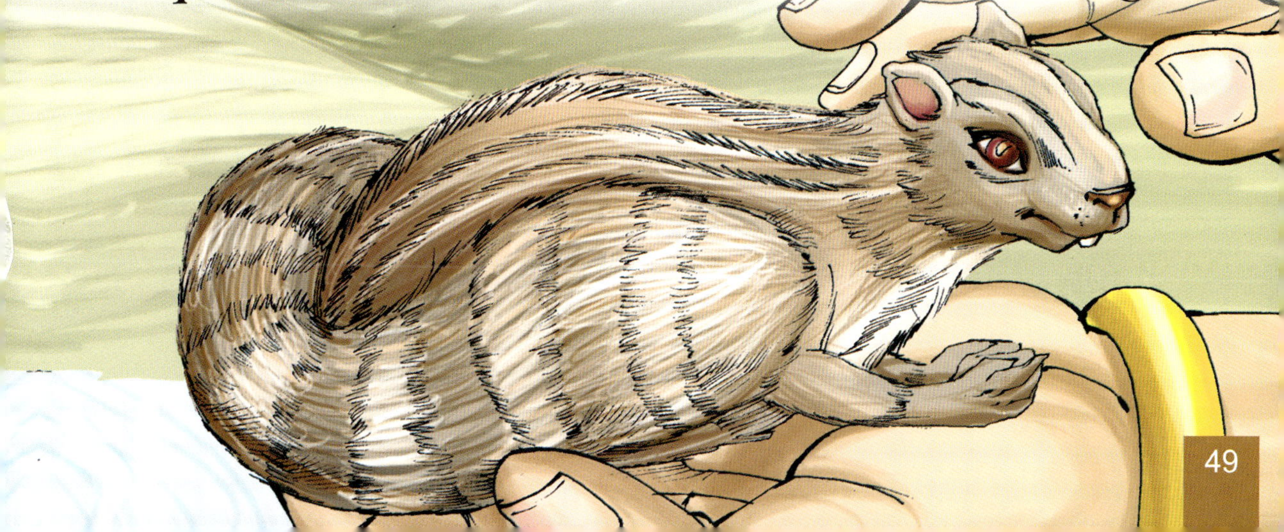

The End of Kumbhakarna

Ravana decided to send his brother Kumbhakarna to fight Rama and Lakshmana.

Kumbhakarna, who was cursed to sleep for six months at a time, grew furious when awakened. Seeing the gigantic Kumbhakarna arrive, the monkeys started fleeing.

Rama blocked his movements with many arrows and finally flung his chakra and severed the demon's head. The monkeys came back once again and rejoiced on seeing the dead body of the demon.

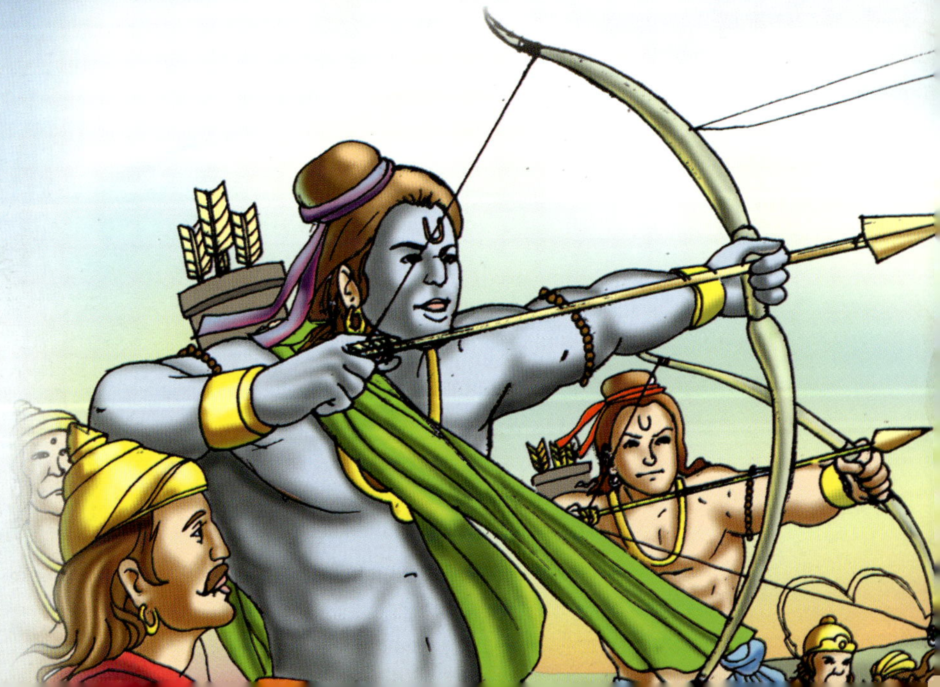

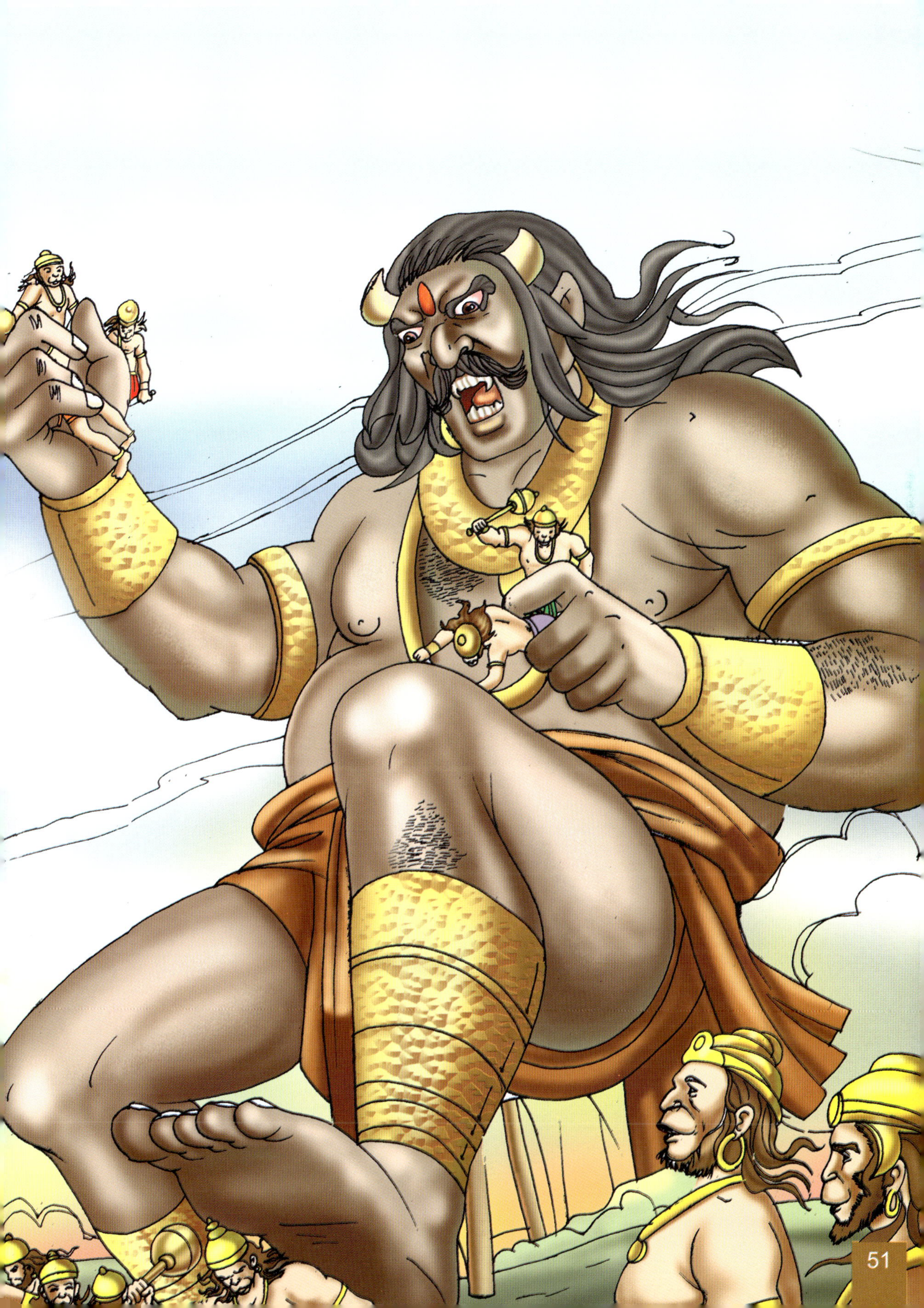

The Battle with Meghnad

Before the final battle with Ravana, Rama and Lakshmana killed six of his demon chiefs and had begun their search for Ravana's son, Meghnad. Lord Brahma had given Meghnad the boon of invisibility. Meghnad started firing arrows at the monkey squad, who failed to discover the source of these attacks. Rama and Lakshmana understood that Meghnad was behind these invisible attacks, but before they could act. Meghnad took out his famous Naag paash weapon and shot at the brothers.

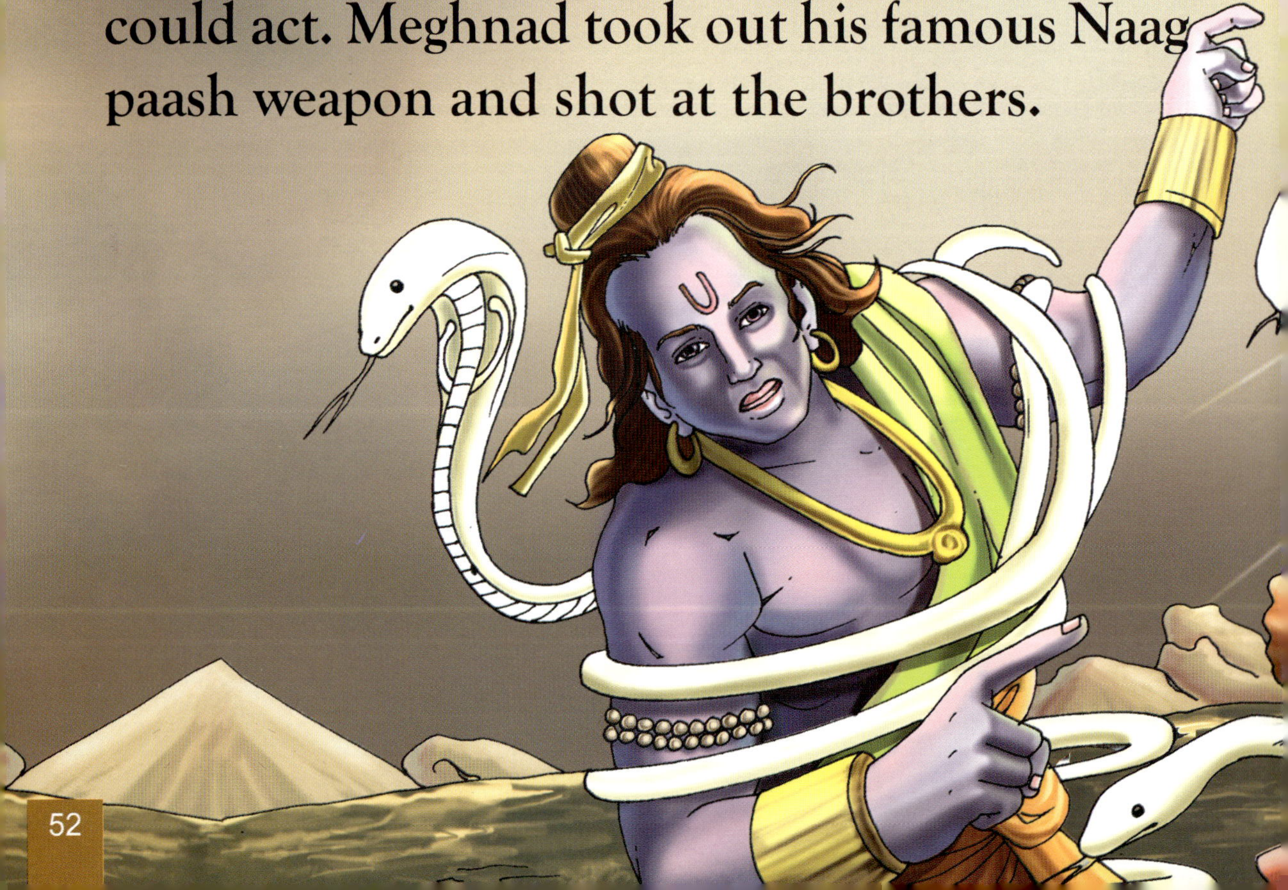

This weapon was a huge snake that coiled up like a rope. As Rama and Lakshmana struggled to be uncoiled, Meghnad shot several snake arrows at the brothers which pierced their bodies, making them unconscious. Thinking Rama and Lakshmana to be dead, Meghnad rushed to his father's court to give him the news.

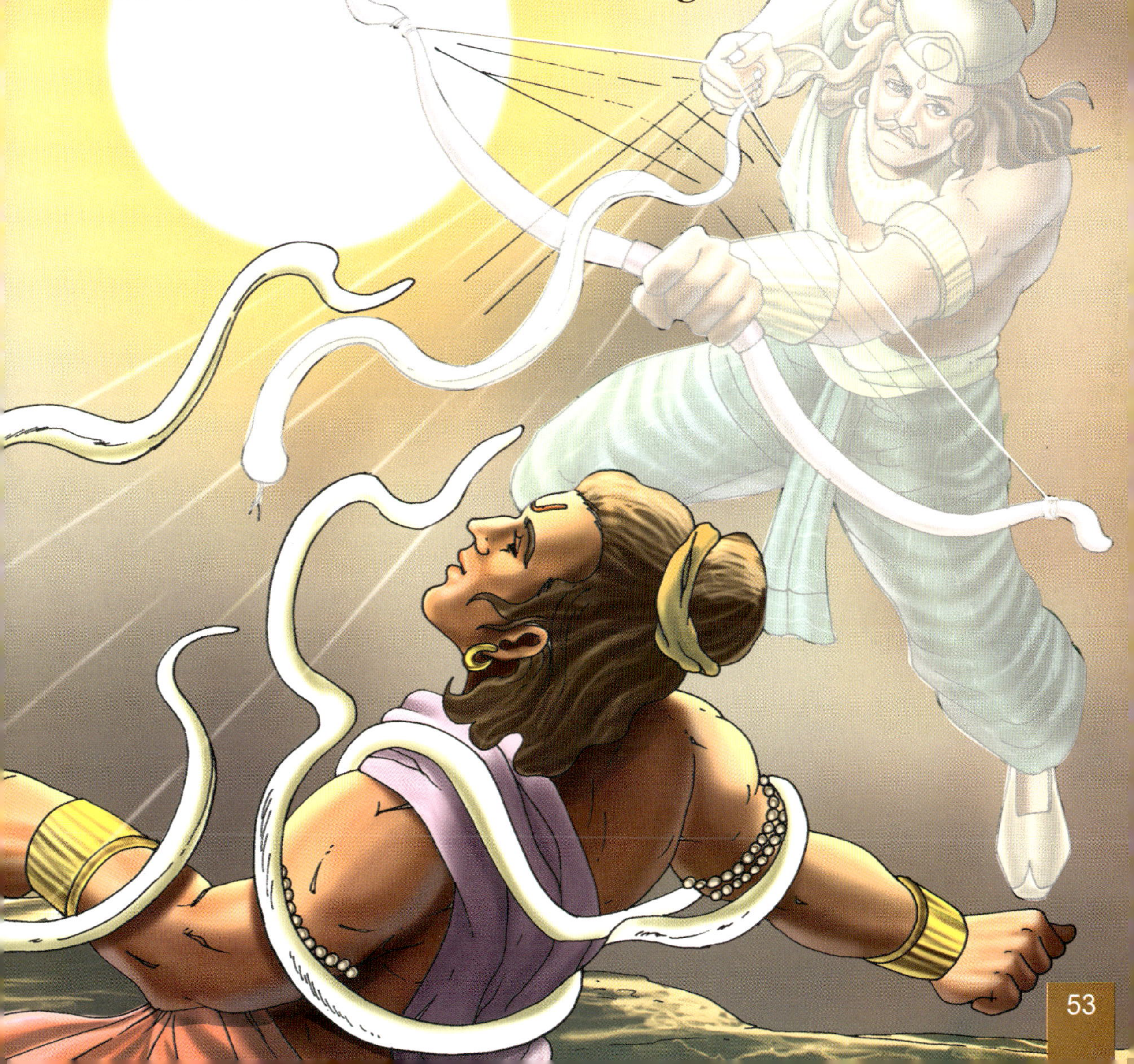

Karna's Promise

The war between the Kauravas and Pandavas was imminent. Kunti, the Pandava's mother went to Karna, pleading, "Karna, you are actually my son. If you fight against the Pandavas, you will be fighting against your own brothers." Karna replied, I am grateful to Duryodhana and can't betray him." Hearing this Kunti started weeping. Karna could not see his mother like that and declared, "I can promise you one thing. I will not harm any of the Pandavas except Arjuna who is my rival. It is Arjun alone who I will not spare. Either he would live or I would. Rest assured, you will always have five sons," Karna declared.

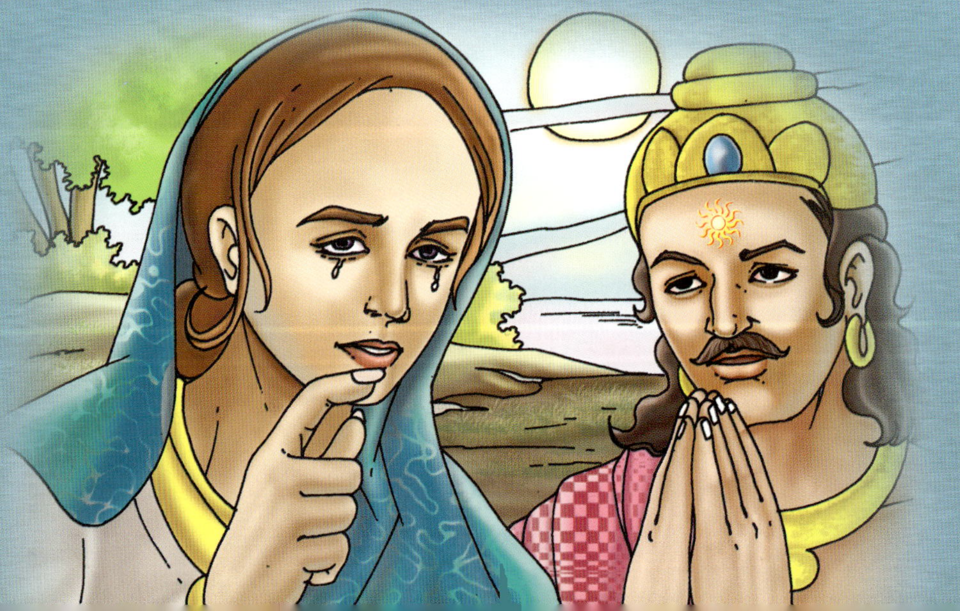

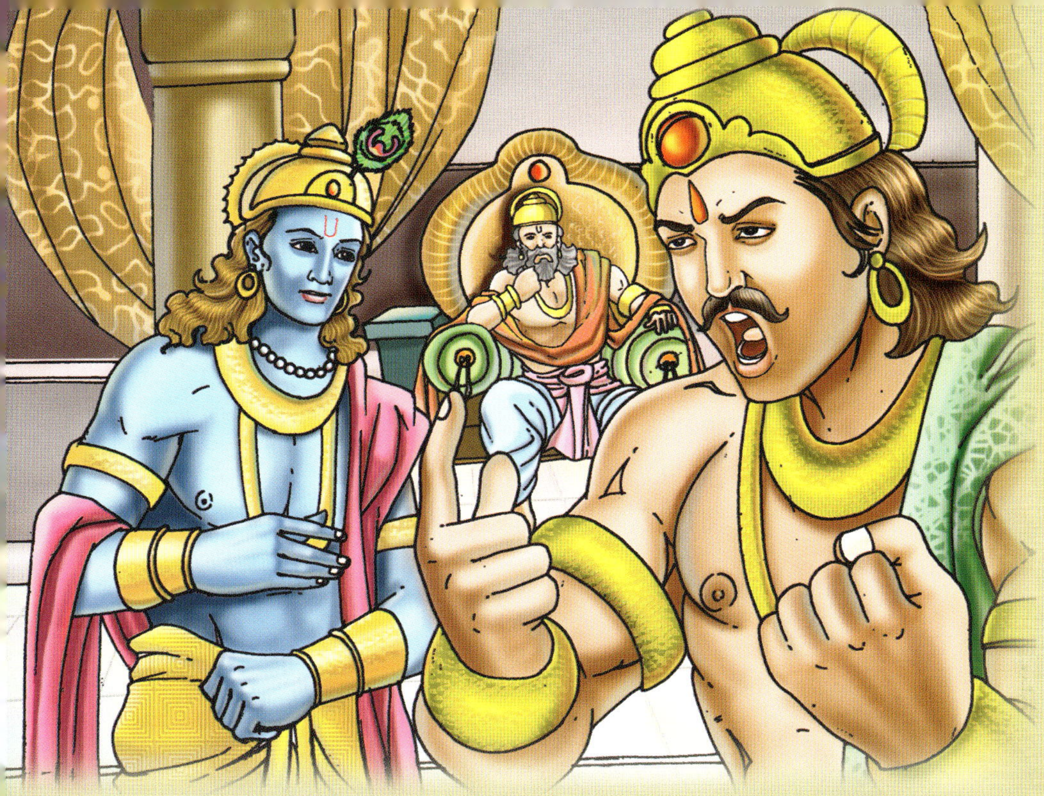

Krishna's Peace Mission

Krishna went to meet Duryodhana in Hastinapur.

"I come with an offer from the Pandavas," said Krishna to Duryodhana, "instead of returning their whole kingdom, they would settle for just five villages as they are peace loving and want to prevent war." Duryodhana scornfully replied, "The entire kingdom belongs to me. I will not even give land equal to the tip of a needle from my kingdom to them. You are always partial to those Pandavas. I will imprison you."

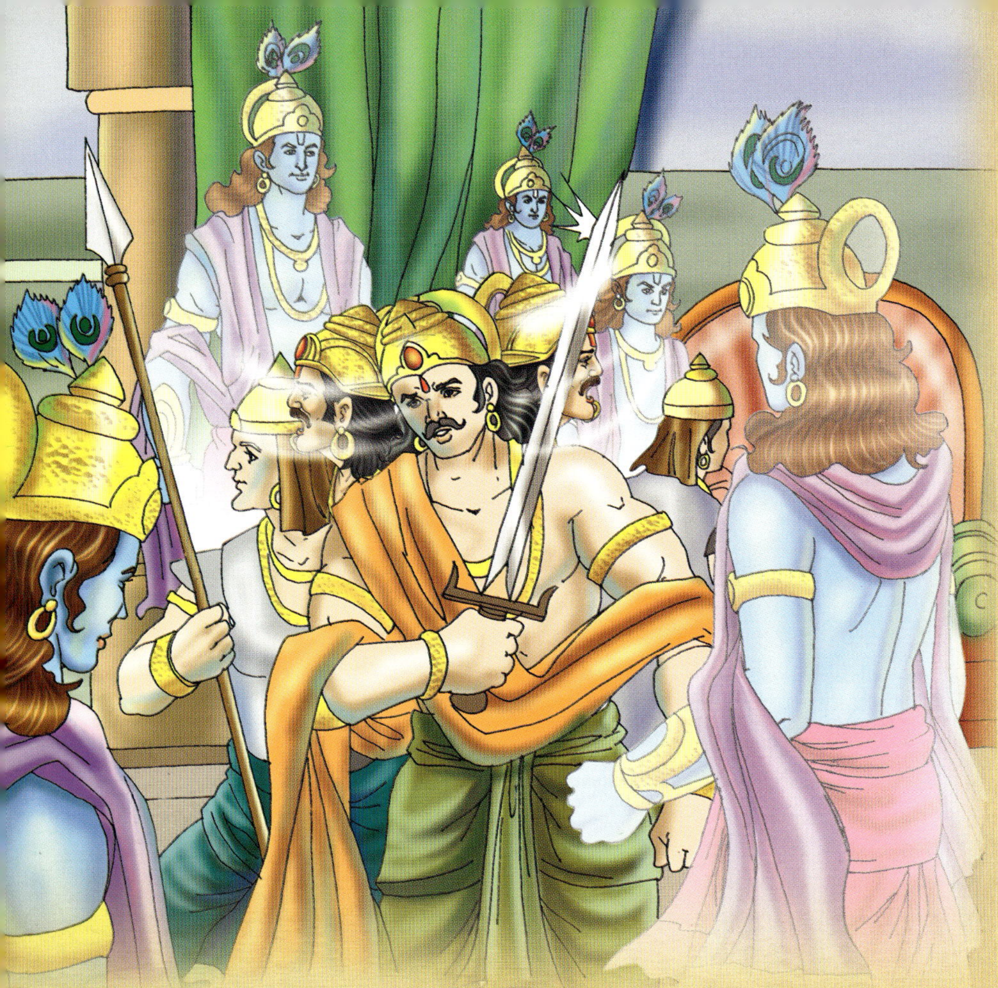

He ordered his soldiers to imprison Krishna. At that moment, Krishna worked a miracle again and suddenly he showed himself everywhere, in all things, even in the hearts of the people. Krishna actually split his image into many figures. Every corner seemed to be filled by a Krishna! Duryodhana and his soldiers desperately tried to catch the real Krishna whom they could not find! Having made his point, Krishna disappeared in a puff of air.

Lakshmana becomes Unconscious

Meghnad, shot at Lakshmana with a powerful arrow. The instant the dreadful arrow hit Lakshmana, he fell unconscious. Rama rushed to his beloved brother and tried to revive him, hoping he had not died.

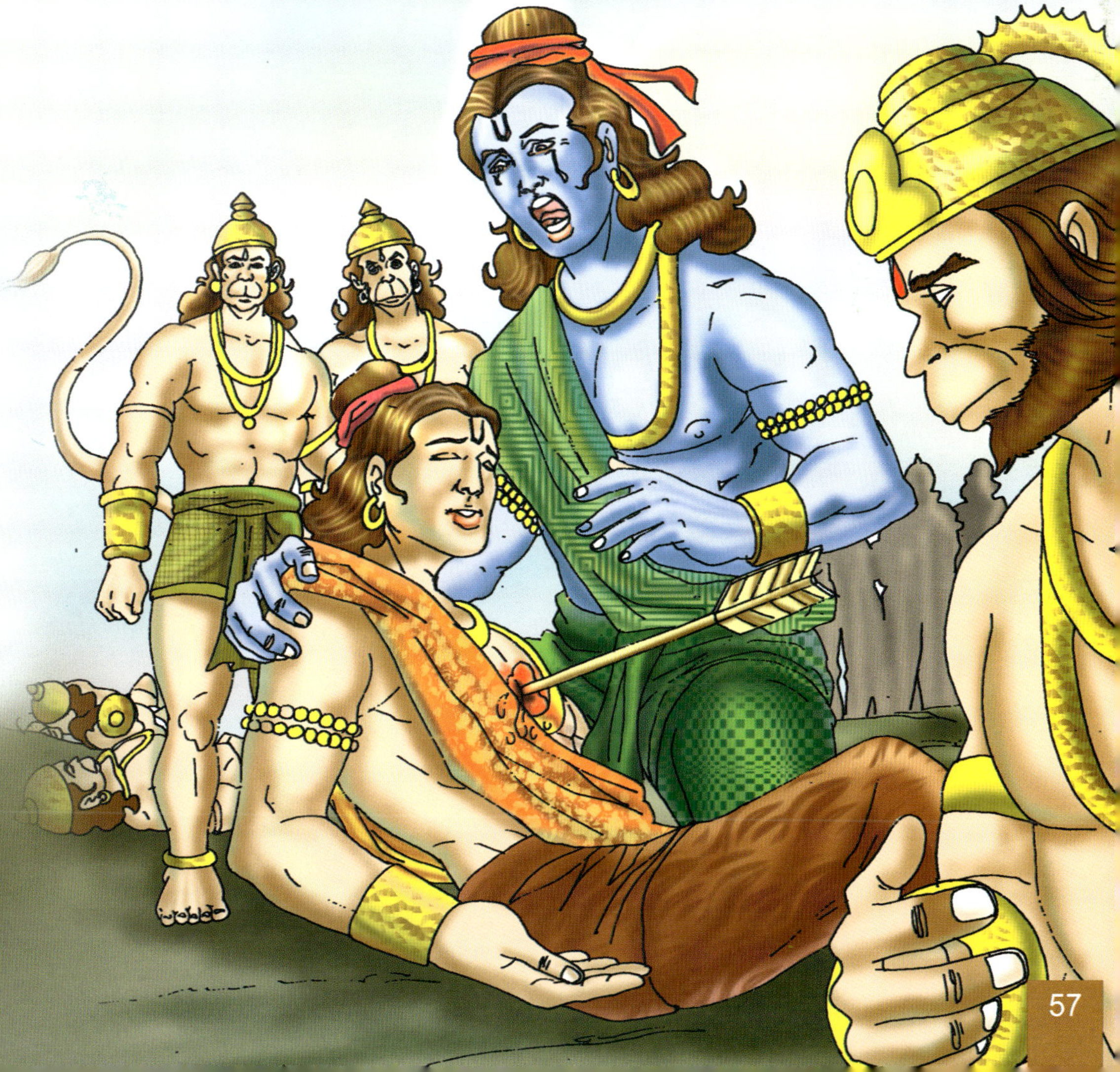

The Broken Code of War

During the battle, Drona, the royal guru to the Kauravas was ordered to capture Yudhisthira alive, so Arjuna always protected him. Once Arjuna fighting some Kaurava warriors left Yudhisthira unprotected. Drona and his soldiers approached Yudhisthira forming a circular military formation known as chakravyuh around him. Arjuna's son, Abhimanyu, had learned how to enter the chakravyuh from his father but did not know how to come out.

Only Arjuna knew how to break the chakravyuh.

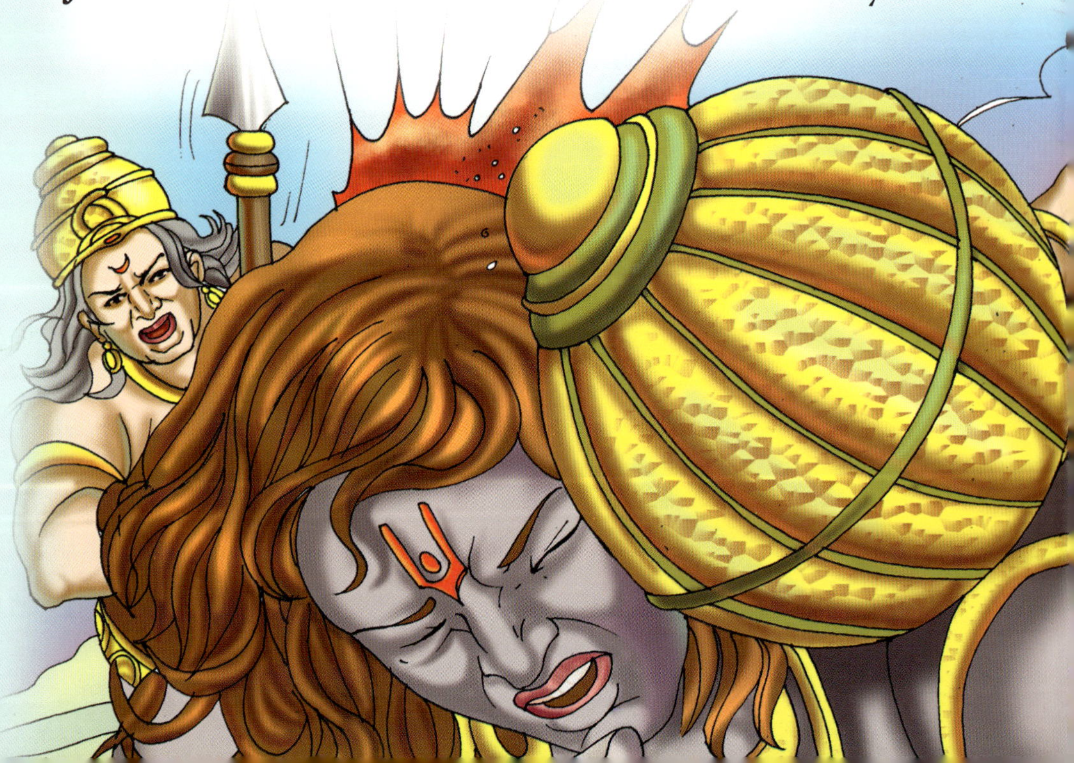

Nevertheless, Abhimanyu decided to enter the formation. Jaidratha, the king of Sindhudesha, who had obtained a boon from Shiva that he would be able to stop the Pandavas for one day, stopped them from entering the chakravyuh to help Abhimanyu. Six warriors including Drona, Duryodhana, and Karna together attacked Abhimanyu who eventually lost all his weapons. Finally, the Kaurava warriors broke the code of war; and attacking the unarmed Abhimanyu, killed him.

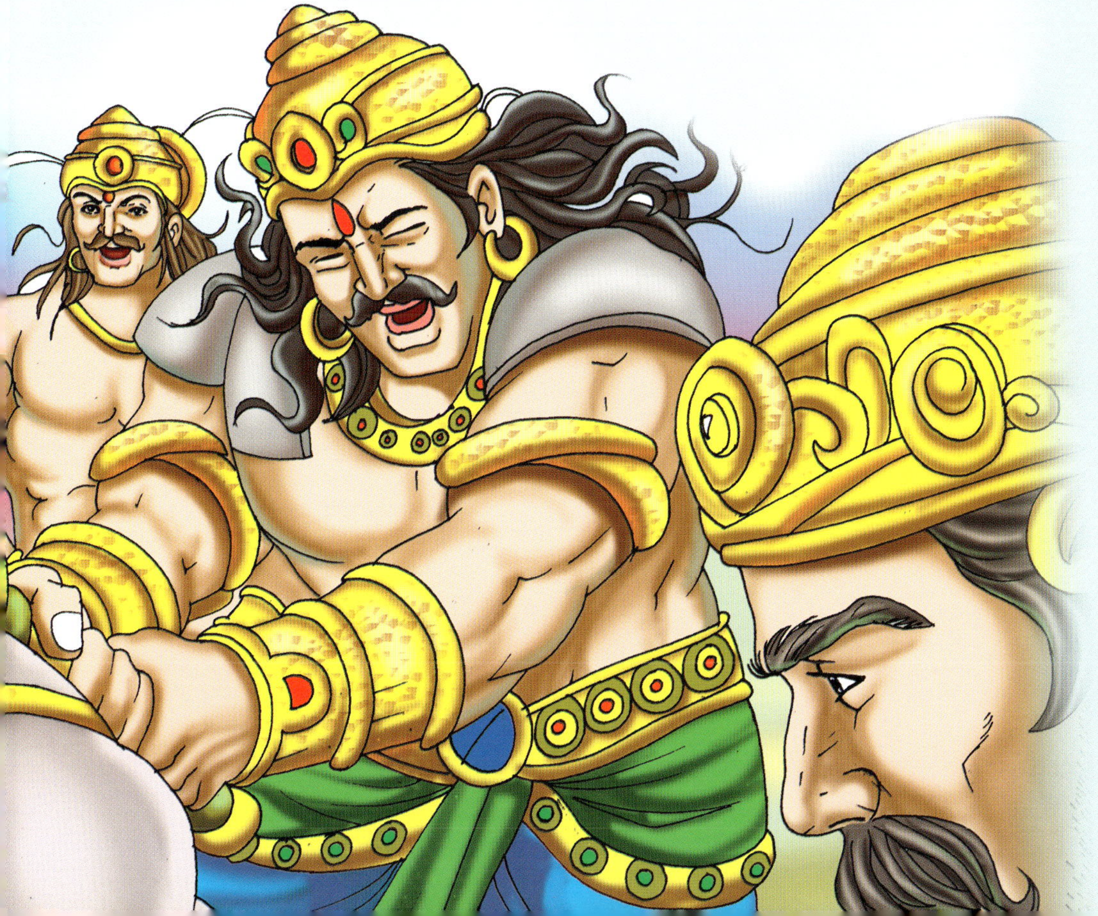

The End of Meghnad

After a terrible encounter, Ravana realized the true potential of Rama's strength. He once again sent for Meghnad, who attacked veiled in smoke from his flying chariot. Meghnad, then using his illusory powers, created a hallucination of Sita and holding her by her hair, paraded her around in his chariot and finally cut off her head.

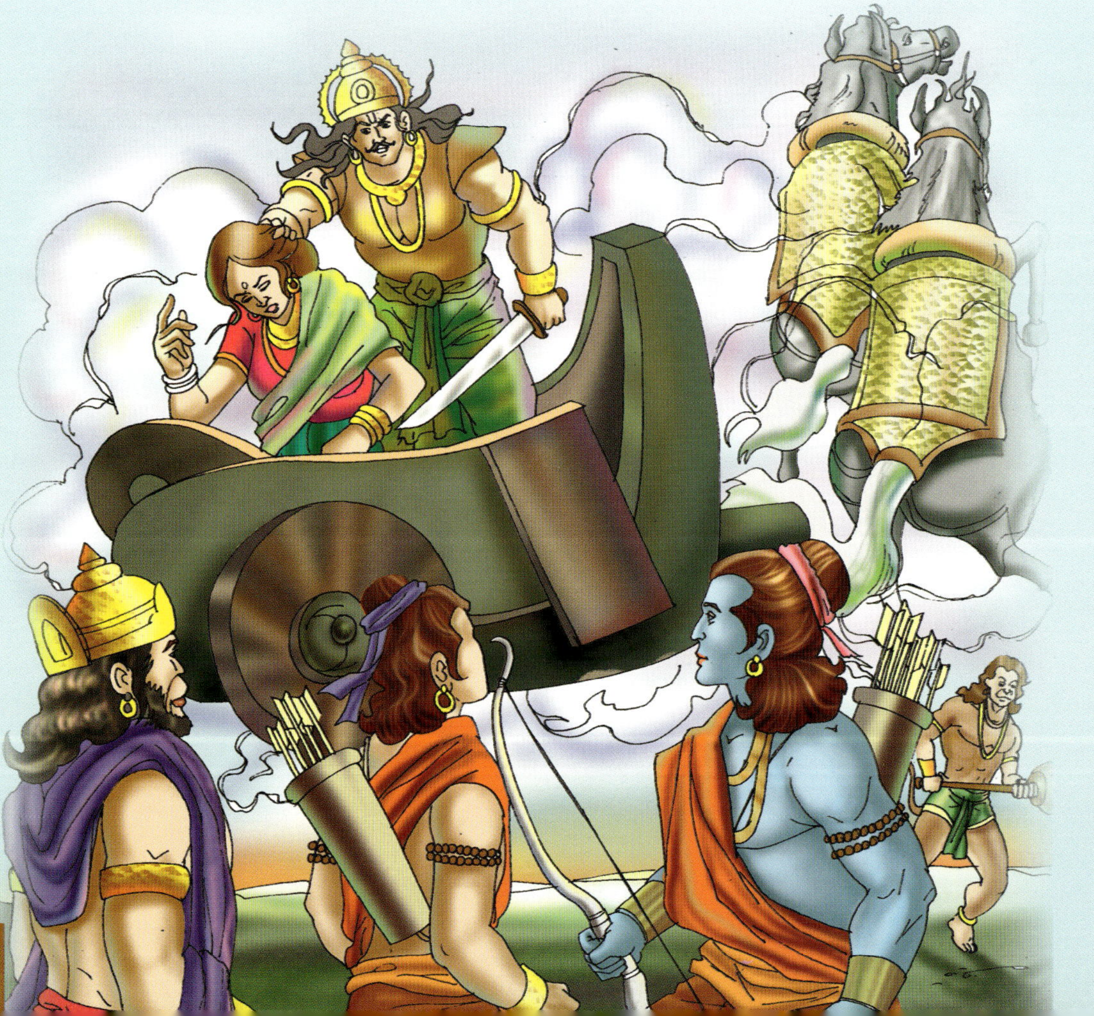

Rama was devastated by this news. Vibhishana saw through this trick and assured Rama that Sita was safe. Lakshmana climbing on Hanuman's shoulders, found Meghnad and launching the formidable weapon, Indraastra, killed him.

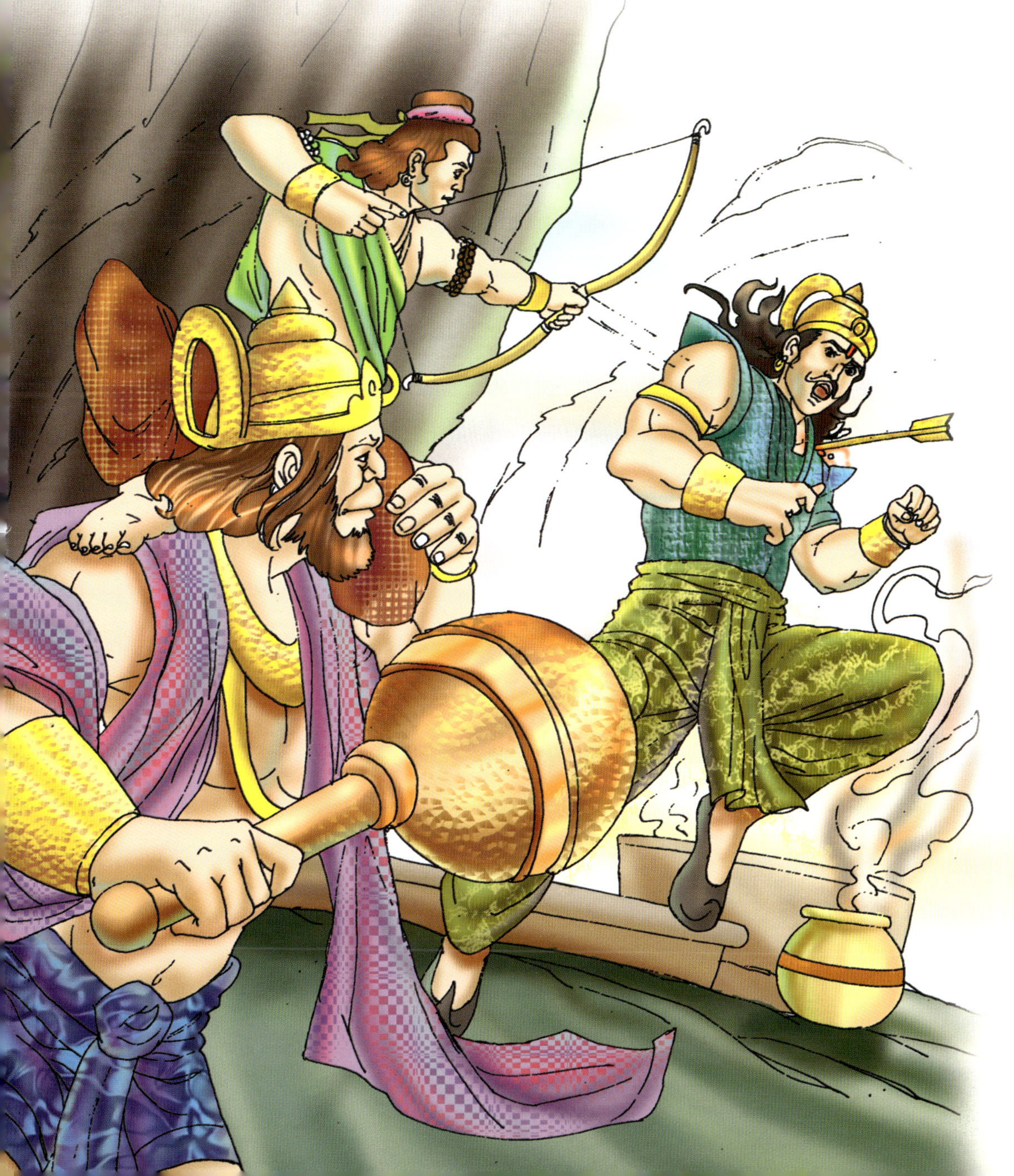

The End of Jaidratha

Arjuna came to know that his son, Abhimanyu, had been killed against the code of war and that Jaidratha was responsible for it. Grief-stricken and furious, he took a vow to kill Jaidratha the next day before the sun set. If Arjuna failed to do so, he would kill himself. On the fourteenth day, the Kaurava army was arranged to give Jaidratha protection. But Arjuna cut through the array of soldiers and reached Jaidratha. And just as he was going to kill him, there was darkness.

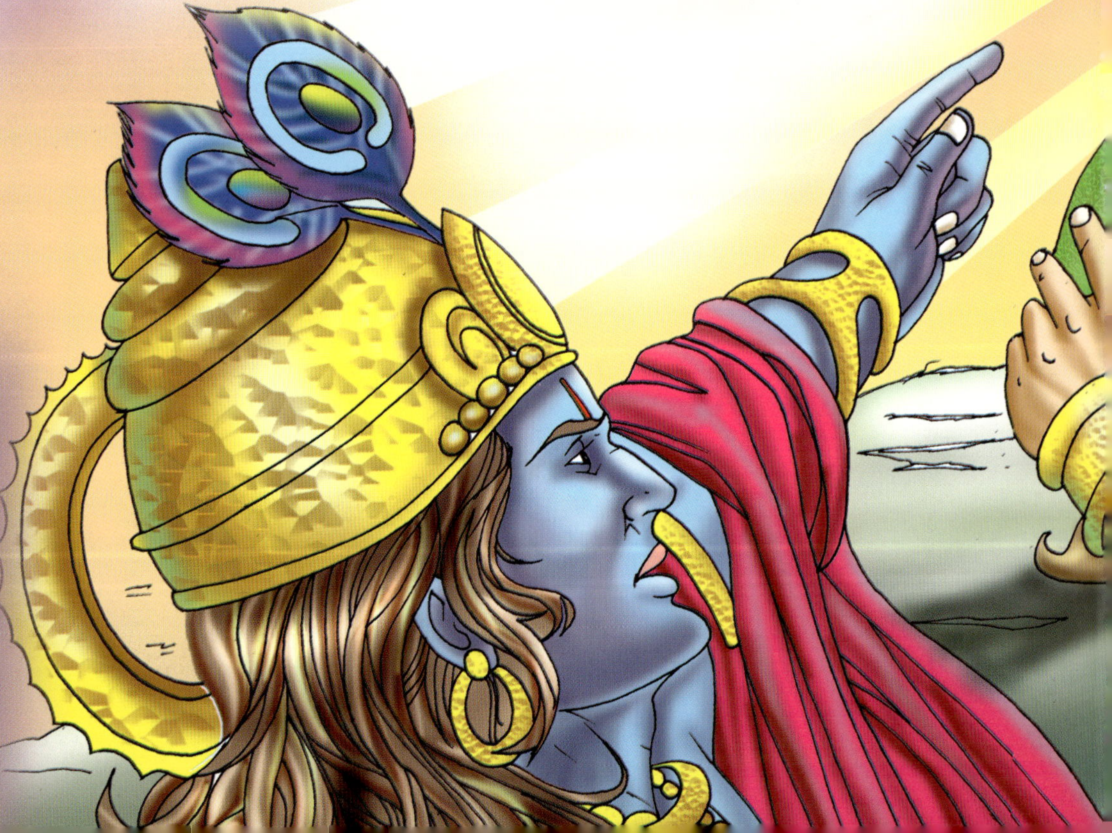

The Kauravas were happy that the sun had set and Arjuna would now have to kill himself. Arjuna was sad but Krishna told him, "The sun has not yet set. I have covered the sun by my Sudershan Chakra (discus). Now is the moment; Jaidratha is looking at the horizon. Kill him!" The next moment, the sun emerged and an arrow from Arjuna's bow struck Jaidratha dead.

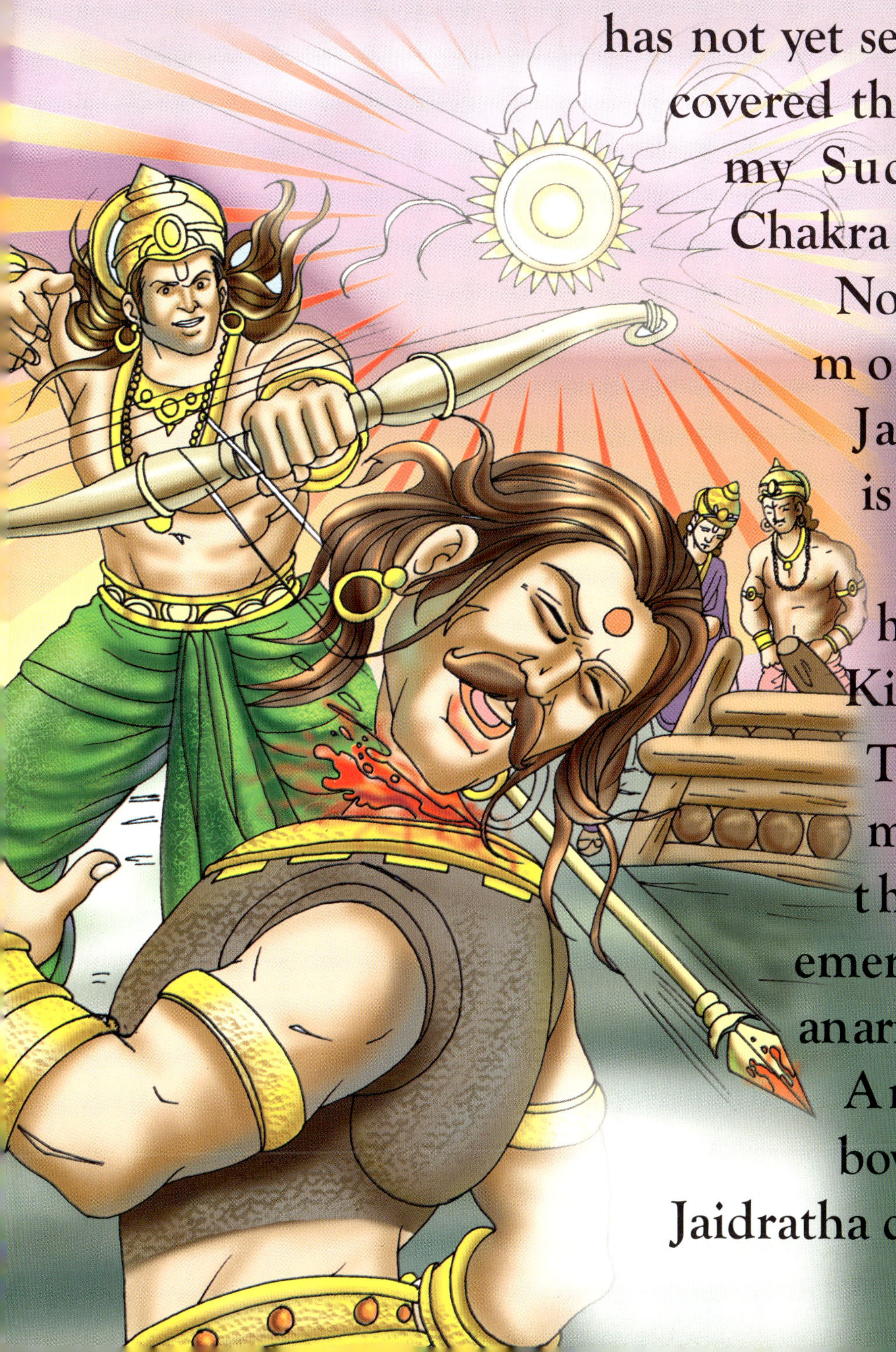

The Fall of Drona

On the fourteenth day of the battle of Kurukshetra Drona attacked the Pandava soldiers with even more vigour. Krishna told the Pandavas that Drona could be killed by a trick. He asked the Pandavas to spread the false news of Drona's son, Ashwatthama, being killed.

Bhima killed an elephant named Ashwatthama and shouted, "I have killed Ashwatthama."

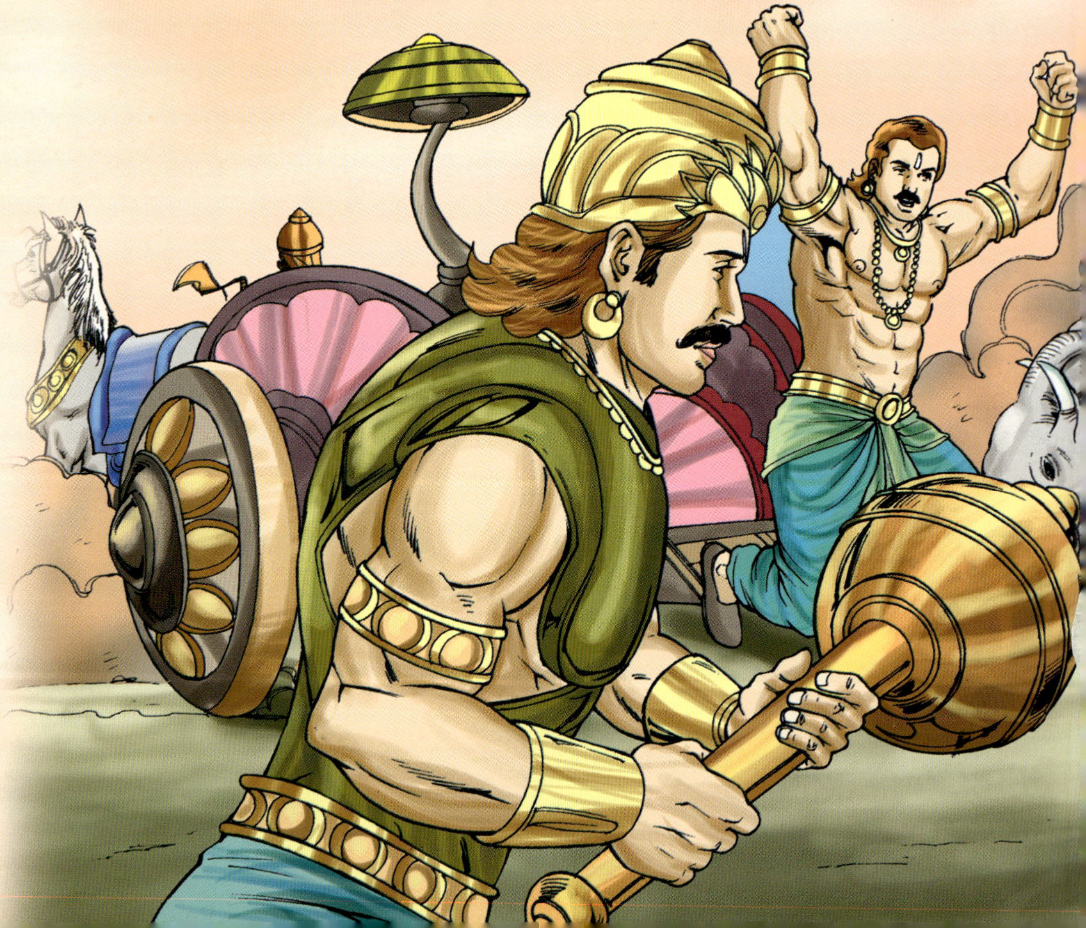

Drona was shocked. He asked Yudhisthira whether it was true, knowing that Yudhisthira would never lie. Yudhisthira replied, "Yes, Ashvatthama is dead, but the elephant not your son." However, Krishna asked the drummers to beat the drums when Yudhisthira spoke the last part of the sentence, so Drona couldn't hear it. As Drona sat mourning his son's death, Dhrish¬tadyumna who had been born to kill Drona, cut his head off.

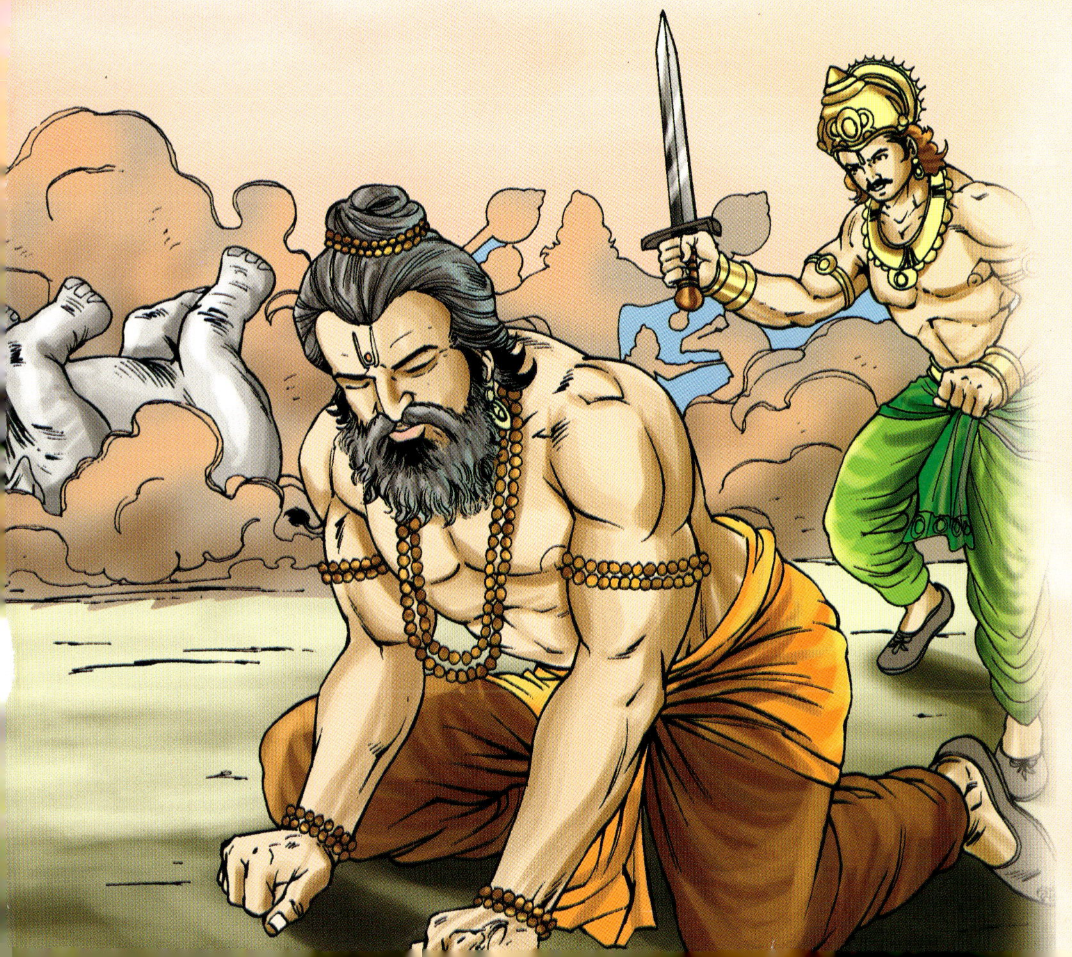

Karna Meets His End

Finally, Arjuna and Karna came face to face and a furious battle ensued between the famous rivals. One of Karna's arrows almost hit Arjuna, but Krishna, who was Arjuna's charioteer, lowered the chariot and the arrow missed him. In return, Arjuna shot numerous arrows at him. Suddenly, the wheel of Karna's chariot got stuck in the mud. As Karna got down to push the wheel, he asked Arjuna to stop shooting, as it would be unethical to shoot at him while he pushed the wheel through the mud.

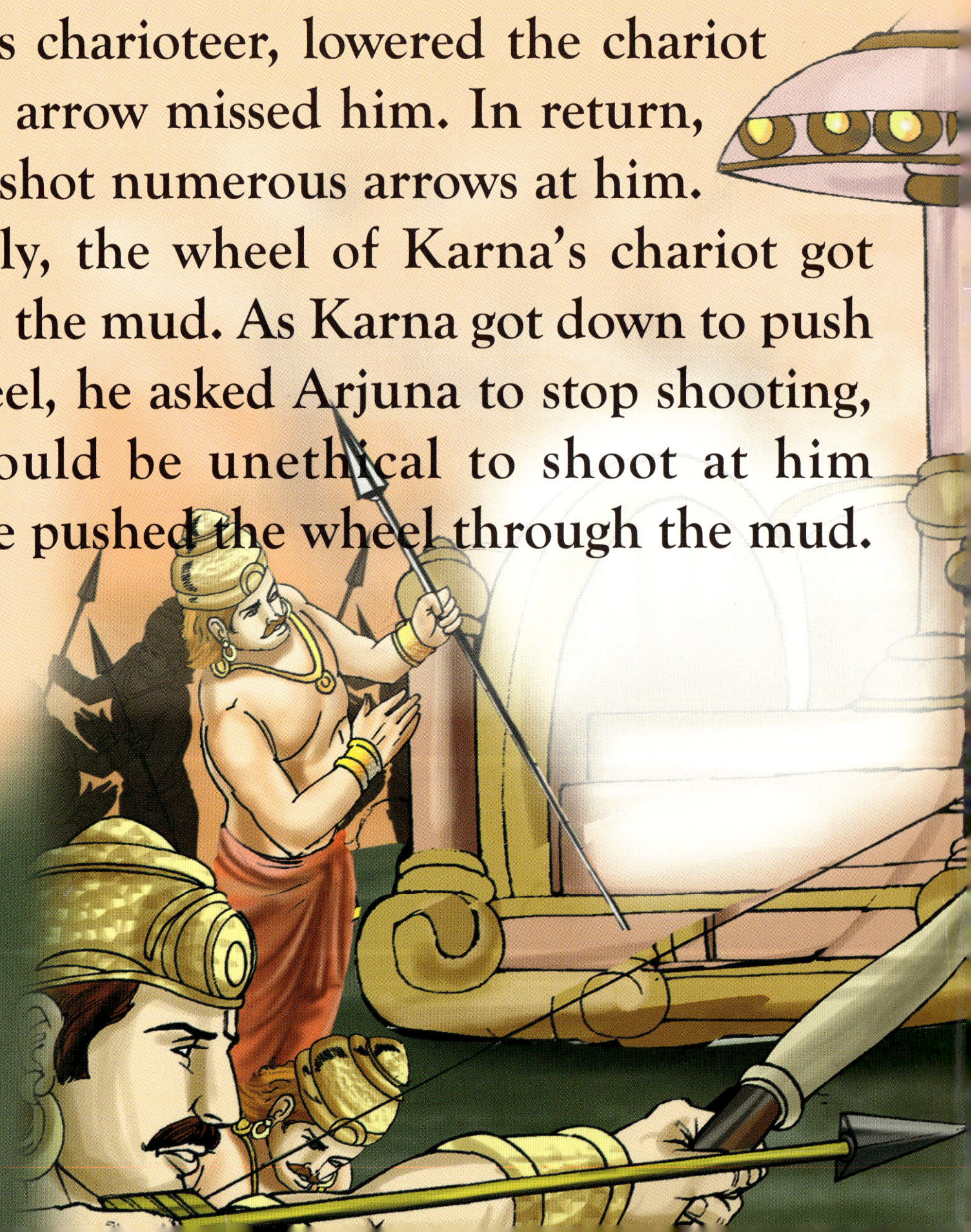

Krishna retorted, "You shot at the unarmed Abhimanyu. Was that fair?"

Arjuna filled with righteous anger, started shooting at Karna. Karna tried to regain his confidence and picked up his bow to counter Arjuna's attack. But suddenly, the curse of Parashurama took effect and Karna felt his knowledge failing him. His knowledge of archery had deserted him when he needed it the most. As the bow slipped from Karna's shoulder, a speeding arrow from Arjuna's bow struck Karna and killed him instantly.

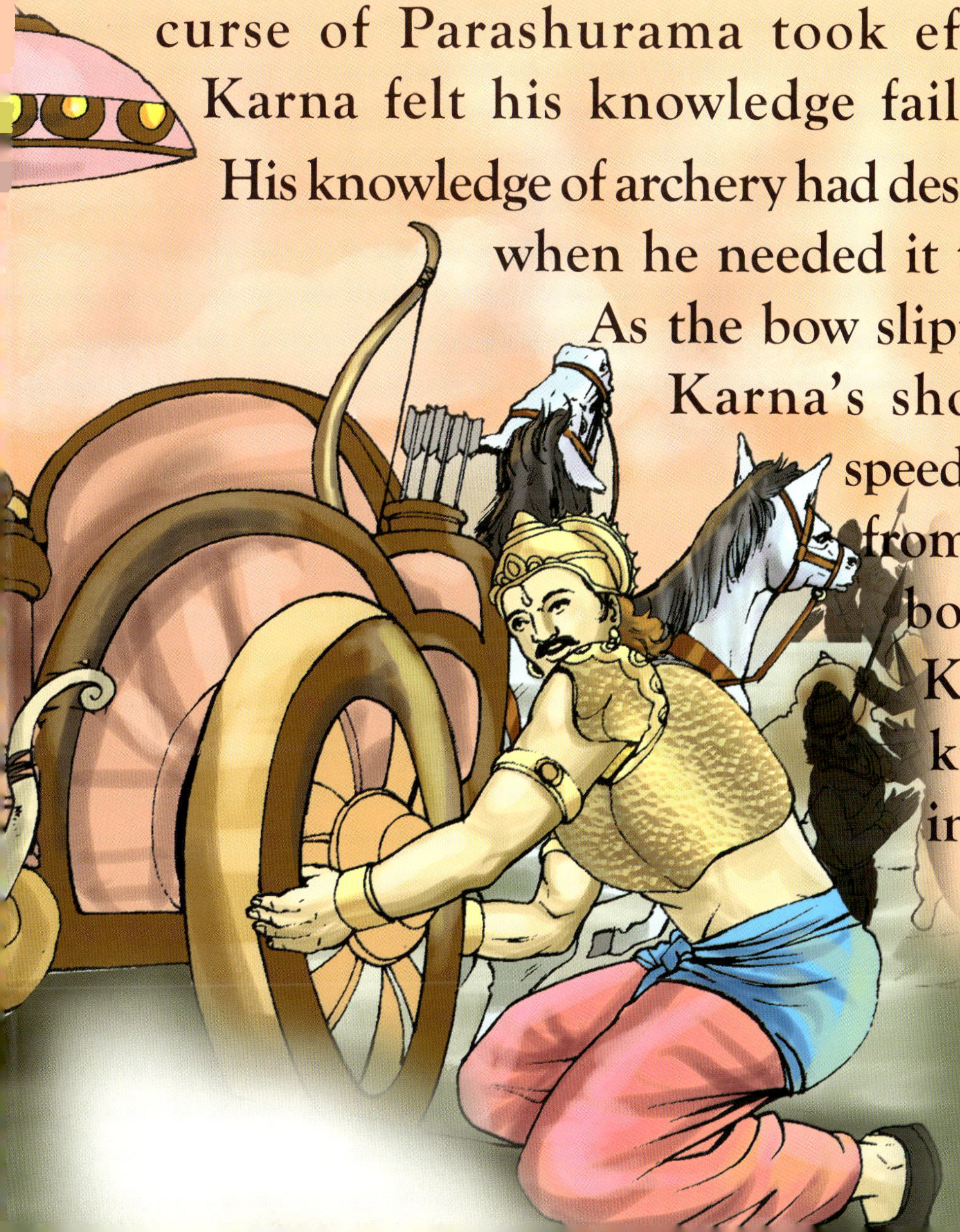

Gandhari's Plan

During the war, Gandhari was worried about Duryodhana. She asked him to take a bath and appear naked in front of her. She would open the cloth over her eyes and cast a look on his body. By the mystic power of her eyes she planned to make his body invincible. Krishna came to know of her plan.

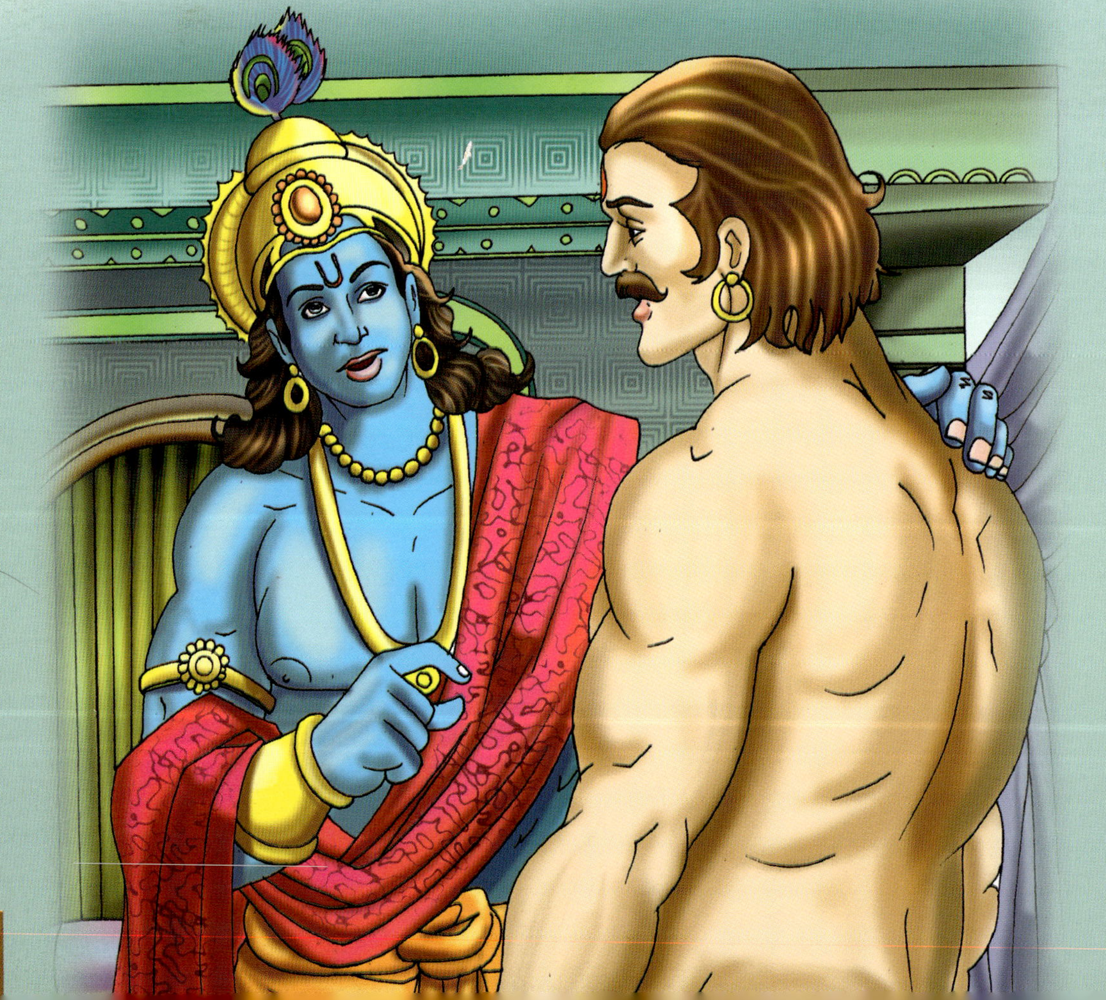

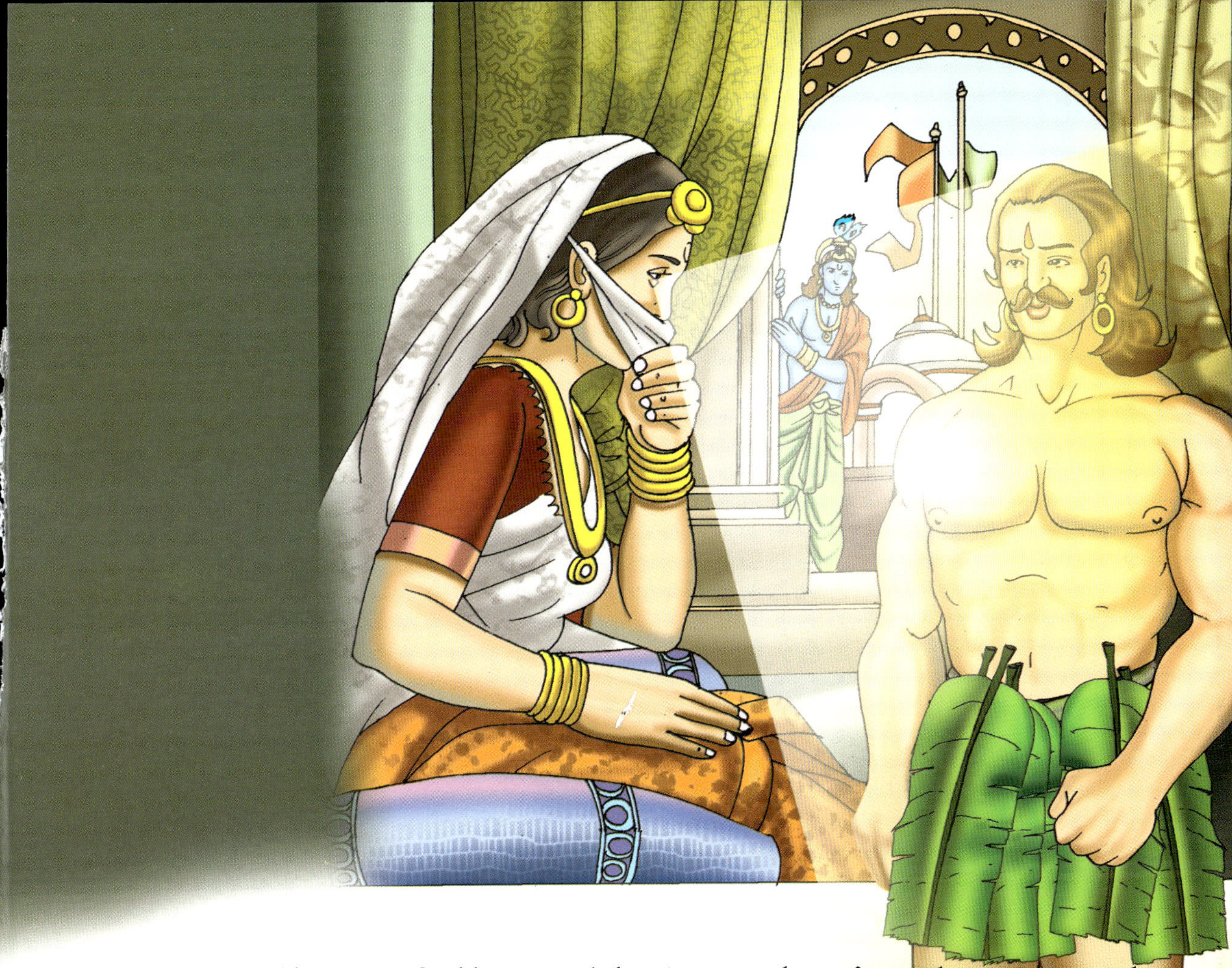

Duryodhana followed his mother's advice, and was going to his mother after a bath. Krishna stopped him and ridiculed him saying, "How can you go to your mother looking like that?" Duryodhana felt ashamed and wrapped a cloth around his waist. Thus, when he appeared before his mother, his entire body became solid except below his waist. Finally, in the battle with Bhima, he was struck on his thigh and being mortally wounded, lay down and waited for his death.

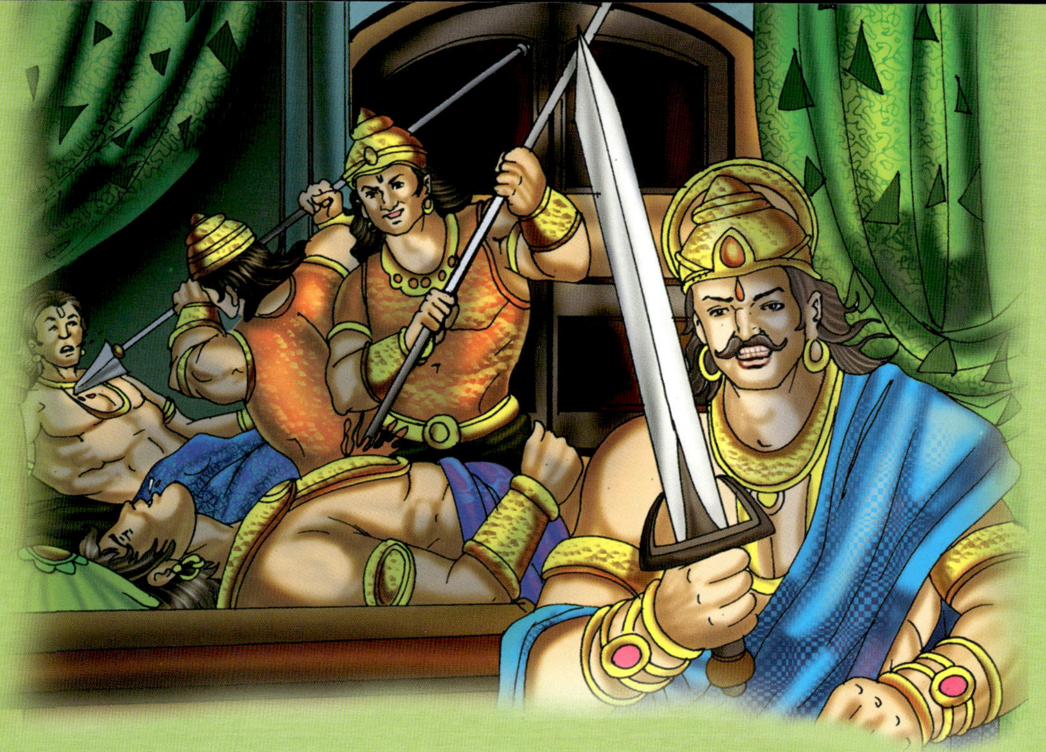

Ashwatthama's Plan

Dronacharya's son, Ashwatthama, vowed to kill the Pandavas. Ashwatthama took two warriors and went to the Pandavas' army camp at night. First, he went to Draupadi's brother, Dhrishtadyumna and strangled him while he was asleep. Then, one by one, he killed all the five sons of Draupadi and finally, Shikhandin, Draupadi's elder brother. The Pandavas and Draupadi were not in the camp at that time. Eventually, setting fire to the camp, he quickly fled to Duryodhana to inform him of his success. Pleased, Duryodhana breathed his last.

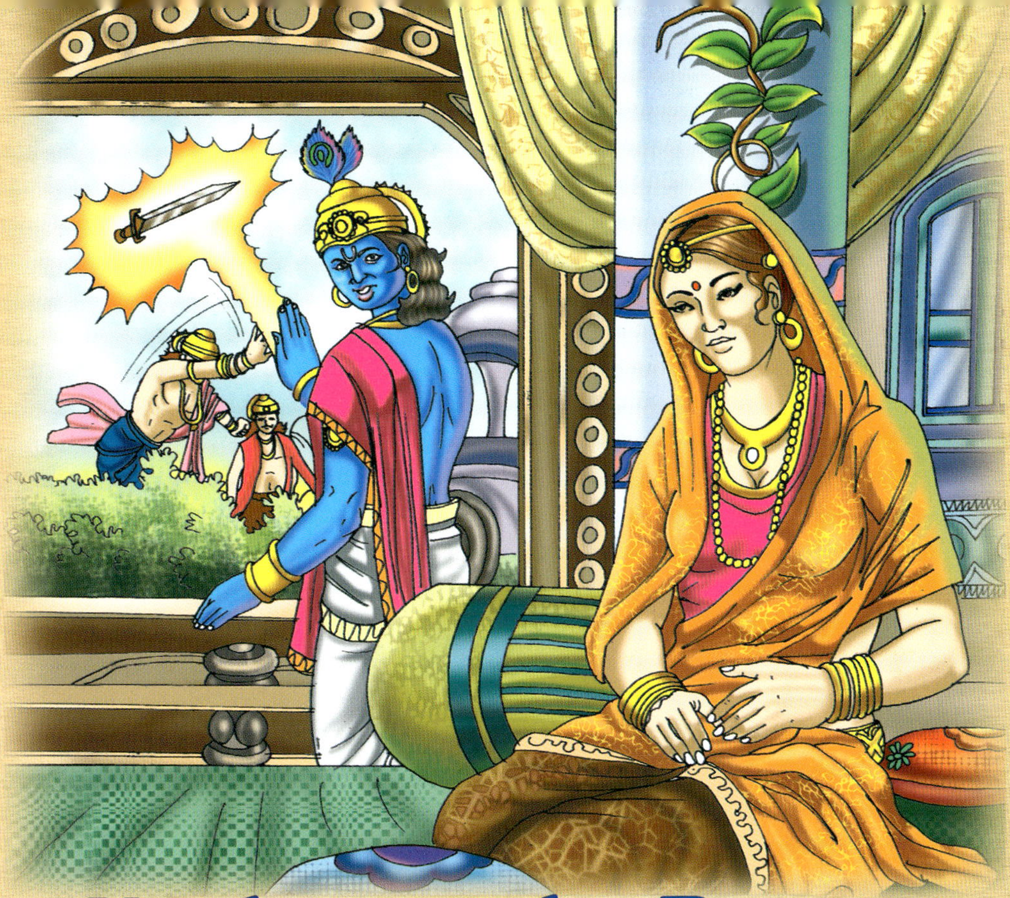

Krishna to the Rescue

The Pandavas were enraged with Ashwatthama, for killing their sons. When Ashwatthama saw the Pandavas approaching, he picked up a blade of grass and ordered, "May this destroy the race of the Pandavas." The blade went towards the womb of Uttara, Abhimanyu's wife, determined to destroy the unborn child. As it took the form of a dagger, Krishna diffused its power. Thus he saved Uttara and her child.

Hanuman's Devotion

Once Sita gave Hanuman a necklace of pearls. With simian curiosity, Hanuman broke the necklace and inspected each and every pearl. "What are you looking for?" asked the residents of Ayodhya. "For Rama and Sita," replied Hanuman. "They are seated on the throne," replied the people.

"They exist in all things. I know they reside in my heart. I am trying to find them in these pearls," said Hanuman.

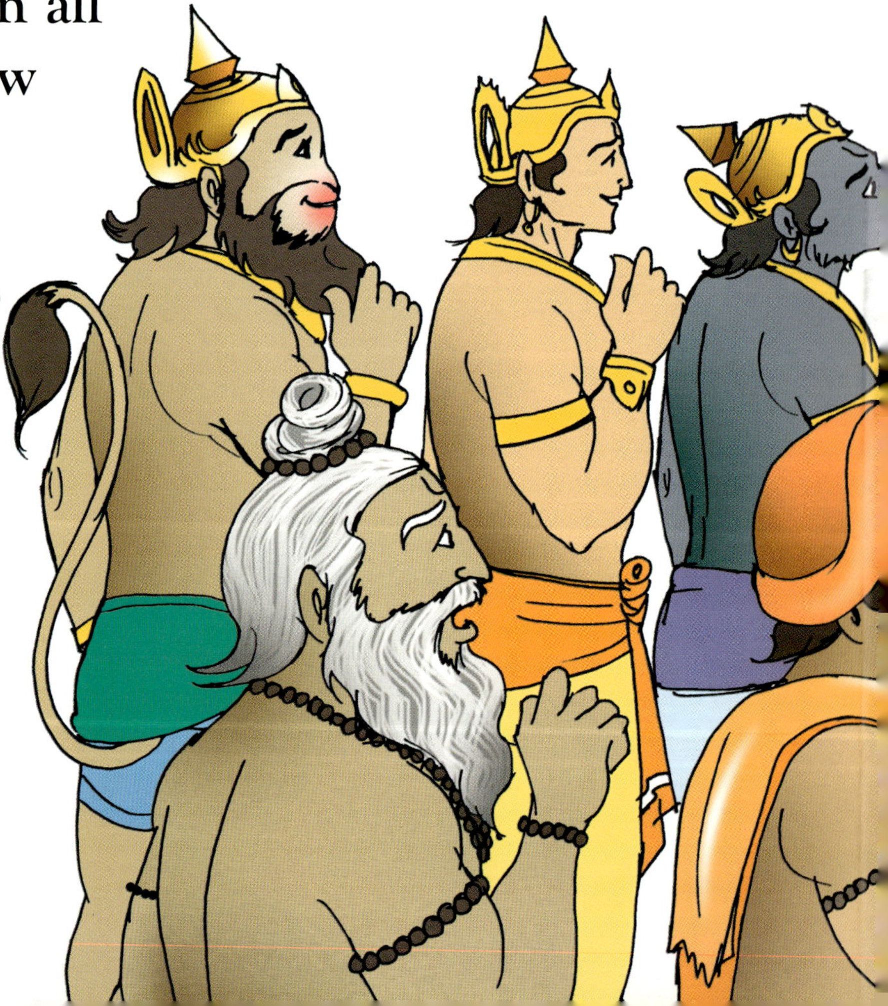

Hanuman's naivety made everyone in Ayodhya laugh. "So Rama and Sita reside in your heart, do they? Can you show them to us," they teased. Hanuman immediately ripped open his chest with his sharp nails. There, within his chest, on his heart, there was an image of Rama and Sita. The people of Ayodhya were astonished. Never again did anyone make fun of Hanuman's devotion.

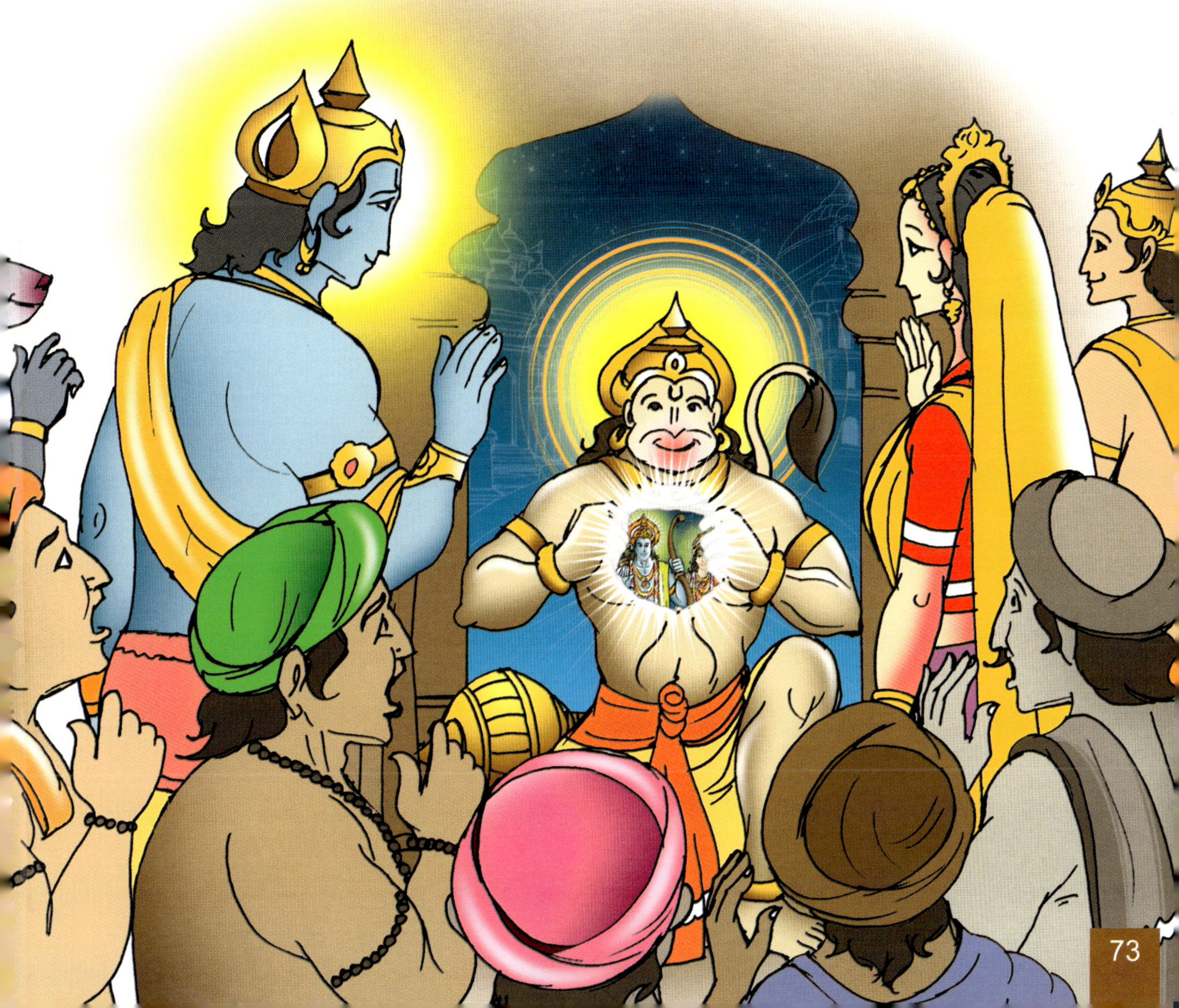

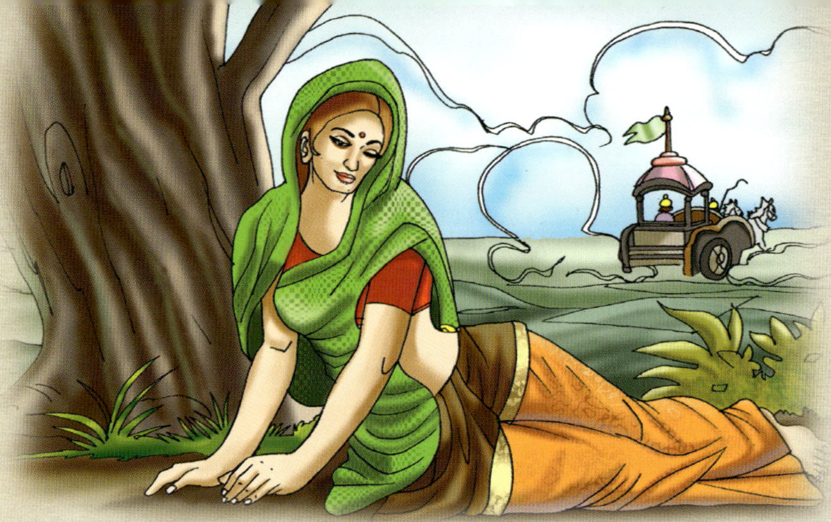

Sita's Exile

Rama was admired by his subjects for his wisdom and strength. One day, one of his spies told him that the people of Ayodhya were unhappy because they believed that he should not have accepted Sita after Ravana had kidnapped her. Disheartened, Rama decided to send Sita away in order to keep his people happy. Lakshmana was entrusted with the task of leaving Sita to the forest. Reluctantly, Lakshmana took Sita along with him to the forest and told her that Rama had asked him to leave her there. Sita was shocked and devastated at this turn of events. But she could not do anything about it. Lakshmana returned with a heavy heart to Ayodhya leaving poor Sita behind.

Cunning Dhritarashtra

The Pandavas returned to claim their inheritance at Hastinapur.

At the royal courts of Hastinapur, the blind Dhritarashtra, father of the Kauravas, met the Pandavas, sobbing with grief. He came forward to hug Bheem. Just in time, Krishna saw a cunning look pass his face.

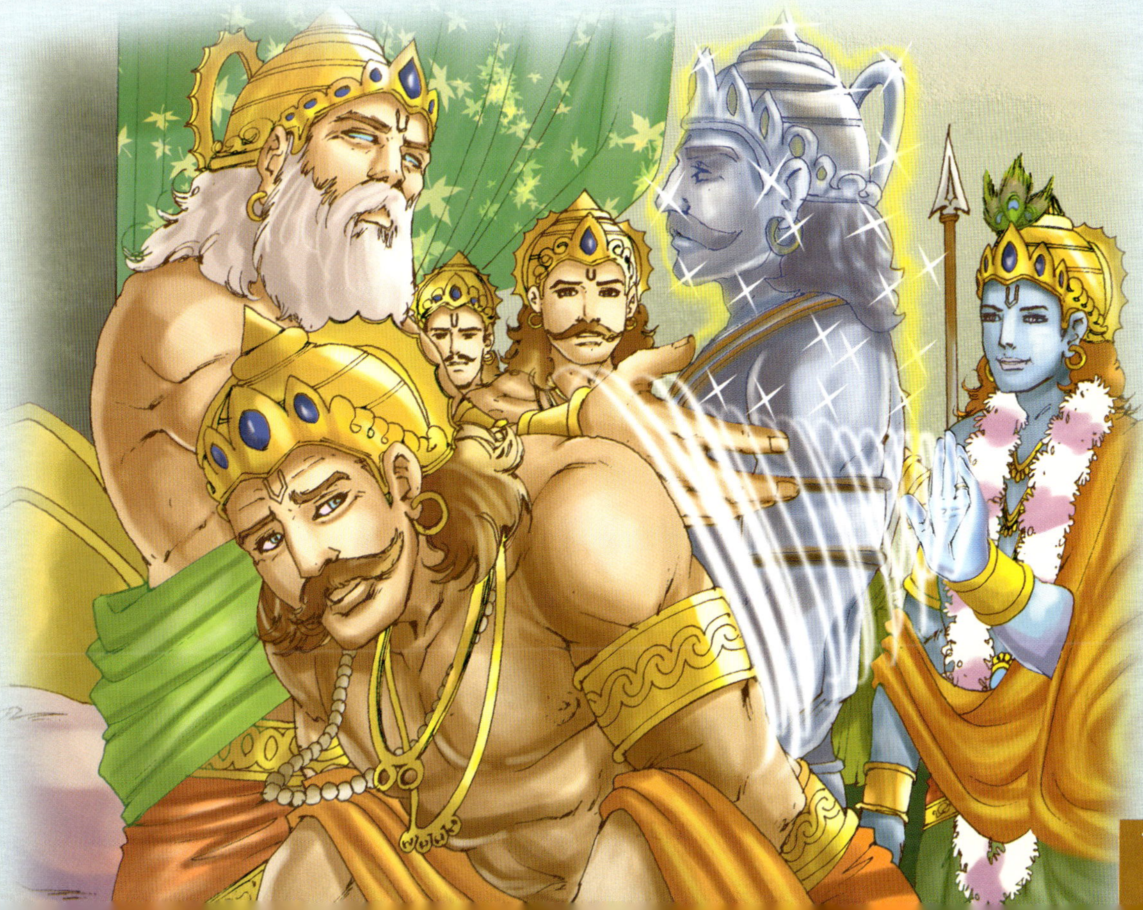

Bheem had killed Duryodhana and Dhritarashtra wanted to avenge his son's death.

Conjuring an iron statue that looked like Bheem, Krishna pushed Bheem aside and thrust it in his place. Dhritarashtra squeezed the statue thinking it was Bheem. So hard did the statue crack that it broke into a million pieces! Even the mighty Bheem would have met with the same fate, had it not been for Krishna. Krishna's quick thinking saved Bheem's life.

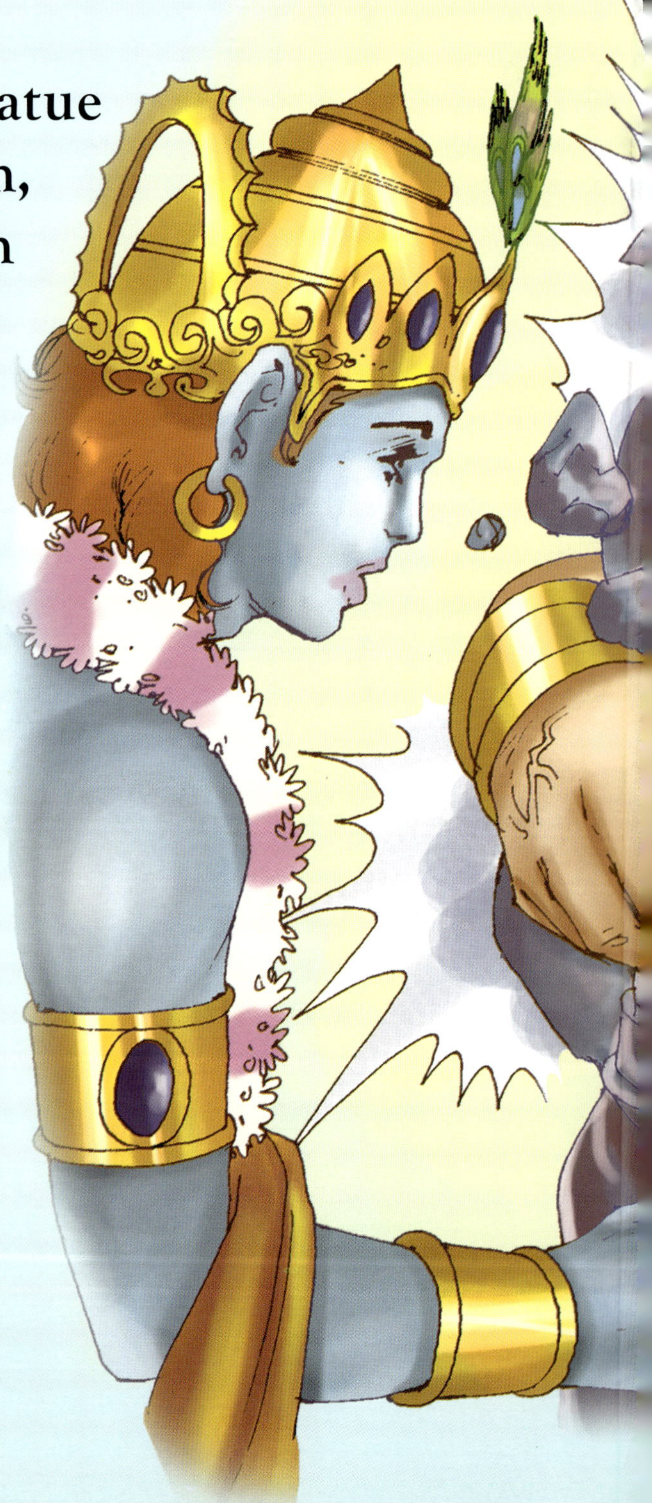

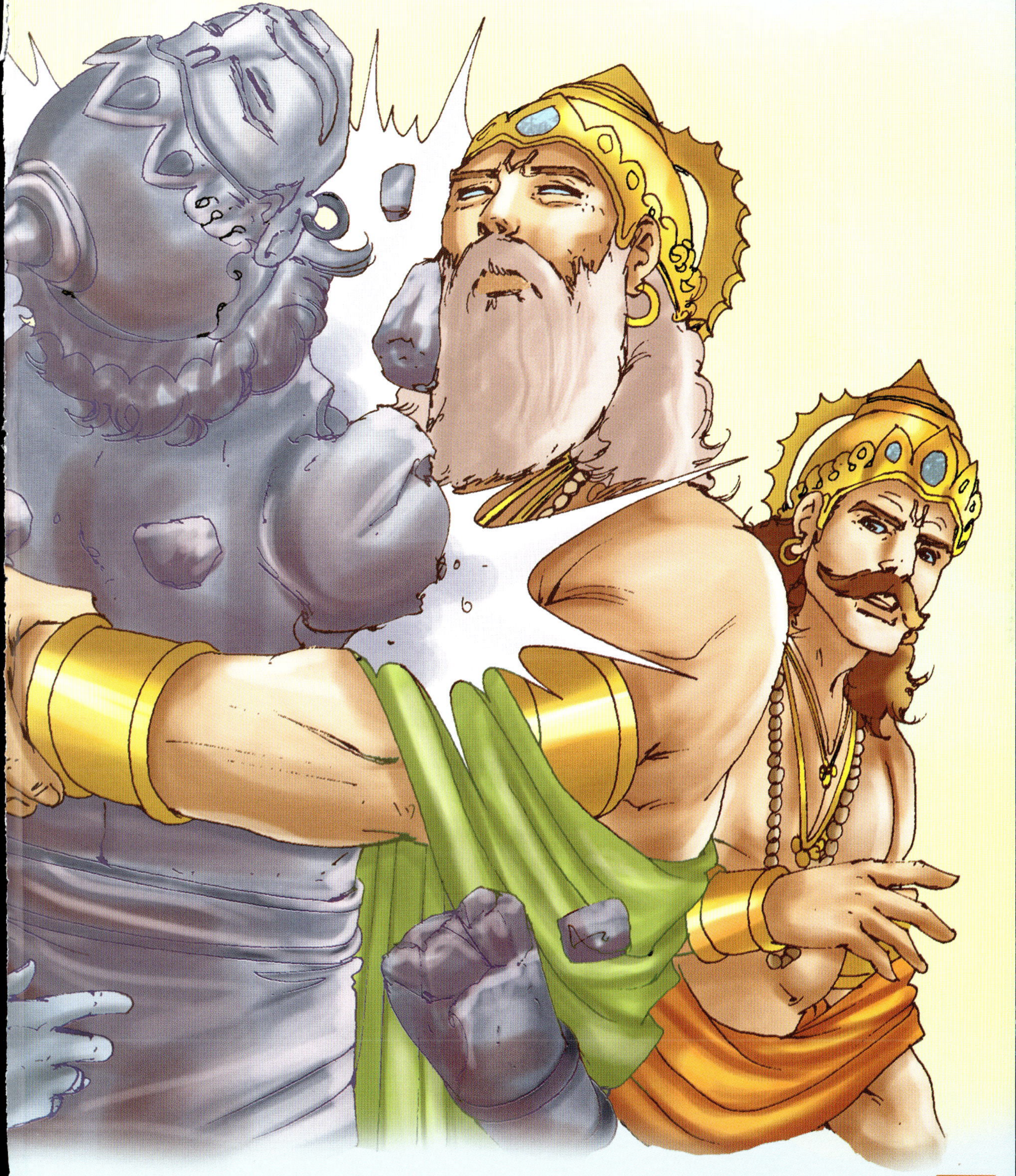

Luv & Kush Fight Lakshman

Rama had released the sacred horse as part of the Ashvamedha yagna. Luv and Kush, the sons of Rama, found the horse and kept it in the ashram, refusing to return it. Hearing the news, Rama sent Lakshmana to Valmiki's ashram to bring back the horse back. However, Luv and Kush refused to part with the horse without a fight. A fight ensued between them and Lakshmana.

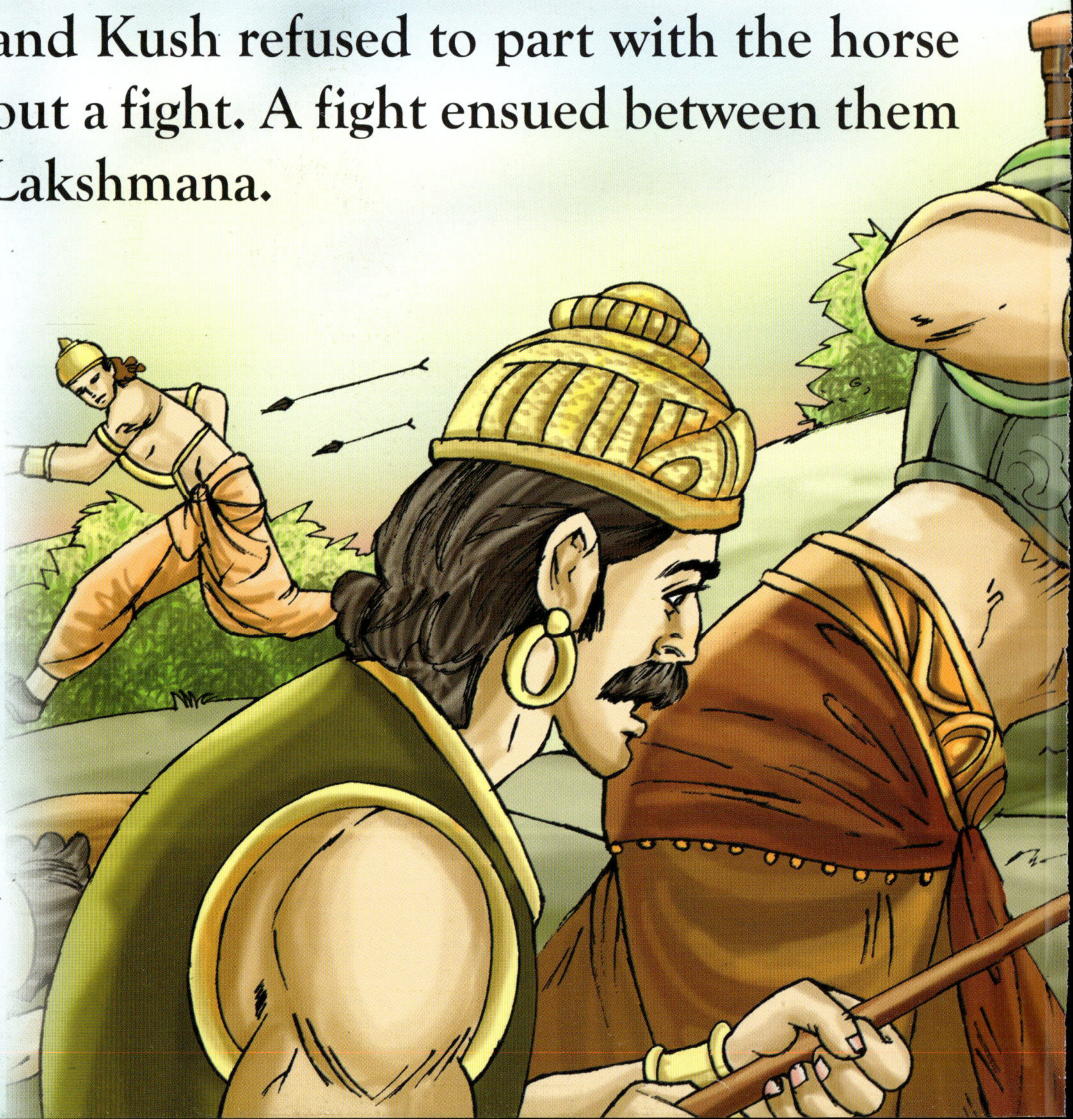